Waiting for Swallows
JIM BRIDGEN

Jim Bridgen. 2011. Bridgnorth.

Jim Bridgen has asserted his right under the Copyright, Designs
and Patents Act 1988 to be identified as the author of this work

This book is a work of non-fiction based on the life experiences and
recollections of the author. In some cases names of people have changed
to protect the privacy of others.

JIM BRIDGEN © 2008
All rights available
ISBN: 978-0-9559556-0-0
A CIP catalogue record for this book is available from The British Library
Published by Bridgen Unabridged
Printed in Great Britain by the MPG Books Group, Bodmin and King's Lynn

In loving memory of Eirian and John Wain
and with special affection to Cari and the boys, as well
as Michael Patrick 'Murphy' a friend if there ever was

With grateful thanks to:
William and Belinda Wain for all their help and support
and Judith Jennings's efforts at converting my pen to text

Prologue

I was becoming restless and aware of a pattern forming which ominously looked and felt like it meant to stay forever, slowly hardening like a concrete jacket around me. I felt vulnerable to any grass seeming to be greener on the other side of the hill and I couldn't bear the thought of the next three years being a repetition of the last three, thence to go on repeating.

In truth, life was good, almost idyllic in fact; I had the Atlantic shimmering right there under my nose and a little wooden hut perched amongst a sea of golden gorse on a cliff. This was Cornwall, Rame Head jutting out away to the left and the great sweep of Whitsand Bay reaching westward to Looe. I had a 'good' job working as a lecturer at the Art College several miles away over the water back in England... Plymouth. Good as it was, it was getting to resemble a 'steady' job, something that I wasn't cut out or ready for. I had itchy feet - nothing to do with athlete's foot, but more to do with a restlessness born of a hunger for exploring new horizons, new challenges that might squeeze me yet closer to 'nature', to the earth and her wildness and make life come as close to a 'natural' existence as it was possible to be. I could taste this burning desire throughout the fidgeting of my restless appetite. I was much too young to be tagged and numbered and putting down roots, life was too short for an appetite like this.

There were five of us, Cari my wife and our three young sons, Spencer, Rowan and Robin, not yet four; the older two attended Infant School some miles away in the village of Anthony and caught the school bus higher up on the cliff road. The nearest shop was a hard steep walk away, down in the valley where a creek came idling up to the little village of Millbrook. Our Spartan life-style hadn't the luxuries of electricity or water; light was provided by candles and a paraffin lamp and water had to be fetched from a tap higher up the cliff. Cooking was done by Calor Gas and so shopping was a back-breaking business carting gallons of paraffin and gas-cylinders back up the long and winding steep hill. All food items were carried in a rucksack, but the drums of fuel had to be tied on to it and dangled freely, leaving my hands to grapple with the heavy gas-cylinder. Mercifully the gas usually lasted for three weeks or so and I only had to fetch paraffin once a week, so I wasn't complaining; after all, this was the life we had chosen and its joys far outweighed its drawbacks.

To ease things, Malcolm, a friend on the ferry down at Cremyl, was giving me driving lessons in his old Morris van. I had always shown reluctance to having those sort of wheels, but having a family changed my mind somewhat. I had to admit that the little van could carry gas cylinders and drums of paraffin with far greater ease than ever I could.

Living perched over a great ocean was exhilarating to say the least: weather came in off the sea without warning and when an Atlantic gale broke upon the place it was pure unadulterated fury, so powerful that it was possible to let go completely and lean forward against the wind till it just held you there, suspended. The problem with spontaneous gales was that of getting the shutters fixed in place before it blew the windows in and the roof off, a nigh-on impossible task. It took two strong people to do this at the best of times, but in a force nine or ten, to be caught outside holding anything large and flat was just asking to be hoisted high, far and fast across distant Dartmoor. But it had to be done and as I struggled grappling with the heavy galvanised wooden shutter against the window, Cari had to firk and fumble around me trying to thread the large bolts through the holes to the inside, then race back indoors to screw on the big brass wing-nuts. This had to be performed on four windows, which took ages and meant we had to light the house with the paraffin-lamp during daylight hours. We always treated this palaver as a fun-thing, a dangerous game that had to be played, like it or not.

The same could not be said for the annual plague of rats, on their migration from the harvest fields down to the shoreline, this really was a nightmare! They came without warning, a whole wave of them capitalising on the rich bounty of cesspits and earth-closets which summer had left. Overnight they gnawed their way inside the hut and ran riot. It took some courage to go fumbling barefoot in the dark, trying to drive them out with a broom or whatever came to hand. They'd taken Robin's soiled pants which were being soaked and had fouled the foodstuffs in the cupboard, tipped the rubbish-bin inside out, knocked jars and crockery over and had discovered the lavatory-bucket in the shed outside, then splattered its contents everywhere and were so bold and brazen that they would not budge an inch when confronted. Very much against my nature I borrowed Malcolm's air rifle and sat out night after rainy night in the ailing paraffin lamp-light, but I never shot a single rat, even though they were darting about everywhere; it was a grenade I needed, not a piddling pellet-gun!

By degrees, the seasons of all things changed, to be replaced by seasons of other things; colours changed, temperatures yo-yoed as did light and dark, tides and moons. Swallows, warblers, terns, cuckoos, black redstarts, godwits and avocets down along the muddy creek, even a short-eared owl in a field at Rame, all had their moment of passing. In winter the adders slept, but on the dry hot days of late summer they basked; the cliff was alive with them and care was needed when walking the wild pathways where the sun had parched the earth tinder-box dry. They sometimes basked on the hot stone slabs of our rockery wall, and I'd seen them between the stones in the high wall that supported our small frontage of lawn. Adders made the business of emptying the lavatory bucket even more hazardous than it already was, as the cliff sloped steeply down through impregnable bramble and gorse, tall grass, towering foxgloves and campions, making it treacherous to keep control of the enormously heavy slopping item all the way down to the deep dark hole hidden away in the thorns. Thankfully, snakes usually got out of the way whenever they felt something coming and so we were spared the venom of their bites. The main worry, in fact, was our staggering infant Robin who would, if he spied an adder coiled and asleep, grab it and stuff it into his mouth; no child was ever so blissfully innocent anywhere under the sun!

Rain was slashing in sideways off the sea, darkness had fallen early, it was one of those evenings best forgotten, just as the entire day had been. A rat was rolling an empty bean-tin somewhere under the hut floor and the boys lay in their beds listening to it and tittering. The candle flames flickered as the umpteen draughts found their way in, twitching the curtains while the old paraffin lamp hissed tiredly. There was a sudden thumping on the outside wall so I grabbed the torch and shot outside to investigate; it was the bedraggled figure of Jerry, an old tramp friend I had seen earlier getting drenched on the ferry-crossing; he was holding something under his mac, a brown paper carrier bag with a cat in it!

He always called me 'Jack', for some reason best known to himself and he called me by that name again as I hurried him inside out of the rain. "Bloody hell, Jack, your place is a sod to find, and on a dirty bloody night like this an' all!" He stood dripping, this tall skeleton of a man with sunken cheeks and goats-beardy whiskers like wire on his chin, a black beret worn like a crash helmet and a long bedraggled gabardine with no belt and wellies rolled down halfway; he was drenched! "Jack! Look what I've brought for yer ... a lovely cat to catch them rats o' yourn wot you was tellin' me about." He held out the bag with two wild flaring eyes burning from it: "This is 'Bootsy', fully housed-trained an' wot's more I 'ad him circumstrated at the cat-doctors! You'll shift them rats of Jack's, won't you Bootsy, eh?" He put the cat down and it bristled and flickered its tail with indignation, glaring about the room menacingly. It was mostly black in colour, with long white whiskers, a little white bib and white front feet, hence its name. The boys were all peeping round their bedroom door, excited at what they had overheard and could now see it for themselves pacing up and down its new surroundings, familiarising itself. "I don't want no money for 'im nor nuffin, I'm giving 'im to you, you'll be glad you've got 'im, Jack ... you marks my word!"

Cari boiled the kettle and made Jerry a mug of tea and some bread and cheese, which he disposed of with canine efficiency, and I could hear the boys all high-spirited and raucous in their room; they'd got themselves a cat and it felt like another Christmas had settled upon the place. Jerry then disrobed his stinking top layer in front of the fire made from driftwood. He stood steaming in his badly discoloured long-johns while he rolled himself a fag and very patiently lit it and re-lit it over and over again. The cat meanwhile had had a mood-change and was now attacking his flattened grimy socks, growling and hissing as it savaged his feet. Jerry wasn't in the slightest bit bothered by this; he seated himself down in the armchair and picked the cat up and petted it. It was now biting his hand and sinking its claws in, fetching blood, the sight of which alarmed me somewhat. Hesitantly, I asked him, "Is ... is the cat alright?" Jerry smiled, "He loves playing, Jack; you've got to give 'im plenty of fuss ... be gentle with 'im ... eh Bootsy, Bootsy, Bootsy, eh!"

He settled down for the night, cat and all. His snoring was so fierce that it silenced the storm outside! When I was woken in the early morning by a new fire spitting and crackling in the hearth, I caught sight of Jerry urgently scraping a pile of cat-shit from the carpet and trying to burn it discreetly. Not wishing to spoil his secret, I stayed back in the bedroom for a while longer before appearing on the scene and judging by the look of relief on his face, I could tell that he was satisfied that his secret was sealed forever; but the aroma was sharp and true, there was no hiding that!

On leaving, Jerry stood in the new wind, a dry man without a cat or a care in the world, a turbulent sky beyond his head and the smell of gorse billowing up deliciously from where the cliff fell away. In his pocket, the folded-up carrier-bag, an item of obvious value to him. He turned and said, "Tarrah, Bootsy!" then climbed the steps before vanishing into the gorse-bushes on his gum-booted way back down to his little hovel beside the creek. It was some weeks later that Malcolm told me that Jerry had been found dead in his shack; it came as a horrid shock and upset us all greatly. He and I had been friends, yet few people would speak to him. I had loved talking with him and that's why he had taken to me and given me his beloved cat, as though he knew that it was going to need a new home very soon.

It was as though he had flung a handful of magic from his grave when, one egg-yolk sunrising morning, the boys all came running into our bedroom bubbling with excitement; "Cari, Jimmy, Bootsy's had kittings in Robin's bed!" Sure enough, the cat had performed the quickest sex change ever, and now we had two more cats... Jerry would be pleased!

Over the next month I managed to fail my driving test, then, some weeks later, passed it. When I went a stage further and purchased the van from Malcolm, it was like developing wings. Life on the cliff was becoming rather hectic: our hut was getting to be a bit of a mecca at weekends for a whole assortment of people, artists, naturalists, athletes, students, musicians, poets, potters, photographers ... you name it, we had them - and usually all at the same time! Minutes were not long enough, hours were totally inadequate, days just blasted by in a blur and weeks tick-tocked away; wings were useful now, so all that remained was for me to get the hang of this new wheeled machine!

I had been born in a tiny cottage by the quaint name of 'Thimble Hall', so this was what we called our hut and it lived up to its name, sometimes managing to seem even more cramped than a thimble. On Sundays, when athletes from London clubs came down, I helped ease our overcrowding by taking them off on long runs over miles of beaches, cliff paths, woods, lanes and tracks, always managing to pass a village shop on the way back where I could pick up a packet of tea. I'd return with my exhausted gang only to find the hut full of others: Malcolm with a large bag of sticky buns, Steve the birdman complete with telescope, tripod, binoculars and notebooks, together with his pal Graham; Murphy, wildman of Dartmoor booming his impeccable knowledge of the Moor. Somewhere else was Chris, one of my students, playing the guitar accompanied by Phil, a writer blowing his gums sore on my tin whistle, with the boys there in the thick of it bashing out percussion on tambourine, tins and saucepans. Squashed amongst them, almost invisible in the armchair, old Les, a lonely little man from the village, blissfully soaking up the company and polluting the air with cigarette smoke, keeping a long-ashed perpetual stub between his clenched gums; with no teeth to bother him, he looked like Adolf Hitler with his solitary bit of hair flat and glossed-down with Brylcreem, or lard perhaps. A painter and his wife and dog came and added to the throng, at which point Bootsy's tolerance gave out and she attacked the dog, causing cuts to the woman's leg in the process; the dog fled with a nasty nose-bleed; then, as if that wasn't enough, my running mate from the village, together with a Plymouth runner and another from the Royal Navy, all crashed in to the tea party, smelling like hunted foxes. Poor Cari, she was murdering loaves and lettuces, tomatoes and slabs of cheese like there was no tomorrow, and I was fetching water as though we had a house-fire! We soon discovered a use for tins of condensed milk, and learned not to throw away our empty jam and honey jars, because they all came in very handy as cups.

News continued to get around that this was a good place to be at weekends. It just so happened that this was where Cari, the boys and myself liked to be at weekends too and so, whenever we could, we'd pack up a nice picnic-bag and escape on long walks with the pushchair and taking turns on my shoulders. Then towards evening we'd go off on a nice easy van drive to Liskeard for fish and chips and lemonade, the boys all sitting snug and singing on an old feather quilt which had now found a new purpose in life.

The cliffs really were magical, always alive with something or other. I regularly saw a fox sleeping early on a kind of bank that sloped away to the cliff edge, beyond my relic of a greenhouse. This was no ordinary greenhouse: This one had been made of iron, by an earlier pioneer who harboured the crazy notion that he could grow tomatoes. But iron alas was no match for the murderous gales that broke over the cruel cliff, and now it stood broken, busted and rusted, half buried in the wild brambles where the stonechats chatted. Each dusk a little owl flew along the cliff and called plaintively from hidden roofs and a barn owl also ghosted like a large moth; while, all along the sweep of the midnight bay, night fishermen fished for bass by lamplight, seeming like fallen stars dotted all the way down to the faint flickering lights of Looe, as too the glow-worms in the grasses glowed in summer. At times it felt too deliciously good to bother about going to bed, and instead I'd wander off with my torch, unable to satisfy the appetite that burned within me. Always I was hungry for more and more, there was never enough of it for me; I just wanted a closer, finer sense of the earth under my feet and all about me, I needed to feel it and taste it, hear its music and all that it was saying. Questions excited me far more than answers ever did, and a greener grass was calling whenever a question hardened into an answer, like a caterpillar into a chrysalis; my own butterfly was forming inside me.

The Green, Green Grass...

I'd noticed a good amount of feral cats on the cliff, week-enders' pets that had strayed, no doubt. The pickings were easy for a cat gone wild and, as I climbed the track up to the road one morning, there were several darting for cover when I appeared on the clearing halfway up. I thought little more of it until evening, when I was haring down the cliff in the half-light on my way back from work and came skidding to a halt before a weird creature with two heads and four eyes burning back at me. It growled before suddenly the top half exploded off and away leaving an agitated Bootsy staring at me before she too streaked off after the other one. I could smell the stink of cat-pee all the way down to the hut and I knew a little more of what the future now had in store for us.

"How does living in a little cottage in the hills of mid-Wales sound to you?" Cari asked, trying to disguise a delighted grin. "Lovely," I sighed. "Why, is there one going?" She had received a letter from back home in Wales informing her that her uncle and aunt had just acquired a small hill-farm which happened to have such a cottage remotely situated on its land. Furthermore it had been suggested that it would suit us right down to the ground. "Blimey!" I gasped. "I don't believe it!" "Well, it's all here in Mum's writing," Cari added with a giggle, which showed that she already liked the idea. It was, after all, the part of the world where she was born and had spent her childhood; it was also near to where we had spent a few lovely idle days the previous summer, fishing in the brook for trout and dace with the relatives in question. Now the grass really was greener on the other side of the hill, I had to find out more and make tangible something I could really believe in.

Letters were exchanged and it wasn't long afterwards that I spoke to Cari's uncle Gareth from a call-box down in the village. He described the cottage to me: "It's tidy like, needs a bit of touching-up on one of the corners ... you'd soon fix that, Jimmy. It's nice and quiet, on a bit of a bank with woods around it, got its own private lane up to it ... that's about it. You can have it if you want it, I don't want anything for it 'cos it's no use to me." That was it. I told him that I was interested and would be up to have a look at it as soon as I possibly could; I'd try to assess what needed doing and sort out any paperwork that might be necessary. "'Don't need no bloody paperwork!" he shouted, "I'm a man of my word, my word's my bond!" "Agreed!" I said and that's the way we left it.

It appeared that our days on the cliff were numbered, as too were my days at the Art College. The hut would have to be sold to provide us with whatever money we could get for it, as this was all we had to our names. It seemed there was no looking back now that this seed had been sown; it all felt like a dream awakening brighter, more glowing by the day. A new challenge was taking shape, that of becoming self-sufficient and living off the land, as near as we could, tasting a little wilderness in the process. The more we thought about it, the more positive we became about meeting the challenge. But I had to go up and see the place first, and check out future schooling arrangements and other important things before finally committing myself to resigning from my job. I didn't anticipate there being any problems, and so we proceeded to spread the word quietly amongst our friends of what we were thinking of doing, and how our hut would probably be coming up for sale.

Once news had crossed the Tamar, Murphy was over like a shot on his push-bike, pockets full of maps of Central Wales and with a sudden interest in the writings of George Borrow, 'Wild Wales' in particular, and with an enthusiasm for following the old drover-routes across the hills. He then announced that his mate 'Greg', a black-bearded badger of a man with an insatiable appetite for antiques, would take the three of us up to Wales in his little van, combining it with a broader search for unsuspected treasures that just might happen to lurk beneath layers of dark gloss-paint in half-open doorways that we passed.

The arrangement was made. On the following Saturday evening I drove Murphy and Chris, who'd asked if he could come too, over to Tavistock where we stayed the night with Greg and his wife and family in their time-capsule of a cottage, with old Grandfathers tick-tocking, music-boxes playing, gramophones grinding, dogs, cats, daughters, stuffed bears, butterflies, oil paintings, china, every conceivable thing! We slept wherever we could on sofas and armchairs and were up not so very bright but very early on the Sunday morning, revived somewhat by strong tea and burnt toast. We made our early start in Greg's cramped and wretchedly uncomfortable van as the frail white mist lifted from the deep dark Tavy below in the gorge.

The journey was long and slow along the main A38 as far north as Bristol, then across the Severn Bridge and all along the Welsh Marches as far up as Craven Arms before heading west into the heart of Central Wales. It was like being trapped in a fiendish noise-torture device, with Murphy's normal excitable shouting voice ceaselessly having to compete with a deafening recorder-marathon being blown by Chris, while big sturdy Greg thunderously and repetitiously broke wind and kept the window shut. Even a whisper had to be shouted and when we occasionally stopped for a stretch and a wee, my throat and head ached from the lost battle of fighting to be heard.

Thanks to Murphy's impeccable map-reading, we found the farm without a single hitch. Gareth was in the yard waiting for us, having watched the little grey van struggling up the long steep hill. We all piled out into a frenzy of handshaking, smiles and hellos. I was greeted like an old friend by the umpteen children and Cari's Aunty Gwyneth and their Jack Russell; it was a lovely moment with friendship flowing and all the patchworked tapestry of hill-country reaching away for miles and miles in a great circle all around. I'd never seen a landscape anywhere so breathtakingly beautiful as this; it seemed to be whispering something to me, something like "gotcha!" We shambled into the kitchen where Gwyneth made gallons of tea and fed us all under a huge din of cackling conversation. Greg managed to swap a tiny bundle of notes for a heavily-lacquered sideboard, and in no time had it roped onto his roof-rack. All that remained was for Gareth to take us over the hills to the cottage! I could hardly wait.

Process was slow because of the dominating panorama, but by slow degrees the farm shrank behind us as another valley and other hills appeared, with an oakwood tumbling away to a willowy marsh in the bed of the valley. Then I saw it, a stone building with double chimneys and a stone barn beside it. It stood alone in the valley, the silence was deafening. We followed a steep track beside the remains of an ancient gnarled hawthorn hedge, down, down, twisting and losing sight of the place, then we levelled out where a little stream had suddenly sprung out of nowhere and a cluster of apple and damson trees continued to hide the place from view. Suddenly, there it was before us ... and my heart sank. The entire end wall and part of the front wall had completely vanished, the bedroom floor was held up by a twisted metal gate that had been wedged there, and the roof was sagging and busted having lost most of its slates; it was a wreck! Gareth hastened to explain that it had formerly been used as a cowshed and that the cows had, over the years, pushed the wall out. Silently we all moved closer, feasting our eyes and unable to speak. I could see Murphy's eyes, fidgeting uneasily and aware of what I was feeling, unable to do anything about it. Gareth broke the silence and said, "It looks far worse than it is, Jimmy; get this owd end wall up and it'd be right tidy like!" The floors were deep with years of cow-muck, and closer inspection showed that the small lean-to back room had been used as a calf-pen, as too had the tiny room where the stairs had once been. All around the walls were the dark smears where the beasts had rubbed their messy backsides. I noticed swallow nests along the beams and evidence of rats and jackdaws too. Beside the decrepit stone barn was a lean-to pigsty with holes in the roof, and beside this a dilapidated lean-to wooden shed. The barn itself was fathoms deep in ancient dung. The sky was visible through most of the collapsing roof, which had large sheets of galvanised tin attached with wire which dangled where the beams had fallen through. Its end wall was cracked wide open from top to bottom and bulged dangerously. A wren flew about inside, agitated at our presence near its nest in there.

We strolled out into the sunlight. I wasn't the only one at a loss for words. There was a kind of clumsy silence as we all stood in the yard waiting for the first person to speak. "You'd soon mend the roof once that wall was fixed, Jimmy ... an' I'd plough you a bit of garden at the front. They's plenty of wood about the place like ... soon get it nice and warm isn't it!" Gareth did his best to stir my enthusiasm back to life, at least that's what I thought he was doing, but he seemed to genuinely believe in what he was saying. So I tried even harder to conceal my shock and be more positive within myself, whilst trying not to be too much affected by the body-language of my friends, whom I sensed were still in a state of disbelief and were closer to bursting out laughing than they were to constructive suggestions right now. "I think you're right, Gareth," I said nervously. "It'll take a bit of time and money, but I think it could be turned into something nice ... and it's a lovely part of the world. Where do the kids go to school?" I changed the subject in an attempt to find air as Gareth firked for his matches to light the pipe which he was biting hard into. "Taint far, Jimmy... quarter of an hour's walk down the bank... bigger ones go into town."

We idled away half an hour in the sun, our voices echoing round the nearby hillsides to add to the feeling of seclusion. Chris noticed this too and started to blow a few notes on his small recorder to start a musical conversation with himself, and Gareth found this highly comical as the notes went bouncing off the hills and melting into the distance. Greg looked at me and grinned, then in a pirate's voice muttered, "You'm gonna have your work cut out if you asks me, Jim Lad!" adding "but it's real 'andsome 'ere, ain't it!" Murphy put his hand on my shoulder reassuringly and growled, "We could do it, Jimmy. I'll give you a hand, it'll be great!" We strolled thoughtfully back to the farm and stood around talking for a while, the children all seeming to have already accepted that I was soon going to be moving in; I wasn't so sure. We piled into the van as the gang in the farmyard waved us off back down the big hill and out of sight.

Once on the road, the previously stifled laughter started to let rip. "It's a bloody cowshed!" Greg roared. "Well it WAS, but 'taint even that no more!" He broke wind again and Murphy almost burst the door open in his haste to open the window. "It's a good job you didn't let that one off in Jimmy's cowshed 'cos you'd have brought the rest of it down and killed us all!" It was like this for most of the journey back, but they all had to admit that it must have been a marvellous little place once upon a time, a small farm in its own right, a couple of pigs, couple of cows, a horse, a few ducks and chickens and a dog, I daresay. I sat quietly nursing my disillusions while Greg settled contentedly smiling under his dense dark beard. He'd done well out of the trip, got himself a sideboard of unquestionable antiquity which would show a handsome profit once it had been stripped; conversely, I was the one that got nowt for nowt!

I broke the news to Cari, painting a true picture and emphasising that the one thing we didn't possess, money, was the one thing it would take to restore the place. It crossed my mind that there would also be no paperwork to prove that the place was ours once it had been restored. The whole thing was given a good going-through and I mentioned how the landscape, the sense of going back in time, was rich about the place, a tantalizing consideration adding fuel to the idea of discovering the idyllic dimension of a more self-sufficient and natural way of life than it was possible to achieve in a modern world. This aspect was fruitful within my mind;

a voice within me was saying, "You only need a roof over your head, the rest is what you make of it, a challenge; stuff the regulations, be free of clerks in offices; go 'gypsy', see what it's like!" I rather liked this call-of-the-wild thing, it felt like the last possibility for avoiding a tamer, more predictable form of existence ...it was showing me the direction that my soul-spirit needed: if wilderness could be purchased, they'd be selling it like bottled water!

Murphy came over, his thoughts of wild Wales stealing him from his beloved Dartmoor. The feeling of going back in time was what had stuck in his mind too. What we discussed wasn't so much to do with the restoration of a cowshed, but more to do with the treasures still to be found in the ancient hedgerows and wild waysides. Ages-old oakwoods still clung to the sides of hills, marshes of willow and alder held the rains for weeks and months before softly draining the sweet waters into the streams and rivers, sustaining a natural upland marsh habitat the likes of which we'd only dreamed about, a natural history of pure fascination.

The more I thought about it, the more restless I became and the greater grew the hunger inside me. Clearing the place out and propping up the roof seemed straightforward enough, and could be done without anyone knowing. Part of the attraction after all was in trying to find a new kind of freedom, away from petty bureaucratic rules and regulations. What's more, doing it in secret was the only way we could ever afford it. Once Cari saw it for herself she was keen on the idea and was more than happy to confront whatever hardships might be involved and the boys all loved the idea of being amongst animals as well as so many relatives. The idea was selling itself; Murphy was eager to give up his job in Devonport Dockyard and live off his savings for a while, move up to Wales and get started. We decided to go for it!

Paradise Lost

At weekends, Murphy and I started going up to make a start on cleaning the muck and rubbish from the inside. We wedged-in freshly cut timbers to support the roof and sagging bedroom floor. I managed to purchase a battered old caravan from one of Gareth's farming friends and had it towed to a spot near the farm in the shelter of a steep wood. Murphy now had a place to sleep and could stay up and work on his own. Meanwhile I took a temporary job in television during my summer college vacation, working in Plymouth as a designer, anxious to raise the vital funds we were going to need and to provide Murphy with whatever he needed to sustain him in the caravan. Each Friday evening I piled the van with his provisions and drove up for the two days of back-breaking work. Once we had created a reasonable dry area in the back lean-to calf pen, we made a trip to a builder's suppliers to load up with several bags of cement and order a delivery of sand, gravel and concrete blocks. I then added a heavy metal wheelbarrow to our armoury, together with ropes, string wire, large rolls of heavy-duty polythene, buckets, a spirit-level, hammers, nails, a stiff yard-broom, axes, trowels, saws, chisels, shovels, pliers, wire-cutters, pick, crowbar, sledge-hammer, nail-remover, ladder, steel toe-capped wellington boots, industrial gloves, plasters - a never ending assortment of essentials, together with a large supply of candles, matches and a brand new paraffin pressure lamp complete with methylated spirits and enough paraffin to fuel it for a month, the only item remotely indicative of a standard of living of any sort!

The 'private lane', as it had been referred to, proved to be every bit as ambiguous as the description of the 'cottage' had been. An inspection showed it to be entirely submerged and sunken back to marsh, more like a canal than a lane, utterly impenetrable, a huge disappointment which would require heavy plant-hire machinery and a damned more stone than ever I could afford to put it right, the only consolation being that it gave the place an even greater degree of isolation. And so, wearily, we had to cart everything by hand across a marshy field and over a slippery steep hill. I thought that the wheelbarrow and ropes might come in handy here, but heavy things like bags of cement very soon sank the wheel deep down beyond its axle, and even ropes couldn't budge it then. Eventually we got all the stuff over, doing it the hard way, and we then cleared an area of grass verge in the lane and marked where the concrete blocks, sand and gravel had to be tipped.

Into the autumn Murphy and I continued to work at clearing the cowshed down to a manageable shell, laboriously carting sand, gravel and heavy concrete blocks across the marsh to be stored under polythene in the back lean-to, which miraculously still had its corrugated asbestos roof intact. With winter now approaching, we decided to stay put on the cliff and make our move in the spring, by which time we should have made a start on rebuilding the wall and I'd still be earning money to pay the bills. Murphy stayed in the caravan a while longer and laid the footings of the new wall, but after a couple of weeks of worsening, extreme weather and abysmal insanitary conditions he was glad to temporarily throw in the towel and bide his time back in the south- west, where Dartmoor suddenly seemed like the South Pacific by comparison.

Time simply melted and I handed in my notice at college, feeling an uneasy lump in my throat as I did so, especially on realising the shock that it caused, made worse by knowing that their expectations were that I was moving in order to further my career in lecturing. How was I to tell them that I was leaving in order to try living in a cowshed?! My resignation was made to seem more like an insult when I tried to explain that my artistic hunger stemmed from the fact that I was still young and unexplored within myself. I needed to feel life raw and rude upon my entire senses and try to discover a kind of wilder closeness and understanding that would help turn life into an art-form in a baring of myself under God's burning eye. This was a thousand light-years from any 'drop-out' ideology; I could never belong to anything that wasn't an essential part of a worthwhile and wholesome greater belonging. I'd never have an idle hour to burden me with its deadweight; all I wanted was to experience a more divine closeness with 'nature', to be part of the questions and not so readily the answers, to discover my own logic before succumbing to the dusty old beast of convention. Nobody seemed to understand this, they just shook their heads and tried to smile, the insult now being firmly upon myself.

It transpired that, when Gareth acquired the hill farm, part of the estate was another smallholding not far from the cowshed. It was a long building, one half of it house, the other half stock-buildings, together with a Dutch-barn, pig-sty and a pond; he kept a few stock cows wintering over there and it was decided that, once the winter eased and the ground dried out a bit, our caravan would be re-sited there, tucked away round the back of the stock-buildings in relative shelter beside the pond. The house part was now empty and was up for sale and it wasn't long before it had attracted the attention of one of Murphy's friends who'd heard from him just what an unspoiled and beautiful part of the world this was, in particular what a bargain the house was. It wasn't empty for very long and Murphy had now got himself somewhere else to stay.

Spring tenderly arrived on the cliff, the kittens were growing and had been given names, 'Tony' after a bully on the school bus, and 'Sorrel' after the herb which we gathered to add to our salads; I commented that this was a girl's name, but the boys wouldn't hear of it, so 'Sorrel' it was! Greg had rather taken a fancy to our hut and jumped in with an offer to buy it, but we weren't going to be tempted by a meagre one hundred pounds, especially when it had cost us closer to a thousand. A more realistic offer came via Laura, a friend of Cari's down in the village; her Buddhist family friends, fresh from Nepal, were in need of a place of tranquillity for meditation, where they might also grow a few things. News of this prompted Greg to increase his offer by a small amount, but we were still not impressed and proceeded with the other, discovering in the process that even Buddhists, with all their inner tranquillity, could rattle out a few decibels when it came to haggling over the price! The 'Guru' amongst them questioned my reason for painting, insisting that this was a form of materialism that I was sadly burdened with. Whatever magical powers and enlightenment they may have possessed, I could never share with them their ability to sit for hours cross-legged on the hard floor doing apparent breathing exercises, making humming noises and smoking what I took to be herbal cigarettes, which must have been in particularly short supply as they all had to share the same one; it smelled more like a vicarage bonfire than it did a cigarette! I knew for sure that I was burdened by a lack of something when the 'Guru' insisted that there was a tiger in the room and that I was clearly the only one that couldn't see it. I wondered what else there might be lurking about the place; I knew that there were rats and adders, but I decided to leave these for them to find, as maybe I'd been seeing things, or perhaps not seeing things!

There were reputed to be dragons where we were going, what's more I knew for sure that snipe and woodcock lived in the marshes and woodlands, and I knew also that we'd be seeing polecats by torchlight and catch sight of the odd red kite in passing; I didn't need invisible tigers or anything other than fresh air to fill me with all the light that I needed.

We packed our spartan possessions, a few books and utility items; my numerous, fairly large canvases would either have to go on the van roof or be given away to friends. As a farewell gift, I offered a large landscape to Laura who surprised me by saying that she could only accept it if I was prepared to let her and the others paint whatever they liked over it, should they so wish, this being a test to determine as to whether or not I was burdened by materialism. I responded by saying that if they wanted to paint their own pictures I would gladly provide them with empty canvases, but my attitude was suffice for them to write me off as another sad materialist devoid of their special kind of enlightenment. She liked the painting well enough, so I left her with it regardless of what its future might be; there were plenty more where that came from!

Other items indicative of my confounded materialism were... cheap binoculars, camera, guitar, auto-harp, a mouth-organ or two and a couple of tin whistles and two bikes, one being my very first old fixed-wheel, hand-built, time-trial bike, the other a really mean road-racing machine with umpteen gears; nostalgia and function together. I loved them both and I guess that cycle-racing was in my blood. Apart from a few jacket-pocketfuls of note-books full of writing, I hereby rested my case and pleaded guilty to the charges against me! Cari's most obvious claim to materialism lay in the cello which I had bought as a present for her from one of my students; she had once played violin with the National Youth Orchestra of Wales but hadn't touched a violin since, life somehow always managing to re-organise the priorities. But I felt strongly, especially now, that life had to be shaped, bullied and fondled into becoming something closer to the needs of our hearts and not be allowed to go stampeding away, dragging us behind it to where we didn't want to be. Whenever I took the boys up into my arms and clowned till they were blissfully helpless with laughter, I saw all too clearly that childhood only ever touched lightly, briefly. I felt compelled to share this precious moment of time with them, learning, growing and sharing in a great broad swathe of all sorts of wonderful things, letting painting pictures, blowing whistles and acting the fool become as normal as breathing ... or riding a bike even!

I started to stock up on artist's materials in readiness for future times of artistic famine, and I paid one of my fine-art student friends to construct and stretch for me five large canvases, each of them five foot square. When I picked them up my eyes nearly popped out as they were far larger than I had calculated; somehow I had to fit them onto the roof-rack and they dwarfed the entire van, making the journey up to Wales rather more eventful than I had planned. I took Chris and my bird-watching mate Steve up for this trip, and we made a very early start on this particular Saturday morning: a long slow drive, top-heavy and aerodynamically destabilised. We passed through Ashburton, heartened by the sparseness of the traffic travelling in our direction. The last thing I wanted to do was to hold other vehicles up by my somewhat slower progress, but, to be on the safe side, I pulled in at a lay-by just to check the load and make sure that it didn't need tightening down. Chris scrambled out first; I thought he was fooling when he said in a yokel-sort of way, "It's gone ... roof-rack, the lot ... gone!" I shot out, not appreciating his humour, and I gawped across the empty roof to his gawping-back face; I was speechless! Steve struggled out muttering, "What's going on out there, you pair?" His first reaction was a low snigger, then he broke into a fit of laughter. I stared back down the hill, not a vehicle anywhere in sight. "Bloody hell!" I gasped. "C'mon, get back in, we've got to find it!" I turned the van round and sped off back down the hill, rounded a bend, then could see stationary vehicles in the distance with figures standing in the road. I pulled over in front of a large tanker-driver who was trying to disentangle my precious fragmented cargo from beneath his wagon. He stood up full-size and fixed me in his stare. "I've been following you for a few miles. I couldn't believe what I was seein' ... this thing just suddenly stood up like a sail, then it took off an' come flyin' through the air straight at me. If I hadn't slapped my anchors on it'd have come straight through me cab. You're bloody lucky, mate! Don't know what it's supposed to be but it ain't no bloody use now ... dunna seem to 'ave damaged me wagon any ...it's your lucky day, mate!"

I didn't feel so very lucky as I helped drag out the tattered and splintered fragments, and the twisted roof-rack which miraculously looked as if it could be straightened out. Even more miraculously, one of the canvases was more or less intact apart from a few small holes scuffed from the road surface. We feverishly set to work straightening out the roof-rack and managed to re-attach it, making double-sure this time that it was screwed down securely before fixing on the one remaining canvas; the rest we bundled into the back of the van, then waited whilst the traffic started to flow again before turning around and resuming the journey. In stunned disbelief we made our way, unable to understand how so big a load could have parted company without anyone knowing it. I hadn't felt a thing, none of us had, no twitch of the steering-wheel, no noise or sudden jerk, nothing; we could have easily gone on quite happily all the way into Wales without being any the wiser. This was a trip well worth forgetting!

Over the cliff, swallows, martins and swifts were coming in off the sea along with cuckoos, warblers, redstarts and hosts of others, a whole tide of them moving inland. I spent a few divinely isolated moments of sadness sitting alone by Rame Head, with the thunderous sea-spray moistening my face and with fulmars circling as I silently cried my farewell to precious memories spent here. There was no turning back now, I was heading where just a handful of these swallows were now heading; the adventure had begun...

Paradise Re-Discovered

We have just arrived from Cornwall, Cari, myself, three boys and three cats. The caravan, our immediate temporary home, is parked for us out of sight, out of the way behind the rancid beast-moaning byres, next to a corrugated-iron implement shed emptied for our use and close by a big shallow pond where a couple of Muscovy ducks have staked their claim on the world, with the uncomfortable appearance of creatures that sleep each night with their heads in a saucepan of boiling beetroot. As we ease ourselves in, it begins to dawn on us that we are in a kind of heaven, the feeling really quite beyond belief: a tight fit but a sense of this being 'something else', mysterious, intangible, everywhere about us. I feel an urge to paint the initial impact of the wildly lyrical up-and-down patchwork landscape; it eats into me, a marvellous relationship existing between sky and earth, as they compete in a most exhilarating diverse harmony, alive and ever-changing. I know that I will have to re-organise my priorities in accordance with the new order of things, try to let just seeing and feeling be suffice, so that my desire to paint might ease somewhat and allow me to paint more with words upon the pages on my notebooks and in stolen moments and more sublimely upon the six strings of my softly spoken guitar. Much as I am cursing the loss of my canvases, I recognise the irony of their loss in assisting me to find the perfect balance amongst these things.

It is cosy in the caravan but not without its flaws: large holes have somehow got ripped into the sides and, when I open the back window to let some air in, the whole window falls away, coming to rest on the cats' box. I soon fix this back on with string, but this is only the beginning. During heavy rain I fall through the floor, and leaks appear everywhere. I cure the main one with polythene, but not before it has soaked our bed; we learn to live with the other leaks and to remain aware that I've only done a temporary job on the hole in the floor. It really is quite exciting, every single one of us feeling a brand new closeness to the world about us, and we haven't even started yet!

The cats are settling in nicely and are looking in really good condition, plump and cuddly. I put this down to an enriched diet of mice about the place, the 'snack-you-can-eat-between-meals' sort of thing. Everything about us seems to be settling with us, getting to be the focus of things; chickens from the farm congregate under the caravan and the jet-black bad-tempered male Muscovy duck is always standing sentry on the milk-crate that we have as a doorstep, his slightly better tempered white spouse never far from him.

I indulge myself thoroughly in the curiosity of the boys by exploring and becoming familiar with this new world about us, listening to the birds and imitating their calls on whistles, selecting phrases whilst at the same time being aware of the vast space shaped and cradled in the bosoms of diminishing hills. We play a musical game: Spencer is the shapes of hills, Rowan is the birds and myself the ballooning clouds; we blow ourselves blue in the face while Robin seems to have his fingers stuck fast in his ears and is grimacing with cats and fowls in close attendance. We wander down the field where the football is begging to be kicked to death; our relaxation is complete after we have raced and chased and are all knackered and ready for a cup of tea. After I have produced the most exquisite brew, all of us go off along the narrow winding lane holding hands and fooling, hidden sweetly from the world, a very happy family.

A gander and a couple of geese arrive on the scene and waddle about the place hissing the whole time as though the world is theirs alone; there are half a dozen ducks as well, so the pond is really muddied now. I notice that on the wild side there are a pair of moorhens too. Our old battered caravan is at the very centre of this growing menagerie, which has now been swelled by a dozen heavy old hens and a brute of a cockerel from next door, together with a farm-dog that has recognised paradise here; the paradise however is not without its moments of nightmare and frustration.

Mankind had already declared himself to be superior to the animals, a smug assumption coming simply from the fact that he ate them, so he automatically considered himself to be boss as a result. I am now discovering a new more involved pecking order, finding out who really is superior and who is inferior. I am rapidly coming to the conclusion that it is these cretins that dominate over me. They can so easily impose their presence on me, but I cannot impose mine over them no matter how I try. It has taken only the slightest smell of food coming from the caravan to bring about a demonstration of this new pecking order that we have got ourselves caught up in and, more importantly, where we find ourselves to be positioned within it.

I chase the cockerel and his chickens out from the sink and immediately become undefended at the rear, allowing mister Muscovy to nip in and flap clumsily up onto the gas cooker where he can peck the porridge in the saucepan. Attempts to coax him out fail as he takes off into the sleeping area, knocks everything off the sideboard and defecates on the beds, pecking me viciously and still refusing to go outside. I can now see all the chickens, cockerel and ducks clamouring as they are back inside scoffing the spilled porridge, while under the grill my toast is on fire and Cari is outside unable to get back in because she knows that, as soon as she makes a move, they'll all join me in the bedroom being savaged by a half-hundredweight duck!

The cats now all want to be part of the action and the boys are having a real battle trying to restrain them as the old gander struts up for a closer look, hissing louder than a punctured tractor. The curtains catch fire as the toast is cremated, and I am in a swirling sea of feathers and acrid smoke as I rip curtains, and the hooks holding them, away from the wall dislodging the window which falls out and smashes on the old ammunition box which is the cats' home! The only species amongst this lot that is experiencing stress right now is 'Homo Sapiens', every other species on hand is totally, blatantly unconcerned and absolutely cool, ready and willing to repeat the performance at the slightest opportunity that we offer to them through our negligence.

Another of their rituals is to congregate inside the implement shed where my two racing bikes and canvases are stored; the hens take soil baths in there and the ducks preen in sprawled-out luxury. A goose has chosen a corner behind my canvases in which to nest on a pile of hay and will not tolerate humans going anywhere near, the boys having all been pecked. Black mister Muscovy is just a sinister old sod, no-one knows what he is thinking, but it's plain to see that he has included us as part of his world, with a disregard so total as to be beyond belief.

There is no mains water in the area, so ancient wells are the order of the day; our water has to come in plastic carriers from such a well down the track towards the lane, while the farm animals get theirs from a well sunk into the hill, and others use the pond. We do our best to conserve the calor gas by gathering wood and making a fire outside on which we can boil the kettle and bake potatoes; food in saucepans is never safe from the animals and their contempt for our neat little twig fire is as great as their contempt for us. Every day is an escalating circus of animalised pandemonium; these are not wild animals, but their behaviour is perfectly wild and without any trace of domesticity. It is something invisible and totally inexplicable that keeps the moorhens from our door, a different kind of wildness. Likewise with the foxes, which are plentiful: not only have I seen their grey-white droppings about the place but have smelled them strongly every day, a reminder for me to tolerate and love my exasperating friends while I can, as foxes don't take prisoners.

This balancing act with animals is keeping us on our toes the whole time, but we're coping and we are all working together, learning to value things anew. The importance of string and penknives, good pockets, polythene bags and a good stout stick; the additional luxury of a pencil and notebook help give majesty to these precious moments in life. The caravan already has ventilation through holes in walls and floor, but it is so cramped as to require additional air to circulate; this can come only through windows and door, both of which give access to invasion from outside. The windows on this battered old thing are not to be tampered with, as I already discovered to my cost, and so 'sentry duty' seems like an option worth trying, the door wide open with someone sitting on the milk crate keeping the animals out while the rest of us got on with other things. Rain soon puts an end to this arrangement and a new problem of washing and drying clothes raises its ugly head. We string up a clothes line in the implement shed, running the gauntlet of our feathered friends ... this is war!

Unable to be wild ourselves, we have to make preparations for Spencer and Rowan to resume their schooling down in the valley once the Easter break is over; it will be daunting for them being amongst so many new faces and with a new infant pecking order to get used to. We are anxious not to have them feeling too much like outsiders, so we make sure that, not only do we take them, but are there also to pick them up and meet their new friends. Meanwhile Robin seems to have found some scissors and has snipped Bootsy's beautiful white whiskers off; he then tries to do the same with Sorrel, but the cat manages to escape halfway through the process and now looks a bit strange.

It occurs to me that Robin has a 'way' with animals and is totally without fear of them. Though he is no bigger than a goose, when an aggrieved goose looks him in the eye it's the goose that backs off, they don't do that with me, that's for sure! He just seems to want to be with animals, close in their midst and free of the disciplines of humankind. It's perplexing as well as frustrating to find him wrapped up in cats, cuddling up to a sheepdog whilst at the same time stroking chickens and with a grin so smug, so big and broad as to dominate everything around. I fear that he may have chosen to become one of them and to abandon the human race altogether, reckoning somehow that he has this choice available to him. I see that I'm going to have to try harder to prove to him that being a human is the best arrangement in the end, but I'm baffled as to where to begin!

The other goose has now taken over the pigsty next to the implement shed, and the gander is a major health hazard, protecting his wives with menacing zeal. Everything to him is quite simply another gander and to demonstrate his unfailing devotion to his ladies, he does his best to annihilate all other ganders, proudly waddling back to each of them to boast and lie through his back teeth that he has just, murdered the bloke-gander, has slain the tractor-gander, put paid to the sheepdog-gander, likewise the cow-gander and the muck-spreader gander; even in the gander-night he brags of having exterminated the moon-gander in his determination to safeguard the purity of his species and to doom it to survival ... provided there are not too many Christmases or red dogs in the night!

Now that we have settled into our makeshift home and the boys have started at their new school, I am anxious to turn my mind to more vital issues and make a start on the cowshed. When I look across the fields towards the marsh I can just catch a glimpse of the chimney peering over the hill amongst the trees, and I long to see smoke coming from it, signifying that we have moved in at last; but I know that we've a lot to do before that magical moment is upon us.

We haven't seen Murphy of late, as he's been preoccupied with helping his friends with their move and going off on trips to buy goats and poultry. Mercifully the goats have not discovered the pleasure of our company and instead have been tethered along the banks in the lane where they are showing themselves to be more effective than any council gang with scythes. The chickens, on the other hand, cannot be tethered and are so blatantly free-range that I expect them all to have their own passports. I have the comfort of knowing that once I do resume work on the cowshed, Murphy will suddenly pop up out of nowhere, if only to point out to me where I'm going wrong! He's anxious to show me how a wall really should be built, so he won't be pleased to know that I've started without him.

Meanwhile a battle of wills is raging between Robin and the gander and I fear that it may only be resolved by the gander falling in love with him, because pecking him isn't making a blind bit of difference and could quite easily result in the gander's beak getting damaged, or perhaps snipped off with scissors. Also a trail of dead moles is becoming a feature between the nettled fence and the caravan door; the cats are bringing them nightly, little gifts for us. The poor moles, they just throw up their castles, sniff the star-smelling dark air, say a prayer clasping their sweet pink hands, then ... Goodnight Vienna! Nobody will eat poor mole in his black velvet suit, there's something about him that repulses even the old sod Muscovy; maybe it's that dark clergyman look that he has, so clerical and funereal. The chickens prod with their beaks to turn the corpses over, hoping to find maggots underneath - no maggots, no business! Nobody will eat the mole. Each morning I bury their little bodies, Bootsy grins with a smile wider than a saucer of cream, and I ask the boys if they know of any reason why nothing will eat the moles. "Probably stinks!" Spencer giggles, setting the others off into uncontrollable laughter. Here am I feeling sad and everyone else is corpsing over the possibility of a mole stinking! I'm vigilant in my effort to remove the corpses from sight because I fear that Robin may well carry out his own scientific research using fingers, nostril and possibly mouth in providing me with the answer to the question I'm wishing I hadn't asked.

There's been a fair amount of rain lately and new vegetation is exploding from the ground, so we get drenched whenever we walk even the shortest distance. Inside the caravan we are finding it snug to listen to the raindrops rattling on the roof, but unfortunately the rain has caused the door to wedge and it requires a thumping hard shoulder to re-open once it has been closed. I fear it is now only a question of time before a hefty blow opens it on the wrong side, because all the remaining screws holding the hinges are corroded and hanging in only by the grace of God, as too is the toilet door which is right next to it and is similarly affected by the wet. This all reminds me to get on with the cowshed, even without Murphy if necessary; I can't wait to get started.

The buzzing, drumming sound of a snipe hung in the air, a

wild and priceless ingredient making space a plankton of magical particles; the warblers are coming through, as are the redstarts and pied flycatchers; the wheatears passed through earlier, just two days and they were gone. By contrast the cows are being given the freedom of the fields once more, after a prolonged winter without exercise or any succulent vegetation. They stagger out like busted deckchairs, stiff and bony and immediately succumb to the ravages of diarrhoea, no longer having to survive on dried-up dusty old hay and the grey pellets of more mysterious smelly stuff, no longer plagued by pestilential worms and mites which otherwise the rains would have washed away. Some of them have calved during their time of confinement and all are unsteady on their feet and seemingly bewildered. As we draw nearer to the cowshed we hear the cracking of sticks over the cows' bony backsides and the high-pitched voices of the farmer and his son driving them to their new sustenance despite the moaning beasts being physically unfit and lacking in the art of movement right now. The working dog is barking for his keep and he's biting for it also, but the cows are placid and have no way of expressing their bewilderment at all this sudden change that has come about them.

We wave to Gareth and he waves back as the ground behind us suddenly shakes and rumbles. We all spin round to see Murphy coming thundering down noisily upon us like a runaway goods train, egg-yolk round his mouth, jacket billowing and a new stubbly beard to show for his absence. Over on the far track down to the marsh pastures, the Hereford bull is snorting the air; he's standing staunchly there, Viking-like in his surveillance, probably more concerned over flies and lice on his shit-encrusted leather than on bigger prey like us. We take some comfort from knowing that the animals don't pose any threat to us, but I feel that we're going to have to keep our wits about us once the bull has got his second wind. He'll be watching possessively over his cows and may well consider in his bull-brain that we pose some sort of threat to him ... after all, he's not there to make the place look pretty ... and it's Spring!

Ringworm is obviously rife amongst the herd and they stop to rub themselves frantically on any available twig, thorn or wire, some rubbing against trees and one kneeling to rub against a bank.

I'm feeling a bit concerned over the supports we have holding up the top half of the place and I know that the sticking-out hacked-off branches will offer the most ideal scratching things. If they go in there and rub themselves on them, there's a good chance that the whole lot will come tumbling down. My priorities are plain and simple: I have to get that wall up without delay, as only then can the cows be kept out.

I see the tiny figure of Robin standing in his red oilskin, dwarfed beside a mountain of sand and concrete blocks, staring in total disbelief up through the bedroom floor and out to the clouds sailing high beyond the roof. He has no possible idea of this ever being a home and I spare him the thought that the small shitted-up calf parlour is going to be his bedroom. It's better that I make progress first and have him so impressed by the transformation that he's begging to be living in it. He and Cari go outside searching about the place for treasures; Cari has the ability to make tiny things seem like treasures, and they are soon amongst the lichens and mosses which encrust the wall in all their miniaturised complexity.

The back lean-to has only a stable-like half-door and the swallows are darting in and out through the open top half like missiles, making it necessary for us to protect our heads whenever we go in there. They are also zooming in and out of the upstairs room, and they make a joyful babbling twitter in their uncontrollable excitement to start work on restoring their old mud-homes and building new ones. We are all in a frantic state of home-building and I can hear scuffling noises in the chimney where the jackdaws have moved in with their crude carpentry skills; starlings are already nesting in several places within the crumbling walls and cannot conceal or contain their exuberance. As I check to see that the cement hasn't hardened in its bags, I see where a wren has built a nest in a hole in the wall, and I can hear the wren scolding outside in the yard.

I fetch water from the ditch to feed Murphy's demanding cuckoo-like enthusiasm and on my second trip I take a shovel with me to dig a deepish catchment area amongst the cress so that I can fill the bucket in one scoop instead of having to top-up dozens of times with a small saucepan that leaks. My mind is now addressing an obvious water problem. I'm thinking of building a dam and having a large water-tub to catch the rain off the lean-to roof. We're going to need as much water as nature can provide for cement and concrete, as well as for washing clothes and bodies and cleaning things generally.

I get the wheelbarrow and Cari and Robin join in to help load it with stones and bricks for the building of a dam of sorts. It's quite a steep and very cluttered bit of ground under the apple and damson trees at the front, and there's an ancient dung-mountain running downhill from the back of the crumbling old stone barn where an even more ancient walnut tree stands crippled and twisted by storms. Only a couple of branches remain growing crazily from a broad and tortured hollow trunk, the fact that it is still alive amazes me. Two single-stranded barbed wire fences line the banks of the lowering ditch, and there are damson trees all the way down to where it skirts the wood. Negotiating myself under the barbed wire and down the slippery bank to the water is not without its hazards; should I slip during the process, the barbed wire is all that I can grab hold of to save me, so it's pure pot-luck whether I rip my hands on it. Robin finds my predicament quite hilarious, especially when my worst fears are realised and I rip the sleeve almost completely off my jacket and go arse-first into the deep hole I'd previously dug, sending up a huge cascade of sludgy water. Robin has never laughed so much and Cari is pretty legless too as I regain composure, smugly proud in a secret sort of way that, even in that catastrophic split-second, I retained the presence of mind not to grab onto the barbed wire and risk ripping my hands. Whether or not a torn-off sleeve, two wellies full of tadpoles and a high-tide line just above my belly-button is preferable to a cut finger is something I don't really want to go into!

When it quietens down we can hear the sound of the shovel scraping as Murphy obliviously mixes cement in the cowshed and I notice the swallows settling on the mud just a short distance away, filling their beaks with it before flying back up to their beams. High over the marsh several buzzards are circling and we watch them being buzzed by crows. The buzzards don't seem bothered by this brawling behaviour, but the crows remain scared, too afraid to confront the buzzards face to face, so they sneak up from behind in a sort of clumsy cowardly dive and then escape, their din echoing all across the valley. We watch this aerial dueling until they drift away, and we are struck by the perfect silence that exists around and beyond all sounds. I put my finger to my lips and whisper to Robin ... "Shhh! Listen to all the different sounds you can hear." I remain perfectly still, up to my welly-tops in ditch-water, the tapestried silence is quite divine. The water in the ditch is tinkling like the frail bells of icicles, a far cockerel utters a sighing, dying lament across the air, a farmer whistles his dog piercingly and faint distant jays squawk deep woodlands apart between songthrush and blackbirds warbling. Pigeons coo like smudged pastel colours, nuthatches pipe, woodpeckers drum and robins ripple all around; nothing is noise, all are sounds held within a great valley of silence. Only the perfect orchestration of nature can produce a silence so sublime. Cari looks at me with the same speechless grin that my face is wearing and a glance at Robin's face tells me that he too is entranced - but also that his nostrils are dribbling stuff that will surely choke him unless someone gets to him quickly with a tissue or a fistful of grass!

Our dam is built: it isn't spectacular and leaks rather badly but we can add to it by degrees, remembering that the higher the water gets the stronger we must build the dam. I feel happy with our tinkling little waterfall and the sweet splashing music it makes. It's really quite deceiving because there's a fair depth of water there, especially after my previous efforts with the shovel, so there shouldn't be too many tadpoles in the cement from now on. The new wall is coming on a treat: we're starting our third row, having laid a strip of asphalt as a pretend damp-course, but we have long since abandoned any idea of having a cavity wall. I can't afford such luxuries: all that's needed is a solid, strong wall which will adequately support the bedroom floor and the roof. When it's finished I will waterproof it, there's bound to be some miracle stuff on the market that can either be sprayed on or applied like tar with a brush. We'll take it one day at a time, no big plans, just a reaping of moments as they avail themselves, inventing on the hoof.

The most dangerous part is not the open end-wall, but the front one which has only partly fallen down. There's an ever present danger of more of it coming crashing down as we try to knit the new wall into it. It has collapsed as far as the old front door, which is jammed solid and twisted, distorted under the tons of stone that have cracked and dropped onto it, making it like a bomb that's waiting to go off. We must be thoughtful and sensible in how we nudge into this unstable mass, to restrain it from coming down on our heads.

With the third row now completed, we can concentrate on strengthening the front wall from the base upwards, knocking out the door as soon as it's safe to do so and getting rid of it completely, then extending the wall right across to where the existing wall is strong, using the stone from the original wall and binding it in with loads of concrete for extra strength.

The tall front window is a write-off, with rot-holes and splits, all the glass having been busted out by cows and I daresay by the odd stone-throwing passing cow-hand over the years; its main function now is that of supporting the wall above it. There are gaps around it where I have noticed bluetits coming and going from a long-established family connection there. I shall fix polythene to help keep out the weather, but the gaps can remain as part of our ventilation system!

The short day has been fruitful and we feel pleased with the start we have made as we stroll back across the lane under a skyful of clouds tumbling over from the west. The cows are standing like statues, their bones protruding like knees under a sheet, as they chew the new grass hypnotically in slow circular mouth movements. This converts instantaneously into dark green slop which explodes huge distances from their back ends as though forced by high pressure hoses. The bull is similarly occupied in perplexed lethargy, allowing us to make it back to the lane at leisure before the threatening rain starts in earnest. Cari and I decide to pick the boys up from school in the van and then drive to a village further up the valley to do some much needed shopping, plan ourselves a nice meal and top up with cat food while we're at it. Murphy ambles back to join his landlady, who is crouching milking a goat further along the lane. I've never seen Murphy so happy - it must be all those new-laid eggs and goat's milk in his tea that he's getting!

All Heaven Ablaze

The lane to the school passes another neighbour's tiny holding, perched right at the head of the valley, a spectacular gaping sprawled yawn of miles upon miles of beauty so intense as to be bordering on vulgarity. Our remote neighbour waves and I toot my horn back; he looks appropriately gaunt and rugged and we comment on how nice it will be to meet him. From here the narrow lane dives down steeply, twisting and winding, passing a couple of half-hidden cottages and old hanging oak and beech woods, high primrosed banks that blot out the sky; down, down past a smart spick and span former school-house, then a derelict old school which has dense ivy clambering all over it and elder trees growing from the walls, even one growing from the chimney. Behind this, an ancient oak wood reaches away hugging the steep curving hillside: I can't wait to go off wandering through it; it looks so inviting, just like I imagined the whole wild world to have looked thousands of years ago. A puddled track goes winding away through another beech wood and vanishes. We see a spring in the forested hillside on the left, rapidly gathering into a crystal torrent that races beside the lane then dives deeply beneath it on a sharp bend before coming out on the other side, taking on the appearance of a proper brook in its urgency to join up with an even bigger one down beside the school at the bottom where the boys will be waiting on a little wooden bridge. Here there are towering Lawson's Cypresses with lots of roosting places for tree-creepers sculptured into their thick soft bark. It's lovely seeing the boys there waving as we pull in, just as the rain starts. They pile in, happy and in high spirits, shouting to their friends and waving as we drive away.

The rain is coming on spitefully and a brisk wind bustles about in the village street as we search for a shop; our luck is in and we land ourselves a large crusty loaf, a rubbery old cauliflower and some battered looking potatoes. I notice another bigger grocery store further down the street, so we head off to avoid the basket of mushrooms which have spent a week quietly dying in the shop window. Once our visit is completed, we return to the hills and settle in to a rain-rattling evening and a miraculous meal of cauliflower cheese and potatoes with thick wedges of crusty bread to polish our plates.

The wind keeps up its pushing and shoving; it's going to be one of those nights with the leaks all starting to reveal themselves again. I busy myself applying sticky-tape to stop the drips before resigning us all to an early night and the saving of a bit of paraffin and candle. Suddenly it's broad daylight, and something weird is happening! I race to the door and Cari snatches the curtains from the steamed-up window. A massive fiery object is racing across the sky, lighting up all the clouds as it passes silently behind them. It's all happening so fast, it's unbelievable, the object is dazzling fluorescent green, almost spectral, and is dripping burning fragments like candle-wax; cloud after cloud just burst into illumination, a frightening tableau all across the heavens from the south-east to the north-west, then there are two loud explosions and it has vanished over the horizon, plunging us into blackness once more. "What the bloody hell was that?" I gasp and Cari is speechless. The boys are all deep asleep and have missed it. We are in a state of shocked confusion, not knowing what to expect next ... a nuclear explosion perhaps ... but all is quiet, save for the sheep on the hills bleating their own dismay. We forage for the small battery radio, but the batteries are so low that it only manages a few tortured squeaks and whines as we despairingly search for a news bulletin which might explain what we have just seen. I make a note of the time and the date, 9.25 p.m., 25th April. At ten o'clock I succeed in finding a faint voice on the radio which says, "We are getting reports of lights in the sky over parts of North Wales this evening. This is believed to be a satellite burning up on re-entering the Earth's atmosphere." Now it gets exciting as further eye-witnesses report forest fires being started over North Wales and a burning object crashing into a bog in Northern Ireland: nothing has ever been this spectacular ... even the rain has stopped!

The boys are happy for us to walk them to school, meeting their friend Joan at the head of the valley where she lives with her grandparents in a hidden-away little cottage with the coincidental name of 'Thimble Hall'. Further down the hill we join up with her cousin Jemma who lives along the puddled track beyond the beech wood. "My Gramps saw God last night!" Joan informs her in a kind of joyful celebration, prouder than ever that God hasn't forgotten this humble little place and is keeping a watchful eye over it. "Norr!" Jemma gasps, "My Dad said that the sky was on fire and that it was Russia!" "God's in Russia as well, you know!" Joan points out in support of her Grandad. Meanwhile Robin demonstrates his powers of observation and changes the subject as he points to a buzzard flying low over the wood. "Badger!" he splutters and the other boys burst out laughing. "That's not a bloomin' badger, it's an eagle!" Spencer points out and Rowan falls about. The girls are still niggling over God and Russia as we see them all safely over the little wooden bridge to the playground, where tomorrow's giants are yet seeds before the dirt of time.

The post-van passes us on the way back and the driver peeps his horn in a 'Hello' kind of way. "That'd be a nice sort of job," I say to Cari; she agrees but has some reservation over the added dimensions of dogs and winter weather. We reach the top where our gaunt neighbour is gathering his post from a biscuit-tin nailed to a sycamore tree. He sees us and we can recognise that we're on a collision course, his body language says it all. "So you're the new people from the 'Wern', eh! Come over for a cuppa?" Much as I want to be getting on with the cowshed, this invitation is more of an order.

He's already leading the way with his large white dog, which is nothing like a sheep-dog, more of an Irish wolf-hound, Jack Russell, Corgi cross, a despicable creature with a slyness that would be hard to match. We are protected from it by the man's growls as we follow his bandy-legged gait over the small field, past a chicken-coop that hasn't got any chickens, across a tiny cow-shitted yard, menaced every inch of the way by this ill-tempered mongrel. "Damn you! Blast you! You bloody bitch animal!" he instructs the thing which is plainly not a bitch. Then I inadvertently put my foot on its bone and I feel a sickening thud like a sledge-hammer blow on the back of my leg. The bastard has bitten me! I yell and the devilish creature lopes off like an india-rubber demon, smiling and dribbling with the bone in its mouth.

Inside there is an old iron range with a fire idling in the grate, and a soot-encrusted kettle is sat belly-aching on the flames with a total unwillingness to boil. Years of mail clog the mantelpiece while, visible through the doorway, is a glass-case containing a badly stuffed cormorant with its head hanging off and foot-powder plastered all over it as a precaution against disease. This item dominates even an old piano with its mouth wide open and live twelve-bore cartridges strewn across the keys along with galvanised nails and a quarter-empty bottle of Captain Morgan rum; a twelve-bore shotgun is leaning against the wall, and I see a mouse strolling across the rotted bit of carpet. Robin is mesmerised by the cormorant in the case, believing it to be alive, albeit a bit sick! I roll up my trouser-leg to display my dog-bite, and ask for something to cleanse it with. I am handed a jar of water with two tadpoles wriggling in it, then am offered a bottle of Dettol and left to get on with it. I notice that already a large bruise has formed.

"Damn, you'll be alright, isn't it!" my neighbour laughs, rinsing cups in more tadpole water. "It's your own fault, if you will go treadin' on 'is bone, what d'you expect, man!" What surprises me is that he is not joking and he defends his mongrel still further, saying, "owd Bob ain't a bad dog ... lets me know when somebody's comin'!" "I'll bet he does!" I say sardonically.

"Did you see it last night ... the 'thing'?" I ask. "Norr! Damn missed it... had your pal round chin-waggin'... owd Thomas at Thimble Hall, he saw it like, reckons it was God. Caught 'im in the wood with 'is trousers round 'is ankles... frightened the hell out of 'im it did!" We all laugh and Dan adds, "I wouldn't mind havin' a quid for every time owd Thomas reckons he's seen the Almighty! 'E's seen 'im down at the pool and in the forest... even had 'im in the house he has!"

The tea is a deep terracotta colour and is made with tinned milk but it tastes surprisingly good. I just have to ignore the tea-leaves in case they might be related to frogs in some small way. "When are you plannin' on movin' in then?" he asks with a whiskery elfish grin that seems to say an awful lot. "That depends on whether the cows go and flatten it first!" I laugh in reply. "Damn, that owd place has been a cowshed for a good many years that I knows of... should 'ave been pulled down backalong ... 'tain't safe!" "Yeah, well... we'll give it a go, do our best; if it don't work out, at least we will have tried." I'm getting anxious to be over there now laying the next three or four rows of blocks and so I get to my feet in some discomfort from where the dog has left its mark. As we all walk back across the field to the lane, we belatedly get around to introducing ourselves: 'Dan' waves us off on our way.

Back at the caravan I bathe my injury and put a plaster on it, then change into my industrial wellies before heading off over to the cowshed. Cari has her domestic agenda to address; Robin has a separate one of his own, while the sky threatens with its poorly concealed plan. As I cover the last muddy yards I can hear Murphy already clattering about inside the place. He appears over his new wall and growls jokingly, "What the hell time do you call this?" "Got stuck over at Dan's place... and I got bitten by that sodding mongrel of his!" We very soon get round to the subject of last night's fiery object in the sky and he is furious that he missed it, but has heard reports on the radio. "They say it was a satellite burning up, Jimmy... what d'you think it was?" I shrug my shoulders: "The old fella at Thimble Hall reckons it was God, but I've never seen anything like it and I don't suppose I ever shall again... it was probably a UFO if you ask me." Murphy's eyes are wild and wide: "You're right, Jimmy... they know when satellites are coming back down, it'd have been on the news, we'd have been warned!"

I look about the place, getting the feel of it once more, Dan's words still ringing in my head, "Should have been pulled down!" I look at what we've already done and feel okay about it, especially seeing the swallows so ecstatic about what is obviously a palace to them. A fresh pile of twigs in the fireplace remind me that it is heaven too for the jackdaws in the chimney and I realise I must block the entire fireplace off so as to deter any person, invited or otherwise, from lighting a fire. I pile the grate up with concrete blocks and as many tools as I can find room for, explaining to Murphy my reason for doing this. He just laughs and shrugs his shoulders: "You and your birds!" "This place is theirs, Murph... it ain't mine, it belongs to them, I'm just a lodger here. I'm not joking, I really mean that. I want to live with them, and for them to live with me, we're all in this life-thing together, we're equals all of us."

Yesterday's bit of new wall is looking good - we're just a little bit proud of it! We'll have to get to town and pick up a couple of new windows and anything else we can think of; it's started to rain, so it's a good day for a bit of planning ahead. We work for a couple of hours until we're ready for the first window to go in. Then we pack up and splosh our way through an inquisitive bedraggled herd and a bull that already looks more than revived and is sniffing the air in a primeval sort of way, warning us to take no chances. There is cow-muck everywhere, mainly in close proximity to the cowshed, suggesting that the place provides some comfort and reassurance for them. I can't say that I'm over comforted by their apparent liking of the place, I feel inclined to rather cruelly drive them away whether they be equal or not, in fact I have a sneaking feeling that they're getting to be slightly more than equal! I notice that there are sheep now coming into the equation, ewes and lambs going wherever they please; their presence is more than likely due to them having escaped, probably from several different farms. "Subsidies, Jimmy!" Murphy chuckles. "Just think of all those lovely subsidies wandering about feeding themselves. The more you've got, the more you gets; bloody farmers, they've got it made!"

A Divinity of Humankind and the 'Max' Factor

Grey driving rain is hitting the windscreen as we follow the lanes into town. I buy two very basic pink-primed wooden windows, a couple of gallons of creosote and a large can of Jeyes fluid, then head back, picking up a large bag of Chelsea buns from a little café, sticky baked heaven no less! This treasure is dropped off at the caravan where Cari and Robin are just returning from a wet walk over the hill at the back, perfectly ripe for one of these precious gems. The day is becoming more and more uninviting and we all partake of tea and Chelsea buns before I give Murphy a nudge.

It's really slashing down with rain now and Murphy suggests that, after dropping the stuff off at the cowshed, we should motor out to a remote place that he's pin-pointed on his Ordnance Survey map, an agricultural Pandora's-box type of place that Dan had told him about last night. It sounds like a good idea, so we do what we have to, then head off for this place. Murphy's doing his impeccable back-seat driving from two inches away, as is his style, and we go up into the hills, into a cold dereliction of a landscape more lonesome than any nightmare. His map-reading is flawless as usual and we are in a Stonehenge of corroding implements scattered over a few acres of mud and fixed to the bellies of punctured clouds by something bloody and invisible. There are elevators, escalators, cultivators, rotovators and things for potatoes; combines, bailers, bee-hives, chicken-coops, tractors, gates and anything that cultivates; harrows, ploughs, prisons for breeding sows, hay-rakes, drinking troughs, sheep-wire, barbed-wire, pitch-forks, scythes and a loft-ladder lying on its side. "Hey Murph, look at this ... my stairs!" It is long, sturdy and heavy, it looks perfect, and I only need half of it. "C'mon, let's go and talk business!"

There are two figures at the business end, a solidly fat man, wild whiskery and tobaccoed, with a filthy shirt plunged agape down beyond his scraggly brillo-pad navel and his wife beside him almost identical, even down to the whiskers; a divinity of humankind here in the tumultuous inhospitable hills. "What can I do for you, gaffer?" he greets me like a brother, at ease with driving rain; people are the very sunshine to him, no messing, this man doesn't feel the cold, his skin has turned to leather. "The loft-ladder back there, I only want half of it." "And what am I supposed to do then with the other bloody half?" "Same as I'm going to do, I suppose!" I reply, watching him shuffling his boots about in the deep mud. "Norr! Can't cut it in half, ruin it that would, isn't it!" "Well at least you would have sold half of it, wouldn't you!" I persist and he shakes his head and turns ponderously away to attend to another of the meandering small bits of dripping gabardine topped with greasy side-slapped caps and purple dew-dropped noses protruding from whiskers at their top ends!

I'm really fascinated by this place, it's like Hell that's been turned into a holiday-camp for lonely farmers, a place where unwanted junk is resurrected into becoming bargains to fit the pockets of the bedraggled poor. But as I think this, I notice that I'm the only one here today that's driving a clapped-out ex-post office van, all the rest are in Land Rovers, Range Rovers and four-track Japanese monsters and a scattering of horse-boxes. Murphy is in his element; it's a bit like parts of Dartmoor up here and, rain or no rain, we are enjoying ourselves, like being in an open-air theatre. "I feel a bit like a caddis-fly larva wandering about amongst this lot; I bet there ain't many of these that bother to take off their wellies or the half-smoked fag from behind the ear when they have a romantic encounter. Yet there's lots of big families about - more of a 'Max

Tractor' than a 'Max Factor'! What do you reckon, Murph?" He is roaring almost out of control, and a drenched sheepdog is shivering in the open back of a Land Rover, watching him with thunderous envy.

"I wonder if he would sell me the loft-ladder for a fiver; I've got the saw in the van so we could saw it in half and come back for the other half some other time ... what do you think?" Murphy is trying to cleanse himself of the giggles as he slowly comes to grips with the thought. "Leave it to me Jimmy, I'll handle this!" We splash back into the thick of the caddis-fly larvae and Murphy confronts the man, puts his arm around his massive wet shoulders and says, "You don't want that owd loft-ladder, it's been rotting up here for years and you know it! Look you ... we'll give you a fiver for it, get it out of your way, what d'you reckon to that?" "Damn, that's a tidy owd ladder that is!" the man says, and I sense that Murphy is winning. "Look you," Murphy goes on, "I'll give you eight quid, that includes the rot ... well, what do you say?" "I ain't gonna get rich doin' deals like this, am I? Done!" I'd got my stairs and firewood besides; we set to work with the saw.

Whilst I'm here I buy several rolls of sheep-wire and a large galvanised water-tub. Then Murphy notices sheets of corrugated iron which have a kind of plastic waterproof coating; these will be ideal for the roof but will have to wait for another trip, as the van is already bursting at the seams and I feel that I'm pushing my luck with one half of the loft-ladder inside the van and the other half roped to the roof-rack. The water-tub is huge and only just squeezes in, while the sheep-wire weighs it all down in the hope of preventing the van from going home like a rocking-horse.

It's a hairy drive back, with some nasty hills to try my luck with; it's not the going up them that worries me nearly as much as the going down, especially when there's a hairpin at the bottom! Murphy is gripping the water-tub and loft-ladder and is keeping an eye on the road behind through the wide-open back doors. I watch out for a huge staircase, roped to a roof-rack, come sliding down in front of me whenever I apply the brakes. It's a slow journey but we make it in one piece and eventually pull in close to the gate beside the marshy field, and set about getting this foul day out of the way as soon as we can dispense with our sodden clothes. But first we have to make several crossings of the marsh, which hasn't endeared itself to us very much in our absence. There's now quite a lake formed down the middle section and the cows have bodged holes into the heavy clay top layer, turning it into a treacherous slimy obstacle course. Thankfully our spirits are still remarkably high, because overall it's been a productive day, we've had a few laughs along the way and met some nice people too.

The cows are thoroughly pissed off with the rain and are remaining close to the old building, as though memory still tells them of things such as shelter and perhaps hay to help stabilise their rampant runs. We have sheep in the pig-sty and lots more in the barn, in fact our family has grown by several hundreds of subsidy-pounds, and this formerly forgotten and derelict ruin is now fast becoming the place to be in these parts!

Murphy is a marvellous friend. I can't thank him enough for the way he has shared the strenuous part of the day: it's damned hard work lugging that stuff through a half mile of muck and mud each time, struggling up steep-sided hills with a ton of old iron that weighs the earth and rips your hands to shreds. This life is the only life, we've got to make it good each precious inch of the way, and I'm so glad of the help that I've had today in making it one to be remembered.

Before leaving the cowshed I check out the blocked gutterings and busted down-pipe of the lean-to, then I take a piece of slate and scoop along the length of the guttering, removing years of putrid rotten stuff that is black and stinks. This helps greatly, and a prod with a stick down the pipe slowly unblocks this too: I can now position the new water-tub and know that we may depend on a much closer water-supply for tomorrow's work. I feel absolutely great, with a sense of somethingness that I've never experienced before. "That's what I call a good day's work!" I say with a satisfied grin, and Murphy bellows his endorsement as we call it a day. We head off back with the sweet sound of our first water tinkling in the new tub.

Our attention is distracted by a cow trotting across our sludgy path closely attended by the bull, who is determined to get his free bus-pass regardless of the weather. This is a dangerous moment for us. We mustn't get in the way of his hard-to-get cow, who is plainly tired out after managing to avoid his clumsy advances for most of the day, but he's desperately impatient to get her ticked off his list. Murphy nudges me and mutters, "Max Tractor!" The bull suddenly ripens to his awaited moment and clumsily mounts her in a frighteningly violent sort of ultimate statement, then slumps back down onto his unsteady legs. "C'mon, Murphy... Max Tractor ain't going to bother us now!"

Cari has already collected the boys from school when I reach the caravan. The wet day has by now dampened the enthusiasm of the chickens, and even the cats are keeping low. I am drenched and grimy, made worse by the fact that I haven't shaved for the past two days as part of a water and gas conservation measure. Now I have a dark growth beginning to itch, and my finger nails, which I had always cultivated for playing the guitar, are broken and black. I feel a very different person from the one I was just a short while back. The boys are boisterous however: Robin is competing for attention as the other two stick up crayoned pictures, which they have done at school, onto the wall above their beds. Finding a place to hang my wet clothes to dry is proving to be a problem as there is precious little space by the small gas-cooker which is our only source of heat. I comment that I'm going to have to buy some spare working clothes and use a kind of rota drying system on the clothes-line in the shed. The boys want me to take them over to the cowshed to see how it's coming along, but it's far too muddy at the moment and I'd rather they see it after tomorrow when the first new window will be in - they'll notice a difference then.

The rain has eased and Robin is eager to show the others all the things he has discovered today. So they charge off noisily outside, allowing me a little space to clean myself up and put on some dry clothing. I notice little jars of pussy-willow and hazel catkins about the place, a jay's feather and a buzzard feather too; and there are dishes of butter-beans and black-eyed beans in soak, a promise of wholesome meals to come. Biscuit-tins used to prove their worth back on the cliff, now we have an even greater need of them, so we make it a priority to get a few more as a safeguard against furred and feathered invaders.

The boys are squabbling as they come noisily back to the caravan; it appears that Robin has found something and will not let the others share it with him. All is revealed when he staggers in, doing an ungainly balancing act with a cupped jumperful of hens' eggs, but he sprawls flat out beside the sink and squashes them instantly! Exasperation registers on the faces of the other two... I know exactly how they feel!

It's another grey wet morning that greets us, the only comfort being the knowledge that the water-tub should have filled overnight. As the van is low on petrol I take the boys to school and then drive on to the little filling-station further along the valley and fill up. There's little point in hanging about as I desperately want to get on with the wall, because I know that once we have the window in, the next stage will be getting the bedroom floor re-supported, and the prospect is already tingling through me. I warn Cari about the bull and ask her to be doubly careful if she decides to trudge over with Robin, and maybe try a different route through the wood. She tells me not to worry as her hands will be more than full keeping up with Robin's demands. Chickens follow me as I head off with my fist full of toast and Marmite. I'm soon stuck into wrestling with the problem of what to use as a lintel over the window, and wondering whether or not the window will fit the height of the hole which the wall leaves. The problem is the size of the concrete blocks, which are three times the depth of normal house bricks, and so there is every likelihood that the window will need some extra packing at top and bottom.

I notice that there are some sheep out in the lane, as the abundant waysides are far more attractive to them than the boring old nibbled meadow-grass on the other side of the hedge. The lane is a damned sight drier too - as I am rudely reminded when I slip my foot into a concealed cow-bodge and have the entire foul liquid contents come squirting up my body and into my face. For safety, I follow the hedge beside the flooded lane and find a long-tailed tit's nest in the rose-briars, a wonderful construction of lichens and cobwebs lined with soft feathers, and I smile to myself wishing that it were that easy for me to make a home so cosy. Once I am past the big sycamore tree, there it is, the cowshed, complete with herd of cows just standing like statues in the rain. I start to whistle, pretending to be both farmer and dog, but they are not impressed and merely turn their heads as though waiting for me to discover that they have knocked the water-tub over on its side! The bull is in the yard with several of his cows and I seize the initiative to show that I am not afraid by charging at them, growling and yelling and slipping and slurping through a whole misery of sloppy splattered shit! They disperse a degree or two and I hear Murphy join me, adding his own far fiercer growls to the air. "Look what the sods have done to the tub... stupid bloody animals!"

I fetch water from the dam and disturb a jack-snipe from the rushy bogland; I am amazed at the speed and zig-zagging flight it can instantly achieve, and I watch it soar out of sight with its secure knowledge of the sky and all the land beneath, until it settles once more and vanishes. The bull is watching me from under an apple tree and I wonder what he's thinking behind those pale-ringed eyes and massively wide horns; I don't trust him despite the reassurances from Gareth that he is a "placid owd boy"!

We mark out where the window will be positioned and start to lay the wall on either side. Murphy has a solution for the lintel problem, having heard of an old warehouse being demolished on the edge of the town, with beams and loads of other old timber amongst the rubble. We decide to go and investigate later, after we have laid another few rows. I tell him of an ex-government junk shop that Cari told me about last night, a place where we can get cheap working-clothes and tools also; it all sounds promising. I set to work with hammer and chisel, splitting more concrete blocks so that we can keep the brickwork alternating as we build around the window; it's all looking good and we can now knock the front door out and quickly extend the wall across the gap to stop the cows from getting in. The old door will be very useful as a platform to stand on in the absence of planks and scaffold; once we get above the window we can concentrate on getting the bedroom-floor cross-timbers secured, and then build the rest of the wall from the inside.

Throughout the morning the swallows are diving in and out, utterly unaffected by the dragging weather which is already weighing us down. Hunger disperses the cows slightly, but they haven't moved appreciably far from the building and are effectively bodging holes in a slightly wider circle all around. Sheep are still cramming into the pig-sty with their lambs; they have a crazy urgency about them, as though the January sales are back upon us and no sooner are they in than they are out again as if searching for some elusive bargain. They're in the barn as well, where the two halves of the loft-ladder are making the place look overcrowded. I keep an eye on the water-tub, making sure that it's still in position and filling up properly this time. With sufficient new rows of blocks cemented in, we gingerly dislodge the heavy stones from above the door and we have to leap for our lives as a whole deadweight mass of wall comes crashing down, together with the slated porch-roof. Miraculously it all lands on the outside, creating a great cloud of dust. We stare at each other with terrified eyes and clenched teeth; the bedroom floor hasn't come down on our heads after all! Our grimaces soften into grins and we shake hands in a daft celebration that hides our relief, then we take time out to admire our handiwork. "Another mix and we'll have that wall across the gap. Jimmy; this place will look like Buckingham Palace before much longer!" Murphy laughs and I laugh with a further picture coming to mind: "Yeah ... shame about 'The Mall' being swamped!"

We check to see that the remaining old wall is secure before venturing on with extending the new wall. It all feels safe and solid now, and I proceed with a steel claw to prise out the massive old blacksmith's nails that are holding the door-frame to the remaining wall. It's like a new window onto the orchard with the door out of the way, but it won't last long. I brush away the rubble and test the new pick by hacking some footings to provide grip for the concrete; Murphy levels it off with the spirit-level before slapping on three rows of concrete blocks, then we call a temporary halt to allow it all to dry out and settle. "Not your actual 'Building Regs', Murph. ... but I don't suppose that Robinson Crusoe was too much bothered about things like that either!"

After a well-earned cup of tea we head off straight for town. It's an ideal day to be looking grubby: I don't feel nearly so bad being whiskery and cow-shitted when the weather's this bad and everybody is looking at the ground. Before finding the demolition site I top up with more grocery provisions, and then we have a bit of a root around the ex-government place that Cari told me about. It's great: they've got every conceivable thing in there and we get ourselves a couple of ex-navy weatherproof hooded jackets and a six-foot-long cross-cut saw that weighs a ton and should make short work of heavy-going timber. I also buy a wind-and-rainproof paraffin lamp with a wick, which should be useful when I work late and have to find my way back across the marsh in the dark. Looking like a tramp, I resist the temptation to pop into the bank just to hear someone call me 'Sir', and instead buy another bag of those lovely Chelsea buns as a surprise. We get back to the van and go off in search of this warehouse that has been pulled down. Our luck is in and the visit proves to be worthwhile: the foreman on the site allows us to help ourselves to the timber, saying that it was about to be burned. It's all very filthy and is full of nails, but we manage to select a sturdy piece and saw it in half and throw in a couple of other heavy pieces as well - nothing will be wasted.

Thus far, diversions have not proved to be interruptions, and we've been lucky in always discovering something useful. Today is no exception, so we're going back to 'Buckingham Palace' with our treasures, wearing our posh new Admiralty jackets with their stiff peaked hoods and pockets that you could hide sheep in! My other jacket is still wet from yesterday so I'm more than pleased to be adorned in this high-specification dry garment. Murphy's fairly chuffed with his too and I reckon we're beginning to look slightly more like intellectuals than tramps now - not that tramps are not intellectuals, I hasten to add, it's just that intellectuals usually are tramps!

I try wearing my industrial gloves but you can't feel your materials so I discard them in favour of the sensual delights of splinters and scuffed knuckles and the complete set of busted nails. We look like one animal crossing the marsh, a huge stick-insect with a black heavy beam for a body; I just hope that the bull doesn't judge us to be either a threat, or perhaps another cow; whatever, it's what's known as a 'no win' situation. It takes three trips to get all the stuff over to the cowshed; the bull is a safe distance away, sniffing the air as he watches his chosen cow grazing ravenously on the sparse short grass, trying to take up miraculous minerals to rid her of ring-worm. He's just there to make sure he doesn't miss the bell when it goes off.

It's been a productive morning on the lean-to roof as well: our new tub is three-parts full, and it hasn't got any tadpoles in it either. We spend a few moments reflecting how we have shaken ourselves out of the grip of each day being a repeat of the previous one, ad infinitum; we laugh in concluding that these moments in our lives are priceless beyond measure. What is 'destiny'? What grand noble plan ever led us to this moment, here of all places- a bloody cowshed and mud up to our crotches? Back in Plymouth there are people walking about with clipboards calling meetings on the further globalisation of introvert thinking... and here we are building a wall, just building a wall in the middle of nowhere. My, oh my, how mysterious are the workings of the Lord!

One of the benefits of rain is that it keeps the concrete blocks wet enough for the moisture in the cement not to be absorbed immediately, and this gives us a nice rate of progress as a result. It's really rather satisfying taking sand, cement, water and stones from the earth and wood from the trees, in the honouring and protecting of the tiny sperm we once were in some faraway forgotten glory. It's no different to the long-tailed tit down in the hedge: there's no real-estate there, as once the family has flown, the house is forgotten. I see that I'm more like a dormouse that has taken over an old bird's nest, past glories blown away like autumn leaves to melt quietly back into the soil of time, unseen and only ever remembered in a fading line that is darkness and light, is wet and dry, cold and hot, is everything and everywhere, eternally nowhere, which is where somewhere is.

We check to see that the window fits, and leave it standing there held tightly by the two sides, so good is the fit, then I mix more cement, using water from the tub this time, to make the previous old doorway safe from cows. It's a wall now and the boys can have fun re-laying the old stones on the outside of it when the weather is warmer. I look at Murphy with a poorly disguised grin and after a brief pause I say firmly and quietly: "There's a tiger in this room; you can't see it, but I can!" He knows what I'm talking about and bursts out laughing. "Fresh air, Jimmy, that's all we need to breathe, none of that other muck! No wonder they can see bloody tigers!"

A quick calculation shows us that the window-height is a surprisingly good fit too and will only require a bit of packing at the top once the sill is in place. We can't nail the frame to the sides until the cement has had time to dry out thoroughly; it's a bit frustrating having to wait, but at least the place is beginning to look as though it's got an inside now, and so we pack up for the day and hope for a nice drying wind to spring up and get to work.

Gareth drops by, having been doing a bit of cow-counting and rounding up ewes and lambs from the lane. He glances over the place: "It's coming, Jimmy," he chuckles in a light-hearted nudge of encouragement and we soon steer the conversation round to the weather which hadn't been part of the original plan. "Damn, there's been some rain: and there's no sign that it's going to stop; th' owd cows don't like it a heck of a lot neither ... the grass is a beggar slow comin'." Before we part company he tells me of a second-hand Raeburn that a farmer friend wants to sell. He scribbles a number for me to ring if I'm interested, offering to pick it up in the Landrover for me if it's any good, as there's no way we'd get one of those heavy blighters over the marsh on a wheelbarrow!

Bodgers, Cretins and Three Bantams in a Sack

Robin is over his egg catastrophe and all the previous protein has now been washed from memory, in fact he's been unusually helpful with Cari today, gathering stinging nettles for their tender young shoots, which are wonderful as greens and only require blanching. No moles have gone into our stews as far as we know, and Cari is performing miracles at the midget stove in the corner, producing right royal stews and golden crispy things from the frying-pan that fair take the breath away. The loaves which I bought in town are particularly good and are on a par with the buns, talk of which brings us round to the subject of bread-making and the Raeburn in particular. After eating we take a stroll to a distant phone-box and I make the call, establishing that it's still available and I can go and see it any evening, with directions on how to find the place.

Walking the lanes is a joy, even in rain: the violets are out, but cowslips are more or less past it, as are the daffodils; coltsfoot and celandine came earlier, hot on the heels of snowdrops and heliotrope, so the year is already racing by. The umbellifers are making their way heavenward, burying the arums which had previous prominence, while the mustard garlic climbs with lustrous leaves and lacy white blooms, climbing, all climbing as the hawthorn sheaths ease open with utter indifference to the weather. The fast gurgling brook is holding deeper secrets yet and spanks its music upon the air. I point out a tawny owl roosting in dense ivy on an ash-tree, and I explain to the boys the nature of ivy: provider of both shelter and sustenance, a blessed evergreen, persecuted for being what man has labelled it to be, a parasite, and punishing it accordingly. The owl, plump and round and chestnutty, has his head on a secret swivel and watches us from its privacy. I promise the boys that I will give them a break from all this rain and mud at the weekend and take them to the seaside for a splash in the sea and fish and chips in Aberystwyth, wow!

Thursday morning, rain rattling on the roof and a school in the valley where another three Rs are waiting to be taught - what more could one ask for! It's odd that a fourth 'R' is not mentioned, especially as it's the most common 'R' in these parts! There's an optimism inside me saying that each day of rain must mean one day less of rain, and soon it will be Blooming May with trees ablaze with blossoms and new feathers borne to the air. I can't get the early start that I would like because the boys need to be dry when they arrive at school for their dose of R's, but with the days lengthening and getting warmer and drier, they'll soon be able to walk with their friends down the hill to school, allowing me to start bright and early and then work on late into the evenings too.

After this first part of the morning has been attended to, I go out into the world of cow-bodges once more, discovering even more deep and devious kinds of bodge awaiting to foul my passage across to the cowshed. The one I fear most now is the 'pure' bodge; this is a deep broadish hole, slightly deeper than a welly, its surface camouflaged under grass fragments so that it looks exactly like the earth; its contents are a mixture of urine, dung and mud. The welly fits handsomely into this and, being the waterproof boot that it is, it won't allow this putrid filth to pass through into the inside... unfortunately neither will it let the stuff out once it has got in over the top of the boot and is squelching between the toes; this way the welly is doubly useful!

I notice that Murphy has beat me to it this morning. The door is open as I splosh bad-temperedly in to greet him and see how he has fared with the wretched bodges. I am confronted by two cows standing on what had been my pile of sand. There is cement everywhere as they have stamped holes into the remaining bags, and to top it all, there is cowshit and piddle splattered over the whole lot. I want to cry! As if that isn't enough they bundle through into the main room and I think for one pant-fouling moment that I am about to see them go leaping through the window-hole. They start bellowing, so I start making little crooning notes in the vain hope of calming them down. Then I notice two stubbed-out cigarettes on the iron range ... we've had visitors, kids from the farm most likely, coming down to have a peep at what we're doing, then leaving the blooming door open when they leave!

I coax the two beasts back into the lean-to, then see Murphy standing in the open doorway with his mouth wide agape. "Move back, Murph!" I bawl, "these cretins have moved back in!" They go teat-swinging gavotte-like down into the orchard where, to my dumbfounded tattered dismay, three more cows are in the ditch by the dam, just standing there slowly and repetitiously cud-chewing and looking at me with eyes that would melt concrete! "This is a fine bloody start, this is!" Murph growls, kicking at the sand and ripped cement bags. "How did they get in, for Christ's sake? We locked the door when we left." "Somebody's been in," I reply. "There are fag ends in the grate... kids, no doubt!" "We can't use this, it's ruined!" he sighs and looks at me in hopeless resignation. Trying to be positive I suggest that we nail down the window-sill then secure the window frame into position. This shouldn't take too long to do, and then it's back to the builder's yard to order a new delivery of sand. We can bring a couple of bags of sand and cement back in the van to keep us going for a couple of days, then with luck we could have the lintel in position and the wall completed up as far as the bedroom floor before we pack up.

It's all sounding hopeful again and we set to work noisily. Soon the sill is in and there are four six-inch nails holding the window solidly in place. We sweep as much of the mess out as we can, then toss a couple of buckets of water down to freshen the place up. Before leaving we drive the cows out from the ditch and do a temporary repair job on the fence they have flattened, but my little dam is a write-off and what once was a pretty little ditch-cum-stream is now a mud-bath, bodged and gouged, flattened and thoroughly shitted along its entire length; and they'll be back, that's for sure!

We go back a different way, along the hill and into a steep wood that follows the ridge all the way up to the head of the valley. We see an abandoned bulldozer standing rotting amongst the tall dead grass and rambling briars and I can see a new blackbird's nest built on its engine. The hillside here is dense with gorse and yellow broom; there is the fresh soil of rabbit burrows piled everywhere, and the call of buzzards just out of sight beyond the steep yellow hilltop. As we pass Dan's place we see his tiny tattered storm-swept figure battling up towards the clouds, with his awful dog scattering sheep ahead of him in all directions; I feel thankful to be spared another hold-up to start the day.

We don't waste time and the little van is soon struggling on its way back up the hill; it has already retired once to my knowledge, but I fancy that this is the hardest work it's ever done in its life and it's still going strong! We stop off by the caravan to transfer the bags of cement into large plastic fertilizer bags which we find in the outbuildings, as we don't want to risk accidents now. It's bad enough with this intermittent monsoon-like stuff, but we still have to run the gauntlet of the dreaded cow-bodge, with each of us carrying a hundredweight on our shoulders. For this reason we decide on yet a different route to the cowshed, one which takes us up a steep bank beside the yellow hill and then along the ridge above the wood where there are no cows. We are like a pair of long-distance coalmen - it's absolute murder! A bolted gate comes as a relief and we save our hearts from exploding by dumping our water-proofed loads to the ground, and gasp in the soothing air to cool our lungs.

It's high up here and we gaze about us over a tumultuous landscape of distant mountains with clouds bleeding their bellies away over them. I'm glad that nobody has yet made carrying bags of cement a necessary penance before God because it's pure hell no less, even on the flat and relatively firm; but we're back in cow territory again and it's getting to be downhill. We pick up speed, both getting speed-wobbles and Murphy starts laughing out of control and comes to grief in a pile; his cement bag bursts on impact, and I'm compelled to hang on in my own reckless descent downhill to the cowshed. "Yaa hoo!" I scream as I manage to drop my bag safely beside the door, and I bellow again so that the whole world hears me and my echoes go crashing off the hillsides all down the valley. Murphy is absolutely plastered in all sorts of stuff and is still laughing like a drain as I stagger back up to join him and I say in false reassuring voice, "Well, Murphy, there's only the sand to go now and then we can start work again!"

Between us we carry the punctured bag which had been saved from ruin by the large plastic outer bag. "I bet the Egyptians didn't have these problems when they built the pyramids!" I joke, trying to keep Murphy from packing up and going home. "Can you imagine those geezers doing ninety downhill in deep cowshit with bags of cement on their backs? No way! There's only two of us and there were thousands of them ... and the weather was nice!" We joke about 'The Cowsheds of Ancient Britain', tombs of scruffy little farmers and their precious artefacts ... string, safety-pins, bacon-butties and agricultural subsidies and we contrive to get the remaining heavy bags of sand over without thinking too much about the discomfort involved.

We construct a platform using the old front door and lay another row of blocks from the inside, then we're ready to fit the lintel into position over the window. It's worked out fine: the lintel is the same depth as the blocks and so, once it's positioned the next row of blocks goes all the way across, which takes us conveniently up to ceiling-height, and the bedroom floor cross-timbers are once more being supported. We need normal house bricks on this rather more intricate row, so I salvage as many as I can find amongst the rubble and clean them up to make them a part of the building once more. It feels very satisfying to have achieved so much after our disastrous start, but our interim sand-supply has taken more of a hammering than we'd envisaged and will require another trip to the builders' yard, unless I persuade them to deliver in the morning. We look over what other things we need which might give our order more importance; the list grows and includes enough new house bricks to build the last triangle of wall above the bedroom window, eight sheets of 8'x4' chipboard for the bedroom floors and several rolls of roofing-felt. I sense that Murphy has had enough for one day, but I manage to persuade him to come with me and check out the Raeburn, which is only a mile further away. So we make absolutely sure that the door is securely fastened, then get back on the road.

They're getting to know us at the yard and we are assured that our delivery will be first thing in the morning. As I part with the money I reflect over the wide gulf that exists between the way it was earned and the way it is now being spent, two totally different worlds; I'll be relieved when I can turn this spending tap off again.

Once more Murphy accurately pinpoints the black and white building and we drive down a bumpy track through an orchard where my attention is drawn to the sight of bantams feeding there; they are beautifully marked and the cockerels are vividly coloured and have crisp ringing crowing calls; I'm really rather taken by them. A little bow-legged man, with his bedraggled coat fitting him like a loose tarpaulin and a slapped dripping cap half hiding his silver hair, stands waggling a stout stick in the air in a "Who the hell are you?" kind of way.

I wind the window down further and shout, "I've come to see the Raeburn ... have you still got it?" "Got it? Of course I've bloody got it, man!" he shouts back in an eccentric sort of antagonistic manner. We risk getting out of the van and trust that his dog is 'all talk'. "I like your bantams," I say, trying to soften his gruff curiosity as he burns his acid little eyes into us and wields the stick about as though all the air were a cow. "Them's 'Dandies'!" he growls without once looking in their direction, and I smile over him in my desire to soften his attitude and ask, "Would you like to sell me a few? I think they're lovely." "You'll have to ask my son... he's the 'Dandyman'!" he says and beckons an awkward looking youth, who sidles across looking at the ground and scribbling a stick of his own into the mud. "Ow much would you sell this chap a few Dandies for?" he snarls and the youth mutters, "Quid each!" and is too shy to look me in the face. The old man is still fixing me with his calculating squint. "You conna teck 'em now, you'll have to come back when it's dusk ... when they're roostin' like ... come back about eight, okay!" I make the arrangement and then ask to see the Raeburn.

He marches us into a dirty old red-brick shed where, in the corner, a badly broken Raeburn is just visible under years of chicken-droppings, bits of string and straw. He scrapes his stick across it to reveal yet more signs of wear: its fire-bricks are either broken or missing and its iron hotplates are badly cracked and its door-hinges broken; it's a complete wreck and looks more like it was blown out rather than taken out. I shake my head and feel a negative nudge in the ribs from Murphy. "No, it's not what I expected," I say. He whacks it ferociously with his stick and shouts, "Bloody perfect, man!" I tell him that I'm sorry and that it requires too much doing to it for my requirements, and I attempt to thank him, but he's really most irritated and hits the stove a few more times to calm himself. I remind him that I'll be back at eight o'clock sharp for a cock and two hens, and he nods firmly and mutters, "Eight!" as we get into the van and drive away.

At eight o'clock I part with another three quid and am handed a twitching sack containing the first livestock of my life. I drive gently back to the caravan, aware of the preciousness of my cargo. It is deeply dusk as we all make our way under lamplight to the cowshed, following the drier route which Murphy and I had earlier pioneered. We have already prepared the barn, blocking the holes under the doors in order to keep them locked in for a couple of days while they get used to their new surroundings; we've also strewn straw about and scattered bread and corn and have sunk a bowl of water into the manure so that they can drink. The boys are well excited, and this is a very special moment for all of us as we walk down the last slope and see the dark shape swelling before us. I go into the dark barn on my own. I don't want the paraffin-light to frighten them, so Cari and the boys stay in the yard as I feel my way to the far end of the manger, then very carefully open the sack and remove them one at a time and gently settle them to perch on the manger. This done, I quietly retreat and fasten the door to keep them secure and safe from foxes; it's a lovely feeling. Then I proudly show everyone our new wall and window. It's all a bit spooky and we wander cautiously back along the ridge, not risking the marsh where the majority of the cows are just barely visible, bodging the night away.

Treasures and 'other things' left by the Tide!

A strange burning object appears briefly in the sky on Friday morning before vanishing behind cloud, reappearing from time to time, sending glowing golden light and racing cloud shadows across the crumpled landscape; it is most odd but really rather pleasant. With having an early delivery promised, there is no need to do my dung beetle impression, so I take it nice and easy after dropping the boys off to school. I wander with considerable leisure and pleasure amongst celebrating yellow-hammers, and find one of their nests in the hedge bottom: I see the small scribbled eggs more precious than any gold or diamond. I feel I have knowledge of something which I shouldn't have, as though I've stolen something, trespassed on holy ground, and I feel ashamed, while at the same time tingling with the absolute marvel of it. I'll only go as far as the gate and then wait there for the lorry to arrive, hoping that perhaps the burning object may show up again and warm my back.

From across the marsh a sound touches my ear which makes me glow with a lovely feeling: it's our little bantam-crock crowing faintly and sweetly like a faraway village wedding lacing across the air telling me that all is well. The postman goes by in his little red van, elbows and arms helloing as he slips away over the rise and under the trees; these moments are luxurious and I feel lucky for being alive.

Cari and Robin are going to give the van a good clean today, to make it all nice for our trip to the coast tomorrow. With this in mind, I tell myself that today is just going to be spent in getting the stuff over to the cowshed. There's no point in struggling beyond that and what's more, I don't think Murphy would appreciate that very much. No sooner has he joined me than the truck appears over the brow and our day has started. Chip-board and roofing-felt are the first things off, then we have to cut the wires holding the bricks into one large intact block. There's no way we can possibly get it over the marsh in one complete unit, it would require a tractor; so we unload it brick by brick and then the lad tips the sand into a big pile and leaves us to it.

Any idea that this is going to be an easy day very quickly turns sour: it takes hours to cart the heavy stuff across, so we're happy to throw the house-bricks into the sand-pile and leave them there until we need them. As it is we have fallen foul of too many 'bodges', and both of us are plastered in the lousy stuff; humour is wearing slightly thin.

We heave a huge sigh of relief when the last heavy chip-board is safely across and as we arrive in the yard with it we are greeted by the sight of my new cockerel up on the barn roof crowing with all the might of the world enflamed in him. "Bloody hell, Murph, he's got out, the little sod!" There's nothing I can do, he's up there and I'm down here with my hands full of chip-board. Murphy sniggers, "Handsome, ain't he," as we lean the board against the wall. He's a handsome bird true enough and an escaped one at that, all I can do is stand and stare and hope that he'll go back inside once he's had a good look over his whereabouts. "He won't go far," Murphy surmises, as the bird throws out his breast and sets all heaven ablaze in a huge statement to the world proclaiming that he is Lord of all things, while the wind has his opulent robes dancing and shimmering like a rainbow at the moment of birth. Then, before our unbelieving eyes, he springs up into the air high and fast and far, so far that I watch him shrinking away high over the wood, better than any pheasant could fly, then across a marshy meadow and then, almost too tiny for me to see, comes down with such speed that he has to run as fast as his legs can carry him for a great distance before stopping and immediately crows again almost too far away to be heard. Both of us are speechless, awestruck before seeing the funny side of it. "I didn't know that they could fly like that, did you?" I gasp to Murphy, feeling almost exhausted by the experience. He shakes his head in agreement; "They've kept their wildness, they're not like chickens." "You can say that again: he'd show a pheasant a thing or two about flying. Hope he can find his way back, he's got two wives in there!" Murphy starts to chuckle and mutters, "Perhaps he hates them. The farmer probably gave him the ugly ones and left all the pretty ones back at the farm. The cock wouldn't have left them otherwise, would he!"

We organise the stuff we've carted over and wrap polythene around the chipboard before storing it in the calf-pen area which will be the boys' bedroom. Then we pile up the hearth even more with the rolls of roofing-felt. As for the new bricks, I know that if we carry two of them each time we come over, it won't be too long before we've shifted them all.

This is practically the only time the sun has shone over the cowshed since we've been working on it and what a colossal difference it makes! The swallows appear to have finished carting mud and are diving through with such a thrilling sound. I think they have accepted us as part of their skyscape and it's obvious too that the addition of cows in the 'kitchen' haven't disturbed the wren or the swallow in there either. Murphy puts our ladder to use and extends it up through the beams of the bedroom floor, then climbs up and stands on the newly supported timbers to test them and to prove that we're actually getting somewhere. I join him. It's marvellous, with swallows buzzing around our heads, but they'll soon get used to us. There's a tiny iron fireplace on the chimney-breast as well, full of twigs that have fallen from the jackdaw's nest. I daresay I wasn't even born when that little grate cradled its last fire. What strange feelings these are, bringing this place back to life. It's possible that someone died in this very space, just as others were conceived in it. As we stand balancing here on the beams, the thin far cry of the bantam-cock tingles from beyond the swampy woodland and I am reminded to empty my pockets of corn and feed the 'ugly sisters' in the barn. And so we descend, lock up, then sneak into the barn and throw down the corn. I make a few clucking noises, believing somehow that it makes a difference, but as I search it becomes obvious that that there's nothing there to feed... absolutely nothing, not even a feather! I look at Murphy with a dumb blankness about me; it's plain to see that they've gone to join their Lord and Master and can fly just as expertly as he can, none of them able to understand or tolerate confinement. I have to break the news to the boys; Cari will understand and may even be happy to know that they have taken their freedom in this grand manner.

It's a sombre evening, with the boys being concerned whether or not the foxes will get the bantams. I try to reassure them that the birds will be safe roosting up in the branches, just like the pheasants do, but my efforts have little effect and the rain comes back to add further fuel to their worries. I am rather concerned myself because I know that this is surely the first time that they have roosted out in the open, and it won't be a very pleasant experience now that the rain is back. What is more I recognise that they do not possess the kind of brain that tells them to go back to the barn and the barn never had time to become even a small part of their even smaller memory.

I get up very early on Saturday, around sunrise, but I'm denied dawn's colours as I head off in dull air that's still damp from earlier rain. I cross over the lane and up the hill to the wood, following the drier route to the cowshed. I'm in the thick of a whole tingling chorus of awakening; even the owls are there still shouting in the woods, complaining about the shortness of the dark hours. Everywhere is song: it is rammed rejoicingly into my ears, making silent thought impossible and also making it difficult to do anything other than stand still and allow it to ravage me. All I want to hear is the cry of the bantam-cock; I'll be best happy then and can take the good news back to start the day. There are magpies rattling everywhere, a gang of them squabbling over the afterbirth of a late lamb; crows are in on the act too; while, almost deafening me, a gang of jays in their gaudy colours are up to no good in the wood around my head where squirrels are also busy thieving. I wander on slowly, knowing that if the bantam calls, I shall pick it out like a needle from a haystack, just as I shall any day now when the cuckoo sounds to let me know he's back.

The entire herd are camped out within a very close radius of the cowshed as I pick my way down the last slippery slope. Almost all of them are sitting cud-chewing, tons of gentleness just watching me go through to where the bull is standing close to his latest heartthrob, between my water-tub and the damson tree, effectively blocking my path. I keep walking just to show him that I'm not afraid, but to my surprise he stands his ground and returns the compliment, then has me reaching for my brown trousers when he suddenly trundles round to confront me. I don't argue but slip smartly off down past my new windowed wall and into the orchard, hoping rather that he might follow me and provide me with a few escape options, but he doesn't and I have to remain amongst the apple trees nervously waiting for him to show. As I'm standing there, I hear the unmistakable call of the bantam-cock coming from the direction of where he vanished yesterday, so I risk a smile knowing that he's safe at least, and that therefore his ladies are also likely to be there with him.

My concern now is to determine whether I'm safe with this two-ton 'Max Tractor' character throwing his weight about up in the yard, and I feel somewhat obliged to have the last word and be the one who drives him away before I head off back. I can't have him thinking that this place is his! To this end, I move as quietly as I can back up through the rubble to the front of the building, and then inch my way along the wall. I take a sneaky peep round the corner into the yard, where the unsuspecting couple have completed their transaction and are standing looking thoroughly disillusioned with the world. I seize the initiative, find my voice and burst boldly onto the scene. It works and they blast off clumsily down the slope and away. At this point I take a quick look inside the barn to check if the two hens have found their way back, but I needn't have bothered.

On my way back I'm determined to make the most of these first ephemeral shafts of golden sunlight and to steal a few precious moments of bird-nesting by following the marsh side of the hedge beside the lane. I strike it rich: not only do I find the nests of robin, wren, dunnock and chaffinch, but one lovely cosy nest in nettles, that of a farmyard hen; seven lovely brown eggs for breakfast!

The first heavy clouds appear as I reach the caravan, where everyone is still sleeping. I shout "Wakey, wakey!", place the eggs safely in a dish, then wander off to the well with the water-carrier, so as to be out of earshot of all the grumblings and groans of pain in the process of severing awakeness from sleep. We're going to the sea today and I know that once everyone remembers what we're doing, there will be joyful anticipation to replace the grumpy moods. When I return they are all back in their dream-worlds, so I boil the kettle and make a pot of tea, then retire to the milk-crate doorstep with my steaming cup and wait for the caravan to start twitching and shaking.

The boost to our dwindling egg supply is appreciated, and we have a lovely breakfast to set us up for the day. I love sandwiches and in particular the making of them: I always feel that a sandwich has to be at least four hours old before it has matured to its very special magnificence, especially in the case of tomato and cheese and the interplay of crisp leaf and fresh herbs; mayonnaise works wonders with time, as do salt and black pepper and a good hearty appetite.

Our little black shiny van is a cocoon, a place of great treasure; we are on our way at last, but only after another major event: Bootsy gave birth to two kittens in the implement shed, right under the tail of Madame Muscovy, astride a nest of her own, pompously sitting eggs. This was all we needed as we were about to leave, and Robin did his usual triple somersault and spoke in 'tongues' too fast for even the birds to hear. There was a sudden trace of reluctance about going to the coast with this unexpected event on our hands, but after a while the seaside won and my sandwiches still have a chance of making their magnificence known to the world.

It isn't long before the wipers are flailing and another dreary day of weather dominates us. We reach Machynlleth with its market stalls along the street, and we stop for a meander among hundreds of others looking for bargains which they don't need. I buy kites for the boys and a football too, a bamboo flute and a mouth-organ for me, while Cari treats herself to a cotton dress, assured by the little Indian lady that it will fit her to perfection. In an antiquey sort of junk shop Cari spies a large metal trunk, which will be ideal for the storage of bulk-foods when we move over to the cowshed and it comes in handy now too. We indulge in another of our weaknesses, that of sampling the bread of a brand new bakery we discover. Bread is one of life's real joys and we can buy more than we need now that we have a tin trunk with handles to carry it all in; so this gives us all something to look forward to, to spite this belly-aching weather. Some rather fine looking greens take our fancy too, as do potatoes, parsnips and carrots. We cart it all back to the van, then set our sights firmly on the coast and trundle off.

The snaking widening 'Dovey', like a poem, is written on our right, grey-ghosted hills beyond and a little railway-line spanning it like a child's toy. Our destination is 'Ynyslas', the dunes and the wide open air of sea-smells. There is a long straight bumpy approach road that cuts through reedy rushy marshland, with willows whispering in the straight wind fresh from the flat sea. Reed warblers are noisily awaiting the arrival of cuckoos, it's a habitat I can't resist, so I pull in briefly and step outside to let it enter me. I immediately see a marsh harrier low over the rushes and my eardrums tingle as the reed-warblers give a massive account of themselves and a kestrel watches me from a pole. I recognise that I mustn't over-indulge myself in what is really an acquired taste, so I cut my pleasure short as the rain comes on more sharply. I notice there are precious few smiling faces behind the windows of cars speeding past in processional windscreen-wipered misery.

Once we are over the little bridge where the sea-trout come in on the tide and the wonderfully structured sculpture of boats excites our eyes, we are there; a few oystercatchers in a field are prodding, before the final junction. A dutiful straggle of escapee golfers trudge the coastal greens, plainly hating every moment of their conscripted duty in the cutting rain and with a crosswind to ensure that, if everything fails, the odd windscreen will be shattered by a stray ball at the very least. The boys can't wait for me to park the van in the dunes and set them free to fly their kites. Others reluctantly parked here are mostly in service of the dog, and I can see dozens of the creatures crazily racing and chasing, defecating and urinating across the wide expanse of sand which the sea will soon submerge as the tide turns and steals back in. Cari's fascination for this place is in the plants and flowers of the dunes, in particular the carline thistles left over from last year and looking beautiful against the golden sand. There are large numbers of rabbits here too and where there is grass growing they have grazed it down to lawn, making it feel like walking on a carpet. Larks are singing and meadow pipits fidgeting low as the wet wind whips the marram grasses and stonechats precariously perch in the buckthorn clumps. Finding sea-holly is an extra bonus of the dunes, where we can feel that we have escaped from the world and found shelter from the wind, which will surely blow our heads off once we reach the beach.

It's an easy place to get lost, so we're keeping a special eye on Robin, knowing that the very moment one of us fails to keep him in view, he'll be off and away over a dune without the slightest care in the world. He practically needs keeping on a string with alarm-bells and distress flares attached, but such precautionary measures would spoil his freedom. It comes as some relief when we reach the other side and confront a vast expanse of beach and a distant docile line of grey sea, too far away for it to look intimidating, but nevertheless deep, dark and deceiving. The weather has effectively thinned the bank holiday population down to a mere handful, tiny specks within the great pale milk of space.

After getting the kites airborne I wander back to the tide-line where I discover some interesting looking timbers that have washed in on the tide. A ship must have lost some of its cargo of planks in a recent storm: I can see lots of long planks strewn and tangled with other junk all down the shore. I'm going to be busy because I'm certainly not going to look this gift-horse in the mouth, no fear! Cari agrees that I should cart it back to the van while she indulges in reckless activity with the boys, so I get started and I soon find it hard going, struggling up and down the unstable sand with these soggy, very heavy 12 foot planks. The cruel sea has kindly provided me with an element of choice in the form of some smaller, thicker pieces, together with other wider and thinner stuff, all of which will become integral parts of the cowshed. I'm really quite glad of the driving rain for making everywhere so inhospitable for the general public in holiday mode.

Kite-play in rain soon loses its appeal and I am joined by the others who quickly enthuse over the search for treasure in this exceptionally rich harvest of storms: flip-flops, babies' rattles, ropes, plastic crates, all manner of containers, polystyrene, oil, allsorts. Robin excels and comes proudly staggering and clutching to his chest a decomposing, completely hairless dead dog. It is grizzly and grotesque and has no eyes and looks as though it is about to explode as we stand gaping speechless in our revulsion. The other two boys run off wailing "Urgh!" over and over and seem about to throw up: worse still Robin is totally reluctant to part with it, but I have to insist rather loudly in getting the message through and I know he's going to be equally resistant to the scrubbing session that I now have planned for him. Cari helps save the day by inventing a game of 'splash football' in a particularly long and fairly deep beach-pool, enabling me to go back to the van and sort out some towels which we had anticipated needing. Soap is also one of our priorities on family travels, so this very special beach-pool will almost certainly become the only one in Britain that contains Palmolive to such levels that it reduces the pristine water to a scummy, milky substance that causes even the shrimps to scream.

Our planned excursion to Aberystwyth for a fish and chip treat is now out of the question and to my surprise the boys don't seem to mind because they can't wait to get back to the new kittens. I'm relieved I won't have to park a van with half a dozen overhanging planks precariously lashed to the roof, so we drape Robin in a bath towel, toss his mucky clothes onto the tide-line, and cart him to the van now that he's sufficiently clean to murder one or more of my sandwiches and slurp hot flask-coffee to warm him through. We soon steam up the inside of the van and have to open the windows, even as the turned tide is driving in a whole busted sky of sagging, dragging rain; but our banquet is coming to perfection as we all tuck in like lords.

It's amazing how quickly the day has flown by and we find ourselves back in Machynlleth, where the streets are wet and deserted, save for one little stall which is very slowly being packed up; it's the little old Indian couple selling clothes. I pull in beside them and hurriedly buy the smallest warm jumper-type thing that's available. It doesn't concern me that it's a woman's cardigan, pink and fluffy, it's better than nothing and will help keep my boy warm until I can get him home. The other two find it hilarious seeing their 'macho' younger brother wearing a lady's cardigan and a bath towel, but I point out that if the wretched carcass had exploded we'd all be wearing ladies' cardigans and polythene bags with their bottom corners snipped off for our pants. Robin sees the funny side now and I think he'll survive the journey back.

The little van eventually makes it up the last long steep hill. I can hardly believe how good this little engine is and I'm eager to unload the heavy stuff and relieve her suspension. There's no need to guess where the boys have shot off to, leaving Cari to get the caravan sorted while I offload the timber and prop it upright against the implement shed, where the rain may help wash the salt off it. Another item which I unload is a long van-seat which Rowan insists will come in useful; I don't quibble, he's usually right.

Inside the shed there is a heightened commotion: the goose is hissing and Madame Muscovy is showing that she has a temper to match that of her notorious partner. She is not amused by the sudden rowdy attention now being lavished on the cat and her kittens and is pecking at anything and everything that comes within range. Without his towel, which has been abandoned long since, Robin is presenting her an opportunity for making a name for herself, while he remains blissfully unconcerned over his naked vulnerability. The cat doesn't seem to mind the pandemonium; even the duck's long stiff tail repeatedly swiping her across the face doesn't bother her, she just blinks and tolerates it. When I see the old duck now taking aim with vicious pecks in the region of Robin's buttocks, I have to intervene and bawl him out of the shed to save him from a far worse fate. But I get no thanks; such are the joys of parenthood!

May Morning Expedition with Chucks and Dickens!

It's the first of May and I can hardly believe what a marvellous May morning it is when I step outside. Everywhere is golden pale and ripe with promise, as the eastern horizon is sore in readiness for the sun. There is enough light rising to snuff out the last stars, for shadowy birds to take wing and for geese and ducks to quietly graze the grass beside the pond before the world grows hard. The birds are ringing deep throughout the land, the world is mine, shimmering and tender raw, with dew wetting the grasses differently from the way recent rains have wetted it. Green growth is becoming rampant where man has not touched. Only the fields have the look of bareness still. It seems odd to see geese feeding by the pond so early, especially so as there are late foxes still abroad; perhaps a dawn fox is a tired fox, too tired to bother risking getting soaked over a goose so close to bedtime. Over these tender awakening moments, the whole deep sky is in a constant state of change. Each time I blink it is a different sky, as the sun inches up into the far low dense mist that squashes the murky distance flat. High trailing ribbons of cloud are gilded in glowing light, while lower bands bleed. A vapour trail is scratched as though by a fine needle, coming from the north-west, miles high and silent; a metal tube built in a factory and bringing travellers from far America, unaware of tiny me down here looking up as the sunlight illuminates their trail of fumes. I thought the world was mightily mine but now I am a speck of nothing, part of that scratch up there, not a goose or a fox or a blackbird, but one of those creatures that invents incredible things that fly. When I lower my gaze, a round ball the colour of a poppy is sitting like Humpty Dumpty on the wall of the world beyond the marsh, and I know that my day has started.

I catch sight of myself reflected in the caravan window; for a moment I'd forgotten that I have a beard coming on. It gives me a shock and I vow that now it is coming off; I can't properly feel the morning air on my face and I am losing out because of it. After making a cup of tea I use the remaining water to address the problem, and suddenly I feel clean and clear once more. I'll grow another one next winter when it will have greater functional justification.

As I sit quietly writing in the sun, Rowan emerges and I make room for him to sit beside me on the milk-crate. He doesn't say anything but I feel his fingers softly stroking my face and I put my arm around him and smile. "Better, hey!" He agrees and I can tell that he's glad I've got my old face back again. "Fancy a stroll across to the cowshed?" I suggest. His face lights up. "Yeah!" "Do the others want to come?" I ask. He grins cheekily. "You must be joking, they're all fast asleep!"

We take the most direct route, partly because I'm carrying a very heavy plank and also because it gives me an opportunity to point out the treacherous nature of the 'cow-bodge' and the importance of being vigilant over the whereabouts of the bull and not to trust him no matter what others may say. Old 'Max' appears to have gaps in his work schedule, he's sitting down and cannot be bothered to even turn his head. His lethargy is mountainous and we are thus able to pass by fairly closely without cause for concern, although I do sense there being an idle thought yawning across his fatted-up mind ... "What's the point in spoiling a lovely morning like this!"

We stand for a moment admiring the old shack in front of us. It really looks good in a wild kind of way and makes me hungry to resume work on it, but I resist the urge because I plan to spend the day with Cari and the boys: I thought it would be nice to stroll over to the farm, take the football and have a kick-about with all the farm kids. Rowan is keen on the idea even though he'd be just as happy to work on the cowshed with me. We can hear the bantam crowing faintly, not having moved appreciably far from where he was the last time I heard him, so we don't give up hope of getting them all back. Instead we start to plan an expedition to try and track them down and see if we can drive them back this way without frightening them even further away. It all sounds exciting and we want to start now, but we feel that Spencer should be with us. Also it would make sense while we're at it to grab a bit of breakfast and bring some corn back over to throw down in the orchard in an attempt to hold them close to the place once we have driven them back. The plan seems simple enough - what are we waiting for? I quickly check over the barn, making sure there are no cows hidden away inside it; everything's in order, with the water-tub brimming full and the swallows buzzing us for good measure as we return to the caravan, taking the track through the wood so as not to spoil our good luck so far.

It's still very early, so it's no surprise to find everyone still fast asleep. Spencer cringes and squirms when Rowan whispers down his ear, "Wakey, wakey! We're going on an expedition to find our banties … c'mon!" I get the toast rolling and leave them to sort out something between themselves. By the time I'm slapping on the marmalade, a bleary-eyed Spencer brushes past, groans and wanders off outside to start his day. Once we have eaten and had a cup of tea we set off back across to the cowshed, another plank under my arm and a pocket full of rough old corn. Spencer eventually starts to enthuse over what we are planning and is really most surprised to discover sunlight at this ungodly hour. Rowan shows off his knowledge of the 'cow-bodge' and they both pick their way in exaggerated fashion beside me.

I throw the corn amongst the apple trees and toss a few handfuls nearer to the barn, from which we conclude in our wisdom that this should do the trick, so we gather close to work out strategy. The first thing we have to establish is where the bantams precisely are and then to find a way of getting behind them without panicking them too soon. To this end we must go where we have never been before, through wood, marsh and open meadow, trespassing on another farmer's land, not that we are worried over this part because not only is it very early but it's Sunday as well… besides, they're our bantams. We head off up the hill into Gareth's oak wood and follow it slowly and quietly around the hillside, listening all the time for the little cockerel's crowing call and resisting the temptation to explore an ancient agricultural tip, where at a glance we can see old horse harnesses with buckles and brasses, lots of jars and little bottles, bones and skulls of horses: a veritable graveyard here on this wooded hillside where pied flycatchers are newly calling in the soft new oak leaves. There are badger earths and fox holes, rabbit scratchings everywhere with burrows dotted about the entire wood floor. Following the edge of the wood we come across a lightning-damaged ash tree with only its burned-out hollow trunk and a couple of defiant splintered short branches remaining. Someone at some time has somehow managed to wedge an old rusty oil drum into it; a starling has converted this into a home and flies out when we investigate, which gives us a bit of a fright and we feel sorry for disturbing it. At this point we hear the bantam crowing, still some distance ahead, but we're getting closer and feel a tingle of excitement as we take ourselves very seriously over what we are doing.

The woodland slips away still further and we are now trespassing, following the big round hill until it fringes marshland with water springing out from the ground under the trees and oozing silvery across the earth, downhill to an eventual stream. Somewhere amongst fathoms of mud and tangles of aspens, criss-crossing hedgerows and reed beds, bits of risen drier pasture, are our bantams. We pause again and take stock of the situation, I don't want to risk any of us sinking up to our bellies in mud, it wouldn't make us very popular back at the caravan, but the boys are eager and willing to try anything. I suggest that we climb back up to the top edge of the wood and follow it until the call of the bantam is behind us, then we can drop down again and hopefully we should be able to spot them and put the science of our plan into action ... we proceed.

There are old holly-bushes amongst the trees and, as we are brushing past one, a tawny owl bursts out from its prickly denseness and almost takes my head off in what seems like an aggressive gesture as it swoops away; I can't be sure that it wont repeat the act, it plainly doesn't approve of us being there, so, rather excitedly and somewhat gingerly, we make our way past. The boys are both giggling discreetly, having just witnessed me flapping, I hear them quietly chanting, "Bantam!" Suddenly, a movement catches my eye and I halt the boys in their tracks. It's the bantams, all three of them below us in the wood. "There, look!" I whisper ... "Our banties!" We crouch and watch them feeding, scattering the leaf-litter energetically, one tight family group being watched by another. As quietly as we can, we creep amongst the trees until we are beyond them, then slip down to the bottom edge of the wood and begin our planned drive. The bantams leave the trees and run out onto the wet hillside fringing the marsh, their wildness is very apparent and we can see that it's not going to be easy to impose our will upon them, they patently have minds of their own and are watching us like hawks. There's little we can do other than to trust in our positional judgment, it's obvious what their intentions are the very moment any one of us makes a movement in their direction. They don't even bother to wait for us to move, the cockerel has an even shorter fuse than I had thought and, whoosh! He is up and away, rapidly followed by his womenfolk and all we can do is stand and watch them vanish across the marsh. "Wow!" Rowan gasps, rather more in admiration than condemnation, while Spencer is plainly gob-smacked, eyes like saucers and mouth wide open. We allow our laughter to put it in perspective; there's no way we are going to find them now, not until we hear the cockerel crowing again; I have a sneaking feeling that they'll be a whole lot nearer to the cowshed no matter what, so all isn't lost!

The first of May is still very young when we stroll by the cowshed; it's been a beautiful hour and pause here to get the feel of the place on the most perfect of mornings. I am especially thrilled when a redstart flies from the damson tree up into a hole under the eaves of the barn roof and there's a pied wagtail enjoying the sun up on the roof too, both no doubt have nests in the old building. Rowan asks why we can't have the caravan towed over here and we stroll about trying to find a place for it to be sited, the main problem at the moment being the huge piles of rubbish surrounding the building and also the deep mud which will need to be dried out a good deal before the tractor or Landrover can tow it across. It's lovely sharing the problems with the boys because it's essential to me that they are a close part in the making of their home, I want them to feel that they have built it just as I feel that I too have shared in the process myself. The heaps of rubble will need addressing soon, re-cycled into a wall or something, but I know that there's going to be a whole lot more junk going to add to it when I start on the roof and also when I strip-out all the old plaster and wattle. So there's little point in us getting over here too soon, I haven't even had time to consider the drinking-water situation because this will require the sinking of a well of sorts; there's plenty to think about.

"Jimmy!" Spencer whispers loudly... "I heard the banty cock!" He points across the lower marsh beyond where a spinney grows from a thousand natural water outlets and an ancient hawthorn hedge has been allowed to grow into individual trees. The lane separates this from a huge hill, the very looking across which makes me feel so very glad that I came here with my family to live. We all stand utterly still listening to the silence and it isn't long before we hear the sound which we are waiting for as the little cockerel stakes his claim, like an old pioneer settler over new territory stolen from someone else; in the bantam's case it is 'sharing', and doesn't require genocide as in the case of Homo sapiens. "They've been disturbed enough for one day, don't you think," I say... "let's leave them to settle down a bit before we try again, what say you?" They agree with me and we amble back to the caravan.

The morning broadens and the ducks and geese preen, having filled their crops with grass and weed; the chickens all gather sun-worshipping around and inside the implement shed, Madame Muscovy is once more astride her clutch while the old sod himself squats menacingly down keeping an eye on the world. A huge peace exists, then Robin appears in the caravan doorway, one welly on, one welly off, cat in his arms, honey and crumbs around his mouth and his nose dribbling. "Nice morning, Jimmy!" he greets me with a wicked grin and I likewise return the greeting and point out that he'll need pants and trousers on because we're all going over to the farm to play football. Cari emerges, fragrant as a tangle of honeysuckle, and we stand with our arms around each other's waist, silently letting the light pour over us and the gentle warmth of the sun sink through; we're all so very happy, it defies description and can best be said only in silence. I leave it to Spencer and Rowan to tell the story of the morning so far and it is only now that both Cari and Robin notice that I've shaved my beard off... Spencer still hasn't noticed. A cheer goes up and I recall and relate what one of my old lecturers at Art College once said to me regarding beards on young people:- "I don't see the point of struggling to cultivate something on my face which already grows wild on my arse!"

While the boys are playing, Cari and I get our sleeves rolled up as we tackle a mountain of dirty clothes, good drying days are not to be ignored and I have to make several trips to the well and also string up another clothes-line under the Dutch-barn before we are free to go off for our football get-together up on the high hill-farm. There's no sign of Murphy or anyone else as we noisily head off down the track, they've obviously gone off for the day, having already re-staked their goats on a fresh bit of council verge. Fenced-in sheep restricted to anaemic meadow-grass look on in envy as the goats stuff themselves on clovers, vetches, sorrels, dandelions, docks, assorted grasses, nettles, campions, hedge-garlics and a myriad of other herbal delectables. I comment on this; "Why not just keep goats ... get rid of sheep, get rid of chemical grassland cultivation and let it all go back to what this abundant verge is now. Milk the goats, make cheeses, eat the goats just the same as the sheep are eaten ... why not?" A ewe with two fat lambs are coming down the lane towards us, having escaped from one field or another and, very much spoiled for choice, cannot decide where to stop and eat their fill. "Wool, that's the difference!" Cari says, and it does seem obvious to me that, if goats grew woolly coats they would very soon replace sheep in the agricultural landscape. The other advantages would release themselves in the emergence of greater species abundance, provided of course that the goat could be managed and not set free to eat everything out of sight. "One day there'll be a 'Geep' or a 'Shoat', it will have thick wool and will require milking just as cows do, you mark my word!" Cari immediately seizes upon my comments and turns it to humour' "Chucks and Dickens, Higs and Porses?" Dan appears as we are in fits of clowning, hybridising every conceivable thing, "Butterpillars and Caterflies!" Rowan chirps, as old Dan grows before us, a thousand years of ancient granite in his chin alone and he shadows like the whole sky as we hold our sides, aching with laughter. "Something's amused somebody!" he growls in his blankness, there's no explaining to him what it is, even though we want to. The boys are bouncing the football and Dan's dog is excited by it and threatens to burst it, but fearless Robin takes the ball from him and clutches it safely to his chest, the dog knows who's boss. "Well, ain't you gonna tell me the joke?" Dan insists with a graveness that defies the delicate nature of this May morning and I try to appease him as best I can; "We were just having a game of crossing animal names, a duck with a chicken and a pig with a sheep, that sort of thing." "And what did you get?" he asks somewhat seriously; "Spam!" I reply and Cari bursts out laughing again and confuses him even more. "You're bloody mad, all of you!" he growls searching for a smile... "Taking the football for a walk are you?" "Yep;" I reply... "we always celebrate May Day like this ... last year we took a tennis racket for a walk, the year before, a snooker cue!" "Bloody mad!" he growls... "some of us 'as gotta work!" I feel awkward with this silly situation that has suddenly come about, and when I invite him to come and have a kick-about with us, it hardens him even more into pretending that he alone is working to keep the wheels of industry turning. The dog gives me a black look as we move on and I can tell by those sly half-closed eyes that he means to get me when there's no-one looking, I show him my teeth as a parting gesture.

Jackets for Goalposts

We meet another of our distant neighbours at the gate by the head of the valley. He is standing solemnly gripping a chromium pipe between his gums and wearing a slanted cap and a glistening dewdrop under his pointed bronzed nose. He makes a tiny round chimney-hole at the side of his lower face and puffs out a little cloud of sweet-smelling smoke and sucks and says a kind of 'hello' with his weasel-eyes. He is glowing with an aura of pleasure at this moment of knowing us, yet not a single word has spilled out of him, just this penetrating eye contact and regularly spaced puffs of scented smoke. He's on his way up the hill to have a dumb sort of chin-wag with Dan who will no doubt tell him that the mad artist and his family are off taking a football for a walk ... some sort of lunatic custom of theirs, having already crossed chickens with frogs and bats with owls, 'Frickens' and 'Bowells'... damn, what's the world coming to! It's difficult to get away from this silent man who is beaming all over us; if only he would say 'goodbye' or something. We feel that we are rude by our moving on when not a single word has come from him, not even 'hello'. From this moment he is known to us as 'Weasel', simply because that's what he reminds us of; deep, secret and silent.

He watches us out of sight as we round the bend by a forest where the lane ends and a farm-track takes over and is tunnelled beneath high hawthorns, crab-apple and ranks of youthful beech trees on one side, oaks on the other. At the high end of this timbered bower, a meadow gate frames a rectangle of light beyond which a high field crowns the polished world; it stands there, a verdant paradise with woodlands fringing it and tumbling away lushly down valley sides all around. The horizons ride like far green seas with galleons under full sail and the grass underfoot is of a dazzling green, tender and growing sweetly under the sun. Recent rains have left a small lake in a dip and will require time for it to dry out; there are black-headed gulls squawking around it having not yet realised that it is only a temporary feature on the landscape. We cross diagonally to the far corner where mostly hidden amongst trees, the farm nestles.

Our arrival is greeted by a cacophony of barking and a sudden litter of children who come swarming from ricks, bales, sheds, pigsties, everywhere. There are seemingly dozens of them, all ragged, rough and sweet, from school-leaving age down to nappies, an army all gathered to greet us in this sloppy cow-shitted yard. A short-legged terrier bitch is trying to wag her tail but it's been removed and so all she can do is wag her entire back and contort in a kind of submissive demonstration of low-order status, while an aging sheepdog has dirty matted fur and is plainly smiling; chickens are scratting wherever I look and an old rooster is almost continuously thundering into the sky and treading hens with the appetite of a tank. Amongst all this, a huge sow is wandering about quite freely and has a large growth of some sort hanging from her stomach, while bedraggled cats looked wretchedly miserable in an obvious loathing of muck and mud that stifles their manners and separates the rat-riddled ricks from the saucers of milk. Robin's eyes light up with all this animalised anarchy dancing before him and I realise that we're not going to have a clean child for many moments longer and so I try to accept this right from the start and move on to more serious issues, like having a game of football for example.

The ball is already being booted around the yard and has left a big splash of cow-muck on the kitchen window, bringing Cari's aunty Gwyneth out, baby in her arms and looking totally worn-out and deliriously happy at the same time. "Oi!. What's going on out here?" she shouts from the doorway, helpless to have any influence over the boisterous mud-bath that her vigorous offspring's are now engrossed in, not that she has any influence of any sort over anything about the place anyway. She beckons Cari inside to join her where the teapot is always full and the table never cleared because eating is a continuous thing where there are too many mouths and not enough hands. There are washing-lines strung up everywhere and clothes-horses weighed down with clothes that won't dry outside, even the Raeburn is piled with steaming, drying clothes. With there being dogs, cats and so many kids milling about the place, I find it somewhat surprising that there are mice and apparently the odd rat as well for good measure.

The gang have all migrated into the field and the air is alive with screams and high screeches, the cork is off this May-day champagne and everywhere is fizzing and sparkling. Hugh, the eldest of the sons, has sneaked away from his work of sweeping the sloppy excrement from the cow-parlour and is haring about in his hundredweight boots that are ten sizes too big and are laced-up with orange twine; the white shirt that he's wearing is brown and has lost its buttons; his trousers are 'hand-me-downs', many sizes too big, worn out and gathered in a bunch around his thin rib-cage where a leather strap is strangling him; the big greasy cap that he is wearing keeps blowing off as he rediscovers the 'boy' in him and he forgets all drudgery over these blossoming moments. A pile of jackets has been thrown down as goalposts, but no-one is in goal because they're all chasing about frenziedly trying to make contact with the ball. There's Hugh, Elwyn, Arthur, Barry and Dewi, who's not much more than a toddler still, and there are the girls; Beth, just a teenager, Mary and tiny Lynda; added to this formidable army are my own three wizards, all of them having the time of their lives and with the terrier getting as stuck in as any of them.

Gareth, back in the farmyard, is showing signs of irritation at having lost his slave-labourer; every day is Monday in his book and I can see him striding about whacking a stick at things and biting sideways at a pipe that looks and smells exactly like the one that 'weasel' was sucking, as though the 'Ministry' had supplied them in bulk, part of a hill-farming package. I think it best to keep out of his way for a little longer whilst he rides-out his private storm. He's a smashing bloke and has a heart of gold, he works like a slave and has a fondness for horses that goes back to his own childhood; he and another farmer have shares in a race-horse somewhere, according to the lads, nobody has actually seen it, he just tarts up and slips away for a day once in a while; knowing Gareth, he's probably the jockey as well as part owner of it, I wouldn't put anything past him!

I join Cari and Gwyneth in the kitchen and it isn't long before Gareth clatters in, takes his cap off and gives Cari a big friendly hug and is a new man. Smiling over to me he says, "Th'owd ouse is coming along tidy, Jimmy! Fair do's, you're getting' on with it; it won't be long before you're in it!" I use the opportunity to ask if he might help by towing the caravan across as soon as the ground is dry enough, and he readily agrees and has a grumble about the recent weather, saying how it has set him back with all his jobs. He says that he is waiting for the threshing machine to do its rounds and get round to his turn; I offer to help out when it does arrive and he says that he'll give me a shout as soon as he knows. It's good to know that some old-fashioned things like threshing and cutting the corn with 'binders' still exist in remote areas. Combine harvesters are not ideally suited to small hill fields where the gradient almost tips even the tractor, so both binder and scythe are still used. The old threshing machine with all its belts and wheels and droning noise brings a rare beauty back to life.

Beth comes running in, rosy cheeked and out of breath... "They want you to come and have a game, Jimmy... c'mon!" She grabs hold of my arm and drags me out. I shout back into the room, "Sorry folks ... duty calls!" Another dozy-looking lanky youth with white curly hair has arrived on the scene; he's wearing wicked looking steel toe-capped hobnailed boots which are tied up with wire; he's not very high in the pecking-order around here and submits readily to a barrage of insults from Elwyn who is in the same class at high school. Elwyn is the 'tough guy' of the gang, small, wild, sharp and secretive, a brilliant footballer, good at most things in fact, a total law unto himself. His main preoccupation now are the boots that 'Curly Jenkins' is wearing. Steel toe-caps don't seem appropriate to Elwyn, he feels that Curly and his flabby reflexes will pose a danger and will trample the tiny ones underfoot and, should he ever commit himself to having a go at actually kicking the ball, is likely to close his eyes, shut off his brain and just get that lump of steel airborne with no control over its terrible weight or direction. "Teck the bloody things off, man!" Elwyn hisses icily. "Can't!" Curly replies sluggishly. "Why the hell can't you take them off?" Elwyn snarls impatiently. "Sweaty feet!" Curly mumbles nervously fidgeting his ice-pale eyes in my direction; the girls all yell, "Come on you two, we'll beat you all!" Robin is there with them puffing his chest like a grinning mud-pie. He's already totally plastered and he hasn't even started on the 'animal-course' yet! "Me and Jimmy against the rest of you!" challenges Elwyn... "Jimmy in goal ... and if you once kick me, Jenkins, you'll be goin' home without your teeth... orkay!" "I'll just tap it," Curly tries to pacify him, his 'three stinking pairs of socks' secret still intact... heavens knows what he is wearing for pants! "We're allowed to catch the ball, touch it with our hands!" Beth declares; "Fair enough!" Elwyn concedes... "Right... who's in goal then?" "I will!" Robin shouts excitedly. So it's father and son in opposite goals in this sludge-bath of a football-cum-rugger match that has no referee or anything resembling rules... wonderful!

After a while, during which time Elwyn has streaked about with the ball apparently glued to his toes, we decide it fairer to swap goalkeepers; mercifully Curly Jenkins still hasn't touched the ball and his prematurely old body is groaning, such deadweight feet were not meant to be raced across slimy turf. Spencer and Rowan are likewise gasping, neither of them have any appreciable foot-skills, football doesn't run in our family like noses and legs do! The re-organisation has changed things a bit and I am leaping about everywhere in trying to stop Elwyn from scoring and I'm soon as plastered in mud as Robin is. They all love it and our side starts to steal the occasional goal. A cheer goes up when Gareth ambles over to join us, followed by the two women who wish only to be spectators; Gareth joins Elwyn in trying to get the ball past me and, the very moment he lets fly a thunder of a shot, it almost snaps my hands off. I've never been hit so hard by a football before, it's like a cannon-ball, but I manage to save it and everyone is cheering. The battle is on! No longer are there sides, it's now a game of 'let's murder Jimmy', but Hugh remains loyal to me and staunchly comes back to defend and bone-crushingly gets in his fathers way, seeming to like this opportunity to be against him, no quarter is given either way, they either love football or they hate each other, I can't tell which at the moment! At this point Dan's figure looms over the hill, thankfully minus his dog, the ball is booted high in his direction and he spurts into a bandy-legged trot in pursuit of it and connects disastrously with a thumping butcher of a left-footed kick which skies the ball in the opposite direction, way back over the barnyard and in the same instance loosing his footing and coming to grief in a spectacular reverse somersault and showing his backside to the sky. There are screams of laughter as he grovels in the mud, Gareth has tears rolling down his cheeks and the women are in fits with Gwyneth desperately struggling to keep safe hold of the bewildered baby. The whole hillside is shaking with laughter as poor old Dan tries to brush himself down and regain some composure Hugh plods off to retrieve it and eventually returns over the dilapidated galvanised iron fence, then, nonchalantly, as in the manner of goalkeepers he's seen on 'Match of the Day', attempts to kick the ball from his hands; he takes a run, tosses the ball up, then 'thump!' The ball goes backwards over his own head and sails high and down onto the barn roof; he has done exactly what Dan has just done in the slippery mud and now Dan is laughing but, nicest of all, Hugh is laughing most of all. Curly Jenkins is lying utterly legless and making strange noises, prompting Elwyn to sneer down at him and mutter: "Don't know what your laughing at, Jenkins ... you ain't even touched the bloody ball yet, man!" Curly remains wobbling like a jelly; unaffected and oblivious of the remarks as Elwyn walks away, more frustrated than amused by some of the footballing skills here on display.

The game concludes when Curly is eventually blessed with an opportunity to swing his leaden boot in the approximate direction of where the ball was when he last had his eyes open, and he manages to just 'tap' it clean through a thorn hedge and away steeply downhill, putting the peewits to flight, bouncing on and on all the way down to the reedy marsh at the bottom. There is a sense of silent resignation all around, a muted recognition that, that crude kick was the final kick. Elwyn angrily tells Curly to go and fetch it, but is confronted by a solid bone-idleness stemming from a life of forever being allowed to say 'No' in a mollycoddled up-bringing; Elwyn responds to his refusal by whacking him on the nose and then grasping him by the collar and seat of his pants and pushing him through the hedge, sniveling and whimpering, being forced to do something against his idle will. All the children are watching this battle with great excitement while the elders unconcernedly drift back to the farm for the well-earned tea to flow like wine over this unexpected change in the weather. Elwyn meanwhile, doesn't let up and refuses to be beaten by a Jenkins with his brakes on; his efforts are rewarded when the gradient comes to his assistance and sets Curly off striding for his life, out of control, down the steep hillside and with too much suddenly pre-occupying his mind for him to cry for his mammy. Elwyn stands and watches his reckless progress as pewits dive-bomb him all the way down with his arms frantically flapping and flaying until the mud of the marsh slows him down and he crouches, as the birds continue to skim angrily over his skin, to the huge excitement of the children gathered in the stumps of the hedge. Curly is now only a couple of strides away from the ball as a final act of spiteful defiance wells in him in the form of another of his condoned tantrums and, in a brief snatching together of his wits, produces a final rebellious outburst and runs up to the ball and boots it even further away. He then splashes for his life to a tiny meadow and vanishes over a hill which is quite close to where he lives. "I'll bloody get you, Jenkins! I'll get you ... you'll see!" Elwyn screams across the whole valley and then calmly strolls down under the whirling birds and gathers the ball, examines it and strolls back.

I feel a bit like a Pied Piper, Alpha-Male kind of creature with all these children swarming around me in what is a curious mixture of adoration and frustration; it's obvious that I am providing a diversion for them, an island where they may steal sanctuary from the constant sludge of things; they follow me wherever I go, buzzing effervescing, just one big beautiful family. This must be the first time that they have ever seen their dad playing like a child and sharing the fun-part of himself with everyone and laughing till he cried, just as the mothers were doing; then seeing old Dan melting from his granite-like isolation and playing like a pup again. Our football game has been a May Day miracle here on these lovely open hills while, many miles away in Moscow, trailers were parading ballistic missiles, and a million conscripted children were goose-stepping in a colossal military display of fist-power to ring-in the Spring in Red Square.

We wait for Elwyn to come back up the hill, puffing. "Punctured, Jimmy!" he sighs and tosses me the ball for me to confirm. "Never mind," I say, "we've had a brilliant game ... we'll get another one to replace this ... and we'll use Curly Jenkins as one of the goalposts next time!" They are in no rush to be back where their backsides get leathered and there's nothing much else to do other than to stay dry and keep out of bother.

Arm in arm we saunter back to the farm. I tell the gang of our dawn expedition to find our bantams and Emlyn tells me that he's seen them in the wood whilst climbing to look into an owl's nest; I mention how I was swooped on by an angry tawny owl and Spencer and Rowan join in to confirm that what I'm saying is true. "It nearly took my head off it did!" "I'm going to tame an owl and keep it as a pet," Emlyn says, in a way that tells me that he already has a plan and that nothing's going to stop him, no matter what! I tell him that I don't think he should and to be content in just learning about owls and enjoying them, like I do, leave them to be free and wild, just like he wants to be free and wild; but it goes unheard.

We go on a tour of the farm and Hugh starts-up the David Brown tractor and demonstrates what it will do and he is determined to see me sitting in its seat and driving it. I comply and drive it a little way down the yard as though a rock-star. Compared with my little formula-one ex-post office van, this is a barge and I don't feel safe on it, despite it being fun and not the first time that I've driven a tractor. Memory takes me back to a time when one tractor in particular graced the soil like a ballerina, the Allis Chalmers, a pale orange insect of a tractor, thin and spidery while all the others seemed like dinosaurs. I feel less safe now than I did when I drove the Allis into a ditch after it's back tyres got snaggled-up with the chain-harrows when I was turning round at the end of a field, the rest is history.

Looking down across the valley a pool is sparkling amongst the trees. It seems to beckon to us, so we find ourselves wandering in its direction; it is one of those treasures they like to show off to Uncles and Aunties, believing that, because they can see it, it is theirs to have, a beautiful bird-logic that doesn't involve greed in any way. It is a goodish sized stretch of water, very peaceful and comfortably nestled here with a delightful rusting old boat-house full of swallows' nests, but no boat. A pike swirls out from its shaded seclusion and leaves a cloud of muddied water as our figures suddenly appear; the children all gasp believing it to be a monster. "Uncle Mostyn reckons he's seen a pike swallowing whole ducks down at that end... 'reckons there's one of about fifty pounds in here!" Hugh says, prompting the others to laugh because their Uncle is well-known for boasting. Out in the middle, a pair of great-crested grebes are courting and I can hear wigeon and mallard amongst the splashing of the noisy coots; further over still, a pair of swans are nesting.

Our attention is drawn to a fat female figure charging like a goose down from a bungalow beyond the opposite bank; she is waving a rolling-pin and is shouting in a high-pitched voice; I keep hearing the words "trespassing" and "police" as she flattens the buttercups and turns red in the face across the placid mirror of water. Spencer and Rowan take cover behind me, they know who she is, it's their school cook, self-appointed guardian over the water. "Stupid old bitch!" Beth hisses quietly and I can hear the others mouthing nastier stuff, revealing an already well-established hatred of her. "What a beautiful day!" I shout in my Sunday-best posh voice, "... is anything wrong?" "You're all trespassing ... that's what's wrong!" she screams hysterically, almost taking to the water. "Thank you for your concern, my dear ... there's no need for you to worry ... my family own the pool!" Perplexed and visibly seething with mistrust, she waddles off back to her incinerating beef and chained-up husband and we move out of her sight. "My dad owns all the land down to this pool!" Hugh chunters, ... "and anyway what harm are we doing?" "She's a trouble-maker," Beth chirps ... "everyone knows that round here!" There's always one, that's all it takes to cause disruption and disharmony in an otherwise harmonious situation.

The floor underneath us is a crunchy mass of pine-cones and the pool narrows and bends in a kind of dog's-leg and visibly shallows to where it overflows, forming a little waterfall that splashes divinely down to where a tiny stream trickles secretly away to the river. This is one of the loveliest places that I have experienced so far, one that I shall come back to, to sit and write in the early mornings by the boat-house. It has a very special feeling, just like the spot on the cliffs by Rame Head back in Cornwall had for me, a deep and soothing peaceful feeling that left me quiet inside.

We get back out into the sunlight and pick our way through the soggy earth close to a particularly old hawthorn hedge that has long outlived any function of being a dividing line of any sort and now provides only summer shade for sheep and cattle and winter berries for hungry birds, neither services of which hold any value any more, alas. This is a natural marsh where good numbers of peewits are nesting all across it, so I am anxious that no-one shows an interest in them and so I make back for the hedge, suggesting that the ground will be drier there. It's hard to imagine some soul planting this line of hawthorns so many years before any of us were born. Most hawthorn hedges at sometime in their lives have been layered and crafted into effective barriers, but this one has never felt steel at any stage of its long, long life; each hawthorn is a separate tree with its branches just touching those of the next one and with ancient remains of crow, pigeon and turtle dove nests. Even in their old age there is a bounty of blossom struggling to bloom, and dog-roses too have intertwined their long searching barbed fingers throughout, promising a pageant of loveliness to welcome June. Added to this lovely prospect, many years of starling families have sown the seeds of elder trees in their droppings as they have settled here after feasting, and there are very old elders scattered all along the length of this ancient relic of a hedge. We leave the peewits undisturbed behind us and are climbing the hill back up to the farm.

Slowed down to a dawdle, mud-stained and rosy-cheeked, the children head for the farmhouse to wallow in oceans of sweet milky tea and to further character-assassinate the school cook and allow an even more widespread dislike of her to emerge as both Dan and Gwyneth relate an assortment of spiteful things attributed to her. She's even reported the postman for being late one day and used to be especially deadly when it came to unlicenced dogs and televisions illegally being watched, her power viperishly sucked from innocent hungry children in her dinner queue. "Oh... 'got a colour telly have you... I hope you've got a 'colour' licence and not just a 'black-and-white' one! And you've got a dog as well... they need licences too... I hope you've got one!" Child:- "We've got a licence for the dog, but the telly hasn't got one... that's why we don't watch it... we sit around in the evenings and watch the dog instead!" "Impertinent boy! I shall report you to the Headmaster, you see if I don't!" My mind is buzzing with possibilities and, even though my acting is terrible, there is an eruption of cackling laughter; the poor woman's ears must be burning fit to set her head on fire.

Amongst this raucous distraction, Elwyn gives me a nudge and beckons me to follow him as he hurries off down past the grunting sow, then darts into a building which isn't being used and halts in front of a pile of draped sacks and turns to confront me: "I lied to you before, Jimmy ... I've already got them!" He removes the sacks and reveals two fledgling tawny owls huddled in a corner of a pen that doesn't smell very nice. My heart sinks, I am lost for words. "They need their mother," I eventually sigh... "they're wild, they need their mother to teach them as well as feed them." "That's what I thought, Jimmy, I tried to bring the mother as well, but she escaped; look at these!" He tears open his shirt and proudly shows me the claw-marks around the top of his arms and on the backs of his hands: "Damn, she was fierce!" "I'm not surprised," I mutter... "How long have you had them?" "Two days... doing well aren't they!" My only concern now is how best to keep them alive and adequately fed until they can be released back into the wild, it's too late to take them back to their nest now. I am just about to ask what he is feeding them on when he reaches and takes a bundle of newspaper from a shelf and unwraps it to reveal the bald corpses of baby starlings which he's stolen from their nests. I once more cringe and he hastens to remind me that starlings are pests and need keeping down, adding that he also steals meat from the fridge and is eagerly awaiting the arrival of the threshing machine because the rick is full of rats and mice and will provide him with a good supply of both. He feeds them as I watch, it all seems to be working and they accept what he's offering, even though it isn't what they are accustomed to, and he further tries to pacify me by saying that the sacks covering the pen serve two purposes, one to stop people from finding them and the other to make them think that it's night. "Don't tell Dad, will you... he'd kick my arse!" I promise not to mention it to anyone, but insist that, as soon as they are ready and able to look after themselves, I want him to release them back in the wood where he found them.

Elwyn is totally obsessed with his owls, his schooling is the very last thing on his mind right now and he is off sick with an invented type of 'flu; he hasn't fooled me though and I also know that some of those baby starlings which he's feeding the owls on are in actual fact carrion crow chicks and I fear that his 'flu' is likely to threaten all other bird-species too; I hope that the threshing will start soon and that the terrier will be up to his expectations and provide him with the rat supply of his dreams!

We rejoin the others, who are now showing little signs of restlessness, as gifts of bags of old potatoes and hard round cabbages are showered upon us. There are hugs all round and promises galore; Dan has suddenly remembered that he's got work to do if only he could remember what it was, but he's more than happy even though his Sunday-best trousers are encrusted in an even mixture of mud, grass-stain and cowshit; he's as daft as we are underneath and I'm growing to like him enormously. We leave a huge pile of appetites behind us as the children wave us off, excitement racing through all their expectation and with hope in all their eyes; I know that we are going to have lots of happy times, all of us.

The daftness of morning has faded as we stroll somewhat fulfiled back over the field and down the shady track to the lane where we find old 'Weasel' leaning on a gate, slightly too far away for another of his silent conversations; he waves but doesn't risk shouting for fear of losing his pipe. Even the persuasive powers of a wave are as blossom is to a bee and I have to fight to make sure not to fall into the trap and hurry ahead so's to be safe and to distract the others from the lure. The air is suddenly rich with the scent of gorse in bloom and I throw my arms out wide and feast on the rich vapours. "Smell that!" I gasp, "that's the colour 'yellow' that you are smelling; there's no red or blue anywhere that smells like that!" It's even stronger than scented foot-powder on a stuffed cormorant; I'd smelt it before like this whilst running on the Cornish cliffs... absolute heaven to experience when running; I used to burst the seams of my lungs in trying to cram it all in. They all pause to fill their lungs and I can hear Dan proclaiming, "Damn, that's nice!" and refilling as he shovels his nostrils at it on realising that it's as priceless as manure and just as free. It's fortunate that the hillside it's growing on is far too steep for any tractored type of machine to venture on, or for any farm animal to find a foothold; yellow-hill belongs to yellow hammers as was intended; thus it is providing us with such treasure.

We linger awhile under the great sycamore before pointing the conversation in the direction of feeding hungry bellies and bathing grimy bodies, not even bothering to mention the scrubbing of clothes. Dan has an appointment with a chip-pan and half a bottle of 'Captain Morgan', on top of which, his swine of a dog needs his companionship. So we part company in an invisible liking of one another. Further down the lane, the goats are all idling as we take to the track beside the well and the long building into which Murphy has somehow disappeared.

I take the boys wood-gathering while Cari tends to our culinary needs amongst gluttonous throngs of chickens and others and it isn't long before my team are back with our arms full of dry kindling, which visibly reduces as we break it into small pieces, making us realise that we've got to go back for more. Cari meanwhile is rinsing a mountain of succulent young nettles and already has a casserole of some sort in the oven. After fetching another load of wood I get the fire crackling in its cradle of bricks and stones and I clean the potatoes and wrap them in foil ready for baking. Once we've established a good bed of glowing embers, the potatoes go in and I can now start on the business of boiling kettles for the bathing of bodies; it's a rather hectic hour but, by the time the boys are all sparkling clean our food is ready, a lovely black-eyed bean casserole with finely chopped sorrel and jacket-potatoes stuffed with cheese-melted nettles, a hint of mint and parsley and thick wedges of lovely bread to polish plates clean; simple! I really can't wait to get our own garden started, it's a dream that is so painfully slowly hatching as I take-on the ripe evening's weight and peg washing on the line under the shed in the late tired utterances of the setting sun, and I settle myself on the milk-crate with my beloved guitar and feel the music of my heart and play quietly into the first pale stars, my way of saying thanks for the most beautiful first day of May.

'Old Sod' shows his True Colours

It's another Bank Holiday and, much as I need to work on the cowshed I feel that other things must take priority, especially on seeing that this is another beautiful day. We have a relatively lazy start; none of the boys are in any hurry to part with their cocoon of drowsiness and I pretend not to notice that Sorrel has somehow found a way in and is a willing prisoner in Robin's bed. Unusual for me I am lying here, hands behind my head and it's coming up to six-thirty; I'm mulling over all the things that we can possibly do without spending money or repeating yesterday's mud-bath; I also feel a sneaking selfish urge to steal time off to go off on a really long run. I haven't had one since coming here and I sense the withdrawal symptoms plaguing me as the runner-inside shows signs of rebellion. Outside, it's the usual free-for-all with the big cockerel noisily boasting his challenge across the entire world and the pond-water is thoroughly muddied as I walk past and climb the north hill and go down into the dense wood where I can scrape a hole in the deep leaf-litter and make the function of going to the toilet a moment to treasure before washing myself in a willow-marsh where marsh marigolds radiate a wealth more precious than the Crown Jewels. I feel very much in tune with life, at harmony with sense and so very lucky to be alive. A woodcock breaks from cover as I explore the wild wood and I feel sorry for disturbing it as it crouched shrouded under grasses and brambles, giving me a fright with its sudden thunder of wings and an impeccable negotiation of dense overhanging tangles of branches. Everything just happens to be whatever it is, nothing, absolutely nothing chooses, every single speck of life is just precisely what it is, everything equal for having not chosen.

I wander slowly back to where my own kind are stirring and I can see that Robin's secret has been discovered and Sorrel is sitting disgruntled on the milk-crate. 'Old Sod' Muscovy is tidying himself up after his earlier showing-off session with geese and ducks on the pond and there are feathers breezing about the place; he has a sinister look of slyness about him and I sense myself being secretly scrutinised and more than a few degrees despised. In the implement shed, where last night's washing is hanging to dry, Madame Muscovy is back on her clutch and once more flicking her tail across Bootsy's nose, it does appear that the cat actually likes it. I notice that Tony has joined her in the nest and the whole family look deliriously comfortable and purring like a pond full of frogs. The same cannot be said of Sorell who is so obsessed that he cannot conceal the fact that Robin's bed is all that matters to him and is blatantly waiting for the slightest opportunity to sneak back in and hide. When Rowan and Spencer come out to join me, the cat sneaks back inside and I watch him hide beneath the cooker in the corner where he thinks no-one can see him; Spencer goes in and gathers him up and the cat protests and wriggles free of his grasp, plainly irritated.

Trouserless and wearing Rowan's school-shoes on the wrong feet, Robin appears and graces the air, his presence I feel may help pacify the cat, but to my surprise, the cat ignores him and instead sneaks back in and once more hides under the cooker; it's very odd, as though something outside has frightened him. I look at old Muscovy and I have my suspicions as he waddles to take up a strategic position under the caravan. I can hear Cari calling "Shoo! Go outside, cat!" and Sorrel is once more looking wretchedly miserable on the milk-crate while Rowan is meeting fearful and uncouth resistance as he grapples on the ground trying to remove his school-shoes from Robin's feet. Spencer has to lend a hand, so determined is Robin to hang on to the shoes, and all the chickens gather to watch the way humans behave. I stay out of it whilst our own pecking-order gets sorted, hoping that this is the simplest, most natural way of resolving the issue. My patience is stretching to the limit and my body-language being totally ignored. I snap, "Robin!" At this point, a miracle begins to happen; not only has Robin suddenly stopped fighting, but he's making no noise either. Sorrel has crawled inside the milk-crate and is starting to have kittens! This is the second tomcat that's done this on us and we watch on in dumb silence. The chickens gather round to watch and the ducks waddle over, even Tony has made an appearance and watches closely in what seems like another proud moment for him. Then, to my surprise, the 'old sod' himself emerges from beneath the caravan with a look of utter delight as the first kitten is born and, with a distinct smile shaping his large bill, takes an even closer look... and in one sudden lightning thrust, gobbles the firstborn whole and stands waiting for the next! All hell is let loose; Robin discharges Rowan's shoes at the devilish creature, missing wildly and smashing the caravan window; chickens and ducks are flying about everywhere in uproar as Cari comes rushing out to see what all the commotion is and catches sight of me diving full-length trying to catch hold of 'old sod', but he slips away back under the caravan as I crash my head against it. The second kitten is on the way as I yell for Cari to pass me the broom and the boys try to guard the cat. I catch the broom and swipe furiously under the caravan trying to make contact, but 'old sod' just backs out of range. I scramble up and tear round to the other side but the wretched duck simply waddles back to the front and promptly eats the second kitten. I grab hold of the milk-crate with Sorrel inside it not knowing what the hell's happening as she gets on with delivering number three. The gander has joined-in the skirmish and is in a total rage as he comes charging head down and hissing furiously; I fend him off with an outstretched welly but he pecks Robin before backing off. Rowan produces a cardboard box and, between them, they manage to extricate Sorrel and a final little grey kitten and take them inside the caravan for safety.

A kind of calm returns as I tend to a cut on my forehead and the realisation of the last hectic minutes sink in; there's a sense of horror that two kittens have just been eaten by a duck of all things!

We all sit round on the beds and I notice the curtain billowing where Robin busted the window and I take up a jagged piece of glass from the bed and show it to him. "Now look, Robin, you've got your own shoes and wellies, so I don't want to catch you wearing your brother's, okay? He's not going to nick yours, so don't you nick his... that's fair, isn't it? ... and something else I want to say... you're a lousy shot!" I give a big wink across to the others as Robin lowers his head and scowls to show that he'll go on doing things his own way regardless of my silly rules: I think I'll try getting him some extra large footwear, the same size as Rowan's just in case it is the size factor that's troubling him.

It soon becomes apparent that Sorrel isn't happy, even with all this attention that she's getting, and she suddenly takes up the little grey kitten in her mouth and, to our utter disbelief, squeezes through the newly exposed hole in the floor and escapes back out into the hostile world where large cat-eating ducks lurk; we are lost for logic. A quick search ensues, but there is no sign of her; old Muscovy is back under the caravan digesting his most recent snack and all the hens and ducks are dispersing to their finer interests, making it slightly safer for us to ease the door open a fraction while I bodge-up the window with polythene and heavy-duty sticky-tape.

During these reflective moments, Robin re-joins the animals, trouserless, but at least he's wearing one of his own wellies this time. I find his missing one and extract from it five disgusting socks all crammed and crumpled up into the toe end. I now realise why he so readily gave up on wellies and chose Rowan's shoes as being the easiest option. The mud that we've had to cope with has caused problems for us all, it's nothing like the firm golden sands of Whitsand Bay! The uneasy silence is too good to be true and is riotously broken once more from the vicinity of the implement shed, the insignificant little place where washing hangs, two bikes are stored and a pile of my canvases adorn the walls the wrong way round; it's become a place of far greater significance than the Taj Mahal or the Great Wall of China even. Robin is becoming airborne with excitement because he's just discovered Sorrel and her kitten in with Bootsy and hers, all the cats are together. Madame Muscovy is once more taking advantage of Robin's disregard for clothing and is frustratedly pecking him, but to no effect and, such is his delirium and usual lack of any control whatsoever, overbalances backwards clutching the tiny kitten to his breast and comes to a catastrophic end in a heap on the aggrieved duck's back, squashing every single one of her precious eggs in the process!

In her desperation to escape, Madame Muscovy doesn't even bother to check whether her bones are all intact and in their right place and she rockets into clumsy instinctive flight and explodes right through the washing-line with such electric force that the garments simply part to let her through as she bullets upwards and high towards the pond. 'Old sod' goes rushing into the shed intent on further savagery, but is distracted by the sight of the squashed eggs and addresses them with the efficiency of a vacuum-cleaner while Robin is being subjected to Spencer screaming at him to give the kitten back to it's mother. Rowan comes out to join me, rolling his eyes in a gesture of utter hopelessness, an expression that's becoming all too familiar. I'm surprised that the goose has controlled her bad temper and is still sitting her eggs in the secluded shade of one of my larger canvases and I'm guessing that she has her regrets at having chosen this place for something so important. 'Old Sod' is unceremoniously sent packing from the shed as Robin protests at being forced to do what his big brother tells him and I have to step in to reinforce what Spencer has said and insist upon Robin that he must stay out of the shed while the goose is trying to hatch her eggs, his having just destroyed the Muscovy's hopes of raising a family. It all seems to go in one ear and out of the other with him, a kind of battle of refusal to be at the bottom end of a pecking order of his own making.

Cari and I lean on a gate for a while and try to work out a way of not wasting this lovely day and I confess to having a somewhat selfish desire to go off on a long road-run and really unwind my mind and body, whereas she feels a similar desire to follow the brook all the way to the river and then to walk down-river to where a flimsy suspension-bridge spans it; she feels that the boys would like that too, especially if it meant that they could wade in brook-water that was deeper than their wellies and then build a dam to dwarf the one that I made. It all sounds lovely and I add a top-up promise of fish-and-chips from a tiny place which Cari swears is the very best in the whole of Britain, a certain little Mrs. Pryce who fries them in her terraced-cottage kitchen; her peas and pickled onions were known to be on par with the Elgin Marbles and it sounds like a pretty good way to round-off the day.

A glance over to the pond shows us that Mr. and Mrs. Muscovy are coming to terms with their setback and are allowing the good water to cleanse away their pains, assisted by their supposed short-term memory... unless of course that's just what the Homo-sapiens think and that in actuality, the duck is a most deeply philosophical animal way beyond our own powers of reason. One thing for certain, a duck is a duck and thinks duck-thoughts in a duck-world; who are we to intervene?

We can assist in the restoration of calm about the place by leaving the scene for a few hours, it will also serve the causes of tranquillity within our own minds and remind me once again to give all available time to making the cowshed habitable. We all need more space, that's why for me the thought of having a long run is so desperately delicious, likewise for Cari the thought of following the long winding brook to its bigger sister, the broad, fast flowing sparkling river. All of us need some moments of escape from our cardboard box confinement and give the word 'cosy' a revived preciousness of meaning.

I change into my old 'City of Plymouth' running strip and wear my best Japanese marathon-shoes, light as a feather and the nearest thing to barefoot running imaginable. Cari helps me to work out a route of about twenty miles and I know that there'll be farm dogs to contend with but I have to push that to the back of my mind as I begin to experience the attack of nerves that for some reason preceded all long runs, a sort of ' runs-before-the-run' sort of thing. Then I'm off into divine oblivion, freedom in the slippery silky air, lost in an exquisite expression of all my energies. There are no words that can express the absoluteness of joyful feelings that running brings to me; I wish I could share it but it's not mine to share, I'm just lucky to have discovered it at all. Two hours of more or less effortless bliss; fast, hard running up into the hills and along lanes and tracks, hardly seeing a soul and not being over-troubled by dogs, they don't seem to know what to make of me, so surprised are they, but I know that once I become familiar to them they'll be lying in wait with their best bum-biting dentures at the ready!

Once I am down from the hills I meet up with a familiar, wider, straighter road and run the last few miles of the river valley glowing with satisfaction and feeling absolutely marvellous. I cross over the brook and can hear the unmistakable babble of the boys further downstream, so I climb the stile and swish through the meadow grasses beside the tinkling water and I surprise them all as they murder the silence in their building of an ambitious-looking dam. The brook has eaten its timeless story onto the meadow and has cut deep winding gorges where the sand-martins are busily excavating ever new nesting tunnels. There are vast banks of shingle and larger round stones that only time itself could have crafted; scars mark the many meanderings of the tireless water cradling its crayfish and dace and speckled brown trout. Excitedly the boys tell me of the kingfishers that have flashed by and the huge grey heron that flew away when they arrived. I can hear kingfishers as they speak and catch sight of one entering its nesting hole only a little way further downstream. Directly, I point it out to Cari who has the benefit of binoculars, but I don't think it wise to tell the boys, for fear of Robin's likely response; even now he's showing-off to me and performs another of his seemingly obligatory, 'fully dressed, dried and all smart ready-to-go-home' walking underwater routines. He eventually resurfaces draped in weed and spluttering, immensely proud and totally oblivious to the fact of having impressed absolutely no-one! Earlier, Cari had decided against venturing down river because the water looked ill-tempered due to the recent heavy rains and furthermore, couldn't take the risk of having Robin doing his dog-act and chasing after a thrown stick!

He's going to find it very cold and uncomfortable walking back home in soaking wet clothes and mud filled wellies; I'm starting to feel the cold myself now that my body has stopped working and my sweaty clothes have turned icily cold. I have to try and keep my engine running and contrive jogging games to keep the warmth coming. Once we are out of the meadow and back onto the lane, we all jog along, but it takes a good half-mile before Robin stops leaking a dribbled trail on the road. The long hill helps us to build up a good head of steam but we must be careful not to get ourselves immobilised in hypnotic wordless conversations and not to stop until we are safely back in our own cardboard-box. My promise of fish and chips proves to be all the blackmail necessary to see us safely through the quaint old-fashioned minefield and no-one is more pleased than Robin is to be wearing dry clothes again, I've never known him to be so appreciative!

I make a welcome cup of tea and have to re-boil the kettle in keeping up with the demand; my own thirst is enormous as a result of my long run and I drink five cups more or less straight off. We spend a kind of languid hour with little to do other than kill time as we wait for Mrs. Pryce to get her oils ready before producing more of her masterpieces in golden brown.

Idle moments quickly pass and we pile into the van, each of us rude with hunger and eagerly anticipating our special crowning of the day. Across the marsh, the chimney of the cowshed peeps over the hill, a peaceful sight which stirs as much anticipation in us as the fish and chips that are driving our digestive juices berserk. I don't rush, it's a twisty up and down lane and has a technicolour panorama of the world on a wide screen along most of it, so I take it nice and easy, much to the annoyance of the boys in the back who are chanting, "Food, food, we want food!" Cari suddenly gasps and interrupts them; "Oh, I've just remembered … she's closed on Mondays!" A stunned silence hits the van and it stays this way as I roll into town and park in a dark side street beside old warehouses. "You all wait here," I say … "I've got an important phone call to make!" I hurry away out of view and, after a couple of corners, come into the street where the terraced cottages are and I vanish inside the one that I'm looking for. I'm just in time, I've beaten the crowds and I place my enormous order and ask for it to be well wrapped for taking back home to eat. Mrs. Pryce is a sweet, very gentle little lady and she makes sure that I get generous portions, her way of thanking me for my large order. I tell her that she'll be seeing me again and then race back to the gloom-filled van and open the door on Cari's side and hide the bundle by her feet. "Was he in?" she asks, and I nod and reply, "Yes, but I only just caught him, he was just about to go to Liskeard!" As we are going up the last hill with our little engine flat-out and coming to the boil, I try to comfort the boys by saying that we still have a piece of cheese and a crust of bread that we can have for tea, and that, maybe we can find a few eggs and boil some nice nettles; they're not amused! We pile out and I give

Cari a wink and a nudge and I tactfully ask the boys if they will come with me to see if the hens have laid in their old nest under the hedge down the lane. Unwillingly, they agree to join me and are soon kicking hell out of the nettles. I can't believe it, there are six lovely brown eggs in the old nest and we sneak back with them, the boys want to give Cari a nice surprise. As I open the caravan door for them, the smell of fish and chips comes deliciously out to vapourize on our noses and Cari calls out, "Dinner is served!" It's a priceless transformation, all etiquette goes out of the window as my new young pigs wallow in their troughs. Cari was right, these really are the best; how could so many fish and chip proprietors have got it wrong?

Flaming Jackdaws and Elasticated Earthworms

After this we need some light exercise, we can't just go to sleep with our bellies so distended, so I suggest that we take a stroll to check the cowshed over, make sure that the cows haven't invaded the place and to see if our bantams have returned. There is agreement all round and so, after tidying up our mess and storing what hasn't been eaten, we stroll out nice and leisurely, taking the short route down the field beside the Dutch-barn. The evening is coming over bringing dark clouds and there are faint spots of rain speckling us as I keep bull-watch across the marsh and up on to the dome of the hill. The herd are doing a bit of lethargic late grazing, some have already collapsed; I sense their tiredness and feel no threat of any kind.

We reach the cowshed and go inside to where we can watch the fine rain falling from the sky; everything's okay. I take Cari up the ladder where we can do balancing acts on the beams and we hear the voices of the farm children and can see four of them racing down the wooded hill-track, making for us; Beth, Arthur, Barry and Hugh. We hadn't spotted them amongst the trees, but they'd seen us and now they are all downstairs on the floor beneath our balancing-act, yapping and barking like a pack of terriers. I'm trying to give Cari an idea of what it's going to be like and to get a better understanding of the work that's still to be done, whilst trying not to disturb the swallows that seem anxious to come in to roost.

Amongst all the din, I fail to notice the fireplace being cleared of all the stuff that I've piled there... too late, they've started a fire which almost instantaneously sets light to the jackdaw's nest and there's absolutely nothing I can do to stop it! We suddenly have ourselves a chimney-fire and it's belching like a furnace and all the dry twigs and years of rubbish that the jackdaws have accumulated are now tumbling down the flue in flames, while the chimney-pot has never known jackdaws leave it so fast, as the flames rocket high over the place sending a dark dusty cloud across the marsh. Jackdaw eggs come smashing onto the piled grate and splatter all about the hearth; I try not to see if they have young in them as the inferno increases and starts roaring louder than the wild yelps and screams of excitement of the entire gang who thinks this to be the best thing they've ever seen! It's not the way I would have ideally chosen to have my chimney swept and it's too late now for crying over spilt milk; all we can do is wait for it to die down, then I can lock up and we can all go home. There's no sign of the bantams when I check the barn, they'll no doubt be roosting up a tree somewhere down the marsh on what threatens to be a wet night.

The farm-gang wend their way back up the hill-track, turning to wave every few paces and we stand in the gateway at the top of our own hill and wait to wave them out of sight. The cows are sitting down in rows facing us all along the dome of the hill, somewhere amongst them, the bull. They've been watching an old film, 'The Blazing Cowshed', and nobody's told them that the show's finished as we, the stars, trip our way back home in the softly falling rain.

There is soft rain pattering on the roof when I awaken to the new morning, and already I can feel myself being pulled over to the cowshed; it's as though the old ghosts that I've reawakened there are calling me to share my body-warmth with them and let them stretch once more amongst the lost delights of the old place. It isn't heavy rain, but the gentle sort that the plants love and can drink at the same pace that it's falling, so I shan't be too concerned that the boys will have to walk to school, I really need to be hard at work long before them. I try not to disturb them as I rise to the day and prepare myself a flask as quickly and quietly as I can, remembering to put some matches in my pocket so that I can start burning some of the rubbish now that the farm kids have 'swept' the chimney for me. It's going to be sad without my little friends in the chimney-flue, but I take some small comfort from knowing that there is still time for them to re-nest somewhere else, but I can't have them back in the chimney now and must discourage them by trying to keep a bit of a blaze going. I'm anxious to check that the swallows were not too disturbed by last night's inferno, but it's no use my thinking that they'll have forgotten all about it by now, not when they blow my mind with their marvellous ability to remember where this infinitesimal wreck of a place is, and have already successfully flown without compasses, maps or any form of assistance from the R.A.C. and have found it as easy as winking, all the way from south of the Sahara; now that's what I call a good memory!

As I set out in my heavy industrial steel toe-capped wellies, I am exquisitely sandwiched by two other cretins with mind-boggling memories. From the oakwoods left and right of me, two cuckoos fill my soul with a most rapturous tingling and, with not being of equal distances from me, one sings slightly higher than the other. Whilst delighting me, they are probably ringing fear into the memories of dunnocks and meadow pipits all across the great green cradle. I feel happy in the sweet rain, back in my old working clothes again as I walk amongst the cows and sheep, alert should any male of a species decide to disrupt, as is the somewhat general nature of the gender. Maybe the bull is getting to remember me, I shout "Good morning" to him and all he does in response is to show me that his eyelids are yet heavy, and pisses!

I hear the bantam crowing down the marsh as I fill the bucket with water from the tub, then get to work clearing up last night's mess from around the hearth, the bloody splashes of busted eggs and all the charcoaled remains. I'm relieved to be buzzed by swallows in the lean-to and can see the others diving in and out of the bedroom; I suspect that the wren in the lean-to is sitting eggs. I don't know what it is precisely, but this place is magical, every little inch of it. It's going to be extreme hard work and long hours from now on, and I haven't the funds to do it by the 'book', so it's going to have to be a good, solid, honest bodge outside of the law, but glorious nevertheless; this dream isn't going to be compromised by little grey men in suits and carrying briefcases full of paper, no way!

I cart a new load of concrete blocks up the ladder and stack them on the chip-board in readiness for the next leap upwards; by tomorrow evening the bedroom window will be nailed into place and I can start thinking then about the roof and making sure that the timbers are all sound and cleaned-off thoroughly before being creosoted. My mind is racing on, I must be patient and take things one step at a time. Today's wall-building will be done from the inside, so I concoct a trestle arrangement out of concrete blocks and driftwood planks, then mix the first cement of the day and hope that Murphy will show up after his break. Whilst I'm waiting, I kill a little time by starting a fire, he'll know that I've beaten him to it when he sees the smoke.

It isn't too long before I hear him coming singing down the slope, I knew that he wouldn't let me down and he's his usual archive of information once he steps inside and can't wait to tell me of a company on a new factory estate less than half an hours drive away and who have loads of wooden pallets free to anyone willing to collect them, so now, when we are held up waiting for cement to dry, we can shoot off and load the van up. I daresay they'd have other uses too, apart from making ideal cross-pieces on the roof on top of the roofing-felt, providing a solid base for the corrugated galvanised iron to be nailed onto. Seeing my feeble fire spluttering in the grate doesn't impact on him, he saw its big brother blazing away last night, as apparently so too did Dan, 'Weasel' and old Thomas, it's quite a talking point already and, once the postman has passed through, news of it will be widespread and could even get into the local newspaper, depending on whether the county has anything more newsworthy, such as a dog sneezing somewhere, or maybe a vicar's wife breaking a cup. The only person that I really don't want to know about it is the school cook... now that would spell trouble! I explain how the fire started and he concludes that it is better to have the chimney cleaned out now when the place is still a skeleton than it would be for it to go up in flames when there's a whole lot of stuff that can catch fire; I agree.

We are both re-charged and ready to go and soon the wall starts to climb as the space for the window gradually begins to emerge. After several hours of hard work we position the window frame and tentatively secure it before deciding this is a good time to go off for a load of those wooden pallets, if they're no good we can always burn them and give the ghosts about the place another chance to glow; there's really nothing to lose, so we lock-up and stomp merrily back over to where our bread is buttered and let it be known that we are going, then blast off down the lane. We find the place and are met by the boss who is somewhat amused by us in a kind of bemused way and gives the impression of being rather refreshed by our acquaintance. As for the pallets, they're perfect, not nearly as big as I feared and will fit into the van in good numbers. The wood is very splintery, but once it has been treated with wood-preserver, we'll have ourselves a roof for next to nothing, solid as a rock! "Come any time, lads," he says... "you're always welcome!" and we drive off waving, remembering his smile all the way until he is out of sight. Thus the pattern for the next few days is set and we make half a dozen trips to the factory, easing their space problems to such a point as to be invited in for coffee and becoming on first-name terms with the office staff; I get the impression that they're going to miss seeing the little black van and the two crazy geezers inside it.

It looks a whole mountain of wood, but once the pallets have been dismantled and relieved of their nails then sorted into pieces, it doesn't look nearly so formidable and can easily be stored in the barn along with the two lengths of loft-ladder and other stuff. I'm working late into the evenings now, chipping out the old plaster; Murphy doesn't stay late but Cari and the lads come over to keep me company. I've draped heavy-duty polythene over the beam above the fireplace so that they can burn rubbish and keep dry at the same time. They construct a long seat using the big van seat which Rowan salvaged from the beach and then perch it on concrete blocks; they all sit in absolute heaven watching the flames all fizzing and crackling, we even fill a container with water that's bubbling out from a spring and boil a kettle for our very first cup of tea. The enjoyment that I am feeling from all this slogging work is beyond description, despite the fact that my nails have split and busted again, my knuckles all knocked off and I have blisters, burns, cuts and assorted splinters. What is proving so wonderful is the paraffin pressure-lamp which I have hung from a sturdy nail under a beam; it is providing a lovely soft light while my family all sit into the late hours in the fireglow as I bash away with lump-hammer and heavy chisel at the ancient plaster, rain slowly drenching me but effectively keeping the dust down.

When we walk back by lamplight through the wet grass, we discover hosts of earthworms out from their holes and, when the lamplight falls on them, they spring backwards at unbelievable speed, like bits of elastic and vanish back into their holes. This is really quite a revelation, earthworms are blind in that they don't possess eyes... but they have just reacted to the light of the lamp, therefore they must have some visual awareness and it's instantaneous. We proceed quietly and repeat the discovery a hundred times more, it's an automatic response and they certainly know light from dark and can apparently only see their way in total blackness: the mind boggles!

This has been a fabulous week, the bedroom window is in and all I have to do on the wall now is to lay normal house-bricks up into the last triangle, but I shall get the roof on before doing that and I am reluctant to risk disturbing the swallows, so I'm in a kind of care-warp and must instead use the time up by forcing on slavishly day and night stripping plaster and creosoting timbers and doing precarious balancing acts on the rain-drenched beams by lamplight. I am in a dreadful state of grime, my hair is all matted and clogged with plaster-dust and particles and I have sore eyes from all the creosote splashes; all my pockets are full of dirt and grit, I've never been so filthy in my entire life!

The cows all gape at me with reservation written all over their slobbering dumbness as I keep appearing with the wheelbarrow mountained high with rubble; one minute I'm wearing goggles, the next I'm wearing a red hanky with white spots, my lower face hidden; after that I'm in sunglasses and have an old wartime warden's steel helmet that's suddenly appeared from somewhere. Whatever marvels of memory these beasts may have, I'm confusing it good and proper for them. I've tried all manner of ideas in the hope of protecting my face but I end up discarding them all because I find them restrictive to the point of being distractive. The mountain outside is rapidly growing and it's much worse now that the old plaster is piled on top of it; small comfort it is for me to realise that, when I scrub it all down and then point it up with cement, it will take me a whole lot longer than this stripping is doing. Of greater comfort is the fact that the roof will be on by then, and it will make a whole world of difference. Seeing the way that the driftwood has already come in useful, my thoughts wander back to that beach and I wonder if there's any of it left buried under the wrack, rubbish and kelp. The more I think, the clearer it all becomes and I really feel also that my lungs would benefit from a good blast of sea-air. So that's settled it, I've decided we're going back there!

Cari is more than glad of a bit of space too, especially on a wet weekend, so I tell the boys that we need more driftwood for making the house and they're all eager and ready to go. Having a mission makes it a whole lot easier, they are focused and feel very much part of everything. So, with ropes, towels, bags of sandwiches and flask, we set off along the twisty grey road which is hedged with a whole celebration of flowering hawthorns; paradise never looked better, all the hedges are like cauliflowers, cumulus cauliflowering, acre upon creamy acre; who cares if the windscreen-wipers are labouring, the comfort I feel is that there'll be berries in abundance for the birds in winter. The only thing we stop off for is, bread, butter, cheese and a toasting fork, then we head straight for the dunes and get started. When I see those small hands all working and eager to please, I feel deeply proud of my boys, and when I glance at Cari, all I see is an angel carrying a heavy plank. This time we have no need to worry over our rebellious cherub, I think perhaps that our recent late nights of sharing in the home-building process has made an impression on him and so I need only to watch over him with one eye! Whatever cargo it was that came ashore here, we have erased all traces of it now, and our little van is labouring once more, carting it inland to be cared for again and put to use in a cowshed.

The rain has eased as we briefly stop to unload by the little marsh meadow gate, our plan for later is to have another late session working on the cowshed, but first we must have a little break and freshen up a bit before changing into our work-clothes. Cari and I prepare a hamper containing two loaves, butter, bread-knife and new toasting-fork, potatoes for baking, a big wedge of cheese, marmite, milk, tea and honey, then a heap of utensils which can be kept permanently in the cowshed; it's just like we're going on holiday! I make sure that the paraffin lamp is full of fuel and that

Robin's wellies are not full of socks, then slip candles and matches into my pocket and we're ready, a slow gaggle of latter-day marsh-gypsies doing our best not to fall foul of cow-bodges that have been refilled by recent rains, urinations and defecations.

The fireplace is getting to look really quite tidy now that it is being put to use and has Cari working away at it with a wire brush. The oven door unfortunately snaps clean off at the hinges when she tries to force it open and it almost breaks into pieces as it clatters heavily into the hearth. After a bit of fiddling about, we manage to prop it back into its somewhat precarious position, wedging it with the iron poker; we'll keep our fingers crossed that all isn't lost.

This old wall is revealing evidence of many years of rodent infestation, it's a whole labyrinth of chambers and tunnels with harvests of ancient hazelnut shells, each of them having a single round nibbled hole in it. There are various small bones too, more evident of rats than dormice and I daresay there are fleas here, suspended in a sleep spanning dense dark years up to this moment of light once more. I'm feeling itchy already and it's only my umpteen other bodily discomforts that are preventing me from scratching obsessively. The boys are outside gathering wood from the pile and I can hear their frustration sounding once more as their organisation is being ignored by Robin, he just doesn't like taking orders from anyone. I shout at him to come and help me by loading the plaster into the wheelbarrow, this should give the others time to get the fire started; reluctantly, he comes in. He can lift the shovel, but only when it's empty, he's a great help!

The blaze is going at last and there's enough wood in the hearth to keep it going; our evening has begun. Spuds are placed in the oven and the kettle hanging on its hook and chain blackens as the fascination of naked flame revives something light-years old within our deep dark ancestry. The farm gang suddenly come swarming in like rodent-ghosts in search of isolated precious memories. I pause for a moment to stretch and rock my head gently back on my shoulders and look up through the ribs of the roof and can see that the sky has cleared, it's only the remaining light that's holding the stars away. I greet the gang, then carry on working while Cari copes and the planks that spilled overboard in a storm find farmer-kid's bums in crescendo sprays of sparking, cracking, fizzing, dying of other far, far older wood. My boys have the luxury of the van-seat and remain glued to it, fascinated by their distant blood-relatives. It's a joyful sound that's babbling all about us as I bash on chipping the old plaster away; Beth is helping Cari to prepare food for us all and I steal out for a break before dark and cross the ditch and find the freshwater spring and slowly fill the container with sparkling water; the teapot's going to be busy tonight.

We feast on buttered toast and marmite with cheese and drink honeyed tea in a kind of procession, passing the few mugs that we have amongst us. It's a bit later before the potatoes are ready, our oven has worked even with a busted door while the first stars are sparkling above us. Appetites have been ravenous, every last crumb of the two loaves has vanished, similarly the spuds and cheese have left no trace. Cari and I think it is best to walk the kids back to the farm, there's still fuel in the lamp and I give it a few pumps to raise the pressure so's to give us enough light to see us home.

It's ghostly when we walk back under the tunnel of trees. There's an eerie silence broken only by owl-sighs and a few rustling noises, and far across the black gaping valley, the thin lights of cars twinkle as others pick their way home. We pass by Dan's place with his fancy hi-tech electric light showing off with sight of Murphy and others breaking his early-to-bed pattern of years. His dog suddenly scales the fence and menaces us, but I manage to keep him at bay with the pressure-lamp and I permit him to make the mistake of touching it with his nose which sends him packing.

Sunday comes slowly, it's dry but cloudy and, after a leisurely breakfast, it's back to the cowshed. Spencer and Rowan sort out all the wood from the rubble while Cari and Robin clean out the sheds and try to re-claim the pigsty for use as a lavatory area, one which the sheep have already turned into theirs; I just press on mindlessly with hammer and chisel, then, halfway through the morning, Gareth comes by in the Landrover and pulls up. Gwyneth is with him and they pop in to say hello and to tell me that the threshing machine will be arriving on Tuesday to set-up and they'll be threshing all day Wednesday, if I'm still available to help out. I give Gareth a big thumbs-up and a grin that tells him I'll be there. They have a good nose about the place and can see the progress that I have made, Gwyneth is particularly impressed and they have a laugh over the chimney fire which the kids have told them about. They find it even funnier when I tell them how I'd piled the entire fireplace up with heavy stuff so's to prevent just such a thing happening, and that I was trying to allow the jackdaws to breed successfully before having a fire. "Damn, you don't want them beggars in your chimney, they soon block it up those devils do!" Gareth light-heartedly advises, and I look at him and laugh; "You don't have to tell me... it was like bloody Cape Canaveral in here! There were a few sore arses in the jackdaw world, I can tell you that!" They are really tickled by this and Gareth has to remove the pipe from his mouth for fear of laughing it down and setting off another blaze. I point out all the nibbled nut-shells and what looks like rabbit bones which are showing in abundance behind the plaster, and I comment; "This place has seen some rats and mice in its time; I'd be a rich man if I could have a pound for every one!" "You'd be a millionaire twice over I shouldn't wonder!" Gareth mutters, wiping his eyes and fidgeting in his jacket for matches to re-light his pipe, then he changes the subject and says between puffs; "We're puttin' potatoes in th'owd top field on Thursday... I've got you a few, Jimmy... I'll put three rows in for you!" I can hardly believe it, that's just the sort of bloke he is and to top it, he reiterates his intention to tow the caravan over as soon as the ground dries out sufficiently. I mention that I'm going to concentrate on getting the roof on next and that my funds will not run to having slates or tiles, but corrugated iron instead, and that I have already seen the ideal stuff which has a coloured thick plastic-like waterproof coating which should help silence the rain on it, as well as giving it a more 'up-market' appearance. I don't tell him about the splintery pallet-wood that I'm also going to use just in case I get him round to thinking that he's harbouring a tramp!

Gareth and Gwyneth drive away leaving deep tracks in the soft ground, they're on their way over to the other farm building, Gareth has sheep to count and has to check on the rest of the stock in the hills over to the back of our caravan. We're all getting to feel a bit thirsty and I'm ready to take a breather away from all the plaster dust, so we all wander off with the water-carriers down through the fruit trees where a couple of cows are vigorously and ecstatically rubbing their ringworms against the trunks, watched closely by the bull who is also keeping a pale eye on us. I boldly request that they move away and, to my surprise, they go trotting off up the slope following the tracks left by Gareth and vanish beyond the hedge. We then cross the bridge over the ditch and follow the other little ditch which comes tinkling down off the hill. I realise that I shall soon have to be thinking of making a well of sorts, and this spot at the foot of a holly-bush, where spring water is bubbling out from the ground, seems to be ideal. It will require fencing off whilst remaining accessible; it will also need to be safe, not more than about three feet in depth and four feet diameter, just enough to hold a daily supply of water. When I've dug it, I shall cover it with the porch roof which is lying upside down in the orchard; it's all beginning to make a pretty picture in our minds, especially with honeysuckle and roses rambling all over it. I'm eager to make a start on it without letting it disrupt my priorities too much; it's got to be the kind of job that I can combine with whatever else I'm doing and preferably when it's not raining. As we stroll back we hear the bantam crowing, hidden away somewhere in the marsh wood, a whole lot closer than he previously was, it brings smiles all round. Soft sunlight breaks through and I feel just like sitting down with a nice mug of tea and idling away a few moments before the clouds swallow it up again. I quickly light the fire and get the kettle hanging over it, but the old saying, 'a watched kettle never boils', proves to be aggravatingly true and the sun goes back into its big grey blanket and stays there.

After we have had some tea and have almost finished off a catering-sized tin of baked beans with crunchy toast, I attempt to make a start on stripping the plaster in the lean-to, but I am driven out by the swallows, four of them who are making it plain to me that they will not tolerate my interference, and so I beat a hasty retreat, because they really mean business. I recall when, one day back in December when I came up and climbed and looked into the old nests on the beam, one of them still had four pale speckled eggs in it, laid too late for them to hatch; it was a sad little moment at knowing the parent birds had been forced into making the decision to abandon them and fly away. Here they were once more back up on the beam and sitting new eggs, full of new hopes, new dreams.

We feel just as excited over our own renovations and, just as the swallows are darting in and out, so too are the boys and for similar reasons. The old nests up in the beams in the barn however, have not been re-claimed, sadly the long journey had probably proven too much for the old swallows that had built them, and they must have perished over the burning Sahara sands. Whatever their fate, each little mud nest marked a heroic journey for, the birds that built them had to have just flown all the way from south of the Sahara Desert, and then to have gathered the mud from these very marshes where I am now hoping to utilize its water. We're all sharing this planet, a fact that is being made abundantly plain to me by very small things.

'Dai-the-Death' and the Banging Starts!

Late in the afternoon we get a visitor of sorts, a short, stubby, bandy-legged man with a cap, a grin, two dogs and a twelve-bore; he's not really visiting in a full committed sense, but simply airing his curiosity in a 'just-happen-to-be-passing' sort of way. His grin is kindly and filling his face, his wellies are rolled down and his shabby mac has felt more thorns in its time than his pockets have felt money. He's another purveyor of the 'silent conversation' and we all stand around smiling at each other, waiting for someone to plunge into the unknown. I make the first effort and ask if he's out hunting, and he encounters a moment's difficulty in attempting to say "Squirrels." He's apparently not quite used to his new dentures and I notice him having the same problem as he attempts, "Pest controller for the Forestry Commission." He wipes the saliva from his substantial chin and, with some relief, resumes his broad grin. "Oh," I reply, "not much fun being a squirrel in these parts, then!" "No!" he snaps, tapping his gun, . "I don't miss a lot like, I can tell you!" "Would you like a cup of tea?" Cari asks, and he shuffles in a way that shows he's pleased to have been asked and, good manneredly takes his cap off and we all go inside, dogs an' all, and he seats himself on the van-seat in front of the idling fire. I quickly liven it up and get the kettle talking; meanwhile the dogs have discovered Robin and our friendship is consummated! I notice that one of the dogs, a collie-cross, has strange eyes, one of them being a rusty brown colour and the other a very pale blue, it looks most odd and I am told that its mother was exactly the same. It transpires that his daughter goes to school with Spencer and Rowan, which probably explains his curiosity and the fact that I don't need introducing to him. He tells me that he is 'Dai', and I tell him that I guessed as much, having heard Dan and Murphy speak of him and the lovely little cottage in which he lives, hidden away in the woods down the big hill on the way to school. I notice him looking up through the rafters and out to the sky beyond and I know that he's searching for something funny to say and will blurt it out the moment he has found it. "Do you find them sort of roofs let the wet in?" he chuckles eventually, and I do my best to reply in similar spirit: "No, not a drop! It's a new design, it's amazingly effective!" He's taking me seriously and I can tell that he's wishing he hadn't mentioned it. I continue:- "It's the same company that invented the string vest… similar principle!" He's hurrying his tea now, sipping it as though he's ripping a blanket in his anxiety to be on his way, and I glance at Cari and see that she is facing the other way, trying not to laugh. I walk with him back out into the yard and I do my best to reassure him that he hasn't gone mad by admitting that I'm going to attempt to get the roof on over the next couple of weeks, bedroom floor as well, and I detect a relaxing of his facial muscles and a sparkle of devilment back in his eyes.

I ask him if he's doing 'official' work now, or whether it's just a bit of Sunday 'sport', and he shows some pride in explaining that, so long as he can produce the tails of squirrels and foxes that he's shot, he gets paid. He gets a petrol allowance because he has to cover a big area and his dogs are all working-dogs and so, have to earn their keep and that therefore, Sunday is no different to any other day… "Squirrels and foxes don't know its Sunday!" Suddenly and without warning, there's a terrifying explosion just inches from me, he's just blasted a wood pigeon clean out of the sky and there's a plankton of grey feathers dusting the air and a heavyish thud as the body hits the ground; he grins… "That one's for my ferrets!" We're all quite speechless as the dogs race to retrieve it and we watch them all slip away under the fruit trees; our day has been spoiled.

It's a strange half hour that follows; I somewhat aggressively load the wheelbarrow and cart out the plaster while Cari is quietly attempting to boil another kettle for washing-up and the boys are all standing in the yard muttering amongst themselves. After a little while, Robin comes up to me wearing a frown and asks, "Jimmy, why that man shooted that bird?" and then the other two come across to hear my explanation to something that has just shocked them rigid. It isn't something that I have a ready answer for and I'm crucially aware of this when I venture to say ... "It's his job to shoot them, and to shoot squirrels, foxes, rabbits, crows and magpies as well." "WHY?" I'm in deep water now because I don't want to suggest there being any difference between so-called 'pests' and other creatures when an animal only becomes a pest if it threatens Profit-margins and is seldom considered for any other reason of worth, just as are 'weeds' so termed, when in actual fact they are simply plants that grow where someone wants something else to grow for reasons of profit ... or sometimes prejudice. I search my mind thoughtfully and try again: "Well boys; things like pigeons and squirrels don't fit in with farming, they're not like cows and sheep, they're wild and the farmers can't farm them and make money from them, and, because they have to eat, just as we all have to eat, he shoots them because he thinks that they're stealing the food from him." Spencer is frowning and asks, "Do pigeons steal food from the farmers?" "Sometimes they do," I struggle on... "but they usually eat berries from the hedges, a few tender leaves and corn that has been left on the ground; sometimes, if the winter is hard and they're starving, they eat the cabbages in the fields to stay alive, but really, there's enough food for everything in Nature, it's only when people get greedy and try to control Nature, that's when more and more things are called 'pests' or 'weeds'. "Squirrels are okay, they don't steal food!" Spencer continues, and I have to be honest and tell him that they do cause damage to the trees in the forest when they strip the bark, but I add too that they're lovely to watch and that such pleasures are also valuable in other ways, different from money and that I think it important that we should remember this. Rowan isn't going to let me off the hook and he firmly states:- "We don't have to kill animals or eat animals!" I put my hand on his shoulder reassuringly and agree with him; "You're right there, sunshine; we manage without meat and we're all strong and healthy, in fact I think we're even healthier than most people who do eat meat!" A glance at Robin shows me that he has lost interest and is picking his nose and smearing it across his cheeks. "Doing a spot of gardening are you, Robin?" I ask. The other two laugh and our day is back on track.

The fire has been allowed to die, we've had a full day and have all worked very hard, so we call it a day at the cowshed and leave it to the swallows and to the little wren tight on her nest in the lean-to. We now have to get the boys all shining clean and their clothes neat and ready for school in the morning. They are all hungry again regardless of the huge amount of beans consumed at lunchtime, so we migrate back over the marsh meadow and settle ourselves to a new round of jobs to do. When I walk to the well to fetch water, I meet Murphy coming up the track, we have a chat and I suggest to him that we make a trip in the morning, back over the hills to the 'holiday-camp for lonely farmers' and get a van load of the coated corrugated iron stuff for the roof. We try to work out the measurements to give ourselves a rough idea of how many sheets we'll need, we're in agreement that its certainly more than one van load, so our estimates don't really matter at this stage. He suggests that we take a stroll over before dark and take measurements, so this is what we do.

With the last twenty minutes of light left in the sky, we put the tape-measure to work and, while we are up on the roof doing this, out from the half-light come three small figures. It is Hugh, Elwyn and Beth, each of them with a bantam clutched under their arm. "Got your bantams back for you, Jimmy!" Elwyn calls, trying not to shout for fear of distressing them still further … "we'll put them in the barn," he whispers as loud as he dares and I just nod and signal for them to go ahead. The darkness settles quietly, saturating everywhere like a black drizzle; I'm not going to be enticed into any candle-lit, chimney blazing chin-wags tonight, regardless of how thrilled I am to have the bantams back in the barn. I'm becoming aware of a rather delicate situation emerging in that the children consider the cowshed very much to be theirs and therefore can go inside and do what they like whenever they like; I have to let them see that that's not quite the case anymore and is now becoming home for Cari, the boys and myself. Murphy is grumbling, "C'mon Jimmy, let's get back over to the other hill!" but I just want to be sure in my own mind that the gang will not simply go inside and smoke fags around a roaring fire once we have gone, so I take my time in putting the ladder away, testing Murphy's patience almost to the limit. We eventually all head-off back our separate ways and I then explain to Murphy my reason for dawdling, reminding him of what happened on the last occasions when they let themselves in. I don't want cows in the kitchen or chimney-fires once I've closed the door for the night and he is in full agreement with me over this, especially as there is now a trunk of provisions being stored there. As we settle for the night, I tell the boys that the bantams are back and so they are happy as they drift off to sleep.

On Monday morning I am awakened by a cuckoo calling over by the pond, everywhere is feathery grey and cool. I have decided against going over to the cowshed at my normal early hour so's to allow the bantams time and space in which to get used to their new surroundings; this means that I can take the boys to school in the van and then fill up with petrol, by which time Murphy should have surfaced. When I return he is sitting on the milk-crate talking to Cari, so we make a prompt start and drive off through the white parsley'd lanes and up into the broad hills. It's amazing how a place can change when there are a few shafts of sunlight beaming from the patchworked white and blue, but our old friend still looks the same, everything about him look distinctly unchanged; his grin speaks volumes, a kind of "what are you looking for this time?" sort of silent communication. We both shout "Good morning!", then persevere with our own body-language which says, "We're just looking!" We're in luck, Murphy finds a huge stack of the stuff we're looking for and, as he's testing the weight and the quality of it, the man saunters over to join us. "You ain't gonna be wantin' me to saw them in half for you, I 'ope!" he chuckles and, after we've all had a bit of a laugh and a yarn, we do business. I try not to overburden the suspension, guessing roughly how many of these sheets would equal a person, and at around ten people, I call it a day. Whilst I am here I buy a heavy bag of galvanised nails with washers attached, then we seat ourselves gently inside the van and very slowly ease away through the pot-holes and sludgy undulations, nursing the engine and springs with all the care I can muster, listening intently for any little sound that tells me there are too many people aboard. We take a slightly longer, more winding route back, thus avoiding the long steep hill up from the school. I really didn't think that we'd make it up that brute of a hill.

We've made it back and quickly unload onto the sand-pile by the gate, deciding it best to go straight back and fetch another load, then, after we've had a bite to eat we can spend the afternoon carting it all over to the cowshed; I must remember to take more corn over and throw it about the orchard in the hope of giving the bantams a good reason for staying, that is provided of course that they haven't gone already. Our calculations show that we'll need the same size load again, plus another smaller one to finish, so it makes sense to halve the last two and save the van from further punishment. It's fortunate that our friend stocks the ridge-pieces too, so we get five lengths, reckoning this to be sufficient.

I'm beginning to wonder what Murphy and I have in store for us, bearing in mind that we have no scaffolding with a platform of planks and a rail along the top for safety; ours is going to be simply two blokes, one ladder and two heads for heights! My mind is an anarchy of electrified speculation; "Penny for your thoughts!" Murphy says in a low mutter, and I prematurely age a few score years as I reply, "It'll cost you a damned sight more than a penny!" Murphy is impetuous by nature, but he is sensitive too and I can see that my reply isn't resting easily in his mind, and so I spell out my concerns as we drive back, even discussing the possibility of us having to rope ourselves securely to the roof. Murphy laughs this off; "You worry too much, Jimmy... it's a piece of cake!" So I struggle free of my negativity and go sailing once more in the raucous air, two old rooks with bullet-proof vests one of the rooks however, has just started sprouting grey feathers.

After a brief lunch we apply ourselves to the task of carting the heavy galvanised sheets one at a time across the marsh and prop them against the cowshed wall, their weight is a warning to us that, getting up onto the roof will not be the 'piece of cake' that Murphy said it would be and I'm rather glad of the fact that there are other jobs to do before tackling that one, laying the last triangle of bricks above the window being one of them and I shall also check over all the roof timbers and finally creosote them before the felt goes on. Another job is to prepare all the pieces of wood from the pallets and give them another thorough creosoting; I want to make sure that we've got enough to finish the job in one go.

Our appearance and constant re-appearances cause the bantam-cock to eye us nervously, his two ladies by contrast don't seem in the slightest bit concerned and go on scratting and pecking, if they fly off, it'll be him that gives the order; we try not to make too many clattering noises and just hope that they'll remain on the ground under the apple trees. By the time we have carted it all over, the afternoon has slipped by and we've left a muddy trail that is quite visible, but it's a job that we're glad to have out of the way, especially so now that the rain has returned with a dullness that plainly tells us that it isn't simply a shower, giving us notice to call it a day while we're in front and hope for a better day tomorrow.

I take advantage of a bright dry start the following morning and am over in the cowshed soon after six setting to work on the roof timbers. A major change will take place today when the roofing-felt is nailed on, the place will be dry again for the first time in twenty years and more; it will be interesting to see how this affects the swallows, I'd like to think that it will improve their lot in them not having to depend on a couple of busted slates still grimly hanging on for shelter, their ancestors knew of better times and, hopefully, these better times will be returning today. It's also going to be a whole lot darker inside the place and it will at long last begin to dry out; to assist this I shall put polythene in the windows, leaving only those which the swallows and wrens use, this should help it feel more like a house again, and a lot warmer too when we get a fire going; I can hardly wait.

I look rather worse for wear by the time Murphy has joined me, I've finished creosoting the roof-timbers and have sorted out all the wooden pieces from the pallets and treated them too; my eyes are sore and burning from where the stuff has splashed into them. The swallows were certainly not happy at having me banging about with the ladder, so I spared them as much disturbance as possible and steered clear of their area, the sooner we can get the roof finished the better, they won't be disturbed after that and hopefully, will be able to raise their family in peace and might even manage a second brood.

With the rain still holding off, it seems like the right time to make a start laying the roofing-felt and so, like a couple of monkeys, we each carry a roll of roofing-felt and brave the rickety ladder and clamber up onto the roof. I'm surprised that the cross-pieces which had formerly held the slates, are not rotten and will take our weight, but quite a few pieces are missing having parted company together with the slates during past storms; we can patch over these gaps with the wood from the pallets, thus avoiding having hidden holes under the felt which we might crash through. I make several more trips carting the remainder of the felt and a box of tools together with piles of pallet-wood which is still wet with creosote that has refused to be absorbed. Whilst I am attending to all this, Murphy is weighing the situation up with the intensity of a high-pedigree thoroughbred badger, a latter-day Brunel figuring out a new order from the old; he is happiest whilst assuming the role of 'Chief'. Which means that, for the sake of peace, I use diplomacy and become an 'Indian'; it doesn't really matter so long as we're in agreement, but, if I do have occasion to disagree, he usually comes round to my way in the end and has the knack of making it all seem like his idea anyway and I'm happy with that and he can wear the eagle-feather head-dress for as long as he likes, I'm more than happy simply being a 'brave'.

We could ideally do with two ladders, not only would it make things easier but a whole lot safer too, but we'll have to make do with what we've got and try not to get in each others way... something that's easier said than done when bundling about on a roof with Murphy! I've taken the precaution of having his industrial gloves at the ready, just in case the wet creosote on the wood triggers-off a bit of temperament in him; he's a changed man now that he has a landlady fattening him up and washing his pants. It takes a little while in getting used to hopping about on the roof and it seems a hell of a long way down to the hard ground, it doesn't bear thinking about. The chimney stack provides a handy place for preventing the heavy rolls of felt from rolling off; if one should inadvertently go over the edge it would crash clean through the lean-to roof, as would either of the two monkeys who are trying desperately to come to terms with a slippery forty five degrees world. Gingerly we start patching up the gaps and the shouting of the hammer resounds all round the valley, echoing as it bounces from hillside to hillside making it seem like we're really working hard doing 'men's' work in a tough men's world, when in fact it's just noise, that's all; the noisier it gets, the greater grows the illusion.

When the job is completed, I take great care in rolling out the first roll of felt, having first had to temporarily shift all the stuff resting against the chimney stack, then I inch my way across to the far end and mark-off the first length and cut it. Once we have it level, Murphy starts hammering again, laying the strips of pallet-wood to fix the felt down These strips provide us with our first safety feature and we now have something to wedge our feet against and stop us from slipping off. Gradually we progress up towards the top of the roof and by early afternoon we have the first side completed; it looks great and the swallows now have a standard of living again.

The sun has come out and, as we squat down to enjoy a few moments of its warmth, I can see the distant figures of Cari and Robin picking their way amongst the cattle in the marsh meadow, Cari's carrying something, it looks like a bag. I do my best to imitate a cockerel and it's amazing how the sound stains all the hillsides around us; Murphy is fascinated by it and sets up his own clarion-calls and very nearly topples backwards over the other side of the roof as his laughter takes control of him. Cari and Robin appear close-by, they've heard all the noise but haven't spotted us precariously perched on the roof; I give another blast and Robin spots us and points us out to Cari, who bursts into shrieking laughter, then shouts:- "I thought you pair of cockerels might need feeding and watering... or have you gone to roost?" "Roost, my arse!" Murphy bawls... "I could murder a cup of your lovely tea!" "Well, you'll have to come down and get it then, 'cos I'm not bringing it up there!" They slip from sight and we carefully shuffle on our bums and then make our way down the roof to the ladder and back down to the ground where the cows are giving us funny looks as though not being quite certain as to whether we are cockerels or those other weird 'things'; the bull is far more philosophical and shows no interest, having concluded that cockerels don't pose any threat to him whatsoever!

Cari has done us proud, hot jacket-potatoes with ripe cheddar and tomatoes and a flask of tea to wash it down; she would have brought bread as well but the boys polished-off the last of it over breakfast, so, somehow I've got to make time later to do a bit of shopping. It serves to remind us just how important the baking of our own bread will be to us, and the exciting thing is that we're getting closer to that marvellous moment with every nail that is driven in.

Working on the roof is a job that cannot be rushed, it's far too dangerous, what's more, the front side which we're now about to start, has no lean-to to break a fall, it's a long way down to the concrete and rubble ... not a roof to be falling off! It's the laying of the first length that's the problem, I have to crouch facing downhill at an acute angle which makes it all too easy to overbalance forward; Murphy's okay, he's up on the ladder for the first length, happy as a lark banging away even louder now that he has an audience on the ground. Cari and Robin are most impressed before wandering off up the hill track on their way over to the farm. This 'making a noise' thing applies in nature too, it's the noisy ones that get noticed. The dawn chorus has nothing to do with music, it's all about making a noise; any cock-bird that doesn't thunder it out gets absolutely nothing; risk-taking carries no brownie-points and is either ignored completely or dismissed as plain stupidity.

It occurs to me that, if this part is proving to be hard and dangerous, then the next stage of applying corrugated iron sheets will be far worse; anyone can hammer nails into wood, that's child's-play, but a nail into metal is different altogether, especially when the metal sheets are very heavy, awkward and slippery; so much will depend on that first nail going in, better still will be the second one. With having no chimney-breast on this side of the roof, the remaining rolls of felt have to be wedged between the thin cross-pieces higher up the roof; Murphy assures me that they are not likely to come loose and knock the pair of us off the roof, but I'm not convinced and take it upon myself to relieve him of the hammer, a couple of pieces of wood and some nails and I lay a section of double-thickness wooden cross-pieces just to make absolutely sure that they'll not suddenly roll away; Murphy grins wryly, he knows I'm being sensible but he won't admit it. We have a minor hold-up when the large box of nails which Murphy has entrusted to behave in the way he assured me that the rolls of felt would, suddenly goes crashing over the edge of the roof, dislodged by the vibrations of his hammering, it makes a thunderous crash as it hits the deck; he's not amused at having to return to earth and gather them up!

Mercifully the roofing-felt lasts out and we finish the job with the very last roll, giving me a fighting chance in a late dash to find a loaf somewhere. I ask Murphy if he fancies a trip to town, but he declines, he already enjoys the luxury of home-made bread; but secretly, I rather enjoy the thought of a few moments on my own after what has been a long and hazardous day's work; slipping off quietly to buy a loaf of bread seems to be the perfect tranquilizer.

Seeing as tomorrow will be taken up in threshing at the hill farm, it seems a timely breaking of the week in that the swallows will be allowed vital time to re-settle into their new dimly-lit five-star accommodation, and it will enable my lungs to swap their plaster dust for corn dust, a change being as good as a rest kind of thing, but I really am looking forward to it with all the enthusiasm that it triggered in me as a boy when the threshing tackle came to the village. These idle thoughts drift leisurely through my mind as my little beloved Morris van and I roll back home with two sturdy loaves, two tired cabbages, two sore eyes and two aching ears; I'm in no immediate hurry to be back risking my life up on a roof with a wild man wielding a lump-hammer!

Return of the Potato-Eaters

Wednesday arrives polished, alive and glowing; the big red rooster is throwing his noise up into the golden air, so long as he's nearest he's got to be the loudest even though fainter faraway cocks are doing exactly the same and for the identical paranoid reason. With all the hefty hens he has to shout over, his flesh has turned to timber, all tenderness long since sown to the sky, all energy burned in a rage of procreating bedlam: if cockerels laid eggs, their yolks would be granite. Geese and goslings are on the pond and a moorhen has dared to entrust a nest in the fingers of a submerged branch; everywhere is peaceful and I am held in stillness, not daring to allow a ripple of myself to ruffle any part of it. The ripe rubbery stink of a fox suddenly brushes across my senses, it's unmistakable and I am compelled to send out my first ripples across the morning and make myself known. Then I see him, a big dog-fox stalking down towards the pond and I feel tingles racing throughout me as I become the protector of my feathered compatriots and pick up the first thing that I can lay my hands on, a small red welly, heavily stuffed with dirty socks and I throw it with all my might, missing the fox by a whisker but sending him effectively on his way. For my efforts I am condemned by the geese and the two Muscovy ducks eye me with undisguised resentment, only the chickens seem to be aware of what I have done and they clamour and cluck nervously amongst the nettles, with their cockerel now turned to teak with the sudden acceleration of his stresses. I spend a little time in broadcasting my own scent about the place and, with no-one watching, I walk around peeing my own mark upon the world, anyone seeing me would take me for a pervert! As I walk back I am met by Tony, the only genuine male cat remaining and I take him up and walk slowly back with him on my shoulder, purring. This nudges me into checking to see that the rest of the family are okay and there's no way I can avoid taking the tin-opener and opening a tin of food for them and blessing their new day in the best way I can.

Even though no-one else has stirred, I don't feel that I can relax with fox-smells still smarting in my nose, and so I bang about the place and generally let it be known that I'm abroad. Two cuckoos seem to be squabbling in the tree over the pond, one chases the other away before he himself glides away calling his noise, the only noise he knows, trying to make it the loudest. I'm wondering why it is that I don't feel the urge to shout or make a noise before others, I think it's that I feel silence to be more effective and easily identifiable, far better than noise in this amalgamation of reason and flexibility known as 'humanity'. Noise, I feel, is probably more evident of insecurity or inadequacy, rather than dominance. Constructive noise in the form of music is a whole separate dimension to enrich the magnificence of being human. Were a lark given the brain-size of a human, it would require a wingspan in excess of ten metres to get it airborne before it could ever be a Vaughan Williams in the sky!

The day has started and I'm eager for that old threshing smell, anxious for that drone of belt-driven machinery made of wood, the fat sacks filling, the corn spilling, the sand-dunes of chaff, the baler baling, the backs bending carting it away, the mice scurrying and the bottom of the rick where the rats all start shooting out in all directions: I'm glowing in anticipation, there's just something about threshing that's impossible to do justice to in any form of description. Cari will be coming over with Robin later, and I'm rather apprehensive over the prospect of his exuberance overflowing; he's going to need watching over like a hawk and I must warn the farm kids not to let him start showing off and to be 'firm' with him if necessary, I don't want to find him as part of a bale.

On my way back from taking the boys to school, I meet old Thomas from 'Thimble Hall', he's on his way over to the hill-farm to lend a hand with the threshing; it's amazing how the news spreads and how folk gather to help, it's really quite beautiful, a really lovely 'gathering round' kind of joyful thing, priceless in two ways, one in that it is a treasure in itself; and secondly, nobody gets paid; it's all done for love, simply that! I expect to see old 'Weasel' on his migration too, but I recall what Dan told me earlier, he'll be leaning on a shovel in a lane somewhere, working for the Council. Dan himself will certainly have his own agenda, patting his cow, kicking the dog and then walking to the top of his steep hill and back, twice, before making the postman an hour late; I expect to see him at some stage, but I don't expect to see Murphy, something else is eating him.

When I arrive at the farm there's a lot of activity, Gareth and Hugh are getting the tractor into position, lining it up with the belt connected and at the right tension, testing it, adjusting and re-adjusting, wedging blocks behind the wheels then checking to see that all belts are working: oil is squirted here and there, everything ready to go. A sturdy man wearing loud heavy boots and with his buttonless shirt agape all the way down to his strap, comes clomping into the yard, his slapped-on cap is precariously perched onto his sparse wiry hair at the back of his head and a stained stub of a cigarette is jabbed into the far corner of his mouth, enabling him to spit whilst smoking; this is Gareth's farmer neighbour 'Bryn', they've been pals from way back in schooldays and go everywhere together, he's going to take charge of the baler. Hugh and I climb up under the roof of the Dutch-barn, our job is to toss down the sheaves to old Thomas on the 'drum', who then cuts the twine with the penknife that he cuts his tobacco with and then feeds the loose corn into a gaping dark hole which it is not advisable to tumble into. Elwyn, who is still absent from school with his 'bad back', is on secret 'owl-duty' and is closely attended by the terrier, he'll also be a floating worker responding to any calls for assistance, but mostly on the lookout for rats.

The droning has started and Gareth is dashing about checking that everything is working properly, everything is and soon the first bales are excreted from the baler and a rick of them is started, much to the delight of the high-spirited children. Cari and Robin have joined us and Dan too has found his way over and is humping sacks of grain to a store in an outbuilding. Up on top, old Thomas stands God-like, slightly stooped, peaceful and solid, at total harmony with everything about him; he doesn't hurry, he just chugs along making no noise other than farting, even these sound more like doves croodling; he's done this kind of work throughout his life, all three score years and ten of it, and he tells me that he's now living on 'borrowed time' and is ready and waiting for the angels to come down and take him away; he seems very happy over the prospect.

Mice are now squirting out from almost every sheaf that a pitchfork lifts, the rick is full of them and the scraggly farm-cat and a couple of others are spoiled for choice. Robin is in his element with a hat full of blind baby mice which he's drooling over and is lovingly stroking them to their inevitable death. He gets wildly excited when we eventually reach the bottom of the rick where the rats are, all mayhem breaks out, the terrier can't cope, rats are streaking about in all directions, they're running over my feet making me more than glad to have my trousers well tucked into my wellies. Poor old Thomas almost topples into the black hole when the sheaf that I toss him has two rats in it; he avoids being threshed somehow, but his cap doesn't, and is now destined to becoming part of a straw bale; he looks half naked without his beloved cap, all pink and tender and wispy silver. Elwyn meanwhile has struck it rich, he's going to have the fattest young tawny owls in the principality and is forming a gruesome pile of dead rats while the children all shriek and scream, both terrified and electrified together, a strange ecstasy all crammed into the same bubble-bursting moment.

The first rick is finished; there's a gallon of tea brewing over in the farmhouse together with a table laid for a potato and bread feast, a whole mountain white and steaming, awaiting the dying of the groaning wheels and the last slap of the belts, then the sound of laughing babbling voices of a menfolk dusted and grimed, well-satisfied to see half a barn full of light once more.

We are all gathered around the long table, it reminds me of Van Gogh's painting, 'The Potato Eaters' come to life with all the chatter and easy laughter; everyone is in fits over poor Thomas's cap getting threshed, and when Dan adds, "I thought you was doing a jugglin' act with them rats ... I never see'd a man look so scared ... I thought your teeth was gonna come out an' get threshed an' all!" There are tears rolling down every cheek, tears of a different kind however from the toddler under the table who thinks it great fun to pinch old Thomas's testicles, only to have the old man's heavy boot flatten his fingers to the cold hard floor. Thomas doesn't even bat an eyelid and carries on being laughed over as though sweet nothing has happened; the noise of the child's crying is lost in the din, it's all to no effect. I've never known boiled potatoes and bread to taste so good, it's the salty golden butter that makes all the difference and is making the tea seem like champagne and is keeping the kettle on the boil; only when the table is bare will the afternoon start. I glance down at Robin to check that he's okay and his glistening slippery top lip and big crumby grin tells me that he's having the time of his life.

It isn't worth the time and effort to re-position all the machinery into better alignment with the new rick, so we adapt a conveyor-belt system with me tossing the sheaves down to Hugh, he then tosses them up to Gareth on the 'drum' and he throws them across to Thomas. Dan is now glad of some assistance from Elwyn in the bagging and carting of grain, while big Bryn diligently threads the baler with long wires, knowing that Hugh will be there to help if bales start coming too fast. Everything slows off when we get down to the last bit where the rats are and there is a letting off of steam in a crescendo of blood-lust; rats are simply not tolerated at any cost and are despised without any mercy whatsoever. Somewhere bound-up in a bale, is old Thomas's cap, more importantly so too are his National Health spectacles, he didn't tell anyone about these because he knew they'd still be laughing, but he's not complaining, he won't be needing them in heaven.

I watch Elwyn eagerly stuffing dead rats into a bag; "How many?" I shout. "Twenty seven!" he squeaks back, trying to hurry away with his wretched harvest before anyone becomes suspicious. He needn't worry though, everyone is preoccupied with the rounding-off process and are generally letting off steam and feeling well-satisfied.

The last bale brings threshing to an end, the farm-cat is puking and I'm summoning-up the diplomacy of a saint before trying to persuade Robin to part with his bald blind mice. Without his cap and glasses, old Thomas has the look of frailness about him as he shuffles about; I recognise his problem and ask him if he can see alright, but he calmly assures me that they were only his reading glasses and that he can't read anyway; as for the hat, he tells me that he's got seven or eight spares back in his cottage, but that he won't be needing them either where he'll soon be going.

There is a slow drift back into the yard once the tractor has died and all the moving bits within the great threshing beast have sunken into stillness; this is when three hard sets of elbows lean on the pigsty wall as Gareth, Bryn and Dan partake of cigarettes and are contorting into extravagant postures of relaxation, gabbling away and showing their weather-worn laugh-lines. There's a rough kind of raucousness throughout their gentleness, it doesn't include Thomas though, his softness has steered him into the farmhouse to join Hugh and the women, which all allows me to slip off discreetly to see what Elwyn is up to. I find him gazing devotedly at his owls, telling them in a whispered voice that he's got some nice rats for them. I point out to him that the corpses will very soon turn rotten and that owls need their food to be very fresh and so his supply will be useless after a couple of days. "I'm gonna put about ten in the deep-freeze," he says, ... "nobody's gonna be any the wiser, honest,

Jimmy!" A broad smile warms his face and he says quietly "Lookin'
good ain't they, I feeds them pretty good… bacon, sausages, steak,
starlings and crows… better than I'm bloody getting'!" "What, no
jelly and custard?" I laugh in exasperated resignation, pointing out
the risk of contamination and the prospect of being served rat on
his dinner-plate; he sees the funny side whilst dismissing the other,
my only consolation coming from the fact that the owls are almost
ready to fly and that he'll soon be back in his classroom learning
useful things like, on one hand, how the Universe was created by a
'big bang', an eternity of 'nothing' spontaneously exploding and
creating countless millions of 'somethings' with ever more
countless trillions of smaller somethings orbiting, balancing,
journeying forever outwards and containing unimaginable variety;
then, on the other hand, a 'God' proclaiming, 'Let there be Light',
and somehow manufacturing an 'Adam and Eve', (others had their
Kevins and Traceys), and a way forward was shown to be a
bewildering minefield, a jungle of unspeakable hell right up to this
very day. All this Science Fiction stuff, yet not one single mention
on how to keep an owl as a pet!

Our small gang make our way back across the hill, the boys
may be back already from their 'house of the four R's', but Cari has
left them a note to say that we wont be long, as we aren't; they've
hardly sampled a moment of unadulterated bliss before we all pile
in, Robin first, hardly able to contain himself in the spilling of his
day's beans. Cari and I decide that the occasion calls for something
like Fish and Chips, eaten out in the open somewhere; the
suggestion is met with wild approval and, after tidying ourselves up
and making sure that Robin's fingers are absolutely spotless, we
take off in the van and head for town.

Later, the boys all wrecked in sleep, I reflect over the day,
telling Cari about Elwyn's owls and in particular his plan to store
dead rats in the freezer and fridge, it seems both hilarious and
frightening at the same time but, what surprises me is that Gwyneth
told Cari about Elwyn's owls, so she is also in on his secret; I'm
beginning to wonder who else knows; all I hope is that there is not
a sudden outbreak of the Black Death up at the farm! Elwyn's dream
is for them to settle on his shoulder whenever he whistles them, be
it day or night; he wants closeness with them because he loves them

and this is his only way, his only chance in life to give it a go. Tomorrow I have to go up on the roof, no wings, no safety-net, no anything; I can't wait for the weekend to arrive.

At a loss to know what's Welsh, for...HELP!

Thursday morning, an indifferent sky that's been chalked white over charcoal, no real clouds, just smudges and smears that don't say one thing or another, all heaven is playing it cool and I can hear the sheep without any 'A'-levels, complaining over the meteorological inexactitude confronting them. The grass is growing, its richness pacifies the two-stomached cows wrecked heavily in a blissful ignorance before excreting mountains mightier than mole-hills and far more numerous. I have to present myself to the morning and begin to turn this heavy iron page, dependant on my old pal Murphy who now appears to be seeing the world heart-shaped and is finding it increasingly difficult to stay focused on the job; all we need is one big last effort to get the roof on, everything else I can do myself and look forward to with an appetite that's acquiring the dimension of a disease.

It's strangely dark inside the cowshed, a bit of sunlight would make all the difference, but there's no sign of that this morning, no sign of rain either and the swallows seem to be happy as they sail in and out, always from the direction of the barn. The bantams seem to be settling too, with pied wagtails and redstarts most certainly nesting somewhere between roof and wall of the barn. The starlings in the cowshed wall are now, with the warmth of their bellies alone, transforming the insides of eggs to blood and veins in the shape of themselves, only the odd scuffling noise betrays their vigil. Everything and everywhere is waiting, a kind of yawning pregnancy; there's not much that I can do and so I'm caught-up in the waiting-game too. To kill time, I burn some of the rubbish and allow the chimney to advertise my presence, it also serves to dissuade the jackdaws from their suicidal tendencies as well as giving me a morsel of luxury to start my day.

I hear Murphy charging down the hill in response to my smoke-signal, he's in high spirits as he clatters to where I am seated sampling a little of the promised life. It's obvious that he's eager to make a start and this is confirmed when he growls, "C'mon, Jimmy; the sooner we gets started, the sooner we gets finished!" I fear there's the risk of a few corners getting cut during the course of the day, which means that I'm going to have to be doubly watchful, even though this means getting called a few uncomplimentary names. I watch him rush off up the ladder like a monkey, then scuttle across to the chimney-breast where I've already placed the box of galvanised nails and lump-hammer. Whilst he's there waiting, I grapple with the first large sheet of corrugated iron and inch my way up the ladder sliding it ahead of me, it isn't easy without help and I have to distract him from his waving across the marshy valley to his dark-haired goat-herd who's waving back at him. It makes sense for us to concentrate our efforts firstly into getting a dozen or so corrugated sheets up onto the roof and propped against the chimney, the reason being that, once we've nailed the bottom row on, the ladder will need to be up on the roof with us, hooked over the rooftop so's to stop it from sliding off and leaving us stranded. This seems to focus Murphy's thoughts and there is a spurt of productivity as the plan is put into operation; should we lose the ladder, our last resort then would be to make a hole in the felt, remove a few pieces of wood and lower ourselves down into the bedroom, hoping to land safely on a cross-beam or piece of chipboard.

We very quickly learn that driving nails into corrugated metal is a hit and miss business and requires the maximum of force; the very first nail that Murphy hits goes shooting off like a bullet, its point unable to find any purchase on the curved, hard, slippery metal and I can see that it's going to be a long, hard job, one that's soon going to make Murphy want to give up the hammer and have a go at holding the sheet in position instead. Several more nails go whirring off and I can sense his frustration beginning to boil, erupting to a head when the next nail flies off and the hammer brings blood from his thumb, splattering the corrugated sheet like a Jackson Pollock painting in red. Murphy bellows in pain, I can feel it myself but I can do nothing because I'm holding the bloody heavy thing, stopping it from knocking him off the ladder. In an explosion of anger he forgets his pain for one split second and throws the hammer as far as he can, screaming "Bastard!" all around and down the valley, blistering everything in its path. I shuffle across the roof with the corrugated masterpiece and prop it against the chimney, leaving poor Murphy slumped and moaning on top of the ladder.

Apart from showing sympathy, I have to remember roughly where the hammer went and I take little comfort from knowing that this is what it's going to be like until the job is finished. Back on the ground I consult the first-aid kit and the pair of us wander off in search of the hammer with the first laughter of the morning just beginning to trickle out from where the throbbing pain had been. After searching through the grass for what seems an age, we conclude that it must have landed in the hedge and so we concentrate our efforts in examining the tangled branches and, sure enough, I spot it wedged in a hawthorn fork. We proceed and I take my turn with the hammer, eventually succeeding in driving some nails in, but not before I have splattered my own thumb and forefinger several times. The valley resounds with hammering and foul language and the completion of the first row has cost us dearly, I'll certainly not be playing the guitar for a few weeks.

We decide against taking a lunch break and to press on whilst the weather is holding, hoping to complete one side before evening. This is the stage when we must bring the ladder up and hook it over the rooftop, first making sure that we have enough corrugated sheets up here with us. It's a laborious and bloody process, Murphy is lying face-down on the ladder beside the sheet which he is holding in place while I crouch down beside it on the other side, gingerly but firmly intent on forcing the nails into breaking the surface of the metal and then driven hard into the wood beneath. Once the first two nails are in Murphy can relax, something that's hard for him to do and so he watches me with a growing impatience, constantly snatching the hammer away from me in trying to force the pace, resulting in more nails flying off like bullets in a cowboy film. Then he splatters his thumb again and I have to snatch the hammer from him before this too goes flying off the roof.

Once the pain has eased, Murphy has to get off the ladder and slide it carefully across the roof into position beside the next one to be nailed down, making sure not to detach it from over the top. As I am turning to crawl down to fetch another sheet, there's a high panic-stricken yell and a sliding sound, he has impatiently tried to bounce the ladder across without getting off it and has unhooked it, he and the ladder are sliding off! My split-second reaction is to leap sideways face-down and at full-stretch, grab the rooftop with my fingers whilst at the same time stabbing my toes down between the last rungs of the ladder, halting its race to earth. I can hear Murphy screaming some distance behind me, but I've miraculously managed somehow to hold the ladder with my hooked feet, Murphy is hanging from the bottom of it high above the ground, I can feel it bucking and jerking wildly as he struggles to get back onto it. I don't know how much longer I can hold on, my fingers are giving way and my toes are hurting. "Hang on, Jimmy ... don't let go for Christ's sake!" The jerking movements tell me that he's inching his way back and the yelling stops as he clambers his way back up the ladder before I feel it suddenly become lighter and I know that he's back on the roof beside me. I yell at him to take hold of it and not to let it go, my body is being stretched apart and the last thing I want to hear now is the ladder clattering away down to the ground leaving us both stranded up here. He complies and, with much relief, I roll over onto my back and we both burst out laughing.

I have to admit it was luck and not judgment that saved him, I could never do that again even if I tried a hundred times. "Somebody up there is looking after us," I say with my head back taking in the whole of the sky. "It bloody well looks like it!" he sniggers, thrusting his blood-stained bandaged thumb in front of my eyes, and I shake my head in resignation, knowing that Murphy's impetuosity remains intact, safe even from God's interventions; nothing will ever tame Murphy! Just as I'm thinking this, a change suddenly washes over him and I am compelled to eat the very words of my last thought; he's caught sight of his landlady wriggling seductively along the hedge in this direction and, without any explanation he slides the ladder over the edge of the roof and lowers it to the ground, leaving me with the words, "I'll be back in half an hour!" I watch him race off, 'Max Tractor' has nothing to compare with this and I watch them both slip away into the dense dark foliage.

There isn't a lot one can do sitting alone on a tin roof for close-on two hours; watching low-flying jets and a couple of buzzards loses its appeal after a while and, like it or not, an alternative has to be found. It doesn't take long for me to calculate how many more corrugated sheets will be required to finish the job and I check on the nail supply, bearing in mind the current rate of loss; we're going to need some more and I think it might be a good idea to try holding them in place with the pliers next time instead of finger and thumb, this should eliminate some of the pain as well as conserve the nails. There's still no sign of Murphy, so I very carefully shuffle down the roof to the ladder and make it safely back to the ground where I kill time pondering. Looking at my damaged hand, I consider it best not to touch it until later, it's congealing nicely and I don't want to disturb the healing process at this halfway stage, but I will attempt to ease an industrial glove onto the hand in the hope of it minimising further damage. Killing more time I forage like a hen and gather up a few of the nails that have rained down, every one of them will be made to count; then I find my ex-government heavy pliers and optimistically make my way back onto the roof and wait for the earth to stop moving.

Rosy-cheeked and ruffled, Murphy reappears, green knees and with cuckoo-spit and bits of clover littering him; a cat that'd just found two kippers couldn't match the smugness of his smile; I don't know what she's done to him but he most certainly hasn't had his palms read! He looks at me with bloodshot eyes, pathetic as a hamster on a wheel; I'll be doing the banging from now on! My new method of gripping the nails with the pliers prior to driving them in proves successful and compensates for earlier losses; I just have to make sure that Murphy doesn't slide blissfully off the roof again, as for bouncing the ladder across to the next position, he hasn't the energy available so I feel relatively safe, taking full advantage of his blatant smugness. We make surprising progress, it's amazing what difference a little 'siesta' makes!

By degrees, Murphy gets round to feeling a trace of guilt, in part over the fact that I'm doing all the hammering and I have to insist that the system we've got is working okay and that I think it best that he continues to hold the sheets in position and to remain lying there thinking of England; I know that tomorrow will be different, he'll be his old wild self again and I shall need to be on my guard. I still can't believe that the rain has held off, a shower now would make the roof treacherous, emphasising the importance of bashing on while it's dry and, the nearer we get to completion, the greater grows the expanse of slippery plastic-coated metal, making me reconsider having an anchor-rope of some sort when we start on the other side tomorrow, but I know what Murphy's reaction will be if I do raise the subject. As a crowning gesture, I invite him to be the one who drives the nails into the last sheet to round-off our day in celebratory fashion, an invitation which he snatches greedily, disregarding use of the pliers, resulting in the first three nails flying off into the unknown, then whacking his thumb again and slumping once more into the missionary position and wailing. I know it must be hurting, mine is now throbbing unbearably and requires dressing, but there's no way I'm leaving this roof until the last sheet has been nailed down, so I request one final act of masochism: for him to hold the wretched thing in place while I hammer a conclusion to our day of ups and downs.

Friday dawns noisily on the caravan roof, the weather has taken its brakes off with a boisterous breeze underlining the fact. My first job after driving the boys to school, is to go off and pick up the remaining corrugated sheets, I won't need to disturb Murphy and, hopefully the rain might have stopped by the time I get back; I'm in no rush and I know that Murphy most certainly won't be in one either. I have a bandage and plasters on my cuts together with an almost complete set of deep purple fingernails. No doubt Murphy will be similarly adorned to help dampen his enthusiasm to complete the job today, weather permitting of course. If the wind wins, the rain will stop; if the rain wins, the wind will stop; it's too much to hope for both of them to stop and for the sun to shine warmly on us.

I have an uneventful trip and return with my windscreen-wipers switched off, the wind has won and I unload by the marsh meadow gate just as Gareth is passing in the Landrover. He notices me about to carry the stuff across and he stops and shouts, "Don't struggle over with them, Jimmy; if you hang on ten minutes I'll pop them over for you!" I'm more than glad of the suggestion and show him a grateful thumbs-up and rest my elbows on the gate and enjoy the fresh wind on my skin. The postman shoots by in his little red van, peeping his horn and showing me his elbow; I feel I have become a close part of all the land about me as I contentedly wait for Gareth to return. I don't have long to wait, when he says 'ten minutes', he means ten minutes, and we load the corrugated sheets into the back of the Landrover and, to my surprise, he opens the gate, deciding it sufficiently firm to cross over the marsh at this point. It's amazing, the Landrover makes relatively easy work of it and flies up the steep bank at the other side, prompting Gareth to say, "Damn, I reckon we could get th'owd caravan over sometime at the weekend, Jimmy; it's dryin' out real tidy... and about bloody time!" I can hardly believe what I'm hearing and my batteries suddenly feel charged-up for the day, all I have to do now is to keep my fingers crossed that Murphy will turn up.

Once we've unloaded, Gareth and I wander around the place trying to decide on a suitable site for the caravan, choosing a spot on the front corner next to the lean-to, it will need clearing of rubble and a few bumps taken out to get it level, but that won't take me long to sort out. I wave him on his way and set about getting organised for the day; what rain there had been earlier has dried now and the wind promises to keep the air swept dry for the rest of the day. I realise that we'll still need to have half of the corrugated sheets up on the roof with us, propped against the chimney as before, which means going up and over to the other side to fetch them each time, an interesting prospect in this gusting wind. Then, true to form, I see old 'lover-boy' coming down the slope, a bright white bandage prominent on his thumb; I wave to show him that he's not alone and he comes laughing into the yard. "Bad luck, Jimmy!" he sniggers... "it looks like it's gonna be a nice day!" I nod in sympathy, knowing that he would have dearly loved it to pour down all day. "Don't worry, Murph," I say, ... "if we stick to the system that we worked out yesterday, it'll be a piece of cake, no more of your bouncing the ladder across the roof though, and if we hold the nails firmly with the pliers, we shan't lose any more and neither should we bust our hands... it's the wind we've got to watch out for today!"

After exchanging notes over the state of our injuries, we get started, carting the sheets up onto the roof first of all, then the remainder round to the front. Murphy goes up onto the roof as I do my balancing act of carrying the first sheet up the ladder ahead of me, a strong gust at this point could easily blow me and the corrugated sheet flying way over the muckheap; Murphy grabs it and hauls it up onto the roof without mishap, we've made our first mark on the day. The bottom row is completed inside three hours and the ladder is hauled up onto the roof and hitched into position over the rooftop. With there being no chimney-breast on this side, and with the ground diving steeply away down to the ditch below the orchard, it feels so much higher than the other side and the sense of danger is heightened thus. It doesn't help having military jets stealing silently along the valley floor and then, suddenly exploding across only feet above the chimney pot, scattering the flocks and herds into total bewildered diarrhoea panic. Buzzards and crows fly as high as these things and could so easily get sucked into their jets with catastrophic results; how we manage to avoid being blasted off the roof is a miracle and it isn't going to make the washing of our pants a particularly pleasant task either.

We make a start on the final row and I pray quietly that I shalln't be left killing time for two hours like I was yesterday. It helps with having to keep our wits about us in the unpredictable wind and focuses our attention towards staying on the roof rather than escaping from it. I'm glad of this because our progress is higher than yesterdays and there's a growing sense of achievement as we slowly but surely inch towards the final sheet. With the end in sight, I can sense a growing temptation in Murphy's mind, to have another go at bouncing the ladder across and he gives me a wry grin when he notices that I have read his mind; "It's a long way down, Murph; ... and it's hard concrete on this side ... it ain't worth it!" Patience wins and he gives me a rueful glance as we set about nailing the last sheet down. It then takes a further half an hour to nail down the five ridge-pieces, only now are we able to relax and celebrate. We straddle the rooftop precariously and shake hands in triumph; "Yippee!" he bellows and, in a momentary lapse of concentration and balance, dislodges the ladder and sends it vanishing clean over the edge and crashing to the ground: we are stranded! Eventually, we allow ourselves to look each other in the eye, but only briefly, one glance says it all. It's much too risky to try leaping down onto the lean-to roof, it wouldn't support us, so, there's only one thing we can do ... "Help! Help!"

With having the wind coming strongly now from the west, our

voices are not carrying back over to either Cari or Murphy's lady and are instead blowing to waste down filtering valley-sides in the opposite direction. A late spate of military war-machines rocket across deafeningly, their futility even more exposed within our thinking now, but it's really rather nice to see the swallows still going in and out!

Half and hour dawdles by and we fail dismally to attract any attention whatsoever; then, an aging halfwit pushing a bike with a spade tied to its crossbar, pauses a moment to pee by the gate, we wave furiously and scream for help, he waves back at us then slowly goes on his way, unable to comprehend our plight. "Shit!" Murphy curses ... "what's Welsh for HELP?" I burst out laughing, it's hilarious, we're up here making all this noise and it's having no effect whatsoever, it doesn't mean a thing. "Perhaps it's got a double 'll', Hellp!" I blurt, trying to demonstrate my Welsh pronunciation-skills and dribbling disgustingly as a result. Murphy catches my laughing epidemic and he too tries to say it in what he considers to be Welsh; we laugh and laugh and laugh until tears are silvering our cheeks, wetting the corrugated sheets and making our ribs ache. Reality once more begins to balance and I comment rather sardonically, "It's a pity that your lady-love couldn't have chosen this moment to come and lure you away to the woods; I don't reckon much to her sense of timing!" Murphy goes very quiet, I've touched on a raw nerve in him and he visibly droops into a worried-looking heap and mutters... "He's coming back tonight!" "So?" I question; "I love her, Jimmy; I loves her and she loves me, and tonight she's going to tell him!" "Bloody hell, Murph!" I whisper sympathetically... "You're better off staying up here!" I put my arm around his shoulders and give him a reassuring hug as he droops his head and I can hear him sniffing like a steam piston before the crisp voices of the boys tingles in our ears; help is at hand.

My little gang come up the track beneath the wind-filled fluttering sycamore and they come to an abrupt halt when they see us waving our arms and whining for help. Cari thinks we're acting the fool, it hasn't sunk in yet but, when it eventually does, her hysterical laughter puts birds to flight all down the wooded hillsides; never did any moment contain such power for her as this and she indulges in its fortuitous offering tormentingly and playfully, keeping us awaiting her pleasure, but she does by degrees get round to rescuing us and it feels absolutely marvellous to be back down on the ground. Murphy has long since lost all grace and patience and doesn't bother over niceties as he hares off into the wind, desperate for a few precious moments before 'he' returns. I tell Cari of Gareth's intention to tow the caravan across sometime over the weekend and she's thrilled as too are the boys and we all sit round a crackling fire, very much aware that we now have a solid roof over our heads as we start to work out a list of all the things we will need to bring over in advance of the caravan. The atmosphere is really buzzing; to know that we're on the verge of a brand new adventure is thrilling beyond belief and we will be able to share now in the shaping of our home; the major structural problems are behind us at last, it may not look too pretty but it'll stand up to anything the weather chooses to throw at it and has my blood, sweat and tears spilled throughout it for good measure.

Eager to get started, the boys look at their dung-smeared calf-parlour, unable to properly grasp that this will soon be their bedroom; I can hear them giggling and making 'Urgh' noises over the smears and smudges on the walls and I reassure them that it's all going to change and that I shall soon make it cosy for them. They rush off outside excitedly, re-familiarising themselves with the pig-sty which will be our toilet, the shed next to it which the cats will have and where we can store potatoes, gardening implements and the like, then off into the barn which is fathoms deep in ancient dung and where the bantams roost. As I'm sitting here watching showers of sparks exploding, it occurs to me that the provision of drinking-water has now risen on my list of priorities, and so, once the fire has quietened down sufficiently, we all wander off through the orchard and along the track to take another look at the freshwater spring under the hollybush to get a better idea of what's involved. When we turn round to come back, our new roof is shining there before us and the wisps of smoke staining from the chimney makes it feel cosy and inviting, even the bantam-cock contributes to the homely feeling by throwing out his breast and crowing up into the wind to show that he too has claimed it as home.

Keen as I am to begin work on preparing the site for the caravan, my battered hands are sorely pleading with me to attend to them and give them a rest until morning at the very least. I am more than happy to flop-out obligingly and succumb to the pyromanical tendencies of my three offspring; the innocent and dangerous beauty of their fascination with flame, a very primitive echo throughout time; their bright eyes dance as I wisely watch and Cari casually points out something frivolous and of no real worth at all; today has been 'Friday the thirteenth'... I should have known!

Smelling of Roses

From the frail tenderness of Spring's growing, the year inexorably surges to the call of the planet's angle; despite the rain, the roses bud-up while hawthorn expires in a fit, prematurely aging the year before its hardly got started; it wasn't quite the same with coltsfoot and snowdrop, these were part of winter, leaving neither haw or berry: when was the last flower and the first?

I watch the chaffinch braving the rain bringing her eggs to ripen, wondering when the dialogue begins between old and new when all is continuity, never ending and never beginning. The acorn takes from the tree, the very tree, the always tree that ever it has been, same tree, same moment of eternity. Within the magma of the chaffinch eggs is written of mosses, of good things and bad, of colours, of song, just as it is with us and every other living thing. The fourth 'R' of the curriculum restricts, is rigid and does not release in the search for reason deep and true. For every conceivable thing there is a reason and to go in search of that reason is to go in search of something Holy. Heaven is the body of which we are all but an infinitesimal part, less that the tiniest speck. The body is 'God' and is without beginning or end; infinity is a flower.

The dandelions are already showing me their science and are waiting for breezes to take them, dreams an' all, on white umbrellas flying far and high, but the last two weeks have brought about a return of wet weather and I too have been awaiting breezes and for the caravan to be towed across. Our migration has been slow and gentle in the late spring rain, see-sawing back and forth across the marsh carrying baskets, bags, brooms, brollies and bikes; cutlery, crockery, clothes, paintings, preserves, pots and pans... just where has it all come from? I've nailed down the bedroom floor and bricked-in the last triangle above the window and the ladder has been put to use as a temporary stairs. My fingers have healed as a result of waiting and now the first dog-rose is flowering down the hedge and the sun has returned; everywhere is warm and polished and today our waiting is over, the caravan is by slow degrees breaking to pieces as it is being towed by the Landrover; encounters with gate-posts have scraped and gouged the sides, the back window has fallen out, the door has burst open and the chemical-toilet has spilled. It looks a very sorry sight coming over the marsh, bottoming out on the mud with its wheels vanishing into deep holes; but it is on its way at last and being closely followed by enthusiastic cows and sheep who mistakenly consider it to be something for them; even the bull has joined in and I have to restrain Robin from getting involved in the thick of it, I don't trust the old bull when he shows such high spirits ... neither do I trust Robin.

The Landrover revs and smokes as it hauls the twisting, buckling caravan up the steep hill and there are several more metallic scraping noises before the last gatepost has been knocked skew-whiff and the Landrover comes trundling down the last slope to the cowshed. All the cattle and sheep have come to a halt as they watch Gareth manoeuvre the caravan backwards into its final resting place. The boys all cheer as he unhitches the tow-bar and Hugh comes striding down the field carrying the window which has fallen out. I help to get the caravan level, wedging rocks under the tow-bar and securing the wheel so's to make sure that it can't roll away. Whatever damage has been incurred will have to be fixed with string, wire or sticky-tape, we're going to be busy and with the disinfectant too!

The scent of tobacco laces the air, a moment to savour as Gareth stokes his chromium pipe, sucking and puffing pleasurably, praising the turnabout in the weather and scouring the skies for signs of cloud but finding none. A swallow almost knocks the cap from his head as he enters the lean-to and comes into the room which now has a new bedroom floor above it as well as a new roof above that. He notes the changes and, after a few wild humorous outbursts over the sudden demise of the caravan, restates his intention to fence-off and plough a small strip of land at the foot of our garden. I gratefully add my own intention to dig a well of sorts, talk of which draws us back out into the sunlight and to wandering down under the fruit trees, then following the ditch up to the freshwater spring so that we can take a closer look at it. The sparkling water is unbelievably clear as it forces out from the dark earth, then races away beneath the sedges; it looks delicious, irresistible in its purity. "There's plenty there for you, Jimmy... damn nice water too!"

We saunter back somewhat aimlessly under a whole fanfare of chaffinches and a pale blue heaven with a sun that's newly-hatched the roses all along the rambling hedges. Any notion I might have lingering inside my brain, that I can indulge in this gift of weather is rudely denied me as I confront the mountain of rubble that has spewed down the orchard slope, it's an absolute tip and I must deal with it, disperse it neatly somehow ... not the easiest of tasks to confront, but the treasury of promise all around is indefinable. I can feel it, sense the little bubbles bursting and fireworks exploding in my warm-fingered sons touching and in Cari's eyes dancing and her voice tripping over itself; we are so very glad for this moment in our lives.

Whilst it's all an adventure, a fairytale of sorts, nobody knows of my growing concerns over the dwindling finances; I wasn't rich to start with, but now I'm getting to worry over it and somehow must find a way of injecting vital funds before confronting an autumn and more importantly, a winter; long-term thinking is essential and I must not be lured into any false sense of security just because everywhere and everything just happens to be bathed in rose-tinted sunlight. There's no immediate panic, but I know what I must do to keep this dream on the road.

The smell of disinfectant lingers throughout the night, sleep is playing hard-to-get and some thunderously huge beast is rubbing a patch of ring-worm against the jagged corner of the caravan shaking it rhythmically and monotonously and I can hear the 'splat', 'splat', 'splat' of group-crapping, knowing that, just outside the door, stands several tons of utterly idle beef, still unable to fathom out what this new 'thing' is in their midst. The cats are safe and snug in the wooden lean-to shed beside the barn, they'll be more than glad to stay there until they become more familiar with their new world. While the swallows are sleeping, all I can hear is breathing, rubbing, 'splatting', with the occasional outcry of an owl and the jabbered unintelligible words spoken in sleep in the jet-blackness all about me; I feel so very far removed from the world, separated from it by colossal distance and I can understand even more deeply how these night-noises can produce a silence greater by far than soundlessness alone. As I lie here I wonder what are the dreams of swallows, do they have pictures too? Do they cart memory-pictures and have nightmares when all the pictures get muddled up? My own thoughts readily spring pictures to illustrate them, and all of these are archived within my brain available at the very tickle of a thought, just as here at dead of darkest night, I can be bathed in sunlight. A steam-train can be racing like a dragon over an ink-black night landscape, scooping up water at great speed, filling its tanks and with the flickering glow of the flames of the fire in the cab illuminating the water frothing, foaming, overflowing in an explosion from the tanks. That memory picture is always for me a dragon in the night, as clear now as it was then when I was a small child.

As the first robin breaks from the dark in a glitter of tingling sound, my drowsied mind has already resolved to later walk with coins to the kiosk and attempt to sell myself once more to a Television Industry, it's what I did before and is what I must do again. Confetti -spending has come to an end, every single penny must count from now on because I know all too well that winter will be long and hard as well as dark and cold up in these hills. I draw the curtain slightly and wipe away the condensation and a huge disgusting backside is smearing flush against the glass and I can see at a glance that we have a statued solid multitude of cud-chewing gentleness completely blocking our immediate access. I instinctively rise, snatch on my trousers, bodge my feet into wellies, grab the broom and try to open the door only to find another massive backside in the way. I wake everybody up as I bash the door against this huge bum, then it suddenly shoots forward and I'm instantly in their midst wielding the broom. Even the bull is surprised by my sudden appearance and there is a bundling clumsy panic and a whole lot more 'splat' noises and snorted silvery slobber flying everywhere. I hardly dare move, the ground all around me is a sea of green 'yuk' which I must somehow clear up if the boys are to arrive at school smelling more of roses! The beasts don't disperse very far but stand gawping with expressions of utter disbelief, the occasional one snorts somewhat defiantly and I don't feel over confident about my containing the situation. I know that I must persist regardless of how long it takes and be careful not to arouse the bull's temper; with luck, things might drift back to normal once their curiosity has been satisfied.

Before getting too engrossed in dirt, I wander off down to the spring to fetch water to start the day and I'm pleasantly surprised by how the mud is firming-up after only a short spell of sunny weather. The heavens are cloudless again and there's hardly any breeze at all, it really is a delightful young morning. A flock of this year's long-tailed tits are flitting from tree to tree, excitedly feeding on the newly abundant caterpillars, while the bluetits in my front wall are likewise carting beak-fulls of the same to their ravenous brood. All around is a feeding frenzy, the starlings are waddling amongst the grass digging up the grubs, some are pecking at the dry cow-pats, they're spoiled for choice while the bantams have struck it rich on the old dung-heap. When I return, a semi-circle of cows are suspiciously eyeing me, uncertain of what to do next; I have no such doubts as to what I must do and I take up the stiff yard broom and set about cleaning away the mess whilst at the same time trying to work out how to prevent it from becoming a regular nightly occurrence.

Our day has started; my persistence pays and the cows gradually disperse amongst the growing grasses; stomachs require filling, itches need scratching, gaps have to be forced into hedges and fences need flattening to the ground. As for the boys, from now on they will have to carry their school shoes and wear wellies to cross the marsh meadow, changing footwear in the lane and hiding their wellies under the hedge, where Robin can't find them. I accompany them to start with, we'll soon discover where the dry areas are and find alternative routes for when the bull is present. It all seems like great fun, especially on this marvel of a morning; even at this hour the sun is hot as I wave them on their way and amble back to where I have an appointment with a freshwater spring and a pick and spade.

The cats tentatively emerge to their new surroundings, providing Robin with a revived sense of purpose; with having a family of cats to counsel, he's less likely to be getting under our feet and it allows Cari and I to discuss the money situation. The conclusion of which finds us in total agreement over my suggestion to find a few weeks freelance design work in making safe provision for autumn and winter. We'll need a thoroughly well-stocked larder, loads of dried foodstuffs and other bulk items such as honey, yeast extract, oil, cheese, cat food, candles and all manner of stuff besides, so it seems right and proper that I sacrifice just a small part of summer in addressing the problem.

Before starting work on the well, I fill all available containers with water knowing that our supply will take some time to clear once I have churned it up. I have no idea where those long-ago previous dwellers had their well, even Dan doesn't know and he's spent most of his life hereabouts; my guess is that they probably took their water from the stream, it was surely clean enough at that time and probably had crayfish and trout in it too for good measure. After stringing-up a clothes-line under the fruit trees, I head off for the spring and set to work. Frogs start leaping about in all directions as I begin to probe the sludge with my shovel and there is soon an ancient stench of years of rotted leaves, rushes and other decayed matter, together with rocks, roots and other fragments of fallen branches, all of which require the pick and brute force to make any progress at all. I'm very thankful for the sun burning down on my back because I'm absolutely soaked to the skin and the sludgy water is not only dripping from my brow, but is creeping up my wellies; I shall be forced to stop as soon as it starts to overflow inside them and then continue my dredging from the bank. If I dredge it about two and half to three feet deep I shall be well satisfied, to go any deeper could be dangerous.

Cari and Robin come to see how I'm getting on. I can see our cat, Tony, following them, tail in the air, apprehensive, pausing frequently to double-check on his whereabouts. What I have done doesn't impress them, it looks an absolute sludgy mess, and it smells a bit, which doesn't help. I try to reassure them that it will take a little time to settle and for all the muddy clay and rock around the sides to bed-in and for new vegetation to grow, adding that once it has settled, I shall fix the old front-door porch roof over it and give it a rustic look ... they're not taken in by any of my reassurances and I gather up my tools and scramble up the bank under the barbed wire to join them.

The morning has gone and I feel reasonably satisfied with what I have achieved regardless of the indifferent responses, it's bound to look a mess at this stage and it's true, it will settle down and begin to clear once it has filled up and is overflowing. We must keep an eye on the time today, not only do I have to make a phone-call, but I also want to meet the boys on their way home from school so that I can help them to familiarise themselves with the new system; I don't want them forgetting that they have wellies under the hedge and so come across the marsh in their school shoes. I also want to get them to make a regular habit of checking to see where the bull is because if I'm going to be working away, I shall need a little peace of mind. To simplify things, Cari suggests that we go in the van to make the phone-calls, there's a kiosk down in the valley about half a mile from the school, we can pick up the boys on the way back. This is what we do and I make my call and am assured that there will be some work for me, probably in July and August, replacing someone on holiday. I am obliged to give them Dan's address, a timely reminder to get myself a biscuit tin and to nail it to the gate-post, same as everyone else.

In the meantime we have a miracle of a heatwave and it becomes all too obvious why this marvellous month is known as the 'Month of Roses'. Every hedge is decked in rambling briared celebration, a whole crazy palette of pinks from pale to deep; everywhere I look is a sea of roses. What was previously mud is now solid baked clay and cracks are appearing over the entire earth, it's an unbelievable transformation and the grass is growing quicker than the animals can eat it. Obesity has changed the lambs from cuddly toys to butchers joints, and thick oily wool is causing the old mutton to pant and seek out shade. Each time anyone visits the new pig-sty toilet, it is crammed with sheep and lambs, it's the same in the cat-shed and the barn, any old shade will do; their droppings are everywhere but it's easier to clear up than the other stuff.

The starlings left their nest this week and are free in the bounteous air, joined up with other families that hatched and flew at the same time; great flocks are just floating from field to field, gobbling and gorging, ridding the farmers of pests whilst at the same time becoming one, and for no justifiable reason. Nothing could be more joyful than a flock of starlings feeding in June; it seems sad now that they have gone from the wall.

Irresistible as the weather is, I'm missing it, slaving away inside the cowshed till I'm grazed and bleeding again and my lungs full of plaster dust; it's a hard slow job and it's a sweaty one too in this heat. I keep wanting to be further ahead than I am, but I must remain patient in getting to where I want to be: I can't make a staircase out of a loft-ladder until I've concreted the floor and I can't concrete the floor until I've cleared it and put hardcore down and I can't make a hardcore until I've sorted bricks and stones and have smashed them into small even pieces with the lump-hammer; I then have to cart more sand and gravel for the amount of concreting that's to be done and I have to keep making new dams in the stream now that the water-tub has been emptied. Patience, that's what I need! I never thought that I would be wanting a heavy downpour so soon after the last lot, but there's comfort in knowing that, now that we have a roof, the tub will soon fill up after a storm.

Under a perfect sky, Cari takes a bowl of washing down to the stream to wash, Robin helps her, garlanded in a daisy-chain that she has made for him; needless to say that it doesn't last long and he's soon muddied the water and caused the cat to sneak back and join the others. I take a well-earned breather and stroll down to join them, then carry the heavy bowlful of wet clothes back along to the orchard and watch our clothes line fill up with colour. I comment to Cari that we really should have a few hens about the place, our own egg supply; I'd fancy a couple of ducks as well. It could be that I'm missing those cretins from back over at the other place I suppose, it seems so quiet here without them. We meander up to take another look at our new well, but it is taking a little longer to settle down and to clear than I thought it would, but I must be patient, good things can't be rushed, and in the meantime I must trudge back over to Murphy's place to fetch our drinking water, hoping that I might bump into him and find out how everything worked out, but I don't see him anywhere; I do hope that the 'other' man hasn't thrown him down their well!

My constant companions as I chip away at the bedroom wall... the swallows; they've accepted me as being just a friendly old animal in their midst and are in no way inhibited by my repetitious industry and the clouds of plaster that I'm choking in. They make a most lovely twittering babbling sound whenever they enter, and they seem to hover in front of the nest excitedly talking to the old swallows sitting eggs; they're a really marvellous family, bonded by something exquisitely precious and private beyond my comprehension; this house really does belong to them.

With having lovely long light evenings, we have fun working and playing, 'I' being the working part, but I have provided the boys with more kites, badminton rackets with lots of spare shuttlecocks, and have also fixed them a fantastic rope-ladder swing in the great sycamore tree; even old Dan comes over in the evenings for a game of badminton and a swing. The good news is that he has seen Murphy. "Oh! Very smart... nice new pullover and corduroys!" This observation of Dan's is one of great significance to him, even though he isn't going to take the subject any further; the rest of his thinking can best be conveyed with winks and grins and the odd cough and elbow in the ribs. He has a marvellous sense of wickedness beginning to show, springing anew from long seasons of loneliness in these ever-so quiet hills. The sound of children laughing in the fields once more must sound better than skylarks and old Dan is becoming a child once more because of it. There's never been a woman in his life apparently, but if he keeps going the ways he's going, I shouldn't wonder there will be Brylcream and aftershave in his grocery delivery soon!

Each dusk, woodcock take to the air and make strange quacking, squeaking noises as they leave their hiding places in the forest undergrowth and head off somewhere wet to feed by darkness. It's usually in the late evenings too that the farm children descend on us like a flock of new starlings; they bring me the news that I've been waiting to hear... the young owls have escaped and are now free and living in the trees behind the farm; I just hope there are no forgotten rat corpses still hidden in the freezer, that's all!

It seems a waste to be burning our wood now, but it's no doubt cheaper than Calor Gas in producing all the pots of tea that the gang drink so ravenously, and old Dan shifts a fair bit himself before finally heading back to his dog and cow. Truth is, it's all so absolutely beautiful, all of us gathered round a blaze laughing and joking and swilling tea, eating baked potatoes from the busted oven and buttered toast done the old-fashioned way with a fork in front of a glowing fire; so simple.

June's flame continues to burn unabated, flowers cover and colour the hedges, meadows and waysides and young birds find their wings and leave a million nests empty everywhere. After a hectic climactic few days, the wrens have suddenly vanished from the lean-to although I can still hear the old wren shouting about the outbuildings showing that he's got more than one string to his bow and an appetite for more yet. The bluetits by the front window have also flown and the wagtails are carting insects back and forth under the barn roof at such a frenzied pitch as to suggest that they too are about to be liberated. The redstarts are more secretive and reveal only occasional glimpses even though they too are at the penultimate stage. I've noticed that we have a colony of pipistrelle bats living in one of the deep cracks in the barn wall and the late evening air is finely pierced with their calls. I can hardly hear them but Cari and the boys have no difficulty at all, this is probably a sign that my head is becoming rather clogged-up with plaster dust and a warning for me to stop.

We make a trip to town in the van, it's getting a bit too hot for walking the ten miles or so there and back weighed down with provisions and a boy on my shoulders, and it gives us an opportunity to visit a house-clearance junk place and get ourselves a few essential items of furniture, chairs, a kitchen cupboard and a small table. We also pop into the ex-government store and buy a couple of old army camp-beds with two hard mattresses and I fix myself up with a sledge-hammer too whilst I'm at it... every home should have a sledge-hammer!

On the way back, whilst discussing the likelihood of having chickens, more in particular the possibility of reprieving some old battery-hens, I come across a mountain of bulldozed hedgerow where housing development is about to spread; there are good fence-posts among it and long strands of barbed-wire too, so I stop and help myself to what will be very useful in my battle against the cows. The van is once more piled to capacity as we wind our way back along the lanes, almost driven speechless by the abundantly beautiful world about us and the joy of realising that we are here in the midst of it all, free and rolling along so easily. Conversation returns to those poor old hens imprisoned in their battery cages, what an absolute hell of an existence it must be and what a lovely thing it would be for us to release a few and see them actually becoming chickens at long last before they may die of old age.

We roll down the last little hill beneath a dense oak, ash and cherry canopy; ahead Murphy and his lady are out walking the goats, taking them on a nibbling stroll amongst the wild herbs. They look rude with health and well-being the pair of them; Meg, radiant as a raven and with an old-fashioned beauty that shines from the polishing affect of being in love; Murphy is likewise affected and has the 'kept' look of a well-polished antique sideboard. They have such an over-abundance of leisure that they are tripping over it and have nothing better to do right now than to take goats for a walk. I pull-in onto the verge by the gate and unload whilst at the same time attempt to hold a conversation. My humble items of furniture have a somewhat degrading effect upon the landscape and seem to be saying, "beggars can't be choosers" in a sickeningly constant apology. "That's a nice jumper you're wearing, Murph!" I comment, and I detect a warm flush of a smile on Meg's face, and a ripple of a cringe pass over Murphy's, hinting at there being a kind of 'fly in the spider's web' situation, with him being the willing fly. I'm wickedly tempted to remark on his smart new trousers too, but back off the subject somewhat ashamedly and talk instead about chickens. "We're thinking of having a few battery hens ... set them free to retire gracefully ... what d'you think?" "Great!" Murphy growls, more like his old self. "You need to get 'Warrens', they're the best layers, aren't they, Meg?" Meg nods knowingly, then adds, "Your best bet is that 'Chukie-Chicken' place at Craven Arms, back over the border in darkest England ... that's the only place that I know of. We're off to Craven Arms on Thursday, there's room in the van if you all want to come." I jump at the suggestion and Cari pauses briefly from feeding hedge-garlic to one of the goats and smiles her agreement, while Robin I notice, is tied-up in an embrace with the other goat which is trying to eat his hair. We enjoy a good yarn and catch up on events generally and set the world to rights. I tell Murphy proudly of all the work I've done in his absence, in particular the new well and the huge difference it will make to our lives; I don't need to invite him, he'll be over I know, if only to tell me that I've done it all wrong! They go idyllically on their slow way and we load ourselves up and trudge our way back across the rapidly baking marsh, through buttercups that have grown knee-high in our brief absence and a lethargic herd that's well scattered with not a single one of them standing. It takes four more trips to shift all the stuff, resorting to the wheelbarrow and the others in harness for the kitchen cupboard, fence-posts, wire and sledge-hammer.

We shan't be winning any design awards with what we've got but, for us, it means a whole lot of difference; beauty really does have to be 'function' and function, beauty. Our main problem at this stage is where to put things; half a century of compacted cow-shit hardly seems to be the ideal place for anything, but it's all we have available to us at this moment in time and it prompts me into giving priority to getting all the concreting done and the loft-ladder fixed into position, enabling us to utilise the upstairs as a storage place. Cari's cello, which I've discovered has the name 'Stradivarius' vaguely visible inside it, this is now in the relative safety of the cat-shed, not so fortunate my guitar and harp, these must continue to rough-it along with wellies, mice and mildewed clothes in the cramped caravan cupboard. Music, however, is everywhere; we don't need to make it so long as we remain part of it, part of a symphony of the folds of fields and hump-backed hills with hanging woods intricately leafed and feathered; swirling air amongst the colours and smells of earth and the same air everywhere whispering like the brook in secret whispered song to the sea. I break free from the monotony of drudgery occasionally and blast a jig on a mouth-organ, bringing forth laughter and bodies in motion, knees and elbows in courtly disarray; who cares... divine anarchy graces us but for seconds before the illusion is gone!

Bull in a Cotton Frock!

Pretty curtains, flowered dresses, scarves and assorted shirts contribute our best colours yet to this magnificent air under the fruit trees. Cari has slaved over an early hand-wash and has pegged an entire rainbow out to dry and has taken Robin off somewhere for the remainder of the morning, leaving me to bash on in subdued grimness clearing and cleaning the upstairs of the piles of plaster debris and dust. I hear Murphy's barking voice in the room below and then his merry face appears in the far corner where the infamous ladder reaches up. "Hey, Jimmy... this place has changed a bit since I last saw it!" A swallow comes in, coughs and immediately goes out again. "It's a slow job, Murph... and I'm missing all this lovely weather an' all!" I reply through a slow swirling pale dust-cloud; "but I'm getting there little by little, it all takes time." Careful not to dirty his new trousers, he steps up into the room, his attention drawn to the completed wall. "I see you've finished bricking that last bit of wall, Jimmy... it looks alright." He goes across to examine it more closely, just as I knew he would... "Pretty good!" he concludes and we both make for the old window in the front wall, gasping for a bit of fresh air. "Oh, shit! Damn! Bloody cows!" I explode in a stifled rage. There are three cows in my well, just standing up to their bellies, urinating, defecating, slobbering, cud-chewing, just standing there beside a flattened fence. As I cast my poor eyes downwards through the orchard I see old 'Max Tractor' vigorously rubbing an itch against the damson tree which has our rainbow of washing attached to it and, somehow, adding insult to injury, the clothes line has got itself twisted around his massive horns as he contorts his huge head backwards in an attempt to reach something that's itching beyond reach down his filthy shit-encrusted back. I almost go head-first down the ladder as my rage reaches volcanic proportions; Murphy follows trying to soothe me with sympathetic animal mutterings, all of which are instantly fried before reaching my ears as I burst upon the orchard scene screaming blasphemy and startling the bull into spontaneous panic. There's a loud snapping sound as the clothes line breaks and the bull goes charging off up the hill with the entire washing draped across his massive back and trailing out behind him as he vanishes through the gateway. I can't believe all this is happening, Murphy is speechless close behind me as I advance at speed upon these three sent angels from hell that are so mindlessly at peace and obliviously unconcerned over my explosive fury about to burst upon them. I have to physically push them and whack them with my bare hands, almost busting my wrists and becoming royal blue in the throat and inwardly deafened by the shattering-to-pieces of my heart, it's like a cathedral being blitzed. I watch their animated legs and feet uproariously churning up the mud and obliterating every last trace of what I had so painstakingly made right here before my unbelieving eyes. My yelling suddenly becomes crying and I drop my head and cry and cry. Murphy puts his arm around my shoulders and says quietly, "Come on, Jimmy, don't let the bastards get to you ... you 'ain't having much luck, are you?" "I'm more concerned about what poor Cari is going to think... that bloody bull has gone off with the clothes line, all the washing and her lovely dresses an' all!"

The only positive thought emerging from the mess is the realisation that my priorities have been scattered into confusion and I haven't a clue what to do next. Cari and Robin are out there somewhere and there's a bull with a temper and disguised as a clothes line; there are also three aggrieved cows with very selective memories, I know that they will only remember the nice bits! I detect a certain restlessness in Murphy, he constantly peeps at his watch as though afraid of being away too long; this helps me to piece together a positive thought of sorts and I nod for him to follow. I'll see him back across the hill and over the marsh, save him from his anxiety, maybe I'll find our washing along the way.

From the hilltop I can see Cari and Robin returning through the wood on the next hillside and, below in the marsh meadow, the bull with the clothes-line still in tow; it's obvious from his wild swishing head movements that his adornments are getting to irritate him. After making some approximate arrangements for our chicken-trip on Thursday, I leave Murphy to make his own way over to the lane and I walk back to meet Cari and Robin and explain what's been happening while they've been enjoying the sun.

I'm getting to understand cows in leaps and bounds, two of the same previous three are already back in my well, the third is standing beside it trying to remember the significance of my thundering feet and ear-piercing voice. Cari and Robin stand back in stiff astonishment as the beasts splash clumsily out from the well with one of them getting its back legs entangled in the barbed wire making an even worse mess of the fence before disentangling. "I haven't told you the worst bit!" I despairingly try to laugh as we both stare down at the disgusting mess which had once been a well; my words fall on deaf ears and I repeat them slowly, adding... "and we 'ain't got a clothes line anymore either... that sodding bull's gone off with it, clothes, the whole lot!" Cari thinks I'm joking and we walk along to the orchard. "What have you done with it?" she asks, thinking that I'm playing a joke on her; I walk off up the hill and beckon them to follow... "Come on, if you don't believe me, we're not going far." They join me on the hilltop and I point down across the marsh ... "there, now do you believe me!" To my astonished relief, Cari explodes into screeching laughter and I let out a long sigh, she's never before seen a bull in a cotton frock... can't say that I have either, come to think!

I don't feel nearly so bad now that my priorities have repaired themselves and I'm more than eager to christen my new sledgehammer and spend the rest of the day enjoying the sun, fixing a stronger fence around the well then completely emptying it and reconstructing the sides; this time I shall fit the porch roof onto to it in the hope of deterring the cows still further; I refuse to be beaten into submission by cows!

I have to take a break from my work soon after three thirty and go to meet the boys from school, but I have by this time already emptied and thoroughly cleaned out the well and dug it a further foot in depth, down into very solid reddish earth which has provided me with the material for a much more substantial dam-wall. As a precaution I have temporarily covered it with the fence-posts on top of which I have plonked the upturned wheelbarrow. In addition to this I've managed a quick repair job on the fence and am just hoping and praying that this will be sufficient in holding the beasts off until I get back and can finish the job properly.

I return to the caravan to pick up the water-carriers and both Cari and Robin join me. We haven't gone very far when we come across the bull, he's totally in the nude now and plodding heavily and slowly beside the hedge back in the direction of our big sycamore tree; we watch him pause and sniff the air rather menacingly, he's obviously got other things occupying his mind now. We discover our washing in the marsh meadow, trampled, tattered and utterly filthied; it's a very sorry sight as we gather it up and drape it over the gate ready for picking up on our way back. We wander up the lane and along the track to the well, then we hear the voices of the other two ringing out and, with our carriers full, we all meet in the lane. They're drowsily tired after their long hot walk up the hill, Robin by sudden contrast is bursting with energy and is insistent on going with the others to see if the hens have laid in their old nest under the hedge, and so I agree and we proceed with the hedge separating them from us as the three of them go pushing and shoving on the blind side, already squabbling and trying to outdo each other while there's no one watching. It's apparent that somebody's had some success when a chicken comes hysterically streaking across the lane in front of us and vanishes cackling through the opposite hedge in a mad panic to find safety in numbers back at the farm. Robin's having another of his territorial confrontations and I can hear the others trying to reason with him, pleading with him to be sensible and to share, all to no avail. I am reluctant to raise my voice too much, I don't want to attract attention and find myself accused of being an egg-thief. Cari and I appeal to them through the dense thicket, but there's a full-scale battle going on now and we're helpless in having any influence on it whatsoever. Robin is being very loud, a mixture of shouted crying and screaming, it all sounds physical and ugly. We hurry down the lane to the gate where our little van is parked and, as I open the gate, the pathetic wailing figure of Robin comes stumbling like a ruptured bagpipe, dripping and dribbling from a whole catastrophe of smashed eggs in his hair, while coming up slowly behind him, the ashamed and dejected figures of the other two with some slimy mess plastering their pullovers and shirts. "He started it!" Spencer booms, pointing firmly at Robin. "It was my nest... I founded it first!" Robin blarts back at him. "What's it matter who found the nest, Robin?" Rowan groans in total exasperation, "we only wanted to help carry them, that's all... then you threw a wobbly and started throwing eggs ... you great baby!" "No I not a baby!" "Yes you are!" "No I not!" It goes on and on and I look at Cari and she slowly shakes her head despairingly and gathers the line of washing from the gate, giving it a cursory glance before bundling it up. I relieve her of the water-carrier, other issues will have to wait until my temperature has lowered, the look on my face should be sufficient for the time being. I'll be having my say later, for what it's worth!

We have an unscheduled washday. Robin isn't allowed in until he's been cleaned and, after relieving the others of their soiled clothes, I instruct them to take Robin and give his hair a thorough scrub, either down in the stream or, alternatively in the galvanised water-trough which I've discovered hidden by brambles in the dip beside the adjoining willow and alder-marsh. First though, I have to check to see where old 'Max Tractor' has gone, then I spot him some distance away down by the stream making clumsy overtures to a very disinterested cow, he's definitely not to be interfered with right now. So, drinking-trough it has to be, provided there is water in it of course!

Surprise, surprise! Not only is there water in it, but its running-water too! It's obvious that these cows enjoy a far higher standard of living than we do, they have a well of their own hidden away in the hill somewhere, the realisation of which makes me boil when I recall what they've done to my own humble attempt at making a well! Theirs is clear, what's more, clean enough for it to support a couple of newts which I can see swimming about at the bottom of the trough. "Hold it, boys!" I say... "one of you go and get your dirty clothes from Cari, we'll give them a bit of a rinse in here before we deal with Robin's hair." Rowan races off back to the caravan and is very soon back accompanied by Cari who wants to check it out for herself. We have to bear in mind that this is the cows' drinking water, therefore we cannot use soap and spoil it for them, even though they haven't shown us this consideration over ours. The very last thing we want now is for Gareth to see us, he'd automatically assume that we were contaminating the animal's water supply with soap. So, I have a good listen and scour my eyes around the surrounding hill, then throw all caution to the wind and furiously rinse all the egg-mess from the clothing, rapidly followed by an absolute pantomime as we try to wet Robin's slimy yellowed hair; it's like trying to hold a rabid hyena down; it's crazy, when we want him to stay away from water, he submerges himself in it and now, when we want his cooperation in wetting just his hair, it's taken four of us to hold him anywhere near it, each one of us is far wetter than he is as a result. It's no good trying to talk to him, he refuses to listen and I'm more than relieved when the job's eventually done and a semblance of peace has returned.

After fixing a somewhat higher clothes-line under the trees, I spend the remainder of the evening driving-in fence posts with my new sledge-hammer, then, before attaching the barbed wire, Cari helps me cart the extremely heavy and awkward porch-roof on the wheelbarrow and I grapple precariously over the watery hole trying to get it firmly positioned and supported on a level base of rocks and pieces of wood, only then can I re-wire the fence and try to turn my back on what hasn't been the most enjoyable day that I can remember, not by any stretch of the imagination!

Sleep cleanses all traces of yesterday away and Wednesday slippers her long, cool sparkling light across the dawn-dewed grass. I'm out early, hungry for what I know deep down is precious, priceless, transient. I really don't relish the thought of having to go away to work and I'm feeling homesick in advance and it's taking a big effort in fighting against it. It's gratifying to see that the bit of fence which I hastily strung up around the caravan has had its desired effect and has kept the cows away, for the time being at least. I stroll down to check that this is the case by the well also and can see that this too has been spared; this means that I should now be able to press on with concreting the floors and so I set to work sorting out bricks and stones for my hardcore.

The bantam cock is up on the barn roof absolutely yelling at the perfect sky, his echo is pure and clear and it must make him feel good, king of the valley no less, unless of course he thinks he's being answered, challenged, in a similar manner to the robin in the lane when he discovered another robin challenging him in my van's wing mirror, and he fought it almost to the point of death. I had to intervene and put bags over both mirrors in order to save him from committing suicide. The bantam cock flies down and I release the others so that they may join him in an on-the-hoof copulatory breakfast; it'll be interesting to see what this gaudy little stud makes of a gang of clapped-out old battery hens when I present him with them tomorrow. Old 'Max' is still on the trail of his ugly moment, he's now got thistles to contend with and they're fighting fit, testicle height, the perfect aperitif if his timing's to perfection.

I keep an eye out for foxes during these tender hours, they probably feel that I'm trespassing on their preserve, especially with the darkness being so short-lived as the longest day draws rapidly upon us. It hardly seems possible that the year has crept unseen to its halfway mark right here under our very noses. This is summer, it's autumn next; for the boys, time is like thick sticky treacle, but it's already running through my fingers like water, talking of which the stream is beginning to look a bit tired, not good news for the concreting job which now confronts me.

It's a lovely feeling to be working in the early morning amongst cows, sheep, bantams and all the birds; there is nothing discordant anywhere, only the thumping of my hammer and the rasping calls of excited jays in the oak wood seem remotely at odds, but even these are part of the gentle music of it all. There's not nearly as much birdsong now that the nesting ritual is as good as over and earlier crazy wild romantic infatuations have once more returned to the sober plane of mere co-existing; there's nothing to shout about now that the eggs have been laid and have hatched and the baby birds all flown away.

The sun climbs beyond the trees and shadows shorten; reluctantly, I now have to leave the world outside and set to work preparing the foundations in converting the calf-parlour into a boys' bedroom. I'm soon blowing sweat droplets from the end of my nose, it's warm work wielding the pick and shoveling mountains of muck and rubble in readiness for the hardcore. Cari pops in with a welcome mug of tea shortly after eight, but there's hardly time for chatting, she's left the flat-iron hotting up on the calor gas and the ironing-board is blocking the gangway in the caravan where our two young scholars are impatiently waiting for their shirts to be ironed. It all sounds a bit overcrowded in there, especially with the cats sneaking in and getting underfoot. A little while later as I'm tipping a barrow load of rubble at the front, I see the gang all wandering up the hill and I shout "Bye!", they wave back and are gone.

After covering the floor area with heavy polythene, I discover that I need lots more hardcore, what I have been bashing away at for the last few hours has gone absolutely nowhere, so I have to return

Jim Bridgen

once more to sorting bricks and stones from all the plaster rubble, then smashing them to pieces. Half the morning has gone and I finally complete the first stage; now comes the laborious part, that of mixing concrete without the use of a concrete-mixer, it must all be done a little at a time, making frequent trips to fetch water from a dwindling supply and carting sand and gravel that's been well and truly fouled by the cows; I notice too that the cats have been finding the sand useful and have peppered it with little presents for me to sort out! Little by little I press on, it's a slow and unrewarding labour, whatever I mix and put down just vanishes, only by mindlessly persevering shall I salvage a morsel of satisfaction. What I do recognise though, is that this is a job which I shall be more than glad to have out of the way, it's holding up my progress on other things.

Dan pays a surprise visit just as we're having a cheese and watercress sandwich in the sun by the pigsty wall. "Postman's been!" he cackles, waving a letter in the air, "... I thought it looked important enough for me to bring over." It's not so surprising that he's impressed, the envelope is emblazoned with the name of the television company and, people like Dan have been seduced into believing that T.V. is God. It's my contract for a total of five weeks work and requires my signature and returning. "Blimey, five weeks! They didn't take long," I say to Cari, scanning my eyes over the dates, noting that I have four weeks before starting work, just time, perhaps, for me to knock the cowshed into better shape, even the water in our well might have cleared by then. By now, Dan is biblically involved in his own cheese and watercress paradise, almost choking as he splutters, "Gettin' some worn-out old chickens, I hear... an' you've had Gareth's cows in your well an' the bull goin' off with your washin' an' all ... that don't sound none too good to me, that don't!"

News travels faster here than ever it did in the city, and it's all too easy to slip into the suction trap of talking and talking while the sun shifts the shadows around us. I thank him for so kindly being our postman, then I excuse myself and return to my work knowing full well that, for a while at least, he'll be hovering over me chuntering that I need a concrete-mixer or a delivery of ready-mixed stuff, neither of which are feasible and both of which I don't want to waste time haggling over. The sooner I'm able to get on with it, the sooner I'll get finished! It's the old adage of there being 'too many Chiefs and not enough Indians' airing itself again, and he goes grinning off on a tour about the place with Cari and Robin; it's the last I see of them until sometime later when the whole gang returns, no egg-fights this time, just hunger and thirst.

Having now been reassured over our finances, some of the pressure is suddenly off and I relax my grip on miserliness and suggest that, when I go to post my signed contract, I treat us all to a fish an' chip extravaganza with mushy peas and plenty of bottles of pop to help conserve our water; there's not a single objection to the idea! It makes a most welcome change, it's been all work and no play of late and, I for one, am ready for a moment of pure, unadulterated decadence. On our return, Murphy and Meg are out milking the goats on the bank and I stop briefly to arrange a more precise time for tomorrow's trip to their van. This done, we go on our way, eat like pigs and I then settle down into an evening of shoveling concrete while the others creak the swing in the sycamore tree and laugh and scream a million echoes which seem to set an entire geography of sheep to bleating well into the dusk; I wonder, is sheep-bleating at night foretelling a change in the weather?

Hi-Tech Refugees

Strangely, the following morning is dull, cool and misty with no sign of the sun; we've all been tricked into thinking that's it's much earlier than it actually is. A breeze is dislodging the rose-petals and a huge quietness hangs everywhere. There's a last minute panic when it eventually dawns on us that it's a lot later than we thought; by contrast, everything outside is just taking life nice and easy, just as it comes, it's only humans that are battling against it. "What are you doing at school today, boys?" I ask. "Oh... a bit of reading, a few sums and the Bible." "Do you ever learn about the birds and the flowers?" "No... it's all the Bible and sums mostly." "Don't you play games or go on nature walks?" "You're jokin'!"

I see them on their way to where their mates are suffering the same sago pudding mixture. It seems such a waste when the only thing that they can expect is to be able to read a bit, write a bit and be able to do sums a bit and be blessed with a degree of confusion over the fourth 'R', a confusion which was demonstrated a couple of days ago whilst talking of suitable names for the new kittens and the names 'Arthur' and 'Alfred' were suggested. I questioned this and Spencer informed me that it was the Lord's Prayer that had triggered the idea. Being none the wiser, I asked him to explain what he meant and so he started to recite the Lord's Prayer:- "Our Arthur who are in Devon, Alfred be thy name..." I choked on my toast, he was deadly serious, the fourth 'R' was really hitting the mark with a vengeance!

The sun's earlier prank has made everyone late, as though out to prove something; it's going to be a talking point in every nook and cranny of this sparsely peopled hill world and could well dislodge cows in my well and a bull in a cotton frock from the number one spot. I knock Meg's door till my knuckles hurt before I eventually hear Murphy's voice booming in the bathroom and a bedroom window creaking open with a resplendent wild Meg voluptuously bursting half out of it, still clouded in another world. "What time is it?" she yawns. "You did say half past nine," I call up to her and can hear Murphy's gruff voice in the background shouting, "What time d'you call this... have you shit the bed or something?!" I realise that we don't need to apologise for being ten minutes late ourselves, and I feel uncomfortable as though we're intruding. "What's happened to the sun?" Meg asks, frowning at the whiteness confronting her. "Having a bit of a lie-in as well, I think," I answer and we start to move away, "We'll be back in about half an hour or so."

It's deathly quiet as we stroll past Dan's place, suggesting that he too has been fooled by the sun's failure to show. There's not a lot that we can do in half an hour in these misty surroundings, so we turn round and wander back as far as my van; it draws my attention to a dislike of being dependent on others for things, far rather I rely on myself, it's much simpler that way. I almost feel that I am pestering when once more I knock on their door where, this time, I am confronted by a wild-eyed Murphy with egg-yolk all round his mouth and a 'Desperate Dan' sized piece of cold gammon in his fist. "What have you done to the weather, Jimmy?" he splutters, battling to keep the food in his mouth. "It's caught a lot of us out this has, Murph," I smile back, "... it's just a little reminder for us not to take good things for granted, that's all it is... it'll clear away, you see if it don't." He invites us in and skips off, almost colliding with Meg who's suddenly appeared brushing her hair in the kitchen doorway. "Whatever must you think of us lazy so-and-sos oversleeping... 'don't usually stay in bed this late." She is blushing apologetically and turns away back into the kitchen. "I wouldn't worry too much about that, Meg... we've all overslept as well, it's a nice thing to do once in a while, it helps remind us that we're not machines." My remarks are intended to make her feel better about it and Cari does her bit to help by saying, "Aren't you lucky having a 'proper' house... it's beautiful, what a lovely room this is." They both return to the room to share in Cari's enthusiasm. "We gets the sunrise coming in through these front windows, don't we Meg?" Murphy boasts proudly, and Meg tops his remarks adding, "We get it all through the day, and you can see twenty miles and more down the valley through the gap just to the left of your place... shall we have a cup before we go... it'll be with goat's milk, mind you!" This isn't so much a question as a statement of intent and she is already off to make it as she's speaking. "It's better for you than cows milk... no chemicals!" Murphy booms, getting excited and giving me a friendly thump on the back to emphasise his point. "Can't say I'm over familiar with goats milk, is it nice?" I ask, and he gives me a funny look which seems to say that he has no choice in the matter and is obliged to drink it whether he likes it or not: "You get used to it," he mutters barely above a whisper, and I laugh and say, "It must be the same as sheep milk, I suppose... can't say I've had that either... good for cheese-making though!" He walks off into the kitchen to help or at least to show willing and they both emerge with steaming mugs, our initiation has started.

I have to confess, I prefer cows milk in my tea, the difference being that I can't taste the cows milk, whereas I can taste the goats milk, just sufficient for it to put me off slightly. "I think I prefer cows milk," I rather bravely announce, adding... "but it's a close call," as the coward in me attempts to be diplomatic; then Cari boldly declares, "That was delicious, is there any more in the pot?" She follows Meg into the kitchen and I can hear them enthusiastically gabbling away together, enabling Murphy and myself to get off the subject, but not before he has noticed that Robin hasn't even dared to touch his drink and has relieved him of it and slung the contents out through the window.

We drive off as the mist shows signs of lifting and a pale circle ghosts over the grey wood. Meg toots her horn as we go past Dan's house, but there's no sign of him or his dog. I'm relieved to know that Murphy isn't driving, the last place he ever looks when he's behind the wheel is the road ahead, but it's only a degree or two of greater comfort to have him in the seat beside the driver because he has a tendency to snatch the steering wheel without warning when he gets a bit excited. He's done it with me and in a large part accounts for my premature greyness! Something tells me that he'll be on his best behaviour with Meg driving.

I learn that, apart from a load of old hens, there'll be a couple of beehives in the back with us on the return trip; it's going to be a bit cramped because there's less room in this van than there is in mine and it's already feeling claustrophobic in here. We tootle along at a lively pace and Murphy keeps us all occupied with a ceaseless barrage of statistics, rights and wrongs, bests and worsts associated with every conceivable thing under the sun. It comes as a great relief when we eventually reach Craven Arms where the sun is once more shining and Murphy's impeccable map-reading has pin-pointed the place where an old man wants to get rid of all his bee-keeping equipment. While they are doing their business, Cari, Robin and I ravenously refill our lungs with fresh air and stretch our legs, we couldn't have lasted out much longer and we're not relishing the thought of the return journey, especially if we discover that there are still a few bees in the hives! We take full benefit from Murphy's marathon discussion with the frail little old man in dangling braces, that can't believe he is talking to, or rather listening to, the world's greatest authority on bees and the nutritional properties of honey ... we haven't started on the chickens yet! Two hives are piled in together with a large sackful of accessories, then we squeeze in once more and head for the chicken 'factory' which we passed on our way in.

It's a rambling place and the grubby little van picks its way amongst wagons before pulling up outside an office where faces are watching us through a window. We all tumble out and enter the office where we are confronted by a friendly man who asks us what he can do for us. I clear my throat an am just about to speak when Murphy pitches in; "I've heard that you sells-off your old knackered battery-hens when you can't get them to lay enough eggs for you... my mate here wants to buy some, don't you, Jimmy!" I nod to indicate that this is so and the man asks, "How many are we talking about, 'cos I've just got rid of a load?" "I don't want many... about a dozen would do if you could spare them," I reply, he asks us to wait and vanishes through a door. In the meantime, Murphy is going on about keeping chickens in battery conditions, then switches to the relative egg-laying performances of the various breeds. "I have 'Warrens' myself," he goes spouting on and tells them how many eggs he's currently getting per bird. I chuckle to myself knowing that his figures are deficient of all the eggs that the boys have found under the hedge, and also that he hasn't got any chickens at all ... they're Megs. The man returns and gives a grin; "I've managed to sort out nine for you... 'hope that's alright, they're putting them in a sack for you." I thank him and settle my account, they're a lot less than I thought they would be; I then ask him if there's anything I particularly need to know about them, emphasising that they're going to be pets. He's amused by this and laughingly says, "Damn, and I thought you wanted them for dog food!" He goes on to tell me that they are 'Sykes' hybrids and that I mustn't expect any egg-laying gymnastics from them as they're more or less past it and are at the end of their egg-laying life; then he wishes me luck with them and we all go outside where another man is standing with a lumpy looking sack in his fist. I glance down at the lovely expression on Robin's face, I feel exactly the same... we've got our own chickens... yippee! The daft thing is that we haven't even seen them yet, it's more important that they be kept in the darkness of their sack until we get them home. Being cramped up shouldn't be a problem for them, they're well-used to that, so I carefully take the sack and gently place it in the back of the van propped against a beehive, then we squeeze in through the front doors and hope for the best doing a battery-chicken act ourselves.

On the way back, Meg starts to feel sick and has to make frequent stops to put her head out of the door, then, horror of horrors, Murphy takes over the driving! Thankfully, Meg's repetitious throwing-up comes as a blessing and permits our blood-pressures to settle after each squealing of tyres and the wild swerving and swaying with the chickens beginning to squawk and the beehives toppling. "Go easy, mister!" Meg warns him firmly, and I watch Murphy's fingers restlessly off-loading the electricity of his frustrations; he reminds me of 'Mr. Toad' in 'The Wind in the Willows', wonderfully impetuous and beyond the reach of reason. "There's no race, so just calm yourself down, I can't help it if I'm feeling a bit sick!" At her very next sign of a retch, Murphy slaps on the brakes and we skid to a bumpy and abrupt halt on a pot-holed lay-by. We're all projected forwards and Meg instantly throws up over the dashboard and bumps her head; even Robin isn't enjoying this, and he's a masochist... Cari remains silent. Fortunately the chickens are providing us with distracting alarm calls and I add my own diversionary sounds in trying to calm things whilst a mopping-up operation goes on in the front. I can hear Murphy grieving like one of the hens as he fusses over Meg, he's oblivious to the fact that his erratic style of driving isn't helping the situation any; she flips him away and I'm sure she'd scream if we weren't here. Murphy takes a bundle of soiled tissues off to a littler-bin, allowing Meg to say how sorry she is; we laugh it off light-heartedly and I admit that I have been on the point of throwing-up since we set out earlier and that I'm still keeping my fingers crossed. "We're nearly home now," she says as though in a kind of prayer, just as Murphy returns, none the wiser, jaunty, his wild curls bouncing and his smart jumper making him look new.

It occurs to me that I'm going to need some hen-food and I persuade Murphy to stop off at the suppliers in town so that I can pick up a bag, regardless of how it's going to cramp us up even more. This extra item almost proves to be 'the straw that breaks the camel's back', and the little engine almost expires in a cloud of steam and smoke on the last hill and only just makes it back to Murphy's place. Meg has vanished to the bathroom and Murphy is showing distinct signs of wanting his own space. He doesn't need to worry, our most pressing concern is to get back home and to introduce our new old hens to the real world for the very first time in their lives, our bag of corn can wait until later, we've still got a bit to be going on with. I take hold of the sack of hens and proceed carefully with them on their very last twenty minutes of bewildering over-crowdedness. Nine old hens in a sack are surprisingly heavy and I don't feel inclined to toss the sack over my shoulder for fear of banging them, so Cari and Robin do their utmost in trying to distribute some of the weight as we swish our way through the high grass and thistles down the sloping field to the marsh meadow gate.

The world is ours once more and the sun is high in the blue and laughing at having fooled us earlier. New rose buds are breaking open and the elder is showing that she's next in line to take the stage and sweeten the air as we carry our little cargo of heartbeats over the final strides, noticing to our dismay that the cows have disregarded my bit of fence and have knocked the water-tub over again in our absence. Sheep with their fat lambs stampede clumsily out from the pig-sty loo in response to our sudden appearance in the yard and two cows go trotting off down into the orchard leaving a good account of themselves all over the ground. We decide it best to release the hens in the barn and to keep them in there for a while until they get used to it and are feeling their feet a bit, so, before opening the sack, I check to make sure that there are no gaps anywhere for them to escape through, or worse still, for foxes to get in. With the main door being in two halves, we can keep the bottom half closed during the day and, if the bantams want to roost early, they can enter through the top half; I can't imagine that these old battery hens will have either the strength or know-how to fly up and over the closed lower part.

The moment arrives; eager anticipation has set Robin to skipping and Cari to a fervour of spectacle-cleaning while I fumble nervously trying to unfasten the knot; it's a bit like lighting my first firework, I'm half expecting an explosion of feathers... instead it's a damp squib; they remain crouching with bewildered eyes eyeing me. One at a time, I gently take them out and place them on the floor where they stand for a second or two, then crouch without a clue in the world as to what to do. 'Pathetic' is the word that immediately springs to mind as I think of all the umpteen thousands of eggs that these have laid and graced the breakfast stomachs of people far and wide; these old hi-tech egg-machines, their exploitation over, have another life yet, beyond the dictates of economics. They're supposed to be white but they are absolutely filthy, half-bald and have outrageously long claws from never having been able to scratch. I realise now why I didn't have to pay much for them, they're nothing like the robustly healthy specimens over at Murphy's place, these look like they've suffered from having been conscripted into prostitution prior to their necks being pulled. Robin races off and returns with a saucepan full of corn and scatters it amongst them, I provide them with water, then we leave them to settle in peace and quiet; their next major shock will be the return of the bantams to roost, it'll no doubt be somewhat of a shock for the bantams too.

A quick check of the well tells me that I'm in luck, the old porch roof is working a treat, even I can hardly see the water, but it's there alright, I can hear its soft tinkle as it overflows. It's a lovely sweet sound, and the fence beside it looks good and is doing its job perfectly. I mend the bit of fence by the caravan and tidy up the mess left by cows, then once more resume mixing concrete, leaving Cari to begin her magic preparing the evening meal. Robin sneaks away to heap his affections on the kittens in the shed, alternating this with periodic peeps through a crack to check that our chickens are still okay but, the appearance of 'Max Tractor' with a new girl friend makes me decide it safer for him to come inside and help me. After a while an exasperated Cari comes in to tell me that the gas cylinder has run out halfway through cooking, this means making another trip into town and a timely top-up with bread and any other items which spring to mind. We'll pick the boys up on the way; it's just one of those sort of days that don't seem to hold together properly.

My body feels like it's broken in a hundred places by the time the day's burdens have eased and we have gas, drinking water, provisions, two more bags of cement and a hundredweight of corn safely over to the cowshed. Cari bought Robin a new fishing net which had taken his fancy and might, with a bit of luck, keep him occupied and out of mischief for at least a minute down at the stream before the fascination dies.

Once the new gas cylinder has been connected, Cari revives her culinary masterpiece while Spencer and Rowan, after satisfying their curiosity over the new chickens, let off steam on the swing, leaving Robin to swank about with his new fishing net and a jam-jar with a string handle. Dan's intrigue gets the better of him and he feels obliged to hobble over the hill to check out our new livestock, he's never seen battery hens in the flesh before and he's not impressed. The boys are called in for their meal and I detect a certain un-hurriedness that's out of character with Robin, he's usually the first to start and the first to finish and with an unendearing habit of raising his plate above his head and licking it, hence the gravy, beans and custard in his hair as so often is the case. I've guessed that he's more concerned about where to hide his fishing net out of sight of the others and he can't do this until they're safely out of the way. The other two have already worked this out for themselves and are guessing where he'll have hidden it as they wash their grubby fingers in a bowl. "It's got to be the cat-shed" Spencer giggles; "Pigsty!" Rowan competes and we all start to tuck in without him. Dan has kicked off his rolled-down wellies and I'm wishing that he'd kept them on, it's stopping me from smelling the herbs in this lovely stew. Eventually our sludgy cherub, dripping wet, graces us with his presence, grinning smugly all over his face. He protests somewhat at having to wash his hands, but he makes a token splashing gesture before joining the rest of us. The other two nudge and titter as they shuffle to make room for him, we're 'battery humans' at feeding time, with Dan leaning back on our bed noisily slurping stew from his spoon, his good mannered appreciation being best expressed in decibels.

It'll be a miracle if the boys manage to get through the meal without a squabble breaking out and so I look at them each in turn, fixing them firmly in a penetrating stare, hoping that this might be sufficient a deterrent; Robin grins back wickedly and I feel helpless. "Well ... did you catch any monsters, Rob?" Rowan asks with an edge of sarcasm which sets Spencer off giggling, setting the scene for the next skirmish. Robin surprises me by not rising to the bait, he just grins and gives me a big wink, taken aback somewhat, I return the wink to show my appreciation. It's largely thanks to Dan's presence that the awaited skirmish fails to ignite and he dominates just a little with a warning of some authority that we can expect a few rats about the place now that we've got chickens, adding that he's noticed rats back at his place now that he's replaced his last lot of hens which were taken by the fox. I discretely ask Spencer and Rowan not to go searching for Robin's fishing net, and so they gallop off instead for a boisterous game of shuttlecock, enabling Robin to skulk off sheepishly to the cat-shed while Cari and Dan come to pass judgment on my floor-laying efforts. After a short while Robin joins us, a cheeky smile idling on his face, he's also being excessively polite and helpful, I can distinctly smell a rat. I look at Cari and can see that she too has her suspicions. "Show Dan your new fishing net, Rob," I say, trying to prompt him into a more revealing body-language; my words fall on deaf ears. I continue;- "You knows a thing or two about what's in the streams around here, don't you, Dan!" "Awgh!" he fidgets, "... it's a long time since I dabbled in these ditches, isn't it; but I does remember them bull-head things, real ugly they was... an' there was crayfish as well, lots of tiddlers... you'd get one or two trout... taint the same now, not with all these new-fangled chemicals they're usin'." Robin still makes no attempt to produce his net, it's obviously well hidden and so I don't pursue the matter any further.

The tired evening draws across and the woodcock go over making their easily recognisable squeaky sounds and the bats come out to dance amongst the plankton of moths delighting in the heavily-pollened dusk; a delicious tiredness settles achingly and, boy, do I ache! It's comforting to know that after tonight's work, the floor will be finished at the weekend and my attentions shifted to the constructing of a staircase out of the old loft ladder.

Shortly after black sleep has made us invisible to ourselves, a blood-curdling scream almost rips the roof off the caravan; it's Spencer yelling in the most animal of ways. There isn't a switch that I can touch, no sudden electronic wizardly thing there for me to see what's going on. I shout to comfort him as I fumble clumsily for feel of a torch or rattle of matches. I find the torch and can see the blinding whites of eyes all around. Spencer is still making wails of revulsion and trying to distance himself from himself almost to the point of levitation. I try to calm him in the torchlight as he struggles to speak: "Something cold and wet crawled over my face ... it scratched me it did!" A sickening thought vomits through me ...rats! I really don't believe it and I strike a match and light a candle, it's like the air-raid shelter I so clearly remember from my own childhood. There's a huge safeness here within these walls, and the candlelight helps to spread this good news; if there's a rat in here, I shall catch it with my bare hands and will protect my family until the end of time: brave stuff this, coming from one whose knees are knocking like a diesel and worse besides. "Take it easy, boyo," I mutter quietly, scanning my eyes around the startled faces before the realisation has sunk in that one little person is still miraculously fast asleep. Spencer yells again and leaps clean out of bed; a newt is twitching on his pillow … and I know that we haven't got rats… we've got Robin!

I feel sorry for the newt, I shan't let it die, but half of me is already seeing the funny side, with the sudden relief of knowing that I haven't got to catch a rat after all. I unveil Robin with a swift snatching-away of the sheet covering his face and he gallantly attempts to continue acting the role of sleeper before his acting skills catastrophically fail him and he becomes helpless with laughter. Spencer doesn't see the funny side however and I have to intervene in stopping an ugly brawl from breaking out. "Get rid of it, Robin!" I growl. "Get rid of it immediately … back to where you caught it!" He fumbles about before producing his jam-jar that still has some water in it, and, as he's reaching across to pick the newt up, Spencer whacks him and, quicker than lightning, Robin stuffs the newt down Spencer's pants: if this doesn't frighten the cows away from the door, nothing will!

The following two weeks are a bizarre bedlam of retribution and counter-retribution taking on surrealist overtones. An earthworm appears in Robin's spaghetti, a drowned mouse in Spencer's pencil-case, large black beetles in Rowan's socks, maggots in the salad cream and dead flies in the tea to mention just a few things which were actually discovered. In the dark pigsty-toilet, holly leaves on the seat are impossible to detect, but you certainly know when you've sat on one! It rapidly gets to the point of no longer being funny and I beg them all to call a truce, the only losers in all this are Cari and I, we're the ones that have to pick up the pieces and go on providing. I tell them that, if they want to play tough, then they have to have it tough and I take them on energy sapping expeditions into the woods, combining the process of identifying things with pushing them beyond their old physical boundaries and making them glow like they never glowed! We return one happy gang with the feather-treasures of jay, buzzard, tawny owl, magpie and pigeon; they have the appetites of hogs and the ability to sleep like logs as soon as they hit the hay.

Over this same two-week period, our new old hens take their first virgin steps upon the planet proper. It's hard to grasp that, seeing as only life can produce life, these decrepit old ex-battery refugees have existed for just as long as I have existed here as part of the Universe; size doesn't matter, status is artificial, all life being equal. It's totally fascinating just watching these old hens experiencing for the very first time, this new concept called 'space', thence to discover within themselves functional body-parts by which to address the whole perplexing puzzle of it all. Even though they've never scratched before, the natural notion of scratching is abundantly obvious, as too is the searching for food, recognition of which is beyond my comprehension. I have to really force myself into remembering that these old fowls have never before seen a single thing in the wild, they could never have been taught by their mothers and have already used up nine tenths of their lives in prison cages, their time for learning long past, and yet here they are confounding me, demonstrating something which I can hardly believe possible... they're just stepping out and doing it!

It's become apparent that they are all individuals; whilst they may all share the same colour, there the similarity ends, each one is different from the next, but there's one that's more different than all of them and we have christened her 'Sykes'. She's ugly, somewhat out of shape, hysterical, spiteful and has perpetual diarrhea. Unlike the others, 'Sykes' is not adorned with a floppy pink comb, she's taller than she is long whereas the other are longer than they are tall; 'Sykes' is an absolute pain! The only other one which has been given a name thus far is 'Gerty', a heavy old bird, companionable and will eat out of the hand, but it really hurts. She is also partial to drinking tea from my mug when I inadvertently place it on the ground beside me whilst taking a break from work. They will all have names before much longer, it's just a question of us recognising their individual peculiarities.

What has surprised us most of all is they are actually laying eggs quite regularly, but it is anywhere rather than somewhere as yet, but they go into the barn to roost quite naturally as though it's always been their home, perching on the manger which is over two feet from the ground, demonstrating that freedom and exercise are already making them fit. Their constant scratching for food has begun to wear down their long claws and they're already getting to look more like normal chickens again, albeit a bit on the bald side. The bantams don't appear to have been troubled by the new arrivals, in fact I have observed the little bantam cock attempting a highly ambitious encounter with 'Gerty' who simply walked away with him a bit like a jockey on her back; he's tried it on with our cat 'Sorrel', frightening her into a new land speed record for cats and also something similar to an altitude record as well, requiring me to get the ladder and rescue her from the sycamore tree. Rowan found an ancient wooden-soled boot up on the agricultural tip in the wood and I could hardly believe my eyes when I saw that randy little banty cock mounting this too. Nothing is safe from him!

Summer Solstice Surprise!

I've noticed the lovely soothing calls of turtle doves in the afternoons, it's a joy to hear them deep down in the hedges, it's like a bit of yesteryear calling from another life. This is a glorious time; the longest day brings the swallows flying over the cowshed at ten minutes to three in the early morning, before both dawn and cockerel, what's more, at the other end of the day they're still flying in the late dusk along with the bats. Cari celebrates the longest day by sleeping out in the field under the crystal stars, braving the bull and whatever else might be lurking on this balmy midsummer night. I'm more than relieved when I awaken her with a cup of tea at daybreak and find her completely happy and feeling richer for the experience. There's a tinge of sadness with the passing of the longest day, a realisation that it's downhill now all the way to winter; we're moving from the very best to the very worst, all this wonderful light and warmth to be turned round into dark and cold. Our darling swallows away back in Africa, as too the warblers and cuckoos, pied flycatchers and redstarts, nightjars and wheatears; it doesn't bear thinking about.

There's a problem with the loft-ladder; what I thought would be straightforward, isn't. It had previously been positioned at only a slender angle which made it easier for carrying heavy sacks up and down. I need it to be positioned at a much steeper angle which means that the steps are sloping steeply downhill, making walking downstairs an acquired art to say the least! Due to the confined space involved, there's not a fat lot I can do about it, I need every inch of space for the boys' beds. I weigh up my options before philosophically concluding, "Sod it!" We are just going to have to get used to it!

At least we've now got a stairs of sorts, murderously heavy and equally life-threatening when attempting to go down them, the acute downhill angle of the steps tend to make breaking into a gallop all too easy; crampons might be a good idea... and maybe a mattress nailed to the wall to soften it. I'm not happy with this particular bodge and I have a feeling that sooner, rather than later, I shall be testing my carpentry skills and replacing it with something made to measure. What does please me however, is that Cari's cello is no longer being used by the cats for sharpening their claws on and is breathing once more, along with my guitar, paintings and posh racing bike up in the bedroom, albeit under siege of swallow-shit. The upstairs has become a vital storage place and the inside of the barn is once more looking like it belongs to the animals, with only my very old racing bike being stored in there.

Realising that chickens too need comfort, I provide them with straw, hoping maybe that their 'eggs anywhere' routine might be replaced by an 'eggs somewhere' arrangement, it also looks a lot nicer with a bit of straw about the place. As for the quality of the eggs when we do manage to find any that haven't been trampled on by cows and sheep or, worse still, used as a football by 'Sykes', they are remarkably good, white-shelled and with yolks of a wonderful deep orangey-yellow. I've never tasted eggs as good as these anywhere. The egg laying idea seems to have caught on and I've spotted the little pink bantam sitting eggs high up on the very top of the barn wall, tight under the eaves, she's barely visible hunched over her clutch. There's nothing even remotely domestic about these bantams, they're wild through and through, never to be tamed; it would be a brave man that tried to put his hand under that little broody hen, she'd have his veins as spaghetti!

As the elderflowers come into full glory along the hedges, our thoughts turn to wine making and Cari has found some very old recipes to set our minds buzzing over the prospect. We make a seemingly never-ending list of all the things we are going to need, then, when we're ready we head for town and spend a fruitful couple of hours trudging between chemists, hardware-stores, grocers, bakers and, of course, the ex-government menagerie junk-shop. Somehow we succeed in filling the van with everything that's on our list, with the addition of a dozen and a half old brown and cream earthenware jars with rubber-washered screw-tops; it's amazing what treasures are just waiting to be unearthed in that marvellous place. I don't know what Cari is planning to do with so many jars, but she definitely has something up her sleeve.

We eventually get everything back to the cowshed where, any idea that we had about utilising the lean-to as our workplace is very quickly ruled out by dive-bombing swallows, so I have to try and organise some space in the main room which is totally cluttered with all my concreting stuff. Whilst I am pondering over the problem, Cari and Robin go off with baskets to gather the elderflowers, chickens and cats follow them in leisurely procession up the hill to the first hedge. It's such a delightfully simple picture and makes me feel good inside.

I soon clear some space by the fireplace and arrange a good work-surface then lay out the new demijohns, plastic bowls, buckets, measuring jars, funnels, scales, filter-bags, bags of corks, airlocks, sterilizing solutions, yeast, siphon and more sugar than I've seen in years; I can hardly move for the stuff and I'm going to need vast amounts of water for both sterilizing and wine-making. This all means that we are going to need a fire for boiling endless kettles of water and I'm rapidly discovering that, even pleasure here is damned hard work! Our own water supply is still cloudy and I'm not happy to start using it until the well has had sufficient time to really settle and for the water to be sparkling clear, so I'm going to have to repeat my cart-horse act and get back into harness, christen the brand new water-carrier and take the old one also and trudge back over to the other place; anyone would think that I had a herd of camels if they saw me carting all this water. How my arms manage to remain attached to my body I'll never know; there are few things heavier than water as my fingers dragging on the ground will testify. I still can't believe it; here I am doing all this while those cursed cows that created my water problem have got theirs on tap!

The divine fragrance of elderflowers fills the cowshed, it hasn't known so glorious a scent as this for a hundred years. Nothing marks high summer more poignantly than the elderflowers... apart from Wimbledon of course and, as anyone in the country knows, with Wimbledon cometh the horsefly... nothing's perfect!

A roaring fire and a midsummer heatwave seem strange bedfellows as we toil in the burning heat like bees; theirs is for honey, ours for wine. The kettle doesn't know its spout from its handle and is almost melting out of shape under the pressure. Wine making demands that every separate item be spotlessly clean or the wine will be vinegar or even worse. It's going to be a late night under paraffin-light, but the thought of sampling the wine of this particular wonderful afternoon, on some dreadful villainous day in winter, such a magical thought just sparkles and fills me with excited feelings, knowing that, by then we shall also have the elderberries bubbling away in their fermentation jars. It all feels so promising, squirrel-like and cosy.

When the boys come home from school one afternoon with the news that their friends Kelly and Joan will provide homes for Bootsy's kittens, I'm really rather relieved, casting my mind back to that wet dark night on the cliff when Jerry the tramp brought me a 'tomcat' in a carrier bag, a gift for catching rats... some tomcat! Robin is a bit upset, so I sit with him and have a bit of a heart-to-heart, explaining as best I can that he should really be happy that they are going to good homes and will be well looked after. There are a few hot and heavy tears and I jokingly try to comfort him, saying, "You'll be able to visit them... Uncle Robin's come to visit you," they'll say." I'm driveling on with all this sloppy stuff and he's blubbering all over my shirt when, silhouetted against an evening sky, three figures come walking slowly down the field. I can recognise one of them by the bandy legs and rolled-down wellies, but the others are a mystery. Robin is up and away, his broken heart has miraculously super-glued itself back to health, he's closely followed by the other two with Cari running a close fourth. I wait by the caravan as the air resounds under a cacophony of laughter; it's my sister Rosie and her Canadian friend Elly taking a breather from university life in Sussex, fully equipped for roughing it in Celtic upland swamp country and weighed down with lumpy rucksacks, rugged footwear and a big tent. Dan is plainly feeling important at having bravely chaperoned them over the crocodile infested marsh, they are not to know that the bull is totally disinterested and knackered, that the cows are all virtually asleep and that there are no lions or wolves lurking about the place. Sykes and Robin pose far greater threats to their wellbeing.

There's a carnival atmosphere as they all let off steam; Sykes is wary and streaks away hysterically and with no apparent sense of direction and making a most fearful din; I'd swear that she had a bit of ostrich somewhere in the rabble of her genes, she's a bit like an-out-of control formula one bumping car and I fear that it'll end up with someone getting pecked.

It's rather fortunate that our eight gallons of virgin elderflower wine is now beginning the long fermentation vigil up in the relative safety of the bedroom along with the rest of our priceless treasures. This means that I must reorganise the downstairs room into a jacket-potato, cheese and beans, toast and tea factory furnace with adequate parking spaces for both invited and uninvited bums. To this end, the planks that we salvaged from storms at sea earlier in the year are really worth their weight in gold now, as are the surplus concrete blocks left over from the wall, so there isn't likely to be a seating problem to concern us.

I've really got to get my brain into gear now that we have our special visitors and I am compelled to work feverishly and discretely, emptying the Elsan toilet somewhere out of sight behind the barn and then magically turning the pigsty into something resembling a glossy page from 'House and Garden' and smelling seductively of Jeyes fluid with a spare candle for extra luxury, together with the artistic touch of one on of my canvases to wedge against the doorway for privacy. Whilst I'm doing this, it sounds like a circus up in the field beyond the cowshed where Rosie and Elly are trying to erect their tent somewhere, their problem is that of finding a small patch of ground that's flat and isn't encrusted with partially baked cow-muck. They are being rather more than ably assisted in this by clowns who are almost certainly luring them into pitching on cushions of the dark greeny-brown squelchy stuff; even Dan is about as much help as margarine upon which to strike a match... they'll get no light from him while he's in this crazy sort of mood.

I don't interfere, they're big girls now and this ain't Brighton; at least they'll have the facility of a 'normal' toilet as a result of my efforts. As I emerge from the pigsty I bang my head on the low beam over the door and I see a few stars before I am attacked by Sykes who comes claws-first up at me like a mad shuttlecock before rushing off into the barn and setting all the others off cackling and clucking their disgust. I bolt their door and set about the business of providing firewood for the night ahead; if this is summer, what the hell's winter going to be like!

Gareth and Hugh drive up in the Landrover and, together with the Jack Russell bitch, join in the general mayhem; there's certainly no shortage of 'helpers' out there. Whilst all this is going on, I get the fire started and fill the oven with lovely big King Edward potatoes and set the first kettle to wheezing in the licking flames. Over all the crackling, spitting fireworks of the fire, I distinctly hear two barrels of a twelve bore boasting up in the wood and I know that this gives notice of yet another visitor in the form of Dai-the-Death Morgan, pest controller. Sure enough, a glance through the window up into the hillside where the setting sun has left a burning golden glow, two dogs and a ferret of a man come jolloping down to join the circus; it's only now that I notice Meg and Murphy are there in the thick of it too. The babbling troupe slowly but surely head for the cowshed where smoke from the chimney is belching a colossal welcome up into the sky where our late swallows are still trawling the vast ocean of evening air, wondering why some of it is making their eyes run.

Bootsy's eyes are flaring like lorry headlights and her fur is standing up on end when she senses the dogs approaching. I'm afraid she might attack them in protecting her kittens, so I coax her back into the shed and hastily fasten the door so's to keep the peace and not a moment too soon either as the herd of jokers drift noisily into the yard. The air is scented with pipe-smoke as Gareth stokes up a huge cumulus that's as idle as are his strides, with no breeze to persuade even the gnats to a livelier dance. Rosie and Elly are feasting their eyes on the entire picture, hardly able to believe what they are experiencing. There's a raucous gabble of voices, shrieks and screams; the boys are in high spirits with Robin showing-off in overdrive. Murphy is practically exploding with his enthusiasm about to pop all his rivets; he's always excited when Rosie appears, he's got a soft spot for her and he could be risking getting a black eye from Meg if he isn't careful. By contrast Dan, Dai and Gareth boringly allow their seniority to get them muttering stuff about the weather, the hardness of the ground, the need for rain and how, according to the postman, a brief shower was recorded only seven miles away last Thursday afternoon. They chew over this just like the collapsed cows chewing their cud, punctuating it with the occasional "Oh, ah!" Dan and Dai remove their caps in anticipation of going inside in the same anticipatory way that the swallows in the lean-to have stepped-up their diving in and out as a kind of warning to us. Regardless of aerial bombardment, I have to keep going inside to check that the kettle hasn't melted, only to discover on my return outside that Robin has used the opportunity to show-off Bootsy's kittens and all hell is let loose there before my eyes. Everything that I feared is happening; the poor dogs don't stand a chance and Bootsy isn't intent on taking prisoners. There's a fearful yelping and squawking and a state of total gob-smackedness all around as animals streak in panic amongst us. Dai's two working mongrels vanish scratched and bleeding over the hill like bits of paper in a gale... we'll not be seeing them again. Gareth's bitch terrier leaps off in another direction whimpering and no doubt cursing the shortness of her legs; fortunate for her that Bootsy took-on the bigger dogs first, thus allowing the little terrier to escape beyond the wood above my well. There is laughter now as it begins to sink in what has happened and Bootsy comes swaggering back, bristling and still very wild-eyed, edgy and constantly turning to check that she's successfully seen them off. Robin is mauling the kittens and I tell him to take them back, having to repeat myself several times before he decides to get the message and at this point, Gareth gives Hugh a nudge and they depart with broad grins and bounce away down past the well and up the steep track back to the farm.

Evening settles and, when the potatoes begin to smell, this is the very first realisation that we're about to have a feast. I light the paraffin lamp and we get candles flickering in jars and the table laid with milk, mugs, honey, salt and pepper, butter and some rather lovely Ceylon tea from the Co-op. The atmosphere is brilliant and, between the laughter and chat, the wine in the upstairs room is bubbling away ferociously. Dan thinks we have ghosts, while Dai discovers that there isn't room in his mouth for a King Edward as well as his false teeth and his face suddenly becomes the scene of a Cavalier and Roundhead get-together. By now my tin and bamboo whistles are having potato and cheese blown through them, while Murphy and I let rip all the songs which I wrote back in the deep and lonesome winter. I play my guitar and Murphy sings, everybody joins in, voice, whistle, bean-tin, spoon and mug, it's orchestrated anarchy, and not a single drop of booze in sight... we're just drunk on life, a treasure beyond measure. In the midst of all this, Dai's dentures are on the floor somewhere, gums suit him better, he looks like he's eating a piano with those other things wedged there. I unhitch the pressure-lamp from the beam, give it a few pumps to bring the pressure up and the light brighter and we grovel about for his national health biting things. Dan is in stitches, he refuses to wear dentures and continues to depend on his sepia-stained stump and a bit. All's well, we find the teeth and not a moment too soon either because it suddenly occurs to Dai that, with the dogs arriving home bleeding and without their master, it's going to set-off alarm bells and he's yet to negotiate the marsh in darkness and with a twelve-bore over his shoulder. As he gets up to go, the others decide to join him and they go noisily off into the dark, allowing us to have a more thoughtful hour in the firelight.

Everyone has had a lovely time and the girls now have to find their tent. Cari wants to join them and so I round-up my sleepy sons and get them settled, happier in my mind to know that this place will be buzzing with activity whilst I am away and I don't feel nearly so bad as I did a few days ago.

Morning brushes the darkness away together with all traces of yesterday. I light the calor-gas ring, put the kettle on, then stagger out into the new day and pee in the tender morning sunlight down the field. There are twenty cows, one massive bull and about a million sheep obliterating the tent from view as I advance with three mugs of tea in my fists. This strange canvas 'thing' with even stronger snoring noises coming from it is a source of uncontainable intrigue to them, they know that it's 'something' and that it's different, but that's all. They reluctantly disperse, permitting me to see that half of the tent has collapsed and has been quite extravagantly fouled, but the occupants remain in wrecked oblivion; how they can possibly have escaped from getting trampled is concerning me as I stand here in the midst of this great beef-brotherhood, calling the names of those within, not venturing to proceed further because of a logic that reminds me that a girls' dormitory contains as many post-digestive smells as does a mans. I respect their need to be smelling like flowers and so I wait and keep calling. Eventually Cari comes to my aid and I point out the collapsed end, where, to my great relief, Elly is still snoring and breaking sweet wind in exquisite oblivion. I leave them with their tea and disperse the animals, I even surprise myself by man-handling the bull and slapping him firmly on the backside... but they've crapped everywhere as usual.

University life, all hygienic and intellectual is a far cry from this but, even now, this to me is perfection ... there's no mud, no whipping rain or that dreadful grey gloom you'd swear was stolen from a cathedral roof. Whatever we've got certainly isn't contrived, it's absolutely real, sufficiently distanced from that which is so taken for granted as to be revelation itself; a timely reminder that we are frail and that the only boss we can ever aspire to be is in that of managing an individual survival and sustaining an understanding which includes all other things, visualising this in a holy way and finding a gladness for being alive, pure and simple.

Backwards into the Machine

With my little van serviced and re-shod with remoulds, I set forth on the long and meandering trail to Plymouth; my heart feels like it's choking me, memory lane is a lonesome place no matter how noble the cause. It's early evening when I arrive and I head straight for the television studios and acquaint myself once more with the security staff and let them know that I shall be sleeping in my van in their car-park overnight. It's fortunate for me that they know me, better still that my old friend Brendan will be on duty through till morning. After we've had a good old yarn, I decide to unwind by going off on a long run, culminating in a touch of real luxury, a shower followed by a stroll into town for a bag of fish and chips before settling down in my sleeping-bag and escaping from the feelings of loneliness.

At first light, there is a tapping on the van window, which is totally misted up and I un-zip myself from my sleep-cocoon and discover old Brendan with a cup of steaming tea for me. It's a beautiful moment, here in the dawn light, a city still sleeping and a father-like friend making sure that I'm okay, looking after me as though I were his own son. I emerge into the youngest sun imaginable and stretch in the divine engineless silence of the new city, Hitler flattened the old one that had character and charm. I never knew it and I love Plymouth for what it is now. Idle gulls call from rooftops and Brendan laces the air with cigarette smoke and coughs to demonstrate the damage that forty fags a night have done to his lungs.

My week has started and, before the world has awakened and the army of early morning cleaners have settled on the scene, I steal silently through the corridors with my toilet-bag and towel. I have to be quick about it, the last thing that I would wish for is a twenty two stone goddess in curlers, rolled-down stockings over her ankles, fag in mouth, mop and bucket in hand, bursting in on my nudity; I'd have a twitching corpse on my hands... not so easy to explain. I know that Brendan, for pure devilment, wouldn't warn anyone that I was there and would sit chuckling waiting for the screams.

It's lucky for me that this thought crossed my mind when it did because, on my way back along the corridor I pass that very twenty two stone specimen shuffling flat-out on her way to the place I have just vacated. Our greetings echo merrily all about the place and when I turn into another corridor there are half a dozen more of them babbling and smoking away beside their buckets. I briefly shock them into silence as I go tripping past and I hear them burst like a dawn chorus as I speed along the next corridor beyond the double-doors and, when I turn at the far end they are all clamouring to get a better look and I wave back at them, setting them off hooting and howling enough to crack the plate-glass windows. When I reach the reception area, Brendan is leaning back on a chair in front of a small switchboard; sight of me springs to life the diesel engine of his cough as laughter hits the starter-button of his face, leaving him chugging helplessly, still gripping a smoking stub in his brown-stained fingers. "You old leprechaun," I laugh... "that's the closest shave I ever had!"

I have time to kill so I bravely step out along memory lane, up the hill to the 'Hoe' passing our old flat in Holyrood Place where we lived when first arriving in Plymouth all those years ago. Sweet, sad memories haunting my every step of the way before the great slam of the sea hits me with the same unbelievable force as it did then, when the entire 'Sound' was crammed with naval shipping as the Fleet were there all gathered for a Nato exercise. This time only a handful of ships are idly at anchor while little fishing boats chug out from the Barbican leaving glistening lines of broadening waves in their wake. I could stand here upon this priceless moment forever, never tiring of its exquisite tenderness. Across the water to the west, old Cornwall with more memories ghosting amongst the slender undulations; it's a battle trying to contain all the aches that are re-awakening in me so I hurry across the Hoe and down the winding steps to the waterfront, then briskly head beyond the 'Citadel' to the 'Barbican' and lose myself amongst trawlers and fishermen, under a clamour of shouting gulls and the smell of fish and nets.

The pattern of all my mornings is here set; just as last night's long run had set the pattern for my evenings. All that remains for me to do now is to fill the bit in between with another pattern that will speed the weekend into my grasp so that I can make my Friday night dash across the miles, back to the cowshed and to those I love.

I follow the pattern, careful not to drop a stitch and I make it back to the marsh meadow gate before the darkness has properly settled. I toot my horn to announce my return and, in a flash, the gang are galloping joyfully across to greet me, wild with excitement, showing that, not only have they survived without me but, more so, have thrived in the rearranged free-for-all pecking order of things. The horseflies have also had a good week by all accounts and everyone has been thoroughly bitten and have taken to crushing vast amounts of garlic and smearing their bodies with it in some quaint old belief that the stink will offer protection, but, as I have learned, the horsefly bites first, then shouts "Garlic!"

Everywhere is bone dry, the drought is really biting now and the cracks across the earth are noticeably wider and far more numerous. It is a great relief to hear that the well is still intact and my fence not yet battered into submission. We sit up late in the flame-flickering dance of a small twig fire and two candles in jars. It's pure magic, made better by having an envelope fat with paper-money in my pocket and with the assuredness of four more to come before September is out.

Rose and Elly are having the time of their lives and are looking bronzed with health, not having experienced too many holly leaves in their bums and are both definitely leaner and fitter than they were a week ago. In my absence, the new swallows have hatched and thus there has been increased traffic through window and door. The wine is still bubbling away in the bedroom where the floor is getting splattered with swallow droppings. I check the water-levels in the air-locks and discover that it's been evaporating in the intense heat, but I catch them in the nick of time and top them up, taking the extra precaution of covering them loosely with a flimsy tablecloth as protection from swallow-turds and fruit flies. The boys simply melt into sleep and we take them gently to roost then return to the languid gorsebloom of yellow flames, finding such simple clarity in our easy talk, cocooned in comforting darkness all around. It's a lovely moment for taking up my guitar and letting it play me, pluck and pick the strings of my heart. Everyone listens because they are part of what is being expressed, a more perfect way to round-off a long and tiring day, I've yet to discover.

Saturday is mine as soon as it shows its head above the alder-marsh. One week away has resulted in a bucket that's asking to be emptied and so I disregard the prettiness of the morning and grovel about in the pigsty man-handling the unpleasant heavy item, then struggle off down the slope beyond the barn and dig a grave to bury the memories of food eaten, while everyone else is sleeping unrestricted and without any trace of an agenda of any shape or form. Saturday means that the boys can wallow in the hot sludge of sleep for as long as they like; as for the girls, only discomfort will influence them into emerging to the light. I don't feel that I have any such luxury and I have a natural desire to both provide for them and protect them whilst not interfering in the delicate nature of preferences.

There are things that need attending to as a matter of urgency; a cylinder of gas, three or four loaves of bread and an army-sized slab of cheese will do for starters. I think on and the list goes on growing; candles, bog-rolls, paraffin, matches, margarine, butter, olive oil; I decide to deal with this now before the others are stirring. I'm all too aware that tomorrow I'll be driving back to Plymouth, so I wander over to my trustworthy little van and slip silently off to town.

On my return, a horsefly bites me while my hands are full; it's going to be a baking hot day, that's for sure and I'm glad for having made my effort early. Carrying a heavy gas-cylinder in this heat is no joke and the iron doesn't soften any as it rests against my skull with all its weight pressing down on my collarbone. Thankfully the heat has more than subdued 'Max Tractor' and his girls and, even at only ten o'clock on this Saturday morning, the sheep and their adolescent lambs are gasping for air and clamouring for shade; it's a heavy day, that's for sure.

After returning to the van to pick up the remaining loaves and other items, I stroll down and have a good look at the well and note the difference that a week away has made. It's settling beautifully and the water is at last beginning to clear and has whirligigs and water-boatmen already claiming it as home. I decide that this is the moment for me to sample the water, so I stroll back to pick up the water-carrier and jug, then return and fill up; we're going to celebrate our new well with a nice cup of tea!

It feels strange my being the 'visitor' with just thirty six hours before having to leave again; it's a bit like being another swallow, with their urgency to breed being echoed in my own urgency to tend to vital things. I'm just hoping that we might happen upon a patch of pure leisure and lie amongst the dandelion clocks and listen to the sighing of their moments; one thing for sure, with heat like this, it's going to be hard to do much more than that.

The hens are still laying their bright white miracles about the place and I'm heartened to notice how they are getting some organisation into their lives, making cosy nests in the straw into which several of them choose to lay. They also indulge in the luxury of dust-bathing, ridding themselves of mites with enviable ecstasy under the burning sun. In total oblivion they lie wrecked all across the dung-heap, bruising the air with dust as they flip the infinitesimal particles amongst their feathers. Robin has decided that he's a chicken and has made his own dust-bath amongst them, so intoxicating is the nectar of their bliss upon him. I let sleeping dogs lie, asking him not to do anything is always a fruitless exercise.

Seeing a bowl of hens' eggs in the caravan is a lovely sight, there are white ones, dark brown ones and creamy ones; the colour variation is because Dan's hens are now providing him with a surplus and he's glad when our gang drop in on him to buy eggs. The dark brown ones are those which the boys continue to find, laid by independently-minded escapee fowls of the Meg and Murphy flock; it seems strange how hens that all eat the same food, lay differently coloured eggs, it makes our pure white eggs even more miraculous. Whatever their colour, none of them taste as good as our white ones, I don't know what it is but they're easily the best.

Sykes continues to baffle me with her anti-social behaviour; she's frightened the hell out of the cats and has made the discovery that a contented cat often walks with its tail in the air, thus exposing a tender target area for her to peck at. It really must be purgatory for a cat with this old git stomping up behind it. She also eats the eggs which the others have so painstakingly laid and has never herself been seen to do anything which might suggest that she too lays eggs. Having no comb and perpetual diarrhoea, she gives no signal that she's a layer but, on this particular scorching Saturday, after going into the barn and being once more attacked by her, I find a tiny white egg, about the size of a blackbirds, it's obvious to me that Sykes has actually laid. I pick it up, it's still warm and I take it into the caravan and place it amongst the others ... it looks like a joke, it's so tiny and my curiosity persuades me to crack it open into a saucer. I can't believe what I'm seeing... there's no yolk in it, it's just white, nothing else. How her complete uselessness was not detected at the battery-farm is a miracle; this cantankerous old sod is an imposter, but more than that, a survivor! The bantams remain independent from the rest. One ruffling of the cockerel's rainbow is all it takes to keep it that way, and he too has learned that Sykes isn't worth losing a nights sleep over and is now avoiding her like the plague.

Miraculously, Robin still has his fishing net in one piece and I stumble across an old glass-fibre fishing rod of my own, complete with reel, line and an ancient haversack containing floats, hooks, weights and spinners; boyhood memories flooding back at a glance. Having forgotten to include cat food on my early morning shopping trip, it occurs to me that the pool beyond the farm might be just the place to idle away an hour or two, not to mention the unscheduled bath that Robin needs after his earlier chicken dust-bath. Thoughts of the much talked-about giant pike gives me the idea that the cats could possibly dine a bit more up-market for a change, food couldn't come fresher. My subsequent suggestion seems like a brilliant idea to everyone, even the cats join in, tails in the air as we all head off smelling of garlic. Up through the wood, skirting the hill farm and slipping down through another wood before crossing the dried-up marshland with its meandering relic of old hedgerow prior to the woodland in which the pool is nestled. The cats are loving it and I'm even getting concerned lest their purring awakes the school cook. The girls soon settle down to deadly serious sunbathing, well smeared in 'Ambre Solaire'. Robin dabbles with his net while I try spinning for the monster, but the density of weed is making it virtually impossible to make a clean cast, so I ask the boys to help me find a big red worm and we all root about under the clumps of turf bordering the pool, eventually finding a very large specimen which is closer to a snake in size then it is to a worm. Try as I may, I cannot bring myself to attach it to the hooks, inflicting pain upon it so blatantly. Without realising it, these are the moments that stop me from ever fishing again.

At the shallow end of the pool, weed growth is minimal and I am thus able to resume with the spinner, making cast after cast to no effect; I lose interest and decide to call it a day, the only bites I am getting are insect bites. I wind the line in and suddenly the rod is almost snatched out of my grasp... I've hooked a pike! The boys jump up and down with excitement as they watch the water being thrashed and the rod bending double; I can hear the line whistling as it stretches almost to breaking point. Eventually I haul it ashore, it isn't the monster by any means, but a five-pound pike will feed the cats in the meantime. I ask the boys to look the other way while I hit it over the head with a large stone and kill it, the very act of which fills me with shame and revulsion, precisely marking the end of my fishing days right here this very moment of time.

We rejoin the others who are having frantic battles with biting insects and are far too preoccupied to show any interest in what I've caught. I lay the pike down on the ground and the cats stare at it before cautiously sniffing in trying to establish what it is. They are not interested but I know that once I've cooked it and left it in a dish where it may be stolen, then they'll eat it right down to the very last bone, no doubt about it!

The air is now heavy with clammy heat that's difficult to breathe as we laboriously head back under a torment of horseflies and little black thunderbugs. It isn't much cooler under the shaded canopy of trees where sheep are panting in desperation, regardless of having been shorn over the past week. We're all suffering from the heat, dehydrated and gasping for another celebratory brew from our new well. Whilst I'm tending to this, the gang flop-out in the shade of the sycamore tree, too weary to even laze to and fro on the swing. Only the swallows seem still to be toiling, but they're not having to fly nearly so high to catch their flies and are catching them close to the ground, an ominous sign which is underlined by a haziness and the first sign of imperfection in the steep sky.

We sit around drinking tea and singing the praises of powdered milk on a day like this when even the cows' udders have turned to cheese. Having no electricity is not without its drawbacks, especially when it is combined with having no water either; lack of sewerage or drainage systems, no access whatsoever. These are the very things which Rosie and Elly are so inspired by; it all seems so heroic and so gloriously defiant to them, recognising that, despite the drawbacks, we have the most marvellous quality of life which is based on getting out of it only that which we are prepared to put into it. A romantic notion to say the least, but with some substance of truth, albeit small. Truth is, right now this is the absolute height of luxury for us. The blessing of dried up parched ground cannot be quantified in any terms of measurable value, just as mud and cowshit up to your crotch cannot be quantified on a minus scale of any sort; heaven is heaven and hell is hell, it's as simple as that.

Four pots of tea later, I am compelled to deal with the stiffened pike which has begun to attract big flies by the million, so like it or not, I have to get it and remove its head. Inside it I find the part-digested remains of a roach, it's like opening the pages of a book that my Mother told me never to read. I feel really bad with myself, even more so when I confront the fact that I'll eat fish from the chip shop as enthusiastically as the next man, the difference being that somebody else killed the cod, while I alone it was that killed the pike, just in order that the domestic cat might eat. These thoughts thunder away in my mind as I hurry to erase the memory once and for all, but I can't escape the thought that I never wanted to be part of the domestic cat culture in the first place, recognising that the wild birds had enough problems to cope with already, what with modern farming methods that destroyed both food supply and habitat. Nature itself could never prescribe or condone such a high density of predators per acre as that of the domestic cat and I, for one, didn't want to add to the problem.

On my way back from the well, sucking at the air like a fish on land, I am confronted by the most delightful sight; the little pink bantam has at long last emerged from inside the barn and has a tiny golden chick chirping beside her. I look for others but this solitary one is all there is and has survived the great leap from the top of the barn wall. I stand and watch this touchingly beautiful mother-and-chick-relationship, all the delicate considerations and the immense sense of pride being shown. I ease away, fearful of alarming them in any small way, but pleased in my heart to know that already so many little lives have awakened here since our arrival.

It's like an oven inside the caravan, but the pike is back in water with a goodish amount of salt and is looking more like food than murder now, its head and its guts are under the caravan on a plate ... first come, first served. I add to the temperature by lighting the small oven and popping the pike in for a short transformation, then return outside into the primeval electric air where nature is conceiving something nasty. The first thing I see is Bootsy with the murdered bantam chick in her mouth, hurrying slyly back into the shed and all I can do is stand gaping full of horrified feelings impossible for me to find reason with. Anger is no use because I know that I am no better and I stand there for some time before realising that the sun has been buried beyond mountainous mysteries of stuff sucked beyond logic from fish-riddled seas light-years beyond my comprehension. I hear the faint far rumble of furniture being shifted in the sky and I know that God is about to remind me just how tiny a thing I really am. I shout for the others to come inside and they need no second asking as a wicked flickering blue light frightens the hell out of everything. Buzzards, five of them that had previously languished in an aimless merry-go-round, come down like planes shot in a war and are consumed in dense oakwoods as the first pitter-patter of overweight rain-droplets hit the new tin roof, accompanied by terrible dancing light and threatening explosions that are inching closer each time they speak. There's nothing hurried about it and the rain is steady, heavy, straight rain which very quickly brings music back to the water-tub and hens racing back to the barn. Sykes would have been first but she runs right past it for some reason best known to herself; maybe she's invigorated by it.

A brave kind of humour makes itself heard as Rosie comments, "Jimmy... isn't a tin roof going to attract the lightning?" I look back at her with a blank kind of smirk. "Er, yes... I suppose you could be right there, Rosie... the caravan's not much better, it's all metal on a steel chassis. What do you suggest... the tent maybe?" We all laugh nervously as the rain steps up a gear and black water starts to trickle down the chimney and into the hearth. Everywhere and everything is held prisoner in a frightening darkness that's crazed with awesome flashes of flickering light which is faster than imagination can grasp and is accompanied by explosions of indescribable proportions. The swallows are huddled together on their nests and the boys scream excitedly, believing that, so long as I'm here, there's nothing to be afraid of; little do they know that I'm standing here blotting my own copybook!

The terrifying truth is that, every one of those bolts of lightning actually hits something, usually something tall... like our chimney; something on a hill... like our cowshed is built on; something metal ... like our tin roof! This is a big storm and it's wandering about with a kind of aimless menace, like a drunkard looking for a fight, lashing out at everything. When it's directly overhead and the flash and the bang happen simultaneously, screams go up and we fully expect the roof to cave in and the chimney to come crashing through the lean-to kitchen roof. Miraculously we are spared and spared again, knowing that something very close must have been hit instead.

As it eases, I can hear the less fortunate sheep complaining up in the wood and frightened cows mooing far and wide. Tentatively, we venture out into the yard, it isn't over yet and the thunder can be heard rumbling all around and there's steady rain soaking down onto a cleaner earth. The tub is overflowing, it's amazing and I'm wishing that I had a spare one for the overflow. One thing for certain, the elderflowers on the hedges have all been wrecked by the storm and I comment to Cari on just how fortunate we were to have made the wine when we did. The girls' tent looks rather more than a bit worse for wear and is sagging at one end and collapsed at the other ... I have the distinct feeling that they'll be sleeping in the cowshed tonight. With evening drawing on, the thunder returns and we endure another fiery onslaught that continues well into the night, easing our fears through familiarity alone.

Sunday morning sneaks up in golden slippers, everywhere is quiet after the storm and the air is crisp and clean smelling under a sparkling blue sky. I'd expected to find lakes of water covering the marsh and the stream merrily splashing once more, but the ground has absorbed most of it leaving hardly a trace. I wake the boys up and ask if they'd like to accompany me on an early walk before having to start thinking about my long drive back to Plymouth later in the day. Rowan is willing, but the other two squirm and contort in their reluctance to be parted from their beds. I don't persist and leave them where they are while Rowan and I aim for the big hill to the north, from the top of which we may look back down on the cowshed and see endless horizons all around with far distant jagged mountains showing in the thoroughly cleaned morning air. The alder and willow marsh is in succulent revival, squelchy and ideal again for snipe and woodcock. We disturb a heron that's come for a frog breakfast and watch it lift into the sunlight, a wonderful sight as it rises like a grey feather blown by a breeze, calling a bold 'kraak' before vanishing from view.

A tree by the lane has a massive splintered branch lying on the ground and the old ash is split all the way down her trunk as far as the ground. "This accounts for one of those bolts of lightning last night," I say to Rowan, "... it was a bit close wasn't it?" He has the look of astonishment, eyes big and staring and his mouth wide open. "Cor!" This was the tree where earlier in the year we had seen a tawny owl in amongst the ivy that grew on it; now it's not even half a tree and has suffered a terrible butchering by electrocution. We cross the lane and climb a gate leading on to a wild acre of gorse and broom together with a fragment of ancient hawthorn hedge where a magpie has earlier built a fortress. Several magpies are yacketing off as we pass underneath and scramble over a wire fence which borders the great hill. The ground here is warm and steamy and my eyes almost burst out of my head when I suddenly see clusters of bright white mushrooms growing amongst the grass. I'm lost for words and immediately start picking, very soon running out of things to put them in. I quickly convert my t-shirt into a bag and steadily, as we inch our way to the hilltop, we fill it until we cannot possibly squeeze another one into it. Rowan is absolutely thrilled as the pair of us stand like princes high above the world; this kind of feeling cannot be purchased at any price and we just smile letting our feeling come sweetly sailing in. Beneath us the cowshed stands toy-like and without any sign of life while, far beyond, the hills over which I must later drive, the very thought makes me want to cry.

We return quietly with a plan to awaken everybody with the smell of wild mushrooms frying and garlic in there too helping to tantalise the taste buds. We don't make a song about it, but we're excited nonetheless and it suits us perfectly that everyone is still locked in their private dream worlds; we're soon going to alter that!

No breakfast could ever equal the one that blesses this Sunday morning table. Field mushrooms gathered early before the flies have had time to lay their eggs in the base of the stems... wow, how could anything compare with this? When I glance at Rowan, he's enjoying the same feeling as I am as we watch the others replacing their sleep preoccupation with enthusiastic delights of a different kind. Robin and Spencer are first to leave the table, satisfied mostly with having had eggs to assist them in coming to terms with the acquired taste and texture of wild mushrooms; the rest of us keep making room for the next hot pan-full, black peppered and Worcester-sauced with generously toasted bread and lots of lovely tea to help wash it down. Sunday morning; who needs to go off in their best clothes in search of heaven when heaven so divinely graces us with her presence right here under our humble little noses. How could anything so simple, get so fouled beyond understanding? What a crazy species upon this planet we are, alien to it in more ways than we are at harmony with it; I can't think why, it's all so simple.

Regardless of the invigorating and thirst-quenching effect of the storm, July marks the very limit for vegetation and this is reflected all along the banks and hedges; sap can reach no further and a tiredness is beginning to take hold already. High summer is marked by the sudden realisation that the song's been sung and the singer no longer wrapped in passion and poetry; nettles are as tough as old boots and green hips and berries have replaced blossoms. Cress in the ditch sucks up the new water and clogs the space between banks and the winged insects have left eggs to make caterpillars and grubs with one sole aim in their metamorphosis, that of eating. What once was spring, is now a table laid in preparation for next year's flying.

Our mushroom crop marks the first of many such feasts and the damson trees are promising jam, our apple trees beginning to boast of future pies and the dog-rose hips already whispering of syrup for winter coughs. This is high summer, the oven of the year baking us and making us idle with holiday feelings. A new flush of grass growth has ensured a bounty of enriched cowshit all across the earth while, on a brighter note, Cari has spotted the green glow of glowworms down the lane, making late evening walks pure magic under an owl and woodcock fading sky.

The Professor drops in to 'Kiss the Pan'!

I hate having to go away to work when I want to discover the gypsy in me and to become a kind of green outlaw for a while and to learn from it before the machine grabs me and makes me its slave for the rest of time. I console myself by remembering that, even the Romanies found it necessary to take seasonal work, fruit-picking and the like, not that this is of much comfort to me because it simply echoes the current situation where there is always a predominant bureaucracy to choke us with bits of paper and even more and more bits of paper to suffocate any mind that questions. Evidence of this bureaucratic monster is exemplified during the following week when, on writing a letter back home, for a bit of light-hearted fun, I painted a picture on the envelope, using the Queen's head on the stamp as my starting point. I painted the rest of Her Majesty sitting on our chemical toilet, a bog-roll on a piece of string nailed to the wall and a Corgi sitting faithfully at her feet. The stamp itself was not defaced in any way but, on its delivery, to the cowshed door of all miracles, the postman had been ordered to establish the name and address of the sender of such a threat upon the nation in order that I may be arrested and thence hung, drawn and quartered for my impudence. Fortunately for me, Cari pleaded ignorance, and she together with Rosie, Elly and the postman too, split their sides with laughter, coming to an agreement over the letter holding no clue as to who had sent it. Nothing more happened, but I thought it wiser not to do it again... well, not too often anyway.

As I think on a little further I am reminded of something which I in turn find just as hard to handle as my little fun-envelope has proven to be. Few things irritate me as much as the brown window envelope upon which is boldly printed, 'On Her Majesty's Service, Inland Revenue' There's little that can compare with this or can better demonstrate our eternal enslavement to a master and monster of our own invention. I don't relish having this 'Dan's-dog-of-a-thing' forever threatening to suck my last drop of blood when I am anaemically poor and of humble aspirations, although, to be fair, a tax system which is in itself fair and fiddle-proof, I won't argue against. It's just that those invasive brown envelopes scare the hell out of me whenever one appears with my name and number emblazoned in its window... they'll be wanting my photograph next!

July slips by and the house of the four 'R's' closed for business until a time of leaf-fall, giant marrows and the new boy, Robin. Three weeks of my working away are completed and I now have a gap of five weeks before my final two weeks in September. It's during this time that my old friend, John Wain, Professor of

Poetry at Oxford, informs me that he's going to be in the vicinity doing something with the University College of North Wales and suggests that we meet up and, in particular, for him to come over and give his blessings on the cowshed which, until now, has been a source of considerable intrigue and amusement to him; he's in for a shock. We're all thrilled at the prospect, although Rosie and Elly unfortunately are about to move on and so will not be able to meet him.

We have arranged to meet early at an 'Alice in Wonderland' kind of place called Gregynog Hall, a hidden treasure blanketed and cocooned by Douglas firs and Lawson's cypresses, with lawns, fountains and crafted box-hedges. An ornate black-and-white building, once the home of one of the finest collections of impressionist paintings anywhere before death duties sucked the priceless treasures away. It is with some reverence therefore that I venture inside where John introduces me to the man in charge, Dr. Hughes, who has obviously been briefed by John regarding my background and is ready to talk art and show me over the place, which he so plainly loves. We get on most amicably and I am invited over tea and biscuits to exhibit my own paintings here in the big hall where van Gogh, Monet, Picasso, Degas, Cézanne, Renoir and many other such giants have graced the walls. I feel an unbelievable thrilling humbleness thundering throughout me and I tingle as I tell myself that I'd better start painting again, a thought which seems as impossible as finding room for a single mushroom more on that marvellous morning of our mushroom feast.

We drive back sedately at fifteen miles an hour whilst conversing at ninety like hyenas at a corpse; our carriage is too small for all that's muscling to be said in it. The little van glides down the last stretch of almost hidden lane and gently comes to rest beside the marsh meadow gate. I open the gate and the professor makes a grand ceremonious occasion of it as he steps out measuredly with walking stick and feasting eyes, sipping the young morning air as though it is French and bottled at a thousand quid a throw. It is pure theatre as he pauses frequently to bless the ground and to absorb the atmosphere of this insignificant gem within the principality. With delightful eccentricity he partakes of the smells, the colours and the sounds, like a conductor about to begin the first performance of a Symphony of Life, here live and spontaneous, too learned by far as to know what the particular birds are that are calling further down the marsh, but aware of their textural significance all down the echoing valley. "Jimmy, Jimmy, this is marvellous!" He stands in a more sober appreciation, fascinated. "What is that bird?" There are two birds in actual fact, John is abstractly merging both into one, part of the symphony within his blossoming. "The near one is a nuthatch and the more distant one is a green woodpecker calling from the ground, a sign of rain on the way, or so I've heard it said." He looks at me, gives a wry grin then a big friendly hug and says quietly: "You're so very much part of all this, aren't you, Jimmy?" In the absence of an answer I feel a bit of a bashful smile straddling my face rather awkwardly as we stride out once more, he leisurely with his walking stick, and me close beside him clutching his holdall that's every bit full of, clean pants and string vest, toilet-bag and numerous heavy books, spectacles, mouth-organ and plastic mac, the very things you'd expect a Professor of Poetry to be carrying.

He puffs a bit as we reach the hilltop where, through the gateway the cowshed stands like a defiant cry against the forces that dominate our lives. Glad of a breather, John pauses to take it all in, the symphony is resonant and raging as Cari comes tripping up the field like a soprano while the boys all melt and mingle amongst the sycamore leaves high above their swing, watching every movement like hawks, not quite ready to swoop down upon the victim ... their moment will come.

The cowshed is given its grand seal of approval, being categorized more as a kind of birds nest than a dwelling house, this conclusion coming from the recognition of there being no electricity, water, drainage or sewerage facilities in the nests of birds; somehow these too seemed to manage okay without such things.

It is a delight having John about the place, his brand of wisdom is always a revelation to me. He seems to bless everything he knows with a warmth of caring and compassion and, what's more, spells 'intellect' with a small 'i', something I find particularly refreshing. He's very much one of the family and we bestow on him our wild Oscar in the form of Keemun tea made with water from our well, wholemeal bread that Cari has baked, all hot and fresh from an early oven, and two beautiful white eggs specially laid for the occasion. It is over the frying of these that I discover one of the poet's culinary eccentricities when he becomes somewhat hysterically insistent that the eggs must merely "kiss the pan". A phrase which he keeps chanting from the moment that the olive oil has bravely begun to warm, obliging me to let him fry them himself. I was fortunate earlier in finding a few more field mushrooms to add to his delight; I never did see a man enjoy a breakfast so much.

Our early start has been arranged in order that we may all go on a trip to North Wales and deliver John back to his own wild fold in their cottage at Rhosgadfan, an eyrie on a Snowdonia hill overlooking Caernarfon and the sea beyond. Summer seems to be a time of reunion, celebratory and somewhat sad with every greeting followed by a parting; some moments I just wish would last forever, a measure of the treasure we find in others. Our reunion with the Wains-folk is boisterous to say the least; boys meeting boys is a bit like dogs meeting dogs, while adults, more resembling elephants, bellow and hoot their Hello's in an effervescent sort of over-indulgence in the building of an instantly self-protective layer upon which to contrive moments where only the very cream of themselves expresses itself; this is why holiday moments ever exist at all. Be that as it may, our reunion is spontaneously joyful for no reasons of inhibition whatsoever; we just pull the plug out and let it all go!

John's wife Eirian gets along with Cari like a gorse heath ablaze; their sons William, Ianto and Toby get along with Spencer, Rowan and Robin with greater ease than strawberries do with cream; we're a formidable team and find each others' company just perfect. We're staying overnight, so we can take it easy, use past headaches as pillows and, as John so constantly mutters, "take it easy." Cari suggests that John and I go off with the boys for an hour or so, enabling her and Eirian to catch up on things and to confront domestic issues.

We don't matter anyway, the macho gang are already letting steam off, ready for anything, booting a football about in the lane somewhat dangerously. After a few moments, John re-emerges minus his 'professor-look' and we all head off on a guided tour of this tiny village. At the hilltop we come to a playing field where a gang of local lads are playing football somewhat lethargically. On seeing our gang, a bold youth comes running over and challenges us to a football match, a challenge which we are unable to refuse for reasons of honour. There are eight of us and ten of them, so for the sake of fairness, the youth offers us one of his lot to even-up the sides; he's a pale, small skinny lad wearing wire-framed National Health spectacles with alarmingly thick lenses. "That's very sporting of you," John says politely, casting a wink in my direction, then starting to chuckle quietly to himself as he decides on whether or not to play with a walking stick or to risk wearing his best glasses. There's little time for any tactical considerations, these Rhosgadfan lads are intent on a quick kill and we just happen to be the sacrificial offering hitherto missing from their day. I tell the boys to simply get stuck in and fight for every ball, to generally get in their way and to swarm over them like flies... it's our only chance. I shall play in goal in an attempt to keep the score more resembling football than cricket, while John decides that his best position is that of playing a sort of benevolent role on the wing from where he can offer advice and encouragement, rather than any fancy stuff with his feet. Everyone else is centre forward, excepting of course our guest player who remains a mystery, but I have a strong suspicion that those are his reading glasses and that he can't see the ball anyway.

The match starts and, as expected, they come swarming all over us, their intentions are plain to see... kill them! I hold the fort at the back and the boys all start cheering with every save I make. Robin is inspirational in his tireless terrier-like pursuit of the ball and is utterly fearless and devoid of any skill whatsoever as he goes crunching into tackles, suffering pain and physical abuse heroically while our other warriors are showing the locals a thing or two about cussed determination. It's having an effect and I can sense a degree or two of demoralization coming over the local wizards who must be finding us more like a disease than an opposition. Jolly John is hopping up and down having touched the ball only once, and that with his walking stick. By half-time, unbelievably and totally against the run of play, we find ourselves leading by nine goals to nil; William's bagged a hat-trick, Toby's sneaked a couple as has Rowan and Ianto and Spencer have poached others. As a friendly gesture we let them have their skinny lad back, then I examine Robin's injuries to make sure that his heroicism isn't concealing an assortment of fractures. I ask him to ease off in the second half, if that is possible, and he grins reassuringly, offering me no such assurances.

Battle resumes and our terriers get stuck-in once more, thwarting any idea the opposition has about the 'passing game' that they have been taught. They do however manage to score four, but we agree to call it a day when our total has reached fourteen. We do our best to laugh it off in a jolly sort of way, treating it all as a crazy bit of fun, but a bold lad comes marching up and asks me who I play for and even argues with me when I tell him that I don't play for anybody. Scowling, he mutters, "Lyin' bastard!" then something else in Welsh before spitting and shambling off ungraciously.

John sprawls out flat and smiling, savouring the moment, his eyes shut tight in anticipation of God settling gently upon him whilst our triumphant sons parade over the blood of the recently slain, and discover new depths in their brotherliness. What I had imagined was just a brief snooze, becomes deep rasping snoring and I suddenly remember that John takes his siestas very seriously, and so we all flop down beside him, idly watching the clouds sail over and wait.

The Itch of Autumn and Empty Nests!

Summer is passing and I have to concentrate my attention once more on getting the boys' room finished before they go back to school and before autumn starts in deadly earnest. Ideally I'd like to have it completed before my final two weeks work in September, so I waste no further time and get stuck-in building two sturdy bunk-beds across the end of the room opposite the stairs and panel-off an insulated barrier between the bunks and the wall. Once again, the driftwood planks come in useful and the room is getting a somewhat rugged sort of 'designer' feel to it, especially so when I hide all traces of concrete under insulating layers of newspaper topped with new straw-coloured rush matting and then fix double thickness heavy polythene instead of glass in the window. When my brother, David, pays us a surprise visit, he can hardly contain his amusement over our primitive set-up and, when he sees the double thickness polythene in the boys' window, he comments, "Ee, bloomin' 'eck, our Jim... that's really modern that is... in the trade they call it 'double-glazing'!" He laughs even more when I tell him that, as soon as the swallows have left, I shall likewise 'double-glaze' all the other windows, and shall remove it again in the spring when the swallows return. He thinks I'm joking but I'm not.

The room is finished and the boys have all squabbled over establishing who's going to sleep where. Spencer gets the top bunk, Rowan the bottom one while Robin gets the camp-bed by the stairs. I insulate and panel the wall separating their room from the main room and attach a heavy curtain over their doorway; it's really very cosy. It's even cosier when I fix another such curtain to hide the loft-ladder stairs, keeping any draughts away from Robin's area. Cari and I fix two camp-beds together and move into the upstairs where the new swallows are now flying and are whizzing in and out of the window, coming in at dusk to roost on the old family beam. The floor beneath them is splattered and I have to use a shovel to hack their droppings away.

I have completed the work with a couple of days to spare; the caravan is now empty and it feels sad seeing it standing there at the end of its life, having served us well over some trying times. "It may still come in handy for putting up visitors," Cari says; "Or growing mushrooms," I reply. For the time being at any rate, we decide to let it remain as our main cooking area because there's still work to be done in the lean-to where the swallows are still in dispute over who owns it, persuading me to postpone any improvement work until they've left for Africa.

I leave for Plymouth and complete my contractual obligation, leaving Cari and the boys to cope on their own for the two weeks. Fortunately the weather holds as an 'Indian Summer' settles over the land, providing ideal conditions for the swallows to put on final fat reserves prior to their mammoth migratory journey. Spiders are getting in on the fly-catching act too and have cast their intricate nets all along the hedges, millions and millions of them; who'd ever want to be a fly! Red admiral butterflies are gliding about the place and tortoiseshells are coming indoors where they spend their entire time trying to get out again; I find their little rainbow fragments under where spiders have capitalised on the new harvest.

This is a time of harvest, and on my return from Plymouth, the mystery surrounding the earthenware jars that Cari bought is solved; she's harvested the rose-hips and has made syrup from them, every jar is full of the stuff. Unfortunately, the occasion provided a window of opportunity for Robin to put his wickedly creative skills to improper use when he discovered that the fine silky hairs inside the hips was a natural itching powder every bit as useful as a newt, and that his brothers' beds were ideal places in which to put it to the test. On seeing everyone furiously scratching, Cari concluded that a plague of fleas had invaded the place and so, walked to town to purchase flea-powder. This, together with having to wash and change clothing and bedding, set her back somewhat, yet she still managed to pick all the damsons which were breaking the branches with their weighty abundance, and now we have literally scores of jars of jam filling the cupboard and cluttering the bedroom floor where another surprise awaits me in the form of two brand new gallons of fermenting elderberry wine; they really have been busy while I've been away.

Summer's idleness has been forgotten, this new season means business; there's a revolution of activity in response to the call of ripeness. Idleness has left it almost too late for the corn to be harvested and there's a panic into getting the ancient binder into working order and the barn to bulging before the rains return. I lend a hand helping Gareth reduce the faded gold corn to stubble as rabbits go bounding and the guns blast while the terrier chases voles in the busted secret of the whiskered field. Farm sparrows in a great flock have left the buildings and are feasting in the shorn fields, rising and falling then darkening the air as they settle to rest in the reddening haws along the old hedges.

Already the warblers have left, so too the orphan cuckoos, totally self-taught having never learned a cuckoo's ways from a parent cuckoo, but having to be brought up by hedge sparrows or pipits, neither of which possessing a clue as to how to get south of the Sahara. Little miracles all flying south now, crossing oceans by day and by night and without maps, while the telegraph wires by the farm are bowed under the weight of late swallows and martins awaiting their moment of departure.

So much is happening and I notice that the potato tops are brown and rotting in the ridges where someone has been forking one of the rows in assessing their readiness for harvesting. The word goes out, potatoes will be picked on Saturday; and so, the shabby whiskery army gathers with buckets and sacks on this white-breathing Saturday field, their voices clear and sharp in the mist, just as are the white webs that hammock the thorns before the ghost of sun has shown. The tractor splutters and groans and the tackle behind it clatters noisily as it unearths potatoes, frogs, mice and stones. There's a rattle of potatoes hitting the bottom of buckets all down the field together with a merry barking of voices and a pleasant bonfire smell as the tops are burned.

Halfway through, the gang meander over to the small kitchen where the famous long table is piled with bread, tomatoes and boiled potatoes. Underneath it, the testicle-grabbing lad who plainly still has a fondness for the prank and has forgotten how Saintly Thomas stamped on his fingers the last time he tried performing it in public. Tea steams in mugs as the whiskery gang drowsily set about the food, muttering blurred stuff about rabbit numbers and threshing. It seems like everyone is only a stone's throw away from falling into a consuming hibernating sleep, but there's a sudden rude awakening panic when a military jet warplane deafens the entire world as it explodes only feet above the barn roof, creating a stampede of bodies to the window. Too late, the devilish thing is already miles away and the bumbling bodies are in the process of disentangling themselves and are about to shuffle back to the table when, concealed by its own terrible speed and hidden in the valley, another brute suddenly obliterates the air as it follows in the other one's dark trail to nowhere. Memory should have told my friends that those things always hunt in pairs, leaving everyone standing petrified like pillars of salt revealing the gaping ravine between potato pickers and war technology. A scar to end all scars, widening too fast for any reasoning to settle and change things more to our needs.

The heavy brigade return to the field as though anxious to rub the soil into their fingers again, like a baby is soothed by its thumb and all the children who, until now have been sitting like swallows on the calf-pen gate, shoot across the yard and into the house, eager to polish off whatever has been left for them.

In the evening, Gareth and Hugh drive over with five heavy sacks of potatoes for us, reckoning that, if stored well protected from the frost, they should see us through the winter. We put them carefully into the cat-shed and await the fall of leaves with which to insulate them, it also makes sense for us to start collecting old newspapers for additional insulation and for fire lighting and stuffing into holes where draughts are coming in. Newspaper for us is more valuable physically than ever it is for all the stuff that's written on it.

Our little 'Indian Summer' miraculously lingers on, but the morning mists are lasting longer, altering the face of the year so that earlier glories are fast becoming memories. The afternoons are still providing a flush of warmth, but everywhere is drowsy, tired, sombre and peaceful. There is a magical glow about the woods now, the leaves are slowly turning to gold and bronze and a silver birch in the little wood down the field is already weeping into the stream. Faded cow-wheat and weary looking purple campions linger on as I watch a scruffy little water-shrew hurrying about in a bubbly pool and sadly note that the marsh-marigolds have called it a day.

The spiders are growing fat and their webs have all needed crude and hasty repair jobs from where old clumsy wasps have crashed through them. The repairs are of a thicker gauge of thread now that their owners have grown obese on the rich pickings of craneflies. What were originally finely crafted silken nets are now poorly darned knotted tangled trawls of sticky cobblers thread; old spiders grow idle when their clothes no longer fit them.

The bridge of branches that the boys helped me to construct at what seems like an age ago, is in need of restoration after the cows have satisfied their irresistible fascination with mud. Fungus is taking everything over; it is growing like fans on stumps, like thatched roofs, from the trunks of silver birches, like orange peel from the ground while some on the old birches resembles elephants' feet. There are villages and temples of toadstools clustering the feet of some old alders, puff-balls that smoke like factories when trodden on; there are parasol umbrellas, tall ones, small ones, shaggy ones and saggy ones, others that are sinister, some just plain deadly. I teach the boys to identify the field-mushroom, parasol mushroom and shaggy inkcap; these are easily identifiable and can be eaten. We are gathering the parasols now, they're stronger in taste and tougher than the field mushrooms, which seem to have come to the end of their cropping. I insist on them being able to recognise the poisonous ones too, in particular the lethal 'Deathcap' and the more easily recognisable 'Fly Agaric' which are now appearing in the forest. Other species are too numerous and risky to bother about and I'm happy for the boys to simply regard them as being inedible and to avoid them accordingly.

We are too late for the hazelnuts, the squirrels have beaten us to them. One minute there was an abundance of nuts and the next minute there was an abundance of squirrels; the nuts had vanished and had been carted away into winter larders in secret nooks and crannies in the oak woods. I've even watched squirrels fastidiously burying them in the field, making me wonder if they know something about the coming winter that I don't.

I follow the stream through willows and alders, then cross into the long, low, lovely field where the grasses are bleached blonde and tired Rowan and Spencer are lazing in the silvery haze higher up, swishing their sticks at thistles while Cari with a basket picks the late blackberries. It's a beautiful field with its old hawthorns in a line spanning it, each one of them a tree with crimson haws and the earth beneath them bare from where sheep and cattle have sheltered from the summer sun. There's also a grand old oak that makes me think of times long past; it is stately, noble and ancient with a crown of acorns and a boy asleep in the filtering sunbeams beneath it... Robin.

The swallows have gone and the world seems suddenly empty. It feels somewhat empty in the cowshed too now that the house of the four 'R's' has gained a fifth 'R'. Getting the new boy ready for his first day at school is utter pandemonium, a live eel could be dressed more easily. Our first problem is that of denying him his sudden urge to hibernate; this is soon followed by a desire to migrate wearing Rowan's school shoes and very little else, occasioning a good deal of brawling and bawling until he is brought to heel, but not before Rowan is plastered in unpleasant stuff and

Robin's ears are smarting. The well-groomed item is painstakingly walked to the sweetly ringing playground in the valley, it's like delivering a hive full of bees and we know for sure that he's going to start stinging the moment we are out of sight. We watch him playfully trip a little girl up as they all cross the rickety wooden bridge and can see Spencer having to get physical with him before we slip from view and wander back up into the autumn-smelling silence.

The sap has turned earthwards to its own special hibernation deep down in the root-systems, safe from frosts. Hibernation seems like a nice idea that's catching on, although not having a foothold within my own species. We're more like swallows than we are squirrels in that migration is within the grasp of those of us who are fortunate enough to be able to throw money at things in order to have them; unfortunately in our case, we miss out on both and, to cope at all, must develop an appetite for adversity tinged with a degree or two of masochism.

The bats in the barn wall have already drawn their curtains, I haven't seen them for some time, but I have seen mice that have moved in to take up residence in the lean-to kitchen walls. In their case it's more a matter of migration and not hibernation alas; there are also a couple of fat old dormice in the wall at the back of the kitchen cupboard; this pair seem to want the best of both worlds, hibernation only coming when their migration into my kitchen has eradicated the very last traces of hunger from their fat little stomachs. In the meantime they gnaw holes in what I previously believed were impenetrable heavy plastic food containers, obliging me to try bringing the cats in as a deterrent. A short-lived idea on account of them forcing their way into the cupboard and eating and spoiling more of our food than the mice could ever achieve whilst at the same time showing a total disregard for their litter-tray. I'd swear the mice actually multiplied during this brief experiment, no doubt finding a few idle cats about the place to be the ideal aphrodisiac.

In addition to mice, we are being invaded by queen wasps in search of places to hibernate. They are suddenly appearing in our clothes, our beds, in the folds of curtains and everywhere that they are least expected to be found, causing panic and a ritualistic inspection of clothing before wearing it, sheets, blankets and pillows before getting into bed. More peaceful are the tortoiseshell butterflies which have settled to sleep on the beams above the bed, while downstairs a solitary honey-bee is quietly snoring on the lace curtain in the lean-to window.

Urgent consideration is now given to our own winter larder and it eats the first major hole in the money that I earned earlier. I also spend money on timber to make two new doors for the lean-to and also buy a sink unit minus the plumbing attachments, just a sink plug and a bucket underneath; at least it looks slightly more like a kitchen now, and when I cover the floor with brightly patterned lino, it looks positively palatial! I decide to fit glass into the window in here in preference to opaque polythene, but I am thwarted by chickens, madam Sykes in particular, and all the new putty is eaten. When I replace it, they eat it again, then again. I try placing obstacles in their way, house-bricks and part of a heavy iron ploughshare which I found up on the tip, but they knock them repeatedly to the ground making it impossible for me to fit the glass. I try mixing a concoction of mustard and strong pepper, having read somewhere of it stopping them from eating their eggs. I 'putty' the glass in with this disgusting stuff, hoping that nobody sees me doing it and concluding that I'm completely off my rocker. I don't believe it; they eat every bit of this as well and stand looking at me, red-eyed and wheezing with dragon-like steam snorting from their beaks, waiting for the next course. So, like it or not, polythene it has to be I'm afraid.

For some little while now there has been a baring of things, a revealing of structural truths beyond that which was previously hidden. Revealed are the umpteen old nests for all to see; what once were closely kept secrets are now bare and exposed; twig nests of pigeon, dove, magpie and bullfinch, grass ones of blackbird, mud-lined grass of thrush and various other moss and feather creations that were reasons for all spring singing. Some have been taken over by ginger mice who have done what I have done with the cowshed. The entire hedgerows are spelling out their wealth, their inestimable value to the creature world, what's more, they are concealing other deeper secrets down in the leafy hollows of their roots where the hedgehogs sleep. Another secret that can no longer be concealed is one of the child that Meg is carrying. Murphy hasn't mentioned it, but he's going to be a dad, that's for sure, and it takes me back to that day on the roof when the hay was high and ready for reaping.

Catastrophe of Fallen Stars

With October gone, all remnants of summer pass with it as a particularly hard frost strips the ash trees bare overnight, the floor beneath them is deep with yellow leaves and the trees stand starkly in bare bones now. Gone too are the cows, back to their winter quarters, to dried rations and whatever exercise that life in a shed affords; but the sheep remain out on the hills and can be heard coughing throughout the nights. It's a sickening sound, ill and haunting, as it echoes in the lonesome darkness far and wide.

Storms deliver November and it isn't long before the ground has returned to mud, signalling a new round of hardships with seemingly never-ending cycles of washing and scrubbing mud-encrusted clothes which we haven't a hope in hell of drying. I have no choice as to what I should be doing, keeping the fire going demands that I spend all day, every day, sawing, hauling and splitting wood. It is a continuous task from now until spring, made worse by the fact that the old iron range has no means of being regulated or controlled in any way, it just burns at one ravenous speed, gluttonously devouring whatever is put on it without returning a fair deal in exchange. It is the ultimate in inefficiency, all the heat going up the chimney to be scattered to waste by cruel winds that roar over and through the woods, making branches creak and groan, toppling the weak, thrashing everything and whipping all the air into a fury, denying birds their gift of flight and making our old cowshed a galleon seem, on a tumultuous sea. I'm really getting concerned as to whether our new tin roof will stay on; already one thug of a gust has brought part of the chimney crashing down through the lean-to roof, while another blast has taken a sizeable part of the barn roof, dumping it in the ditch below the orchard.

Cari and I need to sleep in goggles and crash-helmets now because there are blizzards of old plaster, grit and husks being blown all over the bed from the gaps between the roof and the wall.

I never felt this vulnerable back on the cliff when force elevens were smashing into the hut; the gales here are every bit as fierce and I do believe they linger longer. The boys are really enjoying it though, they thinks it's great fun. It's nice and cosy in their room, knowledge of which is providing our only crumb of comfort right now.

Frost and gales are not without their good points and offer us deep drifts of dry leaves which we bag and generously line the cat-shed with in the hope of keeping the frosts away from pets and potatoes alike. By night we hear the plaintive flight calls of redwings, newly arrived little thrushes from northern Europe; here for the rich harvests of crimson berries. There are big handsome fieldfares too, chattering and feasting all along the old hawthorns while, each afternoon late, the sky is darkened by starling flocks, that span the horizons, a regular flight-path to some famous old roost somewhere.

This is a wildly beautiful time, it's hard but undeniably exhilarating; I know where I stand with this tough old sod of a season; it calls a spade a spade and has no time for terminological inexactitudes, no way! When it comes to bonfires, there are no half measures up at the hill farm either and they really do call a bonfire, a bonfire up there. A social event right out of a Brueghel painting. Higher up the field where we played football back in the spring, Hugh is busy with the tractor fitted with a hydraulic grab on the front and is piling a mountain of timbered junk which includes a dilapidated chicken-coop stuffed with oil-soaked bales of straw for starters, together with masses and masses of stuff that fair makes my mouth water when I think of it all going up in one mad burning hour; it would last us right up to Christmas and beyond as well as boil several thousands of kettles. I gaze upon the pyre with such envy. To add to the mountain, Gareth's pal down in the valley brings trailer loads of his own junk as though Guy Fawkes has triggered a premature spring-clean; only a pregnant volcano could compete with this ultimate statement of promised fire.

There's a fever of eager anticipation in the children, an insatiable fascination with fireworks and an intimacy with the danger that it all represents. For the adults it's just a huge excuse to slip back into adolescence one more and to have a good reason for doing stupid and dangerous things which children wouldn't normally be allowed to do. No matter what November may throw down from her skies, nothing, absolutely nothing, will be allowed to interfere with this great two-fingered jibe at winter.

The hour arrives under a splendour of galaxies and a whipping north-easter after a day of driving rain has exhausted itself over the hills. Our gang pick our way in torchlight through the mud, up the track through the wood where owls are hooting as though in protest over our torch beam that's fouling their perfect night. There are thin wild voices in the air once we leave the trees and we are soon joined by the farm children who have spotted our torch and come racing down the hill to greet us. They are bursting with excitement, anxious to accompany us to the farm where cars crammed with Uncles, Aunts and explosives have already arrived. A limousine pulls in and I glimpse a glint of cheap jewels, a fur coat and thick lipstick gripping a cigarette in a long holder, followed by a pot-bellied tweed-suited in-law uncle with a pink pig over his shoulder and gripping a Sherlock Holmes pipe to the side of his mouth, allowing him to call, "Helloo Jimmy, Caroline!" then vanishing into the bedlam of the farmhouse where electricity is struggling to compete. More headlights come up the hill where the gates have all been left wide open regardless of the sheep straying. They all look like limousines in the inky darkness with their powerful beams bleaching cold light like scythes. There are far more adults than children at this children's treat; sacrificial pigs and gunpowder have rather more pulling power than any gin-and whatever ever did.

The 'Guy' is a blue polythene fertiliser bag stuffed with hay that's riddled with agricultural crow-scarers, and has a swede with an old trilby on it for a head, a really sad looking scarecrow character, but with a few surprises up his sleeve when the heat is really on. For the children its all really quite simple by comparison and has all the logical clarity of the fourth 'R', this time it being a celebration of some geezer trying to blow up some house in London somewhere!

The moment arrives and Gareth, pipe in mouth, can of petrol in hand, ceremoniously sweeps all aside, for reasons of safety, and discharges the fuel over the monumental pyre. He backs off a few paces, then casually tosses a lighted match and gets his eyebrows singed as the pyre almost obliterates in a blinding instance under an insane cacophony of rabbled cheering as he staggers back into the crowd.

The night has been ignited, all darkness is ablaze and pandemonium rages as other figures emerge from the darkness. In this dance of sparkling bonfire eyes, I see Dan dressed-up like a smart sack of corn, Meg and Murphy here too with old Thomas glowing like the Almighty himself, and 'Weasel' there wrapped in a best mac, sucking his pipe and beaming silently into the inferno. So many other bodies all waiting for the heavens to explode in fiery fanfares; even the pig that's sweating giddily on a spit has been looking forward to this moment. Suddenly, in a crescendo of engulfing flames, the diminutive Guy Fawkes detonates in a rapid succession of deafening explosions and disintegrates, the swede falls into the fire; Guy Fawkes has got his cum-uppence! In all the cheering, in-law Uncle Mostyn in his tweed suit and pot-belly that he boasts cost him a fortune, is all elbows as he fumbles with a large box, plying to be the star of this night of fire. 'Mr. Gunpowder' himself no less, but nobody gives a damn so long as he pulls his finger out, opens the box and gets on with the business. Meanwhile, sparklers are doing pretty things as the wild farm-boys darkly slip from cherubs to backwoods guerillas, pockets bulging with bangers and their gleeful wickedness bolting free into the sly shadows.

There are gasps and squeals as flaming rockets rush and roar amongst the stars above the farm where the barn bulges with corn, and cascading arrays of multiple explosions shimmer their fire down onto tractor fuel-stores, old wooden sheds and the whole highly inflammable assortment of cluttered things that constitute a farm. It's an anarchic free-for-all mayhem, with boys throwing bangers at aunties in fur coats, tossing jumping-jacks amongst the elderly, while Elwyn is on a personal mission to stuff a thunderflash down the back of Curly Jenkins trousers or, better still, strap him to a giant rocket and shove him into a bottle with his blue touch-paper ablaze. Had Guy Fawkes succeeded it would have been a tame affair compared to this!

I can feel Robin pulling at his leash and sense his frustration turning to anger at not being free to vent his own extravagant desire to hold a Catherine-wheel in his teeth and Roman candles in his ears whilst walking daringly clean through the bonfire; even with my restraining influence, sparklers have already set fire to his gloves and blistered his cheek and there's mud in his hair. I fear that I'll be condemned to his black book of retribution and must await his pleasure.

There are signs of sparks up in the barnyard, triggering a panicked dash as Gareth hares off and sails dog-like over the fence and then tosses a couple of loose bales that have caught fire, back over into the field where they may safely burn themselves out. As he scans about him for other signs of light, there are cats cringing, hidden somewhere, dogs whining, beasts moaning in byres and chickens grieving huddled and perplexed. This is not the darkness they know and trust, this is a catastrophe of fallen stars with imps and demons fidgeting like a plague; even the thrushes flying over in the dark are finding it odd that the air is blistering hot in places. Many hundreds of little eyes are watching this fiery carnival and are none the wiser as to what it is or why it is, just another perplexing reason for their mistrust and avoidance of this crazy species.

Cold November winds are glowing the embers and fanning the sparks, but all to no avail, the glorious hour has withered to a cindered scar upon the night and the gang, all drawn to the smell of the pig that has melted into its own fire of body-fat and is, together with a mountain of bread, pickled onions and a barrel of beer, ripe and ready for the taking. There's grease dribbling from chins and flatulence flying way beyond the means of etiquette to restrain; mouths going at it like hogs at a trough as in some high cholesterol carnivorous thanksgiving ritual.

It's suddenly quiet and very cold as we leave the hill farm behind, cross the hill and drop down through the wood where we frighten badgers that have dared it out and are rooting amongst the leaves; they are not really frightened, just very wary and stop their snuffling and rustling about; they can see us but we can't see them, as is the case with the owls, but the valley is aching hauntingly with their sighs, magnifying the emptiness and hurrying us back to the secluded comfort of the freezing cold cowshed.

The contrast is rather more than stark; at least we had the light of the stars outside but inside there is only total blackness accompanied by a flat battery in the torch. There's no magic switch on the wall, no welcoming warmth of any kind; getting the place illuminated is a major achievement and is of immense value once we have conquered the dark. This is when it all seems worthwhile and the pressure lamp is hissing and candles are kindled with their small golden flames dancing in the draughts. I've made sure that there is a good supply of wood available for a late crackling fire and plenty of water too for warming drinks and the luxury of hot water-bottles. We bring the cats in for their supper, then all of us sit in the flickering firelight and toast bread with butter from the metal bin which the mice can't get into. We re-live the events of the evening which is now blackest night with fresh rain like handfuls of rice being thrown at the 'double-glazed' polythene of the windows, making us glad to be back.

The boys have all thoroughly enjoyed themselves and we laugh rather sardonically over the realisation that it was actually warmer up there on the windy hill than it is now sitting by the fire. As we're joking about this, the rain suddenly turns to hail and hammers against the windows and roars down onto the roof with a revitalised fury, at a stroke turning our little fireside into the cosiest place to be by far. While all this is going on and hailstones are hissing on the fire, Cari is wrestling with Robin, tending to his burns and attempting to clean him up. "You'll survive!" she tells him and he goes staggering off to bed clutching his hot water-bottle and grinning like a Cheshire cat.

With the youngsters all snugly down in their beds, Cari and I stay up for a while indulging our fascination with fire and in particular, the way each individual little twig burns differently from the next. The poetic choreography of the blue and yellow flames, so fine and delicate, flowerlike in their fragility, yet able to reduce the twigs to powdered nothing in hardly any time at all. Sometimes a tiny reservoir of gas within the twig whistles in an escaping plume of finely ruffled smoke before a flame can find balance on it, demonstrating what wealth of invisible power there is in something as insignificant as a little twig that's fallen from a tree; for me this is far more beautiful than any money-spinning Guy Fawkes celebration can ever be.

A Bushman Friend plus two Strangers
in from the Cold

It's another wild and distinctly uncouth morning, one that makes us envious of anything that hibernates. The very thought of getting up just in order to confront cold, mud, piles of dirty clothes that are begging to be washed and a living room that's freshly flooded as a result of rain coming through the new 'water-proof' wall, is plain crazy. It makes more scientific sense and more natural sense for us just to take it easy like a squirrel and not subject ourselves so readily to the forces that undermine us. Alas, that's a dream too far; the house of the four 'R's' is the unyielding, unending force in the valley that dictates against any such gentle drift to be 'natural' and to respond to the various pressures accordingly. Our species just rigidly bashes on throwing machines and money at things in the crude crafting of an 'anti-nature' that fosters the transparent myth of 'Man' being the boss.

With Robin on my shoulders for the first part, I walk the boys to school, trying to share with them whatever discomforts there are on this still-dark morning that's plainly struggling to be awake. I watch them merge into the dim barking crowd then wander back up the hill with my head in a cloud. Low overhead, the warplanes are already screeching and filling the valley to bursting point with their din; even after they have gone, the noise seems to remain trapped. I lengthen my stride up into the beautiful trees and find soothing sweetness in the ringing crystal water babbling from the hill, on higher through denser woodland and beyond. I call "Good morning." to the deathly pale, frail Mrs. Gittens, ghostlike, fresh from prayer and sniffing the air for signs of the postman. Her response to my greeting is miserly and she shuffles back inside and closes me, and the world, clean out from her world.

I leave the valley behind and, when I reach the top of the hill, decide not to walk past Dan's place, but to climb the gate opposite and follow the track where the old bulldozer remains quietly rotting, then slip up into the wood and have a good scout around for old dead branches which I may later convert into the more down-to-earth religion of warming my family and for heating the oven in the provision of our own daily bread.

When I arrive back, Cari has already started to wash clothes in ice-cold water and so I roll up my sleeves and help out, suggesting that, as soon as we've got this lot blowing on the line, we both go off wood gathering, trying our best to share things in the making of everything bearable. We can then get a fire roaring to help dry-out the room and to provide a welcome for the boys when they return. Once the washing is hanging out, we wrap ourselves up warm and go off to the woods and start clearing up after the gales have wreaked their havoc. We spend the next three hours just carting backwards and forwards until there is a huge pile of heavy branches in the yard and smoke once more coming from the chimney.

The rain is coming on again and so I decide to pick the boys up from school in the van, my own machine that I throw at things; it never fails me, it's a real friend. I roll down the wooded valley and draw-up under the towering Douglas firs and wait for the children to say their prayers before all exploding out into the real world which is a whole lot closer than the one of their prayers. I emerge and make myself visible by the bridge, noting that there is some sort of problem between Robin and the others. On seeing me, Rowan comes running, he's furious because Robin has got him into trouble by accusing him of doing something which he didn't do, namely the throwing of a banger into the staff toilet while the Headmaster was seated. There was a very loud explosion which cured the Head's constipation at a stroke, and was then blamed on Rowan. Poor Mister Hughes, his four 'R' curriculum didn't need this formidable fifth 'R' and, on seeing me waiting, decides to somewhat timidly cross the bridge and to have a quiet word in my ear. We exchange tight smiles and shake hands firmly before he coughs out the pellet that's troubling him. "He's a bit of a rascal, is Robin... a little on the naughty side at the moment ... needs a lot of watching." With this off his chest he smiles reassuringly and says very quietly; "He'll settle down, so don't worry yourself about it." His words are really a kind of warning plea for me to use my influence and to do something about it; I look back at him despairingly and apologise for what is already driving the poor man mad. I glare at Robin and he looks darkly back at me with a lowered brow and mutters, "It was Rowan!"

I feel sorry for Rowan. We all know it wasn't him, neither was it him that tripped the girls up in the dinner queue whilst they carried their meals to the table, and catapulted potatoes with a fork all about the dining hall. I'm just grateful that he didn't let the firework off in his bedroom when we were all sleeping, he must have been sorely tempted to. Blue in the face, I watch my stern words go into one ear and come tumbling out of the other; it's hopeless, he can look so angelic at times, like butter wouldn't melt in his mouth. Being wicked is obviously the provider of great enjoyment and satisfaction for him and I don't hold out much hope of him changing.

To our utter delight and amazement, we awaken to a covering of snow, the first of the winter. I take this as serving a warning to us and so I make a trip into town and spend money on a couple of paraffin heaters and torches for the boys in the hope of improving their aim when nature calls in the night. I buy an ex-army all-weather torch for Cari and myself, with as many spare batteries as I can afford. I also repair the hole in the lean-to asbestos roof where part of the chimney came crashing through; it's a bit of a bodge because I don't feel like handling old asbestos and the corrugations are broad and can't be matched up with anything I have lying about the place. All that I can do is to ram a piece of tin under the busted piece and secure it with nails, it should stop most of the weather from getting in.

Having been forced into becoming a full-time woodman, I am discovering in leaps and bounds how saw-blades rapidly become blunt and useless, constantly twisting and getting stuck fast halfway through a piece of wood. No amount of filing and fiddling about trying to re-set the teeth seems to make a blind bit of difference, so I am obliged once more to splash out, this time on a new 'Bushman' saw, with a couple of extra blades to help keep me in good temper. This purchase turns out to be the best money I ever spent; my new little 'Spear and Jackson' is worth it's weight in gold and enables me to really get my teeth into the wood situation.

Our hens have all hoisted their knickers up and have stopped laying; they don't appear to be very enthusiastic about this new invisible cold thing that's ruffling their feathers and making them hungry. They are not moving very far from the back door now and are more dependent on being fed and have abandoned any ideas they had about wandering in search of food. It's the same with the cats, although on reflection, it's always been that way with them; the only thing I've ever known them to catch was a nestful of baby bluetits, a wren and a bantam chick, plus of course whatever could be stolen from inside the place. All of us are getting to feel that little bit extra hungry now that our bodies are having to do more in order to keep warm. To address this, Cari is making miraculous stews and pasta dishes; she's a genius, her apple charlottes with custard are simply out of this world and the plates and dishes are always licked clean in a well intentioned, albeit bad mannered, compliment. I'm playing my part by keeping the hearth aglow with roaring fires and a kettle that's always steaming.

We're getting through an awful lot of paraffin and I have to make a priority of it being used for light rather than heat when we find ourselves running a bit low. In order to save money I have had to cut back on use of the van for shopping and am instead running to town with a rucksack on my back. The route I take depends on what state the mud is in; if it isn't too bad I can pick my way down past the well and over the top, through the farm and down into the valley where I then meet up with the council road. If the mud is too deep, I have to cross the marsh in my wellies and then change into my running shoes and take the longer route round the lanes. Whichever way, I am doing the twelve to fourteen mile round trip with consummate ease, going like the wind over the first part, and feeling as strong as an ox on the return journey weighed down with stuff, sticky Chelsea buns always hidden away as a special treat. I've never felt so fit in all my life, it takes me back to those days on the cliff when I had to trudge down the long steep hill to the village in the creek and then struggle back up again, burdened with groceries, cans of paraffin and a murderously heavy cylinder of calor-gas. I'm getting a few funny looks from people who judge this sort of thing as bordering on insanity. It amuses me to see the look on their faces when I pass; it's always an utterly dumbfounded expression of, "How can he look so happy, sweating like a pig, running with that great lumbering thing on his back?"

Cari manages to fall clean through the caravan floor with a heavy saucepan of stew in her hands, somehow avoiding being scalded and instinctively clutching heroically onto the saucepan. I scatter cats and hens as I burst from the barn in response to her yells and I carefully take the steaming treasure from her and gently ease her out from the jagged hole. It's the second time the floor has collapsed in this fashion and we stand laughing at the crazy humour of the situation, recognising that the old caravan has had it, it's very body-material is here expiring right under our feet. So much life and weather have all contributed their bit in reducing this once jolly little aluminium dream-bubble into a worn out heap of old junk. Few things could ever have lived their lives to the full expectations of their creators as this old caravan has; it's certainly served its time and owes us nothing.

Second snow with frozen raindrops on all the deep red haws, brings us two visitors unannounced from the south, which isn't always the wisest thing to do, Steve, with Chris on the back of his scooter; it was mild and sunny when they set out from Cornwall in the morning! Petrified in ice, they arrive at Murphy's lovely warm wood burning stove of a farmhouse, thinking it a good idea to park the Lambretta in one of the outbuildings there. After a brief 'hello', they leave the warmth and tantalising smells of baking and venture out into the cold inhospitable late afternoon air and cross the marsh which is still crunchy from icicled frosts, and they arrive upon us, two pathetic figures, come to bring a ray of sunshine into our lives and to sample a bit of this 'wild paradise' of ours.

I soon put mugs of hot tea into their cold fists to help thaw them out, and I get them standing, more like prawns than Eskimos in front of a massive blaze. Standing is the only arrangement right now, there's an obvious shortage of recognisable seating, our salvaged old van seat already has three bums perched on it and the driftwood-plank benches are now part of the boys' bunks. Apart from it being lovely to see our friends again, it triggers a bit of a panic over where they're going to sleep; as Cari and I sadly discovered, the caravan is not simply damp anymore, but positively wet, despite the under-floor ventilation system so recently installed!

There is a sudden war of priorities battling inside my head; the hole in the caravan floor must be fixed, the mattresses brought out and somehow positioned in front of a fire that's growling and spitting dangerously and begging, ceaselessly begging for more.

Conversation is a massive distraction as well as being a major obstruction, one that I cannot be lured into at this moment. I leave Cari to indulge in the niceties of welcoming our old pals and set about trying to address the problems in the rapidly fading light.

I can hear the laughter ringing as I grapple with the main soggy mattress, my friends are obviously warming up nicely, quite oblivious to the hard practicalities that I'm having to tackle. As the light fades still further, there comes a slow realisation that there are no such magic things as light-switches or even a bathroom in which to pop and freshen-up. Rowan holds the torch for me while I pour paraffin through a funnel into the pressure-lamps, one of which is in need of repair and is becoming a fire risk. I manage to get them going, instructing everyone that, should either of them suddenly go out and start smoking and hissing, to unscrew the pressure-screw as a matter of urgency. It's the old 'in one ear and out the other' thing again, so I just keep my fingers crossed and hope for the best.

It still hasn't occurred to anyone that the fire only burns if there is wood to put on it and that there is someone available to fetch it and saw it. Rowan comes to help me, not because I have asked him to, but because he's usually the only one that wants to be helping me, the other two tend to plug for the easy option and stay well out of the way. As I saw a mountain of logs and Rowan runs back and forth with them, we are being scrutinised by the hens at roost on the manger and also by the bantams who have had to shift their roost to the high beam at the other end of the barn after the gale removed their old roof. We must get all the wood we need for the night in one go, thus enabling me to lock up the barn and make it secure from foxes, but, the demoralising reality is that, no matter how much I saw, the fire will devour it and go on wanting more; I could be here sawing away all through the night. As it is, I've got both paraffin heaters going full blast in the caravan with two Co-op candles in jars making the place flicker alluringly. What remaining glass there is in the windows is weeping with condensation; there's more steam than smoke coming from this place tonight! As I toil monotonously away with the saw, guitar music rings out and I can hear uncontrollable laughter with Steve in a fit of choking as the crazy word-game that he's playing with Cari touches on bizarre new levels. Tin whistles add to the pandemonium and I sense this as being a night when the cats might actually prefer being in their box in the shed with potatoes for company.

The temperature drops below freezing and the stars begin to shimmer and sparkle all across the broad black heavens. Constellation Orion has become my friend and companion of the night, always low there when the sword of frost lacerates the night air. The night sky is particularly brilliant with there being no other lights visible anywhere to pollute it. Steve and Chris pop out to thaw a bit of frost and are mind-blown by the great swathe of glistening galaxies with the Milky Way in a glowing band sprinkled like icing sugar, with occasional satellites cruising across it all. Amongst all this, the redwings whimper and bold owls hoot and screech like witches over the barking foxes and the odd blood-curdling scream of a vixen. The distant farm-dog doesn't sound nearly so brave in this inky nocturne and I can sense also that strength-in-numbers is playing a discrete part in the bravado close about me.

The oven is once more full of potatoes and the badly neglected mattresses have now acquired numerous burn-holes, being saved from total incineration by their wetness alone. I'm finding it a bit frustrating because I'd dearly love to be having an evening of fun and making music again, but there really isn't time for such an indulgence when other things are so plainly higher in the pecking order. To confuse things still further, the boys are all chanting, "Fish and chips," over and over and I can sense that this is sounding rather attractive to the others, currently unfamiliar with the concerns that are occasioning me to dash about like a hysterical fart with blood-pressure, in trying to make everything right for them and to prevent them from contracting pneumonia, asthma attacks and premature arthritis.

One of the pressure-lamps suddenly does what I feared it might and I trip over a steaming mattress in my haste to reach it before it spontaneously combusts. Everyone thinks it's a great joke as I disentangle myself and grovel for this wretched gadget that's filling the room with paraffin vapour and is hissing and smoking, still red-hot and highly dangerous. I succeed in unscrewing the pressure-screw and we are left in a gloomy stink of half-burned paraffin everywhere. They are still laughing, but they haven't seen where the toilet is yet, this could change things, especially when they realise that I should have emptied it a few days back!

"I want mushy peas with mine," Robin torments squeakingly, triggering off a chorus of, "Mushy peas, mushy peas." It's all having an effect. I glance across at Chris, he's built like a spider-crab at the best of times, but I know from past experience that he can eat three times that which I can, and I can detect from the sudden way that he's playing the guitar that he's now thinking more about fish and chips than he is about Villa Lobos. Steve, meanwhile, having only recently recovered from dysentery after an ornithological expedition to Nepal, is even more subtle and is making discreet circular movements with his hand over his stomach; Cari just finds it all hilarious, she knows exactly what's going on and is relaxing from a multitude of recent stresses... she knows that I'll cope.

I ease myself down from my exasperation and feel that the current state of things requires spelling out in very simple language. "Okay! Two soaking wet mattresses that have to be dried; two geezers here that need somewhere to sleep; an oven here that I've just filled with potatoes; a fire that has to be kept going for roasting them and for drying these mattresses. I've a caravan round the corner with two paraffin stoves going flat out trying to dry the place; we have paraffin-lights exploding, a guitar recital, two clowns tying themselves up in knots playing a word-game and, to make things worse, I have three blind mice here wanting fish and chips!" "With mushy peas!" squeaks Robin becoming the cherub again. I haven't finished yet: "Okay!" I repeat, "if we go out, the fire goes out; I can't leave lighted stoves in the caravan and I don't want Chris and Steve to have to sleep on wet bedding either. So, what do I do?" The boys are all tittering and elbowing each other, I know exactly what they are thinking. Chris puts the guitar away and strolls over to join Steve in examining the mattresses. "Oi!" he gasps in slightly subdued horror, "these feel a bit wet!" Only at this moment has he set foot back on earth after his six-hour ordeal of slow freezing on the back of a scooter, wearing only a thin brown check jacket and trousers. Steve by now is fairly well thawed out too as he shares in the concern over the state of the bedding. I look at Cari and roll my eyes despairingly and she tries to stifle another bout of laughter.

On realising that we've now got ourselves a paraffin shortage, I concede; it's going to be a late night, fish, chips and paraffin have won the day. The mattresses must be dragged well away from stray sparks, the fire left to die down and the potatoes saved from spoiling in the oven, "Get your wellies on!" I shout and, under a barrage of cheering, go out to the caravan to make things safe in there. To my surprise the cats are in there treating themselves to an unscheduled sauna, and I chuckle to myself knowing that Steve and Chris will be having rather more company that they bargained for later.

We all stride off into the biting air making enough din to scare all the foxes from the area. Several meteorites streak down in astonishing silence, silencing us to a greater realisation of our own size and vulnerability; everyone is motionless and listening to the great silence of the skies. We set off again, our feet crunching over the freezing ground and our eyes adjusted to the light of the stars and the lesser light from the thin slice of moon that's riding; I'm feeling thankful that I remembered to put anti-freeze in the radiator earlier in the week.

Night Madness!

This is the first real opportunity that I've had to greet my two old mates and to catch up with all that's been happening in their lives, although it's proving virtually impossible to get any sense out of anybody at the moment. Steve make's a courageous attempt to be serious, clears his throat and says:- "We've had avocets in Millbrook Creek, bar-tailed godwits ... had a snow bunting and a flock of bramblings ... plenty of kingfishers down at St, John's ... the usual!" He dispenses with the subject, his mind now more focused on the Atlantic cod, King Edward potatoes and peas processed and murdered to a froth known affectionately as 'mushy peas'. Chris meanwhile, is losing himself in another world and is consumed in a rendition of 'Under Milkwood' and sounding more like Dylan Thomas than Dylan Thomas ever did ... although not entirely sticking to the intended script! His gangling spider form is booming across the frozen marsh and we are all in tears of laughter at his outrageous performance.

Like a can of sardines, the little van threads its way along the lanes, all eyes are glued to the front into the beam of the headlights on the look-out for creatures of the night, polecats, badgers, foxes and the like. It feels so good being able to share this place where we live with friends who generate such marvellous enthusiasm to it all; every little glint of glass or sparkle of frost brings uproarious hoots of, "Badger!" "Polecat!" Hippopotamus!" "Duke of Edinburgh!" "Purple-faced groveller!" "Wet mattress!" It gets dafter and dafter; what started out a science is now a driving nightmare and I am more than relieved when I pull up outside Mrs. Pryce's fish-smelling terraced cottage. To help simplify things, I ask for everyone to remain where they are and to put their trust in me, it will be chaos otherwise. They agree and so, ten bags of chips, ten pieces of fish, ten pickled onions, seven mushy peas and a huge pile of bread and butter later, I stagger back out to the van, burdened with what would rupture the average camel; then I blast off again to the garage and fill the carriers up with paraffin. It's a race to save all the food from becoming soggy and we skid crazily to a halt by the marsh meadow gate, all expectations soaring as everyone piles out and goes trundling across the marsh, leaving me to bring up the rear with the heavy containers of paraffin.

Welcomed back home by a dimly flickering stub of candle in a jar, Cari confronts the job of sorting out the huge bundle of food whilst I, by torchlight, hunt for the matches and set other candles dancing. I then fumble with methylated spirits and get the pressure-lamps working again; it's all slowly coming together, albeit more resembling Stonehenge than Sellafield... the 'real' thing being so well worth waiting for! Now comes the turn of the fire. It still has the faintest glimmer of red amongst the white ash and I gently place tiny twigs on an ember and softly blow until the dull red begins to glow and there is smoke curling up before a little flame takes hold and we're back in business again.

They are all beginning to tuck in as I slip out to re-light the stoves in the caravan, trying my best not to step off the piece of chip-board that partially covers the hole where Cari went through. As I'm fumbling, the cats suddenly come clamouring around me, purring and squeaking having caught scent of the same delicious smell that I can smell, making me realise that I'd better feed them right away, otherwise there will be an invasion while we're all eating. What am I saying ...eating? I'm the only thing around here that isn't eating and I'm absolutely starving; I do hope they leave a little bit for me!

The evening rolls by and every last little crumb of food has been polished off; not even a single soggy chip for a chicken remains. With food in our bellies, we're not feeling the cold nearly as much, but this could in part be due to the frost having suspended the moisture content from the atmosphere and also the fact that the mattresses have stopped steaming at last, allowing the place to warm up. Cari and I explain how really hard frosty or snowy weather comes as a welcome bonus for us, a kind of rare luxury that allows us to stay clean; it's the mild wet stuff that causes the problems, even when there are no cows to churn it all up.

Excessive demands on the teapot means that I have to make a trip to the well in the dark; Steve and Chris decide to accompany me. "We don't want you falling in!" Chris sniggers and we amble off out into the cold. The frosty air is really delightful, especially with the starlight even brighter now and shining all across the hoary white ground. They are again amazed by the eerie sounds that the owls are making, it's pure music, clear and clean throughout the lovely air. We stand awestruck hardly daring to breathe for fear of spoiling the perfect magic of the moment. As we're listening, distant engines are heard, they're high revving and certainly not hanging about. "Someone's in a hurry!" Steve mutters quietly, then as the sound gets louder, we see shafts of headlights streaking through the distant trees and can hear an engine screaming through the gears, tyres screeching, exhaust backfiring. Then a whole cluster of dazzling headlights sweep across us as a car, travelling at ridiculous speed suddenly appears on the far lane; we're all speechless, the valley's peace has been brutally shattered. In seconds it has reached the hairpin and 'S'-bend by the junction at the top of our lane; briefly there are voices shouting, then a fearful revving and squealing of tyres and the thing suddenly comes blinding like a missile in our direction. Another appears followed by another and another... it's a car rally!

I'm suddenly worried lest my little old van gets hit because it's perched on the verge right on the very edge of the narrow lane, and where the oncoming projectiles come screaming down the hill, into a dip then up again and become airborne, bottoming-out exactly where my van is parked. This is absolute madness, these are public roads, animals stray out onto them and people walk as well as drive on them. We race back with the water and all of us go off with torches to get a closer look at what is going on. It is unbelievably dangerous, the lane twists and turns every inch of the way and there isn't a flat bit anywhere. Despite our morbid fascination, we daren't stand too close for fear of one coming exploding through the hedge; the noise is enough to awaken the dead and will certainly blast old Dan from his cosy night-grave. We lose count of how many there are but it's certainly into three figures and takes until well after midnight for them all to pass through. We wander back, all of us in a stunned state of shock and confused bewilderment.

In the morning, everywhere is white with frost and there is ice on the water-tub; it's bitterly cold and my breath is billowing from me in vast white clouds. I give the hens extra handfuls of corn and scatter most of it in the barn, out of the icy air. Whilst everyone is doing the sensible thing, I spend a vigorous half hour sawing wood for the fire and soon use up the last of the branches, which means that my day has already been planned out for me whether I like it or not; I've got no excuses now that I've got my new 'bushman' saw. One consolation is that there'll be a couple of extra cart-horses about the place today so I could, with a bit of luck, make a start on the little wood at the bottom of the field behind the barn. I've seen some lovely dead oak in there, the heart of which is like iron; woodpeckers love the soft outer wood which is home to large juicy white grubs and the floor is littered with wood-fragments from where they have been pecking.

Lighting the fire on a crisp morning like this is one of the most pleasurable of things, and seeing the first smoke rising from the chimney in a straight unruffled line is indeed a lovely sight and speaks of the weather holding steady. I boil the kettle and make a large pot of tea, taking a nice steaming cup of it up to Cari, then two mugs into the caravan to check that we still have buddies and not bodies in there. I am greeted by barely awake groans and other strange noises that don't require effort, there's also the unmistakable aroma that tells me to be careful where I put my feet and to make a point of keeping a litter-tray permanently in there.

"Your morning tea, gentlemen! Kedgeree and truffles will be along shortly, as soon as I've found my fishing rod and pumped my bike tyres up. Should you require the bathroom facilities, it's the shed on the extreme left, the door's a trifle on the low side, so I'd advise one to take paper and spade and select a nice spot in a wood or, if one preferred it, beside a hedgerow somewhere; it would be such a waste to miss-out on the experience and on such a splendid morning as this!" There are more lethargic groans as I hand them their tea and I can see that it's a bit early to be confronted by a jolly joker; only the kedgeree bit was a joke, the rest wasn't! I warn them to be extra careful where they tread and point accusingly at the half-hidden lumps of purring fur that are poorly concealed, then I reiterate my advice over going to the loo, and stress that I wasn't joking and that I always go off with a spade and paper, then have a good wash in the stream afterwards: I leave them to it.

After breakfast we all take a stroll over to the lane to make sure that the van is still in one piece and to see what other damage there is. The boys are still buzzing over the unexpected thrill of the night before and are charging about growling and crashing into one another. They're quite impressed by the newly scraped road surface and the deep scars where the cars landed after taking off, but amazingly, the van doesn't appear to have been touched, apart from by flying gravel and stones. We wander back along the lane and up the hill beneath the trees where there are lots more scrape marks and large chunks out of the bank. It's the same all the way along towards the old ivy-clad ash tree that was split in half by lightning back in the summer. A mountain ash is smashed to splintered fragments and a great wound of newly exposed earth has been butchered away from the bank where the lovely little tree previously stood. We stand shaking our heads despairingly and look back along where we have walked, it's like a battlefield. Suddenly Rowan clutches tightly onto my arm and says in a hushed voice, "Jimmy... look, what's that down there?" I am looking at the flattened corpse of Bootsy; her blood is smeared in tyre-marks for some considerable distance. Stunned silence hits us, no-one can speak, only one seemingly endless gasping breath is possible. "Don't look, turn the other way, I'll get the shovel, we can't have her lying here."

It's a sombre walk back across to the cowshed; it's hard to

believe that this was the drowsy autumn field of late blackberrying time when Robin slept under the old oak. The air now has the edge of a cut-throat razor and the aldermarsh is stark and silent, unwelcoming and in winter's early grip. Steve pauses to scan the trees with his binoculars and proudly, as though in an offering of comfort to help ease our sorrowful minds, announces; "You've got redpoll, siskin, marsh and willow tits, coal tits, long-tailed tits, blue and great tits, and that's just in those alders down there." A raven flies high overhead exciting him still further, then a flock of redwings and fieldfares take idly to the air as our presence disturbs them from the old hawthorn hedge where they have been feeding.

Sad though the morning is, we're not alone; there isn't time for brooding over what has happened, we must get on with more important things and let sadness fade gently in its own time. I make a bold suggestion; "What do you say to a really hard hour of gathering firewood ... then we all go on to the coast, doing our shopping in Machynlleth; well, what do you think?" I knew that I needn't have asked and as I hurry back over to the lane with the spade, they all go racing off into the trees and feverishly start hauling branches. I dig a small grave and scrape up Bootsy's flattened remains and lay them to rest where wood anemones and daffodils will bloom as winter herself dies. Feeling utterly choked now, I can think of no better medicine than to stand for an hour scythed by the wind off the far grey lonely sea.

Rallying-round and making an Impression!

The day turns out to fit us like a glove and provide us with the space we need to help soften our sorrows. We load up with foodstuffs in Machynlleth, lots of lovely vegetables from the bustling street market, loaves from the bakers, extra milk and margarine together with numerous bits and pieces. Going to the coast is a bit of a busman's holiday for Chris and Steve but, first sight of the great tidal estuary and the far flat line of the steel sea sets my little tribe into fits of excitement and never fails to fill me with marvellous feelings of gladness for being here. When we reach the lonesome expanse of reed-beds, Steve is itching to scour them with his binoculars, and so I pull in, like stopping to let the family dog relieve itself, so necessary is it for him to do a coastal reed-bed birdwatch. Poor Steve, his efforts are being constantly undermined by Chris who is making weird loud bird noises from inside the van and calling out even weirder bird names and stirring the others into a daft holiday mode. I join Steve outside in the wind and suggest a more favourable observation place a few yards beyond the din of my little Morris menagerie, as I know all too well myself, ears are every bit as important as eyes when it comes to finding out what birds there are about. I draw his attention to something that's caught my eye far across the reed-beds: "Marsh Harrier... brilliant!" It's the second time I've seen one here, but Steve's spotted something even more intriguing, a great grey shrike, but the noise from the van has frightened it away and poor old Steve is really frustrated and needs a better sighting before he can be absolutely satisfied.

Time passes and we have to abandon the search and press on into the dunes and let everyone out to stretch minds as well as limbs. Afternoon, at this, the closing of the year, is but a Spartan dash of half-light even on the best of days; urgency is imprinted on everything and the tide is hurrying back in with darkness close in tow. Over the sea the falling sun hastens to its drowning, but we manage to use what light there is and find enough interesting driftwood to inspire Chris's wood-crafters mind to the idea of making a settle and transforming our hearth into a cosier place to be. I readily welcome the suggestion having already made plans of my own for constructing an inglenook but not as yet having been able to find the time amongst more pressing priorities. As he describes what he is going to make, it occurs to me that we've got ourselves another hungry mouth to feed and this he confirms when he announces that he wants to stay for a little while, at least until the settle is completed: I calculate that, at 'craftsman's' pace, this could easily take us up to Christmas and makes me rather thankful for having a good supply of potatoes in the shed.

Arriving back in darkness to a cold house and no magic light switches, brings hard reality into sharp focus once more. Any 'back-to-basics' novelty value has long since been erased, but such notions still exist in the minds and expectations of our visitors who can pick and choose at little 'designer' morsels to take away with them and find entertainment thereby. Candlelight is fairly quick to put into effect, but not so easy when, in the pitch darkness, the rattling matchbox proves to be full of dead matchsticks, a tiresome habit of someone dear, who shall remain nameless. At such times the cigarette lighter is useful, but when it only produces sparks, it's every bit as useful as a dead match. There are matches outside in the pigsty toilet and also in the caravan by the calor-gas ring so, whilst everyone is making eerie ghost noises, I go out with a feebly dim torch and search out those vital treasures of the technological age only to discover that the ones in the toilet are hopelessly damp and those in the caravan equally useless. As a last resort before being forced into trudging over to Dan's with an unlit lantern, I remove the bottom from the cigarette lighter and blow hard into it in the hope of forcing any trace of petroleum fuel down into the wick. Miraculously it works and I very quickly set fire to some old fish and chip paper in the hearth just as the feeble little lighter flame dies out. "There!" I gasp in eventual triumph, "We have light!" Before the racing flames have consumed the paper, there is a ritualistic panic to light candles and to then get the pressure lamps going, one of which I then have to take out into the yard to provide light for me to frantically saw a pile of logs by and to also make sure that our little feathered friends are all safely locked up for the night.

I call the cats in for their meal, but strangely they don't appear, and when I go to light the heater in the caravan, find them huddled in there. They seem to know that something horrible has befallen Bootsy, having sensed it somehow; they look distinctly shocked and devastated and cannot bring themselves to eat the food I've put for them. They seem to be crying and won't even respond to my soft words and warm fingers. I think it wiser not to mention this to anyone for fear of upsetting them all over again; as it is, I can hear them all making a bit of a racket in the glow of firelight and the promise of last night's saved potatoes back inside the oven.

When I return, Chris is busy measuring-up the pieces of driftwood and working out his design for the settle, while Steve is contributing his effort by trying his hand at making us all a most welcome cup of tea, proving in the process that even this most humble of things can be a thoroughly entertaining and hilarious event as well as being a nigh-on impossibility.

For some inexplicable reason the fire is burning really hot tonight, plenty of bright blue in the flames and a sturdy kind of ease about it, as though both it and the frost had struck on the same harmonious chord. We are certainly going to have to keep a close watch on the potatoes in the oven or they are going to burn on one side while staying raw on the other. "Tea up!" Steve crows at long last, heaving a huge sigh of relief tinged with a certain discrete pride; a cheer goes up as he pours the first cup. "Urgh! What's that?" Cari screeches, setting everyone into fits of laughter. The 'tea' is simply hot water with black bits floating on it; worse is to follow when, as he pours a third cup, the teapot lid falls off and smashes to pieces in the hearth. Even he is falling about laughing now and the fact that no-one will drink it saves him from further taunting when I discover that the sugar in the bowl, that he's somehow found in the dark cupboard, is none other than damp sea-salt. "Get it down you … it will do you good!" he splutters before crashing into a heap and knocking the boys off their van seat. "Those black bits spoil an otherwise nice cup of water," Chris jokes, picking out the tea leaves and flicking them at Steve, while poor old Steve, game to the end, manages to cough out, "Trust you lot to never have heard of tea-bags!"

Not wanting to have another failure on our hands, Cari shuffles the potatoes around in the oven, then sorts out a hard cabbage and some carrots bought earlier from the street market and, in some miraculous combination of poor eyesight and flickering candlelight, produces a dish of coleslaw and crunchy orange fingers of carrot. The big slab of Cheddar comes out from the metal bin to take an un-budgeted hammering, as too does butter and large crusty loaves. As though to underline this, Dan's granite-statued figure suddenly appears in the doorway, sore in the throat from having tried in vain to make himself heard above the din. He stands beaming and unshaven: "I wouldn't mind a bit of what you're all on!" he curses and, before he's had time to re-think, Cari rushes before him and offers a cup of Steve's tea. "No sooner said than done!" and she thrusts the cup before his scrutinising eyes, forcing him to back away. "It's a bit early for tadpoles, ain't it?" he growls jokingly in a pushing-it-away gesture, igniting even more noise.

"Dan!" Cari protests, "... how could you refuse a cup of real Grand Duchy Cornish tea?" "Bloody easy," he chuckles, "... my owd ewes pee better stuff than that!" I feel a bit taken aback by Dan's forthrightness, it isn't like him to be so bold in front of strangers, but I seem to recall that he did actually meet both Chris and Steve about a year ago when we came up with my disastrous cargo of large new canvases shredded to fragments ... how could I ever forget! "This is Steve and this is Chris; I seem to recall that you've already had the pleasure." Dan gives a wild and whiskery chin of a grin, then says, "No! ... but we did meet when you first came to look at this place." His innocence betrays him and he hasn't a clue as to why Steve is once more howling and making effeminate gestures to Cari, "Mmm... Ducky!" I discreetly intervene lest Dan feels that he's being laughed at, and I invite him to join us for 'Take 2' of Van Gogh's Potato Eaters!" "Pull up a concrete block and make yourself comfortable!"

I get the kettle refilled and astride the flames, empty every last drop of Steve's 'Real Cornish ' tea into a dish for the chickens to drink in the morning, discovering in the process that the tin lid from the honey-jar is a perfect fit to replace the teapot lid. Everyone has calmed down and there's a lovely babbling sound of voices in the air. It's always a pleasure having Dan around, he's more than just a neighbour, but an intrinsic part of the soul of this rib of earth and I feel privileged to have him royally seated before our flames. "Oh, before I forgets," he interrupts himself, "... had a delivery for you this morning... couple of heavy boxes an' some drums of summat or other." "Oh, thanks Dan; that'll be our honey, marmite and stuff," Cari says with all the gleefulness of a child, and checks to see how the potatoes are coming on.

A real cup of tea settles the minds to a deeper contentment and I thank Spencer and Rowan for their efforts in making it and for clearing the way for Dan to get round to talking about the motor-madness of last night, the main reason for his paying us a visit. The entire hill country will be buzzing with talk of nothing else and, whether I like it or not, the subject that I was trying hard to steer clear of will no doubt come up to upset the boys before they go to bed. Dan clears his throat... "Damn! What d'you reckon to them lunatics last night then?" ... he thunders in a manner that leaves no doubt as to his feelings on the subject. "They killed poor Bootsy", the boys all groan simultaneously, and I add, "Our cat" so as to make sure that he knows what they mean. This stirs up a wasps' nest in Dan's mind and he reels off his list of things to date, with our cat having stretched it still further. "The mad beggars killed the 'Tyn-y-Pales' cow, their pet it was too... smashed its legs... had to be put down. One of 'em overshot the corner at the top and ended up in owd Thomas's muck heap. They snapped the pole down the bank an' brought the wires down by Dai Morgan's, somersaulted onto it's roof it did ... made a heck of a mess. Farmers round here don't like 'em ... bursts the hedges an' the sheep wander out an' gets knocked over; they's enough boy-racers about as it is without them lot!" We have a thoroughly healthy whinge over our food, easing off when there is no longer a crumb in sight, and we round the evening off by strolling out over the frosty earth to see Dan safely back home, then returning weighed down with our new delivery of supplies.

Prolonged dry frosty weather and visitors combined, very soon empties the water-tub and I find myself having to make rather more than several trips to the well each day in keeping up with the demands. I've reached the point where I'm taking more water out of it than is flowing into it; what's more, the constant disturbance is starting to muddy the water. This stark realisation serves to remind me that rain isn't entirely a nuisance and I hate to have to admit it, but I'll be glad to see the water-tub overflowing again, a clear case of wanting the best of both worlds.

The cats are still off their food and are getting lots of extra fuss in the hope of helping them out from their gloom. It's a slow process and shows us that Bootsy meant far more to them than any of us can possibly understand. I have started work quite early on this Sunday morning and need to catch up on neglected unpleasantries. The ground is hard as I hack a deep grave for the toilet to be emptied into; it is bitingly cold and my feet and fingers are really quite numb, but I persevere and soon have the pig-sty smelling enticingly of Jeyes Fluid and looking all neat and tidy once more. Regardless of what the others may wish to do with their time today, I must spend mine down in the little wood and provide us with a wood supply that will last the week. Everywhere is silent and still, nothing stirs and the hoarfrost is thick upon the ground as I head off with my new bushman saw; I'll soon warm up once the dead timbers start to topple.

The little wood is but a small island in the marsh, just a lump that stands above the mud; it's the same humped-backed ridge that the cowshed is built on. No hardwood tree can attain status with the ground here being so wet, rivers are born here; it's because of this that I am able to benefit from dead and dying branches. Oaks only grow here at all because birds and squirrels have planted acorns over the years and the little oaks have tried to grow, only to give up the idea long before reaching maturity; they're ideal for both me and the woodpeckers. It's the same with beech, ash, birch and sycamore, but the alders are at home in it as are the willows. It's a very wild place with dense tangles of blackthorn, rose-briar, hawthorn, holly and bramble, all of it planted by wild creatures.

I see myself as some kind of tree-doctor as I examine the oaks in search of their diseased and dead bits, and I shin my way up them with a lovely feeling of being wild myself again and I amputate those long dead limbs with my marvellous new bit of metal, and cling on as I watch them crash to earth. From the ground looking up, I'm not very high up the tree but, looking down from where I am, it seems like I'm way up in the sky... a giddy height.

Up a tree is a lovely place to be: birds are so lucky being able to strut and sway about here in the branches like this, and then to just soar up into another dimension and go gliding across the valley. From up here I notice that Gareth has put two ponies in the little field that runs down from the higher wood where Spencer and Rowan accompanied me on an expedition to recover our bantams back in spring. I call across to them, hearing my voice go echoing all around; it's like stealing a moment of being a child again, a moment vulnerable and ripe for a bit of 'evolution' to show itself and turn me into a bird. The ponies turn to see where the voice came from. I can see the sun illuminating the great clouds of their breath; they aren't going to be bothered or even slightly impressed by some prat up a tree, and they ignore me.

I'm really glowing with warmth now and I feel absolutely fantastic and at harmony with everything about me. I grapple up tree after tree and the heavy dead branches go crashing down. It's really excellent timber with a heart that is more like iron than wood and will burn to perfection. In my happy state, the hours slide by and I can hear voices back up at the cowshed where awakened souls are wondering what happened to the tea-boy this morning. I climb another tree with a view to viewing rather than sawing and I can now see that nobody has made the effort to fasten any smoke to the chimney yet; they must be freezing. Aha ... what's this? Chris is taking the spade for a walk and there's a flash of white paper trailing from his pocket. He pauses briefly, having not decided yet where to go for this moment of being alone before the Almighty. There must be a queue for the pigsty, unless of course nobody has checked to see that it's all freshly sweet and ready to start trading once more. His long shadow reaches down the frosty slope, then he's off again. It seems like he has chosen the seclusion of the stream out of sight of the others and out of the sun too, it all helps when there isn't a roof. I lose sight of him, then a few minutes later he suddenly reappears coming this way, aiming for the bend in the stream just a few yards beneath me where he crouches and washes his hands. Whilst he is happily splashing about, for a bit of fun I decide to try out one of my birdcall impressions and, with the very best performance that I can manage and not too loud, I call "Cuck-oo" from high up my tree, then remain in a state of absolute frozen silence, trying with all my might not to explode into laughter. He looks like he's just seen a ghost... but he hasn't seen me and gives his fingers a final splash then hurries back to the Cowshed. I let off steam till the tears are rolling down my cheeks, I daren't risk climbing down until my laughter has eased. Suddenly, just as I'm about to attempt my perilous descent, Chris and Steve appear over the hill, Steve looks like he means business with those binoculars. Thinking quickly, I perform another slightly louder "Cuck-oo" while they're preoccupied with where to put their feet. "There!" Chris shouts in the loudest whisper of his entire life... "Now do you believe me?" They skid to a clumsy halt, if they want to investigate further, they're going to have to get their feet wet and cross the dilapidated branch-bridge over the mud fringed stream. It takes a little while for them to decide, during which time Cari and the boys are coming trundling down to join them. Frantically Chris puts his finger to his mouth and says, "Shhh... we heard him again!" They are all hovering in suspended animation, there isn't a sound anywhere ... then one of the ponies breaks wind with all the authority of an Archbishop, and it echoes out across the silence. The boys explode into fits; blue tits, great tits, marsh tits, tree creepers and nuthatches leave the wood in disarray, even a cuckoo would surely have been frightened away by it. They all splash their way over into the wood, failing to notice all the dead branches lying on the ground; then Steve starts to chuckle and breaks into bronchial laughter, letting go of his binoculars and falling into a helpless heap on his back. The game's up and I call my last "Cuck-oo!"

This little wood has never rung like this before, even the ponies have come down to investigate and are snorting and nodding their heads as though they too are laughing. I look down and the expression on Chris's face is enough to cut the tree from under me, the funny side hasn't occurred to him as yet and he's standing with hands firmly on hips glaring up at me in apparent disbelief and very slowly shaking his head, grinding the words, "You bugger!" in almost a hiss. I can see that he's embarrassed and I try to unfasten its grip on him when I say, "What's the matter, Chris... anyone would think you just heard the cuckoo!" I spare him any further revelations and scramble back down from my all too brief flight of fancy and become a human again.

More the Beggar than the Chooser!

Steve is still helplessly enjoying what, for him, must feel like getting even with Chris; after all it was Chris's weird bird noises that frightened the great grey shrike away yesterday and that would have been a really good 'tick' to have had. The boys all start to build a hut from the thin branches blown down by the storms, so I join in with their enthusiasm and we manage to weave a substantial structure that feels really cosy inside, a little place out of nowhere. It's while doing this that I feel the weather begin to change and note to my dismay, the unmistakable twinge down my back, one that never lies. Just above my right buttock, this old sod of an early warning system is a whinge of rain on the way and is normally accurate within thirty-six hours and provides me with the impetus to shift the heavy branches back across to the barn and in getting all available muscle-power into harness.

This weather forecasting right buttock of mine is well known to Cari and has been in the making for a good many years, stemming from an apprenticeship back in Staffordshire and a Grandmother who could pin-point a shower from two days range; she was most impressive. Most people visited their Grannies just for the tea made with condensed milk and served in Spode cups, followed by the usual sticky apple tart. We, by contrast, dressed up and piled into Dad's motorbike sidecar just in order that Dad, who was a house-painter by trade, could get an accurate weather forecast; fresh paintwork could so easily become ruined by a sudden shower. Granny made both a fine art and a hi-tech science out of her rheumatism and broke it down into a multitude of parts according to the colour and texture of the various pains.

I stretch my body and groan indiscernibly, slapping the palm of my hand on my inherited weather-forecasting body-part. "Rain?" Cari casually asks, and I nod my reply and say quietly, "Yeah... early Tuesday by the feel of it... might even be Monday night, so we'd better get all this stuff into the barn while we can, and do any washing that needs doing as well." It's very strange, but a slight unsettled feeling is coming about, it's putting Steve into a bit of dilemma as to when to go back. He hadn't calculated for Chris wanting to stay with us, just as he hadn't expected to find freezing conditions. I give him the benefit of my twinges and advise him that he will be travelling back into rain and that, with there being a lot of frost on the ground, he'll find it dangerously slippery if he goes back today, best for him to set off after a good breakfast in the morning. All the frost will have gone by then and he can take it easy all the way back to beautiful Cornwall. He agrees and I'm glad because I really do enjoy his company, he's a real good old pal to have about the place. This sorted, Cari decides that a good hearty stew is called for, plenty of dumplings and enough beans and pulses to guarantee Steve a strong following wind all the way down to Cornwall. What's more if this new wood is as good as I have promised it will be, she has agreed to bake some wholemeal rolls in the oven to give him a real royal send-off.

Whilst I'm producing a mountain of logs, Chris is foraging about amongst our driftwood collection, getting lost in the process.

Cari and the others with saucepans and vegetables, all move into the caravan where the cats are still in a state of gloom and could well benefit from a bit of noise and cooking smells to help break their trance. I take time out from sawing to fetch more water for Cari's creation, then resume until the last branch has succumbed to the saw.

Throughout all my activity I have an audience of chickens, all gawping at me with something far less than curiosity. By contrast the bantams never seem to have the slightest negative moment in their lives, their independence is most unsettling; even when I throw food down they seem to prefer finding their own. But I feel a strong sense of affection for my old white hens, remembering how their entire world was no more than a metal prison pressing tightly around them not so very long ago; they've done really well, even that old idiot Sykes.

Chris is examining the tools that he has at his disposal. They're not exactly purpose-made for crafting old fashioned settles, everything's a bit on the heavy-duty side, all of it ex-government. He looks around for anything resembling a workbench and I have to tell him that I use the upturned wheelbarrow and, for more intricate work, a couple of concrete blocks. There's a poorly disguised look of disgust in his unconvincing grin and I get the distinct impression that I'm going to be obliged to make another trip to town for carpentry saws and chisels if the rustic old seat is going to emerge from the driftwood. He glares at my five-foot heavy crosscut saw, a brute of a weapon if ever there was and I jokingly say; "You can use that... it's what I would use." I can tell by his smirk that that's precisely what he does believe, and he moves away amongst the hens picking his way, just as they are picking. I leave him to it and set my mind to getting the fire started and the oven sweetly up to ripeness for bread baking, my little contribution to proving that beautiful things may yet be born from crude busted irons.

The new logs are every bit as good as I said they would be and they don't race away up the chimney like some of the stuff we have been burning. With there being rain on the way and a steady log fire that I can trust for half an hour, I race off back to the wood, this time taking the big axe with me, remembering that there were a couple of oaks that stood dead and upright like telegraph poles, about the same size too. I simply cannot resist the urge to lay them down and have them back in the barn before the stew has graced the table.

Already I can detect a slight difference in the air, the dampness is beginning to steal back and it feels colder because of it. Another discernable difference is in the sunlight, it's starting to dazzle in a liquid sort of way, but there's no hurry, the ground still feels like concrete and remains encrusted with frost. It feels desolate and empty in the wood where only a short while ago we were all in stitches. How quickly the moments change in this brief dash of light; what had previously been for me a cosy little wood, is now a lonesome place to be, inhospitable with damp darkness creeping out from the ground. I don't waste time before becoming the wild man again, making the steel speak and the wood-chips fly in a late outpouring of energy that begs expression. As the tree slowly begins to topple, I put so much force into my last strike that the blade goes clean through the heart of oak and the tree crashes noisily. I'm halfway through the last dead tree when the sun becomes entangled in the trees of the higher wood and a rapid shadow darkens the hillside where the ponies are standing. It then races into my little woodland changing what was a lovely place to be, into no place to be, hurrying me along till my muscles are singing and I can feel the solitary birds fidgeting around me in the new darkness, inching closer to their roosts, wherever those little secrets may be.

I fell my last tree but they're far too heavy for me to drag back up the hill and must be sawn into manageable pieces. When I stride back up the field, I note how the ranging north hill is aglow in late sunlight; I have a dark silhouette towering to my left and a glowing hump-back of a hill to my right. I notice too that my chimney-stack is emblazoned with shrinking light and has a smudge of glowing smoke hanging over it, unable to climb the newly dampened sky. I can hear sweet sounds of the guitar being played in the cowshed, while the caravan is ranting like a school playground, as I load up with logs for the fire before making a last dash back down to the wood with my bushman saw.

The north hill now has the shadow of its brother hill creeping up it while the outstretched fingers of the high trees claw into the last of the dying sunlight. It doesn't take too long for me to saw the trees into lengths that I can carry back on my shoulders, and it is whilst I am trudging back with my body bent under the burden, that I hear the exquisite notes of Chris's recorder being played from high in the darkened wood above the well. He really does have the muse upon him and the sounds are echoing all across the valley; anyone hearing it would melt on the spot, it is pure heaven.

This won't do, I must get on before paraffin-time is upon me again. The high clear notes come glittering through the dark wood, no doubt in some confusion to the restless birds, and when I glance about me in response to a rustling sound, I can see the dark shapes of the ponies standing by the hut of branches which the boys and I had made, awakening in me a glow of affection for them and all the mysteries within their inquisitive minds. These are magical moments just before the dark and the dull shape of the long north hill tells me now that the sun has slipped beyond the world and that the first timid stars will soon be trembling before being quietly swallowed by the reason for my nagging back pain.

Our evening is one to treasure, seven of us slurping pure nectar round our tiny, tatty table that's been made bigger by having the old front door laid on top of it and draped with bed-sheets and a floral curtain. The cats have all come in and are sitting by the fire, fascinated by the flames. It's gratifying to see how they are coping with their loss and I'm feeling somewhat sad too that Steve will be leaving when I really haven't had the time to properly enjoy his company. Chris seems to have got over his earlier embarrassing moment and is adding his own rich contribution to this resurrected grave of so many souls that laughed and cried here where we are now rubbing our souls on theirs in this marvellous thing we call 'life'.

It's candles and lanterns, cats in the hearth and old curtains covering the ancient door that once opened to so many memories long since taken to the grave; and now, the smell of bread baking once more in that half-fossilised remnant of an oven. With guitar, auto-harp, cello, tin whistles and percussive crockery, the 'Cowshed Consort' takes to the air in one incredible surge of expression. Nothing was ever so spontaneously beautiful or so simple; and all without electricity, running water, mains gas, access or anything;

nothing at all could ever compare with this!

It's a grey overcast morning as we wave goodbye to Steve; a little of what the cats have been feeling is affecting us now as we confront the space he has left. The boys are all at school and so we take a trip to town in the van, a start has to be made on our Christmas shopping and this seems a good a time as any. The other reason for making the trip is to provide Chris with a couple of quality tools for the 'thing' that he's promised to make; I will probably find a good use for the tools anyway, so it isn't a total extravagant expenditure, just one which hastens me to the point of having to go off and earn some more money before winter has had it's last barbaric fling.

One thing that is occurring to me is that simplicity, no matter how many sacrificial offerings there are in finding it, is as elusive as a piece of string in determining its length. There is always something that sneaks through even the most well thought out of plans, a rude truth that there can be no slipping back into a prior time of uncluttered charm and tranquillity and without complex degrees of bureaucracy; maybe there never was such a nirvana anywhere anyway. Between them, the fourth 'R' and the Inland Revenue seem to do a fairly comprehensive job of shackling any mind and making it pay for every breath breathed thereafter. Going it simple simply 'ain't simple! Meanwhile oblivious to my trepidation, Steve is straddling his tiny engine and spluttering his way southwest, free as a bird and doubtless assisted by a boisterous following wind that mercifully isn't taxed yet!

Chelsea buns provide the answer to so many things and so I convert even more of my hard summer earnings into flour and treacle before somewhat reluctantly placing an order for the Times Educational Supplement in order that I may start looking at the job market for future reference. I'm angry at the very realisation that there have been unexpected holes appearing in my pockets, and now we have Christmas bearing down on us to tear an even bigger hole.

Rain has returned and the water-tub is tinkling once more; the brief days are dark and foreboding as the shortest day rapidly approaches, giving our paraffin supplies a merciless hammering as a result. The pressure-lamp has been repaired at last and is working perfectly once more. Slowly, Chris's 'settle' is starting to take shape and the sound of the saw is heard above the patter of rain and sets me off on my own mission to replace the dreaded loft-ladder stairs before someone does themselves an injury coming down them. I shan't be using the driftwood, Chris has grabbed all of that for his creation; instead I shall have to make do with the odd bits and pieces that I have been saving for a rainy day. The width of stairs and the number of steps it will have, depends on how much wood there is available and has all the indications of being another unavoidable bodge. The wood is neither heavy enough or having sufficient depth to comfortably accommodate a foot and it therefore concerns me somewhat that it may not take our weight. There's only one way of finding out... make the bloomin' thing!

Finding myself more the beggar than the chooser, I soon realise that this flight of stairs is going to be a bit on the steep side and will have somewhat large spaces between the steps due to the shortage of wood but, on a more positive note, the old loft-ladder can readily be converted into firewood; it will make ideal kindling. To be on the safe side, I won't attempt to remove what's already there until the replacement stairs are constructed separately and have demonstrated that they are adequately strong to support us. I don't have the time to piddle about; there is in me somewhere a craftsman, but I certainly 'ain't got time to go in search of it today and, with rain now slashing down heavily, I shall very soon have to pack up and pick up the boys from school. By contrast, Chris is lovingly stroking his wood, sand-papering it and rounding off the edges in a dreamy kind of slow motion. My effort is mostly guesswork and done in a hurry with 'time' not being one of the luxuries available to me. As soon as I have worked out the approximate angles and positions of the steps, there'll be a jolly banging of hammer and nails and the rasp of my bushman saw filling the air.

The day is all too short and it's time to go and pick the boys up. We all take a break, then drive on to the garage for more paraffin before heading for the village shop to buy matches, more candles and something to line our hungry stomachs. The boys have been making paper lanterns at school and are eager to spend the evening making paper-chains to drape across the room. Christmas has begun to kindle its magic in their minds, just as it did with me when I was a child and when Cari was a little girl in these parts. There's nothing quite like Christmas, it beats birthdays by miles, even though it's situated in the gloomiest, most depressing dog-end of the year. It has the magical power to turn a little monster like Robin into an angel in the classroom, occasioning his teacher to pray for Christmas to last forever, cold dark days an' all!

After we've enjoyed a hearty meal of cauliflower-cheese, roast potatoes, carrots and parsnips, we all gather round the fire for a kind of flamenco carol session. 'Good King Wenceslas' had never sounded quite like this and 'Silent Night' is a tremolo-study with the occasional 'Ole' and a stamping of heels on the hard floor. It's great fun and our mice show up from time to time to just to give the odd wolf-whistle to the cats who wave back at them in comradely fashion, best of friends. Upstairs, bits of grit and plaster can be heard falling to the floor as our little wrens fidget in their sleep; a robin and a bluetit roost up there too and sometimes there are bigger, more mysterious scuffling which dislodge larger bits of plaster, while up on the beam, the mud cradle left by the swallows; they'll be basking in the hot African sun now and roosting over lions roaring and hyenas corpsing about in the hungry nights.

My new staircase isn't such a disaster after all, and takes my weight without too much creaking. Once it has been secured into position, it should find even more stability, so I proceed with the removal of the heavy old loft-ladder, creating a whole lot more space in the process. The rule to remember with the new stairs is quite simple, come down them backwards, they're too steep for coming down frontwards and will require a handrail for added safety. On a more positive note, they look a whole lot better than the cumbersome item that I've removed and may yet reveal other advantages as time goes by.

After three days, Chris has run out of wood and there's no way that I'm prepared to lay out more money now, he's going to have to make do with scraps, like I've had to. Being the tiresome perfectionist that he is, he abandons the project, for the time being at any rate, during which time he recycles Cari's inherited three-legged bamboo hat-stand into a series of flutes and pan-pipes. Fortunately, none of us wears a hat and so the loss of this quaint bit of Victoriana isn't really missed and now there are strange and haunting sounds of the Andes and of India wafting about the place, making me realise that Chris and music are inextricably bonded; making music and musical instruments are as one to him.

Stinking Retribution and Pie in the Eye!

Cari and I have a growing problem of knowing where to hide our Christmas presents, somewhere that's safe from the marauding inquisitive minds that are currently being none too subtle in the dropping of hints as to gift-ideas and are blatantly working out every conceivable hiding place. Cari has agreed to go and ask Dan if he might be able to help us over this. We're already receiving our first Christmas cards, prompting me into devoting the evening to making our own. It's something that I always love doing and it's nice to see that I am inspiring the boys into following my example. Chris meanwhile has managed to find a bit more wood buried under the leaves in what was the cat-shed, and he is now cautiously proceeding with the settle, desperately trying to avoid it resembling something that I might have had a hand in making. Sight of the boys all squeezed together on an old van-seat plonked on top of two concrete blocks, must be somewhat offensive to his craftsman's sensibilities, but the boys love it, they think it's great and that's fine by me.

I'd like to be of some assistance to Chris, help speed things up a bit so that we may have somewhere to sit protected from the wicked draughts, especially with Christmas looming upon us when we're guaranteed to have extra backsides wanting somewhere to park. Our patience is eventually rewarded and the completed settle is ceremoniously positioned at right angles to the right hand side of the oven, creating a little corridor to the kitchen door; it really does make the hearth look cosy and, to help keep the draughts off even further, an old heavy curtain has been stretched all across the back of it. I've got to admit, the waiting has been worthwhile.

It's a very hectic few days up to the shortest day; there can be no let-up in my efforts to find firewood and Cari is working slavishly, scrubbing clothes, ironing, cooking, baking, organising and cleaning, miraculously finding a moment amongst it all to bottle the elderflower wine with all the sterilizing preparation that's involved. Chris has somehow acquired the name of 'Indian Joe', according to Dan who knows about these things; apparently he's been spotted strolling about wearing a large trilby with the brim pulled down and the top poked out, and with the little grey cat on his shoulder: and has named her, 'Spibby'. Curious to know why he has chosen such an odd name, I ask him, "Why 'Spibby'?" He starts to laugh and explains that, while walking with the cat on his shoulder, she turned her back on him, tail in the air, revealing what he termed as, "a tiny 'spib' of poo," ... so he called her 'Spib', which rapidly became 'Spibby'. So our little grey cat is now named after a speck of cat-poo; this will be nice to have to explain to people, although I really must be grateful, it could have been a whole lot worse!

The cats seem to be over their upset and are once more raiding the food cupboard, Sorrel being the main culprit, forever sneaking about in the shadows, snatching food off the table right under our astonished noses as well as maintaining a total disregard of the litter-tray. Judging by the look of it, it would seem that they have some horticultural interest and are waiting for something very special to grow from it... misguided good behaviour if ever there was!

Chris's stay with us has come to an end and I have to drive him back home for a Christmas in Plymouth; hopefully he won't be too badly crippled with rheumatism, cat-flu and fowl-pest. I'm hoping that this might present me with an opportunity to do a spot of serious Christmas shopping of my own and with a cheque book which all too soon will be turning to rubber. Another of my priorities is to visit the television studios and let it be known that I'm looking for work, speaking of which, a glance through my new Times Educational Supplement has revealed a part-time lecturing position at Hereford Art College and I have sent off for the application forms, a move which has made me feel strangely sick inside.

I'm not feeling in the slightest bit happy over leaving Cari to cope on her own at this particular time, but she insists that everything will be fine, plain sailing. To be on the safe side I have made a great effort to make sure that there's plenty of wood, paraffin, candles, matches, torches, batteries and toilet paper, and have stocked the cupboard with tins of beans, sardines, pilchards and cat-food. Already we're getting into the damson, plum and blackberry, the rose-hip syrup and bramley apple chutney, as well as our faithful old potatoes. I've also topped-up the metal food-bin with cheese, margarine, muesli and flour, daring to hope for a more stable and predictable period to enable us to ration and plan through the worst of the winter.

Already, on one of his Indian Joe walks round the lanes, Chris has made the acquaintance of the telephone kiosk and has phoned his mother to let her know that I'm bringing her son back. Such is her relief, she's promised to make one of her famous vegetable pies for me to bring back. Her way of saying 'thank you'. Winter returns to see us off and the surrounding hills are all icing-sugared and there are fresh icicles hanging from the tin roof. I don't notice any tears as Chris thumps the caravan an affectionate goodbye, but I do sense a certain sadness when he says his farewell to Spibby. I give Cari a big warm hug and then head for the van; the sooner I get there, the sooner I shall get back.

I have very strange feelings as I drive south as far as Hereford, clocking the distance and the time that it takes, just in case I should at some time find myself working there. I come to the conclusion that upwards of seventy miles is a long way, a bit too long in fact, but I have to admit that it's a lovely part of the country and has a glorious Welsh-born river sparkling through the centre of it. We press on through hollybush and mistletoe country before the reassuring shoulder of the Forest of Dean guides us down beside the wonderful Wye, all the way down to that other Welsh-born watery monster, the Severn, and the mighty wonder of the world that spans it, marking an end to ridiculously winding and up-and-down roads.

It's mid-afternoon when we reach Plymouth, allowing me time to briefly show my face in the television studios where there are no big surprises... no work available until Spring or thereabout. It's what I expected... these cussed old salts down here don't succumb to flu-viruses like the rest of the country does, neither do they become haggard and shrivelled with stress-related disorders; what's more these bumpkins stay sun-tanned throughout the year!

We spend a very homely evening, rosy cheeks and smiles all round as Chris, with a brand new box of drawing pins, converts the family piano into a harpsichord by squeezing a pin into every little cushioned hammer within the dreadfully heavy, highly polished box of cast-iron and a million metal strings; then, before their unsuspecting ears, plays the National Anthem and has them hooting with laughter; it's that sort of family. His dad is the most complete 'handyman', just another of those disgustingly enviable characters that can do absolutely anything about the place. He is currently doing a complete rewiring of the house and has come up with a problem of sorts, he needs to pass cables beneath the floorboards of a large room and doesn't want to have to take the floorboards up. I can't believe what I am experiencing; he's attached the cables to their extremely fat and friendly family cat, puts her under the floorboards, then places a dish piled high with the finest stinking cat-food at the hole where he needs both cat and cables to re-emerge. He calls her and, whether it be love or gluttony, the cat proceeds to contradict all my own experiences with cats, and completes the rewiring job to perfection. I am totally speechless, spellbound; this cat actually works in harness and in perfect harmony with its human counterparts and I watch in silence as the great fat purring lump wolfs what, only a few weeks ago, was a cow in a field. I can see it now... 'Reginald Doddridge & Cat Ltd., Re-wiring Specialists.'

This sets the pattern of my all too brief stay; the pace is gentle and there's a fragrance all about the place, lots of smiles and an easy sense of fun everywhere; it's like walking back into an eternal moment of springtime with a lingering smell of polished wood, flowers and pastry. Even the cat's purring is like a musical instrument being played by the soft and soothing moments; absolutely nothing is in a hurry, time is just a lovely cushion.

It's like a breezy April morning when I leave both friends and Plymouth behind. I am loaded up with Christmas presents, a huge vegetable pie and a pack of sandwiches of some sort, together with a flask of tea. I am determined not to stop for food or drink until I have crossed the Severn Bridge, the spot I have in mind is the car-park opposite Chepstow Racecourse, I'll be really hungry and thirsty by then. I stop at Bristol for petrol, but it isn't long afterwards that

I have crossed the great bridge and am pulling in by the racecourse for the refueling of my body and to give my legs a good stretch. It's a rare moment of luxury, a piping hot cup of tea steaming-up the windscreen as I eagerly fumble to see what I've got in my sandwiches. Perfect! I have cheese, tomato, lettuce and a touch of pickle; they are on lovely moist brown bread and simply cannot be eaten slowly. There's another little silver-foiled pack with a label... "Pudding, Fragile". She has really done me proud and, after polishing off the sandwiches, I decide to go the whole hog and finish the lot in one sitting, before taking a stroll about the car-park and then heading for home. I pour myself another cup of tea before settling to the best bit and I know that I'm likely to get myself into a bit of a mess with having no utensils to eat my pudding with, especially as it has a soft and soggy feel. I console myself with the thought that pigs get by without spoons, so why shouldn't I!

I'm aware of a sudden sickening stink inside the van... it's coming from my pudding of all things! I tear away the last bit of wrapping-foil and to my horror am confronting a stinking old holey sock and it's stuffed with something... a dried up, brownish crumpled thing! Surely not... no, he wouldn't sink so low as to do such a thing! The smell is so foul that I'm finding it impossible to distance myself from it sufficiently... then I notice a small slip of paper protruding and I know that I'm not meant to resist whatever's written on it. It says... "Let's face it, Christmas wouldn't be Christmas without a nice pudding, now would it!"

With the doors and windows wide open, my warm little van is now an ice-box as I desperately try to get the stink out. It's a whole lot cooler here than it was in Plymouth and there's a cutting easterly wind coming from over the racecourse as I fumble all the old wrapping-paper, together with the mysterious 'thing-in-a-sock', into a litter-bin. I don't feel inclined to linger now, but I will make one more stop as soon as I find a phone-box, I'd like to thank Chris's mum for the sandwiches!

By Tintern Abbey, I pull in and make my call; Chris answers and I have the distinct feeling that he's been waiting for the phone to ring round about now. "You dirty sod!" I blast into an explosion of laughter and I have to wait almost until my money has run out before he eases. I can hear the others laughing in the background as he tries to reassure me that it wasn't what I thought it was, but was a Bombay Duck, adding... "They're considered to be a delicacy!" and I growl back, "Not in my van they're not!" and I realise now that I too have just heard the first cuckoo!

As I near home, it occurs to me that the Christmas presents that I have all prettily boxed-up and labelled in the back will not be safe from the boys, and so I must call in at Dan's before going home and find out whether Cari has spoken to him about storing a few things for us. I've made good time and, as I pull in under Dan's big sycamore tree, I catch sight of him emptying his teapot in the yard. Instantly, like a bat out of hell, his mongrel comes bounding menacingly across, making me think it wiser to remain in the van with the windows shut. I can hear Dan bawling a litany of curses as I sit here with the brute's slobbering solid head level with my own as it scratches and beats its great filthy paws upon the glass, totally oblivious to his master's voice. It's definitely not safe to step outside while he's in this ugly mood. Dan hobbles over and wildly lashes out at the dog with his foot and his welly sails high over the van like a Catherine-wheel and is seized by the dog and shaken mercilessly as though it were a rat. Dan sees the funny side and hops to retrieve it. The air is blue with his blasphemy, then he comes to my window where the entire world can hear our shouted conversation. I gather that Cari has spoken to him and that he'll be glad to store whatever I've got in the van now, persuading me that it will be safe for me to come out and that the dog is all mouth and no trousers. I feel somewhat reticent but rather obliged into taking his word for it and so, venture out into the snarling, barking air. Loaded with boxes, we make our way across the small field with the mongrel coming at me repeatedly and with Dan lashing out his foot and lacerating the air with garbled instructions to the awful animal. It's plain to me that I haven't been forgiven for treading on his bone all that time ago, he's determined to make me regret ever having done such an unspeakable thing.

There's a lovely coal fire blazing in the grate, the warmth dominates over the years of dirt and junk piled everywhere and I notice several mice in the hearth... the more I look, the more I see, they're everywhere. Then it occurs to me that Dan hasn't got a cat, in fact I've never seen any sign of one since I've been coming here.

"I've got the very thing for you, Dan, my cat would soon shift a few of these mice for you, you can have her if you like... what d'you think?" He gives a whiskery grin and says, "Little mice ain't hurting me, so why should I hurt them?" I look back at him somewhat in doubt as to whether I'm looking at St. Francis of Assisi, or just stubborn old Dan who's too short-sighted, or can't be bothered, to see them. "Well, the offer's there; it'd be nice to see a cat purring away in your hearth... be a bit of company for you in the evenings, too." I leave it at that as he goes hobbling upstairs with the boxes, and not a minute too soon either because Cari and the boys are coming noisily across the field, not pestered by the dog, it's only the postman and me that he bites.

There's a loud knocking on the door and I hear Cari shouting, "Open up! It's the Ministry Inspectors!" Dan goes cackling over to the door and opens it; "I'll give you Inspectors!" he laughs, and there is a somewhat noisy reunion which more than fills the room, even the dog can't get in. "And to think he told me he was going to Plymouth!" she jokes, "you just can't trust men these days!" Dan is a little bit confused into thinking that he'd better explain and he says in a slightly embarrassed way, "He's only just this minute popped in to drop off a few p..." I give him a firm elbow in the ribs and he splutters into correcting himself; "... just popped in now he has, to see how I was, like." He puffs and gives me a look of relief, at which point Robin pipes up, "Hey Dan, you've got moleses, you 'aves... look!" He points and Spencer jumps to alertness with his eyes like saucers: "Where?" he asks, straining to see where Robin's finger is aimed... then he sees them and rolls his eyes in dismay. "Robin! They not moles... they's rats!" Cari lets out a subdued yell, half in humour, half in terror and Dan rattles back into laughter and growls, "First I've got mice, then I've got moles, now I've got rats! You'll be telling me I've got badgers next!" Cari inches a little closer to the hearth to prove to herself that they actually are mice, then she turns to Dan and says, "What you need is a little cat, she'd soon thin them out a bit for you, and it'd be a bit of company as well... a little cat purring in the hearth." Dan looks at me and almost splutters the last stump of tooth from his gums, and grins broadly. We leave him with his rodent friends and set out into the menacing yard.

The boys all go charging off across the field whilst I run the gauntlet of the mongrel; I'm somewhat preoccupied with trying to keep the foul creature away from me and it hasn't yet occurred to me that the boys are in a mad charge to be first to pile into the van where the very large vegetable pie is wedged upright in the back. Then I suddenly remember and, as I yell, "Don't go inside the van!" I present the dog with the unguarded moment that he's so patiently been waiting for and I feel the sledge-hammer blow of his bite just below my right knee and in a flash, see the cretinous thing go slyly away to savour the marvellous feeling in the privacy of his stinking old hutch. I let out a howl of pain which Cari disregards, believing it to be another of my weather forecasts; "Don't tell me," she sighs, "let me guess... it's going to be a white Christmas!"

There's no mistaking the fact that I'm back home when, only seconds later, my screamed request for the boys not to go inside the van is either unheard or is ignored and there's further pandemonium as an ugly brawl erupts with Robin fighting his unruly way into being first inside. I scream again, but it's too late, and I see Rowan's utter exasperation when he gives Robin a really hefty shove to help him on his way, resulting in him going head first into the vegetable pie, splattering it instantly into the consistency of vomit. Cari stands bemused, I'm in a state of agonised shock and Rowan is tittering as Robin pathetically emerges, his hair and face dripping with diced carrots, potatoes, peas and gravy. "Urgh! Robin's been sick!" Spencer cries out. "I'm not going in there!" "Serves you right," Rowan says sharply "...that's what you get for pushing and shoving!" Cari still doesn't know what's going on and is abruptly swept aside as Robin, dribbling and dripping with the finest allotment vegetables and fragments of magical golden pastry, goes exploding in pursuit of Rowan, hell bent on some sinister and mean revenge. Rowan shows him a clean pair of heels and goes streaking away down the lane, thinking it wiser to give Robin a bit of space in which to cool off and come to terms with his brief encounter with a vegetable pie. On seeing the passenger seat splattered with what she considers to be vomit, Cari stomps off with Spencer, leaving me limping badly and with a rip in my trousers and an imprint of dogs teeth upon a rapidly swelling and blackening bruise. I painfully settle back into the driving seat and can see Dan at his window laughing all over his great rustic face; I give a lethargic wave together with a look of doom before starting the engine and easing slowly back onto the lane until I'm on the downhill part where I turn the engine off again and roll silently down the slope, back into the real world.

Coughs and Sneezes Spread Diseases!

All attempts to salvage the vegetable pie have failed; after its catastrophic accident nobody will go near it and so our hens are enjoying an early Christmas treat, while at the same time erasing all traces of it from existence; it will take a while longer for it to slip from memory because it promised to be so tantalizingly delicious and had aroused the glutton in me to new heights... or depths maybe.

The frost is particularly sharp, having preyed on a deathly dampness in the valley, turning all twigs and branches white. Up in the wood I can hear dogs barking, then a twelve-bore stutters; voices echo as two figures emerge amongst the solemn trunks, one of them is carrying an enormous pole. I recognise the other one, it is Dai-the-Death Morgan, twelve-bore at the ready, they're heading this way. The smoke is ruffling up from our chimney in a steep climb and must look rather picturesque and inviting from up there on the cold hill. I look at Cari and say, "I've got a feeling that we're about to have visitors... better get the kettle on."

Sure enough, ten minutes later we hear dogs barking in the yard and our chickens all clucking rather grumpily. There's a loud stamping of feet which suggests that dirt is being removed prior to the expectation of being invited in, I go out to greet them. I already know Dai, but the other figure is tall, stooped and has a wild 'in-bred' kind of look about him and has an apparent tendency to slobber and grunt; his nose is as red as a haw and has 'stuff' dangling from it. "This is Griff, my Drey-Poker!" Dai announces jovially. "Your WHAT?" I ask, extending my hand for the stranger to shake. "My Drey-Poker ... squirrel's dreys." Dai explains and I nod to show that I understand. "Nice to meet you, Griff!" I greet him and he answers , "Urhh," and sneezes like a Cromwellian cannon and strikes a glancing blow with his forearm across his messy nose, exposing a badly bleeding hand as he does so. "You're bleeding," I point out and get another grunt in reply. "Squirrel bite!" Dai chuckles, "I did tell him not to try handling a squirrel, but no, Griff had to do it his way, an' the beggar nabbed him. Nabbed you, didn't he Griff!" Griff grunts again and offers a trace of a grin before firing off a whole succession of sneezes. Cari appears at the door, radiant and welcoming as ever. "You're just in time for a nice cup of tea!" Dai removes his cap as I knew he would, but Griff's hat has the look of a garment that's long since been stitched to his skull, and any thought of removing it doesn't occur to him. They bundle inside, leaving the thirty-foot drey-pole with its extensions, propped against the house, while the dogs obediently wait, shivering and glancing about them nervously on the look-out for the demon black cat that they remember and who scratched her name on their galloping backsides backalong.

The two men settle down drowsily on our new settle, while the lively fire spits and crackles, with its heat racing up the chimney to waste. It's plainly obvious that Griff has got a filthy cold and I feel obliged to make a note of the mug that he's noisily slurping tea from because his nose is freely dripping into it and so, pretty though the mug may be, I shall smash it afterwards for health reasons. Conversation is a bit stiff and sluggish and so I apply the jump-leads to get it started up by saying; "All the squirrels are deep in hibernation now, Dai; do you mean to tell me that you and Griff here, are walking the woods, waking them up and killing them?" He smiles so broadly that his dentures lose their grip of his gums, forcing him to take lightning action with his lips in order to stop them from bolting free. With a tighter smile, he says, "Aye, that's just about it ... 'best time to get them, this is. Destructive beggars ... got to be kept down!" He already knows how Cari and I feel about things like this, but finds it amusing for some strange reason. I continue ... "So, Griff wakes them up with his pole and, before they've had chance to open their eyes properly, you shoot them?" He's prouder than ever now. "I couldn't have put it better myself!" and, puffing his little chest out he turns to Griff and adds ... "best drey-poker in these parts!" a grin rises up like a sunrise in Griff's wild scrub of a face and he grunts briefly before proudly muttering, "Fostry Hommission!"

I can see that this moment means everything to Griff, it's the high point of his year. Sad as I am for the squirrels, I am glad for him to have found something that he can do and find some semblance of recognition thereby. Dai invites me to accompany them to see for myself how it's done, but I shudder at the very suggestion and hasten to point out that I have to go off in urgent search of new wood supplies, but quick as a flash, he retorts; "Well, damn; you can do both at the same time, we'll soon find you some wood, isn't it!" It's pointless arguing with him because I know that wherever I go, he'll suddenly turn up there, and so I grapple frustratedly with my jacket, at the same time 'accidentally-on-purpose' knocking Griff's mug to the floor in my sham haste to get the garment over my head; at least this part proves to be a success.

The dogs are more than relieved to be working again and go haring off up the hill to the wood, their noses glued to both genuine and imaginary scent-trails. Meanwhile, Griff ponderously gathers his pole and has an animal logic manifest in his stance before the world, in that, size really matters most of all, and to prove it he insists, against advice, on screwing-in the other extension pieces, making it practically impossible for him to walk with his drey-pole. Dai looks at me and gives a despairing grin, before raising his hat in a parting cheerio to Cari. I nip into the barn and grab my trusty Bushman saw, then, before hurrying to join the others, whisper to Cari that I broke the mug intentionally because of all the horrid stuff which was dribbling into it from Griff's nose. She screws her face up and shudders with revulsion and goes back inside.

With the trees all being bare now, the squirrel dreys are easy to see, but what amazes me is that they all look too flimsy and insubstantial to be of any use in keeping a creature warm and safe from the wicked ways of winter, they look more like autumn play places. I soon learn that Dai is an impressively skilful pest controller and reads the trees with all the instincts of a natural predator and not simply someone earning a living. He really was that man to be born with a ferret in his pocket and a lurcher at his heel, with snares, nets, twelve-bore and a penknife. I watch him with some fascination. Everything he does is instinctive to him. Griff by comparison is more of a liability than he is of assistance; a cumbersome, stubborn man, but someone somewhere knows and cares about him and, so long as he's never allowed to be in charge of a twelve-bore, he's happy and everyone's happy for him to be poking his long drey-pole high into the squirrel-dreys and thrashing the little creatures to their doom.

Dai already knows where all the dreys are situated, but more impressively he knows precisely where the squirrels of any given area will head for, once they have been awakened from their deep sleep: he knows every hollow, every old woodpecker nesting-hole, every split and crack and can read the calligraphy of scratch marks that tell him all he needs to know about where squirrels travel; they don't stand a chance with this man!

As we walk amongst the trees, Dai pauses and then lies down on the frozen ground as he listens to the earth around a fox-hole where the dogs are excitedly telling him something. He listens in several places and smells the entrance hole with all the expertise and skill of one addressing a fine wine; what he deduces from his listening and smelling is all a secret part of his mysterious gift and I can't help noting how his brow furrows in silent thought.

Gazing back down to my precious little home in the valley, I can see the white specs of our heroic hens, not wanting to venture far from the barn and I see the smoke rising before being smudged by the blessed hand of Turner himself; my love... my home. Flowering above it all, the little bantam cock inscribes his signature all across the belly of the winter sky, making the valley his and his alone, just for a few precious seconds of time. Beside me, Griff is sneezing so much that he hardly needs a drey-pole to awaken the squirrels but, sneezes or not, he clumsily hoists the pole, threading it through the branches while Dai has positioned himself obscurely and has his gun aimed at the ready, waiting for the pole to find its way and for Griff to be ready for Dai to shout, "Start pokin'!"

Two explosions in rapid succession brings two little squirrels tumbling to the earth far below and, quick and slick, two more cartridges are rammed into the breach and the gun once more into firing position. My heart boils and pounds with shock and I have to gulp in desperation to breathe at all; this is a violation of everything that I hold dear. The next bit really makes me want to throw up when the dogs retrieve the newly-dead and bring them back to Dai who is already opening the blade from his penknife and, in two crude simple movements, has the tails of the two squirrels in his bag and the corpses tossed casually away to slowly freeze, even though they may not yet be properly dead. Griff gets carried away in a frenzied poking spasm and he doesn't stop until every leaf in the drey is floating to the ground. Dai looks at my stunned and speechless face, grins and chirps proudly, "Ain't no more in that one!" I can't stomach any more and I search hungrily about me for signs of timber to save me from this dreadful initiation, and I see the crippled wreck of the cherry tree which storms had brought down earlier and I make for it. All I need to do is to trim the branches and then saw them into sturdy lengths, which I can then haul back and saw them into logs back in the barn. Dai watches me as I reduce the wreck into purposeful items of fuel. He has a slightly concerned look about him as though he's suddenly realised that living the way we have to in the cowshed, is a whole lot harder than he had previously thought.

There is an overwhelming beauty defying me to ignore it, and it persists, knowing that I shall weaken at some point. I don't often stand here at this obscure corner of the wood and gaze with worshipping eyes upon the world that's falling away down valleys and roaming hump-backed hills reaching away in other directions. I have the souls of the two dead squirrels cradled in the care of my own soul and I am confused in an anger and a loving and caring that's been torn apart here before my very eyes. I look into the cherry tree bark and touch it, feel it; it is red, deep red and so round and glossy, far more beautiful than it is useful, because I know how poorly it burns, having not the might and power of oak or ash, simply being a thousand times more beautiful to look upon and touch... that's all.

The cowshed is now obscured behind another little wood and criss-crossing wild, white frosted hedges. Midway between, in the belly of this valley, a great root system is dark brown and risen high in the air where the wicked wild wind toppled the mature ash tree a year before we came here and the massive rib-cage is still lying there where it fell, supported and suspended on its splintered limbs, forgotten. I can take some timber from this too, but I have to be careful not to assume that me and my bushman saw have a licence to go wherever we please and to saw up whatever takes our fancy.

I must confess, I didn't calculate that life here was going to be so hard and that I'd be so basically occupied from morn to night totally adrift from my needs as a painter and writer. The very living of life has become the work of art and thus I believe that the only way of anyone experiencing my art is to nail my corpse to a wall in a gallery.

There are more gunshots in the wood behind me and I hear their echoes from a new perspective and hear Griff's worsening sneezes exploding and dispersing the spores of all his germs, for them to go sailing in search of hosts through which to spread and go on spreading like dandelion-clocks, but without their grandeur. As I turn to wave my goodbye to the others, Dai's voice rings out, "Another four!" and I head off down the valley with as many cherry branches as I can manage, then rise up again into the other little wood, up the hill and then down to where the cowshed stands before me, looking like some rare and precious jewel.

It's true, there is no heat in the cherry wood. It burns a bit like hawthorn and alder, rapidly choking itself in its own white powdery ash. I plan to spend tomorrow, eve of the shortest day, in salvaging whatever I can from the great fallen ash tree higher up the valley. I must provide us with Christmas fuel in plenty, so that our Christmas may be a dawn-to-starlight dance of sparkling flames, an endlessly steaming kettle and an oven that smells like heaven. We gather more closely around the fire tonight and pull the little table as close as we dare in order to eat our meal, everywhere is so wickedly cold. The boys' room is the only place that is protected from it and I'm really glad for having given earlier priority to making their room as cosy and as near to 'normal' as I possibly could. Cari and I meanwhile, we have just about the same that the chickens have to cope with, although I don't think that we are nearly as 'adapted' as they are in coming to terms with these conditions.

As we sit talking around the fire, a tractor engine breaks the air and we all look at each other with questioning faces. Robin dashes to the polythene window and stammers; "There's a chactor coming down the field wiv its lights on!" He races off out into the yard and we all follow, me with the pressure-lamp, as we try to see what's going on. A little grey Ferguson comes trundling into the yard, it's Dai Morgan with a trailer piled with silver birch logs that he's sawn for us with his chainsaw. I turn to Cari and I feel like crying. "This should boil a few kettles for you!" he shouts, dexterously reversing the small trailer through the gap between backdoor and pigsty, without light and hardly an inch to spare. We all start unloading excitedly and I catch a brief glimpse of his proud and satisfied face in my lantern light.

After an hour of rabbiting on about rabbits and badgering on about badgers, Dai remembers that he's got a flock of his own to tend to, and so the boys put warm clothing on and jump aboard the trailer for a bumpy ride in the dark across to the lane. Cari and I run on ahead so that we can open the gate for him to be able to take a bit of a run up the slope and onto the lane. It's started to snow and there's a raw Christmas feel about us as the feathery flakes drift in and out of the tractor's dim lights and make hissing noises on the pressure-lamp. Overhead, the lonesome contact flight-calls of redwings drifting over together with the haunting cry of owls up in the woods, no doubt complaining that it's started to snow. It isn't going to be a heavy fall, this is just a passing flurry, I can tell by the feel of the air, there's no mistaking a blizzard when it comes.

Shortest day; it doesn't seem five minutes since it was the longest day when Cari slept out in the field under the stars. What a difference six months makes. As yet we haven't got a Christmas tree, so better late than never, I take an excursion into the conifer forest to see what gale damage has occurred, and I find not just one tree, but dozens that the wind has toppled in a kind of domino-effect. I only need to nip the top out of one of them and so, bingo...we've got our Christmas tree and I run the risk of being arrested as I charge down the lane back home with it. In the evening, out comes the famous old box of Christmas decorations which has served us well over the years, and the boys take great delight in making it look beautiful while poor Cari feels like she's got a cold coming on...a present from Griff, no doubt, to us all.

Good Old Santa!

My dog-bite is healing, a small scab has formed and the large purple bruise is now yellowing at the edges, but it still hurts and I'm as yet at a loss as to know whether the dog's anger has at last been satisfied or, instead perhaps, his appetite whetted still further. I shall just have to wait and see. Cari's cold has come to full flowering and I've easily persuaded her into staying in bed out of the way, in the futile hope of it not doing its rounds. This gives me the opportunity to demonstrate my skills as a cook-cum-nurse and general scrubber, dish washer and herdsman over three loud lads.

The silver birch logs are already taking a hammering, as too is Cari's small library of precious books with, George Borrow, Walt Whitman, Rachel Carson and Buckminster Fuller enduring their own timely revocation. There's no need for me to open any windows to let the influenza germs go sailing out, our house is one big open window already, with fresh air in bagfuls forever passing through, whether we like it or not. I do however seem to be thriving on adversity, as though something has ignited a booster rocket inside me and I am coping with enthusiasm, an inspiration of a human kind with loving and caring being the canvas at my touch. I have to admit however, that I'm fairly radical with a saucepan, but with a certain vulnerability to the temptation of over complication, finding myself wanting to make a renaissance of stew making, using preserved damsons, pilchards and cheese in the same 'creation'. I race about like some 'super' octopus with eight heads as well as eight limbs, all of which are unfortunately completely useless when the gas cylinder runs out! There's absolutely no way that I can cook my masterpiece on the open fire, simply because the fire is far and away the most artistically temperamental of us all.

Satisfied that my bleary-eyed patient upstairs is thoroughly nourished and has the comfort of a hot-water bottle and is coping okay, I race over to my van and go faster still to town, returning just as quickly with grapes, apples, oranges, lemons, two sorts of cabbage, a swede and a wickedly heavy gas cylinder. I still manage to catch the fire before it has gone completely out and I carefully load it up and coax it back to chattering and offering a bit of warmth once more. Cari seems quite happy upstairs sneezing merrily away. She has the benefit of fine minds, some decent-ish third rate fruit and the novelty of an on-the-hoof chef of sorts to keep her amused and, hopefully, nourished as well.

The logs that Dai brought are now proving to be a Godsend and are enabling me to concentrate my efforts in the home where they are needed most of all right now. Although, I must confess, some of my efforts are not met with the enthusiasm that I had hoped for... namely the 'damson stew'. It's true, damsons and pilchards may seem like uncomfortable bedfellows, and the odd damson stone here and there doesn't help, but I really find it 'interestingly' attractive, especially with garlic, shallots, potatoes, herbs, cayenne pepper and marmite. The only thing that stops Cari from confronting it with a relish to match my own, is her laughter that too soon becomes coughing and sneezing: thank God for beans on toast!

The cowshed becomes a hospital as Spencer and Robin succumb to the bug left by Griff. Strangely, Rowan hasn't as yet been affected, as neither have I; I can only put this down to the fact that he did actually eat some of my damson stew and even confessed to it being really 'quite nice' after all. The cats seem healthy enough and I never did hear a chicken sneeze so I can only assume that they too are well. It really is spitefully cold and, with having to spend so much time at the sink right now, I have refamiliarised myself with the honey-bee that's in a state of suspended animation on the net curtain. I just look on in wonderment; what kind of deep sleep is this right here before me? There's a mug of yesterday's tea on the window-sill and it's frozen solid overnight, an iced lolly with a spoon in it, that's how cold it is, and yet, that little bee remains alive despite being frozen. I simply don't understand; it is beyond me to even begin the process of imagining any single part of a bee's world, a bee's comprehension, a bee's frozen dreams. It's something that I'd dearly like to know, along with a billion other fascinating things, knowing that I must forever remain on the outside of such knowledge. When a boy sneezes in his bed and wipes his nose on the sheets, it serves to remind me that, whatever my longings, I have my own place amongst things and I'm stuck with it no matter how I might wish otherwise.

There's not much sense in sitting round the fire this evening, wasting firewood, paraffin and candles, so I adopt the hibernating instinct and yield along with the others, to the darkness. The extreme cold has prompted me into sorting out a few extra insulating layers in the form of two heavy ex-government coats and a tablecloth, plus a large knitted tea-cosy which I am wearing on my head to help save me from joining the honey-bee. Having never been a pyjama person, I am more than glad tonight to sleep in shirt, pants and socks, while Cari is more than well mummified in bedsocks, nightie and Aussie outback floppy hat. Even with these extra items, the air is cruelly cold upstairs, making me vow to nail another couple of layers of polythene to the windows and to getting another pile of newspapers for additional insulating layers on the beds.

We chat in the dark, trying to decide what to have for our Christmas dinner and also in working out what drinks we ought to have for any visitors that are likely to drop in. Our minds shift to the various parcels that Dan is storing for us and I suggest that I pick them up in the van sometime on Christmas Eve, at the same time giving Dan his present, Up until this point, the boys have all been chattering away like sparrows, but they've suddenly gone very quiet, and so we stop talking too, suspicious that our conversation is being listened to. In the new loud silence, the kitchen door suddenly rattles and Murphy growls out:- "Jimmy, Cari ... anybody about?" I call back down to him:- "We've all got colds ... we're all in bed, Murph; I wouldn't come too near if I were you, or you will catch it for Christmas!" He's glad to take my advice and walks round to the front and begins a blind bawling conversation through the polythene window. It's so loud that it sets Cari off into fits of laughter, forcing me to pull the blankets over her head to try and silence her. It really does seem a hilarious situation, me with a tea-cosy on my head and he, outside in the black cold, describing in detail a book that he's reading, 'Roof of the World', and none of us able to see the other, just these voices in the blind night sky. A crazy, primitive five minutes made worse by the infectious nature of Cari's stifled laughter which Murphy fails to see the funny side of, and so gives up and goes stomping back on his way without saying goodnight, thinking that he was being laughed at.

It's noticeably quieter at first light; nearly all the world's cockerels have had their necks pulled in readiness for the great Christmas Birthday Celebration feast, although our little bantam is still in fine fettle with the wide open air all to himself. We've decided on a really nutty Christmas dinner, although nothing quite as avant-garde as the damson stew! Cari is planning a rich mixed nut roast with finely chopped shallots, aromatic herbs and stuffing. There'll be roast potatoes and a whole variety of vegetables with a lovely rich fruity gravy, followed by a huge pudding, which she has made already and is being stored in the metal bin where it can't be easily got at. The cats and chickens will have their own special treats, which all means that we have to make one last shopping fling before what threatens to be a lengthy period of austerity descends upon us.

With the cowshed now established as a hospital, the final shopping effort is left for me to sort out and requires a strict shopping list to save me from the temptations and distractions of a street market with its persuasive Christmas-spirited traders. Cari would dearly like to accompany me on the trip as well but, with Rowan now going down with the bug, she settles for a place by the log fire instead, with an oven packed with potatoes and chestnuts to help keep the boys ticking over. We work out our list and I make two trips to the well and then load the hearth generously with logs so as to eliminate the need for anyone to go out into the bitter cold. I'm ready at last and so I set off, promising to be back within two hours. The town is crowded, it's like a disturbed ants' nest with everyone carrying something in a kind of frantic aimless panic and under a cacophony of carols, car-horns, banter and bronchitis. As I charge about doing my own ant impression, I come across Dan, scarecrowed on a corner in best cap and coat, a be-jewelled nose, that's redder and brighter than Rudolph's, and his glazed eyes streaming down his face. I get the distinct feeling that it isn't rum that's caused it, but I might possibly be wrong. He's with a straggle of old schoolmates, all of whom have cut themselves shaving, all wearing ties that never have their knots undone and bear the marks of years of dribbling and dripping. In passing, I tell him that I'll be over on Christmas Eve to collect the parcels, but I get no reply, just a huge beaming grin which is echoed in the faces of those statued next to him and I can tell that he most definitely hasn't got a cold!

I follow my shopping list religiously and, only when I have ticked everything off, do I relax a little and allow myself to indulge in additional items, such as three new hot- water bottles and a few other little bottles to redden our noses and warm our hearts. I also take full advantage of the abundance of vegetables, fruit and nuts that the jolly traders are now vocally anxious to get rid of at silly prices, so that they may pack up early and go home out of the biting wind. I really load up with bargains, all sorts of extravagantly silly surprises as I really do feel that I have gone down with a severe dose of Christmas fever!

It is as though I am a gatecrasher at a mouse party when I stagger in with a huge sack of sprouts over my shoulder and with heavily pregnant bags weighing me down almost to the point of bursting the veins in my arms. There's a gleeful cluster of jolly little red-nosed faces with firelight dancing in their bleary eyes, all seated over a whole land-fill of nut shells and chestnut skins; oh, how I love them, my little family all gathered like mice here in the hearth and with the good earth-smell of potatoes ripe in the oven. This moment is good enough reason for our coming here, and I am thankful for all the love that bonds us like rose-briars to a hawthorn hedge.

It is the eve of Christmas Eve and I've invested in a new battery to resurrect the radio and to permit a broader Christmas into our lives. The battery unfortunately won't last long, for Cari has a weakness, an insatiable fondness for having the BBC World service playing all night, and I must admit that it is only sleep that prevents me from listening to it. Nothing in broadcasting can compare with it, it's like having our own little window on the world and makes us feel better about ourselves.

The evening is mellowing in candlelight; the chickens are all secure in their barn home and the ancient door bolted against the vixen of night. Straggling snowflakes ride on the black wind, it's too cold for snow, that's what I learned from my old Granny Russell, wise and comforting before my excited eyes a thousand years ago. "'Taint going to snow, it's too cold for that … it's a night for the oven-plate." She referred to a metal shelf in the oven, not far short of being red-hot and wrapped dangerously in a badly singed cloth of sorts and placed in the bed. I remember having the oven-plate in my bed many times, but it was damned uncomfortable in the morning when it was cold and after a restless sleep had kicked the cloth covering from it, baring a wicked piece of cold hard iron that hurt when it was accidentally kicked. There are three little surprises for the boys when they retire to their sick-beds; three new hot water bottles that I've sneaked in during 'Take 3' of van Gogh's 'Potato Eaters'. I hear their gleeful expression when they discover them and I feel a warm glow inside, knowing that my boys are snug and happy and won't be stubbing their toes on a piece of cold, nasty metal in the morning.

We're just about to retire to bed when a welly kicks the door; I know that it isn't burglars and that only one other person around here wears wellies ... old Dan; all the rest wear boots. Sure enough, a somewhat repaired Dan is standing there in the stray-flaked dark, bearing forth great treasure in his arms, a bottle-shaped paper covered item and a lumpy carrier bag. He looks a picture of Christmas, watery eyes, snotty nose and silver whiskers that have grown since his clumsy confrontation with a razor earlier this morning. Loneliness has brought him over and we are glad to have him around a revived blaze and a new candle. The cats are clamouring around him having sneaked in with him and somehow seeming to know that it's Christmas. I christen the bottled stuff which I bought earlier and the three of us clink glasses and wish each other a Merry Christmas. I have to put my finger to my lips when I whisper to him that I'll pop over tomorrow evening to collect our stuff, and he nods to show that he's heard me this time. At this point, Sorrel jumps up onto his knee, the friendliest gesture we've ever seen her make; more surprisingly is the fact that Dan is stroking her without being aware of it; I look at Cari, it's like looking into a mirror. We soon get the toast broadcasting its wonderful voice upon the darkened world, requiring nothing but its simple self and butter; nothing could be so simple or more delicious than toast done wild on a fork before an even wilder fire.

I give Dan his own mysterious bottle-shaped present from Jamaica and his face glows brighter than the birch burning on the fire. "Damn! How many Father Christmas's are there? I thought I was the only one tonight!" We all have a good laugh, and the thought crosses my mind that he's going to be alone over

Christmas, and so I extend an invitation for him to join us on Christmas Day, eat with us and enjoy himself, but he surprises us when he says that Meg and Murphy have also invited him and that he's had to turn them down too because he's going to spend Christmas where he's always gone in the past. A farm along the valley which he seldom refers to, yet is important enough for him and his dog to go there each time. He volunteers no other details... 'could be family, nobody seems to know: there's more to Dan than meets the eye.

Sour-puss Sorrel appears to have found a pal for life and is playing her cards to perfection, lying luxuriously along the length of Dan's thigh and gripping his knee with measured squeezes, just a fraction short of being painful, keeping him constantly aware of her existence. "Nice little cat," he comments, then to the cat adds, "... ain't you a nice little cat, ay." "She's the one I said you could have... she seems to like you, Dan," I say quietly, trying not to overdo it. "'Er's a bit thin... doesn't he feed you, little cat?" he jokes as the cat goes into dribbling ecstasies over the attention she is getting. "A few of those pet mice of yours would soon fatten her up I daresay, although she's always been a bit on the lean side, but she certainly eats well enough... too well sometimes." I manage to check myself just in time, avoiding use of the words, 'glutton', 'greedy', 'thief' and 'menace'. "I'd need to put her in a bag or summat... it would have to be after Christmas when I gets back, like," he says thoughtfully, seeming to suggest that he's happy about having her. "Don't you worry about a thing," I hasten to add, "...we'll bring her over in a basket when we see that you're back." I say no more for fear of him changing his mind, and so I top-up his glass and toss another couple of logs onto the fire for good measure, keeping my fingers crossed that she doesn't go and spoil it all by puking down his leg or disastrously breaking wind and fouling his trousers.

Eventually, he gets round to his favourite pastime... gossip! I can tell it's coming, his entire demeanour has changed; "I can see that your pal Murphy is becoming a capitalist... 'building great big dog-pens he is at the back of Meg's place, just where you had your caravan. "Gonna breed pedigree dogs he reckons... says there's more money in it; won't be so quiet and peaceful round here no more, that's for sure!" He allows no time for any response and moves quickly on to the next bit: "Owd Thomas at 'Thimble' reckoned he's seen Christ again... come to fetch him this time, so he stayed in bed for three days waitin'. Nearly killed his missus with worry... 'er was in a heck of a state when I saw her, she got the doctor out to look at him, 'said there was nowt wrong with him... silly owd bugger!" He's in his element and goes grinding on with a comprehensive up-date on every unfortunate inhabitant of the area, showing no favouritism and dealing with each of them equally, making me realise that it was curiosity, rather than loneliness, that brought him over, when he already knew from other gossip that our house was full of colds.

I see him back over to his place, his legs seem to be going in different directions from where he wants to go and the ground has a slippery covering of snow making everywhere seem like thin daylight, heightened when the moon breaks through the racing clouds. I try to keep him on a tight rein, but it's like trying to hold a mad carthorse in keeping him on his feet, especially on our way down the hill to the marsh meadow. Several times we are both in a heap and laughing our heads off. It's a miracle that his Christmas present doesn't get smashed and I am more than glad when we eventually reach the lane where the virgin snow in the strong moonlight has not been trodden on by anything until this moment. I leave him under his sycamore tree and retrace our tell-tale tracks back to the cowshed, double-checking that the barn is securely fastened against marauding foxes that are abroad now, hungry and sniffing for anything that can be translated into food.

Christmas Eve: the wind has changed direction and is blowing strongly from the west bringing dark clouds racing and sleetly rain that hurts as it cuts sideways into my face. Any hopes of a white Christmas have gone out of the window and, staying indoors seems like a good idea. I had hoped to make a sledge for the boys today, using the splintery wood that I've saved from the roof, but there's no real urgency now that the snow has gone and it means that I can instead make a start on sawing some of the wood from the fallen ash tree higher up the valley. The amount of wood that we're going through is really quite staggering and, with the boys not being at school and with the house full of colds, the fire has to be kept going the whole time. It's a never-ending job, but at least, ceaselessly sawing wood is actually keeping me warm, so I mustn't complain.

My bushman saw has now seen so much activity that it has finally given up on me; the blade would now find even butter difficult to cut through, so I give her a Christmas present, a lovely new blade which should see me into the new year. It proves to be a timely move and I work slavishly sawing a whole mountain of logs and making many back-breaking journeys back to the barn with the wheelbarrow laden with the fruits of my labouring. By the time I'm finished, there is a distinct deep trail which the wheelbarrow has left and I'm literally soaked through to the skin and acutely aware of a soreness at the back of my nose and throat, telling me that damson stew hasn't saved me from the dreaded drey-poker's lousy bug!

Darkness comes down prematurely and the freezing rain is peppering the polythene; on the radio, carols are playing and candles are all flickering in the icy draughts. Cari has gallantly produced a sturdy meal from the abundance of stuff that I salvaged from the street market yesterday, using up the last of the drinking water in the process and obliging me to go off to the well in the inhospitably filthy wet dark. In my worsening shivering wet state, it's not a pleasant job to have to do, but one that has to be done nevertheless, and so I take the biggest of our water-carriers and go, head down, through the blind mud, feeling my way along the barbed wire fence to the well. A whole host of better moments cross my mind as I delve my jug into the invisible icy water and I laboriously fill the container to overflowing, then struggle back with it over the perilous ground, hoping that this may last us until Christmas day. It's a job that I am more than glad to have out of the way, one which I feel deserves a celebratory pot of tea to help feed some warmth and spirit back into me. I give Cari a wink as I say that I've just remembered that I've got to get petrol and must go off to the garage, after I've had my cup of tea. I give her an extra nudge to help her understand that I'm trying to tell her something, then it clicks and she says, "Oh, yes; petrol of course, they'll be shut over Christmas." She's got the message and gives me a return nudge; our secret is safe.

I'm anxious to get out of my wet clothing, so the quicker I get started, the sooner I'll be finished and only then can we begin the delicate part which requires that all of the boys are genuinely sound asleep while we fill stockings and arrange presents around the tree. First however, I have to chance my luck once more with Dan's dog, and so I have decided it best to really let him know that I've arrived by peeping my horn and forcing him to come out and hear my request for him to lock the devilish thing away, somewhere safe. I'm in luck, the animal is already locked up for the night and so we are able to load the van without menace and even have time for a seasonal slug of Captain Morgan mixed with Stone's Ginger Wine. I feel it burning as it goes down, sizzling and taking my breath away, making my eyes water; Dan swigs his as though it were water; a stray spark is all it would take and I'd swear he'd explode! I resist his attempts to top me up and explain to him that we have a very busy and difficult night ahead. He pours himself another half jam-jar of the stuff and settles down contentedly amongst his mice and waves me off into the dirty night. I give him a final jolly blast on my horn and head back home with my wipers working flat-out.

I have to make three trips across the marsh. It really is a pitch-black night, I can't see a hand in front of me and the ground is now very muddy to make things even more hazardous. I rely on memory alone to get me over the marsh to the gap in the hedge at the foot of the hill, how I miss the stars to guide me on this night of all nights. It's the most inhospitable Christmas Eve that I've ever known; a strong wind is blowing a wall of ice-cold water from the west, no reindeer is going to be happy with this tonight and Santa Claus is going to have a difficult job keeping them happy. It's a huge relief and comfort to see the dim rectangle of light in the cowshed window each time I reach the hilltop and skate my way down to the caravan where I am temporarily storing the rain-drenched parcels. I leave the biggest one till the end, it's for Robin and is really quite heavy and won't fit into the caravan and has to be placed quietly in the shed where the potatoes are stored.

At long last I can peel off my wet clothes and hang them to dry by the fire, noting with some concern the steam billowing from them. In somewhat drier clothes, I join Cari in the firelight, her cold seems to be leveling out and easing while mine is just about to start. She has filled all the stockings with treasures and has sensibly hidden them until we creep quietly to bed. I can now start to bring in the parcels from the caravan; they're sadly rather soggy and I've not had an opportunity to check that the labels and wrappings are still intact. After a few trips back and forth there is a considerable pile of somewhat sad looking bedraggled boxes around the Christmas tree, but it really does feel exciting and worthwhile at long last, knowing that we have made it and that our darling boys are deep in their dreams, having not been awakened by our rustling sounds and the constant clatter of comings and goings. If Father Christmas hasn't caught pneumonia tonight, he's the luckiest non-existent person ever and I'm going to have to be careful myself!

Seeing the cats there sitting smug, cute and lovely by the fire, I realise that it will be disastrous to allow them to stay in where they will certainly rummage through the presents and knock things crashing to the ground; so I must feed them in the caravan and just hope they won't scratch and tear their way back in during the night. I make sure to give them extra food and then lock-up for the night, leaving a night-light burning in a jam jar by the dying fire and another in the lean-to kitchen. We've done all that we can do, and so, very quietly Cari places the lumpy stockings on the beds and we tip-toe up the stairs to Christmas... and the BBC World Service!

There is a glittering sweetness of incredible clarity, crisp and rippling, piercingly sharp, while Christmas morning is still in mourning, dark and dull as an old cathedral roof around us. I rub my eyes, my teacosy still in place keeping my head warm and the radio still faintly doing its stuff. I lean over my snoring spouse and fumble about trying to find the 'off' switch, to save the battery and enabling me to hear more clearly the exquisite sound that has awakened me. There it is again, a robin announcing his ownership of the hedge beside the caravan; he hasn't even waited for daylight to stake his claim. I lie back listening to this miracle, then ... "Happy Christmas, Cari and Jimmy!" Rowan's squeaky voice arises from the darkness as his tender awakening becomes a full-blooded remembering that this is Christmas day! I hear him fumbling and calling to wake the others up. "He's been! Good old Santa!"

I slip quietly out of bed, slide into my freezing cold trousers, then grope my way down the stairs. "Sshhh...! Not so loud. Happy Christmas boys!" I grope in the dark and manage to light a candle, then go feeling for the kindling-wood that I keep with my indoor log reserve and, suddenly, my feet are soaking wet. I know in a sickening instance that the rain has come through the wall yet again, continuing to ignore the fact that it has been treated with several coats of waterproofing solution. My heart sinks, the presents will all have been affected and I am forced into putting the pressure-lamp into use so that I may asses the damage before the world awakens. Not abandoning my original plan, I start the fire and get the kettle hanging over the flames; in the background I can hear the boys all excitedly babbling away, munching chocolates and crunching apples while I confront the damage caused by a confounded westerly wind! As carefully and as silently as I can, I do my best to ease the presents out from the water, hopeful that only the wrappings will have been affected. This done and the fire topped up with logs, I fumble my way into the lean-to for the mop-bucket and mop, then set about the dreary business of drying the place out, while the dawn robin is still having something to say, out there in the dark.

My reason for getting up as silently as I could, was for to make cups of tea for everyone, followed by a breakfast in bed with boiled eggs and hot toast. My plans have been somewhat set back by this unexpected flood, but I'm still cussedly trying to get back on course before anyone realises that we've got a problem. I'm so thankful that the mop-bucket is made of plastic and doesn't clatter like a metal one would, so I can work fast in mopping-up the worst of the wet, conveniently hiding behind the din that the boys are making. When I step outside to empty the mop-bucket, the robin is singing just a few paces away in the damson tree and I hear the cats come scrabbling through the hole in the caravan floor and come running to greet me. The water-tub is overflowing, a luxury too much right now, then our little bantam-cock emerges through a hole in the barn roof and immediately flames up into the black sky, summoning the daylight to appear.

It's Christmas morning and there's a lull in the rain; the air is clear and clean to breath and I stand for a little while just drinking it like champagne, shivering but feeling the beautiful simplicity of everything about me. The cats rush in with their muddy paws leaving a trail to the hearth, where the kettle is up to full steam and the sparks are spitting and crackling, showing the wretched wetness who's really the boss around here!

It's cups of tea all round; little new torches flash their beams searchingly, cats move into boys' beds and Robin spills his tea as a result of Sorrel trying to steal his Mars bar. This single fairly normal act makes me think better of providing breakfast in bed for the boys, instead I shall wait for the daylight and we'll sit around the table and the cats will have to go out and take some exercise. This resolved, I make the exception of a breakfast in bed for Cari, plus a secret little present that I've kept hidden, sometimes in a hole in the wall and now in my rucksack pocket in the bedroom. It's while I'm grovelling in the dark amongst seemingly hundreds of jars of jam and ranks of home-made wines, that I fire off my first of a million musket-shot sneezes; the horrid reality has finally registered on my brain that I have got the same filthy cold that everyone else has got. Fortunately, I made provision for such an eventuality by buying toilet rolls in bulk and we've still got about a dozen rolls remaining, so barring an epidemic of dysentery, we shall be 'covered' until I can get out to the shops again.

Daylight comes, evolved from the dawning; the great cycle goes on repeating. Nobody notices flooded floors or running noses; it's Christmas morning as Cari is coping with a perfectly golden yolk dribbling, an egg that was laid only yesterday by one of our white ex-convicts. She munches the burnt toast-fingers, whilst nervously unwrapping the small gift, a little thing which I bought for her when I was working away in television ... a Swiss wrist-watch, something I've always wanted to buy for her. She gasps ... her heavy cold cured at a stroke as she stares unbelievingly at this tiny golden masterpiece before her eyes. Her gasps collapse into floods of tears and she clings on to me and soaks my shirt thoroughly. Who cares about a little bit of damp!

A joyous bedlam rages about the place; it's anarchy with fighting, farting, crying and sneezing; our own kind of private tornado, one that can be kept within the bounds of our home. All the wrapping paper is now on the floor, soaking up the wet, not that it can absorb any more but because it looks prettier. There are 'Legos', 'Meccanos', a steam engine, dangerously puffing across the floor at speeds hitherto unknown to steam, a Christmas tree sent flying by a Dumper-truck with Robin at the pedals, jig-saws that require patience when there is none, dice being thrown ...and thrown, riots of laughter, riots that require physical intervention. You name it, we've got the whole Christmas Catastrophe!

White Wilderness

The uncouth westerly continues to bleed the sky dry. It is wearisome, but by dusk on the 27th, the last of the empty cloudskins have blown away leaving a tougher brute from the north to start pulling in the slack and making the waterlogged earth its prisoner, and by dark, setting all heaven's candles to flicker and owls to grieve deep in the woods. An even nastier cousin in the east is now muscling in on the act and has rasped and filed the wind down to a scythe and has sent it to slash down everything in its path. It is so bitingly cold that the water I fetch actually comes into the house to freeze. It remains perfectly unfrozen in the well for some strange reason, but has to be broken with a hammer to get it into the kettle for our first warming cup of tea in the morning. Anything that makes mud turn solid is a luxury while it lasts and we are thankful for it, regardless of our frozen fingers and toes, what's more, it seems to be assisting us in getting rid of our lousy head colds.

It is in the very early hours of the 28th that I am awakened by the awareness of something cold and wet in the air. There's a thin fluting turbulent whine of wind screeching from a hundred newly revealed holes between the tin roof and wall, it's a sound that I've never heard before, sinister and threatening and it awakens me still further; something's wrong. All around me there is oblivious heavy slobbering breathing throughout the total darkness. I can faintly hear the muffled, off-tune, 'BBC World Service' terminally squeaking, unable to compete with the immediate howling of the terrible east wind that's wetting me. I attempt to sit upright, only to discover that there's a very heavy weight bearing down upon the bed, forcing me into trying to struggle out from it only to find that my feet have sunk into several inches of snow. The bed is almost completely buried; little wonder that the blankets weigh a ton. Somewhere buried beneath the snow is my torch and this is really not the most ideal of times to discover that, in order to find a torch,

I need a torch!

Clearly my bed-positioning skills, in conjunction with my rheumatics weather forecasting system have failed me on this occasion and I am at a loss to know precisely where my torch is buried; beneath a snowdrift would never be the sort of place I'd choose, that's for sure. I find it by memory alone and, grim and feeble as its dying effort to assist me is, it still manages to shock me rigid with the dimly visible reality of this white nightmare that has overtaken us.

It is a most mind-blowing realisation, made suddenly worse by remembering that my trousers are folded up somewhere underneath it. Clearly this is a situation that requires my urgent action, even without trousers! I must move the bed further across the room, but I can't do this until I have first found my perilous way downstairs and begun the tiresome ritual of getting the paraffin pressure lamp working. Before risking my neck down the steep stairs, an initial attempt to awaken Cari fails miserably and, refusing to part company with sleep, she dispatches me without ceremony. Trouserless I descend the slippery snow covered steps and go fumbling my way amongst deeply sleeping boys in my blind and desperate search for the music of matches rattling and to see the first frail flower of candlelight to comfort me with the power of sight once more. This is no time to be without trousers and the thought now pressing on my brain is that of having to go outside and into the barn in search of wood to combat this brutally cold hell of an awakening. Everything needs doing first; my priorities are all jumbled up in an animated ugly brawl.

The paraffin lamp-light is my only friend, one which I take for granted; I know all too painfully well that I could not invent this device without the assistance of the timeless journeyings of my ancestral fellow mankind. The candles too I similarly accept without question, as I do the matches, making me realise just how completely useless not only have I become, but an entire civilization as well and that, two o'clock in the morning in the middle of a blizzard from the east, is a very bad time to be discovering knowledge of this most revealing kind.

Armed with this hi-tech iron-age gadget and rather more than half naked, I try to make my next priority that of venturing outside into the screeching wind and the most evil scythe-blade of any winter that I have experienced. I open the middle door that leads into the kitchen and I can't believe what confronts my astounded eyes; a solid wall of snow is completely blocking my path. Somehow, the outside door has burst open and there's a howling gale just piling and driving more and more snow in a chest-high drift right across the length of the room. There's nothing, absolutely nothing, I can do to alleviate the situation, my shovel and spade are both out there in the shed... goodness only knows where the cats are.

Quick thinking doesn't so readily avail itself when it is discovered that the head has somehow got itself stuck up a Polar Bear's bum! One thing is slowly getting through to me however ... light the fire! A second revealing thought gets through ... what with? I have to burn something... anything; meanwhile Cari is becoming slowly but surely buried up there under the old swallows nests. I must rescue her, even at the risk of these being grounds for divorce. Once more it is comforting to see that the boys' room hasn't been affected, apart from the odd stray flake that's landing on Robin's bed, but he's buried away like a dormouse, safe and snug in hot hibernating dreams. I scrape the fresh snow from the steps of the stairs with the palm of my hand and proceed by lamplight and am met with the alarming picture of what has hit us. The snow is howling in like confetti and the bed is just a white lump in the midst of it, with a blissfully unaware dreamer dreaming of summers past, laughter and lilacs in flower; lovely things which I'm just about to rudely change.

If I can drag the bed about five paces it will be safe... this is a crisis and I can't stand on ceremony over the consequences of bawling Cari back into the real world, bless her. Her initial response is to blame me, I even want to join her into putting the entire blame on myself, but it isn't easy getting her out of bed and helping me to shift it across to the other end of the room. It should only take a couple of minutes and when I've removed the top covers that have a level three inches of snow compacted on them, she can go back to her dream, although by now I daresay it's been blasted over the borders into England!

It's whilst we are grappling with the problem that an idea suddenly hits me as I am inspired by the sight of the 4x2 ancient crossbeams that no longer support a bedroom ceiling; the bad news is that my bushman saw is in the barn, making me realise that I'm still a million miles from having a fire despite so fortuitously stumbling on the wood to fuel it. What a cruel time to learn that I should have kept so vital a piece of equipment here in the house! Not to be outdone by circumstances, I start emptying my old stored boxes of art materials and, to my great surprise and delight, come across a very old carpentry saw that Dad gave me years ago; it is blunt and rusty, but it is about to be put back into use whether it likes it or not, as too is the claw-hammer that crashes noisily onto the floor... I'm back in business!

Unlike the others, I don't have the benefit of blankets to warm my trembling goose-pimpled runner's legs, activity is all that I have to help me from turning solid in this spontaneous new ice-age; but it hadn't reckoned on me, I thrive on adversity and I'm getting to enjoy each minute, even with Cari currently brushing up on 'alternative' language and whacking me with the occasional snowball on the back of my neck. Hundred year old wood-dust that has passed through the digestive systems of billions of woodworms comes dusting down, triggering fresh sneezing fits as I go 'caveman' up in the roof. Hysterical yells of... "You'll have the whole roof coming down on us!" and... "He's gone completely mad!"... all to no avail, I know what I must do and I'm doing it right now!

I light the fire and bring the radio down to dry out beside it, learning in the process that here in the U.K. it's shortly before 3a.m., and that's it's daytime and blistering hot in Australia where ex-patriot Brits are not only finding that the sun rapidly ages and cancers the skin, but also that sharks not blessed with knowledge or niceties of the 'fourth R', are biting the bums off bathers only yards from the beaches... 'sure sounds like paradise out there!

Our water-carrier is buried somewhere beneath the deepening snowdrift in the lean-to and the snow isn't therefore going to like what I'm now going to be forced into doing to it because I'm about to boil a few kettles of it and revive the cold hot water-bottles in a kind of revenge for what it has done to us; then I shall try making a pot of Keemun tea with the stuff. I retrieve my trousers and hang them to dry in front of the fire... this is the life! It seems so strange seeing the deep track that I've trodden through the snow to the kitchen cupboard; if only I could have afforded to have kept a film in my camera and had an electronic flash to record this, but I have to remind myself that a film is the equivalent of about a dozen tins of beans and there are other variations on this line of thought which keeps photography well down in the pecking order of things, along with my painting; staying alive is all that matters.

Pleasantly surprising and with 'Carnation' condensed milk, the tea made from snow is 'drinkable' and just about exceeds my expectations. Somewhat a human guinea-pig, I test it out on myself before daring to take Cari a cup of it. It's while in the midst of this biological experiment that I remember that a five-foot wall of sculpted solid snow separates the house from the lavatory in the pigsty and that any resulting call of nature will prove to be a further catastrophe. I have no choice, I've got to get a channel through to the loo somehow ... there's no peace for the wicked! A piddling little brass shovel in the hearth is all I have to confront this great engineering project, it isn't much bigger than a dessert spoon, but at least I've got my trousers back on, not dry by any means but hot and I can cope with that. The shovel is a complete waste of time, better by far is the boys' new monopoly board, its shifts twenty times as much snow in one swipe as the ridiculous shovel did, but a metal tea-tray is even better, wow! Eat your heart out Isambard Kingdom Brunel!

Our little hibernating honey bee is still locked in fathoms of bee dreams up on the lace curtain, just beyond the reach of the blizzard; the cats are somewhere else, either in the spud-shed or in the caravan. I know where the chickens and bantams are and I don't envy them one little bit because there are almost as many holes as there are slates on the barn roof, I just hope that they have had the sense to modify their old roosting preferences and to have shifted accordingly.

I concentrate my efforts on clearing the kitchen of snow, at least things should improve somewhat once I've managed to free the door and fasten it securely, I shall have the luxury of a carrier full of frozen well-water too because it's buried somewhere beneath this driving white stuff. It amazes me just how fierce is the wind that's piling it in so relentlessly and I have to work at a frantic pace even to gain the slightest advantage over it; but I don't slacken any and I eventually manage to force the door closed against the solid white wall and hear the satisfying click of the latch holding firm.

I incur the wrath of Cari once more when I am compelled by a wood shortage to return up into the roof to grapple with another two beams. I don't feel at all comfortable now that my trousers have started to freeze to my body and I can far more easily tolerate abuse and the odd snowball than I can the wretchedness of losing my precious body heat. Any lurking notion that I'm doing this for fun is really way off the mark as the daylight will prove once it has eventually dared to show itself.

With my replenished wood supply, I spend the next two hours in relative calm huddled on the settle, bare-legged in front of a very crackly fire, the crackles seeming to come from the long dead woodworm bodies which shower me with their sparks whenever they explode. I can hear the blizzard raging outside where there isn't a single owl that's prepared to comment on what's happening and I daresay the foxes too are thinking it wiser to stay put where they are. Out there, there are a thousand little somewheres where tiny birds are perishing as I indulge in the decadent luxury of writing poetry whilst waiting for my clothes to dry and while the candle inches slowly down inside the jar.

Today I really will make the boys a sledge, what's more we'll make it fly down the steepest hillsides and show the snow who's boss. It's also a day for a big saucepan of stew and a working oven that smells like heaven and begs to please us. I get up from time to time and peep into the lean-to just to make sure that the door hasn't burst open again, glad to find that the five foot drift outside is now protecting it from the wind, reminding me at the same time that I've yet to clear a way through to the pigsty and across past the spud-shed to the barn, or our creatures will surely starve.

I make everyone a welcome cup of tea at daybreak and check to see that the snow in the bedroom hasn't been tempted into thawing as a result of any stray heat from my fire. No such luck; it's well and truly in the grip of winter up there in the bedroom and, as I've said before, the only place that's warm here is up on top of the chimney, as any jackdaw will testify!

Sight of the snow, more particularly the formidable mountain of it outside the kitchen door, brings screams of excitement. The boys have never seen anything like this before and they go skipping and dancing to find warm clothes, anxious to get out there amongst it; I know all too well that for some, it is likely to end in tears. Cari is a brand new person, no relation whatsoever to the one she was earlier and really cannot believe what she has fully awakened to, laughing at all the palaver of the early hours as though it were part of a weird dream and now becoming a child herself in her eagerness to go out and play in the stuff along with the boys. The tea tray is brilliant and I carve out huge cubes of snow, ideal for making an igloo. We soon have a pathway to the lavatory which, apart from that which has fallen through a hole in the roof, has been miraculously spared by some fluke of shelter. I then hack a passage through to the barn, passing the spud-shed on my way where, to our great relief and pleasure, find the cats all snuggled cosily inside an old Channel Islands tomato box, purring away like distant motorbikes. Inside the barn hardly a thing remains visible, snow is plastered everywhere... then two or three lumps of it start to shuffle about and I can hear the faint grieving noises that sound more like complaints than they do greetings. I feed them generously, more relieved than ever to find them still alive and clucking.

At last the snow has ceased, but the easterly wind is not letting go despite it now permitting the sun to rise up above the wood and to blind us with more glowing light than we have ever known; God, how beautiful the world looks!

A gradual calm settles over us as the white world becomes accepted as being normal. I make the sledge that I promised, using the left over wood from the roof. It's a bit on the splintery side but will soon smooth out with all the use it's about to be put to as the boys all converge on the hilltop in excited anticipation of imprinting their presence upon the blinding white fallen weather.

The day, yet young and tender, is but an empty canvas before Brueghel the painter and also Lowry the painter and, as minutes gather into hours, other little figures are painted on to the masterpiece; the farm gang, Curly Jenkins, several dogs, Dan, Cari, myself and many others I've never seen. So many arses are polishing the white hillside into marble. Our little sledge is the only sledge here gracing this gradient, all others are either polythene fertilizer bags or bits of corrugated iron, while some go whooshing away simply on their rears, including Hugh who, unbeknown to us has recently broken his leg and has appeared with it in plaster and is hobbling on crutches. He's here doing ninety on nothing but the cheeks of his backside, heavily plastered leg in the air, Jack Russell in pursuit to retrieve and shake to death his greasy cap. Robin has managed to get himself a nose-bleed and has lost a front tooth and has somehow parted company with one of his wellies and the umpteen socks that were contained inside it; but he is still there in the thick of it and being competitive despite a fit of crying at having missed out on the tooth-fairy. I've never heard a hillside ring so joyously as this one here... it's wonderful.

Meg and Murphy appear quite late in the day when the hillside has been scarred beyond use and its little painted figures all dispersed to hidden places where ravenous appetites are attended to in an agricultural fashion and where etiquette counts for nothing. We sit around the wood fire, babbling like little brooks, all of us grateful that out of such adversity, flowering moments glow like constellations in the night sky, showing us that we're not alone, not ever alone, no matter what.

Crunchtime

The New Year comes like another heavy footfall, a great clomping sound which resonates fadingly for twelve months before the other foot hits the ground with its nuclear explosion. I sometimes wish that there were no measures and we could simply be as old or as young as we felt. We make this rod for our backs and go on for some masochistic reason to torment ourselves with constant reminders of the most fearful conclusions; a most perplexing species to be sure and, more than likely as a result of ignorance rather than design. Instead of the brains being at the front of the engine, we somehow always manage to keep them hidden away in one of the trucks that are part of the convoy, wiser after the event, but sadly, not in a sustaining remembered way. One day follows another in relentless procession; it's only man that puts markers and measures upon realising the cyclical nature of things and their base potential as a device for measuring, thus elevating his species from a ponderous guesser to that of a slick measurer.

The first days of January are stark and grim, successive frosts have hardened the snow, giving it a brittle crust while the roaming fieldfares and redwings have distinctly thinned out the scarlet haws in keeping themselves alive. Whilst out walking the snowy fields, we disturb a hare from its sheltered form in the snow and it explodes away in a frightened panic, into the blinding sunlight and out of sight over the brow, leaving a spectral dust of glittering snow suspended in the air for a precious second before shimmering back down to the dazzling white carpet; what is our hardship compared to his? Fox-tracks crisscross the field, giving a clue to the nature of the hare's grim existence, the fox's too; they all have to eat and keep warm somehow.

When we follow the hare's tracks to the top of the hill, there is no sign of the hare, it has simply melted away; what I do see however, is a horrid sight that suddenly makes me feel sick. Gareth has started to rip out the old hedgerow and there's a huge mountain of partially burned roots and branches and a horrible long scar with the soil all bleeding out onto the snow. I can't believe what I'm seeing, a lovely hedge here being murdered, its dog-roses and honeysuckle, elders, hazels and haws all slain in their sleep, little hibernating mice in old birds nests unable to avoid sudden cremation. The rosehip syrup, which Cari made, came entirely from this very hedge uprooted here before us, making it an even greater treasure now. We go on to discover that all the gorse and broom bushes on the steep hillside by Dan's place have also been burned out of existence. Never again to be the yellow hill, never again to have yellow hammers nesting there or rabbit burrows gracing its slope and providing both fox and buzzard with the occasional meal. We wander back in subdued silence with poignant images of the old bird nests feeling like raw wounds and the new bareness getting into us. Where the hedge still stands, I remove a few old stakes from it, glad to make use of these last late offerings and I carry them back to help warm us back to life.

I am invited to attend an interview at Hereford Art College and this focuses my mind somewhat, especially so when I realise that I don't possess a single item of smart clothing. A pink brushed cotton suit which had been in vogue back in the sixties fell victim to chronic mildew and possible mushroom cultivation in the damp caravan, leaving me with only ex-government heavy duty stuff and with steel toe-capped wellies and running shoes being my only footwear. I don't have money enough to address the problem, hence my reason for applying for the job. Before the thaw sets in, I wash piles of my old clothes in the desperate hope of surprising myself with an unimagined new wardrobe. Alas, there are no such miracles and I am obliged to settle for a pair of pillar-box red corduroy trousers, threadbare at the knees and with the crotch worn out, topped with a green cord coat which has very large bright red buttons stolen from Spencer's old oilskin mac. There's a rip all across the back of this garment and it has obviously been crudely stitched in a hurried repair job. It's amazing what a heavy polo-neck jumper can do in this situation, alleviating the need for a shirt and tie at a stroke. The problem is more or less solved now, my running shoes will complete the job and make it all seem like a conscious dress strategy and not a poor man's attempt to look smart.

The thaw is rapid and heavy rain is once more turning the land around into a swamp. It feels much colder now that the dampness has been released by the frost; everywhere is dark now that the snow has gone and we're back with the problem of having no place to dry the washing and an ever-growing pile of mud-spattered items is in need of urgent attention.

I manage to scrape together a portfolio of work, mostly the stuff which I did with my students back at Plymouth, and topped-up with various pieces of my television artwork; it all looks surprisingly impressive; all I have to do now is to point the van in the direction of Hereford and go! I feel very nervous, a bit like a lamb to the slaughter, dressed like a clown, penniless, starving and without a clue as to where the Art College is. Somehow I manage to find it and squeeze my grubby little van in amongst smart, highly polished specimens, hoping like fury that I'm not being watched.

My ordeal is soon over; so impressed is the principal that I am not only offered the post but am introduced to a group of about twenty students and asked to spend the remainder of the day with them getting to know one another. This is most unexpected and somewhat unusual and the time simply dissolves. I find myself being dragged to a pub where I am introduced to other lecturers in 'rural' mode, - chunk of bread, wedge of cheese and a pint. Inside me there is a growing pandemonium of confusion, this is the very thing that I had previously escaped from; I don't need a job, I just need some money, that's all. I know that my three days a week here are going to provide Cari with a load of problems back at the cowshed and I feel like a traitor, torn and tattered by hard reality. It's okay having dreams, but dreams are always boss and can easily turn into nightmares... that's the nature of dreams. I see so many hopeful faces so plainly showing that they want me to become the wind in their flagging sails and I don't want to let them down.

It all seems so unreal as I wend my way back across the Radnor hills. A bare landscape dotted with the occasional deathly dwelling place that radiates the most ghostly loneliness imaginable. Seeing the cowshed with smoke staining from the chimney is the best sight I could possibly see and I race to it wearing my heart on my sleeve, a 'smart' man doing close on a ton over the marsh, gladder than ever to be back home.

The thaw expires and icicles return like a Norseman invasion; the boys are back at school being indoctrinated, education being something that comes too late to be of any practical use. It's the fourth 'R' that is the problem here in the valley, it dominates as though heaven and hell were both little opposing villages that footballed and darted against each other with the result always rigged so that hell came out the loser. Not a single teacher knows that there are otters here in the brook and that there are firecrests as well as goldcrests in these marvellous towering evergreens: grim, grey people manufacturing grim grey people.

At the point where our money eventually runs out, I receive a small back-dated pay award from a previous job. It isn't much, less than thirty pounds in fact, but it will help put vital food back into the cupboard until I get my first wages from the Hereford job. I also make a trip to see the bank manager explaining my predicament and being allowed a small overdraft to help me buy petrol. We really are right up against the limit and I set about my lecturing job with energy and grim determination, trying not to think of the distance involved and all the time lost each day in travelling. It's dark when I set out in the morning and it's dark again when I return in the evening, but I keep telling myself that three days a week is going to be okay. I shall just have to work harder on the other four in making sure that Cari isn't forced into becoming a muscle-bound mad axe-woman!

Winter never strays far from being a very nasty affair and, over a three-week period, I encounter blizzard, flood, fog, gale, driving rain and worst of all, black ice! I have negotiated my safe passage through deep Radnor snow and I am relieved at last to be safely down from the snowline, crossing over the Herefordshire border into Bulmer's cider country, a longish flat approach road where something nasty awaits me. Suddenly and without warning, the van does it's own thing and goes lurching into an uncontrollable spin, which rapidly becomes a blind, mad ballet: I'm careering down this icy road in crazy circles and there's absolutely nothing I can do. Over my back axle I have positioned a very heavy sack of gravel to help provide grip, but all grip has gone and my world is an accelerating, blind blur, culminating in a fearful and deafening crunching sound, instant pain and the sack of gravel like a blast from a cannon hitting the passenger seat and crushing it under the dashboard as though it were soft putty. I am instantaneously wedged with my knees crushed and my forehead gashed as a result of my seat belt not locking properly on impact. Blood is pouring off the end of my nose and is smarting in my eyes and I am frighteningly aware too that my knees are bleeding. The realisation when it comes, that, had the sack of gravel hit my seat, it would have broken my back, scares the living hell out of me. I'm in a state of utter shock, my van is a wreck, crumpled and steaming in an embrace with a very sturdy, brand new telegraph pole.

A fellow motorist somehow contrives to pull up on the wide verge and comes running to my aid, helping me out and checking me over before going on his way assuring me that help will soon be on it's way. I watch other vehicles spin off the road, luckier than myself in them not hitting anything solid. People are at their doors having heard the bang as I tentatively skate my perilous way across to join an old lady who is concerned over the blood that's making a 'Jackson Pollock' of my face. I ask her if she could possibly help me by phoning the Art College and letting them know that Mr. Bridgen won't be in; she is more than happy to oblige. Other help arrives as a garage breakdown van draws up, soon followed by the Principal from the Art College, looking very concerned and is insistent that I was driving far too fast regardless of my pleas to the contrary. He irritates me as he doggedly insists on my speed being the cause. "I'm taking you into college," he says, adding that I must notify my wife that I shall be staying in Hereford for the rest of the week! I very soon put him right over this, concussed as I no doubt am; my place is back with my family and I haven't the faintest idea as to how I shall get there without money. We stand arguing, my head is splitting and there's a huge lump that's coming up under my fringe. I just want to go home. It's the only clear thought in my mind, while this man here is more concerned over my class of twenty students with no regard as to how I might be feeling. He briefly switches strategy and starts to insist that, prior to my starting work, he takes me to hospital to be checked over. Meanwhile, the breakdown man is wanting to know what he's to do with my wrecked van and I shake the Principal's hand and beg him to leave me to sort out my predicament, a request he reluctantly agrees to and I almost sense a round of applause from the people watching in their doorways.

The breakdown man informs me that my van is a complete write-off and I am hit with a deeply sickening realisation which is all too much to take in; I want to cry and scream and beat something with my fists, but reality is futile and flimsy, haunting as an old sod ghost. I never before realised how much I depended on my little van, I really feel helpless now as I sadly watch it being towed away, having removed whatever I could possibly carry, leaving the rest for scrap-heap vultures. There's a lump in my throat as well as on my head, and I feel helpless and really quite afraid.

Gathering my senses, I explore the possibility of catching a bus, and, to my great relief discover a 'Midland Red' service operates between here and Craven Arms, going on to Shrewsbury; the maddening thing being that I have no money. Regardless of this fact, I stand at the bus stop and eventually a marvellous red image advances towards me and stops. In desperation I explain the situation that I'm in and, to my amazement I am permitted, blood and all, to board the bus, leaving my name and address for them to forward the bill on later; now that's what I call a Bus Company!

My nightmare starts proper at Craven Arms where the bus and I part company and I head off on foot, adorned, stuffed and laden to the hilt with stuff from the van. I've already made the decision to wear my heavy wellies rather than carry them, but there's not a lot that I can do with the spade that I'm gripping. It isn't adding much to my credibility as a hitchhiker, neither is the dried blood blackening my forehead. I'm acutely aware of the pains in my knees and that my trousers have already welded themselves to my healing process. I'm carrying maps, van documents, torch, tool-kit and running-shoes; a walking scarecrow stiffening by the stride and totally out of luck as car after car blasts by ignoring my pleading thumb and causing me to swear and curse at their indifference to one in need.

I've struggled on for several miles with stiffening knees now making it almost impossible to walk; I'm just stumbling along with the pain in my head making me feel sick. It seems like hell. Seemingly out of nowhere, a motorbike with a sidecar suddenly stops and I look with heavy eyes to this saint of a man; it's like my dad come back to life, similar in every possible way. "Jump in!" It isn't easy, I'm absolutely crippled and the sidecar is simply a wooden box... a coffin. This is a surreal moment as I ease myself within it until I am lying flat out and stiff as a corpse, very aware of the symbolic imagery. I'm looking up at the sky, great bare trees outstretch their fingers over me and I glance at this goggled specimen of a man, and, for a brief moment slip into thinking that he really is my long-dead dad. Dad had an old BSA motorbike and sidecar identical to this outfit, this man actually looks like my dad. Too soon, at a fork in the road we part company and I stand in silence watching this apparitional moment slip away forever.

A good many miles agonise under my feet while my hitch-hiker's luck remains unchanged. Over marshy fields I watch a lonesome redshank rise up and fly a great whimpering circle in the sky before miraculously melting into a swiftly moving flock of the same and slipping sadly away to the northwest. I come to a small sub-post office and notice a little white van just about to move off, there's a jolly looking fat lady at the wheel and I stagger up to her and ask if she's going my way. "You'll have to squeeze in the back," she says to my surprise and I do precisely that and find myself sitting beside a dead pig, it's bloody head rolling around the floor. All I can hear are two women rabbiting on about Women's Institute matters while I'm here, spade in hand, bleeding and looking like an escapee from hell while wrestling with a highly mobile pigs head. My presence here is of total oblivion to them, I do believe that they have forgotten that I am here. Eventually they pull in off the road and stop; I clamber out and thank them, 'think' a goodbye to the unfortunate pig, and plod on my way once more, still with some dozen or so miles to go, feeling sore and aching with my legs now virtually locked solid. I've given up on any hope of getting a lift now and I resign myself to a long and painful shuffle but, after torturing on for another miserable and dangerous mile, a vehicle passes me and then pulls up some way ahead; it's someone who has recognised me and my ordeal is as good as over. He drops me off in the valley half a mile from the school, the day has slipped by and the school is silent and empty when I trudge past cradling my sad news over the last one and a half agonising miles. I'm having to fight a big lump in my throat when I at long last confront Cari and the boys and tell them what's happened. I'm completely devastated, the van's gone, the job's gone and I'd be gone were it not through a stroke of luck. I hate this day more than any other I've known, but I must be grateful for I have been spared to fight again another day.

It's an uncomfortable week that follows as my body somewhat stubbornly heals. There are large crusty scabs on both knees which split open each time I bend them; going to the toilet is nigh-on impossible despite it being a most necessary part of each day. On one such ordeal of an occasion, after struggling to dig a hole down the field behind the barn, I find myself having to race with a huge black cloud that has 'trouble' written all over it. Try as I may, I simply cannot hurry and my scabs have already both split open again as the sky's belly bursts and a deluge of torrential hailstones erupts all over me, in less than seconds filling my pants and trousers deep with little balls of ice. Unfortunately my trousers are tucked into my wellies and, when I eventually manage to stagger into an upright position, a million icy hailstones go tumbling down into my wellies, turning my toes into prawns in an instance. I stagger back home stiff-leggedly clutching my trousers splayed and gaping and with feelings of abject wretchedness dragging me down to a new low. Cari dresses my knees once more and I prop myself up stiffly, a very sorry state to have got myself into and made to look worse by the extensive bruising now coming out all over my chest.

Over this period I surprise myself and actually start painting again, utilising the leftover scraps of torn canvas from the ill-fated roof-rack incident of a year earlier. Meanwhile, Cari has taken to the bushman saw and is stoically keeping the home fires burning, taking full advantage of Gareth's feverish uprooting disease which by now has extended up to the hedge close to the cowshed and has provided us with quite a few old oak stakes which burn beautifully. He pops in for a chat and a cup of tea and is sorry to hear of my mishap and is himself somewhat at a disadvantage with having Hugh off with a broken leg.

Sight of Cari out foraging for hedge-stakes triggers off in him an outrageous gesture of generosity with a chainsaw. I cannot believe my astounded eyes, there's nothing I can do to stop him as he sets about felling a lovely large oak tree just down the track beyond the sycamore tree. The air turns blue and whines with agonised noise. I feel helplessly trapped, heartbroken and grateful in one huge clumsy lump of helplessness; he doesn't take long and I watch this fine and lovely tree slowly topple before crashing noisily downhill into a very marshy corner, flattening the hedge that he's uprooting. "There you are, Jimmy, that should keep you going for a while!" Cari comes over and squeezes my hand, she feels the same as I do, shocked, confused, grateful and so very sad to have added to the world's new bareness.

Doggone Scars in a Cruel Landscape

February arrives miserably, but away on the opposite hillside, a mistlethrush has been singing for some little time in one of the trees, reminding us that springtime won't be long. Coltsfoot are flowering on a forest clearing where winter heliotrope has been secretly blooming for some weeks now, but the air is very cold and damp and the ground completely saturated and heavy with mud. The scar of the old hedge is vile and Gareth has removed two more lovely old hedges that previously ran diagonally down the hill to join up with the other one, creating what now looks like an open battlefield, ugly and bare. I hear the word 'tidy' being mentioned a lot in this context and there's genuine belief that the land actually looks tidier without hedgerows cluttering it, the crowning insult coming when wire fences are strung up everywhere and an austere silence begins to dominate.

Fresh blizzards bring a halt to the tidying up process and I am heartened to discover that one of our hens has laid an egg from a great height, unfortunately resulting in it smashing on impact with the hard-packed manure inside the barn. Up on the wall I spy our little pink bantam actually sitting on eggs; there's a definite air of Spring about, regardless of the February snowfall, the creatures can feel it even though I can't.

Feeling a bit more like my old self again, I start to tackle the felled oak tree, systematically attempting to reduce it branch by branch, log by log and twig by twig. It's a very awkward thing to do and I'm high up, generating an uncontrollable bouncing and swaying motion which makes sawing none too easy, getting the saw-blade wedged fast time and time again. On Saturday the boys come over to help me, Robin on his dumper-truck and the other two with the wheelbarrow. We are all well wrapped up because the air is spiteful and cutting, not the sort of day to be standing around in. Taking no chances, I'm adorned for the occasion in a many times too big police-jacket given to me by Cari's dad and is decorated with rows of rainbow-like medal ribbons and has silvery buttons. On my head I'm wearing the teacosy and around my neck a huge brightly patterned cotton scarf made from one of Cari's old dresses. My trousers are ancient and have neither fly-hole or knees and are lashed to my body with brash orange string, in fact I couldn't be more bizarrely scruffy if I tried.

Up here bouncing crazily in the branches, I'm singing any old rubbish that comes to my lips, making it up for the most part, causing the boys to fall about laughing and getting myself completely carried away, oblivious to the fact that I've attracted a considerable audience over in the lane in the form of the 'Lord Davies Hunt'. Lots of horses and riders but no hounds. I suddenly stop what I'm doing, but go on bouncing up and down just the same. A sharp voice spanks upon the air. "I say... you haven't seen the hounds come by this way, have you?" "Lost your dogs, have you?" I bawl back, smiling to myself, suddenly seeing the funny side of all these immaculately dressed people on horses, having lost their hounds of all things. What doesn't amuse me however, is the plain fact that, on the contrary, it is I that am providing them with a bit of entertainment; the marsh meadow gate has fat elbows all along it, just like bums on seats in cinemas, decidedly a better way of spending the day than trying to find a pack of contrary dogs. "The hounds... have they come by this way?" The voice goes echoing all round the hillsides and I shout back... "Sorry, I haven't seen or heard any sign of them!"

I'm feeling trapped and embarrassed up here in the branches in what must surely seem like fancy dress, and I watch to my horror, Robin going splashing his clumsy way over to join them, his face a bubbly mess of stuff from his nose and wearing two left wellies of odd sizes, one of which is left behind in the deep, sucking mud. I quietly curse the confounded hounds for absconding and leaving me stuck here like some rustic old stand-up comedian. Several of the riders go trotting off down the lane, but those leaning on the gate have plainly settled in for the day and are content to be entertained by this clown up a fallen tree, ably assisted by his youngest son with one welly and a snail's playground plastered all over his face. Rowan and Spencer sneak away tittering, while Cari meanwhile remains quite happily baking bread, waiting for me to appear with my arms full of logs. To top it all, I notice Meg, Murphy and Dan on their way to the cowshed, having heard of my van accident and intrigued to know the details. Unfortunately they fail to see me stuck up this tree and are soon all gorging freshly baked bread with delicious blackberry jam and mugs of lovely hot tea to wash it down. I bide my time and slowly disengage myself from the branches, turning my back on the audience and proceeding to load up the wheelbarrow with live logs which I know will not burn. I then attempt to leave the stage but fail disastrously when I slip in the mud and fall face down into the wheelbarrow which spills its entire load of logs. I'm very lucky to have avoided slicing my nose off on the sharp metal edge of the barrow and I hear the old sods leaning back there on the gate, all cackling at my expense; I don't wait for the applause!

With my arms full of very muddy logs and looking rather worse for wear, I join the others in the cowshed where I am welcomed like a long-lost brother. Murphy rushes up and gives me a huge and careful hug while the others cheer to show how glad they are to see that I'm still alive and kicking. I am soon joined by Robin who has lost both wellies now and has left a trail of muddy feet marks all the way up to the hearth, his dumper-truck has been dumped somewhere out in the mud on the hillside. We all have a raucous celebratory and noisy yarn and catch up on recent events, making a joke of it all this time round. Murphy has noticed my four new paintings and is impressed by them as they lean propped against the wall slowly drying. As for the logs from the oak tree, they're just as I knew they would be, virtually impossible to burn, full of sap and they bubble and steam showing no sign of flames whatsoever and more than once putting the fire out.

Dan renews his friendly acquaintance with Sorrel once more and I choose the moment to take advantage of her sugary preoccupation and sort out an old box from the shed and fix a piece of wire netting on top of it. He can take her back with him to help sort out his mouse problem, but I shall have to slip a tin of cat-food in just in case the mice are not quite to her liking. As the dust is settling, they all get up and go; the new logs have put the fire out and it's feeling a bit cold in the room, telling me to sort out some wood that will burn once more and to get the paraffin lamp glowing and Robin's feet in a bowl of hot water. There's never a dull moment I'm sad to say.

Necessity being the mother of invention, I make the discovery that the deep, compressed old manure in the barn makes a very fine fuel, a bit like peat and after re-kindling the fire with twigs and a couple of stakes, I top it up with a pile of this ancient cow-dung and we boil a couple of kettles on it. The boys think it's a great joke and swear never to eat or drink anything that has been prepared on it, considering it still to be very much 'poo'! Poo or not, it provides hot water bottles for them and puts a bit of warmth about the room as well as giving them the giggles as a prelude to sleep.

In the night I am awakened by the chattering of magpies flying with owls; they're all making a hell of a din and I can hear them travelling from tree to tree. It is moonlight and just turned two in the morning; I can only surmise that the moonlight is extra bright and that perhaps they are following a fox or badger maybe.

I've never known anything like this before but I do recall once seeing a kestrel hovering by moonlight along the cliff top in Cornwall, long after midnight. Having never heard magpies making this kind of racket in the night before, it seems likely that something has disturbed them from their roost, owls fighting over mates maybe; they probably won't ever do it again.

I have since officially notified the Art College of my resignation due to having no longer any means of getting there; I don't feel very happy about it but there's not a lot I can do without transport or the money to replace my old van. Our life here is proving to be so hard that I really do have to be here on hand tending to things in what was intended to be an experiment in 'rural' living. I've already discovered that being an artist counts for less than nothing, be it writer, painter, composer, whatever; there's no such category down at the job-centre, nothing whatsoever to help sponsor or encourage future Turners, Shakespeares, Deliuses-name your vice. There's nothing for artists and I don't agree to adding my name to the register of the unemployed because I consider my job to be that of an artist, not out-of-work. Self-employed and hard working, yes, but as yet not reaping any financial rewards or finding any form of assistance whatsoever. In truth, I don't expect any such thing, it's just that I wished that the state would recognise in some way and to value the existence and the place of artists and the richness of their contribution into life.

With having an exhibition coming up at Gregynog, I really must now try to create time for my work and to get a collection of paintings together. I'm beginning to buzz over the prospect, especially now that I have at long last broken my self-imposed exile from the subject and the paintings are once more starting to flow. I'm running a bit low on materials now, with barely adequate paint to last me into the Spring. I need more turpentine but I've still got plenty of linseed oil and a few indifferent brushes, not that this worries me too much because I'm happy to apply paint with whatever comes to hand … hands even. Canvas is my main problem, but I shall try to make do with the various odd pieces that I've managed to salvage until such time that I can find more work in television, I can then get myself stocked-up properly again.

Right now, poverty has got its claws in good and proper. What food there is remaining has to be for the boys and Cari, I don't want what I am facing to affect them in any way because it was I who made the decision to come here and it was I who was a little bit too free and easy with money when I had it, regardless of how small the amount may have been. I've still not properly recovered from the effects of my van accident, it has set me back in more ways than one despite my stubborn attempts to shrug it off. Malnutrition is now starting to show itself on my body and I am gradually gathering abscesses and wounds that refuse to heal and my hair has started to fall out, leaving me with completely smooth bald patches. I've become a van Gogh 'potato eater', desperate for the first signs of new nettle growth and the cluck, cluck, clucking music of hens that have just laid. It's not me that I see in the mirror, this character is pale and thin, not like me at all. I hear the sound of a twelve-bore up in the wood and I do the unthinkable in my response to it and follow Dai-the-death Morgan, gathering up the squirrels that he's shot, I have to eat something. He laughs when he discovers what I'm doing and is more than happy to demonstrate his butchery skills with a penknife, removing guts, heads and pelts. I have to hide this cruel reality from the boys, already they've been in trouble at school for writing stuff in their diaries, stating that I send them out to collect old cow-shit for the fire, and I certainly can't risk their teachers knowing that I eat squirrels as well, they would have me arrested and locked away!

This newly adopted ferret's life of mine is a whole lot better than the human one that I was enduring and these dear little bodies that I am gnawing at when no-one is watching, are all that's keeping me alive at this moment in time. I do hope that the ferrets are not having to starve as a result of Dai's generosity.

After a trip to town to convert family allowance into bread... an old biblical trick, Cari returns with two items of news, one of them being that someone she knows wants to buy my racing bike and the other, that of an elderly and well respected reporter, wanting to come out and write an article about me, in particular my association with 'Gregynog' and with the Oxford Poetry Professor. It strikes me odd how such news travels in these parts, it's like magic, mysterious and a little unnerving, but I have no real objections, especially if it helps point me in the direction of a crust of bread.

I sell my bike for twenty-five quid, it's worth a lot more than that, but I'm mindful of an old saying... beggars can't be choosers. I quickly translate the bike into vegetables, flour, cheese, milk and some nice tea for the old reporter fellow when he eventually emerges from the mud. He duly arrives, accompanied by a photographer and they really have a field-day; it isn't often an opportunity to wax lyrical presents itself to them as this one does and they both allow the 'bohemian' in them to overflow, almost to the point of drowning them. Our life is a huge novelty to them, a rare culture shock, but I'm nevertheless relieved not to be asked where the loo is or where the light switches and fittings are. I try to explain our life here in simple terms, that of 'waiting for swallows', but the remark flies even higher than the swallows above their heads.

A week later my picture appears in the newspaper, nothing like the bloke that I know who's smothered in boils and bald patches. It's a wordy article, thoughtful and slightly ambiguous with little inaccuracies here and there, attempting to explain and examine our reason for being here, but I don't feel bad about it because it's more or less true. They've somehow got my head tilted in the picture, trying to make me look like a film star, no doubt touching-out the bald bits with an airbrush. There's also a fair bit of name dropping in the article, doubtless guaranteeing that the boys will be rather more looked-up to at school, and I daresay that my own passage around the lanes will have the occasional wave from a window now. I've been called a few names in my time, but never a 'Jack-of-all-Arts'; Murphy thinks it's hilarious, Dan just blinks and gives me a new dark, strange look. Nothing however, removes the feeling of hunger from my gut or my longing to see the cupboard full of food again. Miraculously, Cari's rosehip syrup, blackberry and damson jam has kept us going.

The first snowdrop is rumoured to be nodding in the bottom of a hedge close to where dear Bootsy was buried. I can tell also that the mistle thrushes have laid, judging by the way that the bold birds are noisily having to fight off squirrels and magpies who are hell-bent on stealing their eggs. I hear an old dog-fox barking at first light now and have spotted him a few times silhouetted against the cold dawn sky, on the hill above the well and I'm keeping my fingers crossed that he'll keep his distance and not trouble our hens. The bantam cock, now known as Chris, is particularly brave when he emerges through the hole in the barn roof and delivers his challenge to the world; I've actually made a recording of him crowing and the dog-fox barking simultaneously. I hope he's not pushing his luck!

We're scraping through by the very skin of our teeth, not a thing that I ever want to repeat in my life. Even the dumper-truck now has a wheel missing with another one terminally broken and it has now been abandoned... money down the drain, that's for sure, yet it looked so sturdy when I bought it; it had obviously not been prepared for such a phenomenon as the boy-child Robin.

To help ease our situation a degree or two, I receive a miniscule sum of money, the nine days wages due to me from my brief job in Hereford, although unfortunately not before the verminous taxman has contaminated it with his filthy, fat, greedy fingers. Not to worry, what little bit is left for our needs is readily converted into food and we get the cupboard looking fractionally more healthy again.

The valley now yelps with a new sound; Meg and Murphy's new dog-pens have sex-maniac pedigree stud-dogs barking in them, made worse by chauffeured processions of equally pedigree bitches on heat; it's a bedlam of yelping and offal-eating. "Beats telly!" Murphy laughingly boasts, but the very idea sickens me and the ceaseless yapping is beginning to get on my nerves. What little signs of Spring there are, are not to be trusted as Winter keeps coming back to torment anything that is foolish enough to venture out. Fresh snowfalls continue to paint the mornings, not staying too long but nevertheless serving as reminders to trust absolutely nothing.

We have been quite successful with our bed positioning strategy and have managed to dodge most of the snow since our earlier catastrophe. In fact we have become experts at wetting our forefingers and reading the direction of the approaching weather ... not that this hi-tech skill is likely to find a favourable category down at the job-centre, along with that of 'Artist'!

A couple of days of sun lure Gareth into letting the cows out into the fields and they rapidly bodge the earth into a mud-bath before the frail tender grass has had time to grow and wicked

Winter with a vengeance returning. A large, sweet-hearted cow has become ill and dies a most miserable death just down the field behind the barn. Heavy rain, hail, then heavy snow, make her last hours pure hell. I can see that the children have tried desperately to cover her body and have laid little offerings of grass in the frantic hope of saving her; death doesn't usually come this large.

It is blowing the most fearful gale with sleet pulverising down at a slant when the spluttering tractor with Gareth and Elwyn arrive. Gareth dismounts and stands staring down at this poor dead beast that still has its eyes staring blindly nowhere, and icy rain hammering into its mountainous leathery body. He attempts to light his pipe but is thwarted by the very imbecility of the thought and gives up and starts to grapple with a heavy chain, trying to fix it around the great carcass. I try my utmost to be of assistance, it's a disgusting struggle, very messy and slippery. The dead cow's tongue is hanging out crazily and there is bloody stuff coming from the udders. I feel an ancient iron-age arm drop comfortingly across my shoulders; "Mastitis!" Gareth mutters conclusively, then becomes a farmer and applies all brute force into raising the beast's head from the ground, while Elwyn and I risk life and limb in forcing the chain underneath and fastening it securely. The other end is then attached to the back of the tractor and the throttle is opened to the full, triggering the huge tyres into a 'Catherine-wheel' of hopeless spinning, skidding, sliding and throwing up great turfs and demonic splatterings of mud. Eventually finding a degree of grip, outstretching the carcass and slithering it tragically and decisively, flattening the mole-hills and ploughing a furrow with its horn.

This is the most miserable day imaginable, heavy sleet now turned to snow in wild, crazy swirling large flakes. I walk slowly some distance behind the tractor as the death-furrow leaves its trail through our orchard, then laboriously up the steep hill and over the top to where the new hedgeless landscape insults the valley. Other cows are just standing around looking sick and bewildered; it was a mistake to have brought them out so soon and now they have to be rounded up and herded back to their sheds, but not until the corpse has been dumped on the wayside in readiness for the abattoir truck to arrive and cart it away for dog meat. Gareth tries again to light his pipe but once more fails; this weather is nobody's friend.

Presently, out from the wind and snow, the wagon arrives and a jolly little fat man in jeans and a short-sleeved bright red pullover, whistling sweeter than a robin, immediately sets to work. In hardly any time at all he winches the carcass aboard and I hear the sickening thud as it drops into the back of his wagon. It's all in a normal day's work for him, he's in his element, a very happy little man. "Tarrah, boss!" I hear him squeal, interrupting his whistling, and the wagon noisily strains away in a thunder of blue fumes.

Gareth goes ahead on the tractor leaving Elwyn and myself to round up the rest of the herd and ease them back over the hill behind the tractor. The snow is blindingly thick now and Elwyn is plastered and soaked through to his tiny lukewarm body; I feel sorry for him to have to be out in such foul weather. Glancing round, I catch sight of a young bull-calf who, for some strange reason, is reluctant to leave the marsh meadow gate and is sounding very distressed; I look at Elwyn and he tells me that the dead cow was its mother and he is simply crying for her. Sadly I realise that the sentiments that I am feeling right now, have no place in these surrounds ... it is all 'meat' at the end of the day and isn't for crying over.

It isn't easy, but I succeed in coaxing the young animal into following the others over the hill and I come face to face with its father in the top field and I am more than grateful for the lousy weather when I see that the old bull couldn't care tuppence about me, all he wants is a dry shed, some warm straw and a little sweet hay; the business of disemboweling me can surely wait until the weather gets a bit more settled!

Under the holly hedge, a large and handsome white cockerel that somehow survived Christmas, throws out his breast and crows defiantly and I see a plume of white breath come curling from his throat, showing me that inside he's as warm as toast. I watch Gareth bobbing about, appearing and disappearing, dwarfed and surrounded by the great landscaped shapes of beasts. Thick clouds of steam rising up like weather as he cracks his hard stick across their hugely unhurried backsides; the nearest thing to science here in these cold wet hills. He invites me in for a bite to eat but I decline the kind offer, thinking it more advisable for me to get back to my own cowshed and to change into dry clothing before I feel the cold setting in and doing me no favours. He thanks me and I wave goodbye and trudge back down through the mud, glad to get this good-for-nothing day out of the way once and for all.

Cussedly and defiantly I am trespassing on with my painting and writing; keeping such things a secret isn't easy when the air within the cowshed has the strange and foreign smell of oil paint, linseed oil and turps filling it. The nice thing about writing is that it doesn't give off toxic fumes, neither does playing the guitar and, unlike painting, can be removed without trace after being exorcised. The usual heavy chores always take pride of place over all other considerations and I wouldn't have it any other way.

This is a very thoughtful time and there's a great veil of reflectiveness cast out across everything and everywhere. It accompanies me with saw, axe and spade, whatever I do it's there; it's the same with Cari, a kind of gratefulness to have weathered the worst, narrowly avoiding widowhood along the way. We sit around the dying sparks of a late evening and dissect the last year piece by piece and try to work out where things went wrong and, more importantly, what we must do to get things right this time. It all boils down to promises being broken; in all truth they're like confetti and are soon blown too far from memory on the wind, forgotten. I had really wanted to fence-off our patch and make it safe from cows and sheep, but I was told not to attempt doing it myself and that it was a job for the tractor to provide the required tension for the wire, thus preventing the cows from muscling it to the ground. I was also promised a ploughed strip of fenced garden that we could then make good with our own compost and cultivate it. It was a marvellous prospect, but absolutely nothing happened. Promises, promises all confetti long since blown away, and the cows wrecked everything that I did. But I won't be beaten, promises or no promises; we'll have ourselves a garden and shall have it protected from four-legged strolling lumps of Government Subsidies.

This resurgence of spirit within me I realise is likely to arouse the wrong responses. It isn't easy to show initiative in response to those forgotten things. I can't really win, but I'm not prepared to be a loser either; I always keep my word and I expect others to keep theirs too, it's a simple rule and one which I abide by. I've become rather sad and disillusioned by having to constantly explain to the boys the reason why we haven't got a garden with our own green miracles, our own dreams of other lovely things. What we all agree on, however, is that by hook or by crook, we'll have our own garden this year and shall fence it ourselves if past promises have been buried and forgotten.

What is providing a bit of fun over these last weeks however, is our Sunday morning free-for-all with a football, a ritual which we try to contain within the narrow strip which runs between the ditch and the hillside at the front of the cowshed. An alternative to worship, usually involving a wife, three sons and a pensioner farmer all spick and span in his Sunday best, in some quaint old habit that Dan is stuck with, regardless of the vociferous way he believes 'religion' to be at the very best, something between consenting adults. Habits die hard, they're like mud forming around the feet when standing on one spot in the stream for too long; everyone of us has them forming about us without being aware of it. Some habits are good, others bad; I'm trying to make a habit of having no habits, but who am I to know if it's to any effect!

The Sunday morning football fling is becoming just such a habit and it isn't long before news of it spreads and other wild faces appear, and not just on Sundays either; it's now stolen over into Saturdays as well. This suits the boys well until the barbed wire strand along the ditch punctures the ball and I am compelled to leg-it and provide a replacement which, as though by habit, meets with the same fate as the one before it. This eats even more holes into the family allowance; such is the power of habit.

I've at long last reduced the oak tree down to a final massive stump and I'm eager and ready to put my ex-government, five-foot cross-cut saw to use and provide us with some real logs at last, some of which can be seasoned in the barn and used to warm us next Christmas. Nice idea, shame about reality! The tractor beats me to it as Gareth appears out of nowhere, sucking obliviously at his 'peace-pipe' and tows the stump away without a word being spoken. It'll lie about the farm for the next few years, used as a prop or a stop before ending up as a gatepost; it's amazing how useful an old stump is in a farmyard, a haphazard bit of versatility beyond design.

New Life Stirring

Goodbye February! Mad March has come bouncing and blustering in, lifting last years carpeted leaves into a wild wind-dance and flaying the tightly budded reluctant branches. Try as it may, the wild wind fools no-one and the buds remain tightly closed; only the hazel catkins venture out from sleep, requiring the services of the wind to distribute their pollen and set their lamb's tails dancing. The first daffodils have appeared on the pages of the boys' books. "Daftodils is nice, daftodils is yellow, I like daftodils." Not exactly Wordsworth but I would remind any reader that this be the principality of Dylan Thomas, barked and crowed and belling! In one crazy moonless week, the village-school runs out of yellow crayons and a halt is called to the drawing of daffodils ... or is it 'daftodils'?

As though by magic we have acquired our first pair of house sparrows who have taken up residence in the barn. Our starlings have already returned and have been noisily tidying-up their old nest-site in the bedroom wall for some little time now, together with a prospecting wren who's really started to shout and bawl about the place, reminding us that we are but lodgers; unwelcome ones at that, and that he, loud ranting 'he', is the rightful owner.

Things are gradually improving; we're up to three eggs a day now, what's more, the little pink bantam is tightly sitting her own clutch of eggs, almost out of sight on top of the barn wall, all seemingly snug and cosy; she trusts the air so unquestioningly. Breeding is all that matters to her and, so long as old Chris the cockerel can crow, he can also copulate and make every egg an extension of his family. It does, however, seem to me to be a strange time to be hatching eggs, with winter yet hardly out of the frame. I obviously don't understand or perceive what they are able to, neither do I have the courage to put all my eggs into one basket as they so have done; maybe this is the reason why there are more humans than there are bantams!

The mad march wind grows even wilder, provoking our weird white hen, Sykes, into a hysterical brainstorm of activity and she hares about the field on death-defying strides, every bit as crazily as last year's leaves are doing, but with a mad irrationality powering her. So different from the simplicity of the blown leaves which have a certain predictability no matter how far or high they fly. Sykes demonstrates a lunacy not even known to herself, yet she still manages to perform the miracle of finding her roosting perch in the barn each evening, an achievement which baffles me, persuading me into having to admit to harbouring a certain fondness and respect for her, despite my collection of bruises and peck-scars from her more 'intimate' involvement with me!

There's a very discernable comfort being provided for us by this mad March wind, more of a fascination than a distraction. It's a real blousy woman of a wind with a breathless kind of softness regardless of her broad shoulder power. There's an intimacy between her and the sturdy, stolid trunks of timbered life-forms hard to comprehend in mere reproductory terms, but here she is, the temptress, flirting and caressing, teasing the life-giving sap to rise out from the dreadful winter dark chastity-belt of black ironed earth and to leave a thousand billion infant leaves to tenderly cloak forests and for conkers, apples, acorns and a whole bewildering basket-bursting variety of tastes and splendours to steal out from the forgottenness and to dance in the marvellous celebration of eternal re-birth known as 'Spring'.

Everywhere is rattling; by night we hear the roof creaking as it almost lifts up and breaks free of the four walls. The tin on the barn roof incessantly rattles, more slates come crashing down as do branches up in the wood and my morning stroll with spade and bog-roll becomes a rather unsavoury paper chase. It's the sort of weather that the boys all love as they whoop and yell up on the hill with kites, although Robin now seems to prefer cuddling a Welsh collie that has grown too old and disinterested in a working life up on Gareth's farm. He's providing the tired old bitch with a therapeutical rest-home and she in turn provides him with the barrier he seems to need between himself and the reality of the rest of us. His attempts to cuddle Gerty, our largest old hen, have not been reciprocated however, she much prefers the feeling of physical freedom after a life spent in a prison cage, although I must admit that I do have a good relationship with her and share my food and even my mug of tea with her on occasions when I sit out on the bit of concrete at the front of the cowshed.

It's on these billowy mild days that we miss the van most of all, wishing that we could be on the wide open beach, with our hair being torn off our heads and with salt-spray licking our skin in the gull-diving turbulent air. We feel properly stuck without it on these precious glimpses of better days emerging. Spencer has even started to draw sad little pictures of it in preference to daffodils; he's a promising young artist and, when he feels like it, produces some most beautiful work. Rowan by comparison is more of a scientist, a very practical and inventive child, happiest while grappling with 3-dimensional problems, preferably involving the use of tools.

Being an 'artist in exile', as I feel myself to have become, is a bit like being one of our swallows in Africa; they have to come here to breed just as I have to return to my art if I am to survive. I'm rather satisfied with the last few paintings that I've somehow managed to do. They seem to have a sense of urgency as well as that of poetry about them; but I am alas down to painting on paper and bits of hardboard; I've even been reduced to having to paint over the top of existing paintings, convincing myself that it's the 'process' of painting that matters, and not the finished item. I'm not persuaded by this thinking, but it does at least keep me painting. As I bury paintings beneath paintings, I wish that there were a technology which would enable me, still using oil paint, to peel away the layers at some future time and to re-mount them, not necessarily onto canvas but onto any surface I chose. The more I think about it, the more feasible the idea seems to be. 'Mother of invention', here with me now, why can't you turn my idea into gold? "I haven't the faintest idea!" she answers as a Common Market Juggernaut delivers yellow crayons to the village school, soon to be delivering blue ones in readiness for the season of bluebells, as the year begins to explode upon us.

We are more than ready now to get our gardening plan into action, but I can't help harking back to Gareth's generous wave of a hand down some fifty yards beyond the barn, promising to fence it off and plough it for us. Good intentions are not always what they seem and now the cows are out again and lambing is into rather late full swing. I watch, just as I remember doing last year, a carrion crow tormenting a ewe that has just given birth to twins; feeble and frail, they are more vulnerable to the crow than they are to the fox. A pair of crows is even worse. They go for the eyes of the newborns, presenting the old ewe with a nigh-on impossible nightmare. She rushes one way and the mercurial crows just lift into the air then resettle behind her and keep on doing this again and again. Even when I try scattering them they persist, leaving both me and the mother ewe giddy and frustrated. 'Dai-the-Death' does his best to reduce the odds, but it is the squirrel and the fox-tails that provide him with his livelihood, shooting crows has to be a labour of love. The farmers resort to the other method ... strychnine! Issued for one thing but used abusively for anything, all it requires is a signature in the 'poison book' down at the chemists, and then the deadliest of substances passes into the hands of idiots who happen to own land; it's like giving nuclear weapons to the town council! With the poison book signed and with the power of a terrorist, farmer laces a stillborn lamb carcass with the stuff and kills a dozen crows, several magpies, two stray dogs, a pair of handsome buzzards , but not a single mole, for which it was issued in the first place! Even though the fox usually gets blamed for most lamb deaths, on this occasion not a single one fell to this most dreadful of substances, and not a badger either.

Robins are nesting in the bank just beyond the sycamore tree, as also are the long-tailed tits in the rose-briars down our waterlogged lane. It's a miracle that this tiny little fragment of hedge has escaped Gareth's earlier onslaught, but I fear that it won't be long before he makes up for this omission; once a farmer has a bug like this in his system, it usually goes plaguing him interminably, or so I have found.

Our clothes-line has been working overtime as a result of the good drying wind; Cari has turfed out every last item of cloth and clothing in one gigantic spring-clean, taking full advantage of the favourable weather conditions while they last and there has been a statued audience of gormlessly gawping cows and a very much out-of-condition bull, all of whom have once more covered the entire face of the land with a thick green sludge and are now patiently waiting for the heavy rain when they can then bodge it all into an aquatic minefield.

They don't have to wait for much longer, the bold March lion has by now roared itself hoarse and it all ends in floods of tears. The beasts are all thoroughly washed day and night; it never rains here ... it pours. Nothing was really fooled by the mild spell and, with the exception of the larch, the buds have remained tightly closed; the larch pleads innocence by being the only conifer that isn't evergreen, her intricate little leaves open early as do her small bright scarlet flowers. Every other tree here waits, wisely so too, because the rain readily turns to snow once more, deep enough for the sledge to come out again and long enough for the far hills to huddle closer, making the world seem smaller and cosier.

From the top of Dan's steep and towering lump of hill, we all gaze across shrunken white miles and Dan on the sledge, goes daft in his toppling pensioner's years and christens the virgin snow as he diminishes noisily and recklessly down the perilous gradient, totally out of control, losing his hat and very nearly his scalp too on a barbed wire strand as he rockets underneath it, then parts company in a limb re-arranged white cascade, only a split second before the sledge slams crunchingly into a beech tree. I've never seen him look so happy, Desperate Dan couldn't hold a candle to this crazy old fool who can't wait to limp back up to the top and repeat the performance.

Back down at his farmstead where his new furry pet Sorrel presides over a vastly increased mouse population, Dan suddenly remembers that the postman delivered a letter addressed to me. It's just as well that it didn't slip his memory because it's from the TV Company in Plymouth, an urgent request for me to phone them and to transfer the charges. I waste no time and race off round the lanes to the telephone-box where I learn that my services are needed for three weeks to cover their designer who has suddenly been taken ill. I'm full of yesses and readily agree to anything and everything; all I can think of is a cupboard full of food and supplies and some new clothes for the boys. Nothing else matters. It's only when I'm striding back, grinning all over my silly face, that I start to think of how I shall get there to start work first thing Monday morning, and what I shall use for money. My smile melts as I look more squarely at the problem, recognising that it isn't being helped any by the fact that it's Saturday and that the bank is shut. If my luck at hitch-hiking a short while back is anything to go by, I daren't even begin to think what my chances of borrowing money are likely to be.

Gladness and sadness always seem to go hand in hand, as though existing only because of each other, but we are in no doubt whatsoever as to how desperately we need this opportunity to give ourselves a better fighting chance. There's an atmosphere of nervous excitement, tense and with a sadness that cannot be ignored. As I would have expected, Cari insists that she's more than able to cope in my absence and it's only of partial comfort to know that Spring is now really trying to kick Winter well and truly over the hill and for gentler times to settle once more. None of these thoughts however are helping me to resolve my transport and money problems; I dislike borrowing intensely and the possibility of hitch-hiking is now seeming more of a probability, one that I don't relish.

As dusk is rapidly dusting all around, two dark bearded figures appear at the front of the cowshed, when I take a closer look I can see that it's Murphy and Greg; my luck is about to change. With Meg due to give birth at any moment, Greg has driven up from Plymouth in anticipation of the happy event, but has to drive back on Sunday evening, baby or no baby, and will be more than glad of my company to help lighten the journey. This, together with the pound note which Cari has suddenly produced out of thin air, my problems are solved. I couldn't have planned it better if I had tried.

We all spend half an hour by the fire, Greg seems to be a bit stuck for words. I think he was expecting to see a 'proper' house grown up from the former pile of rubble and he can't help chuckling, "You seem to have somehow skillfully managed to keep it as an old broken down cowshed, Jimmy," hastily adding... "while still making it a lovely little house as well, of course!" Murphy bursts out laughing and says, "Take no notice, Jimmy, he's only jealous 'cos he lives in a bloody museum!" There's nothing that Greg can say now, his every utterance is taken as a joke, and we are all in stitches at his expense, no matter what nice things he says to try and make amends. We ask Murphy how Meg is faring, an enquiry that immediately sets him on edge and fidgeting with his eyeballs squashed against the face of his watch. "No sign of it yet," he mutters as he's forcing his way to the door, anxious not to overstay his allotted time. We walk partway back with them like a troupe of baboons as the last of the light is brushed away by a soft wind. I arrange to meet-up with Greg tomorrow afternoon and we part company. Our gang turn to face the dim lamplight dancing on the polythene windows and smell the smoke of our wood fire; I feel a lovely feeling warm through me, this really is home and I love it.

Yesterday's snow has vanished overnight and the morning is still and overcast. The chickens are venturing slightly further afield now as new little succulent morsels begin to appear; this doesn't include Madam Sykes, in fact, when I return from the well she is inside the 'living room', pecking furiously at the red bits in one of my new paintings. Getting her out is as futile as trying to drive water uphill with a stick; give her the choice of an open door and a blazing fire and the fire wins every time! The word 'coax' has lost all meaning, I can find no use for the word 'drive' either, she, or rather 'it', is dependable only in a lunatic kind of way. My only chance is that of trying to blackmail her into believing that I want her to jump into the blazing fire, then, with luck, the cussed old sod might just go bouncing off into the kitchen lean-to where she can see the open door to freedom. Not a bit of it! This peripatetic streak of diarrhea, on seeing the world outside, decides to leap up onto the draining board and to smash her way through the lace curtains, sending flower vases and other objects smashing to the ground. During this catastrophic process she catches sight of our dear little bee that has weathered the winter and is now miraculously beginning to stir again. In one horrid split second, our little bee is no more and Sykes has a cheap snack that isn't worth the trouble. I'm at a loss for words, nothing can adequately describe this cantankerous imbecile... I give up!

Thankfully it's a good drying day and the clothes line is full of colour once more, a small part of it for me, mostly running-gear, plus pants and socks ... I'm not complicated when I travel. As for where I shall stay, I haven't a clue, but I shall be packing my sleeping-bag in the hope of being offered a space on a floor somewhere. When you live in a cowshed, it doesn't make sense to squander overnight allowances on fancy hotels; I need every last penny, the hard ground doesn't worry me.

Rowan has somehow come into possession of an oval brown metal hat-box and is determined to haul us back into the twentieth century at last, by providing us with a 'state-of-the-art', up-market letterbox which he has nailed to the marsh meadow gatepost; our very own mail delivery-box... and only a quarter of a mile from the house at that! Anyone can have a biscuit tin, but, a 'hat-box', an undertaker's one at that... now that's really posh! What's more, he's got the hat that goes with it. It's a big stiff black job with a strange kind of plastic rosette type adornment on the side, it looks like something from the 'Mad Hatter's Tea Party'. So, thanks to Rowan, we've now got a smart new letterbox, which has the printed words, 'Saville Row' just visible underneath it... now that's even posher!

It's an uneasy kind of day, one that I shall not be sorry to part with. I really hate having to go away from my family and it's made a lot worse by having no telephone for keeping in touch. Time cannot fly by fast enough for me right now as the day contradicts itself in that it's dawdling, while at the same time racing by. Four beautiful white eggs were laid this morning, but I have no appetite; there's also a lovely smell of bread being baked in the oven as Cari shifts her attention now that the clothes line is full to capacity. The cows are all gathered ominously in an idle sort of way, while the old bull staggers about the place with a kind of lethargic, 'not tonight Josephine', laid-back demeanour. I do my repeated best to drive them away from the technicolour spectacle of our washing, but it's a losing battle; they'd walk many miles just to stand gawping at such a breathtaking show as this here idling in the languid air.

Amongst the umpteen jobs that require doing, I do my best to find time to spend an hour with the boys, nothing very inspiring, just an amble along the lane down past Bootsy's grave where the bank is now a mass of wood-anemones. Spencer has it fixed in his mind that they are 'wooden enemies', as in the style of his 'daftodilses'; I'm not going to argue, idle time is already too fast slipping through my fingers and I must keep an eye on the clock as I don't want Greg to go sneaking back to Plymouth without me. The only thing that I feel good about right now is the fact that I shall have money in my pocket when I get back and we'll have a lot of fun in putting some of it to good use, the very thought of which makes us feel that it's going to seem like Christmas again.

On the way back, Rowan insists on showing me our new hat-tin letterbox that he's so very proud of, and on which he has painted the dribbled words, 'Jim and Cari'. It's while we're standing around admiring this we hear Murphy's excited voice go echoing all around the hillsides... "It's a girl, Jimmy, a lovely girl!" We spontaneously burst into loud cheering before Greg's gruff voice barks out, "Oi'll be goin' 'bout half past four, so dunna you'm be late now!" I wave back to show my compliance and we go running across the marsh to break the good news to Cari.

What greets us on our arrival is a sight that takes our breath away; the little pink bantam is proudly out walking with an entire choreography of golden chicks that have hatched this very morning. We are speechless. Robin instinctively surges forward devouringly, but is held in his tracks by Rowan, much to his displeasure, occasioning Spencer to intervene in restraining him, together with a few friendly words of advice, all of which are swallowed up under his vociferous protests. The commotion sends the little hen packing and hastily gathering her family back into the barn and to the sanctuary of her cupped wings. I appeal to Robin's thunderous eyes, emphasising the virtues of gentleness, but to no avail, the thunder remains no matter what I say and I get the distinct feeling that tomorrow he'll sneak off to school with a pocket full of chicks, just to impress the teacher. He can plainly see that I'm a bit stressed up right now and, as he brushes past me, he gives the most wicked wink with a grin to match; he's just enjoying winding the others up. How can I not love such a rascal of a son?

Counting the chicks will have to wait; Murphy's new daughter is far easier to count. It's going to be an eventful week on the planet; lots of rearrangements to existing patterns, some of them brief, others forever. So many seeds get eaten, never to realise their true majesty, ending too soon in the digestive systems and ultimately into the crap of things, back into the melting pot of the soil. Life is a sparkling thing to be celebrated, not just at the 'hatching', but throughout the living at every stage, because, to be born is to be blessed and burdened with a responsibility to carry love forward, to carry wisdom forward and to never let greed or any other gross appetite upset the balance. We are always accountable to ourselves and, like the crinkly brown leaves, shall ourselves grow old and blow away.

Four Wheels and a Few Jam Jars!

The time comes when we say our farewells and I trudge sadly over the marsh with my humble possessions slung over my shoulder. I know that I'm on course when, under a bedlam of yelping dogs, I see the filthy little grey van parked in a puddle and with a Welsh dresser lashed to its roof and other partially hidden bulky treasures protruding through the open back doors which are tied together with string. I can see that it's going to be a long and draughty drive, but with the solitary blessing of being well ventilated, a bonus indeed when I reflect on Greg's capacity for farting! Murphy is rushing about in a panic as he fumbles together a bag of things to take with him to the maternity ward; the very last thing that he wants is for us to be getting under his feet, so we hit the road and leave him to it.

It's dark when we cross Dartmoor and creep into the tick-tocking sleeping museum where pleased dogs lick even before the light-switch has been tickled. I'm due for a few dog-fleas and a sofa tonight, but it won't be until after my starving friend has dealt with what's plaguing him most of all; late night gammon and eggs seem to do the trick in pacifying him. He's a really likeable bloke, quietly spoken and somewhat shy, never committing himself into revealing any great depth or clarity as to where he stands amongst things. The smile that occasionally breaks from beneath thousands of years of beard, is aggravatingly mysterious and so very distant. He's a dark figure of a man that gets by quietly and can charm antiques with ease from frail fingers and into his hugely strong and eager hands.

It's a Gunnislake robin that strips me from my cocoon at dawn and, what I take for being motorbikes back on the distant road, are in fact, cats purring here on the sofa. It is the last week of March and clocks are chiming the approximate time as they have done for haphazard centuries, cuckoos and nightingales flooding the dew- dawned shoulders flanking the deep, still gorge where the silent Tamar slippers silvery from all along the last two, or the first two, counties on our island.

No sooner the week has begun, the weekend rears up and swallows it. I needn't have worried over where to throw my sleeping bag, my long time friend and colleague, Lefcos, one of the film editors here, didn't so much suggest that I stayed at his place, but more or less demanded that I did. Our two families have been close for a good many years, each of us having three children of similar ages, friendship in depth no less. They are already quite familiar with my passion for long distance running, thus I have been out pounding the roads both morning and night in all weathers. I like to be of the opinion that it helps ease the overcrowding bottlenecks, furthermore I know that Lefcos and Jeannie are rather partial to eating late in the evening when it's quiet and we can talk over wine, about life, art and philosophy, jock-straps and Pink Floyd.

I'm making sure that Rowan's new letterbox is being put to use and am writing home regularly; wanting to go back home for the weekend is out of the question with having no transport. It's the problem that prompts Lefcos's neighbour, Peter, into suggesting that I might be interested in buying his old van. He operates a greengrocery business, driving around the housing estates with a van-load of produce. He drives me out to a little village where he keeps all his stuff and I see the vehicle in question, a Ford Thames, hand-painted blue. It looks okay, no rust that I can see, in fact it looks like it could be a lot of fun, something between a five-star hotel and a 'B&B'. "Start her up, Pete!" I ask, but the old girl refuses to comply, the battery is flat ... amongst other things, I suspect. "Now that's not a very good sign, " I say, somewhat dejectedly, but Peter insists that it's in good order ... just a little damp and hasn't been used for a little time, that's all. I'm not convinced and he can sense this, so he suggests that he gets it up and running for me to have another look next weekend. I agree.

A letter from home informs me that we have seven little bantam chicks and the boys have christened the little pink mother-hen, 'Jeannie', an honour that Jeannie here finds most touching; there can't be many who can claim that they've had a bantam named after them. They have named the other little grey hen, Bridgette, after another of our friends down here along the creek beyond the big river, where some believe that England ends.

It feels so very strange being back in a world of hygiene, synthetics and electronic gadgetry, especially coming so soon after experiencing what must have come close to being a Stone Age, or at the very least, an Iron Age winter. It raises laughter whenever I make reference to it, it's a huge joke that nobody takes seriously, simply because it's beyond their own experience or imagination.

Plymouth suburbia Sunday; a strange, unreal phenomenon with an enslaving call to Sunday papers, fat colour supplements, supplements for any conceivable thing, all of which have required forests to be felled in providing the pulp, together with a billion salaried researchers and reporters in covering every inch of its vast acreage. Printed words and pictures, far in excess of what a mind can healthily cope with while, at the same time, Church irons ring summoning the faithful to take leave of their sins, at least for the time being, and bringing them to their knees before another God. Despite this, an idle silence fidgets amongst the lawns and driveways, just as I fidget in my growing restlessness to be off running under towering dockyard cranes and military bullshit before crossing the ferry at Cremyll and then slipping like butter into a jacket potato, off down memory lane. I shall not be missed, they take their Sundays very seriously here; it's a dressing-gown and slippers sort of day when it eventually breaks wind; I shall have run a marathon by then and I'll be easy-going and ready to play the game of 'Sunday'.

It's a glorious feeling as I leave Hartley Vale; if the rest of the world knew just how marvellous it felt, they would all be out running. A 'Sunday' thought crosses my mind … "Thank God they're not!" I find nothing lonely about long-distance running; a divine sense of aloofness yes … but never loneliness. Near the village along the wrack-smelling creek, I meet the other person with a bantam named after her; Bridget is out walking two sausage-dogs and two small sons; it's an all too brief encounter because I hate having to stop just when I've settled into a rhythm. I leave her shouting promises of coming up and spending a few days with us, in what she believes, to be our 'cottage' in the country, then I melt away once more. Back into the most treasured remembered footsteps and into the sweet vapours of an ocean laced with the scent of gorse all along the miles of cliffs; I wouldn't swap this for any dressing gown and Sunday Times, not for all the tea in China, or anything else that's equated with the measuring of treasure. A horrid thought has just struck me... I must be growing old, any fool knows that tea comes from the Co-op!

Later, tender, tired and at total spiritual peace, I alight on 'Sunday'. Lefcos is his usual, though rather late, enthusiastic self, quoting Rosicrucian philosophy and expressing what amounts to an infatuation with surfing. He expresses a similar diseased fondness when talking of diving, making constant references to 'the boat'. It transpires that he has a dream in which he is at the very centre of a surfing culture. A film-maker in the midst of some colossal 'ocean-poem'. It's fascinating to just sit and listen to him, hear of his love-affair with a boat, which tomorrow... always tomorrow... he'll be doing up ready for his dream. Hopes and dreams, that's what it is all about; a yearning to be larger than life and to be able to walk on water just for a few marvellous moments. We all need our dreams.

I race through my second week feeling much more lubricated now that I can once more afford to buy a bag of chips and, on our arrival back home on Thursday evening, Peter has got the van parked outside his house. Not only has he got it going but he's polished it too and it looks like it is out to impress someone. It isn't long before he appears at the door and I'm taken for a spin round the estate, being shown the van's peculiarities, the column gear-change and the foot operated dip-switch. It's a bit noisy but it really does seem like a lot of fun. There's an acre of room inside it and the engine is just a big lump in the cab, separating the driver's seat from the passenger's. There's not much protection at the front and there isn't much grip at the back either, especially when trying to start on a hill with no weight at the back. This is best demonstrated when Peter, for some obscure reason, reverses it down his fairly steep tarmac drive; probably because there's no tax disc and that a police car has just driven past. A recent shower has wetted the tarmac and the van uses practically an average year's rear tyre rubber in trying to get it back up the slope and onto the road. I offer him fifty quid for it, he laughs and shakes his head, then grins and shakes my hand instead. I've got myself another van, yippee! He hands me the documents and I tremble in terrified anticipation intermingled with feelings of guilt and betrayal.

I daren't breathe a word of this; tax and insurance will surely cripple my earnings this week and, after filling the tank with petrol, I could well find myself unpopular. It comes as somewhat a surprise when, on Friday afternoon, I am invited up to the Personnel Manager's office and am asked if I can possibly stay another week. I bite his hand off just below the 'Rolex' and am subjected to having to listen to nice things that have been said about me; it's that sort of company, good at what it does while still remaining in touch with all those who work for it. It's more like a family than a company, that's Westward Television!

My first priority on Saturday morning is to get the van all legal and roadworthy, so Lefcos drops me off in town while he goes into the Studio to work on his surfing film, arranging for us to meet up at lunchtime. So, with all the legal work sorted out and feeling considerably lighter in my pocket, I make my way in somewhat tingling trepidation, telling myself over and over that I have done the right thing and that it's just what we need. Even the thought of an extra week's work cannot conceal the traces of doubt that I have gnawing away inside me; I just hope and pray that the thing goes and is reliable like my wonderful little Morris was.

While Lefcos and I are relaxing over coffee in the Studio restaurant we are joined by another of his colleagues. Christine is with her mother, just popping in for cake and coffee, as do so many in this cosy little family of a company. I'm introduced to Christine's mother as being the 'wild man' and 'mad artist', the usual dreary, tiresome stuff. The subject of jam making comes up and I mention all the lovely jams that Cari made from wild hedge-fruits and how it helped keep us all going when things got tough. This prompts Christine into asking me if I could find use for a stack of jam jars that she's been hoarding and now doesn't know what to do with. My immediate reaction is to shrug my shoulders and say, "I've no transport to carry them." Then I suddenly wake up and remember … I've just got myself a van! We're in business! I don't even give thought as to whether we actually need them, so blinding is the realisation that I have transport once more. We arrange for me to pick them up on Sunday morning from her apartment on Plymouth Hoe, just fifty yards from where we lived when we first moved to Plymouth all that time ago … memory-lane, that's for sure.

Lefcos and I head back. I have pressing things to do and he has a very busy domestic afternoon of shopping to come to terms with … the 'boat' must wait until 'tomorrow'. Their regular child-minder arrives from just down the road and there's a sudden feeling of claustrophobia with the kids all letting off steam and making a terrible din because they too want to go shopping. Jill, the child-minder, is trying her best to calm them down while Lefcos booms and Jeannie is looking at me, laughing with teeth clenched and pretending to tear her hair out. I feel that it's time I wasn't there. My nerves are already trembling for other reasons, so I wander outside to the van and sit quietly in it and attach the new tax disc, as Lefcos and Jeannie make their escape and go roaring away down the road. I continue sitting where I am, familiarising myself with all the bits, lifting the engine-cover and examining the great mysterious oily lump. I check the water and the oil, then very nervously start the engine and listen for rattles. I generally test everything to make sure that it all works, then I switch the engine off and just sit back thoughtfully.

Jill comes out with the children, she's not aware that the van is mine, she thinks it belongs to Peter and that I'm just messing about in it. "What are you doing?" she asks, and I look back at her somewhat hesitantly and reply "Just trying to pluck up courage to drive this bloomin' thing, that's what!" "It's not yours is it?" she asks, with a look of astonishment. "Yep, sure is! I bought it from Pete last night." "You must be mad, it's worn out, it's been carting greengroceries ever since I can remember." "So, what's wrong with that, it probably means that it's been looked after." She smiles and very slowly shakes her head before wandering off for a stroll around the estate with the children.

I wait a few moments longer, then take the plunge and, in a rattle of tappets, a plume of smoke and crunching of gears, I'm driving it. Jerking and stuttering I go off down the road, round a bend, past Jill and the kids, who all laugh and wave, then I slow off for a junction and stall the engine. I'm thrown into a slight panic as I struggle to find the handbrake and am just about to start rolling backwards when I regain control. Jill laughs as she stands on the footpath beaming with amusement. "Are you running this on kangaroo petrol?" and I yell back, "don't you worry, I'll get the hang of it, you'll see!" I try to laugh but realise that I'm making a complete prat of myself. "Stand back… I'll try again!" I leave them in a toxic blue cloud and go trundling off round the corner and up the rise out of sight, determined to take it out onto the open road and to really get the feel of it.

I head for Dartmoor, this should give it a good test with lots of hills and bends and with plenty of off-road bits where I can practice reversing and familiarising myself with its length. It's really quite noisy, but I'm getting to like it. It feels a bit masculine and I am able to look over the top of cars in front of me; it really is a good runner and getting to feel like fun. I'm rather reluctant to head back, it's only the flickering needle on the petrol-gauge that makes my mind up for me. So I hit the road back to town and, feeling somewhat exhilarated, pull in at the local filling-station and top-up the tank; then, with growing confidence, pull out again and head off down the road to the estate.

Suddenly, from out of nowhere, a police-car pulls me up and I am confronted by a stern faced officer who looks like he is out to score and I'm obliged to open my window. "And what have we here? Are you the owner of this vehicle?" "I am!" "Would you mind telling me your registration number?" "I haven't a clue, I only bought it last night. Got it from a bloke on this estate, he only lives just down the road. I can take you to him if you don't believe me!" He dismisses this and starts grovelling about examining the tyres while I gather together the documents to prove that everything is legal. "These tyres need keeping an eye on... you didn't indicate that you were turning left either!" "Oh, that's odd, I did indicate, don't say they're not working. Do you mind checking them for me now?" He stands front and back, everything working properly. "They seem to be working this time, have it checked!" He has a good thorough look inside the van and can see quite plainly that it's empty. "What are you carrying?" "Only myself. That's all... just me!" I look at him in total exasperation and ask "Do you mind telling me what I am supposed to have done? Everything's in order, I haven't broken the law in any way, shape or form, so what's wrong?" He shuffles up closer and mutters, "Don't get cocky with me, sir!" then very slowly and deliberately, as though he is addressing an infant, adds "vans can be used to CARRY THINGS!" He then stands glaring at me in an attempt to impress me with the power and deeper significance of this most astonishing revelation. "Oh!" I say, and he swaggers back to his car and speeds dangerously away.

Another Sunday is once more yawning all around me. I have an appointment, not with bowls before an Armada, but with jam jars ... on Plymouth Hoe. I'm like a herring gull that's found a bag of chips as I climb aboard my van and set sail for the Hoe, where I park in the nearby Cliff Road, a sacred spot where Cari, myself and baby Spencer had years earlier dined on a bench in my lunch-hour from work. On this occasion the bench is bare, just a splash of whitewash where a gull has been, and Plymouth Sound is without the mighty HMS Ark Royal, only a frigate carries the flag, anchored along with a huge tanker, mysterious and in solemn silence. Oh, what I'd give for one of those lunch-hours now!

'Nescafe' Sunday morning and I'm in an ultra hygienic, highly perfumed, spick and span basement collecting jar jars, which I don't need. The apartment is every bit as bijou as the lady is herself and I hardly dare breath for fear of disturbing any part of it; no place could be more opposite from my beloved cowshed. She has the jars all boxed and bagged ready for me and we make several trips to the van before the crowning moment of the instant coffee arrives. We sit like two shy, consenting adults, smiling our very best Sunday smiles, neither of us knowing what the other is thinking as we proceed to pay homage to the somewhat indifferent beverage.

We say our good-byes and I am for a while lost for the next thing to do; my Sabbath marathon must wait as I just sit here in my new old van and gaze out over the chimney pots to a lonesome sea that forever caresses and violates the granite out-cropped shores. A heavy melancholy aches throughout me and I cannot escape from it and sit here reflecting, then find myself reflecting on my reflections and feel isolated from the world close about me.

There's an abrupt tapping at my window instantly snapping me out from my trance and there glaring at me is the same bland face that I met yesterday... P.C. Bloggs! I brace myself and wait for it. "Oho, and what have we here then, hey?" "Jam jars, just a few jam jars for making some jam, that's all," I answer tiredly, recognising that he's out to make a name for himself regardless of what I say. "Jam jars, hey," he chuckles. "They are CONTAINERS, sir... they can HOLD 'things'! Now I think we're talking, sir!" He proceeds to play with his electronic talking toy, reporting to a secret Big Brother on what he believes he has unearthed and I can see that he dearly wants to arrest me on suspicion of trading in illegal substances. Feeling rather more than irritated, I have to tread very carefully, so I bite my lip and refrain from spitting out, "Sod off, you flat footed twat!" I attempt to soften him by giving a brief introduction to jam making, all of which goes in one ear and out of the other without obstruction. He really does believe that he's struck gold and is about to bust a major drugs racket single-handed, but a van-load of jam jars is all he's got to go on and proves insufficient for him to nail me to any criminal involvement. His armada is sinking fast and, after spotting the 'Westward Television' sticker on my windscreen, I am reluctantly permitted to go about my business; no doubt being monitored every inch of the way!

A Whole Load of Bull!

The week flies by and I put the van to its biggest test yet by driving home in it on Friday night. Noisy as it is, it's a really good engine and has a fair turn of speed, although is somewhat on the thirsty side; but it's reliable and gets me home safely. It's midnight as I gently ease onto the gravelly bit of verge where my old Morris had previously languished; nobody knows that I'm here. The inky darkness feels damp as I tread the silence that is only broken by the ghostly breathing of cows. With no moon or stars to guide me, the darkness is total as I pick my way blindly, reading the earth through the eyes of my feet, until I feel the hill and know that the cowshed is only a little way further on. I give my special little whistle that's known only to Cari, repeat it a couple of times more, then wait. Out from the darkness I hear her call my name, it's faint and is accompanied by a dim torchlight which is raking about in a kind of excited panic; I home in on it and we've soon got candles flickering in jars and cats purring as we hold each other tightly under a feeble squeaking of hellos coming from the boys' room. Everywhere is welcoming and so very tidy; there's even a couple of glowing embers from an earlier fire of twigs saying hello from the hearth. It feels so good to be back home again and with my own well-kept secret that's parked in the lane. Tomorrow I shall take them all on a surprise outing to the coast, we'll do our shopping along the way in Machynlleth and fill the van with all the things we need... after first removing a few hundred jam jars of course!

On Saturday morning I start work early, taking full advantage of the fact that all the others want to enjoy a lie-in. This suits me fine and I make three trips with the wheelbarrow and shift all the jam jars, storing them in the dilapidated caravan for the time being. I then remove the mattress, trying not to fall through the hole in the floor and I cart it over and lay it out in the back of the van so that the boys will be comfortable; my secret is still intact.

I take a trip to the well then, on my return, start a fire and get the kettle hanging over it. It isn't long before I hear it wheezing to life and see the first breath of steam go bending its ghostly way up the chimney. I can hear Chris, the bantam cock, giving it hell outside, letting his new children know who's boss. He's probably intending that I too get the message, having not seen me about the place for a couple of weeks. A few more twigs go on the fire and we soon have lift-off, the kettle's boiling and I make everyone a welcome cup of tea, hinting that I have a surprise in store for them and leave them all guessing as I slip outside once more to attend to the serious business of digging a grave for the emptying of the lavatory bucket.

With this unpleasant job out of the way, I rejoin the gang whose intrigue by now is starting to bite. They must think that my surprise is here in the cowshed as they forage about in search of anything that vaguely looks like a present. I tell them that they're not even getting warm and offer a completely useless clue... that it's light blue! Frustration sets in now as Cari joins in the search, turning it into a fiasco. "Get dressed, boys and put clean clothes on 'cos I'm taking you somewhere nice to do a bit of shopping, okay?" This seems to have the desired effect and, under cover of a noisy battle breaking out between Robin and Rowan over the ownership of clothes, I whisper to Cari what my secret is and of my plan to drive us all to the coast and to have a shopping spree in Machynlleth. She screeches with delight at the thought and the young morning is very quickly and efficiently knocked into shape, even the battle over clothes is settled, cats are fed, new chicks are checked and we head off. The boys all think that we are walking to town but when we reach the hilltop, my secret is out. The big blue van is there for all to see and they go racing away down the hill, over the scar of the old hedge, across the marsh and up to the gate where Rowan's hatbox 'letter-box' still proudly sits on the gatepost. There they stand just staring at this big pale blue lump of Ford that's parked on the verge. It looks quite formidable after my modest little post-office van and nobody says a word as I open the doors and let the boys clamber excitedly inside and settle in the back. Cari carefully perches herself high on the passenger seat and I ask the boys to position themselves over the back wheels so as to add a little weight in helping the tyres grip, then I turn the magic key and... Vroom, vroom! Thunder! Rattles! Smoke! "There... sweet as a nut wouldn't you say!" I'm shouting at the top of my voice trying to be heard over it; this seems to excite the boys still further, they find it a bit macho, rude and rugged, very much to their liking. I let it warm up for a few moments then ease it gently into the lane, the back wheels sending showers of grass and gravel flying into the air as it struggles for grip. Once on the lane we find traction and our new van shows what it is made of and wins us over.

We fairly fly to Machynlleth, everyone raucously singing in competition with the engine that's ranting away here in the midst of us. Having to hold a shouted conversation is really quite exhilarating and it never ceases to be funny, it's the sort of van that I don't really feel that I could ever entirely trust, but one which I'm growing to love each crazy mile of the way. I trusted my little Morris implicitly and, apart from a brief and intermittent problem with its fuel-pump and another when the right-hand front wheel fell off, it was totally trustworthy. I must add that the fuel-pump was cured by a thump with a fist on the side of the bonnet by a garage-man who understood Morrisses and swore by the treatment, going on to set my mind at rest over the front wheel coming off. "Oh, that's nothing, they do that, it's the king-pins!" I had quite inadvertently discovered the most endearing thing about English cars, and now I had gotten myself another, one that I could really safely never trust.

We move about Machynlleth as though we own the place; it's amazing what a bit of money in the pocket and a clapped-out Ford van does for one. We go from shop to shop, market-stall to market-stall; this is our second bite at Christmas and we're determined to thoroughly enjoy it! An inspired and unlikely purchase is a sofa, one of questionable breeding... twelve quid ain't going to bust the bank, especially for something that comfortably seats three volatile sons and fits snugly into the van. Why, in Potters Bar, such a feature would cost thousands!

Loaded down with fresh farm produce, bread, cheeses, fruits, cereals, jars, cans, cartons, a gas cylinder and new clothes for the boys, we rattle along the coast road to Aberystwyth, into old bookshops, junk shops and a fish and chip palace; then we all squeeze onto a bench on the front where a busted pier lures vast choreographies of starlings to later roost. Here we all gorge ourselves silly on enough greasy fish, chips and mushy peas to feed an army.

This day has turned out to be an absolute treasure; it's been a laugh right from the start and our journey back over the mountains is breathtaking, especially when viewed from our new high vantage point. We climb higher and higher and the engine gets a bit hot, giving me a sneaking suspicion that something's boiling. There's steam coming into the cab and we have to open the windows to save them from misting up, but we are spared when a long downhill comes to our rescue and the in-rush of ice-cold air onto an idling engine seems to calm things down. I tell myself to pull in at the next garage and check to see that the radiator still has water in it.

I find a garage and, sure enough, the radiator has virtually boiled dry. It's a wonder it hasn't melted. There's a slight panic when I have the engine-cover propped open in the cab and we have to sit around waiting for the metal to cool sufficiently before I attempt to top it up with cold water. I fear that we might have a leak but I won't know until I've filled the radiator. It is now that the sofa is proving its worth, as too is the fruit juice and ice creams that I have just bought from the kiosk. The time passes by degrees and I slowly begin to refill the radiator, spilling the last of the water over both radiator and engine, creating a thousand drips and making it impossible to see any leaks. I throw caution to the wind and get back on the road, reminding myself to take it nice and steady and to check the radiator as soon as we get back home.

We arrive back safely, nothing's boiling this time but, when I check the water level, it's apparent that there is a leak. I decide that before unloading, we drive immediately off down to the garage in the valley and get some stuff to pour into the radiator and cure it, temporarily at least. We've only just gone past Bootsy's grave when a most frightening image comes bearing down before us... it's a massive bull that's escaped from somewhere and is charging straight at us! "Hold tight!" I yell, blasting the horn and flashing the headlights in an attempt to distract him... futile gestures all of them! This fellow makes 'Max Tractor' seem like Mickey Mouse! He's going somewhere fast, his mouth is slobbering and his testicles are boiling and about to disintegrate. He avoids a head-on collision at the very last second and bashes into the side of the van, scraping his wicked horns along the entire length before diminishing at speed down the lane where we've just driven.

We're all in a state of shock and unable to speak; I had feared the worst and I thank God for allowing him the room to squeeze past us. Nervously I hurry to the garage, where I ask Emrys, the owner, to phone the police as a matter of urgency and report that a mad bull is on the loose, stating that he could well be heading this way. With my duty as a good citizen carried out and my radiator satisfactorily medicated, I drive slowly away, fully expecting to discover around the next bend, a rampant Charolais bull about to mistake my dented and scraped van for a young cow in season. I pass Dan's place... no sign of activity there; then I slowly coast past Murphy's patch, still no sign of the bull ... then ahead of me I notice that the marsh meadow gate has been smashed and the cows are wandering out into the lane. I ask everyone to remain inside the van while I go outside and investigate further. It all comes clear when I see across the marsh a small cow staggering under the weight of a thrusting tonnage of Charolais bull, and then, to my horror catch sight of old 'Max Tractor' lying on his side, bleeding and gored from having been involved in a fight with this massive intruder. It isn't safe to even think about attempting to go home; it's not even safe to try and round the cows up and get them back into the field. There's never a policeman when you want one!

I decide it's best to drive round to Gareth's and let him know what's going on, but it isn't easy when the lane ahead is blocked by straying cows. I manage to make about a hundred yards before seeing that it's impossible because a police van, with blue flashing light, is trying to come the other way. An opportune time to learn how to reverse a Ford Thames downhill and around a bend with cows all over the lane... and the prospect of a bull too! I said that this van would be fun, but I was really only joking.

The Law and I manage to co-operate as I somewhat bravely steer the cows back into the field ahead of the slowly advancing police van. I would feel a lot safer if I could fasten the gate behind the last cow, but there isn't a complete gate anymore. Whilst I am keeping an eye on the rampant bull still going about his business like some contemptible runaway machine, the police officer is unbelievably checking-over my van; I can hardly believe my eyes! "Just routine, sir! "Routine my arse!" I scream at him. "There's a mad bull in this field, and he'll show you what's routine if you don't help me fix this bloody gate!" He glares at me with a look of shock, he's not used to being spoken to like this. The boys all cheer ands the officer suddenly realises that I have my family inside the van, at which point his attitude changes. "Who farms this land?" he asks, and I tell him and give him instructions on how to get there, adding that I shall block the gateway with my van until Gareth shows up. He thanks me, turns the van around and gives a friendly wave as he speeds away.

Whilst we are sitting waiting, a Landrover appears in the lane and squeaks to a stop beside the van. A man bawls across, "You haven't seen a Charolais bull come this way, have you?" "You're not kidding!" I bawl back, pointing to the field. "He's in there!" He shambles out and squeezes by to see for himself. I join him and point out the busted gate, at which point Gareth's Landrover comes over the hilltop and clatters down into the marsh meadow, pulling up beside the injured 'Max Tractor' who is struggling to get up on his feet but is unable to. The two farmers know each other and are somewhat uncertain about what to do next; this new bull isn't one to be tampered with while he's in this kind of mood. "I think he's finished-off th'owd bull of mine!" Gareth shouts from within the relative safety of the Landrover, and the other man moves gingerly into the field and mutters, "Orh!... 'ain't done your bloody gate much good either!" Gareth lights his pipe and sits pondering his next move, shouting a warning for Jack, the other man, to stay where he is unless he wants a sore backside. The little terrier is barking, eager to pit his ounces against the testosterone tons of animated beef that's plundering this little pasture of virgins. I lean across to Cari and mutter, "They don't know what they're missing down in Plymouth, do they?" We have a somewhat nervous laugh as the police van reappears.

I notice that he doesn't do a 'routine check' on the dung-encrusted vehicle that's not only blocking the lane, but has no tax disc either. It reminds me of something John Wain told me, that of an alcoholic farmer friend of his in North Wales who, when banned for drunken driving, went nightly to the pub on his untaxed tractor, driving back without lights, legless, and never once being stopped by the police, routinely or otherwise. I can't help but smile whenever I think of it; it just shows the high regard in which farmers are held throughout the principality... and probably further afield too.

The policeman is now getting excited and I catch sight of Gareth courageously taking hold of the bull's ring and twisting it until the great beast yields and can be led. Both Jack and the policeman are suddenly brave themselves and I am asked to shift my van out of the way so that Jack, now with a tether attached to the bull's ring, can lead the beast almost triumphantly out through where he entered and to walk him slowly back to the farm from whence he escaped. After skidding a good deal and being pushed by the lawman, I clear the way. I'd swear that that cretin of an animal actually gave me a saucy wink as he swaggered by ... the bull gave me a bit of a smirk too!

The old bull is dead. "Damn, he wasn't much bloody good anyway!" Gareth philosophically concludes as he fixes the gate with string before slowly driving Jack's Landrover along the lane behind the bull and farmer, with the police van ahead of the convoy, blue light flashing. So, with no longer having a bull to worry about, the field is safe for us to cross once more and we start to pick up the pieces of our own beautiful day and cart our treasures over to the cowshed. I return with the wheelbarrow for the sofa and gas cylinder and can smell the dusk settling about me as I struggle in a losing battle to keep my load balanced; who cares!

I hear Murphy's voice go booming all down the hillsides as he calls my name and shouts "What was that all about?", no doubt intrigued by sight of a police van in the lane. We labour over a shouted conversation, which can be heard for miles; it'll go even further when Dan passes it on to the postman.

We're all glowing after our exciting day and I get the boys in harness to help me provide fuel for the fire. I'm surprised to see that Cari has got them into accepting that dried cow-muck is safe to use and is as good a fuel as any; what's more we have it in abundance just across the yard in the barn. I set my bushman saw to work on the remains of the loft ladder staircase and soon we have a lively blaze crackling in the hearth and a kettle proudly straddling it.

Whilst I'm busy about the place, I decide to transfer the calor-gas cooker from the caravan into the lean-to kitchen. The caravan has really had it now; the door won't shut properly, the glass has fallen out from almost every window and the entire window above the sink has fallen away. The hole in the floor has grown dangerously bigger and now the large mattress has become a feature of the new van. To celebrate our newly modernised kitchen, Cari is inspired into creating another of her culinary masterpieces from the lovely produce that we bought from the street market earlier. So we settle to a gluttonously ripe evening with our three budding pyromaniacs on the sofa, keeping the hearth alive with cascading arrays of sparks and flames which entertain cats and mice alike and stains all the black velvet air with aromatic scents.

Out across the dark marsh, Gareth, Hugh and another figure are working by the lights of the Landrover; I can hear their fragmented voices and clanking metal mingled with an engine groaning and straining. After a while we see the lights of the Landrover pass by the window and on down beyond the well, before vanishing up the bank and across the wooded hill, leaving the valley to dark silence once more.

Sunday tenderly emerges from the chrysalis of Saturday; only the marsh meadow gate, lashed together with string, serves as a reminder of what happened. There's no sign of old dead 'Max' and the cows are all once more back intimately close and crapping everywhere, prompting me to bodge together another fence in the hope of deterring them. I glean a morsel of 'black' comfort from knowing that there'll be no bull to worry about whilst I'm away but, discovering the pigsty-toilet crammed to bursting point with ewes and their lambs, I realise that it's case of... 'you win some, you lose some'! Getting them out is all too easy... the difficult bit is in avoiding becoming trampled to death when they explode into instantaneous panic simultaneously, all aiming for the same small rectangle of light, where one unfortunately happens to be standing, a behaviour which makes Sykes seem like a saint by comparison.

The inevitable moment arrives when I have to make my way across to the van. I'd like to think that it doesn't feel quite so sad this time, knowing that on Friday night I shall be back for good, but I still feel lousy all the same. Small comfort to see that the radiator hasn't lost any more water or that the dip-stick hasn't shrunk. I start the engine and the boys all cheer and wave as I head off on my long journey into the approaching night.

Blisters and more Beastly Things!

The van behaves itself, although having a thirst that tends to blight me with a growing obsession with the fuel gauge. I could fill my little Morris on two-star and never have to look at it for a couple of weeks, whereas this brute constantly needs keeping an eye on and requires regular top-ups if I'm to avoid getting caught empty between filling stations. I'm not complaining though and I feel a special kind of cosiness when I pull in and refuel myself with the coffee that Cari has made for me. I've hit rainy weather again and everywhere is dark and cold as I sit here with no radio for company, just this great throbbing beast beside me in the cab; a friend and half no less.

I reach Plymouth well after midnight and decide it best to head for the Television Centre, keeping my fingers crossed that my old friend Brendan will be the security man on duty. When I arrive there's a police car parked outside the foyer, I can see two police officers inside talking to a similarly uniformed security guard. Luck is with me, it's Brendan and they all watch me as I drive past and up into the car park, no doubt thinking it highly suspicious. I quickly park then hurry back to announce myself and clarify the situation. "I'll be kipping in the van tonight," I inform them and jokingly request that the two officers keep a safe watch over me. We spend a few minutes jovially getting to know one another and Brendan provides me with a mug of milky tea with fag-ash floating on it.

"Herbal tea?" I ask as , fag in mouth, he laughs yet more ash into it. "Be Jesus, it improves the taste!" Everyone is laughing as the streetlights bleed their dazzling light into the rain-soaked empty streets; it really looks like a most inhospitable night.

At four o'clock in the morning, I'm restless and fidgeting in a kind of half-sleep, when something sinister freezes me rigid... someone is breaking into my van! My hackles rise and my eyeballs burst out of their sockets and go rolling down the van. In panic, I reach for a voice but nothing happens. I try again... my vocal chords have packed up. I sense this 'dark' thing fumbling about in the driving seat and, suddenly my voice connects in one deafening outburst, causing the thief to crack his skull on the roof and crap his pants simultaneously before vanishing without trace into the night.

I cannot sleep now, my nerves are all on edge and I keep hearing noises, mostly the rain rattling on the roof, together with the occasional heavy shove when a big wind gusts. It gradually occurs to me that, had I been in a deep sleep and the thief succeeded in stealing my van, he'd have driven off with me in the back; I shudder to think of what might have happened!

When I tell Brendan, he spills half of my tea and almost pees himself as laughter starts the engine of his huge cough. "You know what you've just invented, don't you, you've actually hit on a security system that actually works in this car park!" He goes on to tell me that this is now a major problem, with vehicles being regularly broken into. "Why, you could find yourself being offered the job of car park night watchman. Nice little number that, Jimmy!"

The week flies by; I don't sleep in the car park anymore, but leave the van parked at Lefcos's until Friday when I shall return like a swallow back to the cowshed. On Friday lunchtime I bump into Steve, complete with notebook and binoculars and with the news that he's just been out to Rame Head and has observed the first swallows coming in off the sea. My heart sings at the thought that, somewhere amongst them are our own dear swallows and that they know precisely how to find their way back to the beam over our bed. It suddenly feels like I'm in a race to beat them back, but I realise that they'll need to rest awhile and fatten-up a bit before resuming the final part of their journey north.

We sit on the wall beside the car park exchanging notes about life; I point out my new van, telling him what happened to the old one and how it had nearly cost me my life. We stroll across for him to take a closer look and he sees the mattress in the back and grins: "Building a nest?" he asks. "It's my three-star hotel, Steve; hot property this is, I've only had it a week and it's already attracted the attention of the police three times, a mad runaway bull and a burglar!" He laughs, thinking that I'm joking; he doesn't get these problems with a Lambretta scooter.

I hit the road home shortly after six and press on beyond Exeter and on almost as far as Taunton before darkness slows me down. I'm really getting to like this van; it's a bit of a character, somewhat on the wild side... we make a good pair. At Avonmouth, I fill up with petrol, knowing that I'll soon be in no-mans-land as far as filling stations go, then I trundle on into the weary darkness and, for one horrid split second, fall asleep at the wheel near New Radnor, abruptly awakening when my tyres noisily hit the kerb, sending the van swerving all over the road, scaring the hell out of me. I really feel very tired and have no tea or coffee to help keep me awake, so I open all the windows in the hope that the bitterly cold air might freshen me up. I stop briefly in a lay-by and take a little jog down the road before resuming my journey, and it's near to Llandrindod Wells when, to my utter horror, something breaks! I no longer have an accelerator, the pedal has gone completely limp and dead, but the engine is still ticking over as I coast despairingly to a halt.

I sit for a few moments gathering my senses before lifting open the engine cover and foraging about in the dark for whatever it is that's come adrift. The exhaust manifold is almost red-hot and I keep accidentally touching it, prompting me to blasphemous outrage as I blindly search for the carburetor, eventually finding it and discovering a lever which should be connected to the accelerator pedal; the linkage is missing. I discover, after a few more nasty burns, that I can rev the engine by hand if I tug at this lever, and I'm doing precisely that when, like an owl swooping on a mouse, a police car pulls up and I'm not alone anymore!

Shiny buttons glinting in the dark, backed-up by a distant Donald Duck quacking on an intercom don't do a lot for my peace of mind. He attempts the 'routine' stuff and it very quickly lights my fuse. I look at him in a hopeless, pleading way and say, "Cut out the crap will you, please! I need help not hindrance! Pass me your torch would you... bloody throttle-linkage has bust!" Without another word from him, he becomes the Good Samaritan and hands me his torch. I open the passenger door for him and he's soon in the cab with me, prodding about with the engine. It's no use, there's no sign of the throttle-linkage, it must have fallen away on to the road somewhere. My only hope is try and operate the throttle with my left hand and to steer with my right, avoiding changing gear if at all possible. He points out that this would be unlawful as well as highly dangerous, prompting me to yell at him once more. "Look!" I plead... "I won't be exceeding ten miles an hour... and there's no traffic about, I can do it! I've got a wife and three little boys waiting at home, they're expecting me and I ain't going to sit here freezing to death if you think I am!" "Okay!" he mutters quietly, shaking his head. "You're getting away with bloody murder, you are!" "Thanks, mate!" I say and we shake hands. He goes back to his car and waits to see how I cope before going on his way.

My best bet is to try starting in second gear and to stay in it, dipping my clutch on all the downhills in order to cool the engine off a bit and to give my hand a rest. Clumsily, I put the plan into action and the van begins to stagger forward and the police car stays on my tail for a little while, then flashes me and speeds away into the night. Thus, I struggle on with what is proving to be virtually impossible, but I cussedly persevere, blistering my hands repeatedly and burning my wrists, in this contortionist crawl in second gear only. The engine very soon starts to glow like Sellafield... there's no way I'm going to fall asleep with this handful of bother that's about to explode.

It's well after three when I eventually reach the marsh meadow gate; I'm thoroughly knackered and with far more blisters that is sensible. I leave the van aglow and twitching and stagger off into the beast burdened unknown, back to the cowshed under the leisured sighing of owls.

On Saturday morning I awaken to amorous wrens mating in the bedroom and to vigorous scuffling noises from the starlings about their courtship in the wall. There's a merry chirping of sparrows coming from the barn too, making everywhere and everything, except me, seem tender before Spring properly awakens. When I take my first look outside, I'm even more shocked to find everywhere is white with snow as a late itch of winter plays a last trick on sensing the first swallows are once more gracing English air.

It's a lazy start all round; my badly blistered left hand requires dressing before I am able to somehow 'drive' the van down to the garage for its own injuries to be attended to. I refuse to allow anything to hurry me, an attitude made easier by the awakening awareness that I was generously paid for my work in television, together with the promise of there being more to come in the summer ... such feelings can't be wasted. The boys find it odd to see me apparently 'relaxing', they've never seen it before and I think it worries them slightly. I call them over to join Cari and myself, and I show them my blistered lower arm and explain to them what happened. Being of mechanical and somewhat agricultural natures, it grips them as I relate the awful business and the requirements of negotiating steep downhills with hairpins and then steep, snaking uphills, unable to change out of second gear. Steering one-handedly while my other hand reached across the red-hot parts in connecting with the little lever from which the throttle linkage had come adrift.

Sermon over, I ask, "Who's going to make us a cup of tea then?" The silence that follows tells me that there's no water until somebody has been to the well to fetch it. I don't press the issue, experience tells me that an unwilling water-fetcher always muddies the water for several days to come. So, today, nobody is going to have a cup of tea... unless of course I say those magic words, 'fish, chips and mushy peas'!

The snow has more or less thawed by the time I set foot outside where the cows are once more clustering about the place, reminding me to attempt to fence-off the promised bit of land for our garden. The sun is breaking through now, it's going to be a nice day for walking, so we make the decision to do the shopping first and to sort out the van's problems second. It's going to be a rucksack-on-back sort of day, but one with a bit of money to throw about. The difference that having a bit of money makes is beyond belief; I'd certainly recommend it to anyone!

We set off down past the well, then up the steep track beneath the still tightly-budded oaks, then across the dome of a sprawled world where snow-capped mountains beckon along the horizon to the northwest. At the farm, Cari and the boys all slip off their wellies and change into walking shoes; there's six miles of walking ahead of us, then six miles back again. It's a mere stroll for Cari and myself, but it's a long way for the boys. One that really makes them appreciate our having a van again, even though it is currently standing broken in the lane!

All along the hedges the dunnocks are singing, flitting their wings in courtship while the yellow hammers boast and flash their golden promise upon an awakening world. We're all in fine form ourselves, skipping and dancing the miles down to inches until we are in the midst of street traders who started early and are anxious to pack-up shop and go home. Fortuitously, I am able to fill the rucksack for next to nothing; it's just like that day at Christmas all over again, and it's all first class produce that would otherwise go to waste. Sadly though, we're too late for the Chelsea buns, but we do manage to load ourselves down with warm crusty loaves and the most seductive custard pies imaginable.

It's a slug-slow walk back, each of us with our bag of fish and chips, mushy peas and crispy pickled onions. It's a wonder that we can move forward at all seeing as it's all up-hill, but my boys are marvellous, there are no complaints, just an unscheduled farting contest at about the halfway point, one which, for some reason, completely corpses them and reduces them into collapsing legless on the bank amongst the merging new vegetation. It's the mushy peas that's causing the problem, these and too much bicarbonate of soda are a dependable fart-mixture, one that helps keep our spirits high as we laboriously head for that farmhouse perched on a hill where our wellies are stored.

Saturday evening and we're ready for an early night, then Dan arrives, still smart from a Saturday spent on a street corner in town. It's only minutes later when the farm gang invades and, like it or not, we have the full wind ensemble, all blowing their hearts out in front of a revived cow-dung fire and the obligatory bellyaching kettle and an oven full of spuds. The runaway bull is the talk of the hills and we are told this story as though being strangers to it. When they are this excited, nobody's listening to anything anyone else says: what's it matter, everyone is enjoying it and I gather in the process, that Gareth is planning a trip to market in order to buy a new bull. Hopefully not a Charolais because, as Dan insists on pointing out, the calves could well be too large for the smaller Welsh Black and Hereford crosses to give birth to. Adding that similar nasty things have happened with sheep as a result of too much interference by Man, with multiple births causing loss of both ewes and lambs during lambing. I believe it to be more to do with subsidies; more cows and more sheep mean more Government subsidy handouts. These quaint hill-farmers are really quite cute and are prone to turning their stock into each other's fields when the Ministry man calls to count them and accordingly calculate the subsidies. It is, by all accounts, quite a skilful exercise, requiring a timely phone call and cunning delay tactics while the animals that have just been counted are discreetly driven into the neighbouring farmer's field and allowed to mingle with the next lot of animals to be counted.

So much money for old rope; an entire history that has depended on crooked methods and with a class system that has always benefited the rich and powerful, while the starving worker who poached a roosting pheasant in order to keep his family alive, was hanged, or if his luck was in, was sent to Botany Bay. Absolutely nothing has changed; they're all at it still, the bigger they are the bigger the crime; rewards for the rich, punishment for the poor. It's easy to work out why the fourth 'R' has always been so necessary, so vitally important. A terrifying force simply had to be invented in order to control the uneducated, under-privileged so-called peasants, thus allowing the mighty to go about their greed with the appetites of pigs.

We seem to be stuck with this 'Religion' thing which has little relationship with either science or astronomy and has no spiritual dimension, depending on ancient history and magic combined. It's more like Heinz than baked beans are, with varieties spread throughout the planet, all of them preying on the frailty and the nurtured ignorance of people in order that greedy, bullying bastards may forever have their way. "God back in his heaven and Capitalism off the face of the earth, only then will there be peace!"

I have some sympathy with whoever it was who said that.

My van is looked at by Emrys, our friendly garage-man, typically Welsh in that he's typically gifted. He repairs engines as though blessed with something beyond learning. All manner of things come to his little 'casualty unit' in the valley; he welds like an angel, farmers love him and I know that I can safely take my van's problem to him and that he will cure it. The van is fixed and I know that I shall not be having the same problem again; such is my trust in this quiet genius that never went to university, never wanted to... never needed to.

Tuesday morning, the boys are at school and Cari is busy doing housework while I survey the overnight damage to my new bit of fence which has been trampled to the ground by cows. They're all standing facing me under the apple trees, all breathing heavily and slobbering great cobwebs of silvery, snotty saliva. I shake my head woefully, lost for an adequate response. Frustration drives me to the point of charging at them, bellowing stuff that only I understand. Lethargically they shuffle aside leaving me staggering to an abrupt halt, face to face with a brand new bull! He stubbornly stands his ground as I almost overbalance onto his massive head. His horns have been crudely cropped, suggesting a possible 'attitude' problem. Whilst these may have been cropped, his temper most certainly hasn't! He doesn't think twice, but charges at me and, with adrenaline squirting out of all orifices, I streak away up the slope and into the barn; I don't remember leaping onto the manger and up onto the main cross-beam, my heart beating faster than I've ever known it to. The snorting great sod is standing silhouetted in the doorway as I scream across to Cari, warning her to stay inside. Maddeningly, she can't hear me properly and shouts back, "Pardon?" insisting on coming to the door. I scream even louder... "Stay where you are, there's a new bull in the yard! Don't open the door, do you hear me ... don't open the door!" I get no response and I can't tell whether she has heard me or not.

This is not a very happy moment and I glance about me wondering what to do next. Then my fidgeting eyes seem to fix on the far corner of the barn where, to my utter disbelief, a huge and placid cow is sitting on my famous old bike, cud chewing and without a care in the world. I simply can't believe my eyes! Why sit

on my bike for heaven's sake, it must be murderously
uncomfortable! My anger grows and very rapidly overtakes both my
fear and my common sense. On seeing the garden fork propped
against the wall, I drop to the ground, grab it and charge at the bull,
prongs first, causing him to turn tail and go frisking away down
through the orchard with me on his tail, down past the well where I
stop and gather breath and watch him go charging off up the hill.
My bawling screams echo all along the hillsides, as he eventually
stops and snorts defiantly, viewing me from the hilltop. I'm just
hoping that we've established a kind of working relationship, a
degree of respect for each other. As for my old racing bike, this is a
complete write-off, twisted and bent beyond belief. The offending
cow isn't offended in any way whatsoever as I extricate her out from
the barn and she obliges me by emptying her bowels all down the
front of my trousers, before swaggering away to join the others.

I wipe myself down as best I can, then join Cari and tell her
what's been happening, having to conclude that we've got ourselves
a bit of a problem with this unfamiliar bull. We need to be extra
vigilant by meeting the boys when they come home from school and
find a safer way back over to the cowshed.

With having most of the hedges now removed, it's not
possible anymore to sneak back over the marsh unnoticed. I take
this as a timely reminder to press on and lash-up some more rugged
fencing, with or without Gareth's assistance, hoping in the process
that the new Hereford bull will get used to my presence and accept
me as being just another part of the scenery.

I waste no further time and use the trunks of the fruit trees
for my fence-posts down the one side and drive-in old stakes with
the sledge-hammer all down the other. The rolls of sheep-wire are
now put to use but, unfortunately, I don't have sufficient barbed-
wire to string along the top. I utilise every conceivable thing,
including two ancient rusty bedsteads which have been unearthed
from beneath the muck in the barn together with sheets of
corrugated iron and the addition of a few longer branches freshly
cut from the forest.

Whilst I'm doing all this frantic hammering and banging, the
cows all gather to watch; they convey an ominous kind of silence
which tends to spoil my growing feeling of smug satisfaction. Cari

comes out with a couple of water-carriers for me to fill and I bravely scale the new bit of fence and stride boldly in the direction of the watching bull. He and I keep a watchful eye on each other as I fill the vessels but, for reasons best known to himself, he leaves me unmolested this time. I feel slightly easier in my mind as I hurry back to where Cari is waiting to tackle a new mountain of washing.

Feeling a few degrees more secure in my fenced plot of land, I start to turn the soil over in a fresh determination to have a garden of our own. By the time that Cari has pegged-out the washing, I have dug a sizeable area and have raked it and mucked it in readiness for cultivation. We now must take a trip to town and get ourselves plants and seeds, so we decide to pick the boys up from school in the van and then indulge in green issues, at the same time checking to see if the swallows and martins have arrived back in town. The very first twitter that I hear shall have me whizzing back to tear the polythene out from the bedroom and kitchen windows; I really want them to feel that they're home the very moment that they arrive.

There are no signs of swallows yet, but we do go a bit mad over the other stuff; trays of cabbage plants, with one variety in particular that I find intriguing... 'Everlasting Cabbage'. We buy onion sets, runner beans, carrots, parsnips, beetroot and an assortment of salad items. With more than enough to get us started, we head back in high spirits, eager to become gardeners.

On our arrival at the gate, we can't see the bull anywhere, so we proceed cautiously and quietly, approaching the cowshed from the corner where the oak tree was felled for us back in winter. From here we stroll round the hill until our roof and chimney become visible, framed by the big sycamore tree. We're in luck, the bull is just visible up in the wood acquainting himself with a young cow, he pays no attention to us whatsoever.

What we do have, however, is a garden full of sheep, all of whom on seeing us, go charging headlong into my new fence. Some manage to leap over it while the remainder persist in trying to bash it down with their solid concrete skulls. Struggling to contain my patience, I attempt to round them up and guide them under the wire at the bottom by the ditch, but with no success. Calm and gentle as I am, they still prefer their totally berserk mode, sending chickens and feathers flying in all directions and we look on in exasperation as they smash the bit of galvanised fence by the back door, before exploding raggedly away down the hill.

I do a lightening repair job on the fence as a growing pessimism squirms throughout my flesh and a soft logic whispers for me not to panic and to wait until tomorrow, then have a fresh look at things and try to work out a better method of keeping the confounded things out. We all go inside and close the world out for a while, kindle a fire from our dwindling indoor wood supply and get the kettle boiling to set the world straight again.

Having seeds and plants about the place and with the prospect of swallows returning, there's a cussed feeling of spring dancing amongst us. We're certainly due for a bit of this to warm us after all the false dawns and daft winter outbursts that we've been experiencing. So it's with a rare sense of hope and determination that we sit before the lively flames; things can only get better and, so long as we all work together, nothing will ever beat us.

The Swallows are back and New Stars take the Stage!

There have been no jackdaws in the chimney this time, they got the message a year ago when the smoke from this chimney was a stranger, but with the exception of the awaited swallows, all the rest of the cowshed residents are once more back here sharing it with us. Spring is overdue and a vast multitude of tender new leaves are about to burst forth into the world, with blossoms and blooms only weeks from breaking into riots. Alas, the scent of may blossom, dog-rose, elderflower and honeysuckle will be missing from the meadow where the hedges themselves are missing. Late wheateaters are still passing through and I see their white rumps go bobbing low over the earth as they head northwest to breed. The pied wagtails are back on the barn roof, doing a bit of tail-wagging and chin-wagging too, while across the aldermarsh, the willows are all in a silvery cushioned blaze and the call of snipe and the vibrant 'buzz' of their wings has been heard of late, with woodcock venturing out at dusk to partake of supper in the swamp where rivers are born.

With the cowshed now more or less as finished as it's likely to be, I shall now have time at last for sharing amongst the wild growing things and in the harvesting of the free-growing fruits of waysides and forgotten corners in a natural provision of treasure for the winter to come, one that may not be so kind to us as the last one was. Having a garden is crucial and it ideally has to be an on-going, all year round living thing. 'Everlasting Cabbage' would appear to be, according to the packet, an additional wonder of the world; I can't imagine a cabbage that keeps coming on and on, never knowing when to call it a day. It sounds pretty okay to me, but I find it somewhat suspicious that none of the other things boast the same.

I can now give time to getting my forthcoming exhibition together and I don't waste any of the light as it extends around us, lengthening the days. I work fast on canvas, I always did, quickly working myself into an obsessive kind of oblivion as I power on. The paintings are beginning to appear, images out of nowhere, still wet and leaning against the walls upstairs and down, making it seem more like an art gallery, but with the stink of turps filling the air. It comes as a welcome relief when we all go out strolling in between the showers, following the lane down past the school, flanked on either side by growing cow-parsley, hogweed, alexanders and a sea of softly swaying timothy grass. The sun is surprisingly warm and a brief shower soon turns to steam rising from the warming tarmac road surface, veiling the very treasure we've all been waiting for; we simply can't believe what we're looking at... the swallows are back! They are all sitting on the road, excitedly taking the water and feasting on the newly abundant insects that have also been attracted to the wet, steaming paradise.

Almost panic-stricken, we turn about and head back up the long winding hill in a race to remove the polythene from the windows. Everyone's bubbling and filled with a marvellous sense of wonder. "They've made it boys! They've found their way back from Africa, Sahara Desert, Mediterranean, Spain, where nasty little people on Sundays shoot little birds for fun; they've survived all that and have come north over Portugal, France, the Atlantic, the English Channel, over Rame Head and up through Devon, Somerset. They've followed the Severn and the Wye all the way up to us and up onto the beam in our bedroom, and they didn't even have to go to school, and we're supposed to be the ones with brains... could you do it?" There's a huge chorus of "No!" together with a loving admiration for these uncomplicated little dunces of the sky, and with a pride that makes us feel that they are very much part of our own precious selves.

Halfway up the hill, in the small garden of the old school house, Emrys Gittens, braces dangling loosely at his side, is out exercising his jowls beside a miserly inadequate bird-table. I call over to him, spreading the good news that the swallows have returned, and he in turn bellows something about Lenin and Carl Marx, culminating in a jowly, theatrical gesture of dribbly whispered words, that I'm not totally unfamiliar with. "God back in his heaven and capitalism off the face of the earth... then there'd be peace, Jimmy!" He hasn't heard a word I've said about the swallows being back from Africa and the simple fact that they are bringing peace with them for us all to share. He taps his large nose, a kind of sign-language intended to persuade me into keeping these profound words of his a secret, fearing maybe a gun in the night or perhaps a poisoned dart from a passing capitalist woodpecker. I see his frail wife ghostly at the window, breaking the best family china of an attempted smile and somehow managing to wave a spidery white arm in a God-permitted brief intercourse.

We hurry away and on past the hugely fat, and enormously friendly 'Weasel's' wife, together with the silvered glowing image of his scarecrow skeleton of a mother, friendly amongst potted flowers and a cat on the sill. These are the loveliest of people, unburdened by God, Politics or Intellect. We wave back, making their day for them more profoundly than anything. At the top of the hill we climb the gate opposite and take a short-cut back to the cowshed. Past the old abandoned caterpillar tractor and down beside the bare hill that's had it's gorse and broom removed, then on through the little wood and up into the small steep field, only to be confronted by a mating bull in the last gateway! I hurriedly guide my family back, taking a detour down the dip and up the hill into the wood, then along and down past our well, we've beaten the swallows back.

Evening is drawing upon us, the polythene has been torn out from the windows and we no longer have to breath-in the toxic turps fumes. Cari rustles up the magic of cauliflower cheese and macaroni, then we go to bed with a fresh keen wind blowing through, freezing our noses and sharpening the sounds of the night; we really are waiting for swallows.

Our weekend is green-fingered, although somewhat of a brownish shade. I turn over as much soil as I can in extending our promised plot; the chickens think they've found heaven and give advanced warning of their intentions, not only do they find the soil a joy to scrat and peck in, but for taking dust-baths too. The long awaited sun seems to have arrived at last and a cock chaffinch is spelling out his bright and ringing philosophy from the apple buds, where a promised splendour of blossoms await their perfect moment to open their eyes upon the softly sailing clouds. It's when he pauses to take a breath that I hear... the twittering delight of swallows returning over the cowshed; they're home again!

Our labours come to an end as we stand watching them circling above their old family home, unhurried as they re-acquaint themselves with the sights and smells, partaking of the newly emerging insects, the vital ingredients that make the whole cycle possible. Everywhere is warm and dusty; the sun has summoned all sleep to awaken and release all old darknesses and for new light and colour to pour sweetly inside and out, everywhere.

A celebratory cup of tea is very much in order and so we drowsily amble up the slope and into the kitchen, where the newly opened window has allowed Sykes and an accomplice to enter and plunder, smashing crockery and leaving their calling-cards about the floor. There's a brief pandemonium as we attempt to remove them; it's a great game for the boys, especially when Sykes flaps up onto my back and pecks my head. She really does have an ugly side, one that she's more than happy to flaunt. I sometimes put this down to the biological impossibility of her being half male... probably in the process of becoming wholly male; this might help account for the fact that she's only ever been known to lay one egg, and this the size of a sparrow's egg, having no yolk in it.

I light a small fire of twigs and the slow pale smoke breaths in a whisper from the chimney, welcoming the swallows home as it melts silently to nothing. Somehow, quite miraculously, they re-awaken old memories inside them until their picture is close to perfection and they descend to explore the lower air that has trees and chimneys protruding up into it as they glide caressingly over and around the shapes of the buildings, before, in a triumphant fit of babbling, they come sailing back in through the window and straight up onto the beam in the bedroom.

Their joy is absolute and unquestionable as we all stand in hushed silence at the foot of the stairs and eavesdrop as they settle beside their old nest, then, as though over-excited, dive off again. They fly recklessly and noisily around the room a few times, briefly settling on the beam once more, before swooping back out through the window to perform crazy laps of honour around the cowshed. The other swallows have similarly reclaimed the kitchen lean-to and are ritualistically blessing what, for them, is quite simply 'the palace of birth', provoking a wren into audible abuse and physical protest. This has no affect whatsoever; nothing can equal the joy of these newly returned swallows, absolutely nothing can! What's left of the day belongs to them and we watch in amazement, sharing, if it's possible to share, their feeling of celebration. Truth is we're a billion miles and more from what they are, neither understands or knows the other; wanting just simply isn't enough and never can be.

In the black sparkled night, my old friend Orion is falling into other eyes, others' skies and is held gripped in the thorns at the bottom of the sky as though saying goodbye. Throughout the barbaric winter she has been my rectangular companion, glistening in all the powdered milk-light of the moon upon the iron-frosted ground. I have talked to her and she has spoken to me; countless dark hours I've spent leaning my elbows on the pig-sty wall, binoculars in my hands, gazing in wonderment into the heavens, never, ever, able to get enough of it. Orion is the constellation of my heart, none other was ever so companionable.

The sky is such an amazing place and we're all children of it. It's the unimaginable distance that makes something that's travelling at trillions of miles per second, seemingly stand still; things can so easily get overlooked because of this apparent lack of movement. Tonight I'm looking into the northern sky and homing-in on Cassiopeia and I notice what appears to be a faint white scratch against the jet-black background; this isn't normal. I check and double check to make sure that I'm not seeing things, or have anything wrong with my binoculars. It's there alright and I want to awaken Cari, but that would be risking my life; I'm in a dilemma because I think I've discovered a new comet... I really must tell somebody! Risking life and limb, I throw caution to the wind and make my way up the stairs to where both Cari and the swallows are sleeping. I miraculously avoid a wild elbow as I whisper as loudly as I dare, "I've discovered a new comet in Cassiopeia, wake up!" Persistence pays and Cari gradually creaks awake and hears what I'm saying. She's up like a shot and, draped in a nightie and a heavy tablecloth, shoots down the stairs and out into the yard and up to the pig-sty wall. It's bitterly cold as she searches the sky, before eventually locating Cassiopeia, her concentration is deafeningly silent, then she gasps "Jimmy, you're right... it's a new comet!" She stands staring at me in the starlight, her eyes wide and unbelieving, then she adds, "We must let Patrick Moore know about this!" An obscure thought scratches a mark onto the deep black of my own mind... how the hell am I supposed to let Patrick Moore know? Carrier pigeons are all roosting now, my only chance is a long-distance owl... even then I haven't a clue as to where to direct it. "Oh, yes!" I say with a slight trace of sarcasm, "and how do you suggest that I perform this miracle at this unearthly hour?" Somewhat irritated by my lack of sparkle, Cari snaps, "You go to the phone-box, that's what you do... telephonists work all night, ask them to find his number. It's an Observatory somewhere in Northern Ireland, they'll soon find it!" I can't win, Cari is determined to have a new comet named after me, so I wrap up warm and head off into the deep dark night.

I see a polecat in my headlights, it's eyes shine pink as it turns briefly before bounding away, and I catch sight of sheep eyes, like fallen stars, when my headlights sweep across the hills before the lonesome little phone-box comes into view. I roll up beside it and prepare myself for this dialogue with some lonely little person on a switchboard. Tentatively I dial the operator and a voice answers "Operator Service. What number do you want?" The voice is not customer-friendly. I've heard it before, it's usually posh, loud and arrogant. Somewhat hesitantly I say, "I need to get in touch with the astronomer, Patrick Moore." "What's his number?" he interrupts impatiently just as I'm about to explain that I haven't got it. "That's the problem. It's in Northern Ireland, an Observatory somewhere; I thought that you might help me find it." "You must be joking!" he booms, dismissing me as being a 'nuisance-caller'. "Can't you ring one of your colleagues on a switchboard over there, they'd probably know his number? I've discovered a new comet in the heavens and I..." He interrupts once more and in a shouting voice blasts, "Oh, yes... and my arse is a pumpkin!" at which point I'm disconnected. Frustratedly I make my way back; it's turned one thirty and the heavens are ablaze with more shining stars than there are grains of dust upon this planet. One of them a new one millions of miles away thundering secretly and silently to nowhere.

It is two days later when we hear it announced on the radio that a new comet has been observed in the northern sky, apparently discovered by some Japanese astronomer. The comet is now bearing his name forever.

Down in the little wood at the bottom of the field, a chiffchaff is singing and I can faintly hear the sweet weeping song of a willow warbler further away. Everywhere is a gentle breath of spring and the buds are swollen in the pregnant trees before the great green moment of birth. It's a lovely feeling as I stand here with the boys, listening to our little friends newly returned to the woodlands about us. We discover that the ponies have been using the hut which we built with branches last year. It's absolutely piled with horse-muck, which is rather surprising because it couldn't have offered any appreciable shelter, only a sense of confinement, which I suppose must have been reassuring for them in some small way during the blizzards and storms. It's good news for us because the muck will be useful for the garden and the hut may yet provide us with a lot more of the stuff. The ponies are just visible away up the hillside, enjoying the gentler air and sampling the new tender grass. No doubt relieved at no longer having to suffer the misery of a brittle blanket of snow across their backs.

Miraculously, there are squirrels that have survived the autumn and winter purges of Dai-the-death Morgan and Griff, his gangling drey-poker. Cheekily, two squirrels are bouncing over the earth, unearthing the hazels and acorns that they buried during last year's harvest. It's heartening to see them taking their place once more within the awakening tapestry.

Nervously, the spring is emerging; the fieldfares and

redwings have already drifted away to the east, having stripped the hawthorns of last year's crimson time of plenty. Their buds are softly opening now as a new promise opens its eyes all down the ancient line of hedge. There's a sweet and easy birdsong trickling into the air, just like the sparkling water from Winter bog into the Spring flowing stream.

A tawny owl has been hooting throughout the last few days as well as nights and there's a playful kind of shouting from jays and crows all along the timbered hillsides. The ravens nested earlier in the forest, but they still come high across our valley, performing their half barrel-roll punctuated flight and calling somewhat more melodiously than the crows, always finding time to see off the wheeling buzzards from their patch of sky. We just root about in a kind of leisurely aimlessness, indulging in this marvellous feeling of anticipation and expectation that's itching all around us, while Cari finds a little much-needed space of her own.

Following a briared, brambled and tangled line of blackthorns, with blossoms that look like snow-flurries dancing all around their thorns, we watch the water from our infant stream, hear it tinkle for its last time before tumbling down and around the roots, swirling and curling, gurgling, beautifully describing, not so much the birth of a river, but the very conception. Here in the aldermarsh, the earth all around us is now releasing her weathered treasure from the womb, from fathoms of mosses and roots from whence the willows climb and bend in all caressing air, colouring it as it is these very moments, with gold and silver finery laced with the sweet thread of a tiny warbler bearing her name.

We all linger in the midst of this inestimable schooling, looking and talking about everything that we are seeing and hearing. A glance across at Robin shows him to have parted company with his knitted red pom-pom hat and also with one of his wellies, together with whatever socks there were crammed inside it; I notice also a formidable rip in his trousers and a disgusting celebration of snot smeared across his grinning face. I close my eyes in a silent, private scream which Rowan and Spencer hear. "Oh, Robin! Look at the state of you!" I hear them gasp, in a gesture of disowning him and bringing reality crashing down amongst us, scattering our dreams together with the birds.

I wonder why it is that I never see a wild creature so similarly at odds with its environment? Is it perhaps because 'rebellion' is known only to Homo Sapiens, as is the attracting of attention to oneself for reasons other than to entice a mate? A million thoughts condense into a few despairing seconds in my mind, the very realisation that the tiny warblers, the swallows and others have so simply, so miraculously returned. They have flown day and night, over land and sea, quarter of the way round the planet with nothing resembling a G.C.S.E., while my offspring here can't even stroll through a tiny wood without coming out of it half naked and covered in snot! I thank the Lord of whatever it is that has made me no more than dust and for sparing me being interrupted by the first cuckoo of Spring; I couldn't have coped with so full an orchestra today!

Robin's tadpoles are getting to look like dinosaurs in their glass jar on the windowsill, especially when the glass magnifies them. Restriction of space has protected them from natural predators, only to reduce them into becoming predators of themselves. Sadly, we should have learned that, when people are treated like tadpoles in a jar, they do themselves become as cannibalistic tadpoles, although sadly lacking in the tadpole's ultimate escape-route as a frog.

Had not the earth been hit by asteroids, dinosaurs would never have permitted Man to indulge in the luxurious position of becoming something with nothing bigger than himself to worry about anymore. Thus, an ancient beyond ancient, time-old design was smashed because, even God could never have controlled rogue elements that most surely condemned existence at all to be, of necessity, subject to a Russian Roulette dimension before it could work properly. It is a disturbing thought that Man wasn't really intended to be boss, and that it took a gigantic accident, and others before that, for it to be otherwise. Had we kept our 'wildness', then so would we have kept our wits, our very wisdom, as a species at balance and at harmony amongst species.

Some days later, I find Robin's hat caught up on a strand of barbed wire whilst I'm emptying his young dinosaurs back into their rightful aquatic wilderness, no doubt to be cursed and hated for so doing. There's no sign of his welly, but I can't say that I'm really bothered. The good news is that my bit of fence is still standing and is doing its job as intended; apart from chickens and cats, the garden has not been invaded by creatures with a weight or intelligence equal to or exceeding my own.

It's a comfortable world knowing that there isn't going to be a huge foot come crashing down and squashing me accidentally, just as it is for the peewits and the larks who run the gauntlet of not only Man, but sheep, cows, horses and pigs as well. There's no luckier species than Homo sapiens who, with all opposition removed by some astronomical haemorrhoid, then set about being the monster amongst himself and becoming that very foot that trampled his own precious eggs.

The redstarts are back, nesting in the same corner of the barn as they did last year, only four short hops away from where the pied wagtails are once more nesting. The woodlands ring with the songs of pied flycatchers and wood warblers; all other 'residents' are accordingly going about their business too, and the little bantam chicks are not so little anymore as they learn and grow and go on learning and growing. Sykes remains a mystery and, for some strange reason, refuses to roost in the barn with all her 'friends', driving them mad by day, then vanishing at roosting time. Our black cat, Tony, is doing something similar and the boys are a bit concerned over his sudden absence. When I discuss it with them, relating the bull in the lane and, before that, the visiting baritone tomcat at midnight, it's not too difficult to guess what he's up to.

The first blossoms have opened on the apple tree; war-planes are demonizing the entire area at almost treetop height and are bristling with armaments, wrecking our peace with their terrifying explosive invasion upon us. We are helpless, there's nothing that any of us can do that can alter this wretched dinosaur of things, simply because this was the path we chose to follow. Animals scatter in abject fear and Murphy's dogs bark frenziedly at the sky; nothing remains passive to this hell of a thing that unites us through our fear alone.

Very early on Wednesday morning, just as the dawn sun steals into the bedroom, I am awakened by the sublime sound of the first cuckoo, deafeningly close in the apple tree. This awakening is the loveliest one of my entire life and is made even more beautiful when I hear another cuckoo singing in a different key down in the aldermarsh and can hear their echoes bouncing all down the hillside, making it sound as though a whole army of cuckoos have come to raid nests and leave behind their countless orphan offspring for unsuspecting foster parents to bring up. The echoes must confuse the cuckoos themselves into thinking that they have serious competition to be reckoned with, prompting them to sing even louder and longer, while I lie back luxuriating in their confusion, willing it to go on and on and on.

Chris, the cockerel, is irritated into making his presence known and, in a clumsy flash, is out through the hole in the barn roof and is screeching his clarion call repeatedly, using it more as a flame-thrower than a trumpet and flapping his wings to show the cuckoos that he's pretty handy with these too, if he has to be. They get the message and a little while later I hear them faintly calling from several fields away.

They are a bit like nomads, wanderers without a home to go to anywhere on the planet; a strange role for a bird to be burdened with. Darwin would no doubt explain it as a transitory state, perhaps something between a haddock and a mole, but I prefer to believe that, when the Almighty 'Arthur God' sat down with his spouse, 'Elsie God', making all the fowls of the air, they discovered that they had a few bits left over. Not quite enough for them to make a complete bird, they nevertheless felt compelled to do their best with what little they had remaining, right down to the very last feather. "There!" said old Arthur, looking down at his handiwork, "you poor little thing. I can't find much that you can do, I'm afraid; we've run out of nesting skills and I've only got two notes left over to make you a song out of. As for where you're going to live... that's going to be a bit of a problem, everywhere's been taken up. Have you any suggestions, Elsie?" Elsie looked sadly down at the pathetic little bird and pondered. "Why don't we make the other birds look after it... those little pipitty larks and waterywarbler things that we made on Tuesday, and we could ask a few more besides, they'd teach it all that it needed to know if we asked them nicely!" Arthur's eyes lit up. "Elsie, I think we've cracked it! It's a bit like that tree we made, you know the one, it couldn't stand up on its own... Ivy, that's what you called it... remember?" Elsie smiled knowingly and patted the odd looking bird and sighed; "Well, you poor little thing... seeing as we can't find you any skills, no brains or very much else, your song's going to be the same as your name. Just so you'll never forget it, here's a 'cuck' and here's an 'oo'... cuckoo! Now you go off and practice it, okay?" And so it was, the Fowls of the Air were complete and Arthur and Elsie had an early night.

As though to emphasize a certain over-zealous tendency in Arthur God's 'Fowls of the air' assignment, old cock starling is sitting in the damson tree by the back door, more or less choking with verbal diarrhoea; he's like a pound of sweets crammed into a quarter pound bag; so over-filled is he that he can hardly sing at all. He's a mimic and a ventriloquist and I swear that old Arthur in his wild enthusiasm, mixed in bits of parrot, budgie and mynah bird when he created this character of a bird; maybe this was the reason for there being only left-overs for the cuckoo! I know that the curlews are back because the starling is telling me, just as he is telling that the tawny owl has been screeching about the place and buzzards have been 'mewing' over the valley and dogs barking and Sykes cackling. Heaven only knows what Darwin would have made of it all!

More Tidying-up and a Walking-stick to help a Pig!

The spring sunshine brings Meg and Murphy with their babe in a pram out into the lane, along with nanny-goats and a whole assorted rabble of noisy dogs; they look more like a migration than a family. Getting even a glimpse of the new child isn't so easy with these intimidating pedigree canine cretins straining at their leashes and frothing all round their ugly, shark-like gapes. I don't feel easy and find them alien to the gentler nature of things; they almost unearth in me a morsel of affection for Dan's absolute bastard of an animal... but on reflection, that's stretching it a bit!

We're off on a long walk. The idea being to go into the forest and follow an ancient pathway that's now overgrown and very secret, eventually coming out high on Gareth's wooded hillside overlooking the marshland where the peewits nest and where, further down still, the pool lies cradled amongst a blanket of trees. First however, we have to get past Dan's patrolling brute who is enjoying and abusing the kind of liberty that Murphy's monsters are all bellowing for. He may not be a pedigree but, being a so-called 'working dog', he commands a far more highly prized commodity... freedom! These pedigree brats I'm sure would give their ears, even their testicles for even an ounce of what he's got... they've already given their tails!

The working mongrel and I have a bit of eye-to-eye contact. Something which the dog does slyly, having straightway singled me out as being the one he'd most like to bite. I can tell that he's out for his hat-trick as he circles me, teasing, testing my reflexes, waiting his chance to score. Dan remains oblivious to my predicament in a similar way as his dog; he's really quite tickled by it as he pretends not to notice. "Can't you get this damned thing under control?" I call out in frustration, and Dan suddenly pretends to notice and bawls venomously, "Damn you, bloody dog!" and does his customary lash-out with his welly. The dog falls about laughing and it takes two tomcats in an ugly fur-flying brawl over in the yard to deny the dog his hat trick. In an instance he's over the fence and the cats, only at the very last second, flee for their lives back up onto the stack of bales in the shed, where they had previously been matching up, fortunately for me, holding the dog's attention there while I make my own escape.

Dan would rabbit on all day if you let him; he's hard to part company with and he continues talking until he's having to shout and we are all slipping round the corner out of sight. We leave him to begrudgingly trudge back over to his mongrel and to pet it lovingly and tell it what a goody boy it is. Although we didn't see Sorrel, we concluded that she must be on heat and attracting the attention of those tomcats, some of whom have no doubt arrived here with rucksacks and sleeping-bags, only to depart days later with black eyes, ears missing and badly limping, blissfully happy nevertheless.

In the forest we are fortunate enough to see a dog that is truly free and wild... a deep-chestnut coloured dog-fox, enjoying a moment of spring sun, until we appear and spoil it for him. Swiftly and silently he glides away, melting into the wilderness. No trace of human imprinting to have messed him up; this is a dog's dog, persecuted for being that way. What noble arrogance he shows in his disowning of us before distancing himself. Little could he have known that we were looking at him with affection, fully aware of his habitual crossing over into our own lives as a bit of a menace on the odd occasion. We walk past the spot where he had been reclining and a sharp rancid smell wafts across us, unmistakably fox!

Here in the forest, regiment upon faceless regiment of Sitka spruce reach away in an anonymous blanket, which permits no sunlight to touch the earth below, making it a desert, a faceless place, barren of botanical beauty and of little or no use to much else either, with the exception of goldcrests. They seem to thrive and become even more secretive because of the vastness of this suffocating plague upon the face of Wales. There is evidence of heather on odd fragmented bits of bank, suggesting a previous habitat that had skylarks and pipits, whinchats, grouse, harriers and lots more besides. There are also signs of a rich deciduous variety, sadly only the stumps remain, and they have been treated with a chemical to hasten their demise. We are treading on what was once an upland heath with heather, gorse and broom, silver birch, mountain ash and hanging woods of oak, with beech and sweet chestnut flanking the slopes; a very beautiful world gone forever.

We progress along the ancient pathway that's been hi-jacked by capitalism, feeling angry over the gluttonous appetite for paper, the greatest throw-away item of them all, a money-spinner for speculating city men. This is what happens when you lose your dinosaurs! How the footpath has survived at all is a miracle, but it's a forgotten place and is nigh on impenetrable because of it. Ahead should be an old stile and the sunlight again; we grapple on.

At last... space; I can't believe it, there's so much open space and light. Gareth's hillside is completely bare, not a single tree remains; what's more, the ancient row of hawthorn trees that had reached away down to the pool, has been grubbed-out too, roots an' all! There are splashes of grey-black ash where recent bonfires have been; the picture of devastation is such that we can hardly take it in. This hillside was previously blessed with splendid old oaks, beech, ash and chestnut, plus a few holly trees and some cherry, now there's absolutely nothing, just stumps, sawdust and splintered fragments with butchered soil wounds where machines have dragged them away. All to make space for a bit more hill sheep subsidy. It's a whole world lost for tree-creeper, nuthatch, woodpeckers, owls, doves, tits, finches, thrushes, blackbird, tree-sparrow, robin, wren, hawks and a million other little things. This is green terrorism no less, condoned and encouraged just as is this draining of the marsh, quickening the rains into the streams and rivers, surely to cause flash-flood problems to come for those living down-river.

The peewits are greatly distressed. This has always been their home and they have every right to be suspicious of us entering their space, even though we stay close to the neighbouring farmer's hedge. I need the 'other worldliness' of coots and grebes and the soothing comfort of a mirror of water where the upside down sky sprawls at rest. Even with a tyrannical school cook wielding a poker and getting her knickers in a twist on the opposite bank, this pool has always been a safe harbour for my soul; if we're quiet she won't even know we're here.

Suddenly, shrill sounds pierce the air and the peewits all take to the wing; it's the farm-gang, all haring down the hill to join us. They come panting and sploshing through the marsh making a din that's even louder than the peewits, such is their eagerness to be with us; peace and tranquillity will have to wait. Elwyn is first to join us and excitedly says; "Have you come to see what they've done, Jimmy?" I reply somberly that I couldn't really miss it, adding that it was a lovely old bit of woodland and that the hawthorn hedge was the best I'd ever seen, absolutely full of nests. "Not that, Jimmy; the pool! Haven't you heard what they've done? They've drained it!" I can't believe what I'm hearing and I ask him to repeat what he just said. The others have joined us now and everyone is fighting to be first to break the news. "Electrocuted all the fish they did, Jimmy, dumped them in the canal, thousands of them... except the pike, some great big ones they reckon. They dug a hole and buried them alive... it's going to be trout fishing from now on, fly only; what d'you reckon?" A sense of outrage has silenced Cari and me; the others all mill about in re-establishing a pecking order, oblivious to the concerns of adults.

It's true what they are saying, the pool is now a puddle, not the pearl that we remember; money has spoken. A syndicate, which includes Uncle Mostyn, has taken it over, ridding it of its indigenous roach, perch, tench and the famous pool-pike, all of whom for centuries had given this jewel of a place its deep secret magic. Now it's to become a goldfish bowl, re-stocked with a few rainbow trout for the sport and pleasure of a few moneyed halfwits who really don't give a damn about the place; I'm outraged!

The shoreline is now a deep expanse of stinking slimy mud and rotting weed with an assortment of previously submerged things, which are proving to be irresistible to Robin who, adding insult to our injury, goes wading in right up over his crotch. The others all scream at him to come out and stop showing off, frightening a solitary moorhen and bringing the school cook out to investigate. She watches us grapple with our slippery item of disgust, no doubt she's clocking who we are and how many there are of us, what time of day it is, anything and everything in what for her is an amazingly modest display of self-supposed authority. She needn't have bothered, there's nothing here that makes me want to stay. I just feel sick and so I turn away and the rest of the gang follow me through the trees and back out to the other scene of destruction.

I refuse to look at Robin and instead cast my eyes up ahead where, perched on the hill like a sore thumb, the farm stands up stark and isolated. There won't be many owls hooting there tonight, in fact there'll be hardly any birdsong there at all anymore, just the wind, a whining dog and a tractor.

It seems strange how the farm children have accepted the new bareness about the farm without question; the old woodland and ancient hedgerow meant really no more to them than untidiness and my own reaction to be eccentric and somewhat comical. I can even sense a broad swathe of pride in all of them over the fact that men and machines have dutifully tidied up the land and got it looking neat, with plenty of new space and open air to replace all the pests and diseases that trees and hedges to them represented.

Even after a goodish spell of warm Spring sunshine, the farmyard remains a sticky, stinking mess of all manner of excrement. Recent deforestation activity has added dollops of clay and mud to the equation as we pick our way through it all. There's an enormous old sow that has free run of the farm; she wanders at will wherever she pleases, partaking of anything that takes her fancy. Apart from having multitudes of nipples, she has the most evil-looking growth that's the size of a football hanging from her stomach. Nobody seems the slightest bit concerned about this and it doesn't appear to bother the pig much either. On this occasion she is standing up over her ankles in primaeval sludge, while two farmers, one of them with a walking stick, puff away at their pipes and intently watch while a boar with a fearful corkscrew phallus attempts to mount her. The farmer with the walking stick is stooped beside them and is prodding and firking away with his stick, trying to help guide the boar's part into position with the much larger sow; he's bending over so far that his cap has fallen off into the filth. We are witnessing a bit of 'state-of-the-art' farming... real hi-tech stuff. The air is sweet with scented tobacco smoke and the kids are all in an agony of choking to contain their laughter, none more so than Robin who very quickly loses his footing and is writhing like an eel in deep animal effluence, way beyond my ability to have any influence over him. The two farmers go stalwartly about their work and the trusty walking stick eventually proves to be the very love-accessory for the boar, who after an excited initial grunt and an ugly shove, falls fast asleep and remains that way for the next quarter of an hour, before opening an eye, grunting and shoving again, then going back to sleep.

At this point, Gareth comes slowly over, grinning and still biting hard onto his pipe. Rubbing his hands together and in what I suppose to be 'job-satisfaction', he mutters; "every time he grunts it's another piglet... that's what they reckon, Jimmy!" I laugh back as best I can, calculating that, by this reckoning, the boar won't have finished until gone seven tonight. He laughs and I ask him what the growth is that's hanging from the sow's stomach. He crinkles his face up in an agony of trying to avoid the question, then mutters; "Well, damn... it's a bit of summat her's picked up I shouldn't wonder... isn't it!" We concur that that's probably precisely what it is and get smartly off the subject before we're in it up over our own ankles. I steer well clear of the 'other' subject too and shift my concerns on to the state of my youngest son, wishing in a kind of ironic sarcasm, that there were a nice pool nearby that I could throw him in and scrub him down before allowing him to set foot in the cowshed. He's happier than those pigs and he's made absolutely sure that the shit all over his body has migrated into his hair and ears.

We head back across the hill and into the secluded comfort of our own breathing woods and all the welcoming sounds that fill the valley. Our little place looks like a tiny matchbox way down beneath us and we can see all the cows within close proximity of it, as though the grass there tasted better. When we come to the well, it's a relief to find it still safe from animal interference, and I take comfort too from spotting the bull some safe distance from the house. This allows us to organise the boys into making a discreet cattle-drive, easing them to pastures new because, what I have in mind is a bath for a boy in a cattle-trough at the bottom of the field. It will be better for us all if the bull and all his cows are not in on what is likely to be a life-threatening operation upon an, as yet, unsuspecting son!

With all the beasts now safely at the other end of the valley and with new smoke ruffling from the chimney, Spencer and I escort Robin down the slope. He's guessed where we are going and has already performed his rabid chimpanzee act, winning in the process the concession that Rowan stays behind and that no soap will be involved. This suits me too because it's the cows drinking water; it's only the fact of it being their organic matter that I'll be removing from Robin and his clothes, that gives me a conscience that I can live with. How odd it is that he can tolerate foul animal stuff in his eyes, ears, nose and mouth, yet one little bit of soap in his eyes and he's crying despairingly as though his world was about to end. Smirk as he may as he swaggers back up to the cowshed baring all to the world, the soapy bit comes later!

My meteorological rheumatic right buttock hasn't failed me over the past winter, pardoning me from the more usual weather forecasting systems. Prolonged rain is always a pain in the arse, and it's trying to tell me something right now. With an upsurge of warmth and new leaf growth to draw away the moisture, I hadn't really expected the system to still be working, but it's there alright... the twinge that says 'rain'. Normally, this highly sensitive neurological mechanism takes a rest about now to re-charge its batteries, but there's obviously power in the old backside yet. It's warning me of approaching dampness, nothing more precise than that and not entirely bad news either, because the heavy clay soil in the garden has already started to turn solid and the new seeds and plants will benefit from a spell of wetness. So too will the new nettles which are coming good now and will be nice to eat, tasty, tender and not yet plagued with insects, requiring only the briefest contact with lightly salted boiling water to tenderise and nullify the sting. All too soon they will outgrow their tenderness and become tough, as sadly do most things that actually possessed tenderness in the first place.

The weather duly arrives, not so much in the form of rain from punctured heavy clouds, but a sullen, fallen skyful of sad grey dampness, without any trace of direction or any movement in the whole dank mass of it. There's a lot of lingering drizzle before a breeze eventually starts to skip some shape into the sky and rip a few holes for the sun to break through once more.

Spring is a bit of a clown and isn't ever far away; everything looks brighter now that it's been watered, even the birds sound brighter, they're definitely louder at first-light, possibly because there are now more of them. No diamond, or any other precious thing, could ever equal the richness of the rapturous dawn tapestry of birdsong, especially when there are golden threads of cuckoos stitched into its design. Just a few precious weeks, that's all it takes before birds have fought for, and have found, what they've been shouting their hearts out over, and a reality then sets in to silence them once more. Why is it that delusion so often follows illusion, and evasion follows hot on the heels of persuasion? It's the clown of Spring in love-tide; ebb flow, stop go, yes no, ad infinitum; that's life I guess.

The Bramley apple blossom has made our garden look like a van Gogh painting and a chaffinch has somehow found purchase amongst the knobbly twigs for the creation of a soft green mossy nest, a secret that I will not risk into sharing with anyone; little fat fingers would soon put paid to this little dream. I don't miss many nests, finding them seems quite natural to me for some strange reason, even Murphy thinks it is a somewhat uncanny ability. All that I can offer in way of explanation are the words, 'anticipation' and 'intuition', knowledge alone is not the answer, as neither is good eyesight. Understanding requires rather more than that. I know where Murphy gets it wrong, he looks for the actual nest itself, whereas I tend to look for the place where I expect there to be one... simple!

Everywhere is a mass of tender new green, even the oakwoods have a rich greeny golden glow over them now and the stubborn ash yields and is stubborn no more. This is a marvellous time, just over a week before June blasts her trumpets along the waysides to awaken the dog-roses. Already the ancient line of hawthorns, down in the little marshy field beyond the cattle-trough, are in a glory of blossoming. There's so much blossom it's almost indecent, abundance beyond measure. Beneath them, ewes and their grotesquely fat lambs are huddling for shade in a huge over-reaction to the brash, spanking sunlight. No other time of the year races by so quickly as do these moments of tender Spring.

I don't think of Spring as being so much a season, but a fleeting handful of precious moments which, if I should close my eyes, I could quite easily miss altogether. Moments of it are sweetly creaking in the air right now, as the swing in the sycamore tree provides endless idle moments more of pleasure, whilst serving also as a ladder up into the dense green canopy where the boys have fixed a platform for spying on the world below. It's also a place of great daring to be when the low flying jets come screeching across, making the branches sway. Down on the ground, the young bantams are almost as big as their mother, but they show no signs of independence yet, and follow her wherever she goes; a very closely knit family with old father Chris, the cockerel, in close attendance, strutting proudly and showing them who's boss.

Going 'Gypsy'

We are getting reports from school that Robin has taken to going on 'walkabouts'. The moment his teacher's back is turned, especially on sunny days, he slips out into the garden where he can sit amongst squirrels and cuddle an old half-blind cat that's got to know him. On exceptionally nice days he ventures further afield, following the brook upstream into the meadows. His teacher has become fed-up with having to go off to find him and has taken to sending the other two instead. They're heartily sick of it because he doesn't come back without first putting up a fight, resulting in bloody noses and torn clothes. We've discussed the problem with all concerned and, despite Robin's reassurances that he won't do it again, he continues to do it. Finding himself being locked in a classroom all day is something that he can't cope with or, more likely, something that he refuses to cope with, as his mischievous behaviour when he is in the classroom seems to suggest. Butter wouldn't melt in his mouth whenever he is confronted over his ways; he can switch into gushing charm and helpfulness more easily than he can do anything else and has people thinking he's an angel. It causes Spencer and Rowan to want to throw up. He's a law unto himself, forever putting on an act, and in such a way as to make it impossible for any of us to recognise any truth, if anything can ever be true anymore where he's concerned.

Our swallows have been joined by two more, and there's a lot of boisterous activity in the bedroom with a din that sounds more like squabbling than rejoicing. A new nest has been plastered next to the old one and I notice fresh droppings all over one of my large paintings, before spotting another new nest on the opposite beam above it; these must be part of last year's brood. Positioning the bed is once more becoming an acquired skill if we are not to become buried under blizzards of swallow droppings. It was easy when they were only nesting on the one beam, but now we have them in full stereo... it's really quite thrilling.

There's still no sign of our cat, Tony; we're getting slightly concerned now, as too is 'Spibby' who is moping about the place looking lost. To ease our minds a little, Curly Jenkins told Spencer that he thinks he's seen our cat down at his place, fighting with another cat and doing rude things to theirs. Curly has been coming over quite a lot of late, he never has much to say and just stands around all blue-eyed and smiling like a miniature version of Old Weasel. The gang of them have turned what's left of the caravan into their den, a very private place, strictly for 'man-talk'. Rowan has constructed a rude sort of fireplace out of bricks and an old toasting-rack and has positioned it just a couple of paces from the door, with four little stacks of bricks for them to sit on. They are planning to go 'gypsy'; Robin is in his element and is already causing bedlam in his unharnessed eagerness to get started.

I take them all to town in the van and kit them out with a few basic essentials; kettle, teapot, pots and pans, tea, sugar, milk, tomato sauce and various canned items plus bread, margarine, cheese, matches, can-opener and a few more odds and ends besides. This is what childhood is all about; it's the way I remember mine as being, with the exclusion of catapult, snares, ferret, dog and fishing tackle that fitted into a pocket; vegetarianism no longer permits such things.

We haven't been back long when, to add to the general pandemonium, Rosie and Elly suddenly turn up to surprise us; two more gypsies complete with tent and sleeping-bags. Hilarity reigns and rages all about us and, if this isn't enough of a surprise, Steve and Chris nonchalantly appear ambling down the slope, all of them blissfully unaware of the presence of an ill-tempered bull somewhere in the vicinity; proving what I've said before... it never rains here than what it pours!

The high spirited uproar that follows provides the boys with the cover that they need for them to concentrate on getting their own things underway, without risk of interference from adults. Four pairs of hands, thirty-two fingers and eight thumbs all competing to do the same thing; even the smoke rising from their fire doesn't seem to know what it's doing. Rowan assumes the alpha role while Spencer and Curly giggle uncontrollably over some private joke and are of no help whatsoever, leaving Robin to squabble with Rowan for the job, something that he hasn't the remotest chance of achieving. Sparks fly in a thousand directions and the brand new kettle, that's struggling to boil is knocked flying, scattering the hens who mistakenly think this as being something specially laid on for their benefit only; no amount of screaming and bawling has any effect on them whatsoever.

With steam now coming from the fire instead of smoke, Rowan knocks the dent out from the kettle, clips Robin's ear and instructs him to fetch firewood. A request which Robin adamantly refuses to comply with, insisting, under noisy floods of tears, that Spencer and Curly are already doing that job. I neglect my guests and think it advisable to keep my eye on proceedings outside, fearing that the caravan might go up in flames or perhaps explode.

All the air is a cacophony of sounds, with hoots and yells of laughter coming from inside the cowshed, jet fighters screeching about the sky, belly-aching wails of protest from Robin, dogs yapping incessantly in what seems now as being a permanent degrading of the air across the valley. High and hidden up in the top branches of the sycamore tree, Spencer and Curly are not gathering wood at all, but are twittering like a pair of linnets amongst the flickering leaves as they flick pebbles down upon the unsuspecting Rowan, who is desperately struggling to establish some order into life as a Romany.

Having visitors come to stay means one thing above all else... empty the toilet! This I do, noticing to my delight as I do so, a pair of tree sparrows chirping away in the decrepit stump of our walnut tree at the back of the barn. I see also, a spotted flycatcher catching flies, suggesting that we have them nesting in the barn somewhere. I call Robin over to join me and ask him how their gypsy camp is coming along, ignoring the tear stains down his soiled cheeks. "Rowan won't let me lighted the fire, 'snot fair 'cos Spencer and Curly, they got easy jobs!" I give him a comforting hug and a pat, then send him on his way, telling him to help Rowan and not to fight with him. He gives me a thunderous frown, then vanishes round the corner.

I hear Rowan call out, "Hey!" when a pebble suddenly bounces off his head and several more pepper down onto the caravan roof. "'Snot me!" Robin pleads, anticipating a bloody nose before joining Rowan in a rush for shelter inside the caravan as yet more pebbles shower down. I can see what's going on from inside the pigsty and can recognise too, the unmistakable tone of my 'Raphael Morales' guitar pitching its raspingly sweet voice into the rapidly ripening day.

As I'm emerging from the Jeyes Fluid-scented parlour, Rowan struggles by with the ladder from the barn and drags it off down the slope towards the sycamore tree. Robin excitedly joins him and, by some miraculous super-human joint effort, they raise the ladder until it is rested on the branch beside where the rope-ladder swing is attached. In hardly any time at all, and gripping his new secondhand army knife, Rowan climbs the ladder and hacks through the rope holding the swing to the branch, laughing as it falls to the ground in a heap. He then descends to join his smaller grinning brother and together they gleefully drag the ladder away, leaving the two twittering linnets stranded, with their pockets no longer full of pebbles, high and hiding still in the branches. Little do they know that their goose has been cooked and it brings Robin and Rowan closer together than they've been all day; there are no tears now, just laughter as they wait for the food to start sending out seductive messages. I see Robin as I've never seen him, he's actually running errands for Rowan now and pretends not to notice the very last pebbles from heaven as he hurries to the shed to sort out four lovely big potatoes for baking in the red glow beneath their saucepan, which is full of something else holding promise for them.

I continue to hover about the place as invisibly as I possibly can, just keeping a watchful eye on things. The grown-ups indoors are giving a pretty lively account of themselves before emerging noisily with mugs of tea and large hunks of bread, then shambling somewhat aimlessly down onto the upturned earth at the front, which we rather grandly refer to as being the 'garden'. What few chickens are not around the back pestering the boys, are here lying shipwrecked and partaking of dust-baths amongst my rows of struggling little growing things, sight of which arouses laughter; such unbridled pleasure and with such total disregard here being shown by the chickens. There's no measuring the gulf that separates our two very different worlds, despite our breathing the same air and drinking the same water; we're so near yet so far.

I can hear the two 'linnets' in the tree and I stroll round and can now see them standing on the lower branch where the rope-ladder swing used to be. They are too afraid to attempt the last ten feet to the ground and are pleading in vain for either Rowan or Robin to rescue them. They're out of luck, the camp-fire is now glowing like a dream and the two brothers luxuriate on the ground before it, slurping tea and each with a stick for keeping the chickens away; they're not hearing any cries for help!

Rowan has, in true gypsy style, carved attractive patterns into the bark of his long ash stick and the pair of them have darkened their faces with ashes so that they look more the part. Over the inferno they have a saucepan of beans bubbling away with Sykes, our imbecile of a hen, in persistent close attention, hell-bent on having them as soon as they are removed from the flames. Spibby, by contrast, is sitting on Robin's shoulder, dribbling with ecstasy and purring like an old lawnmower, licking everything that he raises to his mouth. There are other chickens milling about inside the caravan, all noisily squabbling over a thick round of bread that failed to attach itself to the toasting fork. All pecking orders have long since gone out of the window, it's a strictly first come, first served free-for-all and very soon attracts the remainder of the hens from down the garden and they come streaking to join in the bread brawl.

The feeble cries for help coming from the sycamore tree attract the attention of the others and, between them they manage to raise the ladder to their rescue. The two former 'linnets' emerge from the smoke like a pair of beggars, prompting smug laughter from the other two as they sprawl with their faces smeared and bulging with beans and with mugs of sickly sweet tea sploshing in their fists. "Where've you been?" Rowan chuckles caustically, giving Robin a wicked elbow in the ribs and setting him off into uncontrollable sniggering. "You've eaten all the beans, you 'ave!" Spencer whinges, his eyes all large and staring. "Well, where's all this wood that you and Curly are supposed to be fetching then?" Rowan replies, enjoying his gypsy life to the full and having gained a disciple in the process... albeit of a very temporary arrangement.

By now, they have an audience as adults start to get involved and the figure of Dan comes rumbling down the field, eager to be part of what's going on. "Ay up!" he shouts, as his whiskery face splits and a grin bigger than a moon-slice on its back, fastens itself over his huge chin. A ragged cheer goes up as he breaks into an ungainly, bandy-legged trot and tosses his cap triumphantly into the air, sending a ewe and her two fat offspring stampeding panic-stricken away in disarray.

Our garden becomes an even bigger joke now that Dan is here and with a gallery to play to. He sarcastically suggests that I borrow his tractor and muck-spreader, and everyone laughs, but I don't find it particularly funny being forever at the mercy of undermining forces in a perpetual 'one step forward, two steps back' routine. He searches for more morsels of ridicule to blast from his blunderbuss, and I ask him why it is that, despite him supposedly being a farmer,

I haven't as yet ever seen him turn a single clod of soil or grow anything at all, anywhere on his land. In fact never knowing him to do anything even vaguely resembling farm work. "I 'ain't that bloody daft!" he chunters, half defending, half attacking; "Why grow it when you can buy it? I gets all that I needs from bloody Masons in town!"

In truth, Dan isn't a farmer at all, he just happens to own a couple of tiny fields, plus a hill, and he has a tin shed with a very old cow, a couple of bales of hay and a swallow's nest in it. He keeps half a sack of corn in a busted chicken-coop and he has an inexact amount of chickens purely for company, a dog for the same reason, plus vermin that he's too idle to do anything about. He makes a penny by letting his bit of land to another farmer for grazing. The most crazy part of it all is that he really does have a tractor, a little grey Ferguson, but I've never ever seen it working, his muck spreader doesn't work either; just a couple of nostalgic old toys I suppose. Today he is here in an essentially advisory capacity, so I must think myself lucky for the wise and helpful suggestions as they are so generously offered!

Our swallows are very much in evidence, making the kitchen lean-to a particularly dangerous place to be and adding extra novelty value for our visitors. I've also noticed a wren nesting in the pigsty toilet where it is all shadowy dark. This tiny bird has a boldness of temper as to put the wind up any unsuspecting bare-bottomed person on a bucket and could hurry things along rather more than might be advisable. For me though, there's still nothing in this line of business to compare with taking a stroll with the spade and finding a secret little spot where I can hear the birds breathing and the grasses growing. Let's face it, few things can be more menacing than to be attacked by a wren whilst crapping in a pigsty!

Sight of the boys grappling with wickedly hot and blackened baked potatoes dribbling with butter, sets our taste-buds into a rage and gives our dwindling potato supply an unscheduled late hammering, which means that a fire must be made and, more importantly, maintained. Whilst I tend to this, Cari, the girls and Dan go off with a basket, gloves and scissors on a nettle-gathering stroll, leaving Chris and Steve to be introduced to water fetching. An opportune chance for them to familiarise themselves with the weight of the stuff and how easily, and all too rapidly, it converts into tea and a mass of other things besides, all of which necessitate constant repeat visits to the well. I know that to ask them to gather firewood will be a dead loss, for apart from them showing no sense of urgency over anything, they'll only bring a few twigs back anyway.

It's all a huge joke to them; even Dan is acting the fool, set solid in his mind that all food comes in cans and is delivered by van from Masons; all fuel for the fire coming similarly, but as hard black lumps in sacks. The dimension of gathering, fetching, making and preparing having no place in his life ... with the exception of the short stagger he makes across his yard to plunge a tin mug into a puddle full of frogs, newts and 'things'. He has for a long time been spoiled by the wonder of electricity, a kettle that plugs in and doesn't require a fire to boil it, together with a light switch that eliminates the use of candles and lanterns. Even though he keeps a cow, his milk gets delivered in cans from Masons; little wonder he finds it all so hilarious when he comes over to be with us.

While it was by choice that we came upon this lifestyle, it is now by necessity that we endure the hard realities of it and must progress our way through the whole experience, getting a glimpse in the process of how life must have been lived in the past when there was no fast-lane as there is now. I can't imagine there ever being a sky without aeroplanes thundering about in it, streams and rivers full of fishes and without pollution, lanes where the only wheels were slow wheels powered by horses. Where the force of the running brook drove the wheels of the corn grinding mill, such wasted sanity, such sensible science gone forever.

When I brave the swallows in the bedroom in order to fetch jam to restock the cupboard, the elderflower wine looks so tantalisingly clear and promising, that I succumb to temptation and take up a bottle, interested to know how it's coming along. I shall have to sample it discreetly while everyone is preoccupied; firstly though, I must find a corkscrew, a tool that never gets used apart for boring holes in conkers. I seem to remember having seen it in one of the drawers in the caravan but chances of my finding it are pretty slim. Outside by the gypsy encampment, a Flamenco-ish festival is just beginning to let rip, with Chris plonked on a pile of bricks beside a freshly-fueled blaze, thrashing the very life out of my beloved little guitar. Amongst the smoke and flames, shadowy figures fresh from nettle gathering, are heel-stamping and finger-clicking, yelling 'Ole' and falling about in fits of coughing and laughter. I slip quietly amongst them and into the caravan which is full of chickens, and I slip again on 'something' as I take evasive action in avoiding the hysterical Sykes who has got a bean tin stuck fast on her head. She immediately explodes into a panic-stricken rage, flying blindly up into my face then ten times round the caravan before vomiting out through the raging flames like a circus act. Miraculously the corkscrew is out on top of the drawer having been recently used to dig a stub of candle from a candlestick for fire lighting. I make my own exit, feeling rather anxious to know where Sykes has gone with her 'Heinz helmet', making her think that it's night. There's no sign of her and so I ask the boys if they'll try to locate her and remove the tin, careful not to frighten her too much; they rather like the challenge.

Back upstairs, with swallows whooshing in and out, I settle myself in the corner where the starlings are nesting in the wall, and I ease the cork from the bottle with a sound like a sweet kiss, then very gently pour a little of the glistening nectar into a glass. I hold it up before me in wonderment and itching anticipation, almost too afraid to go any further. The fragrance of elderflowers is absolutely divine as I slowly bring the glass to my lips, lingering for a few moments more and filling my lungs with the marvellous scent ... I taste it. Wow! We really have wine! Within seconds I feel a flush of warmth spreading across my cheeks, goodness knows what two sips of this stuff are likely to do!

Like a naughty child I sneak downstairs, clutching my treasure; I must find more glasses and prove to everyone the magic of hedgerows and the great bounty they hold in store to be released on moments such as these. When I enter the kitchen, Cari is at the sink rinsing nettles, so I try not to distract her too much before asking her to close her eyes and to tell me what it is that I'm going to give her to taste. She trustingly does as I ask, never for a moment suspecting that our wine could possibly be touched for another year at least. "Well, what do you think that is?" I ask as she thoughtfully and pleasurably swills it around in her mouth before swallowing it. "It's something that Rosie has brought... Armagnac?" "No, try again." "It's ... it's Champagne then!" "Sorry, you're way off target!" "I give up... what is it then?" I hand her the bottle and to my astonishment, she goes into a rage, yelling at me that it isn't ready for drinking yet, and that it takes at least two years for it to become wine. I laugh and ask her what she would therefore catagorise this marvellous substance as being if it isn't simply the most beautiful wine. She calms, then tentatively takes a larger sip and I watch her face slowly light up; "Gosh, Jimmy! We didn't make this... did we?" "We sure did, two dozen bottles of it... and elderberry as well. Not bad for a first attempt, hey?"

She really thinks she's drunk when Sykes goes rocketing past the door with the bean tin well and truly stuck fast on her head, quickly pursued by Robin, with his fishing net which has made a miraculous reappearance. Then the others in a lethargic trail, having been obliged to abandon their more scientific strategy in submission to Robin's no-nonsense, brute force approach. There's a loud clonking noise and a squawk as Sykes slams head-on into the pigsty wall and is immediately pounced on by Robin. Cari's eyes are out on stalks, she can't believe them. Very much in his element, Robin unceremoniously removes the bean tin from the terrified chicken's head. It looks rather gruesome at first, as though her head has remained inside the tin, so hidden is it by tomato sauce and beans. For Sykes, suddenly it's daylight again and she explodes high into the air, clean over the pigsty wall, like a cruise missile, not even stopping to thank Robin, but leaving bloody scratch marks down his cheeks instead. The others all laugh as Robin struggles to his feet, smiling smugly and feeling like a super-star, while Sykes goes broadcasting her hysteria all down the hillside, very much alive and ready to fight another day.

Elder's last Song and Reflecting on Reflections

A growing feature of the cowshed is the nature diary notes that I have written on the heavy wooden lintel that spans the fireplace. It is something that has come about quite naturally and is now spilling over onto the wall and cannot be missed; visitors may now have a good read while they are warming themselves. It isn't always possible to put my hand on a piece of writing paper or my notebook when the need arises, so I scribble urgent little thoughts and observations onto the beam, with the intention of transferring them into my book later. Something that I invariably forget to do, hence this 'huge book' on wood and it's providing a great deal of entertainment right now. For some obstinate, uncompromising reason, Dan avoids it like the plague, believing it to be evidence of madness and remaining more than convinced that it's no more than lavatorial graffiti. Even to the point of threatening to come over with a brush and painting it out when we're not in. My sanity is put under question still further when I quite casually load the fire with old dried cow-dung and set the kettle to boil over it. Recognising his growing suspicions, I attempt to set his mind at rest by presenting him with a glass of our lovely wine, in the hope of softening him into becoming his old easy-going self again. "What's this you're giving me ...pee, I shouldn't wonder!" he growls with a sharp and cantankerous sarcasm. "Try it and see," I say with the most normal of smiles that I can contrive, then add, "It's what Cari made last year, especially for you." With reluctance he takes the glass and immediately plonks it down beside him on the settle, while I hand out the remainder to the others, then propose a toast. "This is what Cari made from the hedge that Gareth ripped out last year... something that can never be repeated because you can't make wine out of barbed-wire fences. Cheers... to the hedge!" There's a brief silence before groans of surprised pleasure and gleeful little twitters of approval sounds all about the room; then Dan begrudgingly softens and takes up his glass. Not in his fingers but in a fat, hard fist and virtually empties it in one gluttonous swig. He's taken aback for a moment, then he looks up with a wide-eyed expression of astonishment and mutters... "Damn... that's nice!" then throws back his head and sucks the glass dry, no doubt being of the opinion that it isn't alcohol, alcohol being a substance that has to be added by some industrial process or other.

One bottle goes nowhere, so I surreptitiously lay-on a few more, aware as I do so, an increased sound of merriment and a few rosy cheeks beginning to show. By the time the potatoes are starting to smell good, red noses and watery eyes have appeared, together with a distinct slurring of words; this stuff isn't to be trifled with! Its effect on me is quite surprising in that, when I try to stand up, my legs have turned to rubber, causing me to wobble despite my mind remaining clear. This reminds me of something I once read in an old country book, advising caution when partaking of the wine of the elderflower, going on to say how it had been known to take the legs from under the most ardent of drinkers.

Whilst I grovel about on my hands and knees trying to re-arrange the potatoes in the oven, a crazy pots and pans, do-it-yourself rock band is clattering up to full steam all around me, utilising absolutely anything that can generate commotion. Dan hasn't as yet tried standing up but is contentedly dolloped on the settle like a cross between Buddha and Punch; his eyes are double-glazed as he blows across the top of one of the empty bottles, producing a lonesome wailing sound like a faraway cow in the night. Other members of the ensemble are wedded in chronic disarray, unblending and seemingly unending, with such deadly commitment as would scare even Pink Floyd. This is serious stuff and with not a single recognisable musical instrument in the entire anarchic alchemy of it all.

Above all this, I gradually detect the sound of a dog barking out in the yard, which is particularly odd because we haven't got a dog. The barking persists then shifts from the back of the house and goes round to the front, then suddenly, a face looms up at the window; "Oh, heck ... it's my Mam!" gasps Curly, stiffening with fear, the first actual words that I've heard him utter all day. The rock-band subsides into a bedraggled collapse and self-congratulatory cheering. Cari yells to the deathly pale face to come in, but the expression that confronts her is one of such rage as to incinerate any posy of welcome. And I fear that, not only is Curly going to miss out on his buttered jacket-potato but is about to have his trousers leathered each step of his frog-marched way into the lengthening evening shadows, back home across the marshy fields. Cari and I see poor Curly to the door, where he is instantly screamed at and asked what time he thinks this is, making him blush in an embarrassed sort of way, before being physically woman-handled and aimed in the direction of home. He's given the first of many such whacks across the backside with the leather strap that his mother has gripped in her fist. "Aren't you going to come in for a glass of wine?" Cari asks, not reading the situation in her normal manner, and the offer is met with a look that would frighten even Dan as she turns and marches off with her growling Jack Russell-Corgi cross, leaving us standing there with the unpleasant feeling of not being approved of.

Driven by the urge to pee, Dan gets up from the settle, only to collapse headlong and loud into the van-seat opposite where the boys are all perched. They are catapulted in all directions and, even the rapidly vanishing Mrs. Jenkins, now but a dot across the aldermarsh will have heard the resultant laughter and no doubt be reckoning that it is aimed at her. Dan is useless with laughter, his brain is working but his legs aren't and he crawls about the hearth trying desperately to get back onto his feet before he pees himself. Tears are rolling down Rosie's glowing cheeks and Elly has to suddenly lurch outside to the toilet having left it almost too late for discovering that hysterics and elderflower wine don't mix ... just as Dan has so done. Chris and Steve do their despairing best to help Dan to the door, but they almost demolish the place in the process and set the swallows and a wren into vociferous disapproval. Not to be up-staged by adults and always skulking at the door of opportunity, I catch a glimpse of the boys polishing off what's been left over, thus ensuring that the ghost of the deceased elderflower hedge has been thoroughly exercised throughout the cowshed.

The curtain of evening draws in around us with a most beautiful and soothing ease of birdsong far and wide. Jacket potatoes with nettles in melted cheese has lain the ghost of the elderflowers back to rest, enough exercise for one day and without a trace of exorcism anywhere in the entire of it.

It is about this time that the woodcock fly over. They are usually heard before they are seen and always manage to beat the darkness by about half an hour, a timely reminder for Rosie and Elly to focus their thoughts on the business of pitching tent. I'm not at all happy about having this new bull roaming about the fields as I don't trust the animal one little bit. I believe that it was almost certainly because of his volatile temperament that his horns were trimmed, and not nearly enough for my liking... having already been chased by the sod! I try to raise this as a serious issue, only to have

Dan ridicule my concerns, insisting, rather devilishly, that the bull is docile and completely harmless. "You wouldn't say that if you'd had him snorting a horn's length from your arse and doing close on ninety!" I tell him. He just laughs dismissively, determined for some reason to be on the opposite side of whatever I say, noticeably so when there are women present. I put this down to an old, deep-rooted macho mating kind of thing... his way of shouting "Cock-a-doodle-do!"

Fortunately, my concerns are shared by those that matter, and a decision is reached regarding sleeping arrangements. Steve and Chris choosing to bed down in the back of the van, leaving Rosie and Elly to do their best in squeezing a bit more life out of the caravan, throwing their sleeping-bags down at the far end where the boys have established their H.Q.

With the woodcock flown and the first stars flickering, the early owls sigh up from the woods and sail out into the dark air. Candlelight dances on faces around the hearth while, up on the beams, swallows sleep in swallow dreams; bedtime is fast gathering upon us. We get up and all wander out with a wobbly Dan and accompany him home across the dampening grass, amongst the statued dark shadowy shapes of cattle, not one of us having a clue as to which dark shape it is that has the shortened horns and an item of jewellery in its nose. Nervous giggles and false brave laughter suggest to me that there's a euphoric state of 'safety-in-numbers' bonding us, which, by pure coincidence, is precisely what is making those dark and watching shapes around us feel at their ease too. We slip amongst the thunder of their breathing, it's their way of finding out what's going on, a kind of friendly contact. I find it comforting and really quite beautiful, although I am aware that others are somewhat nervous and greatly relieved when they see the dark shape of the hedge as we near the lane.

The air is suddenly split by an ear-piercing yell... Dan has stumbled into a drainage hole, striking fear into every living thing within a mile radius; we hear it go bouncing all along the blind hillsides and we hear also the panicked stampeding sound of cows' feet hammering the ground, as they disperse in an anywhere sort of way. It sets all the dogs yelping over at Murphy's and is rapidly joined by the blaring and bleating of sheep and the relieved laughter of the others as they all clamber clumsily over the gate and into the safety of the lane, leaving me to assist Dan out from his predicament. His previous smugness has now turned to bitter cursing and, judging by the noise that he's making, I fear that he might have broken something. My mind eases when he swipes aside my offered hands and mouths words that I don't normally hear him use; it's apparent that it's mostly his pride that has been hurt.

I unlock my two-star Ford doss-house for Chris and Steve to offload their stuff into before Chris leads a raucous, owl-hooting procession along the lane back up to Dan's cottage. The pageant of noise torments a bellowing response from Murphy that halts us all in our tracks… "Haven't you buggers got beds to go to?" His voice can be heard echoing all the way back into England, and it prompts Dan, now limping more healthily, into his own 'cock-a-doodle-doo' dialogue. He shouts into the darkness… "Who rattled your cage? You're only jealous… go back to sleep!" "Sleep, my arse! Some of us have got to work tomorrow!" "Work? You don't know the meaning of the word!" Murphy doesn't answer, and through the sudden pregnant silence we hear the bedroom window slam shut. I look at Dan and say quietly, "I think you've upset someone." He isn't in the least bit bothered and is obviously feeling a bit more like the Monarch of the Glen that he was feeling like earlier. He goes off into another of his antagonistic chunterings… "Why, damn… he's got a woman to do all the bloody work there! He knows what side his bread's buttered. Meg makes him do as he's told now, isn't it!" He's really back up on his high horse now, and I'm tempted into having a little dig at him by asking why it is that, if by having a woman all the work gets done, why is it then that he hasn't got himself one? The question irritates him, but he stands his ground and barks back at me an ill-considered knot of words. "I don't need no bloody bossy woman when I'se got my owd Bob!" It's his uncouth mongrel that he's referring to and, realising this, Steve pipes up… "I've heard about people like you… mmm… Duckie!" This sets everyone off laughing again just as, bang on cue, the dog comes bounding and barking to greet and protect him, prompting Cari to yell, "Oh, look, it's the wife from the kitchen!" This makes Dan smile, but it isn't a real smile and we leave the pair of them and hastily make our way back home before someone gets bitten. A weight seems to have lifted from us.

The Sunday dawn sun squints into our room prompting swallows into chattering excitedly amongst themselves before the divine cool moment of gliding out through the window. The air rings with a sparkling swell of birdsong as the dawning turns slowly into morning and the red sun yellows and inches clear of the aldermarsh. I emerge with the swallows and go off for an early stroll over the dewy grass while the others are all down in their beds. Little daisies slowly open as the sweetest stillness hardly dares breathe, so perfect are these moments of being alive. Simply standing still is the most inexplicable luxury; it's maddening just trying to find something inside of me, anything, that can respond in some way worthy of this overwhelming miracle of feeling. There is absolutely nothing other than to stand perfectly still and become as close to nothing as I possibly can, and let it just swallow me alive and whole.

I thank whatever it is for making the colossal space between me and the tiny silver speck that's leaving a vapour-trail, in total silence, across the impossible -to-mix shade of blue that's labelled 'sky'. Such a massively contrived, complex technology with deafening engines functioning at immense temperatures and in such ice-cold emptiness. An aircraft capsule full of people going about their simple, separate lives, all of them full of private dreams, heartaches and longings. It never ceases to amaze me when I gaze up at this tender hour and see them there scratching a trail across my bit of heaven.

I cast my eyes down and see other flying things, tiny gnats that are just as massive... smaller, that's all. Spectra dances and dazzles on the silky fine fabric of the infinitesimal wings as the sun's magic light touches and they manoeuvre in the vastness of space between daisies, size being only relative to that which we ourselves ultimately are. Space is shapeless and without size and weight is weightless outside and beyond that which our own selves are, just as similarly, time is timeless. Finite things require measures for finite reasons, as phase follows phases, phase upon phase forever.

Where IS the song I hear being sung? If I can hear it and am the measure of a mile from the blackbird that's singing it, then, why does that song not go on forever? It is here all about me but I can't see it or feel it; I don't know where it is or what it is, but it's massive none the less, where does it go? I gaze about me and, on a faraway bank, rabbits are hopping about enjoying the early sunlight and focussing my thoughts on a miracle which I take all too much for granted, and ask the question... what IS sight? Is there anything of me existing in the space between what I am seeing and the marvellous sense in me that's actually seeing it? So many things that are beyond and without measure or explanation, just as Life itself is seemingly as conspicuous by its absence as it is by its presence and is just as impossible to see. It dwells in the tiniest imaginable thing just as mightily as it does in the hugest thing imaginable, and with the same clinical efficiency and effectiveness too. Invisible Life, the magic that powers us all; nothing can be more precious in life than Life itself.

I marvel at this moment NOW, casting my mind back to the very worst of days back in the bleak, cruel winters, aware and amazed by there not being even the minutest trace of it remaining now, even though the power of those moments raged with the most ferocious presence upon us. Demonstrating that every single thing is itself a million things and each single one of those themselves, a million things and more besides, ad infinitum. Transient moments in time, like waves on a stormy sea, only to vanish without trace in the calm that follows; always though, the sea.

Chris the cockerel crows and ignites all air to a fanfare of flaming colour and a distant cuckoo-call lilts on the light, like fish scales of sunlight reflected on ruffled water, while the sycamore tree remains anchored and imprisoned to its only ever place where a long hundred years have passed through her branches. Endless moments of dialogue with the air and I've never heard her utter a sound, nothing at all, yet she's alive or whatever it be that stops her from being dead. I fill my lungs to bursting, taking in the air that's been breathed by dinosaurs and their grannies before them; it's been replenished, that's all. Rearranged, revitalised and breathed, exhaled, breathed, exhaled again and again by every single thing that has ever lived or is likely to ever live... good stuff, this air!

The high north hill is now bathed in soft early morning sunlight and the sheep languish before the blood-letting of the first engines and the relentless demands of eating and breast-feeding great strapping lambs that are old enough now to go off and get themselves a job... not today though, this is a day of rest... Sunday. I compare the song of the crow with that of blackbird and it is easy to come to the conclusion that one crow sounds exactly the same as the next one. It's because of this glib assumption that I have taken so long in distinguishing one particular crow from all the rest. In fact it was as long ago as the quiet frosty days that I first made the acquaintance of 'Old Crow'. He was different from the others because of his call, a 'kaah, waa, waa', as compared with their 'caw, caw, caw', twice heard, never forgotten! I do my best by means of imitation, to communicate with him whenever he passes over, usually chasing a buzzard or just plain loafing about, and he appears to answer me.

We've got a good thing going, but I do worry myself sick whenever I hear the belching of a twelve-bore or catch sight of Dai-the-Death slinking amongst the trees on a mission to make a necklace of crows for Gareth's barbed wire fence. It's always a relief to hear that old familiar call, a kind of tongue-in-cheek shout of defiance which really has a tender place for itself in our lives, even though we know that a crow is a crow and does crow things that don't endear him to the farmer, just as a farmer is a farmer and does farmer things that don't endear him to me; but I haven't got a twelve-bore to help emphasise my preferences and I don't care much for necklaces of that sort either!

Old Crow is the first crow to call on this early Sabbath morning. I can't see him, he's concealed somewhere up in the oakwood above the well, presiding over a rough old shed of a nest, four speckled eggs and a spouse who idolises and sees him through her rose-tinted spectacles as being even more handsome than a kingfisher. Their world holding just as much love in it for them as ours does for us. Glancing back to the cowshed, I can see that Old Crow and I have something in common... neither of us is able to compete with a wren or chaffinch when it comes to building a home, but then, we could both teach the cuckoo a thing or two about home-building. So it's not such a bad thing that we share. We humans are closer to the common wasp than we are to birds regarding this and, as a gregarious species, tend to make homes resembling wasp nests, conglomerate variations on a tower-block kind of thinking, with each hexagonal element identical to the next.

I make my way back to the cowshed, smugly aware of it in no way resembling a wasp-nest; this old shack was more the result of fat bumble bee-thinking than ever it was of wily wasps. It's just a rough and ready hovel, that's what makes it so attractive. No doubt it originally had charm and some style as well as a basic sturdiness, in fact a very normal little farmstead with God-fearing souls, who were more than likely in-bred countless times over and who kept and killed pigs and had a couple of cows, a horse, hens, geese and ducks. It's like an old forgotten grave that I'm making my way back to, one that's alive with new life now and is about to have a fire roaring up its chimney as I set to the business of boiling a kettle for the first pot of tea of the morning and arousing the slumberers into letting their life be heard in the clean, clear air.

Bullish Encounter prior to Pea-Sticking

Today I really must gather pea-sticks and bodge them into position, not simply for the peas to climb up, but to help keep the hens from obliterating the whole pea-patch, as they seem hell-bent on doing. This will have to be a morning job because Steve and Chris will be leaving later. Their trip was only intended to be a weekend break just to make sure that we were alright, but with a crotchety Dan and a lunatic new bull thrown-in for good measure. I'm joined in the hearth by Rowan. It's lovely the way he always turns up to help me when I need it, and together we get the day rolling and cart mugs of tea to wrecked faces about the place, each one still with a trace of last night's elderflower wine aching in it. I fill a flask and take it over to the van, watched closely by the bull, who seems undecided as to whether or not to make me fill my pants. We stare at each other for a few anxious moments before he lethargically backs off, empties his bowels and snorts stuff over the grass. I can never be quite sure about this creature, he leaves me with more questions than he does answers and keeps me forever on my guard.

The sunlit wooded hillside above the van is alive with the piping calls of nuthatches and I can see tree-creepers busying themselves on the stout trunks as they fastidiously search for insects. All along the narrow winding lane, yellowhammers are golden upon hedges, letting themselves be seen as well as heard amongst willow warblers, chiffchaffs and whitethroats. There's a merry jingling of dunnocks and wrens are shouting everywhere; this really is a most splendid morning.

My two bleary-eyed friends grunt and groan in their sleeping-bags like grubs in dung and, judging by the dribbling condensation on the windows and walls inside the van, they will be more than ready for the tea that I have brought for them. They exchange lighthearted insults over each other's ability to snore and make other nastier noises, cursing the van's confined space and booming acoustics. I open the door wide allowing the stale air to escape and for the birdsong to rush in, then I leave them to sort themselves out, reminding them not to take chances with the bull.

When I return, the girls are up and about in the yard partaking of mugs of tea and surrounded by clamouring hens, whilst Spencer and Robin attempt to provide them with a register of each chicken's name. They smirk rather sheepishly when they see me and I guess from the wicked glint in their eyes, they are planning to make a fiasco of it and to invent the names wherever possible. Not wishing to cramp their style, I pretend to busy myself doing other things, but stay within earshot so's not to miss out on their game. It's Robin that makes the first move, starting on a serious note with the bantams. "Dat one's 'Chris Cockerel', dat one is... an' dem two is 'Jeannie' an' 'Bridget'." Before progressing further, Rosie interrupts him and says ... "But we already know the names of the bantams, it's the big white ones that we don't know." With an uncharacteristic spurt of initiative, Spencer springs to Robin's assistance and blurts... "That one's 'Sykes', that stupid one is, an' that big fat one's 'Gerty'... or summat, I think!" He offers no more and is already finding the task to be a drain on his intellectual reservoir and so he withdraws from the limelight and allows Robin to complete Rosie's poultry education. Sniggering and grinning broadly, he rises to the occasion; "Dat one's 'Aunty Hilda' and dat one's 'Missus Jones', our school cook, an' dat one's named after you Elly, dat one is!" "What about this fat old boiler here?" Rosie asks, pointing with her foot to a particularly heavy one who I always refer to as being 'Matilda', but I say nothing just to see what Robin comes up with. He scratches his head and looks to Spencer for a bit of help. "Posh Aunty Rita!" Spencer explodes in a fit of giggles, while Robin rushes to the barn cackling like a hen that's just laid, as Elly turns to Rosie and proudly whispers, "I've got a chicken named after me!" At this point, a noisy white projectile and a mass of feathers shoots out through the barn door, rapidly followed by Robin... "an' dat one's 'Uncle Gladys'!" He folds his arms in triumphant conclusion, but Rosie draws his attention to one that he's forgotten; "What about that big heavy one that's limping over there... what's her name?" Robin is put on the spot and isn't helped in any way by his big brother, but he does at least have a try. "Oh... it's... er... Jimmy knows what that one is called!" Now I'm put on the spot as I emerge from the shadows, and the very first silly name that comes to mind is 'Spirrenger', simply because that's what she looks like. So, 'Spirrenger' it is; the chicken register has been called and, dunces as they may be, they've provided is with a bowl full of lovely white eggs for our breakfast.

Our entire gang is congregated, standing and otherwise, around the rectangle which we fondly refer as our 'table'. Cari has thought it wiser to boil a large saucepan of eggs and to shout "Come and get it!" A kind of 'take it or leave it' philosophy, remembering the precise and painful science that John Wain made of frying an egg. Our last loaf is hacked into chunks allowing individuals to toast them if they so wish while the fire still has a crackle or two up it's sleeve. Cari gathers the last few crumbs for the hens and announces that she will have a bread-making session later. Bread being both basic and essential and, Sunday in these parts essentially being basically a lousy day to discover that you've run out of bread. Visitors, alas, never bring stuff like bread with them, in fact the only thing that they can be depended on to bring are their gift-sized appetites and their arses ... they do, however, make immeasurable joy and leave behind a huge sense of emptiness.

There's a glowing feeling of peace and gentleness in the room now, time seems to be standing still; it's a moment that has always lived here, stealing out from the timeless rocks to warm our souls. With Robin snuggling close beside her, Rosie asks him why it is that she hasn't been honoured by having a hen named after her, and in the brief silence that follows, Chris whispers in a romantic sort of way, "They're saving that for when they get a partridge." "Or an ostrich!" Steve wickedly jokes, killing any romantic notions at a stroke and immediately having to dive for cover under a hail of missiles before being chased out of the house by a rampant Rosie. Their squeals of laughter crash to an abrupt silence when, on rounding the water-tub at speed, Steve comes face to face with the bull that's just trampled my impregnable bit of fence to the ground and wrecked Rowan's gypsy fireplace. Steve stops dead in his tracks and Rosie, who hasn't as yet seen the bull, collides into his petrified back with such force as to almost impale him on the startled beast's stubby horns. There's a weird banshee-like wailing cry and the pair of them are frozen to the spot, clutching desperately on to each other. Mercifully the bull is too shocked to have even thought about pressing his own nuclear button, thus allowing them to have a better-late-then-never gush of adrenaline, which results in the clumsiest of about-turns before both of them explode back in through the cowshed door, slamming it with such force as to almost demolish the entire building. In a continuous collision with each other and skidding on the lino like rabid hamsters. They burst into the room where the rest of us are all standing wondering what all the noise is about, Steve bravely tries to laugh but is far closer to a spontaneous attack of asthma and is panic-stricken as to how to start breathing again. Rosie unceremoniously bundles him into the room and then, with superhuman strength, slams the middle door shut tightly and leans heavily back against it and gasps... "That bloody bull is out there!" Her eyes are wide and wild as she searches for a safer place to be and is totally oblivious to the screeches of laughter from Cari and Chris, which sets the boys into letting-off steam of their own. "You've got to do something about that bull, our Jim!" Rosie yells above the noise, "it's a wonder we weren't both gored to death; that animal's looking for trouble!" She herds the boys up the stairs ahead of her, leaving poor Steve struggling for breath. He looks like he's just seen the devil himself as, staring-eyed and gasping, he pushes past Chris and Cari and staggers into the boys' room and up to join the others upstairs with the swallows.

I stroll over to the hearth and sit down thoughtfully before the dying embers. I have a mad circus going on all around me and I'm hungry to do other things, longing to paint and to write on paper instead of on the wall. I want to be able to sit down and play my guitar and to write a symphony, all in this hopeless eggcup of moments... but I can't! The only saviour I know that can help me to express through these frustrations, is the open road and a long distance run in which to find an oblivion of blissful thought. An intense feeling of being of the earth in all its spirituality, of myself in all my own spirituality whilst treating myself to the most amazing physical expression of joy.

There's a sudden clattering noise coming from the kitchen and the swallows are all complaining, bringing all laughter to a puzzled silence. I stare across to the other two... "Sykes! Somebody's left the outside door open!" I say in a musical way intended for Rosie to hear, then I get up and sneak over to investigate, quietly taking a firm grip of the drift-wood door handle, then snatching it open. The handle comes clean away in my hand; the door was slammed so hard that it has wedged tightly shut. There's no way it will open, we're locked in! I stare down at my artistic door-handle and the gaping screw-holes like craters in the door and can hear Sykes having a field day in the kitchen beyond my reach. Determined not to be outwitted by a chicken, I take up my large screwdriver and the poker and laboriously prize open the door and burst into the kitchen. "Whaaa!" There's a sickening thud that knocks all the wind out of me... I have run into half a ton of highly animated Hereford Bull! It feels like my ribcage has shattered, fortunate nevertheless because it's the animal's thunderous arse that I've been hit by, as it spins crazily around in the cramped space, sending the draining-board flying and knocking the table over in the process. A pair of wrens and several swallows are attacking me to add to my confusion and, to make what seems to be a parting contemptuous gesture, the bull excretes in a fearful jet all across the room, giving me neither time or space to escape the foul blast. I'm aching and screaming at the very limit of my stress-tolerance levels, and the bull's pale rimmed eyes are wide and wild in his panic to escape. It's as though the hand of God has intervened to prevent the back door from fastening shut and for the huge animal to force its way back outside again.

I try to fasten the door only to find that the latch is no longer working, no doubt as a result of Rosie slamming it so hard when she burst in. I don't feel comfortable with the situation and realise that I won't find any peace of mind until I have driven the bull a safe distance away from the cowshed. It's with some reluctance that I venture outside where I can now see the ponderous old sod standing looking agitated just a short distance away, on our bit of garden; he is plainly not in the best of tempers and certainly isn't planning to do a bit of digging! I recognise that this moment calls for extra vigilance if I am to ease him away without making him madder than he already is. I'm hopeful that he might respond to a few kind words instead of mere bawling and shouting. For safety, I take up the broom and cautiously proceed, giving him a very wide berth until I have positioned myself behind him, muttering the softest utterances that I can contrive. "Come on, old boy... there's a good fellow... come on now." I wait a moment or two while he consults his options, one of them undoubtedly being that of tossing me over the barn roof. I remain behind him and continue to talk quietly in the hope of calming him; there's no pressure on him and, in sudden capitulation, he staggers forward tossing his head left and right so's to be constantly aware of where I am. It's working, I have him on the move, no hurry, just steady plodding back up into the yard; please God, stay with me for a moment longer!

My prayer falls upon deaf ears; the swallows are in a rage over something and are dive-bombing both the bull and myself. I raise my eyes and the cause is easy to diagnose, the bedroom window is crammed full of prattling faces, denying the swallows access to their nests and presenting me with the kind of situation that I had feared most of all. The bull stops in his track, distracted by the din and confusing him dangerously close once more to a filthy temper. I want to scream at them to shut up, but to shout at this crucial stage, could prove disastrous. "Shhh!" I hiss with my finger to my lips, but to no affect whatsoever, causing the bull to turn round and face me. Having run out of options of my own, I scream filthily up to them to be quiet, at the same time searching for an escape route, should he decide to lower his huge head and charge. To be quiet is the hardest thing that those up there in the Royal Box have ever been asked to do and, apart from stifled fits of giggling, they comply, enabling me to shuffle discreetly sideways towards the barn door. I know that I can take refuge on the beam, for the second time, if the situation arises. The new silence cools the bull's temper and my own pounding heart eases a notch or two as I resume my whispering dialogue with this massive thing that doesn't write poems. "Come on boy... there's a good boy... easy now... easy there... good old boy." He looks at me and there's a softness in his large eyes, then he turns and walks slowly away; my prayers have been answered. I follow him at a discreet distance as he swaggers with his aubergine-sized testicles waltzing merrily from side to side. His life's not so bad if he did but know it!

I leave him on the hilltop and watch him suddenly and without a care in the world, trot happily away down the hillside to rejoin his heartthrobs in the marsh-meadow valley. I stand for some time watching him in a dumbfound silence before turning about to where a couple of doors have to be fixed and a kitchen completely disinfected and reorganized; such is life.

Bluebells are flowering on Bootsy's grave as we all drift somewhat aimlessly, having originally set out with the intention of gathering pea-sticks; no resolve is so very safe when there are visitors abroad. Already the may blossom has passed and the ancient old hedge is now about to burst forth into a dream of rambling dog-roses, with honeysuckle and elderflowers waiting in the wings. Magpies and pigeons are visibly nesting along the whole length of it, and it's a safe bet to suppose that chaffinches, bullfinches, greenfinches and linnets are nesting here too, as all of them have fallen prey to Steve's binoculars. As he preys on these with his eyes, so too a sparrowhawk preys mercilessly and without waste. We hear him, not a song, just a warning that's all.

There's something alluring and quite magical about this little corner of the world where our dear cat lies at rest. Ghosts of old cottagers breath about the place and the stones of a long ago dwelling are warmed by the sun and litter the ground beneath where the lightening struck and devastated the ivy-clad ash tree where owls always snoozed by day and kept watch by night. There's a sweet babble of a brook in the dingle, babbling because it's tumbling down from springs in the big north hill, hurrying on its way, never straight, always snaking beneath and beside the lush wooded strip that drops away down past Curly Jenkins house.

It's from that direction that the sound of a twelve-bore is

heard; a sound that can mean only one thing... something has lost its life. I can't for the life of me think of a single reason why anyone should go off with a gun on such an easy going, marvellous Spring morning such as this... this being Sunday too. We sit around for a good half-hour enjoying the sun, reminiscing, selecting moments to treasure before they harden into regrets. Steve has spotted something in his binoculars, it's a tiny figure high in the topmost branches of a distant tree, raiding a nest. "The wicked little sod! I bet he doesn't know he's being watched," he curses. He hands the glasses for me to take a look and I recognise the faraway figure as being that of Elwyn, up to his usual wild ways; no doubt getting rid of crows for his dad; he'll never change, it's in his blood.

We follow the lane down in that direction, with towering parsleys in a lace-like dream all along the verges; it's impossible to hurry in all this insect-tingling air. Violets are everywhere, 'milkmaids' too, sweetly pink and without a trace of breeze to sway them. Little pathways of rabbits and voles criss-cross the verdant earth where partridges and pheasants are sitting eggs. There's a lovely falling s-bend that's shaded by aspens, birch and alder, with the smudge of bright blue, where the sun is filtering onto bluebells. Time doesn't exist anywhere in this mesmerizing space that we breathe.

A little way further on, I catch sight of Elwyn stooping beside the brook, he's picking something up from a clump of rushes. In one hand he is gripping a shotgun as he picks up a dead heron in the other. As he turns, he spots us and hurriedly tosses the heron back into the rushes. "The little bastard!" Steve seethes in an angry whisper, hardly able to believe his eyes, and I do my best to calm him and attempt to plead that Elwyn is really quite passionate about birds ... it's just that he shows it in a strange sort of way, that's all. "He needs education, not punishment," I continue and am thankful that the others haven't seen a thing and have been distracted by something else on the opposite verge; I'd hate for there to be an unpleasant scene with Elwyn. He surely must now be feeling a bit like a cornered animal on seeing our gang of relative strangers approaching, having chosen this quiet Sunday morning to steal out unseen with his dad's twelve-bore and to contribute his bit into keeping the 'vermin' under control.

"Come and look at this, Jimmy," Cari calls, pointing down to something amongst the flowering dandelions. I stroll over and am shown something that horribly looks like the flattened remains of Tony, our black tomcat. He's been dead for some time and is barely recognisable and helps to explain his absence and the fact that Spibby had earlier tried to tell us that something was wrong. They all gather flowers and lay them on the flattened remains, till no more is visible and an air of sadness breathes amongst us.

Elwyn has thought it wiser to remain on the other side of the hedge as we move nearer, and I am now able to see what it is that lured him out from his bed. The brook has been dammed with the roots and stumps of yet more murdered hedgerows and now there's a sizeable pool forming, with a ragged waterfall spurting and splashing wildly It doesn't look safe and has as much water forcing through it as there is flowing over the top of it. "Hi, Jimmy!" he shouts, ignoring the others... "'got our own pool now. Dad's put a few big trout in it but the bloody owd heron's been taking them, isn't it!" "So you shot it!" Steve interrupts him, putting him on the spot and causing his small eyes to shift like tiddlers in a jar. "No I never, but I damn well will," he lies, turning to face the other way before getting off the subject. "What colour's a buzzards egg, Jimmy?" he asks, and I answer that I think it to be a roundish, brown speckled one, and ask him why he needs to know, upon which he raises his arm and points. "See that high tree over there... well, I though it was a crow's nest at the top of it, so I climbed it and, damn, I gets attacked by a bloody buzzard. Two of 'em came at me, and when I looked at the eggs there were two white ones, no speckles or nothin'. What d'you reckon Jimmy?" I look at Steve and he shrugs his shoulders dismissively and mutters, as though there was a bad taste in his mouth... "It does happen sometimes." I can tell that he feels uncomfortable being in the presence of this tiny wild figure holding a twelve-bore that's taller than he is, and is breaking the law here and there to say the least. "D'you reckon an owl could have laid in the nest, Jimmy?" I shake my head and suggest that they are just a couple of freak white eggs, that's all. As though rubbing our noses in the fact of his rapidly ripening manhood, Elwyn, with his back to us, fumbles in his pockets and clumsily shoves a cigarette into his mouth and strikes a match. He inhales the first suck right down to his welly bottoms, then blows it out with all the force he can muster and casually tells me, "Dad's put you a couple of rows of spuds in... top field, same as last year; we're a bit late with 'em this time, isn't it." He's surreptitiously signalling me to one side so that we may have whispered words of a private nature, and so I respond and he hisses out of the side of his mouth, "Don't tell dad that I nicked his gun, he'd kill me, right as ninepence he would, Jimmy!" "Don't worry, boyo," I reassure him. "I won't breathe a word, but just you go and put the damned thing back for Christ's sake." He fidgets a last nodule of fear from his small bundle of bones and adds, "Tell Cari not to say anything either... okay?" "Okay!" I say and he skulks away like an escaped mink and vanishes into the bushes, no doubt to skulk back to pick up the dead heron as soon as we're safely out of sight.

The morning is moving on and we haven't a single pea-stick to show for it. Steve is a bit tense and makes frequent references to his watch, not wanting to leave it too late before making the long journey back to Plymouth and trusting that his scooter is still under the shed at the back of Meg's place where our caravan used to be. There's a shadow of sadness over the loss of our cat and the boys are unusually quiet and downcast, even though Chris is doing his best to make them laugh. It's the thought of freshly baked bread alone that is keeping our spirits from failing altogether and so we turn our attentions to finding firewood in an attempt to bring some sunlight back amongst us. With luck we might just about manage an oven-full of wonderful rolls before the intrepid travellers set off, so we move up a gear and are soon carrying items of firewood to get the irons warming.

It must look strange on such a glorious golden day for there to be smoke rising from our chimney; we should be storing wood now, not burning it, just as I would argue that it's far easier for us to buy bread now than ever it is to keep up with firewood demands in the winter. Convincing others of this is simply not worth the breath that it's written with, so I set to and get my bushman saw into action again.

Whilst I'm attending to this, Chris and Steve, plus a little help from the boys, repair the swing and attempt to fix the fence which the bull flattened. I can hear a lot of hammering and screaming as too many cooks are spoiling the broth and fingers are getting in the way of hammers. There's an industrious buzzing all about the place, not an idle pair of hands anywhere. I slip off down to the well where the first dog-rose has chosen this moment to open its petals, making the old porch-roof look as though it has always been there. The water is beautifully clear with whirligigs and water-boatman making it their paradise. It's comforting to hear the tinkle of water overflowing, showing me that the old spring hasn't dried up, as has the previously muddy earth all around this area. I hear Old Crow briefly and he hears me, then, out from the more expansive silence, the thin clear bawling cry of old Dan, at the top of his private mountain, cursing his dog. The words 'bugger' and 'bastard' are as crisply engraved upon the air as are the silvery sentiments of a nearby robin. Dan's privacy is flawed by the uncaring emptiness that so sweetly clothes the gaping miles.

We've made it and the proudly risen rolls come out of the oven, piping hot and almost burnt... but not quite. The tray is put to cool and a marauding Sykes is put to flight, prompting me to fix the door and to leave only space enough for a flying swallow to enter through the window. Last year's blackberries and damsons come out from storage and there is pure bliss here while the bread is yet hot and the butter dribbling deliciously around our fingers.

Murphy drops in for a brief update on events and to know what all the din was last night, obliging me to explain how Dan wasn't his normal self and that our elderflower wine had got the better of him. This comes somewhat hard for Murphy to believe... "I'll have to try some of that," he gibes, "it must be good if Dan can't handle it, his guts are pickled with Captain Morgan!" He gives a growling laugh, sniffing the air in the manner of a ram sniffing for a ewe on heat, as he does so. "Been baking bread, Cari?" He doesn't miss much does Murphy and I ask him if he's detected the smell of bull-shit in the kitchen, emphasising upon him not to take this new bull for granted. "This one's nothing like old Max Tractor ... I've had a bit of a skirmish in the kitchen with him already, ask Rosie and Steve, they'll tell you!" They are happy to make fun of the incident now and relate it somewhat laboriously, prompting Murphy to consult his watch, fearing that this story could well exceed his allotted time. He's glad when I tell him that Steve and Chris are about to leave for Plymouth ... provided that no-one has absconded with their scooter in the meantime. "Don't worry, it's still there, Greg hasn't been up this weekend!" he sniggers, putting Steve's mind to rest and serving as a reminder that time is getting on and that he should be on the road by now. The afternoon concludes and we all make our way across the valley to see our friends off safely after their quiet weekend in the country. Tomorrow, God permitting... I shall gather pea-sticks!

Painting talk, a Brush with Foxes and an Experiment in Oils!

We enjoy a quiet clutch of days as the egg of June spreads her incandescent glow around us. Our swallows in the bedroom are now peppering the bed with their merry droppings and no matter where we position it, it gets plastered just the same. Necessity being the mother of invention, I have resorted to a 'Heath Robinson' kind of arrangement and strung up one of my larger paintings to serve as a canopy. So now we have a surrealist nightmare staring down on us. It's a massive heavily painted and brightly coloured raw carcass, suspended against a very deep sky, and it has owls, magpies and devilish things living in it together with human-like figures seated round a circular table that's perched over an open trap-door. I call it 'Last Supper', one which I started to paint after a sickening visit to a slaughterhouse; certainly not one to have around when the vicar pops in for tea, and it isn't really the most ideal image to greet us when we awaken in the morning either!

After just two awakenings to this disturbing image, I turn it round to face the other way and let the swallows have a sneak-preview of my forthcoming exhibition ... no doubt they'll be passing a few comments on it.

While the boys are at school, the girls go gliding off in their pretty bits of cotton to idle a few hours away with a basket of bread, cheese and Ambre Solaire, leaving me to paint. I don't ask for much and always put myself last in our own pecking order, doing my writing mostly while others are sleeping and only once in a while playing my guitar in a kind of painterly way. A bit like mixing colours and creating textures, usually while everyone else is absent.

There's a broad 'art' that I strive for, one that commits me to sharp awareness, to opinions, theories and plain adoration. I could never think of art as being opportunism to confound and disgust, pretending that a smart idea, slick and sick as it may be, can ever replace the long looking and searching, the love-labouring, ever-hungry process of drawing, feeling, exploring with all the majesty of sight and sense and joy combined. Art is forever, not just a cheap one-off; artists are not manufactured, they are born.

I look around these hills, steep, stately and with grace and grandeur; I see the skies ever evolving, never the same, always tumbling and with 'things' held suspended and yet always going somewhere different from the last. I see the light and the shade ever polishing and darkening and, there amongst the whole crazy mixture, sun, moon and stars, birds flying, sheep and variously patterned cows doing balancing acts around the turbulent patchwork gradients. All kinds of differently coloured trees, big ones, little ones with blossoms, berried fruits and nuts, each with the clasped fingers of their gripping hands deep and clutching the dear earth. The entire landscape is a living miracle that takes my breath away. I don't' simply paint 'IT'' I am part of 'IT' and 'IT' is part of me, another of it's creatures, alive and aware, with ideas and passions, opinions which all must form part of what I paint. It doesn't bother me in the least that our swallows are shitting all over my 'Last Supper', they're part of it; the painting is only alive whilst it's being painted, after it's finished it's dead. Just like the jay's feather I picked up yesterday, beautiful but of no further use. This I fear, tends to make art galleries seem like cemeteries, and the paintings in them, carcasses.

I'm back into the money-famine. Little comfort is to be gleaned from knowing that each nerve-shattering time that one of these devilish war-planes explodes across the valley, it's several million pounds of taxpayers money just burning to waste and all to the wicked purpose of destroying this beautiful world. I loathe and despise the very notion of war, which always results from ideologies at conflict, the very ultimate test for humankind to resolve through the majesty within our very species. Bullies bash boys on noses because they don't know any better. There's always, always a 'better' and it can never be made holy by the power of money, which is itself an artificial measure and causes more blindness than ever looking directly at the sun through binoculars can ever do!

Be that as it may, I'm still worried over this lack of money and I feel that I must spend a little of what I have left of it on making a phone-call to chase up some work back in television. I slip out quietly, without anyone knowing that I have gone, and I follow the line of woods shouldering the marsh, where a year ago the boys and I went in search of our bantams. The woods in June are irrepressible and resound with splendours to excite every sense. Shimmering, flickering greens and with Delius, Debussy, Vaughan Williams and hosts of other wild birds too; all singing before the vivid little splash of colour, the red phone-box in the middle-green of nowhere. How can it be that this solitary little life-saver has pee all over its floor, broken bottles, busted windows and a door that won't shut? What is it about Homo Sapiens that is so vile and destructive... aliens, perhaps?

Faraway voice coming through a wire to this 'lavatory' here; help is at hand and my choosing of this moment to phone has proven fortuitous, because they were just about to send me a telegram asking for me to phone them. I have less than a week before heading off southwest again in the provision of funds to help keep us going; I'm glad of it but I hate it all the same, especially in this most eloquent of months.

It is the pre-dawning of the fifth as I lie beneath the upturned canvas with my head in my elbowed arms, deep in thought. There's a cool breeze breathing in and the swallows are yet sleeping along with other darling souls in this cowshed shack. I'm suddenly alerted to a spontaneous pandemonium of cackling chickens, with Chris the cockerel, giving it hell up on the barn roof. I shoot upright and stare out through the open window; Christ! I'm glaring down at a fox with one of my hens in its mouth! I don't remember my feet ever touching the ground and I've most certainly by-passed the niceties of dress. Adrenaline in orgasmic proportions has ejaculated me out and away down the hill, numb to pain, determined to catch this confounded fox! I don't recall clearing the barbed-wire fence and the brambly ditch by the cattle-trough, I'm running faster than a hare and with the bloody smear of dawn creeping up through the aldermarsh before me. This fox doesn't realise what it's taken on because I'm rapidly catching it and am suddenly upon it, whereupon, after whacking it across its backend with my bare feet, then diving headlong upon it, it lets go of the hen and wriggles free of my clawing fingers, then flees like the very wind into the osiers.

I kneel over my terrified little hen. It's Gerty and she's trembling, wild-eyed and unable to move. My own heart is pounding as I watch the vixen vanish from sight, then, gradually my eyes settle upon something that horrifies me... piles of earthenware drainage pipes, pile upon pile of them; somebody means business! I take Gerty up into my arms, then hurry back with her to where I can still hear hens in distress inside the barn. Two other foxes with hens in their mouths, are racing off in different directions, one is heading off past the caravan and up the hill, while the other has shot away down through the orchard towards the well. I put Gerty down and streak away past the caravan, clear the bit of fencing and blast up the hill, catching up with this fox too and forcing it to release the hen and run for its life. I race back and place this one, Missus Jones, beside Gerty and then power off down under the apple trees and along the well, but I'm too late, this one has escaped and I stagger to a halt.

It is only now that I feel the pain in my feet and realise fully that my mud-splattered body has not a single item of clothing on it. With a sudden flush of embarrassment, I tentatively sneak back to tend to my hens and to make myself presentable before the world wakes up. I tiptoe through the orchard and up into the yard and am met by shrieks of laughter from two women in their nighties, and by a round of applause from three small boys. "Good old Jimmy," the boys all sing proudly. "We saw you chase them nasty foxes away!" Rosie and Elly think it's hilarious and I can feel their eyeballs massaging me as I choke in the despair of having no hiding place. Just my two hands cradling what morsels of modesty that are available as I do a death-defying leap over the two trembling hens and push past the boys and into the cowshed. I can hear Cari upstairs newly awakened from her deep sleep; "What's going on down there?" she groans feebly, while the boys all giggle on seeing my bare buttocks vanishing round the corner. "Foxes... that's what!" I pant, bursting into the bedroom and frightening the swallows into flight before slumping heavily onto the rickety little bed. "We've been raided by three foxes," I complain to her dumbfounded face and clutch hold of my feet, which are raw and cut to ribbons. "I've managed to save Gerty and Missus Jones, but I don't know which others are missing; we've lost one at least, I'll go and check in a minute." I set to work on my injuries and remove a large thorn from the ball of my foot, before hurrying into my clothes and limping off to assess the damage and to try to track down the other fox.

The raw sun is rising through the low trees as I emerge once more to where Gerty is now cradled in Robin's arms, with Spencer holding Missus Jones in his. I ask them to try not to disturb them and to make them as cosy as possible inside the spud-shed, trying to explain that they'll be in a state of shock for a while and might even be injured as well. They tend most lovingly to what I ask, watched somewhat tiredly by Rosie and Elly, who are plainly being seduced back to their theatre of snores. I leave them and hurry off in search of our other little hen and the canine cretin that has taken her.

The dawn chorus is fully underway, totally oblivious to our trauma, as I slip up into the dark shadows of the hanging wood where I know of several fox-holes, the nearest of which has recently been reoccupied by badgers. I'm half expecting to stumble across a late badger as I, the predator now, skulk among the trees, keen-eyed and alert to the faintest whiff of fox. I feel charged with anger and without the slightest trace of fear whatsoever. I must be giving off terrifying vibes in true predator style, a warning to any fox to stay well clear of me. The fox that I'm looking for is not a local one; if cubs had been raised here just above the well, I'd have been the first to know of it. No, these foxes have come from some distance away, but I know that, if the situation arises, they'll not hesitate to take refuge in a badger-earth, as has proven to be the case on this occasion. I need look no further; here before me in the well worn entrance hole, a solitary white feather tells me all that I need to know and I lie down with my ear flush to the ground and listen. There's no sound at all and I crawl to my knees and bellow a growling scream down inside the hole in a final, utterly futile gesture. Nothing can bring my little hen back, even though I have tried.

When I get back home, and with the help of the boys, I read

out the chicken register once more, coming to the grim conclusion that two of our hens are missing, one of them being the recently christened, 'Posh Auntie Rita' and the other one, sadly, 'Sykes'. The bantams are all present and correct, while the two poor dears in the spud-shed are settled as comfortably as possible and have food and water; whether or not they will survive is really anybody's guess. We are hugely sad, it's been a strange few days, having lost a cat and two hens, as well as being plundered by a bull. As we stand reflecting, something vaguely white starts flapping about in the tangled top of the damson tree; to our utter delight and astonishment... it's Sykes. This crazy old tart isn't quite so stupid after all and she disentangles herself with her customary lack of elegance, and flaps down to a loud cheer; I think that a celebratory pot of tea would very much be in order!

The sun is high and hot as I tidy up the van in readiness for my annual migration for work and I see Murphy out leisurely walking a goat. We succumb to the trap of conversation, grumbling in particular over the necessity of money, the way it prostitutes us into all manner of submissions. I talk of the price of petrol and the ridiculous amount that it's going to cost me just to get to Plymouth and back, in order to earn a bit of money for vital things; this van drinks petrol for fun! I wish the damned thing would run on water... not so much a steam engine but, water instead of petrol. My hopeless dream makes us laugh on realising that, if water could be used that way, they'd damn soon slap a tax on the rain and we'd be charged for every single drop of it that fell on our heads!

Murphy shares in my anarchic futility and says... "They ran cars on paraffin during the war... I was reading about it; they did lots of things then that you're not allowed to do now. Take pigs for instance..." "Never mind about pigs!" I interrupt him, "do you mean to tell me that, plain ordinary household paraffin works okay in a petrol engine?" "Yes! It may be a bit rough but it works... might shit the engine up a bit but it was used a lot during the war." My ears really have pricked up; money and me are strangers at the best of times, even I know that paraffin is but a fraction of the price of petrol, what's more Plymouth is a damned long way! I look at Murphy with a wicked grin creeping up my face and I give the side of the van a friendly pat. "This old girls game for anything, aren't you eh, my darlin'? I suppose I'd be breaking the law, wouldn't I Murph?" Murphy frowns and thoughtfully growls... "Look, Jimmy... laws are only intended for the likes of you and me to have to follow, them that makes them, they knows how to wriggle round them... that's why they're rich and we're poor. Simple!"

Law or no law, I'm up for it; I'm going to give it a try, just as a 'scientific' experiment on behalf of the 'poor'. I must waste no further time and get on with my testing in determining the most suitable mixture of petrol with paraffin. It could be that pink paraffin is better then blue ... and that the petrol should be, perhaps a five star mix instead of the two that I flog her on now. There's simply so much to this 'poor mans science' and I'm compelled into thinking of the risks as being part of the thrill!

Murphy's really buzzing; this beats taking goats for a walk, any day. I get the distinct impression that he thinks of me as being his own private human guinea pig over this, but I don't mind because it excites me too. It feels a bit 'outlawish', wild and sort of 'gypsy' in a world of bureaucratic do's and don'ts and where freedoms have all been stolen away, then sold back to us at grossly inflated prices. I don't breathe a word of my intentions within earshot of the boys, it matters nil that I have just rescued the chicken which they so lovingly named in honour of their school-cook when, the real human 'Missus Jones' would have me hung, drawn and quartered, bleached, castrated, boiled and fed to pigs, if she ever got the faintest whiff that I was running my van on paraffin. Come to think, she'd have that done to me anyway, simply for having never seen me on my knees down at the church. We need science, not religion; understanding and not make believe, only then can we start on the building of trust and tolerance and, dare I say it... seeing if my thirsty old van will run on cheap paraffin!

The gang and I head for the forest and we gather pea-sticks, putting to good use the 'thinnings' which foresters have cleared from between the rows in creating access for felling. It's only now that I feel able to talk about what had shocked me when I chased the fox across the aldermarsh; the full meaning of what I saw didn't sink in properly then for obvious reasons. Regardless, like it or not, plans are already underway to drain this marvellous marshland where the snipe and the woodcock live; I dread to think of what other plans these Europeanised farmers have for chasing the subsidy-carrot, at the expense of the natural Eco-system. One doesn't have to be much more than a monkey to understand what are the ultimate consequences of draining upland marsh, the natural sponge for holding and slowly releasing its water to feed streams and rivers over times of drought. Simply, whatever rain that falls, will go roaring and racing back down through a million pipes back to the sea from whence it so beautifully and laboriously came. Multiplied a few hundred times and we're talking of the terrifying prospect of awesome flash-flooding further downstream. Can't anyone see this? My only regret is that I insulted a monkey in saying this... sorry, Monkey!

Our garden looks most attractive now that the pea-sticks are in, and the boys have dammed the ditch again, so that we have a water supply for the garden; it's all started to look hopeful at long last. Seeing people walking in gardens is a lovely sight, a beautiful bonding kind of relationship, holy and perfectly intended to be that way. There's something about the earth that's simply divine... soil in your fingers, crumbling it to dust, knowing that it feeds all the little things that in turn feed us as we in turn feed the earth, regularly and ultimately. All those resplendent colours coming from the brown tilth; all the amazing tastes and smells, the endless shapes and textures, the mind-boggling variety, all coming from, and returning to ... tilth... soil... mother Earth.

Ghost of a Blowlamp and a few Idle Moments

I leave the peaceful scene, grab my paraffin-cans and large funnel, then slope off sheepishly down the sheep-track beneath the sycamore tree and cross the marsh to where I can already see Murphy waiting by the van. He's grinning like an open piano, almost tripping over himself with laughter in his eager anticipation of our old wartime experiment. We climb aboard this sacrificial ex-greengrocery delivery van and drive respectfully, just a little faster than mourning pace along the lanes to the garage in the valley where we fill the cans with 'Esso Blue'. Emrys, the proprietor watches us like a squirrel watches a nut, casually picking his teeth with a bit of fuse-wire and spitting the bacon bits obliviously anywhere in thunderous silent thought.

Our plan is to head off out along the road towards Machynlleth, get the engine nicely warmed up, then, when the road's clear, pull-in somewhere and top the tank up with paraffin. I wouldn't like to start it from cold with this stuff which I remember my Dad having trouble with in his blowlamp. The moment arrives and I skid to a halt in the gateway to a field and fumble the petrol-cap from the tank while Murphy clumsily jabs the funnel into place. I'm full of strange feelings as I pour in two gallons of the stuff, it's too late to change my mind now! We stare goggle-eyed at each other, then Murphy starts to snigger and gives my arm a thump... "C'mon... there's no turning back now!" We race back and jump aboard, then I take hold of the key and give it a twist; I don't believe it... it works! I rev it a little just to make sure that the paraffin is thoroughly circulating and, almost immediately, the smell coming from the engine tells me that it's the new fuel that's being vapourised... it really does smell like the blowlamp that poor old Dad had so much trouble with! I ram it into gear and give it a bootful of throttle and we take off like a Saturn rocket in the most thunderous billowing cloud of white smoke, the likes of which I have never seen. Now, not only smelling like, but looking like Dad's blowlamp, we head off along the broad valley between the high rolling hills, chuckling like two mischievous magpies. Traffic is reasonably light as we thunder along between the snaking hedgerows, smugly excited by our success and feeling a huge sense of relief at last. Nonchalantly, I glance up into my mirror, then double-check in my side-mirrors to make sure that I haven't suddenly developed cataracts... I can't believe what I am seeing... or not seeing, as is more the case; the world behind us is solid white smoke, an impenetrable wall of it, blotting out absolutely everything. "Jesus Christ!... what are we gonna do about that, Murph?" Murphy's response is swift and simple... he collapses forward against the dashboard choking with laughter! "You're a fat lot of good!" I yell at him... "if they can see the Great Wall of China from space, they'll surely be able to see us!" He tries to talk, but the occasion seems to have the better of him; he manages to splutter... "Keep going, Jimmy, put your foot down... get the engine hotter."... then he crumples forward again and is useless.

With all previous self-satisfaction now turned to paranoia, the thing I fear most of all is to come across a police-car; this would really make their day. I'm panicking now and, being able to hear Murphy's head repeatedly bashing against the dashboard, isn't helping. I see an inviting-looking lane to my right, I can't see what's behind and I yank the steering wheel and aim for it. I'm buried in a bower of ages-old hedges and a climb that throws the engine down through the gears. I'm negotiating extremely steep and winding terrain with high overgrown banks and bedraggled sheep straying everywhere. No matter where I go, the ghost of old Dad's blowlamp follows thick and stinking close behind and the engine is sounding a bit hysterical to add to my concerns. Murphy finds his voice again and incessantly rants... "Keep going, Jimmy!" and stamps his feet enthusiastically, craning his head out of the window, looking back on the filthy spectacle, loving every moment of it. We come across a small, bandy-legged farmer with a knobbly stick in one hand and a dead lamb in the other and, on seeing us he staggers back under the towering hogweed. His 'N.F.U.-issue' aluminum-shafted tobacco-pipe falls from his dumbfounded gape as, in one blinding, paraffin-stinking Armageddon, he is consumed in a swirling white cloud, gone from my mirror, gone from the world, sheepdog an' all! "Keep going, Jimmy; don't worry about him... he'll not be taking your number, that's for sure!"

The engine is glowing hot when we level out on the high, wild, open moorland; it's been working overtime and is now screaming for a rest and to cool off, but I daren't turn the engine off until I've come to a good downhill section where I'll be able to bump-start, should it prove necessary. I find the very place and we roll to a stop as the wind blows our dense white cloud past us and away like fog across the tussocky, wet bog, driving larks and pipits before it. I slump forward onto the steering wheel, then slowly turn to Murphy and say... "The things we do for science!"

We sit thoughtfully for a while allowing our pulse-rates to settle and I raise the engine-cover to assist the smelly lump of almost molten iron to cool off. I'm surprised and greatly relieved not to find the radiator boiling over and Murphy jokes that it's probably boiled dry. "Well, at least it works on paraffin... 'shame about the smoke!" ... I go on, trying to ignore his joke about the radiator, and I open my door to release some of the heat. The air rushing in is surprisingly cold, and when Murphy opens his door, it feels like a gale off the arctic. We go outside and lean against the side of the van in the sunshine.

There are cuckoos up here and the whipping wind veils the miles of larksong in waves, interspersed by the shrill, plaintive calls of pipits. It's really a wild and untamed place, lonesome and hauntingly bleak with far mountains majestically riding the rim of the world. Few places on the planet can compare with Wales, and here I am nursing a highly polluting paraffin disaster right at the very heart of it!

Presently my mind shifts from the wild silence and resettles on the problem at hand. "Hey, Murph, it's easy to see what's wrong... we've been running her on neat paraffin more or less. I reckon the mixture should be something like, two of petrol to one of paraffin... I bet that would do it!" He dwells on this for a few moments then, in a revelation of positive thought, comments... "and Jimmy, don't forget that she's been pulling her guts out in low gear... high revs almost the whole time since we filled her up. You're right about the mixture... we need a good flat road, she'll be alright then."

It's getting to feel a bit chilly in the rarified air and so we return to the cockpit and warm our hands over the still glowing engine. I don't feel quite so bad now that we have confronted and solved the problem, knowing that it's downhill all the way back to the garage where I shall top-up with petrol to be on the safe side. I turn the key once more and there's an initial flatulent backfire and another disgusting discharge of smoke but, with the engine now idling, this soon disperses, easing our troubled consciences to levels that we can live with. It's when we are back down from these hills that I'm obliged to boot the accelerator and the ghost of old Dad's blowlamp returns to haunt us.

The garage comes into view with some relief and I roll up to the pump in my vaporous cloud. Emrys is biblically involved welding a muck-spreader, he doesn't miss much even with dark goggles hiding his eyes. He stops what he is doing and shoves the goggles onto the top of his head, weighing us up, then starts to smile; "Running it on chicken-muck?" he laughs in Welsh. "Can't afford that!" Murphy bawls back in English, and no other words are spoken as I top up with petrol; I think it might be wiser to get my next paraffin from a different garage.

Another miraculous Spring morning is awakening, virginal in every way. I'm lying in bed listening to the infant starlings in their nest in the wall; it sounds like they won't be long before leaving home and discovering the marvels of flight. I'm on my own eve of departure, but with no such marvel to delight me on my journey. In my awakening thoughts, I think of possible parallels between my own life and that of a starling with regard to bringing up a family. I have a feeling that goes right through to my bones that I should be a constant and close parent until my own young birds have flown, only then could I ever think of addressing the rest of life and adjusting to it.

If I were that old cock starling, my trip to Plymouth to earn money would be the equivalent of travelling all that crazy distance just for a few juicy grubs and the time that it took me to bring them back to the nest would surely result in the starvation of my offspring. Maybe the parallel should be drawn between learning to fly and that of learning to walk, the difference being that infant human beings remain relatively helpless for quite a long time after learning to walk whereas, when young birds are on the wing, they very soon go on their own way after the briefest of learning periods, which I suppose is the equivalent of our going to infant school.

The behaviour of our different species would be far closer were it not for the concoction known as 'civilization', a clever piece of marketing strategy intended for bringing us into manageable flocks. Starlings do this quite naturally, but for beneficial reasons to do with the welfare of all, ours being for the creation of class-systems and the sanitisation of greed, assisted still further by the invention of Religion as an effective stick by which to herd and hold together manageable, exploitable masses; there are no such comparisons in nature. Birds, bees, weeds, wolves and whales all do it as easy as peeing and are quite possibly possessing of a spiritual dimension and knowing of greater awarenessess than themselves, so very far and so different from Religion... which I suppose is the main catalyst in Man's imperfecting of perfection.

Swallows are joyfully darting about the room as my mind

comes back down to earth and lists all the things that need doing before I leave, with fears of the bull gnawing away like a toothache. Waiting to go is always the worst part; time dawdles, the only trace of comfort coming from knowing that there'll still be a bit of June remaining when I return. I get up and take an early trip to the well in the sweet-smelling air; there's a trace of dew on the grass and a huge sense of expectation breathing all around, tender and terrible, so overwhelmingly perfect is this early morning here holding me.

The little cockerel has emerged from the hole in the barn roof and is filling the valley with his flaming cry; it hardly seems possible for so small a creature to make so deafening an account of himself, he always brings a smile to my face, he's so comical and is plainly enjoying every moment of it. I think it wiser not to release the other chickens just yet, fearing that foxes may be crafty and pay us another visit when we least expect it. Early jays are squawking up in the oakwood, undoubtedly plundering the nests of other birds; magpies are at it too and I can hear a squirrel scolding. There's a whole lot going on up in that deep, dark, secret wood.

We make an early trip into town for a cylinder of gas and to stock-up with provisions which I am hoping may last until I return in two weeks. Even though the van's got petrol in the tank now, it still smells like Dad's old blow-lamp and is still leaving a discernable haze of smoke in its wake; fortunately no-one has noticed it, it's just another smelly, smoky old machine to them. We see Dan in town, standing sentried in his best suit on his usual corner, dew-drop sparkling from the tip of his nose and with patches of silver whiskers that he's missed with the mower, making his face look a bit of a landscape in the morning sun. This is the day he loves, the very day that his pension was intended for; he's the picture in an old book that somebody will always turn to and remember... it wont be too long before Captain Morgan double-glazes his eyes and sets him off ranting.

Aspirations of idleness weigh us down as we trundle home; this day's far too good to be doing something on. Curly Jenkins' mother gives us an extra friendly wave as we pass, this gives us a pleasant surprise considering the temper she was in when we last saw her. I give the horn a familiar blast and return the greeting, which sets their horrid little mongrel into chasing after us... heaven only knows what he thinks he can do if he does manage to catch us.

When we arrive back at the marsh meadow gate, there's a distinct absence of cows, the field was full of them when we left, but I'm not complaining, I've seen enough cows to last me a lifetime... not to mention the male of the species! It makes a pleasant change in not having to be constantly looking over our shoulders... all we have to look out for now is where we put our feet, the sun hasn't had time to bake the wretched stuff to a crust yet. Despite this, the world really is smelling of roses; all along the lanes the hedges were adorned with them, crowning this month as Queen of all the year.

Weighed down with a gas-cylinder and everyone else loaded down with bags, we make our way home where the mystery of the cows is made abundantly clear... they're all in my garden ecstatically sprawled on the peas, having flattened the sticks and also having eaten our everlasting cabbages; they've spared absolutely nothing, crops, clothes-line, fence... the lot! I'm utterly speechless as is everyone else as we just stand staring in silence. The bull is nowhere to be seen... I don't trust this situation one little bit, he's probably hiding somewhere awaiting his moment to leap out at me and get even. I try to remain cool... wishful thinking if ever there was... then my thermostat gives up and I throw all caution to the wind and leap about noisily amongst these great placid, cud-chewing lumps, not a single one of which is even slightly bothered over my hysteria.

The garden is finished! What they haven't flattened, they've eaten and have crapped absolutely everywhere. Robin very bravely checks to see that the bull isn't hiding inside the barn; I hear him doing a pretty good impersonation of me as he hounds about thirty sheep from inside and the girls all scream as sheep explode out in all directions with the precision of headless chickens, influencing the cows into shifting their great carcasses at last and getting entangled in my busted fence as they reluctantly disperse. They make me feel like I don't belong here anymore as I gingerly check to see that the bull hasn't got himself locked inside the kitchen again. I am greatly relieved to find the place empty, but I can tell that the situation has affected my brain when I go to check that he isn't upstairs in the bedroom ... I wouldn't put anything past that shifty-eyed sod of an animal! The girls catch my madness and are afraid to go into the caravan, a place that's just as impossible for the bull to get into; even the boys have contracted the disease now and insist that I go and check the caravan, just to prove to them that it's safe. On my way back, my attention is suddenly drawn to two yellow circles peering down at me from the starlings' nesting hole... Spibby! That confounded cat has raided the nest and has one of the young starlings in her mouth. This really makes my day... there's nothing I can do, the damage has been done, the starling's nest has been destroyed!

Miraculously, the day remains untouched by events, even with a bull hiding somewhere amongst the sunbeams. By contrast, my spirits have floundered and I must somehow summon the motivation and restore some semblance of a fence and get the clothes-line back into service, otherwise there'll be problems here while I am away. With having a new cylinder of gas, there'll be no need to light fires for the next couple of weeks, so I feel a little easier about this part and waste no further time in getting the new supply connected and ready for action. Rowan and Spencer come to help me repair the fence and get the clothes-line strung-up again, but it's all a bit rough and ready, our spirits not being at their best right now... and the day still hasn't reached its adolescence.

None of the others are feeling inclined to break sweat while the bull's whereabouts remain a threat and tends to cloud things, encouraging a fear that any gross sun-worshiping idleness may yet be spoiled by un-divine intervention. After using up precious water in swilling the cow muck from around the house, I conclude that I need to go off for a run about the fields and through the woods, I shan't be happy until I've discovered where the bull is hiding ... what's more, a good hard, grueling run will do me a world of good right now, and I'll be back before the day is three o'clock high. So, while Cari, Rosie and Elly collaborate over the creation of the salad of a lifetime, I slip into my flimsy running-gear, give a nervous wave then take the plunge.

Few things can equal this marvellous feeling of aloneness in the silken air, aware of a sublime sensation of being relieved of treadmill concerns... temporarily at least. Running is my only known way of restoring and replenishing my mithered spirit. After a quick circuit of nearby fields, I take to the path through the wood, then into the other smaller wood close by where the old bulldozer lies at rest. There's no sign of the bull anywhere, he's nowhere to be seen and so, I race back home to let them know that it's safe to go out and sunbathe, then I head off for an exhilarating experience on tarmac roads.

Fourteen hard miles later, I end my run on the wickedly steep hill up to the farm... even Gareth's Landrover makes hard work of this one. It's a great feeling as I attack the murderous yards and triumphantly scale the iron gate into the deep-shitted farmyard where, to my unbelieving horror, I am suddenly standing face to face with the bull!

There's pandemonium in the yard... Gareth flaying wildly with a stick, gripping his pipe with a grip that would frighten a crocodile, while poor Hugh is screamed at as he dances this way and that with his arms outstretched like a scarecrow. "You stand by the gate, Jimmy! 'Gotta get this owd bugger out of sight, isn't it... he ain't been registered!" I'm back down to earth with a bang!

The bull looks confused, bewildered and more than a degree or two mad. He plainly doesn't understand what's happening, the fact that he hasn't been 'registered', whatever that is, and that the Ministry Inspector is rumoured to be doing spot-checks in the area. My heart is beating like a paraffin-generator and sweat is dribbling from me as shit flies everywhere and growling screams lacerate the idle air. Poor Hugh looks like a rustic figure that's escaped from a Brueghel painting, as the bull is bullied into a long shed at the far end of which he may be hidden in the gloom beyond sacks and cobwebs until the danger has passed. I jokingly suggest to Gareth that he get a set of plastic udders and attach them to the bull at times like this. He laughs and irritates a cough which causes him to go naked without his pipe while he fights for his breath; Hugh looks at me in a way that plainly begs... "Help!"

Gwyneth staggers across the yard clutching a hefty child; laughter is a stranger here and she's come to investigate. I get them laughing again when I relate the incident of the bull in our kitchen, going on to express my despair at having lost our garden this very morning as a result of cows and sheep, shit everywhere about the place and the water-supply showing signs of drying up. "You've got to expect that sort of thing when you comes to live in these parts!"

Gwyneth smirks, with rather more than a trace of sarcasm, leaving me in no doubt whatsoever that any earlier promises have long since been forgotten. I should have known that such things were about as safe as a bird's egg in a schoolboy's trouser pocket. "You needn't worry about the bull, Jimmy... I'll keep him in for a while, and he's staying up in the top fields now," Gareth mutters through his clenched teeth, and I leave them all tittering at my expense, then make my way back over the hill feeling a good deal happier about the bull at least... not that I believe in promises any more.

Back at the cowshed the entire herd are gathered in wait under the shade of the apple trees where Cari alas, has hung out the washing. There is a persistent menace just standing there disregarding my presence and I know that sooner or later one of them will make a move and smash my fence again and the rest of them all follow to complete their ruination of our garden dream. My gang are all sprawled out on the concrete at the front, idling the afternoon away; there seems little point in wasting energy in trying to drive the cows away when it's obvious what their intentions are... a crazed obsession with the unfinished business. Maybe they're missing the bull, but I have a sneaking feeling that he'll be missing them a whole lot more.

Since their recent mauling by foxes, 'Gladys' and 'Missus Jones' have both developed limps; in the case of 'Missus Jones' it's more of a stagger. However, they are attempting to settle back into the swing of things and are there along with the others, wrecked in dust-bath paradise on the flattened remains of our garden. Leisure, for us at this moment, has the extra weight of disillusionment in its ingredients... great if you're bone idle, but not so good if you're still riding on the back of a dream.

It's a somewhat uneasy, peaceful sort of afternoon here under threat of cattle and sheep; the sun is just a big soft rubber hammer beating down upon all things, with the effect of rendering everything lethargic... it's only this that is keeping the peace. When I look at the little grey cat sprawled full length and purring like a motorbike, I notice what at first looks like a stomach swollen with her recent meal of baby starlings... then I take a second look and realise it to be more the result of the baritone tomcat that called by this way awhile back, crooning his rag-and-bone-man's aria in the moonlight. I've got the distinct feeling that he found himself a fan for life and a bit of V.I.P. treatment to help him on his tour.

Meanwhile the bantam chicks are growing up rapidly and are now almost as big as their mother. They are a very close-knit family, totally separate from everything around them and possessing a rather noble and arrogant kind of wildness, something that our white hens have had bred out of them; I almost get the impression that these old dears are actually trying to be like us, a kind of self-imposed evolution, on a par with Robin who seems to want to be like them. They occasionally strut amongst us, ever hopeful of a crumb or a sneaky slurp of tea from an unguarded mug, before drifting back to crash-out in the hot soil.

Separate groups of sun-wrecked things; cows in a cluster beneath the apple trees, sheep all gasping and clamouring as tightly as they can squeeze into the groins of the hedge at the back, demonstrating a loathing of the sun, while people and chickens worship it and fall horizontally at prayer in its dazzling light while the sky is a sweet, babbling discourse of swallows. These little darlings are more separate than all the rest, even the bantams cannot compete with these, yet they share our bedroom... or rather, they share their bedroom with us, something that makes us feel greatly privileged.

Lethargy prevails throughout the long afternoon before hunger and thirst begin the undermining process and the first traces of evening touch upon the skin. Cows get up and empty thoroughly all over the ground beneath the clothes-line and they snort and slobber their silvery slime all over the washing. I stand close by, imposing my presence upon them until the balance of their minds has tilted in my favour and their idea of trampling my fence and obliterating what's left of our garden, shrinks as their need for grass and water begin to dominate. A similar drift is taking shape in the stirring bodies sprawled around me, with stretching and yawning, then standing up, shuffling and stamping, exercising, while thoughts of food and drink does to us what it has done to the cows, sheep and chickens; this one thing makes us all equal under the sun.

Sunday has arrived and my long wait is almost over ... only to be replaced by another long wait until I return. For the first time in quite a while, there are clouds a-sail in the Sabbath sky, where insects and swallows are not flying nearly so high as they were yesterday. I've received no meteorological messages from my right buttock to prepare me for any change in the weather, so I can only conclude that the dry spell is set to last, regardless of clouds... either that, or my bum's developed a fault!

Blast-Off!

Over in the lane, my 'Saturn Rocket' stands silently on its launch pad amongst arums, hedge-garlic and bluebells, in readiness for my paraffin mission to the 'Planet Plymouth'. The boys stroll over with me with dustpan and brush, duster and air-freshener, essential tools for vital pre-launch adjustments. Gareth suddenly appears, bouncing at speed over the skyline in the Landrover; he seems to be in a hurry, kind of restless, but not appearing to be going anywhere in particular. He's looking for something but I can't think what as I watch him, trying to guess what's on his mind and very soon give up and concentrate my efforts into getting the space-ship ship-shape and the mattress aired.

We are presently joined by Meg, Murphy with a babe on his back and a couple of nanny-goats in harness; it's a lovely sight to come across in a country lane under a canopy of tender new green and the rapturous birdsong bonding it all together.

"What d'you reckon he's up to, Jimmy?" Murphy asks quietly, watching Gareth, now out from the Landrover and walking amongst the trees in the little wood. "He ain't gathering daisies, that's for sure!" I reply and go on to relate the incident regarding the un-registered bull and how the cows had just put paid to any hopes we had of having a garden. "They're a law unto themselves, you of all people should know that, Jimmy!" Meg laughs, her thick black hair still un-brushed from sleep, but looking radiant just the same. "Are you referring to cows or to farmers?" I ask and Murphy bawls out... "Both!" We all laugh and he goes on to tell me how, according to Dan, old Thomas had seen Christ again... in the garden by the red-currant bush whilst emptying the tea-leaves this time. "Got to get yourself ready to come," God said... "You've had your three score years and ten and you're living on borrowed time now"; that's what he told him. Dan reckons he's been taking strong medicine for his bronchitis and that it always gets him seeing things." We share in a kind of thoughtful laughter, then changing the subject, Meg says... "You're never going to run this dear old van to Plymouth and back on paraffin, are you?" I hasten to push my finger to my lips but I'm too late to silence her as Rowan's ears prick up, leaving me obliged to lie my way out of it. "You must be joking!" I abruptly reply with a frown that's meant to close the matter. I catch sight of Murphy giving her a dig in the ribs with his elbow and Rowan gives me a questioning kind of look and I return it, hoping that he'll think she's mad. Meg looks a bit puzzled and shakes her head... oh, what a tangled web we weave.

As they go on their way, we wander back across the marsh meadow and cross paths with Gareth who's now heading for the gate by the van. He waves hurriedly and gives a gash of a grin, not offering to stop until he's reached the gate where he jumps out, climbs the gate and vanishes under the trees; he's like a man with the problem of not knowing where to bury a tea-chest full of gold bullion.

Back at the cowshed, Cari tells me that Gareth has been strutting about on the wooded hillside above the well and also down in the wood by the aldermarsh. "Did you show him what the cows had done to our garden?" I ask, and she shakes her head... "No, he didn't even stop."

I'm almost ready to go, no-one feels happy about it, but at least we have the comfort of knowing that the bull won't be causing any trouble in my absence and, on another positive note, there isn't a garden to worry about any more, so with luck, it should be quite straightforward. Cari and the girls have prepared me some sandwiches and a flask for the journey; I've packed a Spartan change of clothing, toothbrush, razor and running-gear, my guitar and tape-recorder; I need nothing else... what am I saying... I've got nothing else. It's kisses and hugs all round, then I head off... Planet Plymouth, here I come!

I've worked it out that, if I mix about three gallons of paraffin with six or seven of petrol, I should have saved myself the price of a meal when I reach Plymouth, but I must make sure to end my journey on neat petrol in the hope of cleaning the engine out as far as possible ... I don't want to overdo it at this stage. I won't really be making any savings when I crash-out in my sleeping-bag in the back of the van because this was already part of my tight planning budget; every little helps, wise or otherwise, every single penny has to count in this new-found, old-style living experience-cum-adventure of ours.

My rocket fuel is a pretty shade of pink this time when I pull onto a verge high outside of river valley orbit and top-up for my second-stage burn, this time without cosmonaut Murphy providing moral support. I have yielded to caution with this particular mixture ... space-travel is a serious business and I don't want to get over-confident at this stage, I can always adjust the mixture later when I get down from the hills. The old girl is churring like a nightjar, leaving a ghostly afterburn through a whole galaxy of villages and black-and-white half timbered small towns bathed in the deathly quiet of Sunday late afternoon.

I eventually reach the tiny satellite of 'Redbrook'. Just south of Monmouth, where I pause for some throat lozenges at a shack, where an old friend provides travellers like myself with fried battery-eggs on white stuff known in the trade as 'bread', together with mugs of a tea-like concoction, referred to as being 'tea'. It's a handy stop for a quick 'hello', because there's a petrol station close by where I can dilute my paraffin mixture with petrol once more, in preparation for the black hole of Bristol, where the space-police operate in herds; the last thing that I want to do now is to push my luck with these guys. My old friend has a good laugh when I tell him that I'm running my van on paraffin; I know that my secret is safe with him and I get the distinct impression that he doesn't want me to ask him what he's frying his eggs in either!

I blast off in a cloud that convinces him that I'm not pulling his leg and go on my winding way beside the sparkling River Wye, close by the great Forest of Dean, crossing the river to be buried beneath more dark forests. Then, Tintern, its magnificent Abbey which still hasn't been finished after all these years, then on to Chepstow and the high-flying Severn Bridge. I leave my thinly veiled paraffin trail high across this convergence of bad-tempered tidal waters then, when I'm safely back down to earth and heading for Avonmouth, feel somewhat uncomfortably more at home with the itinerant tinker-folk established in lay-byes along the way, breaking up cars and burning them, violating the landscape with sump-oil furnaces and with free-range elephant sized Alsatians performing like dirty-bomb nuclear deterrents over the cheap diamonds of shattered windscreen and non-precious fragmented metals, while chromium-plated caravan palaces of quaintness turn blind eyes to the hell-hole that they've created.

I don't honestly feel that I'm as bad as that, in fact I don't really see paraffin as being very much different to petrol; petrol's poison is invisible ... mine ain't, that's all! What's more, paraffin is but a fraction of the price of petrol and I'm short of the cost of a crust right now. I'm more than glad to be safely out of this area as I find it intimidating and I pray that I never, ever, have a breakdown here; not only do I fear I'd be robbed, but eaten as well. So I put my foot down and set my sights on Taunton and another lay -by where, after a last calming slurp from my flask, discreetly re-fuel my rocket on the special juice that will carry me over the last long stretch to the planet of my family's bread and butter.

Re-entry is thankfully without incident, but I have taken the precaution of running my tank dangerously low before making a final stop for a top-up with pure petrol to end my journey. I glide-in to land on my bedding-down landing pad in the Television Car Park while there is still light in the sky and this architecturally fragmented planet is in idle mood. The gulls are retiring to their chimney-pots, obese after their gluttonous supper of human sewage that's sailing out on the outgoing tide down at West Hoe. In the past I have watched the foul stuff bubbling violently to the surface in a disgusting example of mans lack of respect for the wild and beautiful sea and all the creatures that live in it, creatures which we in turn catch as food for ourselves.

It's my turn now to turn a blind eye, a deaf ear, limp leg or whatever it takes to preserve and encourage my own obsessed, gluttonous appetite for fish-and-chips which my illegal use of paraffin has made possible for me to afford. I curse my memory for reminding me of the millions of raw-sewage outlets all around our coastline and tidal estuaries. My confounded hunger is like black-out curtains in the windows of a chromium caravan on a lay-by near Avonmouth. I'm as guilty as all the rest, I tell myself disgustedly, but with hunger eating into any real commitment connecting what I'm thinking with what I'm doing... I just feel like fish-and-chips, full stop!

My arrival in the car-park has, unbeknown to me, set off alarm bells. A police car suddenly appears on the forecourt outside the reception area and a security guard, whom I've not seen before, quickly joins the two police officers and points them in my direction; my heart sinks, I'd expected to find my old friend Brendan. Fortunately for me, I'd had the presence of mind to keep my contractual letter in my pocket and, as these uniformed lawmen come racing menacingly up to me, I hop out of the van with my bit of paper and waggle it before them, distracting them from the still present ghost of old Dad's blow-lamp. One of the officers takes the paper from me, examines it then passes it to the other. Both of them stroll up to the van and proceed to examine it, I'm not feeling too happy about the situation and so I stroll to the security man, hoping that the two officers will follow. "Is Brendan off duty?" I ask and he looks at me with an expression of shock, disappointed that I actually know somebody that he does too. Very quickly he mutters... "Brendan's off sick," and one of the policemen hands him my letter of contract and he can see that it's official by the V.I.P. signature. He doesn't look happy, "Oh, ... so you're the 'Jim Bridgen' are you? I've been hearing quite a lot about you... you're the wild-man that lives in a cowshed up a mountain!" This amuses me and I sense the hand of my friend Lefcos at work somewhere, but my smile fades as I catch sight of the two officers giving my van a more thorough going-over. "It's all legal and above-board!" I shout across to them... "that's my space-ship, that is, I run it on chicken-muck... damn, I wish I could! I used to come down here in a little Morris ex-post office van, sweet little engine cheap to run; that thing there guzzles petrol as though it was Ribena!" I get a few more funny looks before one of the officers nudges the other one and they lose interest in the van and, as they come past me one of them mutters out of the side of his mouth, "I suppose a mattress in the back comes in pretty handy!" He makes a rude gesture with his fist and pouts his lips, making him look like a bull sniffing the wind for a cow on heat; he then digs me in the ribs with his elbow and gives a sordid wink: I nod back and smile.

They all wander back to Reception and, after locking the van, I run to join them considering it better to be part of them than apart from them, and we sit around joking in an air of thick, putrid tobacco smoke. I make it known that I shall be sleeping in my van, not just tonight but for the next two weeks, adding that I shall be expecting them to keep a safe watch over me, relating the occasion last year when I was awakened from sleep by a car-thief who was just about to drive off with me tightly zipped in my sleeping-bag in the back. They fall about laughing and the saucy one asks... "Don't tell me... you were on the job at the time... I bet!" Amidst all this merriment making 'Reception' seem more like a Union Street pub, the poor security man has to try his best and answer the phone, performing the role of both telephonist and receptionist, operating from a tiny switchboard on the desk; the last thing he wants now is for the Managing Director to phone in and hear all this crazy racket going on... which is precisely what does happen!" He despairingly gesticulates for us all to be quiet, his poor heart is going like a hamster on a wheel as I hear him trying to explain. "No sir... there's no party going on... it's just that, the Graphics chap, Jim Bridgen has just arrived... we're having a bit of a laugh!" I watch his face soften and his entire body ease as a smile rearranges his mouth. "Goodnight, Sir!" He spins his chair round and slumps into a rubbery, limp lump and lights a fag. The two policemen go quiet... "Problems?" one asks, and we wait for his reply. Blowing out a filthy exhaust of second-hand smoke, he sighs... "No... it's just 'wild-man' there, that's all! That was the gaffer that just phoned... "Oh, so glad to know that Jim's arrived!" What am I supposed to say?" He frowns at me and gives a questioning hard stare... "I don't know what you've got, but I wouldn't mind some of it!" "I don't think you would," I answer and glance up at the clock and ask... "What time do the chippies shut?" "We'll drop you off at one, we're going down to the Barbican now anyway!" I can hardly believe it; I'm actually going to get a lift in a police car to a fish-and-chip shop!

The week flies by, I'm really in a fast lane that's so different to the one I've left poor Cari to cope with. The softly spoken, jolly Managing Director comes to greet me in my little sweatbox and shakes hands with a bunch of warm, raw sausages, laughing in anticipation of my making him laugh. He makes me feel important, that is what I love about this company, it's just big enough and not too big, for it to have lost touch with all those who work for it. He insists that I call him 'Ronnie', and revels in my seeming 'vulgarity', a wild use of words that cut across normal etiquette in their directness of intent, and he knows that I shall do my job well and get along happily with everybody, something that means a great deal here. He takes on a slightly more serious look when he asks me... "Why on earth did you ever choose to live in a 'cowshed' of all things, Jim?" and he shakes his head in despair. I give a bit of a grin and say... "It all started off as a kind of adventure... I needed to find out who I really was, what I was capable of ... what life was really like when you stripped it down to the bones without the distractions of being stuck in a nine to five job sort of thing." He shakes his head and nods in a kind of accepting way; ... "You're a fool... what are we going to do with you! If I had your talent, I'd be a rich man by now, and that's a fact!" "You ain't done too bad without it!" I reply, and he bursts out laughing... "You're incorrigible, Jim!" He gives me a friendly hug and leaves, smiling like a tomcat that's not only just serviced two shes, but has found three stinking kippers as well.

Chris and Steve pop in to see me; Steve has been keeping a big surprise up his sleeve, He's just been appointed Warden of the R.S.P.B. Bird Reserve at 'Ynys Hir', a tiny place in woods beside the magnificent Dovey estuary, just to the west of Machynlleth, next door to the marvellous sand dunes at 'Ynyslas' where we all love to go and lose ourselves. I am absolutely thrilled and so very proud of my friend... recognition at last!

I used to be provided with early morning cups of tea; alas, my old friend Brendan hasn't taught this other guy of such niceties. It's a wonder he tolerates me sleeping in the company car-park at all, so seriously does he take his uniform, the one item that obstructs his pathway to smiling. I've been lunching with my old mate Lefcos all week and he's been trying to persuade me to stay with his family, just as I did in the past, but I have selfishly declined, reckoning my hunger for a long run at both ends of the day too pressing by far. I can take a shower whenever I like and crash-out whenever I like... totally selfish I know but it's the only way I can be right now... even without my early morning cups of tea.

I've been rather more fortunate with van-thieves so far, it's probably the heavy condensation that's on the inside of the windows that's warning them off... or maybe it's the jockstrap on my steering wheel that's doing the trick. I'm deliberately sticking to a very frugal agenda in total determination to maximize the amount of cash that I take home and I end every day with a run, a shower, fish and chips then crash-out into a kind of dog-sleep, still half expecting an unwelcome visitor to my doss-house space-ship in the car park. It's not the sort of routine that's likely to endear me to it and I'll be a little greyer and close to being certifiable by the time my contract comes to an end. To help vary things a touch I spend time over the weekend painting a couple of still-lifes in the Graphic Studio and also varying my fish and chips routine by dining in the canteen where I can pay with the meal vouchers which I get provided with. What surprises me during the following week is that I actually boost my earnings still further when I am persuaded and pestered even into selling the two paintings to people who work here; a 'Still-Life with Mackerel' and the other 'Flower Forms', two fairly large, bold, freely painted and colourful pictures which I had intended for my exhibition, but I'm not going to lose any sleep over it, the money's far more useful right now. If I'd got more of a business-head on these shoulders of mine, these weekends away could prove to be quite lucrative but, their greater value to me is that I'm not using my thirsty old hand-painted space-ship to take me places and using up money in the process. It must seem miserly and somewhat antisocial of me to be sticking so resolutely to my plan, but I know what I have to do and I have the scars to help remind me. What's more, any thought of luxury causes me pangs of guilt.

No matter what I do, the heartaches of being away from Cari and the boys never leaves me and I thank my lucky stars for the fortuitous occasions of having Rosie and Elly coming to stay and helping ease my gnawing concerns over Cari's workload. I've made sure to have kept the engine of the van in working order, but it still belches paraffin fumes whenever I start it up. The radiator has held together and there've been no oil-leaks, bu I do have to open the doors whenever I can to help sweeten it up a bit and to get rid of the condensation.

The final working week has started and a most welcome letter from home provides me with a tonic that I need and acts like a wind in my flagging sails and helps ease my constant anxieties. It's a relief to hear that Gareth has remained true to his word and has kept the bull up at the farm; more predictably though, the cows have finished off their devastating gardening and fencing job which they started earlier. True to form, Dan has been over rather a lot, clean shaven and a bit smarter than usual too, in his 'town clothes' no less and has kept Cari busy at the teapot end of things. All the gang have been over to his place in the evenings to be reminded of one of his best kept secrets... his cooking speciality... Desperate Dan Chips a la hors an carte! Unwashed and unpeeled potato chunks crudely hacked with his trusty, all purpose pen-knife, then incinerated in dark, deep, ages-old lard that's permanently left uncovered in the hearth, in a black, thickly encrusted frying pan where the mice all gather to go skating by night. Surprisingly, these dark, browny-gold metallic hunks of potato taste quite divine; whether this be due to the lavish amounts of mouse turds in the ancient lard or, perhaps the never-cleaned penknife that he uses for castrating sheep and docking lambs' tails... I couldn't really say for sure. All that I can say for certain is that Old Dan's chips are really something else. Not only are they delicious, but the cooking of them is a highly entertaining and hazardous process, one that has more than once resulted in a frightening chimney fire. Cari goes on to say that our old cat, Sorrel, has settled in nicely at Dan's, but is still as thin as a rake even though she is on a diet of corned beef, fresh mice and neat cow's milk. Rather sad news is that Rosie and Elly have now gone back to university, so it will feel a bit strange about the place for a few days I expect. Other odd snippets of news include the fact that Meg's little daughter has chicken pox and that it's become a lot noisier of late as a result of Meg and Murphy extending their canine concern to include Dobermans and Old English Sheepdogs to add to their existing yappy poodles; the noise she says is driving her mad at times.

My week is slowly grinding to an end, I really can't wait to be back and taking the strain again; I know that Cari will have found it pretty hard going, but she'll never admit it, she just gets on with it and never complains, she's wonderful. Friday eventually arrives, it's the busiest day of the week and always builds up to a chaotic frenzy with in addition to the Regional Magazine Programme to get out, all the weekend Programme Promotions need designing as well. Trying to steal a few minutes to go to the Pay Office before it closes to collect my wages is nigh-on impossible. To complicate matters still further, the managing director comes down to personally thank me and to offer me assurances that there'll be further work to come. It's all so frantic, everyone's in a rush and I have to stay cool and not make a mistake; when you're freelance, you're only as good as your last job, that's why it's so well paid; cock it up and they don't ask you again, Phew! I'm all twitching as I say my goodbyes...

I say my good-byes and join the eastbound traffic bedlam that's heading slowly out of Planet Plymouth on this tired old Friday evening. With having a bit of money in my pocket, I decide not to risk using paraffin on my return journey; I feel that I can now really pamper the engine with a bit of pure, unadulterated petrol this time, with the hope of sweetening the old girl up once more. There'll no doubt be other times when poverty drives me back onto the paraffin trail.

It's a long and tiring journey back home and, by the time I have at last reached Wales, the sun has slipped from the sky leaving a red smear shrouding the far hills where I am heading. There's no radio in the van and still no batteries in the tape-recorder and so, apart from the thunder of the engine, it's still pretty quiet in here, and I soon run out of songs to sing through my not knowing the words. "Da, da, daa" is alright for ten minutes but, after three hours is more likely to drive me to sleep than it is to keep me awake. As the darkness folds in all around, the air rushing in through my window turns cold and it is this alone that keeps me awake.

Black hump-backed hills and dim starlight welcomes me back down once more onto the cool, damp grass of home. Scattered hill sheep bleat and an occasional distant cow wails in a leathery tongue, nearer ones breathe and I can smell the vegetation and sense a million small eyes watching all around. I have arrived safely back to my little nothing in nowhere where everything that matters to me waits for the clacking sound of the latch and my little whistled two notes that says it's me, I'm home.

Jim Bridgen

Sign of the Cross

I sleep like a ton of lead beneath the frail ounces of swallows snoozing above me on the beam. My dreams are fragmented geographies full of garbled historic dimensions, each broken fragment a partial truth surrealistically rearranged into a convincing nonsense. I wonder, what is a swallow's dream like? I can actually hear the silence here just as clearly as I could hear the noise back in my van in the city car-park. It's only the occasional hooting owl that provides a handle for me to hold. The cockerel crows and there's a sudden squabble of magpies in the apple tree as though summoning first light to surgically ease the land-mass separate from the sky. I don't miss much after the first robin has yawned and tickled my ear, even though I'm still only vaguely awake.

I tiptoe downstairs, pausing for a moment to look upon my lovely boys all deeply asleep; just listening to their heavy breathing fills me with a glow right down to the soles of my bare feet. I move on and slip into my industrial wellies, then quietly go out into the dawning air and stand awhile just sucking it all in before answering the cock-crow of my bladder. A late tawny owl screeches up in the wood, no doubt irritated by my presence, and the magpies have all gone thoughtfully silent; it's just me and a little robin now, that's all.

How can all this relative silence be so priceless... could it ever become a tangible commodity that could be marketed? Making something out of nothing would appear to be one of Man's more recent achievements; they've done it with food and they've done it with 'Art' so called. A blank canvas is accepted as being 'minimal art', although I very much doubt an empty plate being accepted as a satisfying meal in a restaurant, or an empty glass as being a drink. Silent statement has made a bit of a joke of things in 'Art'; 'empty rooms', 'nothing', priceless works all of them! I had an old picture frame hanging on the wall and, for a joke, I signed the wall beneath it; it made a few people laugh that's all. I did actually write a minimal poem, a serious and thoughtful piece of poetry written in pencil. I then took a rubber and rubbed every single word out, saving all the bits of rolled-up debris as being the poem. Then I asked myself, why write the bloody thing in the first place if you don't want anyone to read it? No, I'd rather look at a Van Gogh than a blank canvas any day, wouldn't you? Dawn's silence is a whole lot more than 'nothing', it's a brand new awakening, rich and ripe, certainly not 'minimal' anything!

Robin has somehow managed to lose his footwear, one badly split school shoe is all that he can come up with, no doubt all the rest are scattered about the fields somewhere; minimal footwear! This is the 'growing season' and all of my boys have grown an inch or two in my absence; this is especially noticeable with Spencer and Rowan whose clothes have been gladly grabbed by Robin. So, whether I like it or not, Saturday is destined to be 'buying-the-boys-clothes-day', and the first onslaught into the money that I've just earned. It's also going to be a 'fish, chips and mushy peas' day too, a rare and long overdue luxury to end on, especially when eaten in the van parked on a high, wild wayside; this moment alone makes my two weeks away in Plymouth worthwhile.

In our euphoric state, we make plans to spend Sunday at the coast amongst dunes and the wide-open beach at Ynyslas, where the new carline thistles will be flowering alongside last year's beautifully dead ones. The dunes are really quite miraculous at this time and the boys are always excited whenever the place is mentioned; it doesn't matter what the weather, the seaside never fails to captivate their minds and it never ceases to be a sad place for them to have to leave at the end of the day.

Sunday arrives; it's the last day of June, sunny and warm. There are no late risers this morning, the cowshed is buzzing with activity and high spirits as everyone gets in each other's way in a race to get ready for our day at the sea. Cari has made a mountain of lovely cheese and tomato sandwiches and I've produced two big flasks of tea; whatever else we may need we can pick up along the way. Good weather and June together make Sunday a trading day that's too good to be missed by traders, and so we plan to do a spot of shopping in Machynlleth before dropping in to see Steve on his bird reserve.

A happy family in a van is a most marvellous life-capsule; everyone is singing while I, the father, just grip the wheel and steer us on our way. There's really quite a lot of holiday traffic, Midlanders mostly, all desperate for air and space; capsules full of kids, dogs and grandmothers, roof-racks with things tied on, trailers in tow; caravans ballooning like blancmanges, swerving and wobbling. Teeth, dentured and otherwise, dazzling in smiling mouths, bare elbows stuck-out like dozing dogs' noses and lay-byes steaming with bursted-for wee, dogs defecating and daughters throwing up while the car radio deafens the world with crazed din. "Not much further to go now"' fatherly comforts for kids that have already patterned his shirt with diced carrots and something resembling custard: "Not much further now."

Chapels look like aircraft-hangars in peacetime, cobwebbed and desolate, despite this being Sunday; their trade diluted down the march of recent years of shouting, as by habit down the ages... "On the Seventh day thou shall not Labour!" 'Thou shalt not drink either!' was another such cry, one which Capitalism and all its backhanded benefits soon put paid to. Someone had to sell us petrol, strawberries, bottles of pop, ice-cream and asparagus, crazy kites, silly hats, sunglasses and breakdown services. Heathens all of us, in a convoy racing to the sea, the grey far horizon that has no smoking chimneys or windows piled on windows on windows on windows on windows.

'Ynys Hir', the bird sanctuary, is on our right and I turn into a little lane, then follow a crumbling, bumpy track down through the woods, eventually coming to a slight clearing and a little cottage with miles of reed beds fringing the far side of this gaping, yawning estuary beyond it. This is Steve's new home now, a temple built by solace for herself.

There's no sign of Steve; the place is deserted. I stand for a while calling his name, then withdraw quietly inside myself, feeling that I've come to the wrong place and that I'm trespassing. It helps having Cari and my young boys beside me, making me feel less of an intruder. I call, "Steve!" I couldn't call louder if I tried. There is a huge hush about the wood; it's like standing in a Cathedral staring up into the vaulted roof, reverently dissecting the myriad murmurings of soft new leaves and the finer sounds of little birds feeding on new caterpillars. Suddenly, there's a rustling noise and the sound of branches snapping some distance away, then Steve appears from a tangle of undergrowth... they didn't wait long before getting him into harness!

He looks completely knackered, machete in hand, face

dribbling with sweat, blood from umpteen cuts and his sparse clothing in tatters about him. He comes puffing across the clearing to take an unscheduled and much needed rest. "Fancy a day at the coast?" I suggest, hoping to make the Sabbath feel more like Sunday to him, but he laughs... "You must be joking! I shall nip down to the local for a quick half tonight, if I'm lucky!" We are taken into his new home, a sort of office bungalow, very Spartan, just a couple of books on the side, a small mammal-skull on the windowsill, a utility chair, a telephone, a map on the wall, a small kitchen and an even smaller bedroom; we weren't shown anything else but I imagine there was a toilet facility tucked away in a cupboard somewhere. "Well, at least you've got electricity!" Cari says jealously, and Steve gives a proud grin and replies... "I've got everything I need here!"

In a sudden rush of excitement, he beckons us to follow on a short guided tour, emphasising to the boys that they must be very quiet in order that he might show them something very special. We all tiptoe down to the muddy shoreline and Steve leads us into a hide that's perched overlooking the great expanse of estuary and reed-beds. I catch sight of a marsh harrier swooping low over the far reeds, then Steve freezes, places his finger to his lips then gesticulates for us all to peep out from the window to where he is pointing. There are two kingfishers, one flies away but the other one stays like a dazzling fragment of rainbow on a old stump that's jutting from the mud. We all hold our breath before the bird darts away. "Not bad, hey?" he grins proudly; it's really made our day.

We take our leave and let him get back on with clearing the overgrown marshland at the edge of the wood, then make our way back to the road. We've disturbed the peace of this quiet woodland and I'm more than glad to hide now amongst the people-carriers on the last couple of miles before the sea fills our horizon.

The day drags slowly across; the tide goes out, then steals back in across the golden expanse where the boys have all spent many hours exhausting their energies and are now drowsily tired, wet, hungry and thirsty. There's a mass migration underway, like lemmings drifting tiredly through the dunes, back to their cars and vans while the racing water snakes and swirls back to fill the estuary and to distance the almost touchable Aberdovey, concealing the treacherous currents that lurk beneath, bringing shoals of fishes in their arms. Cari has caught the sun a little too much; she usually manages to fall asleep for two hours or so, whereas the boys have spent most of their time wallowing in pools where the water is really warm. I've roamed the driftwood shoreline and have found the nests of sandpipers amongst the pebbles and other little treasures discarded by the sea, although how she ever came to have them in the first place remains a mystery to me.

The sandwiches don't last long and even though the tea is now like stew, we soon drink every last drop of it and then just laze about feeling the weight of sadness at having to leave, as are thousands of others just wishing and wishing. Courting couples are most reluctant to leave and seem to be waiting for others to leave first before eventually attempting to put out the fires that the day has kindled inside them. Meanwhile, the steady procession steals quietly away beside the golf course, everyone promising that they'll buy a place here one day and come back to stay. Promises, promises; hopes and dreams, all too easily ripped to pieces back in the cage of reality. On the little river as we cross the bridge, boats are bobbing anew and the sea trout ride in on the new surging tide and race upstream in the invigorating half rain-water, half salt, too wary by far to be caught.

Not many words are spoken over these distancing miles; what few there are tend to be of an irritable nature and drivers' boots seem a degree or two heavier all round. All too soon it's just become a hard slog, squabbles break out and angry silences rage; at the filling-station no-one speaks. I catch sight of Robin leaning out of my window, poking his tongue out at children in another car, prompting a reaction from them before he is unceremoniously man-handled by Rowan and thrust back into the van, starting a screaming match which brings all life down to a sober perspective. I return to the van as the car that was just in front of me drives off, with a dog barking hysterically in the back window and a pretty young girl shoving her tongue out at me and giving the 'V' sign. I toss an armful of Mars bars and a few cans of fizzy drink into the back of the van and witness an ugly brawling scramble in true Darwinian 'survival-of-the-fittest' style. "One each!" Cari booms, bringing my monkeys back to humans with a voice that stuns the forecourt into silence ... and we silently drive away.

It's been an absolutely fabulous day and we're all worn out and ready for bed; our small treasured artifacts are placed on honoured window-sills, little shells, pieces of sea-sculpted wood, bladder-wrack and dead carline thistles. There are glowing faces all around as the dreams all line up in readiness to be dreamed to the full and the dreamers ready to row their little boats into the crashing waves and wishes of deeper dreams yet.

Monday. Moo... moo... baa... baa! It's the first day of July and the weather is miraculously holding true. I give the boys a treat and take them the long way to school in their new clothes, calling in to get petrol on the way. Emrys greets us warmly, egg-yolk around his mouth and a glad smile to catch the day. The van isn't smoking or stinking of paraffin now as I book it in for a service which I hope will last till Christmas. "Any more trouble with bulls?" he laughs, referring to the 'Charolais' beast of an animal that ravaged Gareth's herd some time back. "Plenty!" I laugh... "we had another bull smash its way into our kitchen only a couple of weeks ago... and it's chased me a few times!" "Damn!" he laughs... all we get down here is an owd swan that attacks us... they've got a nest in the ox-bow." I have to excuse myself or the boys will be late for school, so we all wave and head off on our way.

Cari wants to make more elderflower wine, but the hedges that we made our notorious leg-wobbler concoction from, no longer exist and this tends to sadden us into a kind of apathy which isn't good for either of us. Dogs are barking incessantly across the valley, sharp yappy ones, growling gruff ones and bellowing booming ones. A pair of American jet fighter-bombers have mated with Mid Wales and come diving low and brushing the breasts of hills, then delving deeper along the gaping splayed-legged valleys in ear-piercing orgasms of fire, causing us to share with sheep their bewilderment. Millions of pounds burning to waste in mere moments, while it has taken me two hard weeks of heartbreak just in order to scrape together a few pounds to buy shoes for my boys, a rare luxury of fish and chips and a long overdue trip to the seaside. The military are flaunting their costly hardware low over the roof of the cowshed, perplexing our swallows into thinking it's a kind of thunder. "Somebody's in for it!" I mutter to Cari... "you mark my word, the Yanks and the Brits will surely concoct a war somewhere just in order to test all this bloody stuff!" We stare blankly at each other and I sigh ... "Whatever happened to peaceful co-existence?"

"C'mon, let's go for a walk," I suggest, trying to find an escape from the sudden gloom of things. The jets are still roaring in the sky, a hundred valleys away by now, but with others coming up hot on their tails. "Come on, love, let's see some nice things in the forest away from dogs and jets and bulls." We are together and we pull in the same direction regardless of the odd little snatch from time to time. As we stroll up into the wood beyond the well, we note how the water supply is failing under the prolonged dry weather; it's getting hard for the cows too, but they at least have it on tap still, unlike us. "Jimmy, look!" Cari gasps, pointing up into the trees. "Look, there, there... everywhere!" I can't believe what I am seeing; every tree has a black cross painted on it. We walk sadly on and soon discover that the sign of the cross is manifest throughout the wood and I suggest that we check all the remaining woods surrounding us, fearing the worst as we hurry down the steep hillside and across the valley into the little wood. Our worst fears are realised, not a single tree has been spared! We cross the marsh meadow to the lane where our dream blackens; trees are certainly not high on Gareth's list of favourite things! I want to turn all the crosses in swastikas... help!

There seems little point in going on with our walk now; these moments are almost suffocating us with their leaden significance and we lean upon the gate in dappled shadows while nuthatches pipe and wood warblers sweetly lace the leaves above us. The little red post-van comes down the lane and skids to a halt right under our noses and the jolly postman jumps out and passes me a letter; it's a brown window-envelope with the words 'On Her Majesty's Service. Inland Revenue. Private' printed on it. "Thanks very much!" I say... "that's all I need!" The postman laughs and hops back inside his van and races off up the hill and vanishes under the trees.

We amble back across to the aldermarsh, noting that there's still water in the cow-trough, together with a newt; we note also the piles of pipes beyond the willows and then complete the morning's black promise. The circle of black crosses is entirely surrounding us and surely must be the longest sentence that Gareth has ever written without punctuation; I daresay he'll be off sick with writer's cramp now!

Darwin's monkeys have come up trumps! A species of self-proclaimed monkey that actually destroys the very things that it depends on for survival. This seems more of a retrogressive thing than a progressive thing to me; what's more, there isn't a single ape on this planet that works so systematically against itself, not anywhere or anyhow! The mad appetites of Homo sapiens are destroying our planet until the planet itself cannot sustain its place within the heavens.

A Pig of a Heatwave and a bit of Cooling off!

A great gloom hangs over us as, dumb-faced, we aimlessly saunter back to the cowshed. More warplanes blister across almost touching the trees and shaking every living thing down to its bones. It's beyond me to comprehend that there's a young person at the controls of each of these terrible things; the last one was probably called Peter, with a mother by the name of Edna and a dad called Anthony; they probably live in a detached house in Cheshire where they have a large lawned garden and a golden Labrador. Peter has a love-bite on his neck and a passport-photo of his girlfriend in his wallet; he's well mannered and quite good looking ... not much different to anyone else, in fact. The most unbearable thing for me however, is that I actually love aeroplanes and am fascinated by flight technology; a fascination stemming from a lifetime love of birds and those boyhood stalwarts, the Spitfires, Hurricanes, Mosquitoes, Lancasters, Wellingtons... all of them propeller driven before the Vampires and Meteors whistled-in an age of jets. No; flight fascinates me for the same reasons that so intrigued Leonardo; at least he never experienced a Phantom blast his hat off and spoil his underwear!

The most marvellous moments in time are now being experienced in our bedroom ... the young swallows have just hatched. Little pink blobs of giblets with two blue lumps where eyes will be. They're being fed on tiny flying things, gorging them, wings an' all and reducing their incredible technology to white squirted paste. The happiness being shown by these tiny parent birds is measurable, audible, credible, plausible and we are privileged to be witnessing the birth and development of one of life's most amazing flying machines. Nothing in my entire life has been so poignant as waiting for these swallows; they hold the secret that money can't buy, yet all they are is frail little vulnerable birds who simply need flies!

We're into a real blistering summer heatwave now; Murphy comes over all downcast and cursing. "Yes, yes!" I groan... "I've seen all the crosses ... I've seen all the drainage pipes down beyond the aldermarsh." "Money, Jimmy... more hill subsidies, that's what it's all about! Our old 'Hedgerow Song' has come true," and he proceeds to sing a bit of it:- "Oh the farmers are ripping up the hedgerow, hedgerow, hedgerow, hedgerow! They don't give a bugger for the blackbirds and thrushes-o, blackbirds and thrushes-o." I don't feel like singing, not even a protest song, and everywhere slips into silent reflection and I look about me at all the marks upon time that plainly say how we have tried in a grand and romantic way to find through our own fingers and off the sweat of our backs, a simple life of loving and understanding; these are the marks we have left upon the world.

I get back on with my painting with a deep burning that keeps me caring even though my anger is overflowing onto my canvases. Swallows are splattering everything that I do, but I don't mind one little bit, they're part of my palette anyway and I absolutely adore their company, even though on occasions they brush my nose and almost smudge my paint.

Two weeks into July and I watch, unbelievably, a Welsh Collie bitch with a Corgi-Jack Russell cross, completely coupled; it's an unlikely match if ever I saw one, with the 'boy-racer' being unceremoniously dragged behind the much larger Collie. I don't believe my eyes ... they've jumped into my well! That's put paid to the water supply good and proper! Unbeknown to me, the sow from the hill-farm, heavily pregnant and very much a swine, gives me a fright and presents her disgusting self in the ditch close by, distracting me from the dogs; I dislike this horrid animal and she knows of no laws or boundaries whatsoever, a free-range, foul-mannered walking cancer if ever there was one. I'm caught in a moment of indecision as I hear the boys newly home from school, racing to get changed into old clothes so that they can be with our little grey cat, who's just about to have her first kittens on a pile of leaves in the spud-shed. Too late... while my back's turned, the pig has left the ditch and has come swaggering into the yard and shot straight into the spud-shed and eaten the kittens. I can't believe this is happening; first it was a duck and now it's a pig; the damned thing would have eaten Spibby too had she not leapt up onto a cupboard. I scream the monster out from the shed, a highly dangerous thing to do because this animal doesn't take orders from anyone. The boys all scatter in disarray along with the chickens, who had also gathered around the maternity unit; no-one knows which way to jump or where the animal is likely to head for next. I fear it might be the kitchen and I yell at the top of my voice, "Shut the kitchen door!" and I manage to vigorously steer the pig with my foot and get it trotting off down under the apple trees and up in the direction of the well. Robin takes up the chase but his valour backfires when the pig turns on him and instead chases him across the field; I've never seen my boy move so fast in all his life! The pig gives up and heads straight for my well. There's a terrible yelping and splashing as two dogs leap out, parting company in the most painful of ways with the Jack Russell-Corgi streaking off across the marshy hillside howling and barely making contact with the ground; the Collie bitch has left dust hanging in the air as she cleared the hill and vanished from sight. The big fat sow meanwhile has just flopped into the last of our drinking water for a desperately needed drink, acquiring a long bloody gash from the barbed wire fence in the process. I give up!

The boys are all terribly upset; it's like a whirlwind has hit them. They stand silently staring about the place as I stroll over, unable to find words to console them. The poor little cat is in a state of shock too and is still huddled on the high cupboard, peering down at the scattered leaves on the floor. "I didn't know that you could run so fast, Rob!" I try to joke, and he just smirks, unable to shake-off his deeper feelings. "Poor Spibby," Spencer sighs... "that blooming pig took all her kittings!" Then Robin shuffles a couple of steps closer and, with a deep frown asks... "What's dat fing on dat pigs tummy, Jimmy?" and I just shrug my shoulders and shake my head. Cari comes out... "What's all the shouting about?" she asks, noting a sense of gloom about the boys' faces. "Bloomin' pigs been and eaten poor Spibby's new kittings!" Spencer tells her, and she looks questioningly at me for clarification. "Yep, it's true! That cancerous swine from the farm has just polished-off all of Spibby's kittens!" "Where is it now?" she asks. "Robin chased it off, didn't you Rob?" Robin puffs himself up smugly and smirks, letting his body-language do the talking. I turn to Cari and say, "if you really want to know... it's in the well, that's where the bloody thing is and I'm not going anywhere near the damned animal... it's evil... I much prefer the bull any day!"

There are a few silent thoughts, then Cari asks... "and what are we going to do for water?" "Same as we did in the past," I say, trying to ease her concerns... "we'll have to go over to Murphy's and fetch it. The spring's more or less dried up anyway and I'm going to have to clean it all out before we can use it again." "What about the washing... I've got a mountain of it there, I can't move for it!" I have a sudden flash of inspiration. "I know, let's bag it all and go and find a launderette somewhere, that's what money's for... what do you say?" My suggestion is greeted with immediate approval; Cari knows the very place, on the housing estate in town where she spent her childhood.

We are spending a romantic evening in a launderette on a council housing estate; the boys and the cat are all keeping a low profile in the back of the van, out of sight of marauding hostile town boys. I've treated them to their second fish and chips in almost as many days and it is helping to keep them pacified. This is pure memory-lane for Cari; she meets many of her old neighbours and really is quite a celebrity, leaving me to do the washing and getting into calamitous, hilarious confusion, having never been in one of these hi-tech wash-houses before. There's a Spar shop next door and, while the machines seem to be coping without me, I sneak out and hide in there amongst the shelves, where I fill several baskets with 'essentials' that I never knew we needed, making sure to include several huge plastic containers of mineral water, plus enough baked beans to feed an army and tins of pilchards to match. Candles always come in handy, as does a bar or two of milk chocolate, should the wrath of heaven later descend on me for my extravagance.

It's a lovely evening as we leave the launderette; the sun has slipped away and a long burning glow spreads over the darkening town. There's laughter and a babble of voices as we cart our ballooning bags back to the van where our boys are in fits of excitement... Spibby has just had another kitten in the van!

The heat-wave becomes a serious drought and the grass in the fields parches, silver birches wilt and die and the brook by the school completely dries up leaving only puddles here and there, with dying trout clinging on grimly to life and providing easy pickings for tickling farm-boys. The warplanes don't seem to be in any way restricted by the lack of water and it's highly dangerous for buzzards to respond to the marvellous rising thermals and to soar in idle circles beneath the lofty heavens where the toys of war go thundering. Try telling that to a buzzard or a raven, a rabble of jackdaws and 'old crow'.

The joyful swallows go about their life wonderfully separate from anything and everything; if only they knew how much they meant to us. We are so vain to even want to share with them anything of ourselves. Swallows are beautifully swallows, without need of our dimension or intervention upon them. They see-saw between here and Africa as they have done throughout time, never once needing Man, only needing flies, that's all. I look upon them with such yearning but there's absolutely nothing anywhere in time that can bring me a biological gram closer to them, as with a chimpanzee or anything else for that matter. There's a mathematical correctness, a preciseness about everything being what it is. The challenge of existence was for us to discover and to marvel at the unimaginably complex interdependence of every conceivable living thing, nothing, absolutely nothing left out, overlooked, forgotten; every single organism related in some way with everything else. We humans were blessed with a brain that could make this ultimate journey ... but greed got in the way and the fourth 'R' had to be invented to befuddle the human race from all its potential.

The old July weariness dusts into the wayside vegetation; nettles turn to timber, hostile and hopeless. The ground burns in search of a spark to explode it in a kind of marital fulfillment and sheep are sheared in repetitious annual cider-binges that adversely affect the cutting process, which unfortunately includes a highly animated beast component. Dan never washes his shirt, he simply wears it until he has to buy another from Woolworth's... Masons don't sell them or he could have one delivered. Sheep-shearing uses up vital days of an unwashed shirt's life; sheep's blood and other nasty stuff pushes the shirt to its limit... cider does the rest! He isn't gripping the ewe properly and, in one independently minded leap from his embrace, the ewe's back legs rip his shirt clean in half. "Damn! Gotta get a new bloody shirt; two in three years... damn! I'm not made of bloody money!"

We're all in fits at the commotion, the sheep is a damn sight smarter than Dan is as it tears amongst us and the gang of shearers stagger about dangerously drunk, tears rolling down their cheeks and cutters still wired-up to the national grid and revving away at nothing as the sun burns down, flattening the dog to a panting heap and keeping me safe from being bitten.

Cari and I leave the scene. It's the river in the valley that has drawn us out today; crystal-clear, fast running water is the next best thing to the sea and, with our spirits being somewhat bruised of late, dangling our toes in the ice-cold rushing water seems to be just about right. Emrys Gittins at School House has been forced to undo a shirt button and appears to be expiring rather than perspiring. He blubbers something about God back in his Heaven and Capitalism and we give an affectionate wave and leave him panting under the hollyhocks and rush on down till we are caught up in the music of children at infant school, then follow the pebbles and stones of the dried-up brook, all the way to the river.

Horseflies have bitten me through the shirt on my back, another has scored a hit on my arm whilst I am busy concentrating on keeping them off Cari, but we are happy and unable to understand where all this sparkling, rushing water is coming from. It's mesmerizing with kingfishers repetitiously flashing by; dragonflies and a thousand damselflies dance over the shimmering mirror of water where long graceful weeds snake and twist and writhe, trout quiver their tails and eels wriggle, chub idle and salmon remain a mystery. Oh, how I love this upland reach of the wonderful Severn, hardly able to believe that we have no water whatsoever ourselves. We ain't got electricity either... at least the fish have got water... well, the lucky ones have.

It's a small miracle having this new little tiger of a kitten; 'Spibby' is proving to be a doting mother and has found true happiness at last, as too has Robin; he's named it 'Tiger'. It's a beautiful little stripy bundle of fluff, a lethal hunter in waiting, another tomcat unleashed upon an unsuspecting world. Let's hope it's not the type of 'tomcat' that old Jerry the tramp gave me as a gift backalong on the Cornish cliffs!

As we lie in bed on this slightly cooler early morning, we watch with fascination the young swallows raising their wobbly little heads above the mud wall of their nest, then, turning completely around and raising their bottoms, doing as they're being told and producing white, wrapped excremental packages which the parent birds dutifully take into their beaks and transport out through the window, to dump well away from the nest. They're so well organised, so thoroughly clean and tidy, these most magical of birds; they could teach us all a thing or two and they provide me with a timely reminder to empty the lavatory bucket.

After digging a grave for this unsavoury item, I have the sad task of having to dig a smaller grave for our dear old hen, 'Missus Jones', who I discovered lying dead on the barn floor when I let the hens out this morning. Her traumatic ordeal with the fox has eventually claimed her, even though my effort in saving her had prolonged her existence here amongst us. It's a very sad little moment seeing her lying in the small grave and I cannot contain my tears. The burial process is being subjected to invasion by the cretinous 'Sykes', who insists that she's missing out on something and seems determined to dig 'Missus Jones' up to ask her what the hell's going on. This brings us down to five hens now; it's so sad, they are so very much part of our lives, little souls all of them.

The boys are once more being successful in supplementing our diminishing egg-supply with those that Meg's free-rangers have been laying under the hedge in the lane. Those old brown hens of hers are like upper-middle-class country ramblers; well-fed and comfortably off, done-up in brown cords tucked in at the knee into thick knitted socks. Ours, by comparison, are like silvery-haired, rheumatic-riddled pensioners, frail and retired now from a hard life down the mine. They are pets, not working arses anymore, and so I don't feel quite so bad about seeing a few brown eggs about the place. But there's still no way that they can compare with the white beauties that our old dears still surprise us with every now and then.

We receive a letter marked 'urgent'. It's from Cari's sister in Northern Ireland, just to let us know that, whether we like it or not, she and her family are about to come over and spend a holiday with us! Mercifully, it goes on to say that they'll be bringing their caravan with them. After the initial shock, we all start to buzz over the prospect, having spent a most enjoyable time over there with them a few years earlier. From what I recall, we're in for a bit of a madhouse, because, when the two sisters get together, everything turns crazy! I put this down to being the genetic result of pure Irish and pure Welsh mixing together; a wild and wonderful concoction, exhilarating to the point of being terrifying! Connie's husband, 'Nobby', is from south London, a kind of reckless extrovert and is every bit as daft as his wife. Forever rattling a laugh and brandishing a prominent 22 carat gold tooth on the front row of his insatiable smile; I'm really looking forward to meeting him again.

To complicate matters somewhat, I receive another contract from Westward Television, requesting my services in mid-August; there's no way that I can afford to put pleasure before work, it's our vital winter money that's at stake. I can't possibly turn it down, to do so would be to let them down and I couldn't do that. At least I shall be able to spend a week in the company of our friends and, who knows, they may be planning on staying for a while; after all, the fourth 'R' has failed them disastrously where they live, particularly on the 'Love thy Neighbour as Thyself', and the, 'Thou shalt not Kill' parts of the contract.

Murphy comes over, highly enthusiastic about a new toy that one of his friends has brought him back from Australia... a boomerang! What would Leonardo have made of this, I wonder? I stand fascinated as I watch him demonstrate this insignificant piece of curved wood, watching it climb high into the air, seemingly gripping onto absolutely nothing and climbing still higher in a curve, spinning, whispering and then aiming back down upon us at incredible speed, forcing us to dive for cover. "Bloody hell, Murph," I gasp... "that's magic!" He hands it for me to try out but, even after a dozen efforts, nothing happens. He laughs at my pathetic attempts, having had the last few days driving Meg mad as he tried to get the hang of it. Eventually he discovered the knack and here he is now, an expert. This small piece of hunting technology is a highly scientific invention, in no way whatsoever attributable to the white man, but to the beautiful, dreamlike indigenous people of the Australian continent; long, so very long before the white bigot there set foot and jabbed into the soil a Union Jack, greedily declaring... "This is mine... all mine!"

It strikes me as being very funny; Murphy and me here thousands of years later on a hill in Wales, two Englishmen, one of them still trying to teach the other how to throw a boomerang ... and with one of them still unable to get the bloody thing to fly! My persistence pays and, suddenly, everything falls into place and I experience a most amazing sensation and am accepted into this forgotten fragment of Aboriginal culture. Feeling this 'thing' so simply flow from my hand and to seemingly generate its own power, thence to return to the hand that threw it... or at least that WAS the idea! "How could anyone invent such a thing?" I ask, examining what, to all intents and purposes, is simply a piece of wood. "It must have been one hell of a mind that calculated that a piece of wood could behave in this way... it tends to make Leonardo seems a little 'heavy-duty', not to mention a trifle clumsy." I throw it again but my attempt is crude and more than a trifle clumsy and I am obliged to watch Murphy indulging in his recently acquired expertise.

Cari comes up the hill to join us, having become intrigued by the spectacle of two men throwing a stick about the place. "Don't tell me," she says... "you're water-divining!" We laugh and Murphy hands her the piece of wood and asks her to throw it as high and as far as she can. On her very first attempt she equals my own worst effort and she plonks her hands on to her hips in a gesture of bemusement, "... and this is what has kept you amused for the past hour!" She rolls her eyes wickedly and starts to shriek with laughter. "Stand back!" Murphy orders, "...I shall demonstrate!" Whoosh! ... the miraculous thing seems to know that it holds all Aboriginal survival at stake; it seems to know that it's going to be an uphill struggle to educate the scientific western world into believing that the true father of aviation was just an ordinary black poet of a man, with a bone through his nose and wearing a jockstrap crafted from a dried and stinking fish-skin... and at a time when his European counterpart was hunched, grunting and staggering about with a club! The clever little piece of wood seems to be aware of all this and puts on a star performance, culminating in a sudden inspired urge to kill all three of us, repayment for having introduced his country to the Rabbit and to have reduced it to ultimate desert! I somehow contrive to outwit the device and save us all from ultimate recrimination, pushing the other two clear and taking a blow in the ribs myself. Cari climbs to her feet, she's impressed now.

Thunderbolt Re-union and a Man with a Gold Tooth!

July's growing quietness continues to burn upon the land; the sun has wearied everything down to a state of hopelessness. Even without their coats, the sheep are plainly stressed by the heat and huddle panting wherever they can find shade. No birds sing; blackbirds dramatically flatten themselves on the muck-heap, their wings outspread like black feather fans as they wreck with their yellow beaks agape, gasping. I find it impossible to know whether this is ecstasy or, perhaps, agony. It's too hot for any serious sunbathing, but I'm finding it a bit useful right now because it's really speeding up the drying time of my oil paintings and enabling me to work that much faster on them. It's really like an oven up in the bedroom and the poor young swallows must be at roasting temperature. The tin roof is far too hot to touch, too hot even for frying eggs on. I never thought there'd be a time when I prayed for rain, but I've joined the club... everything's praying for rain but nothing appears to be listening to our prayers.

The well has now dried up, enabling me to clean it out at last and to deepen it in readiness for the rain when it eventually returns to dominate. We're now totally dependant on Murphy's well, but even this one is requiring longer arms to reach down to the water. Dan's crude well is just a clogged up tangle of exhausted watercress that's gone to seed, and so he's got 'Masons' to deliver him several large plastic barrels of cider, his cunning way of beating the drought!

We make a trip in the van to the ex-government menagerie in town and purchase a couple of hefty water-carriers, then we pop round to Cari's old neighbour on the estate and fill them up from her mains supply. When they are full they are so heavy that I can barely get them off the ground; everyone laughs as I risk a host of assorted ruptures in my struggle to get them up into the back of the van. Getting them over to the cowshed is going to require the wheelbarrow, a rope and a family in harness, but at least we'll have a most satisfying cup of tea at the end of it, and the chickens will be able to quench their miserable thirsts at last.

The cows are getting to look rather bony; their grass has parched away to nothing and the poor beasts have a pained deadweight of misery over them. It comes as no surprise to discover another one of them lying dead quite close to the cowshed. The flies have moved in with savage efficiency to claim the corpse in assuring perpetuation of their species, a process which happens at unbelievable speed, long before Gareth eventually appears with a tractor and chain to tow it away, maggots and all, to a discreet burial somewhere. This carcass is now far too alive with other things for it to be of any use to the abattoir ... it doesn't smell too good either. The exhausted herd is moved up to the top fields by the farm where they can survive on what's left of last year's hay and silage, plus the modern miracle of main's water.

As our friends in Northern Ireland are about to set out on their holiday with us, so too do the first clouds... it's the clouds that arrive first. This late July afternoon has a sky highly stacked with menacing shadowy giants, bigoted and blasting in hushed disregard, a fiery kind of lurking terrorism exported and transported on some crazed jet-wind off the Atlantic. The very air twitches, charged and trigger-happy; it must be a magnetic minefield for insects and all things that duty drives in pursuit of; an undeniably awesome monster itching for a fight.

By ever increasing degrees, the jet-wind herds the cumbersome ghostly giants till their tempers burst and one of them goes for his gun and fires. The war is on and there are lightwaves and shockwaves, live wires dancing and flickering through every breath of air breathed. Weightless, tiny insects that need suction-pads and little clawing things to save them from being blasted into oblivion, attach themselves to the undersides of leaves, while a gluttonous heaven is forced to abort and release all the sea that it has stolen, sending an asteroid-sized catastrophe of water droplets, faster than bullets and with mesmerizing rapidity down upon the world.

It takes a storm to give relative dimension to the otherwise empty sky. Terrifyingly beautiful, she conjures-up frightening menace and unimaginable power from seemingly nowhere. What was nothing suddenly becomes something; what was nowhere, suddenly becomes somewhere, pure, marvellous, terrible, exhilarating magic. The barn, dilapidated as it is, has now become a shelter from the blitz, with old wild-eyed chickens in a state of grieving bewilderment, having only minutes earlier been sun-worshippers. Everything it seems, knows instinctively when to hide, but nothing apparently understands that there's no hiding place from this electro-aquatic monster of monsters, it'll find you wherever you are. This amazing beast of beasts can magic-up a wind out of a skylark's breath, not just once, but over and over again whenever it so chooses.

Thirsty as everything desperately is, nothing dares venture out to partake of this most vital substance known to life, even though the very sight of it is unbearable before a gaping thirst. The hammering rain is washing the heat from the roof and is gurgling down the pipe from the guttering, filling the tub in hardly any time at all. It's hard to imagine that this stuff was the sea not so very long ago, saltwater into rainwater and without a single cod or haddock getting sucked up and dumped alive and flipping into the fields.

It's a long and lingering storm but, frightening as it is, it's impossible for us to resist as a visual spectacle, and we clamour excitedly at the lean-to door snatching peeps at it; false bravado as water is pouring down the blind chimney close to where our kitchen swallows are huddled on the beam. Our own noise is probably far more disturbing to them than the storm could ever be and the parent birds nervously flit about the room, confused as to know what to do. I understand what they are trying to say and persuade my gang into splashing our way back to the illusion of safety in the living-room. This is swamped now with dark matter that's come down the chimney and more that's dripping through the ceiling as a result of our upstairs windows belonging to the swallows.

There's hardly a leaf that doesn't have a tiny flying thing hanging on for dear life beneath it; larger butterflies too, with Roman mosaic artistry hidden in their clasped wings, all of them hang on in unknown silence. Everything has to find shelter... it's either that, or perish. Birds huddle in thickets, squirrels in hollows, farm-dogs whimpering deep in kennels. The conifer forest behaves as one great sail before the lunatic wind that the storm has whipped up, offering no peace for the wood pigeons, jays and sparrowhawks. For the tiniest of all our birds, the goldcrest is like a mariner lost and adrift on a raging sea in a life-raft; the fury of the green needled branches being every bit as perilous as the wind-demented waves.

Mercifully, no storm lasts forever and a strange mysterious calm returns before dark making it feel as though something played a joke on us. The earth's thirst is so overwhelming that everywhere still looks thirsty with contemptuous steam rising as deeper heat comes up through the soil, generously giving the sky some of its water back. There'll still be no music in the ditch and it'll take a lot more than this for the brook to remember the words of her song and for new trout to venture back and re-stock it from the mother-river. At least we may all sleep more easily now that something's turned the oven down a notch or two, and our swallows are happier too with this more agreeable temperature.

With the air so much easier to breathe now, we take a walk over the high north hill to see far horizons once more and to gaze back down upon our own little home and to see it as the buzzards do, tiny and so very vulnerable there beneath us. Another reason for coming was a hunch that there'd be mushrooms... we're not disappointed! We very soon fill our bags and then race them back home for the Feast of Summer while they are still tenderly fresh and visibly still growing before the little flies have had time to lay their eggs and spoil them. This is the only occasion in the whole year when we are compelled to become gluttonous; the harvest is so short-lived and is a feast for other creatures too, so we have to be quick and as greedy as we can possibly be. With black pepper and a splash of Worcester sauce, nothing can compare with wild field mushrooms... and gluttony presents us with no problems whatsoever!

'Daddy-long-legs' have suddenly appeared everywhere, like miniature helicopters, but lacking their controls. Spiders are eating them by the dozen in webs that are almost invisibly strung-up on every conceivable thing that stands. Big webs, little webs, broken webs, webs that are littered with wing fragments, not just of these craneflies, but of butterflies, moths and a whole lot more besides. It will take autumn mists to really broadcast the webs in all their glory, but the spiders are already into their time of harvest, as we are with the mushrooms.

A twelve-bore coughs two barrels of fire and Dai-the-death Morgan appears under the fruit trees with a large hare that he's just blasted to pieces. He comes grinning up into the yard and throws the mangled bleeding mess down onto the muck-heap, whereupon Sykes is at once attacking it like a vulture, frenziedly pecking at the oozing blood while 'Spibby' timidly looks on, dwarfed and afraid of this gruesome, once beautiful creature that graced the hills and meadows, hunting nothing and damaging absolutely nothing. His two working dogs come running, the cat scarpers, but our confounded chicken refuses to be driven away and will not let go of the corpse and is already splattered with its still warm blood.

The dogs sit obediently by the kitchen door, panting nervously and on the lookout for a certain black cat that left its mark on their memory a sad while ago. Dai's pride at having just shot the hare is beyond question and now he wants me to accompany him for the rest of the day hunting fox cubs. I decline, but he persists nevertheless... "Aw! Come on man... it'll be a nice day out for you... do you good, isn't it!" I don't seem able to get it through to Dai that I have better, more important things to do with my time; he cannot accept that painting pictures or writing a book are 'things' at all... not in the same way that shooting hares, snaring foxes and ridding the world of badgers are to him. His grin hasn't left his face for a second; he is unquestionably happy with his work and is, unfortunately, wickedly good at it. I thank him again for his invitation and try once more to explain that I have an exhibition coming up and that I shall be losing yet more time having to spend some weeks away in Plymouth. He gives me a strange look, then says "Orh! Going on an expedition to Plymouth, are you? Damn... it's alright for some... some of us have got to work!" At first, I take this as being a play-on-words joke of his and I laugh before realising that he's being quite serious. I look at Cari and she discreetly giggles as she tidies up in readiness for our visitors, then she turns to Dai and explains. "You'll have to excuse us, Dai... we're expecting my sister and family from Northern Ireland and I shall need your fox-hunting friend with me today. He's got to run me into town in a minute to buy some food... they're going to be hungry after their long journey."

Dai understands Cari's more direct way of putting it and he proceeds to take the next twenty minutes to put his cap on and move towards the door. He gives us a wave and then stomps off back down the slope and I call after him, "What about the hare... you've forgotten it?" and he calls back, "Orh, that's alright... you can have it!" Then he quickly vanishes into the wood, leaving me obliged to dig another grave, and quickly too, because I cannot bear being confronted by a blood splattered 'Sykes'; it doesn't seem right for a chicken to be behaving in this disgusting manner.

There are hazy, mountainous dark clouds gathering in the stratosphere, like bad cauliflowers waiting to be dumped, and all the swallows have come down following the abundant shoals of their 'baby food' that is now stacked on invisible shelves around the cowshed. We head off for our own stacked shelves in town and, when we return are confronted in the lane by a caravan, a car and a Landrover plus a confusion of yelping voices. Gareth is half hanging out of the Landrover window, pipe in mouth, craning his top half backwards as he 'caresses' the caravan through the rarely used gateway at the top end of the meadow just opposite Meg and Murph's place. There's a kind of high-spirited bedlam with a large and highly physical Alsatian bitch in the thick of things, chasing Meg's chickens and worrying sheep on Gareth's blind side.

As yet unnoticed, we park the van further on in our usual spot, then very gingerly, Cari first, enter the theatre of activity, where on seeing one another, Cari and Connie rush into an embrace. The noise is almost unbearable and for one terrifying moment, I fear that the Alsatian is about to savage Cari. To my utter relief, Nobby has spotted it and growls an ear-piercing order that halts the dog in its tracks. Nobby rattles a low laugh, "Good as gold she is when she gets to know you... ain't you, Ripper, old bitch! One word from me and she'd have your froat out, no messin'... wouldn't you, hey girl!" he proudly boasts, gripping the dog's studded collar with a fist that has gold rings glinting on tattooed fingers, and with a broad leather, metal-studded wrist strap and more tattoos vanishing away under his sleeves, that are rolled up virtually to his hairy armpits. A medallion swings across his gaping, open-necked front as he then walks the dog at-heel across to his tarted-up Vauxhall Estate over by the gate, opens the boot and the dog leaps inside and the boot door fastened.

I'm getting strange feelings of apprehension squirming through me, having just realised that memory sometimes distorts things out of all recollection and, judging by the strained smile that Gareth is trying to hang on to, he's having a few wobbly thoughts of his own.

The caravan has been gently towed across to the foot of the hill where the scar of the old hedgerow begins and is settled into position and levelled. Nobby meanwhile has returned to the car and has driven it somewhat recklessly across the bumpy field and skidded to a dramatic halt alongside the caravan, apparently unconcerned that it's coming on to rain quite heavily now, and with the distinct possibility of the ground becoming muddy. Like a circus showman, he emerges from the car, a sleepy, golden-haired son flopped over his shoulder and his right arm outstretched to shake my hand "Jimbo... good to see you mate!" Never once does his roll-up cigarette fall from his 22 carat rugged grin, and my poor fingers feel like they're being crushed in a vice.

Gareth is temporarily enjoying being hugged by the re-united sisters, while the young blonde-haired boy looks on with a somewhat puzzled expression. The girls are already in fits over absolutely nothing at all, just drunk at having seen each other again, while Gareth has the distinct look of a man who has realised too late that he's offered more than his generosity should have allowed. The Alsatian bitch, meanwhile is trying to figure out how to get the car started and to perform a ram-raid on me, having come to the mistaken conclusion that my vigorous handshake and friendly hug with Nobby, the alpha-male in her life, represents something that she must protect him from... preferably by biting my testicles off! Gareth has a worried look as my pleas for reassurance over the animal's safety are brashly ignored. It's all a big laugh to 'medallion man' here, who, to settle the issue once and for all, stomps over and opens the door. Before I can catch my next breath, I have an Alsatian locked on to my wristwatch and Nobby yelling for the bitch to let go. It eventually obeys and Nobby flashes a golden grin and proudly says... "There... now do you believe me! One word... one word from me, that's all it takes; another word and she'd have your froat out, mate... no messin'!"

Gareth can no longer contain himself and he stutters, "I... I... I think you're g... g... going to have to keep her ch... ch... chained up. I've got several hundred ewes ab... about th...these fields and I... I don't want any trouble, isn't it!" "She won't 'urt a fing!" Nobby growls, "...you take my word for it, 'Gareff'... I've trained her myself. If I tell her not to touch 'em, she'll leave 'em alone!" Gareth is even less convinced by this reassurance and insists that the dog not be allowed to roam at will and be kept under control whilst being walked in his fields. Nobby spits out his soggy fag-end and stamps on it; no more is said on the subject and I catch a glimpse of Gareth's expressionless, squinting eye and I can see that he's aged several years over the last few minutes.

I take my leave of them and rush off to pick the boys up from school, as all heaven's black cauliflowers collide noisily and rain crashes down like an avalanche of dull metal. This is a desperately needed rare moment of peace for me, and my van becomes a shelter for a whole gang of young urchins and angels alike, as they wait for their own parents to brave the weather and pick them up. The little hill lane has suddenly become a river as we all huddle cosily inside the van beneath the towering Douglas firs, lessening our load by ones and twos as the parentfolk appear, highly sociable because of sudden meteorological adversity.

When we pull in by the marsh meadow gate, the boys spot the new caravan vaguely visible through the rain and they become excited; we sit for a while hoping that the storm might ease, and between the rumbles, I vaguely detect a sound that eases my mind a great deal, it's the sound of the dog barking from inside the caravan. Now I feel as happy as the boys are, and we all shove two fingers at the awesome sky and splash our way in a mad dash over to the cowshed. The entire noisy gang are in there, even Gareth; our swallows don't know what's hit them. There's a thick haze of pipe and cigarette smoke together with a constantly colliding fragmented outpouring of family up-dates, with everyone and no-one able to say what they want. A wild cheer goes up when my bedraggled boys enter the stage; kisses fly, hugs entangle and two of my wet paintings fall flat on their faces... there are new puddles forming in this chaos of uncontrolled rejoicing.

The table was laid earlier and is now heaped with fresh bread, assorted salad things and a variety of cheeses... but there's no wine which I feel the occasion calls for. I sneak upstairs and grab a couple of bottles of the Elderberry; the elderflower is much too warm to drink at the moment; then I proceed and discreetly draw the corks and rectify the problem.

The ghosts of the elderberries smile in a host of faces; the two sisters are the first to succumb to red noses, but only by a short head. Nobby has stepped up several gears and is laughing almost continuously and requesting that everyone feels the hardness of his muscles. Gareth remains cool, he's got a few muscles of his own but he keeps them up his sleeve; working arms are like working dogs, they don't make a fuss, but just get on with it. He sprawls even cooler now that the elder is taking it's revenge, and he is quite oblivious to his etiquette having slipped a degree or two and is pleasantly at ease, scratching his bollocks and sprawling his daddy-long-legs into the hearth, where black water is once more flooding down the chimney. The girls are in raucous fits of laughter at it all, any previous irritations have now been buried out of sight.

The boys have all retired to their room and are tittering in a manner that suggests that someone has succeeded in nicking the corkscrew and has tiptoed upstairs to our 'wine cellar'. Then Robin staggers through the curtain and wobbles into the room clutching the new kitten in his dirty, fat little fingers, intoxicating and suffocating it with his love as he takes it on a tour of all the beaming faces. Gareth lets out a sudden loud howling noise as Robin tries to interrupt him to tell him that his pig ate Spibby's kittens, but Gareth is far too preoccupied in a desperation to put out a shirt-fire, which has resulted from his pipe turning upside down and a sneeze doing the rest. There's uproar anew, even Gareth himself finds it painfully funny. Nobby springs decisively into action and tosses his wine all over Gareth's smoking shirt front, killing two birds with one stone and giving me a devil of a wink, and an elbow in the ribs, accompanied by a cackling laugh as he triumphantly writes the figure 'one' invisibly in the air.

Our poor swallows have it coming at them from all sides now; the tin roof above them must be deafening, while the pandemonium from downstairs is surely far worse. At least the rain will ease but, so long as this sisterly reunion persists, it'll remain noisy for some while yet I fear. Nobby clatters noisily into the kitchen dramatically clutching his bladder, opens the door and urinates high into the yard, yodeling like 'Tarzan', and leaving no-one in any doubt as to what he's doing. His return is equally theatrical, making sure that he's still doing up his zip, trying to give the impression that what he's trying to put away is far too big for his trousers to accommodate. I just pray that the heavy rain will continue for a while longer... there's a lot of stuff that needs washing away out there.

Eventually the storm passes, and a tiredness allows a fragile peace to return. Somewhat worse for wear, Gareth departs and our visitors confront the prospect of settling into their caravan while there's still a glimmer of light in the day. Rather begrudgingly they splosh their way over the sodden hill, the holiday for them has started.

Moss resumes growth once more on the school playground as the children are set free for their annual taste of dawdling days. High over the hill, marsh meadow has taken on the look of an outback smallholding-cum-gypsy encampment; no moss grows here and neither do days dawdle while Nobby is at large. There are deep scars where his car has got bogged down in mud and it's taken no time at all for him to acquire a flock of laying hens, a roosting pen, an outside lavatory, a cesspit, a place for the dog to sleep and an outside cooking area. I'd half expected him to sink a well, but he seems content to fetch water from the tap on the wall of the stock-shed adjoining Meg's place. It's Gareth's 'agricultural' supply for the cows that he keeps over there. His chickens roam freely about the place, as does the dog, while Nobby himself pads the odd hour away with an air-rifle and wearing a belt which has a dagger attached to it. His pockets are well lined with pellets and he fires shots at anything that moves and has targets littering the field, all of them peppered with pellet holes. He constantly throws the dagger at things and is highly skilled at making it stick into the crosses on the trees. There are wickets and goalposts that he's hacked from saplings, more stacks of saplings for use as bows, arrows, fishing poles, spears, javelins or anything else that comes to mind. He's also strung up a clothes line that goes halfway across the field. Whatever he does, or wherever he goes, he's never without either a roll-up fag or a matchstick wedged between his teeth... and of course, his ever-loving bitch Alsatian. He's a gypsy, a circus clown, a cowboy and an Apache Indian all jumbled up into one hyperactive lump and we'll surely need a holiday ourselves, just in order for us to recover from his!

As a little family unit they are so very happy, but individually, Nobby and Connie are like unstable gelignite. Periodically exploding into screaming-matches with bag-packing, spontaneous separations and floods of tears, invariably followed by earth-moving, passionate reconciliation that threaten to dismantle the caravan and set the dog covering its eyes and whining with fear. They emerge rosy-cheeked, arms around each other and love-bitten almost to the point of needing surgery, both of them grinning like Cheshire cats.

Every single day is nerve racking, I never knew that fun could be so life threatening, or peace so very close to war. Even as I sit painting in the bedroom, 'friendly fire' pellets come flying in through the windows, arrows ricocheting off the tin roof and stones falling out of the sky, each one accompanied by a distant rattling laugh. Murphy is afraid to come near the place, Dan did try but had his bum bitten whilst running for the cricket ball, only then to have to help separate the dogs from what would surely have been a fight to the death; he too stays away now. What Nobby has attracted however, is the farm-gang; they're both fascinated and excited by this macho, crazy, clown of a man who seems to be in a constant state of showing-off, always having something to demonstrate that he's expert at. He brings the worst and the best out of all those under his spell... he's truly mind-boggling!

The days are thus flying by in a kaleidoscopic fervour of cricket, football, shooting-matches, archery, catapulting, knife-throwing, stone throwing, arm-wrestling, karate, darts, card games, with cheating permitted, deafening games of 'snap', 'quoits', using the rims of pram-wheels as discs, tug-of-war, tree climbing, tree felling; marbles using very large stones... you name it, Nobby's thought of it!

There are black eyes, bloody noses and severe limps all about the place; this is no place for the faint-hearted that's for sure. Curly Jenkins came ghosting over, took one peep and sneaked away again, taking Spencer with him; too timid by far the pair of them. Robin, for the time being at least, thinks it's great. The more plastered with mud, ripped and ragged, scratched, cut and bruised he can become, the better he likes it, but he's become a menace at home where all our kitchen knives have suddenly gone missing and practical jokes have reached obscene proportions. Rowan's patience has expired and our peace alas has been adversely affected by this holiday-camp, anarchic madhouse that's come to spend a holiday with us.

With Gwyneth being aunty to both Cari and Connie, there's a distinctly uneasy kind of tolerance up at the farm and I can see poor old Gwyneth just crossing off the days and keeping well out of the way. In one sense it is probably comforting for Gwyneth to know where all the children are but, in another it must be a bit nail-biting at never knowing whether the whole crazy circus will suddenly descend on the farm and turn it into a rodeo-show with 'ride-the-bull' contests, pig-wrestling, tractor racing and bareback horse riding with horses that haven't been broken in. It must come as a relief at dusk to do a head count and find them all present and correct, counting their limbs being a thing that must wait until morning.

The cowshed has become the centre of attraction each evening and we have resorted to the unthinkable and lit the fire so's to save the gas cylinder from premature death as a result of continuous use. It's total bedlam every night with noisy darts matches in the boys' room and even noisier card games around the fire. The whole place very nearly went up in smoke on one occasion when Nobby, on one of his outrageous clownish trips for a pee, inadvertently headed the glowing pressure-lamp from its hook on the beam, sending it crashing to the ground, shattering it to pieces and immediately filling the room with highly inflammable vapourised paraffin. It could have been our guardian angel that saved us from an explosion and fire, a miracle no less. Nobby has a nasty cut on his forehead and my best pressure-lamp is a write-off and will have to be replaced before the darkness crowds in on us.

I'm hardly missed when I make my paraffin dash to Plymouth, coming back at weekends to get the distinct impression that no-one knows that I've ever been away. On such a fleeting passage, I am in tender first light before the circus has awakened, captivated by the magical moment of the young swallows learning to fly. I risk a black eye as I awaken Cari from her deeply needed sleep and whisper to her... "Our swallows are about to leave the nest." and she responds with a bleary-eyed tenderness of her own and fumbles for her spectacles. We lie watching for almost two fascinating hours, their excitement is beyond belief, a loud and thrilling, babbling, twittering sound, plainly, this is a very highly regarded moment in their relatively short lives; an equally special moment in our lives too as we witness the arrival of the point of no return, not just once but five times over. Our darling young swallows, one by one, are being taken out through the bedroom window into a worldful of sky for the very first time, leaving behind an empty and eerie silence. The nest on the opposite beam was built after the newly vacated one and the eggs in it are only just coming up to hatching.

On the third and final weekend, the 'holiday camp' has a distinctly droopy look about it. Everyone's had enough of it and Nobby's audience has scattered, as too have our young bantams, only one of them remains; it's all very mysterious and we suspect the fox. Somewhat less of a mystery is that concerning our old hen 'Gladys', recently painted in oils by Robin, the master himself, who else! He's nicked a tube of my Scarlet Lake and she's bright red and limping worse than ever. Of course, Robin denies having anything to do with it, even though the evidence is plain to see under his fingernails; it's not the first time he's performed this trick.

I mention to the farm-gang that foxes have taken our new bantams and I am met by a turning away of faces and a sniggering that arouses my suspicions. Later, in a moment when Hugh is separated from the pack, he splutters something about either Elwyn or Nobby having shot one of Meg's heavy old hens with a bow and arrow, and that it had been cooked in a pot over the outside fire. "I suppose that's what became of my bantams as well," I mutter in quiet resignation, and his fidgety face tells me all that I need to know. "Don't tell them that I said anything, Jimmy... he'd bloody shoot me!" "I shan't say a thing, don't worry," I reassure him, "what's done is done."

August has almost slipped by unseen and silver thistledown is adrift on the breezes as a broader silence breathes everywhere. I've agreed to look after the boys while Cari takes a break and goes to Ireland with the others to spend some much needed time with her Mum and Dad, whom she hasn't seen for far too long now. I know now what she must have felt like when I was about to leave for Plymouth; it's a very lonely feeling as I watch her getting ready, joking about having to cope with fangled flush toilets and hot and cold running water, no cows or sheep in the kitchen and no more swallow-shit in her hair. The boys all seem fairly okay about it; I'm glad I've got them and they're no doubt glad that they've got me.

The day arrives and Gareth is all smiles as he tows the caravan back across the marsh meadow to the lane, his feeling of relief is impossible for him to disguise. Nobby has bequeathed his chickens to the farm, a kind of repayment for services rendered. I had hoped that we might have them as compensation for our bantams, amongst other things, but I suppose that, that would involve having to admit to a certain foul deed... not the easiest thing for Nobby to do. The caravan is once more hitched-up to the car and there are hugs and kisses, promises galore, a bone-breaking handshake and they all slip away down the lane waving wildly until they are out of sight.

There was never a silence quite like the one we are tiptoeing into as we trudge slowly back across the empty field to the cowshed. My heart is bursting and tears are silently spilling down my cheeks; I hate to admit it, but I'd give anything now for that mad circus to be here in the hugely empty field right now! Gareth, by contrast, shatters the mud of his crocodile-skin smile and shows a tooth or two as he puffs his peace-pipe and starts to breathe again, elbow jauntily sticking out of the window of the old Landrover, bouncing happily back into his old routine.

We busy ourselves tackling a host of jobs, the most urgent of all being that of gathering up the widespread rubbish and making a trip to the tip with a vanload of assorted junk. It's a lovely feeling of us all pulling together; the boys are marvellous, there's not a moment shirked by any one of them, I feel so very proud. We discover what became of our kitchen-knives, finding them scattered about the field where they landed after being thrown... we don't ask who threw them!

The industry doesn't slacken in any way and there's a fresh smell of furniture polish in the air and the old iron range is glowing having been black-leaded. We still have no drinkable water in the well, what little has started to come through is sludgy and has a layer of scum across it; the well itself looks pretty sound and should be better than it was before once the rains properly return. What water was in the tub has all been used up, and so, this enthusiasm for cleanliness is in danger of flagging if I don't make sure that our water-carriers are kept full the whole time. It really is a drag having to make van journeys, running the risk of making myself a nuisance just in order that our mop never goes dry. I time my trips to town to coincide with the chip shop being open and I have lessened my burden on others by stocking up with large containers of mineral water, keeping my fingers crossed that Robin doesn't decide to use it for mopping the floor. In the evening we take a steady stroll round the lanes to the telephone box and call Cari in Northern Ireland. We can all sleep better once we've spoken and we're glad to know that she's happy and enjoying her holiday; she too is comforted to know that we're all coping well in her absence.

The kitchen swallows have all flown, but the occasion was not without some very anxious moments which required the back door having to be wedged wide open, and the cats having to be locked in the spud-shed. Normally, the parent birds zoom in and out through the very small top window, but this was proving to be rather difficult for the fledglings to negotiate, a tantalising temptation upon the instincts of a cat. Having the door open attracts another problem ... Sykes! Even with a gaping wide open door before her, this cussed so-and-so always chooses to exit through the top window, a physical impossibility to say the least. Hurrying her on her way is never advisable and causes distress to the swallows and antagonises a wren, even though his brood have long since safely left the kitchen. Eventually the swallows are liberated, Syke's signature is washed from things and the door closed once more, sealing a strange silence inside that small dark room.

The farm-gang descend on us in the evenings, squabbling with eagerness to spill the beans over the fate that befell our bantams and, in particular, how good they tasted. Not quite as meaty as Meg's heavy free-rangers, but who cares when it's in a big steaming pot with potatoes, carrots, parsnips and a great hunk of bread! They seem to enjoy slagging Nobby off now that he's gone, even though they were all very much hypnotised by his brand of magic while he was here. "He always had to be the best!" Beth snaps, her frowning mind going over things, such as the games of cricket when nobody could get him out and he just stayed there whacking the ball all over the place, never once offering to retire. The problem now is that they're bored again, just like they were before Nobby came to liven things up; things have returned to normal and the summer holiday is all too slowly dragging to an end.

The weather has broken and the rain is doubly welcome, telly becoming the best option for the farm-gang when it's wet, enabling us to simplify our evening and enjoy a bit of space about us at long last, without having to shout to be heard. I light the fire on these wet nights and find time to reflect over the past tumultuous month, having to admit to a certain nostalgia when I think of Nobby and the marks in the field that bear witness to his having passed by this way. According to Cari, Nobby has been catching brown trout from the brook that runs through their garden and the whole family are living like lords as a result; I can't help having a chuckle when I wonder which method he used for catching them. Was it a bow and arrow, air rifle, thrown dagger or spear? One thing for sure is that he would never resort to rod and line!

We're getting very excited about Cari returning and, when I phone a couple of days before she's due back, she tells me that she's planning to fly from Aldergrove to Manchester. For some strange reason, a horrid feeling cramps up inside of me and I beg her not to fly, but to come over on the ferry instead. Just to pacify me she agrees, and no more is said on the subject. The day duly arrives and the boys are all jumping for joy; they've put jars of flowers all about the cowshed, mostly harebells and campions, plus the odd sprig of late honeysuckle. I put new batteries in the radio so that the BBC

World Service may come through loud and clear to help comfort her homecoming. It's while messing about with the radio that I hear of an aircrash in Germany, no survivors. I feel a terrible shudder go through me; maybe that's what I had felt earlier.

The priceless treasure of a moment arrives. We didn't even hear the taxi in the lane but, suddenly, there, coming down the field is Cari. We all go crazy and trip over each other in our mad dash to hug her, even the swallows couldn't compete with this. She comes back home and sees the flowers that the boys have put for her and I watch the tears rolling down her lovely face as she is overwhelmed by their loving.

It is in the evening when we walk to the phone-box to let her Mum and Dad know that she's safely back that Cari admits to me that she did fly back; we learn also that the plane that crashed in Germany was that very plane that she came over on. She got off it at Manchester and then it took off again and crashed! We are stunned into a state of numbness, it's all too much to take in, but it does unearth from my memory, a time when I was a National Serviceman. I dearly wanted an overseas posting, desperate to use my two years in uniform seeing the world; Singapore or Cyprus would have suited me fine. It wasn't to be, when the new postings came through, mine was a posting to Aldershot. To help me, a friendly staff-sergeant fiddled the books and found work for me as a clerk, in the hope that the next postings would be overseas ones, which he could then try and fiddle to get me on. Unfortunately, notification came through that I was to be posted to an Army Camp in Hampshire. Two days before, a Cyprus posting came up and I appealed to the same sergeant to fiddle the books again and swap me for someone else in getting me on that flight. He tried, but couldn't perform his magic this time and the original person flew on that 'Comet' which went and exploded in mid-air over the Mediterranean, killing everyone aboard it! They say that lightning never strikes twice in the same place... well, you could have fooled me!

Insult upon the Face of the Earth!

It's a very sobering thought on realising that we have both cheated certain death by inexplicable fate and it leaves us in a kind of paralysed deafness. It therefore comes as something of a shock to realise that we can hear again; the entire air is suddenly a deafening busted accordion of chainsaws! There is no tune in it at all, just a ceaseless, moaning whine, coming from all directions, broken only by the great crashing sounds of trees fracturing as they hit the earth. We lean on the pigsty wall in a state of dumbfounded horror; the stately line of ancient hawthorns spanning the aldermarsh meadow is being felled. Further down, a monster of a machine is ripping out the willows, while another one is digging trenches for the drainpipes to go in. It's taken since long before I was born for that magical row of hawthorns to become trees and now, in mere minutes, to be felled and burned on a huge bonfire! The aldermarsh and the willow-beds have met their day of reckoning; instead of holding water for half a year, this mysteriously wild and fertile place is about to shed its water in half-an-hour! Multiply this a few thousand times and, every time it rains it'll be like a tidal wave racing down our rivers and causing havoc. Goodbye jacksnipe, goodbye woodcock, we'll never meet here again, all we'll have is the clay and the windy old hill ... the clay and the windy old hill.

Bonfires glow throughout the night, their crackling can be heard amongst a moaning of owls and under the great silent witness of constellations. Orion isn't properly amongst them yet, but when she does eventually elbow herself over the horizon, she'll go mad when she sees what's been done in her absence. Morning comes like a bad toothache and the woods shake out their birds, as the chain-saws rant and rape again. The oaks in the wood above the well are not even half-old; these woods were the dreams of others long since departed, way, way back before farmers were subsidised for their contribution to the devastation of the planet.

Murphy comes over and we lament upon each other's shoulders at the passing of sense in favour of money. He drifts gloomily back and I go up onto the hill and scream as loud as I can... "MAN... you're not fit for this planet!" and it echoes and goes on echoing; my throat is now raw and hurting from this explosion of myself upon this scene of insanity. There's no way I can paint a 'pretty' picture anymore; these recent days have angered me beyond repair. We can create vast bridges to span rivers, aircraft to fly oceans, rockets to project probes into space, to examine planets... but we have apparently not a single grain of commonsense. Is this not a species with its arse where its brain ought to be?

September; all the swallows are flying and growing strong from the protein of flies. They sail about the sky with intricate economy, building up layers of fat to fuel them way down beyond the Sahara Desert and deeper into Africa. They come in to roost when I come in to roost, our dreams mingle, I breathe their breath and they breathe mine; oh! how I love my darling swallows.

September is also the month when Cari and I were born, a one in three hundred and sixty five chance, both of us born on the nineteenth; Christmas Day conceptions, no doubt. Dad was a ferociously strict non-drinker, no doubt a trifle vulnerable at the magical time of Christmas when a bottle of 'Empire', so-called Port or Sherry traditionally joined the pyramid of sprouts and something else which was most certainly rabbit and not chicken or turkey. Even a thimbleful of port would have laid Dad to sleep... but he must have woken up sometime because I'm here to prove it. What a way to celebrate the birthday of Jesus Christ!

The relentless tortured moans of chainsaws are, by degrees, forcing themselves into my brain as being just another normal noise, just as the daily deafening lacerations of warplanes and howling dogs have done. Added to this, the straining engines ripping out willows, digging trenches and hauling the mighty tree-trunks into piles for collection by even bigger, noisier machines, I am confused into wondering... is this awful mess of noise just a nightmare that I'm having?

'Old Crow' has been watching down on events, I've heard him a few times lately; no doubt he's every bit as shocked as we are at this sudden bewildering onslaught on the world that he depends on to provide him with a home, just as we depend on it for similar reasons. Any ironic benefit of the trimmed-off branches providing us with a winter fuel supply is very rapidly dispensed with because, this felling gang work at devastating speed and immediately burn any wood that is of no commercial use to them. They're not from these parts and are a particularly rough, tough-looking wild bunch, unsociable and appearing to be watching us with scornful slyness out of the corners of their eyes, muttering and sniggering whenever we are in earshot; dual-tongued with the Mother-tongue providing a refuge for their darker thoughts.

There's a lingering smell of bonfires day and night, something that delights Gareth as he stands amongst the glowing embers in the evening, pleased at all the new bareness that's bringing the hills down in size. He's well on his way to getting his upland desert, criss-crossed with barbed wire fences; he won't find shelter then to light his pipe when the wild winds whips and haunts the bare flanks and barren tops that he's prescribed upon this little place, where oakwoods have always rang with birdsong and where heather tops once held wild grouse, larks and pipits.

There is no let-up in the destruction; it has spread now and machines are bellowing and baying all around us. The aldermarsh has been flattened, so too has the little wood up where the old bulldozer has now mysteriously vanished. The wood over where my van is parked is now a hive of activity and the van has picked up some nasty dents, with no explanation being offered by anyone as to why this should be so. It's all looking so strangely bare here where the mature oaks, that previously formed a dappled canopy and a cosy tunnel up the hill lane, are all now lying murdered on their sides as too, the tangled marshy wood that fringed the aldermarsh meadow looks like bombs have hit it. A monster of a machine is bulldozing mountains of dog-roses, bramble, alder, elder, rowan, blackthorn and birch; everywhere is a scene of utter devastation; it's an insult upon the land and all the creatures that live amongst the abundant growing things. What the lightning only ever managed to do to one or two trees over several years, one man has, in a handful of days, managed to do to an entire landscape... and for what?

The lure of the government subsidies proves irresistible; the draining of the upland marsh is just another of the financial handouts to accompany a string of others. None of which ever seem able to stop the farmers from pleading poverty. I'm sympathetic to the opinion that land should never be owned by one person and that it should of right belong to the People. The working of it being just another profession, along with all other professions and, with any one of us suitably qualified, to be able to work it efficiently and in accordance with the standards and requirements of the people. Failure to do so being the same as with any other profession... likely to get you the sack and to make room for someone else who could do the job properly. Let a well informed, well educated people decide on issues such as de-forestation, land-drainage, use of pesticides, nitrates, and so on, land for building, roads and all other aspects that could devalue the soil, landscape, water and the broader natural environment. A limit being put on the amount of land included as being part of a dwelling, anything in excess of it having to be rented from the State. Radical? No... a move in the direction of sanity, I would say! Before becoming swallowed by the monstrous landowner from the East, the American Indian thought of earth as being Mother, provider; a vast and varied treasury never to be owned but honoured. The false god of money and the concocted anaesthetic of a condoning fourth 'R', soon put paid to such divine thoughts about Mother Earth!

To make a bit of extra cash, Gareth has sold a strip of land to one of his drinking mates, and so, instead of having lushly wooded hillsides and a gentle sighing valley before them, Meg and Murphy are about to have a large, utility, modern red brick house and all the 'doing-up-cars' junk that goes with it. Had Meg known that the land adjoining her small garden was for sale, she'd have put in an offer of her own; but the blood of horse-racing mates runs thicker than water and the deal was long-since signed under the blurring whisky of a good day at the races.

Our joint birthday has been swept aside by the march of madness. September has blown to another page... our swallows have gone. A decision of awesome dimensions made here over a cowshed in the hills, and no-one heard a thing; it's worse than having my wisdom teeth taken out! Also gone, 'Gladys', our recently painted scarlet hen; her journey dark and mysterious, while the journey that our swallows are on is one that takes them back to spring and summer again, leaving us to face the certainty of a bleak autumn and an even bleaker winter.

The wagons that take the trees away are wider than the lanes and, as a result, have scraped away the banks and ploughed deep ditches on either side with their huge wheels, together with the colossal weight that they are carrying. This is causing all manner of problems, especially with the heavy rains now adding to it. Anyone driving simply has to stay on the thin strip of tarmac, otherwise they're in one of the two new ditches. Meeting a vehicle coming the other way is a nightmare and, the one who's forced to give way has to reverse around blind, narrow bends... never the easiest of things to do at the best of times. There's no subsidy available to compensate the Council for the extensive damage caused to roads and waysides, no subsidy either for damage caused to vehicles or for the poor parents whose kids have ruined their clothes as a result of slipping into the ditch. Only the farmers win.

With our swallows now gone, I can take down the painting, which, for a while, at least offered us some protection from the swallow-droppings; it was our insatiable fascination that had us move the bed back into the firing line. A good inch of the stuff on the floor directly beneath both nests bears testimony to their tireless devotion; I must confess, my 'Last Supper' painting now resembles, 'Last Trip to the Toilet'! It's time for me now to nail back the polythene to the windows and give us some protection from the wind and driving rain; it'll feel cosier now, not an entirely adequate compensation for the loss of our swallows, but nothing's perfect in this life.

I've noticed that the wrens and bluetits are back roosting in the bedroom but, with the rolling landscape now reduced to a graveyard of stumps, the madrigal choirs of owls in the starlight are now silent from this place where Autumn should be glowing. A ghostly, gloved silence walks the darkness through the lonesome night until the first dogs bark and the day comes blaspheming back to life.

Rosie and Elly pay us another surprise visit, bringing with them an undergraduate called 'Fred'. Fred is here on a mission, that of catching a falling leaf before it has hit the ground; not such an easy thing to do when there's hardly a tree left standing anywhere. For some private, romantic reason he is obsessed with his mission, believing in some deep and undiluted spiritual way that by so doing, he will be granted a wish; strong medicine handed down to him by a Celtic grandmother. We therefore don't see a fat lot of him, he's always prancing about, frisking and skipping, bursting into mad zig-zagging dashes in hot pursuit of odd leaves that fall from the one remaining tree that Gareth has spared or, more than likely, overlooked... our big sycamore with the boys' swing dangling from it. Not only is it we who are amused by his gleeful cavort about the hill, but the workmen too are highly bemused... they've never before seen a grown man twittering like a linnet and spending half a day chasing leaves!

Eventually, with his ginger curls in disarray, a rosy-cheeked and beaming Fred comes skipping in, clutching to his bosom the precious leaf that he has caught and, having made his wish, is now content to wait for it to become true. I can guess what his wish is by the certain glint in his eyes each time that he looks at Rosie. He seems to have settled into a deeper peace with himself and is just about to sprawl back in the comforting promise of his wish, when he catches sight of my new chromatic harmonica. He's a changed man within the breadth of a second and his eyes instantly swell and light up, his trembling fingers snake-tonguing their ways to its cold metal. As in a dream, this sweet poet of a person is once more up on the hill, twizzling, dancing, skipping and blowing the very reeds out of my beautiful, costly new harmonica. Rosie and Elly beam in tender amusement through the window at this courtly dance, and the workmen are once more compelled to lay down their chainsaws and gaze on in utter disbelief, being forced to reconsider their life-long established macho disregard of the existence of fairies!

Cari and I address more domestic realities, such as where they're all going to sleep, and so we leave the others, my new harmonica as well, to wander off to familiarise themselves with the new bareness. Later, when we are carting the water-carriers over to the van, we discover the others engaged in a highly vociferous argument with the workmen up on the devastated hillside above my van. This is probably the closest that these rough-and-ready blokes will have ever been to a University education and the experience is certainly not impressing them one little bit. As far as they are concerned, felling trees is just a job, a skilled one at that, no different from lots of other jobs... except that it's probably a damned sight more dangerous. It's just another way of earning a living and providing for their families. They never thought that they'd be here being screamed at by rather more fortunate young pretenders up from University.

I shake my head in frustration at the futility of directing their protests at these blokes here, they're only the messengers after all; it's plainly obvious that the blame rests way, way higher-up the pecking order than this. I glance across to Cari and can see that she shares my despairs. We are the ones that have to live here after all, and we'd rather not have visitors making more enemies for us than are necessary. I beckon them down from their verbal slagging match and I offer a conciliatory wave to the workmen in a kind of damage-limitation gesture of friendship. Rather surprisingly they wave back and one of them cups his mouth with his hand and shouts, "Gonna find it a bit quiet round here when we've gone, boss!" Just as I'm shouting back... "Ay, and a bit draughty!" he snatches the cord of his chainsaw and my words are drowned under the fearful ranting din, and Rosie, Elly and Fred pick their way back down through the trunks and sawn-off branches. I have to shout to be heard, "We're off to town, fancy a trip?" Gleefully they come scurrying and I try to open the back doors, but Fred's old banger has been parked right up touching my bumper, so I have to ease forward to let them jump excitedly aboard, laughing at the realisation that this is a damned sight more comfortable than the cowshed is!

Watched by the workmen, we slowly drive off up the newly bared hill and I ask the question over my shoulder, "What was all that shouting about?" Rosie answers somewhat rebelliously, "We were just trying to make those idiots aware of what they're doing to the planet, and to pack up and go home, that's all." "And did you have any success?" I sigh in a frustrated sort of way. "No, but we certainly made our point!" There are warm, approving smiles from the other two as I negotiate the hairpin at the end of the lane, then I offer a few words in defence of the workmen. "If those guys were not felling trees, they'd be on the dole. It's not them that you should be trying to educate... you should know that, it's just a way of earning a living; that's the way they see it." Rosie shakes her head despairingly and says ... "In this life you've got to fight for what you believe in ... you're too blooming soft, our Jim ... that's your trouble!" It's an old bit of family 'knock-about stuff', a kind of protective loving and I conclude my part of it by saying ... "Yeah, well ... that's as may be, but you won't find me shooting the postman when the Inland Revenue send me a bill that I can't pay!"

In the early dusk we all amble down the slope to the cattle-trough, then cross the barbed wire fence which, in Spring I had leapt clear over in hot pursuit of the fox that was making off with our hen. Everywhere that I look is unrecognisable now. No longer the row of old hawthorns spanning the little meadow, no longer the willow-beds fringing what was the aldermarsh, no longer the little wild wood on the rise bordering the lane, it's all bleak and open now with ridges of heavy clay soil marking the drainage trenches which are now half full of water. There are numerous blackened patches where fires have been, and I notice in the growing gloom, a pile of sawn-off alder stumps, attempts to burn them having failed; alder never was a good burner, it's wood acting like blotting paper, hence it's flourishing in marshy areas. I'm astounded by the colour of the recently sawn wood; what was originally a golden cream colour, is now a vivid, rusty blood-red, sadly beautiful with the rings of all its springtimes boldly circled upon it. I take an armful of it, not for burning, but for painting instead. It seems fitting for this beautiful wood to look like it's bleeding.

Candlelight flickers in our rapidly crumbling caravan, where Rosie and Elly have chosen to roll out their sleeping-bags, leaving Fred to bravely take over Robin's bed, while Robin wriggles into the end of Rowan's bunk, causing a riot with accusations and counter-accusations of germ-warfare and gas attack. Spibby and her growing kitten seem quite oblivious to the uproar and snuggle luxuriously together on Robin's pillow, purring in perfect harmony, one high and one low. I'm hoping that they'll choose this occasion to lift their boycott of the litter-tray, especially now that autumn is once more upon us, with the prospect of another winter spent in the spud-shed if the boycott remains in place.

Potatoes have been harvested up at the hill farm, nobody told me and so it comes as a pleasant surprise when Gareth drops by in the Landrover and offloads three lovely bags of King Edwards. With all the extensive tree felling that's going on, spud-picking has been reduced to being one of those awkward jobs that have to be fitted in somehow; not to be the pageant of last year with Old Thomas and

Dan with their old backs bended beneath the sky, fondling this bounty of the soil with their worshiping fingers. No gathering round the table for a Van Gogh potato feast, no tapestried reminiscences of times gone by, no communion of glowing smiles and cackles of laughter; everything's bleak up at the hill farm now.

I'm just keeping my fingers crossed that Rosie and the others will steer clear of the subject of tree-felling; the very last thing that I need right now is for this hand of friendship to be bitten by an unscheduled crash-course on the global effect of deforestation. I glance about me and can sense three undergraduate hand-grenades itching for their pins to be removed; so too can Gareth, having no doubt heard of yesterday's verbal skirmish with the workmen... news being the fastest thing that moves in these parts. He doesn't stay for more than a couple of minutes before saying goodbye, easing both his and my own blood pressure, as he heads off on his way.

What better way to celebrate our lovely new potatoes than by having a potato feast of our own! With the weather coming in dull and drizzly now, a crackling fire in the hearth would brighten the place up no end. I drag Fred away from my harmonica and gather him to the task of finding some firewood that will burn. I take up my trusty bushman saw and we head off, not so much in hope as in expectation, following my memory-picture that tells me that there were long dead branches on the oaks that the workmen were felling this morning. I just hope that they haven't burned them already... I hope also that the workmen are not still up there or they'll think us somewhat hypocritical if we ask them for firewood after previously slagging them off for producing it. We're in luck, there's no sign of life anywhere on that desolate hillside, what's more, the dead branches that I had remembered are there all tangled up amongst the pile that's ready for burning. I quickly get my little saw back into action and sort out the good from the bad in the tangled heap before, straining to the limit, head off back down to the lane in the grey-veiled drizzle. The branches that we are struggling with have long since lost their soft outer wood to woodpeckers, leaving just an iron-hard heart... 'heart-of-oak', dense and very heavy, the kind of wood that I always pray that I shall find in the dead of winter; nothing burns better than this, it gives off a wonderful heat and lasts for ages.

Fred is soon puffing and panting and, as we grapple our way across the lane, there's a clattering sound and I catch sight of my new harmonica having somehow slipped out from Fred's pocket and I see it smash onto the hard tarmac. I drop my branch and pick up the instrument, only to see that it has fractured and come apart at one end; it's finished and I've hardly ever blown it. It's true what Rosie said... I am too soft! I look dolefully across to Fred and his lowered head tells me that he's not feeling too good about it. I spare him my true feelings and pick up my heavy branch and proceed through the marsh meadow gate where I notice Dan rubbering his way over to the cowshed.

Dan misses nothing, not even when the sky has fallen down all around us. He stops in his tracks and the devil in him clears its throat and hoots... "And I thought you was against all this tree-felling!" I can't really argue with him when he's got the devil in him, and I can sense, even from this distance, that he's feeling mischievous, his Alsatian bite is no longer bothering him. "There seems little point in wasting it!" I shout back and he just sneers provocatively and fires off another volley. "Cutting down trees suits you now, doesn't it!" I can sense Fred's volcano about to erupt, but I beg him to hold his fire. He's not met Dan before and I advise him that, provocative as the old rascal may be, he's a damned good bloke, one of the best. We struggle nearer as Dan starts up again. "What's all this puffin' and pantin' about... damn, them's only blooming twigs!" Fred gets the idea and we both smile and continue to grapple each inch of the way to where Dan is standing with a grin that's many sizes too big for his face.

We arrive back like drowned rats and I tell Fred to go inside with Dan; I can soon saw this wood into logs and have everyone thinking that fires are produced by magic. For Dan though, this trip over to see us, and in such inclement weather, is a bit like going to the doctors; there's so much that the past month and a half have left for him to try and cough out of his system. Predictably, he lets rip, never once losing his antagonistic streak of devilment, leaving us to guess what he really thinks. Having been involved with farming all his life, it wouldn't surprise me to know that he approves of all the things that have so drastically changed the face of the landscape surrounding us, equally, it wouldn't surprise me to know that he's violently against it; that's the cussedly irritating thing about this lovable old so and so! One thing for certain, he cannot disguise his fondness for well-baked potatoes, strong cheddar cheese and a few of Cari's new pickled onions. He doesn't complain about the tea either, becoming almost silenced by his concentrated enjoyment of it all. "How did you get along with Nobby?" I ask, taking advantage of his preoccupation. An onion shoots from his mouth, like a ball from a canon, as my untimely question turns to gunpowder. Tea spills everywhere as he chokes... "Don't talk to me about Buffalo Bill and that bloody she-wolf of his!" Everyone laughs as I teasingly say... "Come off it, Dan, you only had one tiny nibble of a bite... that great mongrel of yours has bitten me really hard several times now!" "Tiny bite, my arse! Come to think... it WAS my arse!" Even he joins in the laughter now.

His consultation has done him a power of good, he's a cured man as he totters out into the drizzling night. I take up the torch and accompany him back up as far as his sycamore tree, declining his offer of a Captain Morgan nightcap. I shine my torch through the depressing drizzle in shedding what little light I can to help him over the last few strides where his old chicken-shed grain store is scuffling and squeaking with rats. I shout my goodnight and hurry away before the dog is let loose and scores another direct hit.

Memory kicks me down so many lost-trodden pathways, bringing alive once more, early days in Cornwall when Councils adopted the widespread policy of chemical control of waysides. Oh, how it enraged me to see all my lovely flowers and herbs poisoned to a brown slime, small birds and insects robbed of food and homes and poisoned along with the vegetation. Cari and I recall those days, remembering how we went off one night to find where the Council spraying tractors were parked, and then pouring sugar into their fuel-tanks and leaving flowers for the driver. Our babysitter had no idea as to why we took so large a bag of sugar with us.

Our response to the current regime of green-terrorism is sadly lacking in fire-power. There's not much we can do, but when we come across a forgotten tangled pile of roots, we immediately set to examining the mess. There are dog roses, hawthorns, hazels, birch, elder, rowan, willow, honeysuckle, oak and ash; the rose-briars rip our hands as we disentangle the mess, but our bloody hands are borne with pride, as we go off with spade and fork, transplanting every last little root by torchlight, into the good soil of neglected quiet corners. The boys all join in as we make this our nightly mission; they're really excited about it, thinking it to be an illegal thing that we're doing when, in actual fact it's nothing of the kind, just a caring thing, that's all. I feel as guilty as they do, goodness only knows why, but I suppose it's because we would appear to be working against the interests of more powerful people who suppose themselves to have authority over the face of the planet

The disturbance of peace of late has left a weird, threatening kind of tension in the air and there is a stealth in whatever we do, ever being on the lookout for some demon or other about to undermine us and reduce us to silence and ineptitude.

All Hell Let Loose!

Darkness soothes away so many sores, permitting dreams to cleanse away the sorrows of light; but dreams are transient offering only briefly a harbour for leaden sleep. The swallows have gone, the trees have gone and our dear friends are but a memory. The wind has returned, not the usual ill-tempered brief bully, but an October biennial brute of a blast, a westerly of ill intention. Of all the most outspoken of weathers that we've experienced here, nothing has threatened us more than this sudden tumult of enraged air. Overnight, it separates the weak from the strong without favour and, unfortunately, there are no longer any trees to act as a shield and exercise any restraint over it in any way. An invisible tyrant by day, but in the darkness, visually understandable, being both humbled and enraged by knowing that it cannot blow the darkness away.

Everything shakes; no American jets were ever so warlike or sounded as ferocious as this. I'm in awe of this 'Mother in the Sky', that can make frailty as in the wings of an aphid, and go on to flex a muscle in showing another aspect of her awesome overwhelmingness. 'Truth is, size doesn't exist, as neither does any measure beyond the quantifying of our needs. We only perceive bigness relative to our assessment of worth, vanity alone makes any worth, worthless at a stroke; a massive gale like this one now, soon sorts out any lingering ambiguity!

We are in fear of our lives, sleep is out of the question. I feel like going out into the pitch- blackness and digging a hole for us all to crawl into, but this rapidly growing storm-and-a-half isn't waiting for fools and the cowshed is in dire threat of being blown away. The van perched on the wayside isn't a convincing option either and my brain goes into overdrive. All curses are negative and futile but, nevertheless I curse the loss of trees, some of which would no doubt have been blown down, but most would have offered us a degree of protection. Fearing the worst, I calculate that the safest place to be anywhere around here right now, is Rowan's bunk. I built it as though I was building a battleship, and so, Cari and I gather the family together and huddle inside the heavily fortified capsule... the cats can't believe their luck!

There's no way I can imagine our corrugated iron roof will be able to withstand this battering and we all snuggle up together waiting for a catastrophe, totally unable to make any worthwhile or constructive response. Options torment through my mind without stopping, but I know in my heart that I've done the right thing. I even have to admit to having a deep trust in this cowshed that Murphy and I bodged together; why, dammit, that tough sod of a roof has the blood of both of us as part of it! At least we are all dry and warm in here and it benefits us that the candle in the jam jar is but a terminal stub beyond the wind's reach, the jar itself is more at threat that the little flicker of light inside it.

The hours are long and laboured, dark and cruel; it's impossible not to feel afraid, but I have done my best to convince everyone that we are well protected where we are... even if the cowshed collapses and buries us. There's a sudden frightening, heavy crashing noise outside, it's impossible to know what's going on as one noise is rapidly swallowed by another, then another, in a ceaseless catastrophic procession of noise. To top this, an even louder, more terrifying crunching noise explodes on us and we instinctively brace ourselves in anticipation of being struck and possibly buried by whatever it is. I hear debris smashing against the wall protecting us and can only guess that the chimney's come through the roof, or that the kitchen roof has taken off; one thing for sure, I'm not about to go prancing off with a torch to find out which!

The candle dies and is immediately swallowed by the great black denying beast of dark. This monster is so huge that she almost bursts the air with her bellyaching embrace and we pray that she'll cool down, take it easy and allow the Goddess of Light to once more soothe away our fears and show us the way. It's a debatable comfort having the small battery radio with its 'World Service' informing us of rabbit damage in Australia and medical breakthroughs in the war against obesity in America; but right now it's the best thing we've got, even though its batteries are about as useful as a string-vest is for carrying water.

Daylight trespasses timidly, shaping things; the hurricane blast is blowing itself out and a deep wave of sleep has consumed my boys. The last straggling winds of the storm rattle things and cause anything that's busted to flap. Some of the gusts are still fierce enough to inflict damage and set things tumbling, but the most miraculous thing of all is that the cowshed is still standing! Our brotherly-blooded tin roof has stood the test and with Cari in my arms, we lie with the boys in a heavy breathing heap of thanksgiving.

I ease myself gently from my family asleep and venture to face the world that the wind has left. First I tiptoe upstairs... it's a miracle; apart from lots of plaster debris, nothing has been drastically altered. The swallows' nests are still up there on the beams, and our bed hasn't been flattened under a collapsed roof... the roof is still firmly on in fact! I return downstairs where I discover a litter of house bricks that have come crashing down the chimney, the fireplace is buried under lots more. I then carefully pick my way to the kitchen and ease open the door. Immediately a whole pile of bricks come crashing in on me, causing me to skip backwards in avoiding my toes being crushed. I can see sky where I could never see it before, there's a huge hole where the chimney has come smashing through the roof... it's a dreadful mess.

Little by little I clamber over it and make my way over to the door, having to scrape away piles of bricks before I can begin to ease it open. By degrees, I manage to get it partially open, sufficient for me to see a rearranged world with the pathetic figure of 'Sykes' standing huddled amongst the debris of the pigsty toilet; her shabby feathers being ruffled by the tormenting fits of late wind. With a hefty shove, I force the door fully open and the full horror of the storm hits me... half of the barn has been blown down and is just a pile of rubble. This was the end where the chickens and the bantams roosted... there's no sign of them. I hurriedly scan about for signs of life, but, apart from 'Sykes', nothing stirs... I fear the worst.

I return indoors and awaken Cari to break the news; the boys are best left sleeping because it's far too dangerous for them to go rooting through the debris for signs of our chickens. I really need to go in there and assess the damage in determining the state of what's left standing. I must also examine the remains of our chimney and make myself fully aware of the problems we are facing. Part of the chimney has ended up in the hearth, but the bulk of it has either bounced off the kitchen roof, or just smashed through it. Fortunately, my ladder was at the end of the barn that suffered the least damage and so, with care, I am able to retrieve it and return to examine the state of the remaining chimney, concluding that, barring no repeat of the storm, it poses no immediate threat, so I am able to set about the task of clearing up the mess.

Murphy comes hurrying over having feared for our safety and certainly not expecting to see the cowshed still standing, especially so when he sees what the wind has done to the barn, even though it was in the shelter of the cowshed. Together we carefully sift through the rubble, sadly confirming the fate of our dear hens, but finding no trace whatsoever of the bantams; they just seem to have vanished without trace. We salvage a sheet of rusted corrugated iron which was formerly part of the barn roof, and then we perform a very basic first-aid job on the kitchen roof; it isn't very pretty, but it's better than nothing and, with luck, should keep most of the weather out.

Our hammering wakes up the boys and they all come and watch from the living-room doorway, silent with shock. Whilst I am up the ladder, I can't resist taking a peep into the swallows nest which has miraculously survived; in it are two pale little eggs, part of an abandoned hope of rushing through a second brood. I hold one of the eggs up for the boys to see, it's ice cold. "Ahh!" they all sigh, feeling the same sadness that I am feeling and I return the egg gently back to the cradle of its grave. Murphy looks up with a sad smile and says, "It's funny how they never came back to those nests in the barn ... they probably knew that it was going to be blown down!" "I doubt it, Murph," I say thoughtfully... "it's more likely that they didn't survive their journey through the Mediterranean countries; we saw the problem for ourselves when we lived in Spain. Every Sunday, families went strolling out all dressed-up, dads carrying air-rifles for shooting little birds; swallows, martins, warblers, larks, finches, hoopoes. They carried sad little bunches of dead birds like bunches of flowers. Sunday worship wouldn't be the same without a few bouquets of murdered birds! You ask Cari; it completely horrified us, disillusionment beyond measure. I'd gone there to study the guitar and to paint and write; we were so glad to come back... to this!"

I get off the subject before I explode and try to focus my mind more on the problems at hand. On a more positive note, the well is once more overflowing and its water is sparkling clear. It hasn't fully dawned on us that, in the space of a few dark hours we could have been made homeless; when it eventually does, it's a most sobering thought.

The dream we have held on to for so long, is fragile and vulnerable, and is being steadily distanced from our willing fingers, but there isn't one of us that reveals the faintest trace of defeat. We just can't wait to be getting back on with things, and making the most of a bad job. I dig a grave for our dear old hens, being silently watched some distance away by 'Sykes'. She's showing uncharacteristic restraint and I get the distinct feeling that she's experiencing the pain of loneliness. These are very sad moments... it's like digging a grave for our broken dreams.

I ask Murphy, if the storm did any damage over at his place, and he laughs, saying proudly that he and Meg benefit from having Dan's place higher up the hill to provide a perfect shield. Dan, being that shield, took the full force unfortunately, and had his chicken-coop rolled over a few times and part of his stock shed blown in. Old Thomas, however, he apparently had a late shave and put his best clothes on and sat in a chair waiting for the angels to come and take him away. "Dan reckons that they must have been called out on more urgent jobs, because he says he saw Old Thomas talking to a cow this morning."

Over the next few squally days, I give priority to salvaging whatever timber I can. The wood-men have now more or less finished and just two of them are left tidying up. The heavy digger has left the marsh and a battered and scarred emptiness sprawls away to where the woodland that sheltered the little brook has also been brought to its knees, revealing to us, for the first time, sight of the other little lane. There are huge sawn-off trunks everywhere to serve as reminders of what once had been; it'll take a long time for these scars to heal.

Making a ruined barn safe is a laborious job; it feels like having come full circle to be here sorting out debris again. The place that once stole my heart bore no resemblance to the one that is now breaking it. What was once a seed of hope is now a raped and ravaged dream, barren of any song. Nothing subdues the warplanes with their awesome technology that hungers for wars to make the whole investment worthwhile. They never fail to ride across this well-worn and wearied rat-track in the sky, festering all silence into cancers. It's all routine, not just by day, but now by night as well, sometimes with disastrous results when mountains suddenly leap out of nowhere and get in the way, and young pilots are wasted to nothing in a terrible instance.

The cowshed stands up defiantly, just as I remember our little wooden hut on the cliffs had previously done, confronting the very worst of what the weather could throw at it. What I have learned is that, storms cannot last forever and that better things always replace bad things, as is the balancing factor that makes life possible. Someone once said, "To remember is to become blind in one eye... but to forget is to become totally blind." I think that this best exemplifies the balance that I strive for in my own life, never to be totally blinded by the past, but never to forget it either!

Lovely pale mists are bandaging the mornings, preserving little islands of fragmented summer yet trapped in what folk are calling an 'Indian summer'. What I love most is the cool bandaging part which is like the soft white breath of a yawn, painting the spiders webs white and hushing everywhere to a most perfect meditative silence. No longer the unbearable heat and, who'd ever know that only days ago, a gale blew half of the barn away and toppled the chimney stack. These divinely quiet moments of morning here touching haven't even the strength to topple a jewel of dew from a hogweed umbrella.

I've been off walking with my camera along the lanes amongst a million white webs, but the morning has now broken free of its bandages and a soft ghost of a sun is warming the whiteness away. I walk silently past Dan's little acre and can hear him sneezing in a manner that suggests that it isn't too much pepper on his egg or dust that's tickling him, but something else. He, Mister 'Radar' himself, appears in the yard, having detected my silence; his wretched dog has picked up my vibrations too and, in a clumsy flash, is airborne and sailing over the barbed wire fence and coming at me in his usual crazed state of mindlessness. Fortunately for me, I'm carrying a stout stick of ash and I give him warning that I too can inflict hurt. He frustratedly backs off and keeps his distance, not wishing to chance his luck.

Dan staggers over the wet grass and I can see that he's got a heavy cold and has got his own jewel of dew hanging from his bright red nose; I can see also, his leaden, watery red eyes. "You've got yourself a nasty cold by the looks of it, Dan," I say by way of greeting him. He delves deep into his locker of wit and sarcasm, managing to borrow somehow, a smile from somewhere and also a little bunch of words that leave him indebted to something else. "Nor... I ain't got no... aa, aa, achoo... bloody cold! Just a bit of a sniffle that's all!" His chest is bare, white and whiskery and he's wearing the shirt that's got to last him day and night till it rots, coming off briefly on the day that he goes to town. There's still the odd button or two on it, but it remains unfastened all the way down to where it is stuffed into his grimy trousers. Cold or no cold, this is the way Dan likes it, Spring, Summer, Autumn, Winter. This man is made of iron... yet he can still catch a cold. "I'll bring you a jar of Cari's rose-hip syrup ... that'll get rid of it for you," I say as he rifles another cluster of sneezes, then growls... "Get away with you, it's just a bit of a sniffle... a bit of damp, that's all, nothing that a drop of Captain Morgan won't shift, isn't it!"

His contemptuous mongrel whines frustratedly as it watches

me on my way; my ash stick has spoken to him without even raising its voice, enabling me to slip away unmolested; down once more into the consuming emptiness with only a robin sweetly and faintly rippling from over by Murphy's place. As I move nearer, I see the man himself standing in the yard taking the air and looking hungrily and restlessly at the morning. I break the silence and call across to him; he responds, beckoning for me to wait for him and comes charging down the track in his 'admiralty jacket' and thunderously large ex-government boots. Rumbling to a halt and wearing a sardonic smile as his eyes do the talking, sweeping this way and that across the devastated landscape before coming to an awkward rest as he faces me. Slowly shaking his head he says, "Progress... that's what they call it, Jimmy... some bloody progress!"

We amble down past where the big new house will soon dominate the valley, noting that a start has already been made with a huge hole having been smashed into the hedge, just wide enough for a 'J.C.B.' to get through. With a grimace, Murphy moans, "They're starting on Monday Gareth reckons... should be well on the way by Christmas!! I look back at Murphy in silent disbelief and ask, "What are they going to do without a good water supply, how can they get approval without a good supply of water?" "I asked him that, and he says there's a going to be enough in the old farm well across the back to last until the mains water comes." My eyes open wide, "What's this I hear... Mains Water? That sounds a bit posh... when's that coming then?" "He didn't say, but he reckons it's coming... for those that can afford it, that is!"

Down by my van we dawdle to a stop, Murphy doesn't want to go any further because it's too depressing; I've never seen my old friend look so dejected and there's nothing I can do or say to help him in any way. He turns and somewhat aimlessly saunters up through the high dead grass and into the gateway of the field that leads back up to the Dutch barn and home. He's only gone a couple more paces when the air is suddenly split apart by an ear-piercing explosion higher up on the deforested hillside above us; rocks, boulders and roots are flying in all directions and are raining down. In one crazy, mad, spontaneous panic-stricken flash we have instinctively thrown ourselves under the van and are desperately crawling for our very lives as debris clatters down noisily onto the roof and all around us. It's an absolutely terrifying few moments ... then all is quiet. "Bloody hell! What was that?" I gasp, unable to move a single limb, so tightly are we wedged under my old van. Murphy is numb with shock and cannot utter a word. Being stuck fast proves to be a blessing because, just as suddenly as the last explosion, the entire earth beneath us shakes as two more deafening blasts go off in rapid succession higher up the hill, bringing fragmented root-systems and disemboweled earth crashing down in a wide radius all around us. Murphy suddenly finds his voice; "Bastards!... They're dynamiting the tree-roots out!"

I struggle to free my head and try to get a view of the world from under the grimy black belly of the large engine that's dripping oil all over us, we're both plastered in the stuff. Somewhere, wedged under me is my beloved old Canon camera... I daren't even begin to think what state it is in. "Do you realise," I mutter to Murphy, "we could have been killed! No warning... no nothing... just BANG! Is this Armageddon, do you reckon?" "Cunning Celts, more like!" Murphy curses then subsides into a sickly laugh and mutters, "Just think, Jimmy, we'd never have got under your old Morris Post-office van... we'd have definitely been killed!"

There's the sound of an engine and, suddenly, an identical vehicle to the Morris van in question pulls up alongside us; it's the postman. He hasn't seen us and I hear the lid of my hat-box letterbox open and close and can just about see the postman's shiny shoes kicking away the debris. "Give's a hand!" Murphy shouts and I see the feet stagger to a dumbfounded halt as the postman looks about him to see where the voice is coming from. He's looking inside the van now and sees absolutely nothing, even though the voice is still coming from that direction. He thinks he's going mad; this is being expressed through the language of his shuffling feet. There are voices now and other feet have joined in, it's the workmen come to assess the damage. One of them sees Murphy's struggling body and, suddenly there's a row of faces peering into the darkness at us. "What the heck are you doing there?" the postman whimpers, "that artist bloke hasn't run you over, has he?" "No, he bloody well ain't!" I scream, "your artist-bloke's stuck under here as well!"

There's a good deal of laughing and joking as they man-handle us out, goodness knows what damage we have done to the underside of the van, because we both get snaggled up on things, and there wasn't any skill involved in the extraction process. "How the heck did you manage to get stuck under there?" the postman persists, scratching his head, "...problems with the exhaust?" "Exhaust, my arse," Murphy growls... "it's these mad sods here with their bloody dynamite... startin' a world war, that's what!" Still chuckling and faking a look of consternation, one of the workmen mutters, "We're only doin' a bit of root-clearin', that's all." Murphy springs into a rage, his eyes turn wild and his face colours up; he stomps boldly up to the workman and gives him a flat-of-the hand push that sends him staggering into the clutches of his mates. "Root-clearin', my arse! You don't do root-clearin' with a bloody atom-bomb... you bloody morons!" He stoops and picks up a heavy fragment of root and throws it at the cowering figures, hitting one of them in the chest. "Try havin' that come down on your bloody head... and that... and that!" He kicks stone fragments in their direction as the postman takes cover behind me, only now getting to realise what's going on. My own temper is coming to the boil as I am slowly emerging from a state of shock with a growing realization of how perilously close we have come to be being killed. Suddenly, my lid flies off and I'm alongside Murphy, steaming on all cylinders. "You crazy, mad bastards... you could have killed us! My mate here could so easily have been walking along here with his little daughter in a pram ... and the postman here... he could have had a tree root through his windscreen; you need that dynamite shoving up your arses ... you stupid twats!" I notice Cari coming scurrying over the meadow and the workmen turn, one of them muttering... "Ay up... here comes trouble!" The postman hands me my camera, it's a sorry sight and is clogged with dirt and gravel; I'm too angry to examine it. Cari comes rushing up to my side, plainly with an axe to grind of her own, as Murphy still rages... "Ain't you supposed to give warning when you're using dynamite beside a public highway... close-off the lane or summat?" The workmen are on the defensive now and looking for any excuse that they can think of. "Us did put a sign up, well you did, didn't you Merv... you put a warnin' sign up didn't you!" "Orh, yes!" the other one snaps with a firm nod as though his head were an exclamation remark. I turn to the postman and ask... "Did you see any official warning signs, postman?"

Shaking his head thoughtfully, he replies, "No I saw nothing that looked like a warning sign... there was summat down by the school, a tatty, hand-painted thing. Written in Welsh it was... either that or bloody Russian; I took it for a Young Farmers prank or some Plaid Cymru protest or other... didn't mean a thing to me!" Murphy turns to me with a look of abject astonishment ... "Bloody typical! They'll write 'Bed and Breakfast', 'Car for Sale' and 'Private Fishing'... they'll write it in English when it suits them!"

Cari intervenes, she has a piece of rock that she's been clutching in her hand and holds it up menacingly; "I think we're missing the point. See this!" she holds up the rock before them... "this piece of rock just landed on my roof... and there's plenty more besides. Nobody warned me to stay indoors, nobody warned Meg over there, not to put the baby out in the pram, in fact, nobody warned anybody! This is a police matter!"

There's a stunned, deathly silence; eyes move in discrete mad dashes in their sockets as, gradually, our attention is drawn to a growing scraping sound that's approaching from further along the lane. By degrees it advances and then, over the brow of the hill a figure appears, dark and hunched and pushing a bike that is burdened with 'things' from the rubbish-tip lashed onto it. It's Alwyn, a remote lovable soul, the result of close family inbreeding; he's the man that just waved back when Murphy and I were stranded on the roof and screaming for his help. Here he is again, coming slowly down the hill, erasing Cari's threat of police involvement and grunting with every other stride. This poor soul is one of life's natural scavengers; he cannot speak and communicates only with grunts, occasionally attracting ridicule from loveless halfwits which sadly includes a couple of these workmen here now. It must be a daunting experience for this more than half-wild soul to come upon such a gathering of hungry faces. The noise becomes deafening, he's dragging a heavy six-panelled door, a full size tin bath and has a galvanised watering can tied on his handlebars, as he curses the roots and rocks that are littering the road. "Hello, Alwyn; you've been busy!" I say, and he stares back at me with his red eyes spewing tears of weariness and his nose and mouth dribbling ceaselessly. He grunts and I catch sight of his eyes meeting mine very briefly, and a trace of a smile twitching from him. I hear one of the workmen mutter slyly ... "Might as well talk to a sheep!" a remark that sets my blood boiling all over again. I wait a moment until Alwyn has moved on a few paces, then I stomp up to this joker and fix him with my stare, and hiss, "There but for the grace of God go you and I, my friend... he didn't ask to be born."

We watch Alwyn go clattering round the bend and out of sight; he's going to be weary when he gets home because he's still got a long way to go, two cottages beyond old Thomas's where the council road ends and a narrow, winding up-hill track takes over, all the way up to the very top; the most hidden-away cottage imaginable, overlooking the most breathtaking of valleys anywhere in Wales. Murphy turns to me and grins. "At least Alwyn's gonna have a bathroom, Jimmy... that's more than you've got!"

With the passing of this rustic character, we all ease into a space for a little reflection, a cooling-off period. There's nobody here that's really bad, its just that sometimes, we are all capable of making mistakes, being stupid and forgetting to do things; none of us are perfect. "Sorry, fellahs... sorry love!" one of the workman mutters; the other two join in and they all come and shake our hands and we all thump each other on the shoulders, in a kind of affectionate anger-dispersal, fully aware that this day could so easily have turned into a nightmare, never to be forgotten.

The workmen clear the rocks and roots from the lane in assisting the postman to go on his way, leaving Cari, Murphy and myself in a befuddled state of wondering what the hell's happening to the world. My windscreen has taken a few hits but, miraculously, hasn't shattered, even though rocks have dented the roof. I confront my camera that is full of the earlier peaceful sleeping images of spiders' webs; it's in a sorry state, the lens-hood is bent and clogged with earth. When I examine it more closely, I get the unmistakable whiff of 'dog-stuff' and I can see that what I had taken for soil clogging the lens is, in fact, something a whole lot nastier!

Vengeance of a Stump!

By night, the plaintive notes of redwings call down from the darkness. Little newly arrived thrushes flying in the inky blackness in search of one thing only... food to keep them alive... berries.

Wouldn't it be so lovely if there were such an awareness and caring as to provide and safeguard a food supply for these brave little winter visitors... wouldn't it just!

The last Bramley apples fall from the tree and are gathered immediately and converted into crumbles, tarts and pies. Shaggy parasol mushrooms are also making a late showing and we gather them by the score. We've invented a method for carrying them, like stacking saucers, removing the stalks then laying them along the length of our arms. They have a lovely strong rubbery flavour and, as yet, haven't made any one of us feel ill. We're missing all our old hens and the contribution they made to our budget and also to our culinary variety, especially at times when there's a mushroom glut and an egg would make all the difference. Sykes never ever got the hang of egg laying, just as she can't get the hang of being a family pet, bless her. She's her usual obnoxious self in everything that she does; we've grown to accept her as being that way and continue regardless to treat her like royalty, despite her aloofness to such status. There's still no sign of the bantams; I can only conclude that the foxes took them during the night of the storm when they were possibly injured and provided easy-pickings. Oh, how I miss that early morning call from the barn roof; it was the cry that expressed so eloquently what our life here has been like. It's all so very silent now, apart from the bellowing of pedigree stud-dogs and the American jets playing their incurably diseased games of war.

Drowsy days that before would have been golden and leaf-strewn, hang hauntingly about us; late lazy wasps are burned alive in their parchment fortresses by the farm-gang with paraffin and matches. They're jumping for joy with the thrill of what they are doing and have, without a trace of regret, totally burned down our prolific damson tree as a result of them finding a wasps' nest in a hole at the base of the tree. There's nothing I can do to exercise any influence over them whatsoever, in fact, rather more to the contrary, it's getting to seem obvious that our conservation ideas and, in particular, recent confrontations with workmen, have established us up at the farm as being somewhat freakish, weirdo outsiders even. Nothing feels the same anymore, it's all so very, very sad.

With only six weeks remaining before my exhibition, I'm

working flat out on my paintings; I can't afford such luxuries as proper framing, so I have instead chosen to use cheap, thin strips of soft wood and am tacking it around my canvases. It's an honest compromise, very basic; in truth it doesn't look bad at all and I'm growing to feel okay about it.

November brings the first real frosts, an ominous reminder of hardships to come as winter inches nearer and our wood supply no longer there for the taking just outside the door. With the frosts, so too come the sparkling night skies, with my old friend Orion now boldly clawing back above the hill. Saddest thing of all, angels have called to take dear old Thomas to his heaven. He was all dressed up and ready to go by all accounts, in fact he'd been ready for some time; it was like waiting for a bus, a charabanc trip to the stars. His passing has stunned the hills to a new silence. He was such a beautiful little man, sweet, kind and so very gentle. I meet a brooding and deeply thoughtful old 'Weasel' in the lane; he's staring blindly across to 'Thimble Hall', the sad little cottage where the angels had been. He splutters a few utterances around his pipe-shaft, but I cannot for the life of me understand what he's saying, so we just nod in mutual agreement, "Oh aye... aye... oh aye!"

Dan isn't any too good either; his 'sniffle' has migrated to his chest and he's looking pale and gaunt; still with his shirt open down past his belly-button. He's taken old Thomas's death very badly as they had been close friends throughout life and had worked together back in the famous old days of real horse-power. No horses this time, the hearse is undeniably the smartest carriage that Thomas ever travelled in; just a short journey down to the valley and the little church that presides over the ancient river's oxbowed wanderings. A sorrowful gathering of people amongst the towering evergreens, standing best-shoed upon pale rainbowed confetti left strewn from a wedding. Joy and sorrow here expressed under the dull gaze of dozing ghosts, the carved names of old departed friends. Saints all of them, in solemn rows: old flowers, new flowers and salt spilling down little brooks on watching faces. The little widow is grim with grief and is supported by her son Dai, minus his dogs, gun and ferrets. Tears tiptoe as time flows on like the river in a ceaseless searching journey to the sea from whence it came, and will go on coming and going, coming and going forever.

It rubs salt into my wounds to see the mountain of wood that is destined to become ash in just a few minutes. All in the name of the bloke that tried to blow-up the Houses of Parliament, especially when I'm having to grovel, scraping the bottom of the barrel in confronting an escalating heating and cooking problem that's only just starting to come into focus. Gareth has uprooted one of the last remaining hedgerows up at the hill farm, a large part of which is here on the pile that's going to celebrate one of Western Civilization's first terrorists. Some would argue that the celebration was that of good triumphing over evil, but I'm not convinced and am persuaded into the belief that there's a bit of pyromania lurking deep down within the species, and they simply welcome any old excuse whatsoever for a frightening blaze and a whole lot of explosions, the thrill of things being fiercely obliterated into smithereens or burned inexorably into dust.

Having got rid of his trees, Gareth is now having to buy timber from the Forestry, just in order that his 'sheep-prairie' may have its miles of barbed-wire fences. He has piles of Sitka-spruce posts just waiting to be pointed by his tractor-driven circular saw, the most fearful hell of an invention imaginable. The very sound of this thing strikes terror into my soul whenever I hear it; what it does is even more frightening, as horribly proves to be the case. Gareth is working slavishly, as is normal for him, pipe in mouth and this dreadful circular saw under full power before him. As a timber, Sitka is very knotty and one has to be extra vigilant and firm when offering a piece of it to a saw-blade that's whirring round at almost the speed of light. Just one slack moment, that's all it takes for that offered piece of wood to be instantly transformed into a missile. In one blinding flash, Gareth has a large stump of wood, at the speed of a bullet, hitting him flush in the middle of his face!

There's calamitous bedlam; poor Hugh is stuck between prioritizing shutting-off the tractor saw, or rushing to help his father who is lying bleeding in the dirt. He screams for help and Gwyneth, with a baby in her arms, comes running out and she sees red, the same unmistakable red that she's seen a thousand times before. She phones for an ambulance and poor Gareth misses the fireworks.

It's no less than a miracle that he has survived, most others would not have done so; Gareth just so happens to be tougher than timber, a kind of walking resilience that causes even the weather to show respect. Mercifully, news from the hospital says that he's going to be alright, just busted cheekbones and a smashed nose, that's all; he'll still be able to pull a cracker at Christmas and blow cigar smoke down his crumpled nose!

One creature that won't be celebrating Christmas is the old sow, she's miraculously evolved into bacon now, cancerous growth an' all! If animals could speak, no-one would ever eat them; I suppose the same could be said of a cabbage, but a cabbage doesn't bleed like a pig bleeds, or a cow or a sheep, or a hare. Warm, red blood is that which unites us in our somewhat contradictory cannibalistic way, not our language; I could no more converse with a cow as a cow could converse with me, yet all things do converse in ways that are special to them. Ours, by comparison, seems a degree contrived in that it is perplexingly different from country to country, whilst a robin speaks the same wherever it is, as does a sheep. There's no doubting the fact that we are complex and, the more I think about this, the more I am drawn into wondering whether Mankind actually settled here upon this planet. Things go in circles, overlapping, repeating over and over. There are therefore behavioural circles, repetition being proof statement of an eternal pattern. Just as mankind is, through the splendour of mathematics, trying to discover ways of leaving this lovely Earth planet, it is possible therefore, that so too could he have arrived upon it; this is the very nature of circles. It may also help explain how asteroid impacts that caused ice-ages, dark-ages, tidal waves and volcanic catastrophes, wiping out at a stroke, the age of dinosaurs, woolly mammoths and virtually everything else... yet, by some strange magic, spared primitive man from such ultimate wrath. It would make more sense to consider that he was not here at that time. Theories of his having crawled out from the sea and becoming an ape-like something or other, are as far-fetched as 'Gulliver's Travels' or 'Alice in Wonderland'. If that were the case, it would have been equally possible for the dinosaurs to have taken to the sea and, by similar magic, becoming whales. So, what's to stop them from getting fed-up with that arrangement and coming back out onto the land again and 'evolving' back into dinosaurs? The mind boggles!

Why, dammit... we could even revert back to being monkeys, (some might argue that this is already happening!) and then into something else that lived in the sea... after all, things go in circles, circles, ever-repeating in timeless pattern!

November is now dropping over us like a church roof in the night; even the rain feels like lead as it uncaringly saturates us, pausing only so's to allow cruel frosts to hammer nails into things. It's particularly depressing for the boys who both leave and return in the biting half-light and over a gaping, open, hedgeless and treeless world surrounding us. Cari and I are becoming concerned about how their life is now being affected by recent drastic changes, and so, to address these concerns, I am consulting the job market once more, either for work back in television, or some lecturing back in an Art College; preferably somewhere nice.

With Gareth being in hospital, Cari has been helping Gwyneth up at the farm, enabling her to visit him in his facially mummified state. Without having the ferocious gaffer bellowing and wielding his leather strap about the place, there's a new sense of freedom itching to be scratched and the kids are all having a field day. They've turned the 'David Brown' tractor into a nursery toy, all of them having a go at driving it, causing poor Hugh to go out of his mind in just trying to keep them off it, but he has a hundred and one jobs to do and so his back is always turned. Elwyn has taken it upon himself to provide 'vermin-control', and is once more absent from school and prowling the dank, dark undulations with his pockets full to bulging with cartridges, and his thin, grubby fingers clutching the lusty, rusty twelve-bore. 'Billy the Kid' couldn't hold a candle to this rampantly wild young Celt who, beyond any question whatsoever, shoots first then asks the questions... if at all. No robin, wren, tit, finch, thrush or blackbird is safe from him, and he merges into the November gloom, an outlaw through and through.

With all authority here gone, it's easy to imagine how there could be a drift away from the hard-won refinements of our inventive technology, and a sinking back into the grasp-and-grab, dog-eat-dog, free-for-all that's so dispossessed the American Indian, the Australasian Aborigine and others, gunpowder winning every time... and of course, being blessed by some or other version of the 'Almighty', as has been and still is, the case with every such rape, plunder and butchery upon this planet!

Fireworks no longer have owls to frighten up at the hill farm, they've gone along with the trees. The bonfire makes its threatening statement, a kind of nuclear testimony, a demonstration of menacing, awesome power before an imagined alien 'something' that really doesn't exist... unless of course that threat comes from moles or rats, sparrows or starlings. However, moles are sleeping, rats are squeaking, snug as bugs in ricks, sparrows and starlings oblivious and at peace in eaves; the fire rages upon itself.

Blind wind rattles the tin on the Dutch-barn; 'Aunty Rita's' glitzy, fake jewels rattle, 'Uncle Mostyn' rattles boastingly over the cost of his protruding belly, lavishing as much name-dropping as he can muster in elevating him from being a nobody, into becoming a somebody. No-one has ever been able to tell him that fertile brains cannot be purchased and that, Rolex watches on wrists and gold rings on fingers, hold no persuasion whatsoever over the quality of prayer. There is no hiding place for sadness, the painful truth of non-achievement when the desire for status dwarfs all else. And so, with the state of humbleness being totally out of the question, any refuge of worth is hard to find; some choose patriotism, others, money, both of them adequately backed of course by gunpowder, together with the fourth 'R' that best suits their particular greeds.

Driving rain, Gareth in hospital with his face bandaged without provision made for his pipe of peace to reach his hungry lips, a dismal conclusion settles upon the celebration. Late fireworks mutter upon deaf ears and blind eyes, although the children are always able to find fun and they play like kittens play... it's the old cat that has to do the killing. Celebrations sour but, oddly, nobody's really complaining, just gloomily subdued and not really belonging to anything that's being said, as though waiting for a better life, believing that the bus will be along shortly.

It hardly seems possible that, in what seems only like weeks ago, daylight almost circumnavigated this tree adorned heaven of ours; it's all so very different now, with darkness doing what the light had previously done. I cannot see to paint as the foul, cold wet weather eats what miserable bit of light there is; we've even had to resort to having candles burning in the daytime and our precious paraffin is taking a cruel hammering too, as it additionally provides a little warmth as well as light about the place.

Financial hardship is rapidly becoming a monster in our midst once more, making any trip to town a rucksack-on-the-back, long distance slog each time. Next to money, sharing the very bottom line, is firewood. Whether I like it or not, every single day I must find time to go wood collecting... not such an easy job in a desert! I have systematically sorted out all the wood from the part of the barn that was blown down and have bagged the last of the ancient cow-dung... not a lot, but every little helps. In addition to this, I have boldly decided to salvage what wood I can from the caravan and then dismantled the rest of it. Emrys at the garage, has asked for the thin metal outer-skin; he says that he'll find a use for it and I'm not going to argue with that, so I set to work on the messy business.

It's all so very sad; it never was a palace at the best of times, but it's heartbreaking nevertheless, all these precious little memories being surgically cut to pieces and removed forever. The boys are also very unhappy to see it go, it was their gypsy world within a bigger world that's shrinking as they grow up into it.

It's rather ironic that I cannot survive as an artist or as a gypsy either! Honourable failure is really the hallmark of something that's in decline. Honourable though failure may be for some, for me it's nowhere near as good as glorious success. Being the best is far more desirable and satisfying than being second best could ever be, and I take pride and satisfaction from striving to dredge the very best out of myself at all times. I'm not in a race, or competing with any other person other than my own, solitary true self. Being born was the ultimate privilege, life presenting the greatest challenge. I have to be the best, the very, very best that I can possibly be for the sake of my mother and father who made me, and for all the countless trillions of mothers and fathers before them. We here are the flowering blooms of our separate, deep, dark root-system histories; it is we who carry the scent and colour and shape and dreams of what everyone before us has ever reached for. There is glory to be had in roots, the same glory that we sow in our seeds.

New Friends from the South

Dog-foxes bark beneath the dim stars as, thin-veiled clouds race and a half-moon comes and goes, showing us our terrifying place within the heavens; rather more than that of being cocooned and encapsulated in cosy villages, towns and all the things that blind us to the awareness of being creatures of the Universe. Butterflies of tomorrow are but hard-skinned, twitching things suspended in death-black forgotten corners. My mind bursts when I wonder how such dazzling, brightly pigmented rainbow colours are here now being born in total blackness!

I'm starting to get little shivers and flushes of excitement over my forthcoming exhibition at Gregynog, the marvellous place where some of the finest Impressionist paintings once graced the walls and where the composer Holst came to dream about Planets, and where the works of George Bernard Shaw were finely printed on the famous Press. I feel such a glow of pride to be even the minutest dust-particle of the history of this amazing place, even though I'm having to starve my way to this moment and have to work by candlelight. My father would have been so proud; he was an artist too, but he died young of cancer. He endured a miserable life of poverty, winning a scholarship to study Fine Art at the Slade, only to have poverty deny him from taking it up. Instead finding himself being put in what was then known as 'The Workhouse' where, an accident on a farm removed, of all things, his fingers! I owe my beloved dad so much; this exhibition is going to be for him.

I've fixed the old repaired roof rack onto the van, knowing that my largest pictures won't fit inside it. My very large painting of 'The Last Supper'. currently has swallow-shit all over it, as too has my horrific image of souls begging for help at the National Assistance Board, as it was known back in my early Plymouth days. It's an untitled painting showing naked, decrepit figures at the mercy of a mouth in a hole in the wall, screaming out their numbers. In all honesty, I'm afraid to exhibit these, I probably never will. It isn't that I'm ashamed of having painted them, but more of being disgusted at having been driven to paint them in the first place. They're amongst the best, most powerful things I will ever paint in my life, but I feel shall always remain deeply personal and private.

Wandering off to start my day, bog-roll in hand and spade on my shoulder isn't easy anymore; there's no longer any seclusion or privacy, but I still prefer it to squatting over a bucket in a pigsty. Digging a hole and then burying it, is the next best thing to a flush toilet; the very notion of being able to see the motion of the person before you, is both obnoxious and disgusting to me; it's bad enough having to bury the bloody stuff!

When I walk the boys to school, I wear a tracksuit and running shoes, usually managing a ten-miler before properly starting my day. Hard though this is to explain, it's the best, most rewarding hour of my entire day, I'd be lost without it. I simply have to be fit to stay on top of the umpteen heavy demands that living here presents me with, and I count myself lucky that I derive such pleasure from the process of staying fit.

Far hills ride white and the first snow of winter dusts the surrounding fields after a period of frost has temporarily suspended the mud which was getting to be a misery. This is a far nicer kind of cold, even though it's a lot colder than its predecessor, backed by a thinner wind that whistles instead of rumbling. Out from the thin Easterly, a sound that's every bit as heartening as that of the first cuckoo in Spring... "Damn you, you bloody stupid bitch!" The blasphemous song of Dan treading the first powdered snowfall, as he climbs the summit of his private mountain to brush up on his maths in the counting of sheep, assisted to the point of chronic hindrance, by his overjoyed mongrel who scatters the entire flock out of sight in every conceivable direction, producing this heart-rending call that the entire hills and valleys have been mourning for. He's back in business, raw, rough and raucous and we are glad to hear the sweet music riding the air again. There's no keeping a good man down, and I have a little chuckle to myself, a picture of Dan up there on the barbaric hill, wearing only a pair of badly moth-eaten long-johns and wellies rolled down.

Every little such thing helps us in our hanging on to this dream, as too has our continued defiant planting of trees, keeping us sane in the knowledge that, without having any money at all, hopes of having a job away somewhere is a virtual impossibility due to our poverty having fallen below recognised poverty levels. I'm not unfamiliar with this, I've been through it before when, upheaval was a financial non-starter and the cost of getting to work hardly equalled the money earned; with the additional low punch of the Inland Revenue then looming up in what I have termed as the 'State Steamroller'. The only phenomenon known to be able to extract blood from a stone!

Any glory that defiance offers is short-lived; jets with missiles strapped to their bellies and, sinister brown envelopes with windows together make sure that a poor man can't run back and become the gypsy that he no doubt once was, even though he may attempt to do this from time to time. I'm both proud and ashamed of being an artist, and I both curse and love whatever it was that fixed me, as in a disease to a language which isn't largely recognised. It's a disease with no known cure but, fortunately, doesn't appear to be catching!

By now our swallows are back in Africa, it's just a holiday for them, after first having had to survive the massive journey and all the hazards and setbacks along the way. For just a tiny handful of them, their home is now our borrowed home here in the cowshed; we are simply the guardians, keeping it safe until they return next Spring. It's a place that we also share with a tribe of mice, who have moved back into their ancient family home behind the busted iron fireplace. They proudly and boldly come out for exercise periods, providing a curiosity that has rapidly grown into an entertainment for Spibby, and her growing son, Tiger, who watches them with the fascination of children watching television for the very first time. We get the occasional long-distance mouse off on a marathon around the room, cheered every inch of the way by the cats. Robin has placed little feeding stations along the route, pointing out, "If we feeds them, they won't eat our food." He's catching on fast! Another family that has returned to the wall behind the food cupboard in the lean-to, are of a wilder genetic line, being blessed with no social graces whatsoever. They're fit, fast and lean, possessing of a certain hostility, unlike their 'yuppie' cousins in the hearth, who actually have the audacity to come out sunbathing while the flames glow and the irons heat-up and the entire balmy, decadent air full of the health-giving ozone's of food that's being baked in the place which they regard as being their 'cathedral'.

I've never seen Spibby smile or dribble so much; she wouldn't eat a mouse if you paid her to, her feline instincts are brought alive only by birds, alas. The good news is that she's now, as near as dammit, mastered the litter-tray, settling on a comprise that I've been persuaded into accepting, that of crapping on the floor beside it and then scraping the sand from the tray to cover it up... well, partially so.

Poor Sykes, meanwhile, she's roosting all alone in the spud-shed; dereliction could not be more painfully expressed. The only morsel of comfort that I can find comes from the knowledge that she was always an antisocial loner, an antagonistic and cussedly solitary so and so, the very characteristics that prevented her from being crushed along with the rest. The spud-shed is far more cosy than ever the barn was and no foxes can get in once the door has been fastened. Slenderly comforting as this may be, I still feel sorry for her and I wish that I could do more. Bringing her into the cowshed would be disastrous, even Robin would agree with me over this. I've weighed-up all options ... she's a loner and that's the way it's going to stay, perhaps the way she wishes it to remain.

Sad though it is, I honestly can't see her lasting the winter out, she must be feeling the cold terribly because, even at the best of times, she's bald and more than a bit messy around her backside. Her remaining feathers are in a poor condition; it doesn't help them by being white either, not the best conductor of heat. If Robin could catch her, I know she'd be wearing a pair of his old pants by now! Even though she's got plenty of straw and a warm, straw filled hutch to roost in, her preference is to roost on top of it, out in the cold... she's impossible!

Gareth has now come out of hospital; he looks like he's done fifteen rounds in a boxing ring and wished he'd not bothered. To say he's a changed man is an understatement, his nose has been completely flattened and rearranged and his cheek-bones are still very swollen and bruised. He can still manage a smile and is now able to grip his pipe and puff clouds of sweet-smelling smoke for the east wind to lacerate to shreds. He won't be feeling much like taking convalescent recreational pleasure with his twelve-bore thinning crows, buzzards and peewits... not just yet a while anyway. So, Elwyn's plundering of his cartridge store may well go undetected.

It isn't long before he's back to his old self, screaming at beasts and boys once more and breaking sticks over cows' behinds. Poor Hugh, he gets no praise, he never has and he never will, yet his weight and worth could be measured in gold. He's a lovely, honest and hardworking boy who has aged twenty years beyond his rightful place in time. This place offers him no escape or any choice whatsoever; he grafts like a slave from first-light to last-light and well beyond, for seven --- or is it nine days a week? Being the eldest son has done him no favours; his younger brothers will be more fortunate and will have learning to seduce them away to safety and to more fruitful flowerings. The girls don't face these problems, they are beautiful, bright and sensible as girls usually are; it's the male that never performs in the classroom... always preferring to do so at the back of the bike-shed!

Instead of resting as the doctor suggested, Gareth is up and running, albeit in that of a leisurely landowner sort of way, driving around his brand new, gapingly open estate, his 'short-back-and-sides' chunk of Earth. He comes over our way in his Landrover and takes note of the storm damage to our barn, then strangely vanishes without even coming in for a 'hello' or a cup of tea. A couple of days later he re-appears, on foot this time, with a stranger. They're standing some distance away and he's pointing in our direction with his stick, then strolling down to examine the waterlogged driveway, which originally connected us to the lane. I look at Cari and she looks at me, but we say nothing.

Much to our surprise and totally out of the blue, Rosie turns up with two friends plus an aging golden Labrador. We are introduced to Pippa and John, Rosie's colleagues from University, who also happen to live in fairly remote hill-country some twenty-five miles to the south of us. If ever there were two more like-minded people, I'd gladly eat a pair of Robin's socks... these two could never come closer! They have brought with them, wines which they have made and bread that's still warm from their oven, together with vegetables and herbs from their garden, which their neighbour tends to while they're away at University. We just get on like we've always known each other.

There's a lovely atmosphere with the boys at the very centre of things enjoying every minute; it's a carnival of babbling with an old dog called 'Jason', excitedly knocking things flying, even with the weight of Robin astride his back. My open sketch-book, which I had previously been working in, is trodden on by a very large and muddy paw print, right in the centre of what I was doing... it's wonderful. Our life has been enriched by these bursting seeds of moments now.

Their intrigue is drawn to my growing collection of paintings that I'm about to exhibit, and I simply cannot believe their response, I'm not used to handling such praise as this and so I discreetly escape out into the bald aftermath beyond the door and enjoy a long and exquisite pee behind what's left of the barn. My mind full of pleasurable feelings of how ordinary people are able to make life feel so worth living and I glow with a gladness of knowing that our friends could just about be classified as being neighbours. Cold air soon brings me down to earth and a large ewe is standing staring at me, just a few paces away; she's either full of questions or is totally lacking of any question whatsoever, as is the nature of sheep. All I know is that she's got bronchitis, or something a lot worse and she coughs with a disgusting and deep innocence, the awful sound being easily absorbed into the daylight, unlike as with the darkness of bleak night when their coughing sounds awesomely different and echoes far and wide.

Feeling frozen to the bones, I return indoors where my paintings are propped everywhere with an intense interest being shown in them. Dissecting my own paintings on request is something that I neither enjoy or value; I try as best I can to remain a stranger to my work and to move on as quickly as I possibly can. Too many answers tend to suffocate and deny the questions, when it's the questions that breathe life and open the doors; answers simply close them.

John and I are soon trapped in an involved discussion that gets so deep that it requires the others to tactfully come to the rescue with bounteous offerings of food and glasses of crystal wine. Rosie gives me a broad, flushed smile that tells me that the wine has already brought summer back amongst us.

To top things, before they leave, John insists on buying three of my paintings prior to them going on exhibition, putting me into a situation that I'm not familiar with, one which both embarrasses and flatters me. The equating of my brush marks and ideas into money makes me squirm; I feel strange and sort of sick inside. I'd far rather just give them as gifts and the lovely thing is that John understands how I'm feeling and writes a cheque and slips it into my pocket, sparing me the torture of having to see it.

We amble across the inky-black marsh, the pressure-lamp being rudely economical with the light that it's providing for us. It's just enough, not a glimmer more than that, attracting us to comment on it, contrasting this with the vulgar waste of power that turns night into day in towns and cities; providing the alibi for Nuclear Power to go on extracting weapon-grade plutonium for bomb making, while claiming to be the answer for producing electricity that's virtually too cheap for it to be calculated! The paraffin in the pressure-lamp is getting perilously low; I don't normally let it get to this stage for fear of it sucking up bits of dirt from the bottom of the cylinder and clogging it and suddenly going out. We shout our good-byes amid laughter over our predicament, then hurry back across the marsh in a race with the last drops of paraffin. The comforting realisation that we now have some money to buy paraffin is not the same as actually having paraffin, no matter how much of it our money can buy. Just as I feared... PHSsssss! We are in total blackness, surrounded by the bronchial orchestra of sheep. It's hilarious; here's me with a plump cheque in my pocket and it hasn't the power to help us find our way home in the dark! We all hold hands as I try to lead the way, climbing the hill until we're on the level and before it plunges steeply downhill in the wrong direction. Then... yippee... we see the dim glow of a candle-lit window down to our left and the smell of the wood fire that's still languishing in the grate. This place really is a treasure, our little home... it's all we've got and it feels marvellous just to click the latch and enter, then click it again and leave the world and all its problems outside.

Few things feel more decadently luxurious than filling my old van's tank with petrol. Mobility is very high on the list of priorities where the boys are concerned, and I have to respect this to the very best of my ability. Being seen to be up and running along with all the rest is very important to them; it makes things level and it doesn't matter that the van has a bull's-horn scar all along one side and large dents in the roof, from where rocks and roots fell out of the sky. In fact, these could easily pick up brownie points. Going off to town in the van is a great event, it's an act of triumph and we walk the streets with new pride in our step together with a soothing sense of being 'normal' again.

To my utter shock, I see a poster advertising my forthcoming exhibition and we all look at each other in goggle-eyed astonishment. Cari starts to laugh and we all join in with a feeling of suddenly being a little bit important. Having themselves had a good day, the street-traders have started to pack up; some would rather they have unsold produce dumped or fed to pigs, but a couple of others are more than glad to let us have it, rather than for it to go to waste. We load up with carrots, parsnips, swedes, cabbages, a cauliflower, sprouts, onions, battered tomatoes; even potatoes go into our bags... and it hasn't cost more than a few nominal pennies. It's amazing how different it feels to have sold three paintings, even though the cheque can't be paid into the bank until Monday. It's just the knowledge that is making all the difference, an illusion that will all too soon make way for harsh reality again.

The shop windows are full of Christmas things and the lights have come early as we make our way to the car park. On our way, we find Dan looking like he's been waiting to be found and he's more than glad of our offer of a lift; he looks frozen standing there in his town-clothes. Apart from a bottle-shaped lump in his coat pocket, he has no other evidence of having done any shopping; he even makes fun of the fact that we're all loaded down with stuff, reminding me that his trip to town is for purely social reasons, Masons delivering all the things that he needs, a sort of standing order.

In a celebratory gesture of seeing Dan up and about again, Cari says, "I bet you won't laugh at all this shopping if I invite you over tonight to help us eat it... a lovely stew and dumplings and lovely crusty bread with your favourite cheddar. What d'you say to that?" His eyes immediately sparkle, just like the twinkling Christmas lights in the windows, and he eagerly reaches out to take Cari's heavy bags. We both smile and the boys find it funny too; he's answered her question without resorting to a single word.

At this point, just as we are waiting to cross the busy road, I am spotted by Doctor Hughes and his wife from Gregynog... "Ah... just the man I want to see!" They come scuttling up close, making sure to be heard over the traffic. "Can you pop up to the hall sometime, Jim... we need to talk about your exhibition, lists of exhibits, titles, prices... that sort of thing. I shall also need to know how many guests you'll be bringing to the Private View... and whatever else." The sack of sprouts over my shoulder is getting to feel a bit heavy and is compromising me somewhat as I finalize an arrangement to drive out to Gregynog in the week. There are smiles and nods, good wishes galore, as we go our separate ways and I detect a trace of something from the past in Dan, a touch of 'master and servant' sort of thing. It must seem a little confusing to him that here we are chatting away to the people who happen to reside in one of the finest country mansions in the principality while, at the same time inviting him for a bowl of stew in a cowshed! He gives me the cold, questioning look that he's given me before and I try to smile reassuringly from my contorted position under my burden of sprouts, but to no effect.

We reach the van and the boys eagerly scramble into the back and stack all the bags, while Dan and Cari are involved in a light-hearted argument over who's going to sit where; Cari wants Dan to have the comfortable passenger seat next to me and for her to join the boys in the back. Try as she may, he adamantly refuses, causing quite a palaver, a bit like a spider-crab in a basket. Cari gives up as he flays and grapples his way into joining the boys at the livestock end. For them it's all one big laugh, they love a bit of drama, especially when there's a funny side. This is more like the Dan we've grown to know, he's back to form, effervescent in a continuous refusal to comply; when he says "No", he means "No!" When he says, "Yes", he means... "Maybe."

I start the engine amid great cheering then Dan's ranting voice dwarfs even the din that this is making. "What the hell d'you call this? I've been in better cattle-trucks!" There is bedlam, everyone's laughing and having to shout to be heard; it's the first time Dan has been in the van ... come to think, it's the first time I've driven him at all. With this in mind, I proceed at a very considerate and sedate pace, not wishing to provoke him in any way, and to minimise any discomfort he may be experiencing. A couple of cars overtake me as we glide along the tree-lined road and on down beneath stately beeches that tower over a graceful, snaking section of bends. I catch sight of bramblings amongst a flock of chaffinches that fly up from the beech-masted ground; I'm really enjoying this. I should have known better; this new-formed peace is too good to be true as... "You ain't driving to a funeral, for Christ's sake!" "I don't want to crack the eggs!" I reply, hoping that it might satisfy him. Instead it prompts him to bark back, "Eggs my arse! They'll be bloody hatching at this rate... this owd thing's knackered!" I give Cari a nudge as I shout... "Message received, have it your own way. Hold tight, boys... we're going a different way back home!" I turn off into an up and down, winding lane where the rally cars go, and put my foot down, bringing squeals of approval from the boys and an excited scream from Cari. This big Ford engine has a bit of a poke when it's aroused, and it sounds like it's enjoying it. Dan is the only one of us that isn't laughing as we hurtle upon the first hairpin which we take at just under forty, sending sprouts, kids, cabbages and carrots flying from right to left on the first bend, then, Dan, parsnips, onions, potatoes and tomatoes all flying the other way on the next. Cari is in hysterics as I charge along a brief open stretch, then have to drop down a couple of gears as we climb back up to buzzard country then joining another lane and a fast section with bumps and bends before a steep downhill with an extremely tight right-hander at the bottom. This is immediately followed by another steep climb up to a horizon that we're supposed to recognise. I slow off, much to the disapproval of the boys who are all shouting... "Come on, Jimmy! Come on... come on!" Over a quieter engine, I shout back to Dan... "Do you still think this is a hearse?" and he splutters back... "I'll bloody soon be in one at this rate!"

Glad as he is, Dan doesn't show it as I drop him off under his big, bare sycamore tree. Cari gives him a hug, he knows that deep down that we all love him, whatever his confusions. I try to catch his eye because I know that, what may seem like anger in him is just a sham; old as he may be, he's just a mardy kid at times. I catch his eye and he can hide no longer; his smile betrays him comprehensively and he's back to his crafty, wicked old self again. The bottle of rum in his pocket is still intact after his introduction to rallying; I daren't imagine what state the rest of him might be in, but I have a sneaking suspicion that he might have a bit of washing to do before coming over for the banquet that we're going to prepare for him.

A Head of Steam and a Whiff of Fox

Darkness takes no prisoners as she clamps down upon every single thing, requiring neither screw nor nail to assist her overall dominance. We poke little holes with our torches but whatever we may do is futile against this beast that's as big as half the world and bigger yet. We light our candles and I refuel the lamps and clear for ourselves a little place within the darkness and then snuggle into it. My boys are great; it's a joy just watching them rally round in making this cowshed feel like it's the Ritz.

While Cari prepares the vegetables by candlelight in the lean-to, I head off with the pressure-lamp to the well, trusting the boys to get the fire started. I can hear the redwings in the black sky and I wish that I had their nocturnal sight, instead of having to use power-generated light, which I then throw at things. As I scoop up the crystal water, I have a whole load of stuff raging in my brain, wondering why it is that redwings, owls, foxes and badgers can see in the dark while I can't. Surely it would be cheaper to develop infra-red spectacles than it is to make light from the burning of fossil fuels and the costly development of nuclear power; throwing light at things is not the same as being able to see in the dark. Distracted by my thoughts, I get the hood of my jacket caught up in the barbed-wire, just as I'm accepting the fact that the light that we get in the daytime is light that's been thrown by the sun, just as the light that I'm seeing by to disentangle my hood, is thrown by my paraffin lamp.

Cussedly, I make my way back, still wishing I had infra-red glasses to see by. There's a joyful pandemonium when I return; Cari's going great guns with the vegetables in the kitchen, but the sofa's on fire in the other room and... would you believe it... I'm the only one that has the water to put it out! I return to the well.

I'm somewhat less full of beans as I scoop up the water this time, gloomily wondering what we're going to do with our lives that's meaningful, creative and productive. I realise with a growing sadness that, where we are now is but a stepping-stone along the way and can never be an end in itself. I'm mindful that the boys need horizons, without too many obstacles in the way. Truth is, we're penniless; both Cari and I come from a long line of church-mice, a status that cloaks us in unspeakable limitations, no matter how grand our dreams may be. I have no desire to further the mythical belief that successful artists are usually the dead ones! Back at the cowshed, I drag the dripping sofa to one side; it isn't too badly burned, I caught it just in time, even though the mess I have created looks as though it might have been a slight over-reaction. We must now resort to our original seating arrangement, that of the plank of wood across two concrete blocks. I ask the boys how the fire started and it transpires that they had become rather carried away by the different explosive qualities of the various types of wood, a competition that very soon had sparks flying everywhere. The fire in the grate has now been subdued by ancient cow-dung as the potatoes go into the 'mouse-cathedral' to be baked and the boys once more settle with the cats in the gentle flickering firelight as they all engage in a less hazardous dialogue with our hearth-mice.

There's no peace for the wicked! Cari comes up and presents me with the empty water-carrier and I have to trudge off yet again into the inhospitable darkness. It's bitterly cold and overcast and there are no stars tonight. I can see Murphy's light like a mirage ghosting across the valley, tantalizingly conveying to me a picture of a glowing wood-burning stove and windows that have been opened to let some of the heat out. Closer to, my watering eyes fall on the pale, dim smudge of light beyond our double-layered polythene, and a sudden wind whips up and I see stray sparks amongst what's being whipped from the remains of our chimney. Winter is toying with us; there are all manner of nasty little things filling her basket of surprises and I can almost hear the thin, sly wind sniggering as it shakes the solitary bush that shrouds the well.

Dan is fortunate... he's apparently got infra-red eyes as well as a nose for homing-in on a good stew. He and I very nearly collide in the yard when I'm hurrying back from the well. "Damn!" he yells... "you gave me a fright. I thought you was a bloody ghost!" He covers his eyes with his hands, pretending to be dazzled by my lantern. "Sorry, Dan," I laugh apologetically. "I think that all the ghosts moved out of here some while back... too damp and draughty here for them!" He grins as my light catches a devilish glint in his eye as he mutters, "Orh, you think so do you? I wouldn't be so sure about that if I were you!" "Are you trying to tell me there's something that I don't know about?" I reply with a laugh and, just as Cari is opening the door to let us in, Dan replies firmly... "There's a lot of things that I knows that you don't know!"

Cari gives me a puzzled frown and then greets Dan with a welcoming hug and a smile, then laughs, "...It didn't take you long to get changed! The potatoes are in the oven and the stew is on its way." He sniffs the air and I immediately know what he's thinking; the rank smell of the burnt sofa is still dominating all other smells. "We've had a minor accident," I hasten to point out, trying to get in first before he has time to make some derogatory remark about the stew. "The boys have unfortunately set the sofa alight... that's what you can smell!" An uncharacteristic flush of diplomacy briefly trespasses over him and he smiles broadly and chuckles... "Well, I know'd it wasn't Cari's stew... that's always nice that is... 'specially with them lovely dumplin's in it."

We shuffle our way ditheringly into the other room, where Rowan is busy mopping the floor; Robin has claimed his place on the settle, right up next to the oven and with both cats drooling in close attendance. Spencer meanwhile is still utterly mesmerised by the fire and is prodding it inquisitively with the poker, still hungry to see what it yet might come up with. I glance across at Dan and give him a big wink and say, "Dan reckons that we might have a ghost... isn't that right, Dan!" He nods his head as a grave authoritative expression straightens his face. There's an abrupt, loud clanking sound... Spencer has dropped the poker and is staring wildly, mouth agape... he looks like he's just seen a ghost! To add fuel to the fire, Cari makes her own theatrical contribution to the subject and issues forth a witch-like howling noise and does a balletic sort of scuttling dance, arms outstretched, swooping on poor Spencer who is definitely not amused. Robin is in fits... the more ghosts the merrier as far as he's concerned; Rowan just smirks, he knows it's probably going to be another of those nights.

Being aware of Dan's fondness for rum and ginger wine, I

have kept a secret supply hidden away amongst our own diminishing stocks of homemade wine in the bedroom. There's no way that I would risk the last of the elderflower on him, I'd be having to carry him home if I did. Anxious for Spencer's sake to get away from the subject of ghosts, I pour Dan a large glass of his favourite tipple and his face lights up like a sunrise; "Now you're talkin'!" he laughs, as Cari joins him and me by the fire. "Toast!" she shouts, interrupting his first gluttonous swig, causing him to choke briefly before himself proposing... "Here's to the ghost of Cari's cowshed. Cheers!"

Robin's rattling laughter provokes Spencer into whacking him, sending the cats scattering and Robin into a sprawling heap at Dan's feet. "Ghosts ain't funny, Robin!" Spencer yells at him, but Robin just lies back on the hard floor howling with laughter which sets Dan off barking his own dog-laugh, in turn triggering Cari and Rowan to complete the pandemonium. "Come on, Spence," I say offering a comforting arm around his shoulder; "Take no notice of Dan; there's no such thing, ghosts don't exist... he's just making it up." My words arouse a response from Dan, and he growls, "Oh, and what do you know about it, mister know-all?" His face still has a trace of a grin amongst its ruggedness, he's been itching to have a bit of a go at me for some time and he's not going to stop now, until he's adequately satisfied. He proceeds, "I've seen it with my own eyes... not just one, two of 'em there is." Cari's owlish ghost-noises temporarily interrupt him, but he presses on regardless... "One of 'em's an owd grey-headed woman... red flaring eyes an' crooked fingers... and no teeth. The other one's a hound... a great big grizzly owd dog!" I grin and say, "That sounds exactly like you and your dog, Dan!" and Cari shrieks with laughter, touching Dan just to make sure he's real. "Dan's not real... he's a ghost!" she jokes, bump-starting his own laugh again and causing him to spill what's left of his drink. Poor Spencer looks more confused than before and keeps muttering ... "It's not funny," over and over, as I take Dan's glass and refill it for him.

Having already mopped the floor and cleared some of the junk away, Rowan's interest shifts to the model steam traction engine, which was a previous Christmas present, and has been an ornament ever since. Spencer is glad to join him and together they fill it with water. I provide the meths which I use for starting the pressure lamps, then they get it lit and kneel quietly waiting for something to start happening. Lovely food smells are emanating from the kitchen as a more peaceful atmosphere settles around the hearth where Dan has at long last got himself settled on the plank as he watches in anticipation; it's gone so quiet that I can hear the cats purring.

Still feeling a touch nervous, Spencer timidly whispers, "It's gone a bit quiet in here," his large eyes fidgeting slightly, prompting an immediate response from Robin who rasps an ear-splitting fart and takes on the look of a cherub. "Robin!" Spencer scolds, showing his disgust, and quick as a flash, Robin shouts back, "It wasn't me … it was the ghost!" Dan hoots with laughter and almost overbalances, then suddenly and without warning, the traction engine explodes from the starting grid in a great hissing plume of steam and goes rocketing at almost the speed of light across the room, making straight for Dan. There's a spontaneous, raucous cheering as it goes scorching underneath a startled Dan, unceremoniously up-ending him, arse-over-tip from his plank, before crashing head-on into the fender! Cats fly absolutely anywhere amidst a din that would awaken even the ghosts from slumber. Cari comes rushing in to see what she's missing and sees a wild-eyed Spibby halfway up the heavy curtains, clinging on for dear life; the very next thing she sees is Dan, groveling about on the floor with a plank on his back. The boys are all in tears of laughter and finding it necessary to hold on to anything that's handy to save them from collapsing; this is the second glass of rum that Dan has spilled!

The noise gradually abates, but there are so many ribs that are aching, Dan's unfortunately being the only ones that aren't aching from laughter. Over the cow-dung fire, white steam is sweetly celebrating from the spout of our blackened kettle; the crashed steam engine remains intact but is still steaming as Rowan attempts to rescue it. It's still far too hot to be handled and so he resorts to shoveling it up, then putting it to cool off on the ice-cold floor over by the window. I drag the table over to the hearth and Cari brings in a large saucepan of steaming stew, followed by a basket of bread and a large slab of cheese. I remove the broken oven door and the smell of baked potatoes is as friendly as an Indian Summer, as the pungent heat-wave makes the entire hearth so very cosy. We settle to a most marvellous, simple meal in the candlelight as the mice come out and sunbathe.

Dan has shed his old antagonisms and is at peace, sombre and thoughtful, revealing for the first time his dislike of all that's been happening hereabouts over the last month or two. In particular, the big new modern red brick 'thing' that's being thrown-up between Meg's house and his. "Poor Meg, dammit; her's had all her driveway dug up... turned it all into a mud-bath they have, never did see a house thrown up so quick. Owd Murphy's been bawlin' and shoutin' at 'em... but that don't do no good. They've got the downstairs windows in already... Owd Thomas'd turn in 'is grave if he knowed what they was doin'!"

I've never seen Dan so serious or so thoughtful; it's plainly his world too that's been hi-jacked by events that have taken the birds away at a stroke, leaving behind an emptiness that offers neither beauty or comfort. "There's always been trees 'ere for as long as I can remember... damn, it used to be real nice!"

I never saw Dan looking sad before; his deeper concerns are revealing a more lovable person. Be that as it may, he still thinks of me as being mad, especially where 'Art' is concerned. "Damn! Why can't you paint summat proper... summat real?" he curses, and I do my best to explain that, that's precisely what I try to do. He just laughs and there's nothing that's ever going to change him over this. He even rages on to say that he thinks that the person who's just bought three of my paintings is every bit as mad as I am. As for my exhibition that's coming up in a few days ... this is all the proof he needs to confirm that the world's gone completely mad! What both irritates and throws him into confusion is that Cari loves what I do and readily identifies with what I try to express. Not just in paint but in my writing too, whether this be on the wall over the fireplace or in my books. She has been an unfailing source of support and inspiration throughout our somewhat 'off-centre' passage through life.

We all wrap up warm to see Dan back home safely and I give the lamp a few extra pumps to bring the pressure up and make sure there's enough paraffin in it to get us there and back. In addition to this, Spencer has a torch to help ease his recently troubled nerves. Normally, there'd be owls hooting all about the place but, as we stand listening in the yard, the only sounds breaking the deathly silence are the occasional bronchial utterances of sheep, strewn far and wide across the bare blackness... it's all really rather spooky.

As we are slowly making our way up the slope, I catch the unmistakable whiff of a fox; Cari has picked up on it too, a rubbery, rancid smell and we all briefly stop so that everyone may latch-on to this elusive stink. As they are all sniffing away like 'Bisto-kids', the most eerie, blood-curdling scream violates the air from over in the direction of my parked van; it's the most sustained and terrifying noise imaginable, especially coming out of pitch-blackness. I am very nearly enforced to let go of the lamp as my entire family come clutching on to me, stiff with fear everyone of them. I stagger in regaining my stability, noticing that Dan has been struck dumb and stiff. There's a brief stunned silence before, only a short distance away on the opposite side, three loud, shrill barks of a dog-fox. We can clearly hear his heavy breathing and the pounding of his paws, as he comes in a race up the hill and streaking phantom-like across our path, barking again as the awful screaming starts up once more, deep and long.

We stand all ears and hearts pounding. "It's the ghost!" Dan mutters, "now do you believe me?" There's a lot of fidgeting and Spencer stutters... "I...I w. want to g.g.g.go home!" almost tugging me off balance. I hasten to set his frightened mind at rest and say, "It's alright... it's okay Spence; take no notice of Dan. It's only a vixen, that's the noise they make when they are mating ... think yourself lucky to have heard it." He remains petrified and hasn't a clue what a vixen is anyway. "Vixen, my arse!" Dan mutters barely above a breath, while surreptitiously back-tracking until he's so close to the paraffin-lamp that I have to suddenly snatch it away for fear of his coat catching fire.

The barks are now getting closer to the source of the screaming, and then all suddenly goes quiet. We stand listening awhile then I say quietly... "I don't think we'll be hearing from them yet awhile ... they're bonking, not barking now! Come on you lot, this won't do, we've got to see Dan back." I try to move but Spencer's firmly rooted to the spot and he won't let go. "I ain't going! There's no way, no way!" Robin is nudging Rowan, starting him off sniggering, and they too won't move. Cari is most decisive. "Give me the lamp, you take the torch and see Dan safely back; I'll go back with the boys … it's way past their bedtime anyway."

They hurriedly say goodnight to Dan and go scurrying back down to the safety of the cowshed, leaving Dan and I to follow the rancid trail of the dog-fox. My torch is none too good as we plod steadily on across the blind marsh. I can tell that Dan is a bit scared, his bravery left him when Cari turned back with the boys. I'm enjoying a secret smile over the fact that I've not managed to coax a single word from him all the way over to the lane; something which turns out to our advantage when, on sweeping my beam across the opposite hillside, I fasten onto the four shining eyes of a pair of foxes stuck fast together, unable and unwilling to budge an inch. Dan gasps, "Well I'll be buggered! If I had my owd gun I could get them both with the same shot!" I try to distract him as I mutter; "C'mon Dan; a fox's got to do what a fox's gotta do, don't be a spoilsport," and I head off up the lane before he thinks about foraging for a stone to throw.

Kippers at an Exhibition
and the final Broken Promise

It's another stark grey morning as I drive out to the Hall for my meeting with the Bursar. Over coffee and biscuits we get everything sorted, it's a load off my mind. I take the opportunity of having a long look at the Music Room where the exhibition will be hung; it really does feel rather daunting that I shall be filling this large space where really great paintings once hung and it occurs to me that getting everything hung properly will be no easy job. Much to my relief, Dr. Hughes points out that there'll be someone laid-on to assist me, setting my mind to rest still further by saying that we'll have two whole days at our disposal.

It's a somewhat crazy and hectic time at the cowshed, a weird and wild mixture of ingredients dominated by always having to provide firewood and, with all of our own stocks used up, this means going much further afield to find it and to cart it back. On top of this, I somehow must find the time to get on with my painting, getting everything ready for hanging. It's been nerve-racking as well as a trifle on the cold side to say the least. For the boys, going to bed a bit on the early side has certainly helped them keep warm and conserve fuel, but also has rather hindered the situation. I am awakened at death-black dead of night by a sudden fracas downstairs and I discover my wide-awake son, Robin, a white paper-bag on his head and a torch fixed somehow down his pyjama top, shining light upwards, making his disgustingly contorted face seem like the very ghost that Dan dreamed up, awakening Spencer and his sickening yell then waking everyone else up.

Robin is certainly back in his element, he loves a bit of devilment... so long as he's not on the receiving end... it's a whole new ball game then. It isn't much fun for Spencer, but I can't help seeing the funny side and it's helping us all forget about the cold. I'm really having to reconsider my priorities and I question the sanity of having this exhibition at all. Providing warmth for my family is far higher up my list than hanging pictures on walls ever could be.

I'm in a confusion of guilt and nervous trepidation as Cari and I begin the process of loading up the van with canvases. All this 'weird', brightly coloured stuff pouring out from a dark and forgotten cowshed, while a northeast wind shows no respect whatsoever for the larger canvases, as we cart them, one at a time, across the marsh; making us aware of the awesome power of wind over sail, forcing us to tack our way, just like a sailing boat into safe harbour. After a while of struggling against the elements, I catch an opportune sight of Murphy, and I whistle him to assist us in securing the largest canvas to the very same roof-rack that failed me before. He comes galloping with the grace of a carthorse, down the slope almost finding it impossible to stop, having misjudged the steepness of the hill in his eagerness to help. It's almost like a circus act as he narrowly avoids going through the large canvas and thumps noisily into the side of the van. "This wind's nobody's friend, Murph; it certainly ain't helping us get this big thing up onto the roof," I laugh, relieved that the canvas is still intact.

It's a lot easier with the three of us and we soon get the big picture secured and all the fastenings double-checked before predictably engaging in an enthusiastic exchange of ideas and experiences. "Here, Murph, guess what I saw in my torch-light... two foxes mating... actually mating!" His response isn't what I expect and he curses... "Don't talk to me about f... ing foxes... they've just killed six of our best hens!" He updates us on the progress of the new house and we have a good grumble to help us feel better about things; then he stomps off back up the hill, leaving us to get on with our own mission. If this lot blows off like a load once before did, it'll be because of the power of the wind and not the speed of my driving because I shall not be exceeding twenty miles an hour, no matter what.

We set off on our snail-slow meander around the up and down, twisting lanes, gently easing our precious cargo, till at last are entering the gates of the great estate. We reverently proceed until we are shrouded and surrounded by towering evergreens along a jay-squawking track that's like a tarmac lawn, before the most exquisite and immaculate gardens imaginable. We already feel we're in a different world, either a forgotten one or a very secret one. It's a grand and beautiful fragment of loveliness that holds us as we roll to a halt on a car-park that's more or less empty, apart from a boisterous parliament of magpies in uproarious debate over something or other. They disperse noisily as I race off across the gravel to make sure that the huge oak front door is open, before dashing back and starting the process of transferring the humble contents of a cowshed into this shrine of great art.

Thankful at having arrived without incident and the leaden sky having spared us a drenching, we don't risk pushing our luck any further and begin offloading the big stuff that's unprotected up on the roof-rack. We're fortunate in having trees providing such solid protection, were it not for these I'm sure that my large pictures would take off across the lawns. We proceed with caution, my knees are knocking, even the ghostly faces on my largest painting seem to be blushing as they enter the reception hallway, where several small Rodin figures respectfully acknowledge them.

It's amazing how much smaller they seem when I lean them against the wall in the huge gallery; back in the cowshed they looked enormous and completely overpowering. It's really rather refreshing being able to step back and see them from a distance for the first time. They look like totally different paintings; equally, the smaller ones look tinier yet, making me want to race back for the next load and the next, in the hope of making the gallery look less empty.

It's no good my complaining about the wind, because it's only this that's keeping the rain off, enabling us thankfully into completing the transporting part before the wind has dropped and rain is once more miserably closing in around us. During the course of our driving back and forth we have spotted some lovely old hedge-stakes in a neglected hedge, along a remote stretch of lane, so, not being ones to look a gift horse in the mouth, we stop on our way home and load the van with enough wood to last us several nights. This is a huge help as it frees me to spend the next couple of days getting all the paintings positioned and properly hung, without having to waste precious time in trudging off to another of Gareth's woodlands that's being felled, way over the hill to the back of Murphy's place.

The stage is now set. Cari has shaken out all the moths from my only remotely respectable clothes and the foul weather is proving to be a blessing, because it means that I can wear my very old fisherman's sweater to help hide my worn-out shirt. As for the boys, they'll look fine in their school clothes but, in all honesty, they loathe the very thought of having to come at all. They've already seen the paintings till they're sick of them, what's more, the very thought of having to be on best behaviour in the presence of 'posh' strangers, is making them more miserable than I've ever seen them. "It'll do you good," I say, trying to encourage them... "you'll probably see some of your school friends there." I do understand how they feel, but we don't have much choice in the matter.

We make a late trip into town to buy food, I haven't eaten for two days and this prompts Cari to seize the initiative and prescribe kippers, of all things, as we gaze down upon the humble fare in the dull window of 'R.Gittens, Fishmonger'. We enter and the proprietor comes swirling up before us like a moray eel, tobacco-teeth smiling, almost eating us both in an instance. "We're looking at what you've got," I say, trying to spot something that looks remotely like a fish. Then I catch sight of some flabby-looking things masquerading under the name of 'bucklings" and I ask what they are. "They're bucklings!" he informs us, leaving us none the wiser. "Oh, Bucklings... I go there every year for my holidays... Bucklin's

Holiday Camp!" He has no idea whatsoever that I'm joking, even with Cari's outburst of laughter, and he slaps one of them before us. "It looks sort of 'fishy'... smells a bit though!" I say, and he retorts... "That's the way they's supposed to be... a bit like bloaters, isn't it." "We'll try two of them," Cari decides with a snap. "What are your kippers?" "They're kippers... Manx... very nice!" he replies, with all the authoritative flatness of a flounder; he's not a man to joke about fish, or anything else for that matter. I can't help but have another prod at trying to make him smile. "Oh! Isle of Man kippers, hey; aren't they the ones that race around the streets on motorbikes... or are they just the ones that don't have tails?" He shrugs his shoulders and mutters, "No I don't think so... not to my knowledge anyway; they're just ordinary kippers... nothing fancy like!" I look into his glazed eyes and see the ghost of a man that's destined to sell some fish or other until the day he dies. Cari is doing her utmost best not to explode with laughter all over him and perilously orders a couple of pairs, then we race out into the street and let it all out.

Mission accomplished; we now have to hurry back to pick up the boys from school, and then start getting us all ready for my big night up at the Hall. I'm a nervous wreck, not enjoying this one little bit. To make things worse the lane ahead of us is blocked by sheep, all coming out from Murphy's drive. I can see Hugh wielding a stick and bawling instructions to the excited dog that's driving them down the lane where we are anxiously waiting to go. The Landrover then appears with Gwyneth, infant in arms, sitting next to Gareth. Cari jumps out and goes over to say hello, then comes running back with a smile on her face. "Problem solved!" she announces. "You boys are all going to spend the evening up at the farm, watching their new colour TV!" There's a deafening cheer that drives every former trace of gloom from their faces, and they keep up the din all the way down past the rapidly growing new house, as we follow the Landrover as far as the marsh meadow gate, where the flock are steered to new pasture. I can't tell whether the sheep are cheering or jeering, every single one of them is making exactly the same comment as the next one, we can't hear ourselves speaking, it's so noisy.

Cari insists that I starve no longer and that I stuff myself solid with kippers, pointing out that I need to build my strength up for the ordeal ahead... making it seem more like a dental appointment than the opening of an exhibition. I do as I'm told, forcing the kippers down till I am disgustingly bloated; not only am I a bundle of nerves, but I'm now on the verge of vomiting with every step I take. I don't think that this was such a good idea.

The farm gang come noisily crashing in, they've come, mud an' all, to collect the boys and to save us from getting sludged-up before going out to the Hall. It's a really kind and considerate thought, I wasn't relishing the prospect of walking them all that way through the mud, before having to race off to Gregynog. The boys are all letting off steam in their crazy excitement, making me wish that I could catch some of it for myself; I'd far rather be going with them than to be going where I'm going. They all go off noisily into the darkness and we stand in the yard listening to their fading laughter as they splash through ankle-deep slime, leaving us in a sudden silent, cold and kipper-smelling, empty cowshed.

Our new friends, Pippa and John, have arranged to come over, bringing with them a couple of friends, in what they refer to as being 'rent-a-crowd'. It's their way of making the place look busy and saving me from any possible feelings of disappointment, should there be no-one else there. I don't feel nearly so bad when I remind myself of this, having earlier hoped that Meg and Murphy might be there, babysitting problems preventing them. I did ask Dan but, predictably he just laughed at the suggestion... much to my relief.

Our 'rent-a-crowd' friends arrive, mud-spattered, but otherwise in good spirits. I notice them all sniffing and John asks... "Have you been painting kippers?" "I wish I had!" I reply. "I've just been force-fed a shoal of the bloody things... I never want to see another sodding kipper as long as I live!" They all laugh and it helps lessen the shock for our newest friends, 'May' and 'Alan', who could never have imagined that anyone would live in a freezing cold and totally un-serviced cowshed.

I forage about in my old pockets in a panic to find my van keys. "Damn... I nearly forgot these!" I gasp, my nerves beginning to get the better of me again. "You'll not be needing those, Jim; we're taking you there in style. We figured that you needed a bit of comfort to go to such an auspicious event; we're going to drive you there!" I can't believe it; two new friends plus two total strangers... and they treat me like this!

I turn the paraffin lamp off and search for new candles to replace the ailing ones; I don't relish the prospect of returning to a pitch-black freezing hovel after previously being roasted and dazzled by electricity. So, with a little yellow flame flickering in the hearth and another in the kitchen, we leave, every step I take being a kippered nightmare and my heart skipping the odd beat or two... going to the dentist is, on reflection, less of an ordeal than this is; I know now where Spencer gets his bad nerves from.

My torchlight illuminates a lovely, shining Volkswagen van, with windows all round and with seats in the back; it's the very vehicle that I wished I owned. We all make a joke about scraping the sheep-muck from our feet... but we're not joking really because we're plastered in the stuff. We climb aboard and the trusty engine in the far distant back, rumbles to life and we glide away like Royalty; I'm shaking like a leaf.

We've taken the precaution of setting out a bit early just to be on the safe side but, good thinking as this may have been, on our arrival, the car-park is chock-a-block with all manner of better vehicles than I can afford. There must be something else going on, something to do with the University no doubt. I point out that this is sometimes the way it is out here, visiting Professors, all manner of famous people, politicians attending secret conferences, with helicopters landing on the lawns... it's no ordinary place. My friends are impressed, especially so after where they've just come from!

My kippers are playing up; my digestive system is busy converting everything to gas... and it's showing. As our feet crunch across the gravel, I begin to shudder from the shock of what I'm seeing; the curtains of the Music Room have not been drawn and I can't see a single painting... people are in the way... the whole place is heaving with people! "Bloody hell!" I gasp. "There must be some mistake... I've got the dates wrong!" We rather hesitantly force our way into the entrance hall, deafened by the babble of voices, then Dr. Hughes, who has been keeping an eye out for me, suddenly appears through a coral reef of encrusted wives, his eyes bright and a look of immense pleasure beaming from him. "Come in, come in!

Come and help yourself to a glass of wine and some food." I simply cannot believe what I'm seeing... I've never seen food like this. There are tables laid with the kind of stuff that I only ever dreamed of, and with wines that bewilder me with their pedigree. My own little group of people get thoroughly stuck-in, leaving me standing, stiff as a dead penguin, with kippers frothing acid in my throat, showing me that they think it's bonfire night.

As a child, my Mother told me that my eyes were always bigger than my belly; she was right, so very right! I want to eat everything in sight, but I can do absolutely nothing about it because I'm so stuffed to bursting with bloody kippers! My poor eyes need pain-killers... they'll never forgive me for this... not ever! Hundreds of mouths are eating at an unashamed gluttonous pace that I'm not accustomed to and Cari comes gushing up to me, exotic food particles dribbling from her words. "Jimmy, isn't this absolutely wonderful!" I give her an 'R.Gittens, Fishmonger' look and groan... "Kippers!"

A sharp clap of hands summons everyone to silence; Dr. Hughes is taking the stage. "Ladies and Gentlemen! I'd like us all now to retire to the Music Room." Everyone follows as he steps out proudly through to the adjoining room, settles everyone, then says; "Ladies and Gentlemen, welcome to Gregynog!" I'm a trembling mass as I listen to him babbling about the historical past and the old family association with fine impressionist paintings, then to my absolute horror, he invites me to emerge from the shadows and to be introduced to everyone and to give a talk about my pictures! There's loud applause as I come shuffling out into the light. I'm completely stuck for words; they're all waiting for me to say something that's worth remembering as I stand trembling before their hungry eyes and ears. After the applause has died, the silence is worse than any kippers; I can't think of anything to say and I can feel myself blushing. Somehow I manage to break the silence and I blurt... "Thank you, thank you for coming out on such a nasty night to see my pictures here. I can't really speak for them, I want them to speak for themselves; thank you, I hope you enjoy them." I'm applauded back into the relative anonymity of mass, whereupon I am immediately seized by Dr. Hughes, eager to tell me that the University wishes to purchase four of my paintings. He then proudly takes me to point out which ones they are and puts red stickers on them to show that they're sold.

Kippers apart, I'm feeling a touch easier and I can relax a little; people are coming up to talk to me with such warm enthusiasm about art, making me feel that it's all been worthwhile. It's lovely just looking about me and seeing various little groups of people standing in front of my paintings, pointing out things, totally engrossed in what I've struggled to produce in a cowshed. I watch as more red stickers go on to pictures making me suddenly realise that this is probably the last time I shall ever see quite a few of them. A sadness sweeps over me, the lump in my throat most certainly isn't kippers, and I can feel hot salt smarting in my eyes. "Don't be upset," Cari whispers, as a red-hot tear breaks free and splashes on the floor. "He hates parting with his pictures... they're like his children!" she tries to explain to the others but, the reasons for me are more complex than that, true as her sentiments may be. I'm just overwhelmed emotionally, humble with gratitude and touched to the very core, by the warmth of people. I've never had my hand shaken so much in all my life; Murphy's never going to believe this!

I make my way discreetly to the far end of the gallery and take a long look, wanting for Dad's eyes to be looking out through mine; he'd be so proud if he could see this now. "This is all for you, Dad," I choke, fighting to regain composure, and the others come over to join me and jolly me up a bit. "Well, Jim," John says with a smile. "I'm glad I bought my paintings when I did... these vultures would have had them!" He throws an arm around my shoulder and says... "Come on, there's still some food and wine out there, that's where they're all heading!"

My poor eyes can't take this torture. I'm still in a delicate state of kipper-metamorphosis as my eyeballs wallow in self-pity, aching with grief and greed, lusting over the diminishing banquet. I can contain myself no longer and I force my way round to where Mrs. Hughes is clearing away the empty bottles and dishes, and I discreetly say to her, "I do hope all this lovely food is not going to be thrown to waste... I'll happily take some of it back with me... if it would help!" She deals me with a thud of a smile before saying... "Don't you worry yourself about this, Jim, there are plenty of mouths around here that can deal with it; thanks for your offer all the same!" I'm choked, Cari is embarrassed; my 'village' upbringing has let me down. "I can't take him anywhere!" she jokes, much to the amusement of the others as a final round of handshaking brings the evening to a close. A happy Dr. Hughes comes and thanks me. I thank him in return and say... "Just think... if it wasn't for John Wain, this wouldn't have happened."

Cari has asked Alan, our driver, if he'd mind calling in on our way back to pick up the boys from the farm and he's more than happy to do this, then Cari makes a quick phone call before we leave the hall, warning Gwyneth that we're on our way and for the boys to be ready.

We follow the trail of red rear-lights out of the estate, all of us in high spirits and letting off steam, especially over the wonderful food and wine that was provided. They think it's hilarious that I never managed even a crumb of it, inspiring John to confidently predict that my next painting will be, "Man who's just eaten Kippers". I laughingly reply that, this particular memory will be far too painful for it ever to be re-lived in a painting.

I'm glad of the soothing splash of cold night air when I hop out to open the gates on our steep climb up the track to the farm, and I take in long swigs of it to help calm my kippers. The farmyard is a slimy mess as Alan very carefully turns the van and reverses it up to the farmhouse where, dancing in the doorway, the boys are all in high spirits. Cari supervises as they climb inside the spotless carriage, minus muddy wellies which are in polythene bags. I quickly jump out to explain that we can't stop because our friends have a long drive ahead of them, but Gareth has something on his mind and is fidgeting in an agitated sort of way and is beckoning me to one side. Satisfied that no-one is within earshot he starts to stammer, "Jimmy, I..I..I know I said you c..could live in th.. that owd p.. place down th.. there f..f..for a..as long as you w..wanted to; b..but I.. I've been offered r..real silly money for it, m..money th..that I'd be daft to refuse. He's gonna p..pull the whole l..lot down and b..build a b..b..big new house w..with a road up to it. So I want you to g..get out, n..no rush, just as s..s..soon as you can like, isn't it!" I stare at him for a brief stunned moment, then throw-up profusely at his feet. "A..a..are you alright?" he asks, and I spit a few times, then mutter... "yes thanks, I'll be alright in a minute... I knew I shouldn't have eaten those bloody Kippers!"

We drive back round to where my old van is parked and we say goodnight to our lovely friends and sadly watch them slip over the hill and out of sight. This has been a strange, 'hand-grenade' of a day, one that I can't wait to dispose with. I'll say nothing to Cari till morning, we could all do with a good night's sleep.

Eventually, morning emerges; it's raining hard as I lie back listening to it slashing against the polythene, looking sadly up at the swallows nests on the beams. I'm trying to do a mental calculation of our current financial state and how recent painting sales may have altered things. I conclude that this is not an occasion for euphoria, recognising with a sickening reality that, what pictures I have sold are roughly the equivalent of three weeks works in television. It seems crazy, it's taken me blood, sweat and tears to produce these painting; it doesn't make sense.

Cari stirs and notices my grim expression and asks if I've had a bad dream. "You could say that!" I reply, then I quietly break the news to her. "Don't breathe a word to the boys... it'll only upset them." She goes very quiet as the rain continues to thrash down... then she says quietly, "What are we going to do?" I shrug my shoulders and sigh, "I haven't a bloody clue; it's all I need now with my exhibition on and Christmas galloping up! It's not the best present he could have given us, that's for sure!" We lie deep in thought, like a book open at a page we're on and then a spiteful wind coming and blowing the pages backwards then forwards till we lose our place; what's already gone representing not so much what we have read., but rather more, that which we have written. "Gonna have to write a few more letters to television companies, I suppose... let's face it, the small amount of money that we've got won't last five minutes and that's a fact!" I stand up and give her a look of grim defiance as I snatch up my ice-cold damp trousers and buckle my belt. "You stay there in the warm, I'm going to make you the best cup of tea you've ever had; nothing's going to get the better of us, do you hear. Nothing, nothing, NOTHING!"

I go bouncing off in my socks, determined not to let things get us down, as I sing... "We're all going on a Summer holiday, no more workin' for a week or two..." I don't know the rest of the words, but it stirs Cari into her own defiant effort... "One wheel on my wagon and I'm still rolling along..." while the boys all show a cheeky silence as they try to figure out what's prompted this outburst of awful singing. I put the kettle on the Calor-gas, then, while I wait for it to boil, I saw a few of the hedge-stakes and get a lively fire started in the hearth; it's amazing what difference a fire makes!

After luxuriating over a cup of tea and having given an airing to our problem, we don't feel quite so bad after all; I even have to admit to feeling a sense of relief beginning to settle over me. What was becoming a fungal burden upon my growing self, has suddenly eased and I feel a sense of glowing pride returning. We shall leave this place of dashed dreams and broken promises with a dignity like that of the swallows before us, and like them, we shall go when we're ready and not a moment before. I shall honourably burn every single item of wood that we have put into the place, walls, floors, ceilings, shelves, doors, furniture, the lot, and we shall leave this place as we found it, but in a blaze of glory!

Full of fire roaring through me and with yesterday's dark clouds blown clean away, I stride out into the new day's dark clouds and driving rain, to fetch more of the hedge-stakes from the van, anxious to never let the fire go out again and more than glad of the open space, the open air in which to vent my anger. Not mincing my thoughts any more I gaze piteously over the sad and mutilated, murdered landscape, my mind haunted by paradise pictures of what it was when we first came and fell in love with it.

I'm sad, so deeply sad... but I'm glad, so glad that we can no longer stay, for the sakes of our precious dreams alone; it's time to move on to better things... we can't stay here waiting for swallows... the swallows won't be coming back here ever again.

Standing On Stubble

The War Years; *all fathers were mysteriously stolen away and sent overseas to fight and kill other men.* The book spans the years between 1937 and 1950 and is set in the heart of England on a wild heathland next to an army barracks, just two miles from an RAF aerodrome. The book is a tapestry of characters and events which evoke, in the most colloquial of ways poetic, a detailed social event of the time.

The language emerges as a flower from a seed that grows and grows beyond gardens and heathland, with laughter and tears going hand-in-hand as in life itself. It gives a raw perspective on the American participation, which prompted an old village-man to bluntly proclaim, *"If they aint braggin' they're shaggin'!"*

The title 'Standing on Stubble' refers to the moment when the corn is cut with a horse-drawn 'binder'; grandads are standing around with their dogs waiting for the rabbits to bolt out from the corn and the children are standing in the short stubble. The 'Stubble' in this case being an allegory for 'life' itself in which every child thinks that it will support their weight. They never stop believing this, because they always trust that it will... but sadly, it never does.

This is a book crammed full of character and characters, dreams and dreamers and it concludes in late adolescence, the mysterious threshhold of manhood; a new world awaiting there, where the old one is lying, slowly dying. Poignant and vivid, this book will make yu laugh more than it will make you cry; a child's perspective entertains no blurring bureaucracies and is raw and very real in a most refreshing way.

The Aspiring Alchemist

Like Jim Bridgen's other books, this one pulls no punches in bringing High Art down to where it may be dissected and all bullshit removed.
Life and Art forever remain as one, integrity and honesty being key words running throughout this most penetrating search. The artist and the philosopher run along parallel lines at times and as surrealism provides images of weird impossibility, the author provides equally way-out ideas of 'probability', even by suggesting that the searching for 'oranges' is more fruitful than the futile search for 'origins' !

This is an art student's dream of being able to perceive and discover a measure of worth beyond that of the purely monetary. The Aspiring Alchemist is a voyage of discovery into 'Art', a revolutionary journey into a conceptualised world, where pure gold can be possibly manufactured from chicken-shit and something else to be found in the humbleness of ordinary living.

This book is a journey that you've most probably been on yourself, when you felt that you knew all the answers and were at odds with the measures of worth that existed at the height of your journey.
A radical book, utterly down to earth as you would expect from Jim Bridgen; deep meaning, hilarius, poetic and hugely entertaining.
Another 'original' from an 'original!

White Coal for a Queen

Between Art College and manhood there existed a two-years' wide, highly dangerous 'adventure-playground' known as 'National Service'. Most young men of te 1950s after leaving school, college or apprenticeships, were conscripted to 'do their bit' inside this compulsory briar-patch, supposedly for their Queen and country, the author being one such victim.

Jim Bridgen really does call a spade a spade, with an honesty that might cause the reader to blush at times, in this painfully hilarious account of what was generally considered to be a complete waste of time, a major interruption-cum-obtruction coming at the most crucial stage in a young man's chosen career. Hugely entertaining and vividly evocative, this book paints a raw, rude and randy picture documenting a State Bureaucracy at odds with a meek humanity and that humanity fighting back with both dexterity and cunning. Never a passive conscript, Privat Bridgen 'does' the Army his way; this was another kind of war within a war.

These characters and events are entirely real, right down to the last impeccably observed detail- the hallmark of this great writer

Two-Legged Camel

'Two-Legged Camel is a reflective journey through both time and space and uses as its structural base, the length of Great Britain and the step-by-step walking of it, sleeping in fields and under hedges, quietly documenting the very nature and character of the land out of which the writer was born.

John O' Groats to Land's End is often thought of as being a publicity-seeking 'charity walk' undertaken by 'celebrities', highly publicised and organised with lavish back-up facilities. This journey most certainly is not to be confused with that sort of venture; it is instead a most solitary, virtually reclusive undertaking of somewhat spiritual dimensions and leaves the reader in no doubt whatsoever how it feels to average thirty miles a day in all weathers, your house on your back, kitchen-sink, the lot and, more often than not, no money in your pocket.

As with all Jim Bridgen books, the attention to detail is second to none and you'll cry with laughter and sometimes perhaps, just cry. The picture he paints is of an island people and of a passionate sense of being one of them, immensely proud and loyal. *"I want to feel every painful inch of my own beautiful land beneath my tender feet; only then can I say that I truly belong to it"* To read this book is to experience these very sentiments and to be thoroughly entertained every painful inch of the way.

"The pain got worse, I was in serious trouble and slowing-off drastically because of it. If I peed myself I'd stink; if I did it in the gutter I'd be arrested; all I could do was to 'delicately' shuffle on, put up with the pain and pray that I didn't explode. A high speed train sped by, its carriages were all empty, the thing was carrying air at high speed to empty it somewhere hundreds of miles away. It was of no consolation to know that at least sixty vacant toilets had just shot past at ninety miles an hour!"